The Economic History of Japan: 1600–1990

VOLUME 1

The Economic History of Japan: 1600–1990

VOLUME 1: Emergence of Economic Society
in Japan, 1600–1859

Edited by

AKIRA HAYAMI
OSAMU SAITÔ
RONALD P. TOBY

OXFORD
UNIVERSITY PRESS

OXFORD

UNIVERSITY PRESS

Great Clarendon Street, Oxford OX2 6DP

Oxford University Press is a department of the University of Oxford.
It furthers the University's objective of excellence in research, scholarship,
and education by publishing worldwide in

Oxford New York

Auckland Bangkok Buenos Aires Cape Town Chennai
Dar es Salaam Delhi Hong Kong Istanbul Karachi Kolkata
Kuala Lumpur Madrid Melbourne Mexico City Mumbai Nairobi
São Paulo Shanghai Taipei Tokyo Toronto

Oxford is a registered trade mark of Oxford University Press
in the UK and in certain other countries

Published in the United States
by Oxford University Press Inc., New York

©1999 by Akira Hayami and Osamu Saitô

English translation rights arranged with Akira Hayami through
Iwanami Shoten, Publishers, Tokyo.

The moral rights of the authors have been asserted

Database right Oxford University Press (maker)

First published 2004

British Library Cataloguing in Publication Data
Data available

Library of Congress Cataloging in Publication Data
Data available

ISBN 0-19-828905-7

1 3 5 7 9 10 8 6 4 2

Typeset by Newgen Imaging Systems (P) Ltd., Chennai, India
Printed in Great Britain
on acid-free paper by
Biddles Ltd., King's Lynn, Norfolk

PREFACE

This volume brings together in English translation a selection of ten chapters on early modern Japanese economic history that first appeared in the series *The Economic History of Japan* (Iwanami Shoten 1988–90).[1] In the expectation that this work will be most useful to readers who do not have access to scholarship in Japanese, we decided to make the work more than simply a translation of the Japanese version—an introduction has been added, and several changes and additions have been made for readers unfamiliar with the history of Japan, including the Appendix for those who are not familiar with early modern Japanese history.

We have also included a glossary: with these additions, we hope to provide readily understandable explanations for the administrative and monetary systems, as well as the systems of weights and measures, the calendar, and other features characteristic of early modern Japan, as an aid to readers not yet familiar with the history of Tokugawa Japan. The references are also listed in a standard Western format, rather than using the format of the original Japanese.

Economic history as a field in Japanese scholarship has a history of nearly one hundred years. As with other social sciences, economic history in Japan began with the introduction of methods used in the West. Initially, early in the last century, research focused heavily on institutional history, and German economics of the historical school, but the interwar era (1920s and 1930s) witnessed a factional split in economic history between a methodology based on one specific ideology, Marxism, on the one hand, and a variety of other factions that were primarily descriptive, but lacked any clear methodology. This ideological and methodological division strengthened in the postwar era, a trend that continued until the 1970s.

The 1970s, however, saw the rapid introduction of various new methodologies, reflecting the intellectual ferment characteristic of the advanced industrial nations in the 1960s and 1970s, including "New Economic History" and "Business History" that were increasingly fashionable in American academic circles, and "Historical Demography" developed in Europe, and most often identified with the French "Annales School." These various approaches differed markedly from the traditional

---

[1] *Nihon keizai-shi* (8 Vols, Tokyo: Iwanami Shoten, 1988–90). *Emergence of Economic Society—17th and 18th Centuries*, Vol. 1, Akira Hayami and Matao Miyamoto (eds.); *The Initial Movements of Modern Growth*, Vol. 2, Hiroshi Shimbo and Osamu Saitô (eds.); *The Opening of Japan and the Meiji Restoration* Vol. 3, Mataji Umemura and Yûzô Yamamoto (eds.).

methodologies of economic history. One impetus for these new developments was the strong influence of a session entitled "Searching for New
Historical Images of the Edo Period" held at the 1976 annual meeting of
the Socio-Economic History Society, at Waseda University, Tokyo, Japan.[2]
Another stimulus was the initiation in 1972 of a series of conferences, held
nearly every year, for researchers who had become dissatisfied with the
conventional techniques used to study the economic history of Japan.
A broad spectrum of researchers were invited to the conferences, regardless of their subject of study, and conference results were published in a
series of volumes.[3]

This research group is called the "Quantitative Economic History (QEH)
Research Group," but its goals and methods are not necessarily the same as
the movement in the United States that has come to be called "cliometrics."
The objective of this group is to make correct and accurate use of statistical
data, including the evaluation of historical source materials, and the society
is not based solely on the framework of the neoclassical school of economics. However, members of the group do include specialists in development
economics, so we do see more influence of modern economic analyses,
methodologies, and concepts here than in traditional research in economic
history. Another characteristic of this group is that it also considers areas
such as consumption, demand, distribution, transportation, and population, while conventional economic history research in Japan almost entirely
focused on production and supply.

In 1984, Iwanami Shoten approached us about the possibility of publishing a book on *Economic History of Japan* (Nihon keizai-shi). Numerous
preparatory meetings were held the following year, 1985, during which
we examined the fundamental objectives, details, narrative methods,
number of volumes, and the authors. By the end of that year, we had
hammered out the drafts for all seven volumes. However, further investigation indicated that the drafts for the "Age of Industrialization," which

---

[2] Published the following year as Shakai Keizai-shi Gakkai [Socio-Economic
History Society], ed., *Atarashii Edo jidaishizô o motomete*, (Tokyo: Tôyô Keizai
Shinpôsha, 1977), with contributions by Akira Hayami and almost all authors of
this volume.

[3] *Sûryô Keizaishi Ronshû* [Collection of Theses on Quantitative Economic
History], Tokyo: Nihon keizai shimbunsha. Nihon keizai no hatten [The
Development of Japanese Economy] Vol. 1, Mataji Umemura et al. (eds.), was pub-
lished in 1976. *Kindai ikoki no nihon keizai* [Japanese Economy in Modern
Transitional Periods] Vol. 2, Hiroshi Shimbo and Yasukichi Yasuba (eds.), pub-
lished in 1979. *Puroto kogyokaki no keizai to shakai* [Economy and Society in the
Proto-Industrial Period] Vol. 3, Yasukichi Yasuba and Osamu Saitô (eds.), was
published in 1983. Vol. 4, Kônosuke Odaka and Yûzô Yamamoto (eds.), *Bakumatsu
meiji no nihon keizai* [Japanese Economy at the Last Years of Tokugawa Era and the
Beginning Years of Meiji Era] was published in 1988.

covered the initial era of modern industrialization, were simply too much for one volume, so the articles were reorganized into two parts, or a total of eight volumes in the work.

The authors in each of the volumes were drawn primarily from the membership of QEH, but as they could not possibly cover all aspects of Japanese economic history, approximately half of the chapters were assigned to other authors. In all cases, the authors were asked to present their volume editors with a preliminary outline of the proposed coverage of their chapters, and proceed with the writing only after the editors had examined the proposals. Volume 1 was published in November 1988 and the final volume (Volume 5) in February 1990. Publication was achieved relatively quickly for this series, the result of the dedication of the authors, editors, and publishers.

A Chinese version of the *Economic History of Japan* appeared in 1997, including translations of the entire series of eight volumes. This achievement was extremely surprising and gratifying to the authors, who were very eager to hear the response of economic history researchers in China to their work. With this English publication of *Economic History of Japan*, the work will now be available to people throughout the world, the greatest honor that we could hope for.

I would like to point out that we do not present the information contained in these volumes as the final word on the subject, precluding all other ideas and concepts. Each of the authors was aware of this prior to publication and strove for objectivity, but recognizes that dealing with historical questions always entails interpretation that emerges from the author's stance and methodology, as well as the inevitable choices about coverage. We realize that there will always remain elements which cannot be settled definitively, and that there are numerous methods of approaching a subject. We would like to ask the reader to evaluate this work in that same spirit of frank and honest inquiry. Readers may also wish to consult the English-language review of the Japanese version of this work by Kozo Yamamura, an economic historian at the University of Washington, which appeared in the *Journal of Japanese Studies*.[4]

In this work, the Japanese names of contemporary persons are listed in the Western order, with the given name first, followed by the surname. However, for historical persons, who appeared before the Meiji Restoration (1868), the surname comes first followed by the given name.

This English version is not the same as the Japanese edition. Since we had to condense eight volumes into four, some chapters have been left out. Chapter 3 in this volume, written by Kazui Tashiro, is the translation

---

[4] Yamamura, Kozo (1991), *Journal of Japanese Studies*, Vol. 17, No.1, Winter: 127–42.

of an article that appeared in the other book. Also Chapter 10, by Ronald P. Toby, was not included in the original Japanese edition. Not only did he contribute the chapter, but also read through all the chapters and gave us a lot of suggestions and comments. I am greatly indebted to him and to Osamu Saitô, who helped to edit this volume.

The English translation of this work was made possible largely through the efforts of Professor Alan Christy, University of California, Santa Cruz, with financial help from the Daidô Foundation. The editors and authors would like to express their deep appreciation to Professor Christy and the individual translators who worked with him on this project, and to the Daidô Foundation. We would also like to express our appreciation to Kiko International Co., Ltd., Kyoto, particularly Ms Kiko Matsuura there for putting the draft into shape, for making arrangements for the spelling and style, and for giving me many suggestions, too.

I would like to express to Mr Stuart Fowkes, at Oxford University Press, my deepest gratitude for having him as an editor. Without his very patient cooperation, this book would not have appeared.

Finally, I am very grateful to Ms Miyuki Takahashi Ph.D. and Ms Masako Unosawa, who worked hard on all the chapters, including checking the contents and digitalizing numerous tables and figures. Indexing was done also by Ms Takahashi. Their impressive computer literacy was displayed fully in achieving this. We are also grateful to Mr Kanetarô Saitô Ph.D. who prepared the complex reference.

We are sorry to have to write here that Professor Hiroshi Shimbo, one of the most active and key people involved with this series, sadly passed away before the publication.

December 2003 *Akira Hayami*

CONTENTS

LIST OF FIGURES

LIST OF TABLES

1. Map of Japan (Region–Province)

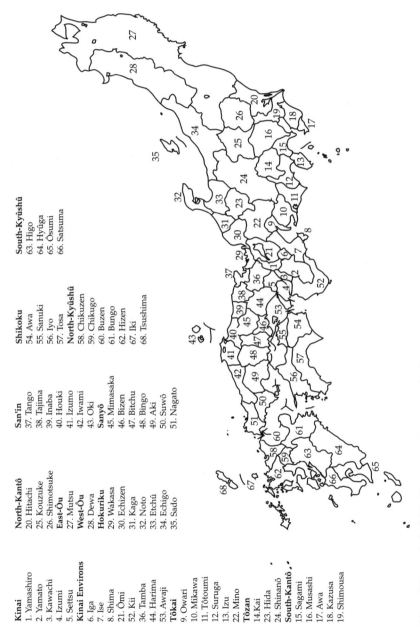

Kinai
1. Yamashiro
2. Yamato
3. Kawachi
4. Izumi
5. Settsu
Kinai Environs
6. Iga
7. Ise
8. Shima
21. Ōmi
52. Kii
36. Tamba
44. Harima
53. Awaji
Tōkai
9. Owari
10. Mikawa
11. Tōtoumi
12. Suruga
13. Izu
22. Mino
Tōzan
14. Kai
23. Hida
24. Shinanō
South-Kantō
15. Sagami
16. Musashi
17. Awa
18. Kazusa
19. Shimousa

North-Kantō
20. Hitachi
25. Kouzuke
26. Shimotsuke
East-Ōu
27. Mutsu
West-Ōu
28. Dewa
Hokuriku
29. Wakasa
30. Echizen
31. Kaga
32. Noto
33. Etchū
34. Echigo
35. Sado

San'in
37. Tango
38. Tajima
39. Inaba
40. Houki
41. Izumo
42. Iwami
43. Oki
Sanyō
45. Mimasaka
46. Bizen
47. Bitchu
48. Bingo
49. Aki
50. Suwō
51. Nagato

Shikoku
54. Awa
55. Sanuki
56. Iyo
57. Tosa
North-Kyūshū
58. Chikuzen
59. Chikugo
60. Buzen
61. Bungo
62. Hizen
67. Iki
68. Tsushima

South-Kyūshū
63. Higo
64. Hyūga
65. Ōsumi
66. Satsuma

Note: Names in bold indicate a region as applied to a province.

2. Map of Modern Japan

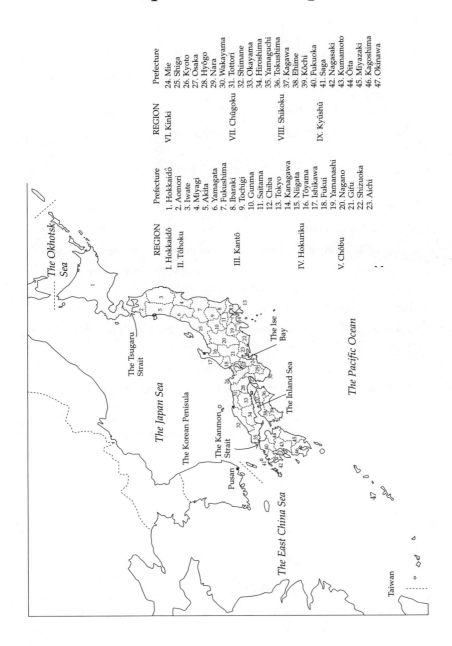

REGION	Prefecture
I. Hokkaidô	1. Hokkaidô
II. Tôhoku	2. Aomori
	3. Iwate
	4. Miyagi
	5. Akita
	6. Yamagata
	7. Fukushima
III. Kantô	8. Ibaraki
	9. Tochigi
	10. Gunma
	11. Saitama
	12. Chiba
	13. Tokyo
	14. Kanagawa
IV. Hokuriku	15. Niigata
	16. Tôyama
	17. Ishikawa
	18. Fukui
	19. Yamanashi
V. Chôbu	20. Nagano
	21. Gifu
	22. Shizuoka
	23. Aichi

REGION	Prefecture
VI. Kinki	24. Mie
	25. Shiga
	26. Kyoto
	27. Osaka
	28. Hyôgo
	29. Nara
	30. Wakayama
VII. Chûgoku	31. Tottori
	32. Shimane
	33. Okayama
	34. Hiroshima
	35. Yamaguchi
VIII. Shikoku	36. Tokushima
	37. Kagawa
	38. Ehime
	39. Kôchi
IX. Kyûshû	40. Fukuoka
	41. Saga
	42. Nagasaki
	43. Kumamoto
	44. Ôita
	45. Miyazaki
	46. Kagoshima
	47. Okinawa

The Okhotsky Sea

The Tsugaru Strait

The Japan Sea

The Korean Peninsula

The Kanmon Strait

Pusan

The East China Sea

Taiwan

The Ise Bay

The Inland Sea

The Pacific Ocean

LIST OF CONTRIBUTORS

Amano, Masatoshi, Professor of Economic History, Kobe University

Hasegawa, Akira, Professor of Economic History, Momoyama Gakuin University, Osaka

Hayami, Akira, Emeritus Professor, Keio University, Tokyo

Iwahashi, Masaru, Professor of Economic History, Matsuyama University

Kitô, Hiroshi, Professor of Economic History, Sophia (Jochi) University, Tokyo

Miyamoto, Matao, Professor of Economic History, Osaka University

Nishikawa, Shunsaku, Emeritus Professor, Keio University, Tokyo

Ôguchi, Yûjirô, Emeritus Professor Ochanomizu University, Tokyo

Saitô, Osamu, Professor of Economic History, Institute of Economic Research, Hitotsubashi University Tokyo

Shimbo, Hiroshi, Late Emeritus Professor, Kobe University

Tanimoto, Masayuki, Professor of Economic History, The University of Tokyo

Tashiro, Kazui, Professor of History, Keio University, Tokyo

Toby, Ronald P., Professor of Asian History, University of Illinois, Urbana–Champaign, USA

Introduction: The Emergence of "Economic Society"

AKIRA HAYAMI

1. Context

When the Muromachi shogunate breathed its last in 1573, it was the culmination of a long process of disintegration at the center, and reorganization in the provinces. For more than a century, daimyos (regional lords) had worked to build militarily and economically coherent domains; for the last quarter-century, they had sought to use their provincial power bases gradually to expand their influence toward the center.[1] With that, the social and political system that had somehow managed to survive from the seventh and eighth centuries lost its foundations. But Japan in the latter half of the sixteenth century entered a period characterized not only by political and strategic crisis and chaos, but equally by the urgent need to establish new principles of rule that could replace the previous system.

The international environment surrounding Japan was also seriously unsettled. The merchants of the port city of Sakai (south of Osaka) were enjoying a golden age of international maritime trade, traveling as far as southeast Asia in pursuit of both markets and commodities. Meanwhile, Ryûkyûan merchant ships brought the Ryûkyû kingdom to the peak of its own "Age of Seafaring," moving far and wide throughout maritime east Asia, and bringing unprecedented prosperity to the kingdom. The merchants of Ming China were likewise so deeply engaged in trade as to render moot the Ming dynasty's ban on maritime trade. In the wake of the terror of the *Wakô* pirates, the east Asian seas now revealed a flourishing maritime trade on a previously unheard-of scale. But into the midst of these merchant ships came strange and grand ships that people of the region had never seen before. The first of these were the galleons of the Portuguese, and later the Spanish, who had crossed tens of thousands of miles of hitherto uncharted seas to reach east Asia, bearing huge cannons and muskets, merchants and missionaries.

One of the interesting things about history is that in these encounters of a number of societies, each of which was moving in independent directions, we can see how the direction of development of each one changed, how each society's movement was regulated, and how these encounters cast a large shadow on their subsequent histories. In particular, it is important to consider the question of timing; that is, at what point in a society's transformation does the meeting occur? We must give due consideration to these kinds of exterior influences, quite apart from the internal elements of historical evolution. In other words, we should recognize the "Age of Encounter" as a kind of global cataclysm that significantly changed the histories of all its participants. Japan in the late sixteenth and early seventeenth centuries experienced an age of extraordinary historical interest, an age in which internal and external transformative elements overlapped. The events described above do not lie precisely within the framework of the economic history that is the principal focus of this volume; yet the point of departure for our economic history was precisely this period of enormous transformation.

The final quarter of the sixteenth century was truly an age of violent change. Within those twenty-five years, Japan's medieval era came to an end and the early modern era began. The first of those twenty-five years, 1575, was the year in which Oda Nobunaga used a small number of troops armed with guns, arrayed in rotating rows of three, to defeat the experienced cavalry troops of Takeda Katsuyori at the battlefield of Nagashino. While firearms were a European technology that had been imported from Europe only thirty years before, Oda's strategy for using them was entirely original; nothing like it had yet been seen in Europe, and thus this battle constituted a significant moment in the history of warfare (Parker 1988). The forerunners of those guns were a few arquebuses brought to Japan by Portuguese merchants in the early 1540s. Within a very short time, however, Japanese smiths had figured out how to manufacture them, and began producing guns domestically: Japan became the only gun-manufacturing country in east Asia. In the end, the threat of guns not only changed battle strategies, but also made possible the separation of warriors and peasants, and the construction of castles on plains.

The century closed twenty-five years later with another momentous battle, at Sekigahara (15 ninth month 1600), which came to be known as "the watershed of the realm." When the smoke of battle cleared, the realm belonged to Tokugawa Ieyasu and his heirs, who would rule it for the next 268 years. In the intervening years, firearms had not only been decisive in Japanese domestic warfare, but had become the tools of expansionism abroad: When Toyotomi Hideyoshi, driven by what can only be described as insane ambition, sent his armies to invade Korea in 1592, his armies' tactics were those of massed musketeers. Their early successes owed more to the overwhelming firepower of these new weapons, and the massed tactics in which they were deployed, than to sword-wielding elite samurai in hand-to-hand combat. The invasion ended in failure, and while the defeat may properly be attributed to insuperable logistical problems and fierce resistance by both Korean and Chinese armies, Hideyoshi's failure also owes in part to the opposing Chinese–Korean alliance's masterful use of a different kind of firearm: field and shipborne artillery. The Japanese use of firearms drew international attention; the very fact that Hideyoshi attempted what he did may have been due to the intimidating power of guns.

In the arena of international relations these twenty-five years witnessed a great change in the relations between Japan and the European powers. Japan's relations with Europe, which had begun as the monopoly of the Portuguese Jesuits and merchants,[2] changed with the shifting fortunes of power in Europe, as well as with the evolving international environment in east Asia, and in domestic Japanese politics. As the Spanish king took over the Portuguese throne (1580), as the Netherlands gained independence (1581), and as the Spanish Armada was defeated (1588) by the English navy, Japan began to have contact with new European powers whose representatives found their way to east Asia. First to follow the Portuguese were the Spanish, who had established their base in Manila in 1571. Later, on the eve of the Battle of Sekigahara in 1600, a Dutch ship found its way to Japanese shores for the first time, introducing the Japanese to a new kind of European—Protestants who were interested only in trade, not in seeking converts to their religion.

This age of violent change continued outside Japan in the seventeenth century. On the east Asian mainland, the Ming dynasty met its demise in 1644, and was replaced by a non-Han dynasty, namely the Qing dynasty, the Manchu, which ruled China until the early twentieth century. To the north, Russian power made slow but inexorable inroads across Siberia, creating repeated friction along the ill-defined northern borders of the Qing empire, with stability achieved only in the eighteenth century. In Japan, however, the founding of the Edo shogunate, the obliteration of the last remnants of the Toyotomi house in the Osaka campaign (1614–15) and the suppression of the Shimabara–Amakusa Rebellion (1637–38) brought an end to large-scale internal disturbances. For the next 200 years and more, Japan enjoyed what the Tokugawa regime eagerly called the "great peace" (*tenka taihei*), both a celebration of the end of civil war, and an ideological claim to political legitimacy. At the root of this *Pax Tokugawa* was the attempt to limit the influence of China and the West to the smallest scale possible, and to cultivate a native social system and culture.

In world historical terms, this was a rare (and unconscious) experiment. After two and a half centuries, when Japan encountered a West which had passed through an industrial revolution and possessed overwhelming military and economic power, had Japan not been in a position that enabled it to respond to the West, modern Japanese history would have turned out decidedly different than it did. In that sense, the salient questions are two: first, what stock of social, economic, and cultural assets did Japan build up during these centuries? And second, how did that legacy hinder Japan's ability to cope with the Western encounter at the end of the

Tokugawa era? These two questions form the undercurrent to all of the chapters in this volume.

As a final note on the context of the early modern era, I would like to touch upon the geographical situation of Japan. First of all, Japan is a narrow island country stretching along an axis from northeast to southwest, for a total distance of nearly 1,500 km, with a mountain range running approximately down the middle. To the north and west, Japan is separated from the Siberian coast by the Japan Sea, one of a chain of inland seas that run along the eastern coast of Asia, from the Bering and Okhotsk Seas to the East China Sea. At the southwestern end, however, it is only a few miles from the Japanese island of Tsushima, to the Korean port of Pusan. From north to south, the islands of Japan span 10° of latitude. This is longer than any European country, save those of Scandinavia. The average annual temperature of the northern city of Aomori is 9.6 °C while that of the southern city of Kagoshima is 17.0°C. The lowest monthly temperature averages in the two cities are the January figures of −0.2°C for Aomori and +6.7°C for Kagoshima.

Turning next to rainfall, the annual average in the interior, at Nagano, is 1014 mm while not far away on the coast at Owase City (in Mie Prefecture), the average is 4,158 mm—this is a significant difference. Seasonal differences among regions are also quite substantial, largely due to the barrier effect of the central mountain range. Rainfall along the Pacific coast is concentrated in the months of June to October, standing in clear contrast to the dry months from December to February. On the Japan Sea coast there is heavy snowfall in the winter, making it one of the heaviest snow belts in the world; but the mountains keep this moisture from reaching the Pacific coast, where winters are quite dry. Compared to the other countries of east Asia, the precipitation is heavier, and the mountains accumulate enough snow to form a natural reservoir of water.

In this way, Japan is long on its north–south axis, and climatological conditions on its Pacific and Japan Sea coasts differ greatly. As a result, it possesses a highly varied geographical appearance and a range of local ecologies, given its relatively small area. In terms of topography itself, Japan has an extremely long coastline, as may be expected of an island country. The islands are crisscrossed by mountain ranges and lack broad expanses of plains; the largest alluvial plain, the Kantô, which surrounds Edo (modern Tokyo) is only about 7,000 km², about the size of Connecticut. As a result, the country is easily divided into small regional units. A highly varied landscape and climate gave birth to products particular to each region, and stimulated the development of a regional division of labor. This in itself was an important element in the development of commerce. Overland transport is complicated by the steep mountain passes that were part of every major road, and by short, swift rivers that flooded so frequently and violently that permanent bridges were often impossible. For the same reason, even river transport was often unfeasible, for the steep slopes meant that inland boat transport was dangerous floating downstream, and extremely difficult going upstream; it should be no surprise that inland water transport was not highly developed. In contrast, coastal shipping achieved a remarkable degree of development that made possible the shipment of a high volume of products across long distances.

These natural conditions were a blessing for Japan and, of course, were by no means limited to the Edo period. However, natural conditions were a far greater determining factor for economic activity for societies prior to industrialization than after. Moreover, very few of these natural conditions functioned as inducements to economic development for preindustrial society prior to the Edo period. Still, I would argue that from the Edo period, as the processes entailed in the emergence of economic society (which I will discuss later) proceeded, Japanese frequently used natural conditions to great advantage for the expansion of production and improved circulation of goods.

For example, agriculture was impossible along the Japan Sea coast from Tôhoku through Hokuriku during winter because of the heavy snowfall. But this snowfall also provided the water that was necessary for rice production. In these conditions, the region specialized in rice production, and the people of the region were able to achieve a high level of productivity. In the mountain regions of Honshû, which were also ill-suited to rice cultivation, the people took advantage of high summer temperatures to develop a relatively high quality sericulture industry. This provided the foundation for the further development of this region after the opening of Japan's ports to world trade in 1859. Cultivators along the Inland Sea coast took advantage of sandy soil to expand the production of cotton, thus providing clothing material for the masses, and an important industrial commodity. Other commodities to arise from specialized regions included rapeseed, safflower, indigo, vegetables, paper, sugar, and salt. Food processing industries that made their mark as regional specialties included *saké*, soy sauce, and *miso* manufacture.

As the production of these commodities developed, producers sought higher earnings. In addition to the fertilizers they had earlier been able to supply themselves with locally, farmers began to use fertilizers purchased from outside sources, that is, the market. The use of dried fish fertilizers, made from dried sardines or herring, and residues from vegetable processing (from *saké*-brewing, for example), became an important element in the development of the fishing industry and a by-product of the development of the brewing industry. In other words, the use of these fertilizers was either a prerequisite to, or an after effect of, the development of other industries. Fishmeal fertilizers produced in Ezo (modern Hokkaidô) and the Kantô or elsewhere were carried all the way to the central market in Osaka and used in the cotton and rapeseed production of the Osaka area and Inland Sea region.[3] The manufactured cotton goods made possible by these fertilizers were then sold in the Kantô and Tôhoku (northeast). In this way, a national network for the distribution of goods was formed. This kind of economic integration was not possible prior to the Edo period.

One characteristic of coastal shipping is particularly worth noting. The best-known routes were: the "eastern route," from the Japan Sea coast, through the Tsugaru Straits (between Honshû and Hokkaidô) to Edo; the "western route," from the Japan Sea to the Kanmon Straits (between Honshû and Kyûshû) and thence through the Inland Sea to Osaka, and the Higaki and Taru (barrel) ship routes between Edo and Osaka. But in the actual practice of shipping along the eastern coast of Honshû, especially from Ishinomaki (a port at the Pacific side of south Tôhoku) to Chôshi (a port at the mouth of Tone River, in Kantô), the ocean currents were complex, vision was frequently obscured by fog, the six months of autumn and winter were dominated by a strong northwest wind, and there were very few good harbors in which to take refuge. For the Japanese ships of the time, this was a very difficult passage. The logical solution to this problem was to carry products from Tôhoku around the "western route" to Osaka. Thus, many of the products bound for Edo had to pass through Osaka for its geographical location. From there they were traded on the wholesale market established in Osaka, which came to be called the "kitchen of the realm," while Edo, the city with the largest population in Japan (and by c. 1700, in the world), emerged as the dominant consumer market—the end of the line for many of these commodities.

A thorough analysis is still in the future, but it appears that, compared to its neighbors in east Asia, Edo-period Japan possessed three important products of relatively superior quality: iron, wood, and paper. The development of iron production was centered in the San'in (the provinces along the north shore of the Chûgoku Region) region through traditional forge techniques (*tatara seitetsu*). This method, which employed a bellows and furnace, was inevitably displaced by the high productivity of iron production processes resulting from the industrial revolution. Nor could one say that the traditional processes sufficiently met the demand for iron in Edo period society. Nevertheless, the traditional forge techniques for iron achieved relatively high levels of productivity and could by no means be ignored in northeast Asia. Furthermore, charcoal, which provided the fuel for forging, was indispensable to the success of the traditional iron industry and charcoal depended, in turn, on a supply of wood, which was its source. One reason that Japan's iron industry did not suffer the kind of dire fuel shortage experienced by England's iron industry prior to the Industrial Revolution, was the plenitude of forest resources in Japan. The sufficiency of forest resources was itself probably due to the fact that the climatological conditions of high average temperatures and high humidity made the growth of forests rapid.

Lumber was also a decisively important construction material. As urbanization advanced and the lumber market was firmly established, the cutting of forests proceeded in every region. In places like the Kii peninsula, where the growth of forests was quite rapid, the growth of the lumber industry was aided by the convenience of shipping to the Edo market. These factors contributed to the fact that planned cultivation of such woods as cedar and cypress was begun during the Edo period.[4] Perhaps one could say that this was the result of wisdom gained from high temperatures and high humidity.

The raw material for paper production, paper mulberry, was grown throughout the country, but the production process requires a tremendous amount of water. So the clear streams of the mountain regions provided appropriate sites for paper production. Paper was occasionally a commodity subject to domain monopolies, but because paper was generally made available in large quantities and at low prices, Tokugawa Japan produced a volume of documents rare in world history. This volume of paper production also made possible both the publication of a large number of books and the high rate of literacy.[5]

In this way, then, the Edo period was a time in which the natural resources and climatological conditions were comprehensively put to use in production and distribution. Such practices as the use of fish-meal fertilizers and the planned cultivation of forests revealed utilization of natural resources to a degree rarely seen in the world at that time. The development of industrial technologies unique to Japan was a result of demands arising from the "economization" of Edo society—the emergence of what Robert Heilbroner calls "economic society" in early modern Japan. Even if many of these demands were washed aside by the wave of modern industrialization, they taught the people of Edo society about the kinds of effort necessary for effective production and distribution. Japanese after the Meiji Restoration quickly understood the meaning of the rapidly expanding productive technology of the Industrial Revolution. One of the reasons why the Japanese made such concerted and conscious efforts at technology transfer, and one of the reasons why they were so successful, was the experience Japan had had in the preceding period.

2. From "Medieval" to "Early Modern"

From the fifteenth century, Japan experienced a socioeconomic transformation that had been preceded by a political transformation, particularly in the central region. The payment of *shôen* taxes in cash may have been one of the causes of this transformation. But cash payments also transformed the cities where the proprietor class lived—limited at the time to Kyoto and Nara—into places of densely concentrated population, where residents used cash to acquire the commodities necessary to daily life. Prior to this, cities had been relatively self-sufficient places where the resident's daily needs were met almost entirely by goods remitted as taxes in kind from *shôen* to their proprietors. As cities came to depend more heavily on cash, they underwent a decisive transformation in terms of function.

In addition, the trade with Ming China that had developed during the Muromachi period stimulated the formation or expansion of trading cities such as Hyôgo, Sakai, and Hakata. These cities developed rapidly as centers focused quite specifically on economic activity born of international trade. On the other hand, as Japan entered the Warring States period (1467–1568), castle towns were formed as administrative centers for even small-scale warlords, both in the center and in the most distant periphery, setting in motion nationwide processes of urbanization.

But while the economic changes of this period had led to a massive imports market, there were still many limiting conditions. First of all there was no domestic supply of currency, particularly coins, so Japanese society was dependent on imported coins. A profit from the import trade in coins was an important financial resource for the Muromachi shogunate, so much so that the various *shugo daimyô* (provincial military governors) fought amongst themselves over the division of this profit. One of the decisive points of difference between the Muromachi and Tokugawa shogunate was that the central government of the Muromachi period lacked sufficient authority to mint its own currency.[6]

Although the ancient *ritsuryô* state and *shôen* estate systems had disappeared as effective administrative and legal systems, they remained the sole principles for a system in Japan. Without them, the political control of the Muromachi shogunate and the *shugo daimyô* could not have spread throughout the country. As long as the principle of these systems survived, it was unthinkable for the estate proprietors and military governors to control their territory autonomously. Instead, their extraction of wealth was inevitably expressed as a *tokubun* (a "gain," or "revenue" entitlement), which referred to the division of the rights to collect yearly taxes on a parcel of land into a series of layered claims, each attached to a particular *shiki* ("rights" or "role"). This made the self-contained rule of territory impossible. Consequently, when the political authority that supported this principle disintegrated, a state of near anarchy ensued.

Japan's "medieval" world differed from that of Europe in that, while the framework of the state as a political system continued ostensibly to be patterned after its Tang-dynasty model in China, the land and revenue systems that sustained it economically were no longer consistent with the patterns of the Tang-style system with which it coexisted. Meanwhile, the regions saw the rise of local proprietors who personally controlled their surroundings and eventually came to proclaim their own ruling principles. The rise of these local proprietors, and competing networks among them, made Japan's medieval age one of increasing instability. What made it possible to sustain this instability over time, however, was the fact that, as an island country, Japan was relatively isolated from its neighbors and, apart from the Mongol invasions in the fourteenth century, was not subject to external tensions. As a result, its domestic history was able to develop at a relatively leisurely tempo. If we measure Japan's history with a European yardstick, there are long periods in which change is difficult to label. Those periods with a clear, easily defined character, however, are relatively brief. Europe's dynamic development is only one historical pattern. Although historians—especially since Marx—have often measured the histories of African and Asian peoples by the degree to which they match or deviate from the pace or patterns of European history, Europe is only one of the many patterns that can be found across the peoples, countries and cultures of the world. There is no reason why we should expect to find the European mode of historical development anywhere else.

In summary, "medieval" Japan was characterized by an unstable political authority, with a social structure replete with contradictions and tremendous regional differences. This society was in no way capable of forming a "national economy." The weakness of the central government was such that it left absolutely no economic indicators that cover the entire country. As this condition continued, a state of anarchy developed which brought on a "crisis."

At this point it is worth stating the basic perspective from which we take up the study of economic history in this volume. We call a society— or more accurately, the people who live in it—which engages in basic economic activities an "economic society."[7] These economic activities refer to activities based on an economic view of value in which there is an attempt to acquire the greatest utility at the lowest cost. When human activities are predicated on this kind of inclination, "economic rules" are born. Human beings possess many different views of value, economic values being only one of these. But to take the example of contemporary Japan, daily activities, whether performed as individuals or as a group, are carried out primarily centered upon an assumption of economic value. This is truly the meaning of an "economic society." A market economy is a concentrated expression of an "economic society," in which both the providers of finance, goods, and services, and their consumers, act to the greatest degree on the basis of economic values.

The major topic for economic history is explaining when and how this "economic society" came into being. This is because the experience of an "economic society" is not that old when measured in terms of the history of humanity; perhaps not older than the last couple of hundred years. Moreover, in spatial terms, the period and method of its establishment has varied greatly. There is even a question as to whether it is universal in human societies. At the least, it appears to have arisen under very particular conditions. When the appurtenances of economic society have disseminated sufficiently, modern industrialization, operating on the principles of a market economy, becomes possible. Without this dissemination, modern industrialization takes place via a planned economy directed by the state. This results in the present discrepancy among various countries' economic systems.

What Heilbroner called "economic society," however, is not uniform, but as varied as the historical experience of the countries where it is found. Even in countries where industrialization emerged on the basis of a market economy, the resulting economies, and the styles of their "economic society," display characteristics peculiar to each. In the contemporary Japanese economy, the market economy takes precedence and Japan is counted one of the "advanced industrial nations." But could one really say that Japan is absolutely on par with the other industrial nations? Not at all. But this is not limited to Japan. Each of the "advanced industrial nations" has its own particular characteristics, to one degree or another. That is the reason why serious disputes occasionally arise at the annual summit meetings of the G8 Nations, which are then resolved through agreements that recognize the particularities of each nation. Therefore, the investigation of the process whereby this "economic society" formed has meanings beyond simply knowing the past.

Of course, the above discussion is no more than an outline of our economic world view, and we must recognize that it leaves a number of important questions unresolved. It seems doubtful, even today, for example, that economic activity is completely divorced from other value perspectives, at the level of individual behavior. Nor can we ignore the "country" when we engage in economic activity, in spite of the word "globalization." Regions and industries, or regions as an element in the composition of social groups, all often engage in noneconomic activities in the pursuit of perceived self-interest. Economic activities have not superseded all other human activity.

Nevertheless, the following matters may be accepted as facts. Once the process of the economization of society begins, producers, for example, seek efficiency in production; that is, both to achieve lower costs and to maximize profits. It is expected that consumers will buy the cheaper of two identical items and will seek information on price and quality. In pursuit of their respective interests, producers seek the improvement of productive technology, while both consumers and producers seek better methods of information gathering. The introduction of competition produces winners and losers. Winners may accumulate economic wealth, but losers are forced out, giving rise to the need for means of social welfare. These conditions inevitably accompany the rise of "economic society."

The economization of society shakes a society to its very foundations. It stimulates people both in their appetite for a higher level of material culture and a rise in the standard of living, and in their quest for the means to achieve these goals. In some cases, as a work ethic takes root in society at large, what was once seen as a very strenuous form of labor may come to be seen as less painful. In this situation, the greatest problem is the question about which part of this society is indicated by the term "the people." Even if there are gaps of greater or lesser degree between the people who compose the members of a society, in a society in which all its members take economic actions, the expansion of demand stimulates production, raises the level of technology, lowers costs, and raises purchasing power. This cycle gives rise to a spiral that encourages economic development. All of this comes from the existence of an "economic society" and the particular character of its social composition.

The most important factor is whether power is concentrated in one stratum of society, or dispersed. In a society in which power remains concentrated in one stratum, the wealth that is produced by economic activity is concentrated in the politically ruling class and the economization of society does not extend to the entire society. Rather, the gap between rich and poor grows wider, obstructing the economic development of the society as a whole. Even in the present day, where the acquisition of advanced technology is possible, there are many examples of this kind of society—societies that are unstable and have been unable to start sustained economic development.

In contrast, in societies where power is dispersed, particularly where there is a clear separation between politics and the economy, economic activity functions as a domain independent from political control. Wealth does not become concentrated in one stratum of society, but rather produces even greater demands, further stimulating economic development.

When viewed from this perspective, European feudal society comes to mind as a clear example of a dispersed society. The societies of the ancient Orient (Assyria and Persia, for example) come to mind as representatives of the concentrated social pattern.

In Japan, there was already a considerable flow of goods and currency in the Kinai region, centered around Kyoto, Nara, and Osaka, by the late "medieval" period, and the formation of markets had advanced significantly. Merchants traveled among these markets, and between these central markets and the provinces, engaging in a lively trade. Land sales were transacted in cash, and financiers penetrated into the agricultural villages. The activities of merchants, artisans, and farmers—who were not subject to political power, even if there were still remnants of ancient rule—have been vividly described in recent studies. Regional towns emerged as centers of commercial and artisanal activity, in contrast to the essentially unipolar, aristocratic nature of the ancient capital of Kyoto. In that sense, the late medieval period saw the birth of the phenomenon of the "economization of society," though with some regional limitations.[8]

However, when we turn to look at places outside the economically developing Kinai region, we find many regions in which economic activities had not yet developed, but a new political system of territorial control was emerging, as outlined above. In other words, in late "medieval" Japan we see, on the one hand, the development of "economic society" in the central region, which was growing politically weaker, but where older forms of political control remained. On the other hand, in the peripheral regions, "economic society" had not yet formed, but new systems of political control and land proprietorship were developing, which were fundamentally different from the old *ritsuryô* (administrative) and *shôen* (estate) systems, and unrelated to the power of the Muromachi shogunate. The daimyos of the Warring States era who had eventually brought these regions under their control, then turned their attention to taking control of the Kinai region— where the capital city and symbol of state authority, Kyoto, was located and, moreover, where there was the highest concentration of people possessing monetary wealth.

In the midst of this estrangement between the world of the economy and the world of politics, we can find the gestation of the "early modern."

3. The World Historical Place of Tokugawa Japan

There are two methods of situating the history of a country within the broader context of world history. One is to do so by discussing the role played by that country at particular times in world history—its involvement in the wider world. Another is to discuss in comparative historical terms how that country might be placed within world history. These two methods are not completely unrelated and it may be that it is only in blending the two that we are able to draw a true historical image. But for the moment, I would like to deal with the two separately.

Kazui Tashiro relates the first perspective to Chapter 3 in this volume. Therefore, I will restate her argument here very simply. The traditional view is that Japan in the Tokugawa era was a closed country with its economy cut off from the world. In that vision, one speaks of trade in the period, at most, as the trade with Dutch and Chinese merchants, centered in Nagasaki. The standard textbook version is that the volume of this trade was not high and was rather more important as a conduit through which Western texts were acquired in small numbers, and through them, new techniques and ideas. However, as Tashiro suggests in her chapter, recent research has shown that trade during the era of supposed "seclusion" should not be underestimated: first, the trade was of such a volume as to have a significant economic impact; and second, the trade also had a qualitative effect on the economy. Tashiro, that is, gives us a positive assessment.[9]

If we expand our period to include the years just before and after the period of "seclusion" (1638–1858), we can see that Japan clearly played a particular role within the "world economy" that was just forming at the time. The sixteenth-century Portuguese poet Camões wrote in *Os Lusiadas* that Japan "produced good silver and received the light of God's law." In other words, while he praised Japan as a place that had been converted to Christianity, he also reminds us that by the latter half of the sixteenth century, the silver of Japan had already captured the mind of a Portuguese poet.[10] In fact, from the latter half of the sixteenth to the early seventeenth century, Japan was the largest silver producing country in Asia, with an output rivaling that of the mines of Spanish Mexico and Peru (Atwell 1977). Merchants in virtually every region of Asia—whether European, Japanese, Chinese, or others—carried large volumes of Japanese silver. Silver even became the goal of the European powers in their approach to Japan. Once the Dutch East India Company (VOC) began to use Japanese silver for payments in its Asian trade, especially in connection to its trade with Japan, there was no longer any need to send precious metals from Europe for use in Asia. It is important to note here, however, that Japan's silver exports were rarely destined for Europe, even when carried by European vessels; rather, they went to slake the insatiable thirst of China for silver, a demand that was the result of both Ming tax policies, and rapidly developing domestic market forces.

Similarly, Japanese copper production rose dramatically during the seventeenth century, and while much of this was incorporated into the domestic money supply as copper coins minted by the *bakufu*, vast quantities were exported as a trade commodity, in payment for import goods. Arai Hakuseki, a senior *bakufu* official in the early eighteenth century, estimated exports over the previous century at more than 1,500 tons annually. And, as John Hall has shown, imported Japanese copper was the mainstay of China's copper coinage in the early years of the Qing empire, only displaced by the development of mines in Yunnan late in the seventeenth century (Hall 1949: 444–61). This was the first time in history that Japan was an exporter of mineral resources in such large volume. When we further recognize that Japanese products came to be well known in foreign markets, not only in Asia, but as far away as Europe, we are left with no choice but drastically to re-examine the image of seclusion connoted by the term *sakoku*.

Of course, we must not be too quick to conclude that this export of mineral resources took place on the model of modern trade. As we can see in Chapter 3 by Tashiro, it would be more appropriate to call this "traffic" (*kôeki*) rather than "trade" (*bôeki*). Some of this traffic was conducted without a view toward economic profit, while other transactions were, in fact, part of "tribute" shipments sent to China (*chôkô*) from Korea. The regulations and prohibitions of political authorities took precedence over profit, and we have no lack of evidence of these laws and systems. But no matter what the system for exportation, once an export commodity had left Japan, it became completely independent of the will of Japanese rulers and began to circulate and be consumed as a financial asset. Likewise, once import items entered the country, they were exchanged on the market as economic property. It is in these areas that we can find a point of contact between Tokugawa Japan and world history.

As I stated before, silver performed an important function in the Asian market. But Nagasaki was not its only port of exit. The greater bulk of the silver flowed from Tsushima through Chosôn-dynasty Korea, or from Satsuma through the Ryûkyûan kingdom to be absorbed by China, the great consumer of silver. Some Japanese silver went to China as tribute from Korea and Ryûkyû and some went to China as an item for exchange in the trade that accompanied tribute missions. In other words, Japanese silver was an important medium in the formation of the tiny, fictive "tribute world" that Japan constructed during its period of "seclusion." At the same time, it functioned as an important factor in the formation of the real tribute world centered on China. We should also take this fact into account when we examine the later histories of Ryûkyûan and Korean struggle as they were caught between their powerful neighbors, China and Japan, during the period of modern Japan's formation.

From the Tokugawa period, silver was exported in the form of coins minted at the shogunate's mint. Keichô silver coins, which were 80 per cent pure and stamped with the mark "approved" were, of course, precious metals whose quality was guaranteed by the government. Recently, scholars have argued that these coins came to be exported as a kind of "commodity."[11]

The situation with copper was even more complicated. From the late Heian period (eleventh and twelfth centuries) through the Muromachi period, Japan did not mint any coins. But after the thirteenth century, Japan imported a huge volume of Chinese coins and copper cash minted by the Song, Yuan, and Ming. They minted a tremendous amount of copper currency, much of which then flowed out of the country through foreign trade. The volume of Chinese copper cash entering Japan was large enough to give rise to a currency-equivalency system known as the *kanmon* system. But by the seventeenth century, political instability in China, as well as the exhaustion of domestic supplies of copper, brought a halt to the production and export of coins. In fact, China slipped into a state of severe coin shortage. At the same time, Japan was experiencing a boom in the output of copper, and Japanese copper cash minted from the Kan'ei era (1634–44), as well as copper ingots, began to flow back to China. This situation continued until the discovery in the late seventeenth century of copper in Yunnan in China (Hall 1949).

The fact that the Kan'ei coins also circulated widely in southeast Asia means that we can say that the Tokugawa mints in the seventeenth century functioned not only to supply money for the domestic Japanese economy, but also as mints for east Asia as a whole. Indeed, the late Seiichi Iwao recalled that, as late as the 1930s, when he visited Bali with a colleague, more than half the cash he received from a money changer in the local market was Japanese Kan'ei coinage.[12] But so long as we are unable to determine the volume that left the country or the ratio used in foreign markets, we risk overestimating its importance. Furthermore, as Tashiro observes in Chapter 3, the flow of silver reversed after the mid-eighteenth century from a net outflow to net inflow. Moreover, we should note that as Japanese copper-mining became increasingly unable to supply both domestic currency needs and export demand, Japanese marine products, such as kelp and dried sea-cucumber—highly prized in China and in overseas Chinese communities throughout southeast Asia—came to displace copper as an export item in the eighteenth century.

However, it is also true that Japanese copper played an important role in the Amsterdam market up to the first quarter of the eighteenth century. An important reason for this was that Sweden, a copper producing country, had adopted the copper standard around that time. As Swedish influence extended to the south, the Netherlands strategically used Japanese copper imported by the Dutch East India Company to manipulate prices in Amsterdam, Europe's central market. Japanese minerals thus functioned as a global commodity for a time, affecting markets half a world away. Viewed in this light, there is no way that we can say that Japan was a "closed country" or that its economy was completely cut off from the outside world.

At the same time, we should recognize that by pre-industrial standards Japan had one of the world's largest mining industries, and that the development of this industry in Japan was largely spurred by exports. Japan was an exporter of raw materials—primarily precious metals—and thus it is not surprising that Europeans, in their passion for ever greater supplies, went to great lengths to gain access to Japan and its resources. But Europe was separated from Japan by a great distance requiring a long and dangerous ocean passage; distance, therefore, was one important reason why Japan was able to avoid the direct European control experienced by other places that were closer to Europe.

Nevertheless, for better or worse, the image of Japan as Marco Polo's "island of gold and silver" faded during the seventeenth century. As precious metal resources dried up and Japan lost export power, the Europeans, who still sought precious metals, suddenly saw Japan as a country of little economic attractiveness. In the eighteenth century, international activity directed toward Japan fell to a meager level. As trade with Europe through the VOC (the Dutch East India Company) declined in value and economic significance, the meaning of Europe came to be limited largely to matters of culture and technology. Both directly through the VOC and through Chinese translations, Japan learned of European culture and scholarship, while in Europe, Japanese items such as porcelain became objects of curiosity. But the economic relationship declined to utter insignificance. Largely because of this, Tokugawa Japan was able to

continue the slumber of the "great peace," and to discount the significance of European developments to its own future.

Japan's principal imports, prior to the Tokugawa period, were Chinese
copper cash, guns and cotton, silk yarn and fabrics, and medicines. Cash,
in particular, played such a major role that it transformed the Japanese
economy. Guns not only changed warfare; they also made possible the
separation of warrior and farmer, which was one of the defining socio-
political characteristics of Tokugawa Japan. As the domestic production of
cotton spread in the Edo period, it spawned major industrial changes, on
the one hand, while precipitating a kind of clothing revolution, transforming the clothing customs of the masses.[13] The superior absorbency
and durability of this material undoubtedly had a positive effect on the
health of those who wore it.

But comprised mostly of Japanese imports in the early modern period
were Chinese raw silk and silk textiles. Raw silk in particular played an
important role as the raw material used in the silk textile industry of
Kyoto's Nishijin district. So large was the trade in raw silk that it gave rise
to an organization of silk merchants in Nagasaki, the *itowappu*, whose primary goal was to set prices. Until domestic Japanese silk production
improved in quality and quantity in the mid-eighteenth century, the high-
quality silk textile industry of Nishijin relied almost entirely on imported
raw silk for the majority of its raw materials.

The pattern of Japanese trade throughout the seventeenth century
involved exchanging silver, as the main export item, for raw and woven
silk as the main import goods—though of course there were other significant import and export commodities. In world historical terms, the Silk
Road extending to the West from China had a counterpart in another silk
road, perhaps equally appropriately called a "silver road," extending to
the East, linking Japan and China. Though the immediate trading partners varied—Chinese and Dutch merchants traded in Nagasaki; Japanese
merchants traded in Pusan (Korea) and Naha (Ryûkyû)—Chinese silk
remained the dominant Japanese import and, until quite late in the
century, Japanese silk the major importing item.

The later decline in trade was due to at least two factors: Japan's silver
sources were depleted, while domestic demand increased, leading to a
rapid loss of any remaining export power. As silver became unavailable,
copper and marine products became Japan's main export items. But
these were a mere shadow of the former exports, so the volume of imports
also fell. The merchant population of Nagasaki fell rapidly, eventually
dropping from its peak in the early eighteenth century to a mere 40 per
cent of that just prior to the opening of ports near the end of the
Tokugawa period. This, too, was a result of the decline in trade.[14] The situation in Tsushima, whose economy was almost totally dependent on
trade with Korea, was similarly grave; consequently, the search for ways

to compensate for the declining volume of trade was a major preoccupation of the domain (Tashiro 1986).

But there is also a fascinating link between foreign relations and domestic history in this change in the volume of trade. As intellectuals of the time well knew, the massive volume of silver outflows caused deficiencies in the domestic circulation of currency, and hence became an obstacle to the lively economic activities of the time. One response to this condition was the devaluation of silver currency in the Genroku and Hôei eras (1688–1711) carried out by Ogiwara Shigehide, the Shogun's Finance Magistrate. The 1711 issue of Yotsu-Hôgin coins, at 20 per cent purity, marked the lowest-grade silver coins of the Tokugawa period. If we compare these to the 80 per cent quality coins prior to the devaluation of 1695, we can see just how far they had been devalued. These policies increased the nominal money supply—the face value of coins in circulation—but also brought on rising prices, and resulted in policies in the daimyo domains based on the theory of monetary supply. On the other hand, it brought into play Gresham's law that "bad money drives out good"; namely, that devalued currency eliminates good currency from circulation. Economic thinkers of the time, like Miura Baien, recognized this principle, stimulating the birth in eighteenth-century Japan of economics as an empirical science (Nishikawa 1979: 94–113).

In fact, the situation was even graver, for most domains found themselves forced to issue domain scrip, which scholars today call *hansatsu*. This scrip served as local currencies, or domainal notes, in order to make up for currency shortages within the domains. But the *hansatsu* were paper currency, with no intrinsic value, whose exchange value was fixed by the decision of the political authorities, so they can be considered a form of "fiat money." At the same time, of course, *hansatsu* did not circulate at the value set by the domains issuing them, and some of them caused a severe degradation in prices.[15] However, whether we call them low-quality paper currency or domain currency, is it not likely that the social accumulation of experience with these currencies during the Tokugawa period meant a great deal to the Meiji government in its early crisis period? Lacking gold and silver reserves, the early Meiji government was prepared by the currency experiences of the Tokugawa era to issue bank notes and have them circulate at face value.

Another area in which the decline in trade had an impact on domestic history was the production of silk. The demand for good quality domestic raw silk rose in the middle of the Tokugawa period as import volumes declined. As a result, the production of good quality raw silk began in every region. Once consumption habits were formed through imports, the decline in import volume led to a rise in demand for domestically produced materials in order to maintain the accustomed quality and quantity. The development of high-quality domestic silk production was extremely important because, when the ports were opened near the end of the Tokugawa period, raw silk was perhaps the only commodity Japan possessed that could compete on the international market; it was Japan's principal foreign-exchange earner from the opening of the ports in 1859 to the start of the Pacific War in 1941.

The above discussion should make it clear that one cannot simply treat Japan during its era of so-called "seclusion" as entirely separate from the rest of the world in economic historical terms. Of course, it is risky to overestimate Japan's international economic links, but Tokugawa Japan was quite firmly situated within the world economy that was formed in the sixteenth century, and continued to be affected by its involvement in international trade throughout the era.

4. The Comparative Historical Investigation of Tokugawa Japan

In this section, I will compare Tokugawa Japan with European feudal society and look for points of comparability and contrast in a comparative historical methodology.

On occasion, Tokugawa Japan is unreflectively called a "feudal society." *Hôken*, the term now used for "feudal"/"feudalism," was originally an ancient Chinese term designating those regions in which governance of the land was left to the great families of the region, in explicit contrast to *gunken* ("prefectures and counties"), a term that referred to territory under the direct rule of the central government. The word was grafted into Japanese history by the popular historian of the late Edo period, Rai San'yô (1780–1832), who argued that with the establishment of the Kamakura shogunate, Japan entered an era of *hôken* polity.[16] No matter how one looks at it, Rai's use of this term was a mistake. But Rai's work, *Nihon Gaishi* (An Unauthorized History of Japan), had a tremendous impact on the Japanese intelligentsia with its elegant prose and its periodization of Japanese history; with Rai giving these periods their names. In the Meiji period, the entry of European scholarship gave rise to the problem of translation. Meiji-era intellectuals, eagerly translating the scholarship of contemporary Europe into Japanese, used the term *hôkensei* (*hôken* system) to render into Japanese the European historical term "feudalism," and the word that had once been mistakenly used by Rai San'yô now had additional meanings added to it.

What set the confusion firmly in place was the belief of many postwar historians that history evolves along a more or less fixed path from ancient slave systems, to feudalism, to absolute monarchy, to bourgeois revolution, and then to modern capitalism society. Despite the fact that this kind of historical development can be found nowhere in the world, historians had come to embrace the fiction that this was the universal principle of world history. For example, European feudalism as established by the Carolingian Franks had not developed out of an ancient slave system, whereas regions with ancient slave systems—such as those of the near- and middle-east—had not developed feudalism. As for history after the establishment of feudalism, there is a subtle problem as to whether or not a modern society can develop only after the experience of a bourgeois revolution. In my view, bourgeois revolutions did not end with the English Revolution of the seventeenth century and the French Revolution of the eighteenth century. Those political transformations should be understood as the beginnings of a series of changes that still continue.

Reviewing European history once more in this light, we can see that feudalism was born and cultivated, and came to an end, under historically unique conditions. Its birth came from the contact between the simple and clannish Teutonic society and the highly developed, more advanced Roman civilization with its provincial system and universalist religion (Masuda 1959).[17] In terms of the economy, the Mediterranean was dominated by people of another religion, Islam, who European Christians felt would not be received into Heaven. Because of the struggle between Islam and Christianity, a great economic depression ensued in which long-distance trade stagnated, commercial activities declined, cities disintegrated, and highly-valued metal currency ceased circulating.[18] In this kind of society, land was the only asset and a self-sufficient economy was the starting point of everything. Feudalism was a form of social, political, and economic organization that emerged in response to these unique local conditions. Consequently, the linkage between land and people, whether at the level of the lord or the level of the farmer, was extremely strong. The lord granted land to his vassals and expected loyalty in return. The lord himself lived on his land, supplying all his own needs from his fief, which he operated by exploiting the labor of his villains. For that reason, the lord forbade his peasants from leaving the fief.

The peasants lived on the land and in return for cultivating their lord's lands through weekly corvée labor or by performing a variety of other functions, they were allowed to cultivate their own land and raise their families. The tying of the peasants to the land, coupled with various other restrictions on their rights, placed them in the status of the unfree and segregated them apart from those of free status. Feudalism, that is, was premised upon maximizing economic activity during extreme stagnation. It has even led some to describe it as something that appeared as a necessary evil.[19]

What brought change to this condition was economic activity. The lords who possessed the power of political rule took yearly taxes from the unfree peasants by whatever means possible. But the gap between the lords and the peasant class was not as great as that between rulers and slaves in ancient society. In other words, medieval European social relations were unlike the relationship between rulers and slaves in ancient societies, where the former were endowed with full rights and the latter with none, and the rulers did not concern themselves about the lives and reproduction of the producers. The relationship of lords and peasants in European feudalism presumed their equal humanity before the Christian God both worshipped, while the feudal aristocracy took strength from the support of the Church.

The decisive difference was the fact that their rule was founded upon a certain limitation. In ancient society, the rulers were all-mighty, wielding absolute power in both the sacred and mundane worlds. The physical vestiges of this kind of society, represented in the pyramids or the engineering marvels of Rome, in their overwhelming size, and in the scale of labor required to build them, today challenge our imagination and cause us to wonder what motivated the construction of such massive monuments. In comparison, the architectural remains of medieval Europe, while they may be exquisite, are markedly smaller in scale than their archaic predecessors. This is because there was a division of power between the sacred and mundane worlds in medieval times. Moreover, the political rulers of the mundane world may have dominated the political world, but they were, in a sense, economically neutral; that is, purely economic activities were left to peasants, merchants, and artisans. Consequently, medieval cities were generally located at diocesan seats, or in sites where merchants and artisans gathered. These latter types of cities came to be known to history as "free cities" which were independent of the political control of feudal lords.

One further special characteristic of feudalism was the class system in its vulgar side with the king at the top, the nobles and their vassals, and the peasantry below them. The exchange of loyal service and protection, rights and obligations, took place only within a limited range, between those classes close to each other in the system. In other words, it was limited to the range of personal relationships. The huge gap that existed in ancient rule simply did not exist. This explains the relative weakness of rule in feudal society. Ancient society survived for thousands of years, even though there were changes in dynasties, and even in ruling institutions.

Feudal society necessarily crumbled after several hundred years. Moreover, the collapse was not due to an outside force, but came about because of the interior accumulation of economic and political contradictions. Governing power was relatively weak, so the classes that depended on economic activities, which accumulated wealth and then further developed their activities, eventually noticed that they would be unable to achieve their own goals under the existing system. With that, they sought a social transformation and, under political leaders who responded to this appeal, feudalism was negated. In other words, feudalism had its life cut short by a demon that its own existence made possible. Its very existence contained within it a contradiction that eventually manifested itself in the formation of a new society.

In this sense, feudal society was not at all a stagnant society. At the time of its formation, it was a society in which economic activity was immobile. But when the opportunity arose, it was a society that possessed a dynamic power that revived economic activity, and this economic activity eventually overturned society at its very foundations. This was because feudal society was divided both horizontally and vertically. When the majority of people who composed its members were given the opportunity to participate in economic activity, the result was the accumulation of economic power, that is, wealth.

The debate over whether the feudal society of the kind that Europe experienced historically—or perhaps the concept of feudalism—was universal to world history goes back at least to Montesquieu and Voltaire. But as the histories of most regions of the world become clearer today, European feudalism appears not to have been a stage in world history, but an experience unique to Europe. To put it in terms of global scale, feudalism had a unique existence at the far western edge of the Eurasian continent from the eighth to the fifteenth or sixteenth centuries. It was particular, and historically contingent, and did not occur everywhere.

The usual periodization for Japanese history locates the beginning of "feudalism" in the Kamakura period (1185–1333) yet even then the ancient state and the *shôen* system continued to define the framework of society. The Kamakura period did not see the development of a new political system that completely negated the old system and covered the entire territory of Japan. It is far too superficial to see the birth of warrior power as marking the establishment of feudalism in Japan.

I myself believe that if we are to look for a period in Japanese history that resembles European feudalism, the era of civil war in the fifteenth and sixteenth centuries is the best candidate. Above all else, this was an era in which the great daimyo families ruled substantial territorial domains which they themselves called *kokka*, the modern Japanese term for "state"; contemporary Europeans called the daimyos "kings," and their domains, "kingdoms," in which the lordship system was strongly tied to the land. With the military and agricultural classes not yet separated, there was at least a class system of lord, vassal, and farmer, and relations of loyalty and service, protection, and servitude were formed. Economic activity could not be called vibrant, save in one region (the Kinai), and while currency circulated, coins were not minted domestically, their supply was unstable, and it was easy for exchange activities to be conducted as barter in the goods themselves.[20] But this era of civil war lasted no more than 100 years, without ever being able to produce a stable society.

In contrast, the Edo period (1603–1868) differs from European feudalism in a number of fundamental respects; and in any case, it endured for 270 years. First of all, the lord's tie to the land weakened, and in principle, he could be transferred or dispossessed at any time by shogunate fiat. In

fact, transfers and attainders were quite common for the first century of
Tokugawa rule. There was no thought of direct daimyo management of
the land as was the case with medieval European manorial lords. With
very few exceptions, vassals were gathered into the cities through the
policy of the separation of warriors and farmers, so that only a tiny number
of warriors lived in the villages. In the beginning, there were cases where
daimyo vassals were given fiefs in the form of administrative authority
over a particular piece of territory within the larger domain.

But over time those became solely titular, changing into a retainer's
salary, expressed in terms of volumes of tax rice (*koku*). In other words, for
both daimyo and vassal, the domain was something that they happened to
hold for a time. Daimyos came to speak of themselves as holding their
domains as "fiduciaries," entrusted with them by the Shogun. They did
not live in a specific place in which they had deep-rooted baronial rights.
It is important to note that this was recognized by the lords of the time and
that they were no more than the "military constable of the moment."[21]

As Iwahashi shows in Chapter 2 in this volume, the *kokudaka* system was
the indispensable prerequisite condition that made possible the existence
of baronial rights of the character described above. It is the *kokudaka* system
that holds the key to the differentiating between the daimyo system of
Tokugawa Japan from the European feudal system (Wakita 1975: 297–320).
It was Hideyoshi's national land survey (*taikô kenchi*) that brought the
kokudaka system into being; thus, we must recognize the significance of the
land survey as the instrument that made possible formation of a new
system in Japan that differed from European feudalism.

Through the *kokudaka* system, the domains of the daimyo and their
vassals could be expressed in quantitative terms, as lands assessed as
having the capacity for a specific annual level of production, and hence, of
taxation. That meant that domains need not be expressed as unchanging
and particular territories, and that they were commensurable to a unified
standard. For that very reason, there was very little resistance from the
daimyo when, in the aftermath of the Meiji Restoration, the new government converted their baronial rights into public bonds. This fact by itself
reveals that Tokugawa Japan was decisively different in character from
feudal European society. This is also supported by the fact that in Europe
the abolition of feudal barons' rights had to be carried out through a social
revolution that meant the spilling of a tremendous amount of blood.[22]

The structure of society in Tokugawa Japan was also systematically
premised on the development of a certain level of money economy. That
is precisely why the shogunate, from its inception, established and simultaneously began the minting of gold, silver, and copper coins. A portion
of yearly taxes was paid in cash, and over half the tax paid in rice was converted into cash. Once converted into cash it was used to purchase necessary goods. With that in mind, we may see that the common description
of Tokugawa Japan as "a rice economy" cannot be taken literally.

Moreover, apart from the intentions of the shogunate and the various domains, socioeconomic conditions in Tokugawa Japan were ripe for the development of a money economy. The policies of legally mandating the separation of farmers and warriors, both constructing castle towns as administrative centers, and requiring samurai to relocate to the castle town—of which Edo was the largest—in effect stimulated the growth of urban populations with massive purchasing power in the form of money. Until then, the formation of true cities had been largely restricted to the plains of the Kinai region, where they had grown only to a limited scale. But now numerous cities formed rapidly across the country, on a scale roughly commensurate with the economic size of the domain as measured in *kokudaka*.

But urbanization was not limited to the castle towns. The lively economic activity generated regional market towns, post towns, and ports, which were established in a variety of forms. This was the first time in Japanese history that such rapid urbanization had taken place and naturally it had a major impact on surrounding areas. In fact, seventeenth-century Japan may have experienced the most remarkable spurt of urban growth anywhere in the preindustrial world: By 1700, there were five cities of 100,000 to 1,000,000 inhabitants, and literally dozens with populations of 5,000–10,000,[23] and about 15 per cent of total population dwelt at the urban sites.

Furthermore, the system of alternate attendance (*sankin kôtai*), which required all daimyos to divide their time between their domains and Edo, and to maintain lavish residences and retinues in the city, within a century made Edo into an enormous city of one million.[24] Osaka developed as the hub of the national distribution system, the city that provided consumer goods to the residents of Edo, inevitably involving it in the circulation of goods from across the entire country, as well as import goods from abroad. This transformation was unprecedented in Japanese—and world—history and, the extent of its impact cannot be overemphasized. No matter how low the standard of living, the necessary daily goods consumed by a population of one million—the food, fuel, clothing, building materials, and so on—alone reached a substantial volume. Osaka, too, which functioned as the market center, and the base for provisioning Edo, grew to have a population exceeding 400,000.[25]

What was different in the process of urbanization in European Countries is that in Europe, most cities were based on economic activities, and became autonomous, self-governing entities developing outside the framework of baronial control. In Tokugawa Japan, on the other hand, the moment of urban formation was creation of the castle town, which was created by fiat, in the first instance, with greatest weight placed on the strategic and administrative interests of daimyo rule. Castle towns therefore, of course, were never by self-governance under the authority of the commoner (merchant and artisan) elite, as had been the case in cities like Florence or Venice. This issue has long been emphasized in scholarly debate, and has often been linked with the issue of differences in modernization between Japan and Europe, focusing especially on the question of whether or not there was a "citizenry" or "bourgeoisie."

But recent research suggests that the medieval European cities that were free from the feudal baronial system or were self-governing did not necessarily grant modern freedoms to their residents. Now, to the contrary, recent scholarship on medieval European cities points to the existence of urban aristocratic rule, or the existence of a class with special rights within the city.[26] Moreover, these cities declined briefly at the beginning of the early modern period and so cannot be said to be directly tied to the modern city (Gutmann 1986: 21–56). Further, in functional analyses of the cities, as we can see in the urban class system, the question of what conditions made their formation possible is a secondary issue. Instead, the focus in most studies is on the class composition and distribution of the urban population.

Whatever the case for European cities, Tokugawa Japan experienced urbanization without a precedent in history. This urbanization was based on the fact that Tokugawa Japan systemically made possible large concentrations of consumer populations. This could not help but have the effect of fostering the development of a market economy. The great demand stimulated the growth of agricultural villages and the production of daily necessities. And this, in turn, swept commodities, money, and people into a whirlpool of circulation.[27] On the surface, strictly as legal fiction, farmers were pressed to produce only for taxes (*nengu*) and their own subsistence, and were forbidden from leaving the land, but in reality these laws were completely ineffective. There is a great difference between investigating Tokugawa society through the laws and investigating its actual practices. Once we acknowledge that it was a society founded upon these kinds of economic activities we can see how different Tokugawa Japan and European feudal society actually were.

But does this mean that Tokugawa Japan and feudal Europe were absolutely different, that there were no common points whatsoever? Not at all. Tokugawa Japan resembled Western Europe in a number of ways. The similarities are found in those common points that industrialization was achieved relatively smoothly when founded on the principles of a market economy.

First of all, we must point out that both Europe and Japan were societies with a division of power. Both societies could be characterized as having a separation between the sacred and the profane, and between the political and the economic. Of course, this does not mean that the daimyo had no economic impact at all. Furthermore, both the mercantilist European countries and the Edo shogunate interacted with the economic world through such practices as the regulation of trade and prices, the minting of currency, or the granting of special rights to merchants. At times, these states even acted as economic subjects.

The European system of agrarian lordship (*Grundherrschaft*) and the domainal monopolies—daimyo domains that controlled the marketing of products in which they had a strong comparative advantage (see Shunsaku Nishikawa and Masatoshi Amano Chapter 8, this volume)—in Japan were both examples of this. But despite those examples, economic activities were essentially relegated to those outside the ruling class. In both Japan and Europe merchants handled the lords' finances; at times both European lords and Japanese samurai even went bankrupt. For example, the Fugger family handled the finances of the proud and politically powerful Hapsburg dynasty and feudal lords, in the same way that the finances of every daimyô and *hatamoto* (shogunal bannermen) were absorbed by merchants in Tokugawa Japan.

In other words, the lordly class was organizationally unable to manage its domains, or the country, by themselves. Such phrases as "a samurai will flourish a toothpick even when he hasn't eaten," and "samurai don't count coins" reveal the conventional wisdom of the Edo period that samurai were lacking in economic sense. The ruling class in Europe likewise lived extravagantly as lavish consumers, giving little thought to meeting their expenses except through taxes and loans from merchants. These are but a few indicators of the division between political rule and economic activities in both societies.

We can also find common points in the process of urbanization. Western Europe and Japan possessed similar patterns in the scale and the population distribution of cities just prior to industrialization (de Vries 1984: 262). The urban hierarchy was not top-heavy. Rather, small and middle-sized regional cities were highly developed. It goes without saying that cities were nodes in the flow of goods and the networks of information. The pattern of their distribution shows that urban economic activities were vital across the country and, moreover, developed in a bottom-up pattern. This also shows the possible existence of inter urban networks and a single economic system.[28] Much remains to be seen as to the particulars, while the process of industrialization in Western Europe and Japan may have differed in a number of ways, their common pattern of urbanization may prove the key to the fact that both achieved industrialization on the pivot of a market economy.

We can also find common points in the experience of demographic change in Europe and Japan. The national population of the Edo period over the long run was characterized by rapid growth in the seventeenth century, followed by stagnation in the eighteenth century and a slow revival of growth upon entering the nineteenth century. However, there are significant regional differences, but the population of Western Europe also grew in the sixteenth century, declined in the seventeenth and grew again in the eighteenth century, all one century earlier than Japan, but on the same pattern.[29] In other words, the populations of both Europe and Japan changed in ways that stimulated the economic change. If the rate of increase is too high for a preindustrial society, the population becomes a kind of pressure that weighs upon the standard of living. On the other hand, if the rate of increase is zero, the population will not serve as a stimulus to economic development. The population changes in Japan and Europe were in neither category, so I view them as "appropriate."

What are most important in these situations are the conditions of population change just prior to industrialization. Whether the population grows so much that it puts pressure on the standard of living, or whether it is linked with resources and employment to create new demands, the implications are entirely different. The latter was the case in western Europe, excepting Ireland. In England in particular, the population increase acted as a magnet to raise the price of wheat, which in turn served as a stimulus to the development of new, highly productive forms of agriculture (Umemura 1969: 138). This is a sure sign that the population increase was "appropriate."

The relation between the population and the economy must be considered in both directions, but Ester Boserup's famous theory—that population growth can in itself be a resource for economic development—is not applicable in all cases (Boserup 1965). We must not overlook the fact that Boserup's theory is only valid for cases in which the rate of population growth is appropriate and population density is not too high. But in both western Europe and Japan, the rate of population growth just prior to industrialization was mild. That the rate of population growth rose rapidly after industrialization began, is a good example of the way that population growth can contain an element that propels industrialization.

A contrasting example may be found in China. Prior to industrialization the population of China quadrupled over a span of 300 years.[30] Again, the population of Ireland grew at the highest rate of any European country from the beginning of the eighteenth century, until the great population decline in the middle of the nineteenth century (the "potato famine"). Although both countries experienced population growth, they were quite slow to industrialize.[31]

However, the problem of population must also be viewed in connection with customs concerning the age at marriage and practices of inheritance. It is too simplistic merely to link the speed of population growth with industrialization. In western Europe, it was common for children to live independently from their parents once they married. But such was not necessarily the case in Japan. Consequently, in Europe the economic environment was linked to population growth or decline through the age at marriage. In Japan, no matter what the economic environment may have been, the child who was expected to succeed to the family headship would have been married. So the link between the economy and the age at marriage was weak.[32]

But the following appears to be true. In Europe, especially on the continent, the unit of agricultural production was the peasant, as it was in Japan, and the peasant made operational decisions. Of course, in both places, the peasant would have to obey a variety of rules. In Western Europe, agriculture under village community regulations went from free three-field law to regulated three-field law, thus becoming more restrictive.[33] In Japan, by contrast, the need to use water as a common good for irrigation meant that the village community came to dominate over the productive decisions of individual households. However, small peasant households in both areas, composed of the lineal family members, supported themselves either on their earnings from agriculture or on earnings from non-agricultural activities.

But in Japan, the amount of arable land was small compared to the population. After the seventeenth-century boom in land development came to an end, the only way remaining to increase production was by focusing on how to maximize the output from any given parcel of land. Methods for solving this problem included increasing the frequency of cultivation of a parcel of land (double- and triple-cropping), utilizing the vertical dimension of farmland through deep plowing, and heavy utilization of fertilizers. All of these made heavy demands on the labor of farmers. Family labor proved the most effective way to respond flexibly to this demand. This was because indentured or hereditarily bound labor, was unsuited to the heavy, intensive, and strenuous labor demands this type of agriculture entailed. Wage labor, on the other hand, was hard to match to the seasonal character of agricultural work. Therefore, from an operational perspective, the family was the most appropriate labor unit. Thus, the unfree labor of hereditarily bound servants (*fudai* and *genin*) that existed up to the early Edo period was gradually replaced by the labor of the family and wage laborers.[34]

Now, it is important to note that this backbreaking labor became the basis of a work ethic. A comparison of data from the area around Nagoya for the late seventeenth and early nineteenth centuries shows use of domestic animals in farming declined so severely on the plains of central Japan that they virtually disappeared.[35] Yet production does not appear to have fallen during this period, so the labor formerly performed by domestic animals must now have been performed by humans. That is, there was a shift from horsepower to manpower! Behind this shift lies the most significant economic experience of the Tokugawa period.

Difficult, time-consuming labor was morally configured as "industriousness" and an ethos everyone was called upon to respect. People expected that industriousness would result in a rise in their material standard of living. In general, peasants at the beginning of the early modern period saw their lives improve from a state in which they used a variety of fibers to make clothing that could not stand up to washing, ate a variety of grains and lived on mats spread on dirt floors, to a state in which their clothing changed to cotton, and even occasionally silk, rice was the main grain they consumed, and they lived on raised floors. The average life expectancy also extended five to ten years, even before the arrival of modern medicine and knowledge of hygiene, to approximately forty years of age.

Moreover, literacy rates rose to surprising levels: Before the introduction of a modern school system, more than 50 per cent of adult males in late Tokugawa Japan could read and write.[36] Perhaps the most significant reason why this ethos of industriousness became so firmly entrenched in daily life, without the sort of religious sanction that Weber argued in *The Protestant Ethic*, was that people's rising expectations—for an improved standard of living—were satisfied to a certain extent. Demanding work was the price they paid for becoming independent and being able to act as economic subjects.

In any case, the "Industrial Revolution" emerged in an island country off the western coast of the Eurasian continent, entailing a reduction in labor and intensive use of capital. Off the continent's eastern coast, there was an "industrious revolution," in which the society sought to increase production through greater investments of labor.

5. Agrarian Taxes in Tokugawa Japan

During the Edo period, the greatest flow of goods and money was found in the movement of annual agricultural taxes (*nengu*). The act of collecting taxes is by its very nature of a noneconomic character—the ruling class forcibly expropriating from the ruled classes. Therefore, to the extent that this activity was the source of the movement of goods and currency in society, the society could not be said to have been modern. There were many ways in which Tokugawa Japan was an era that paved the way for modernity, but on this point it was decidedly not "modern." But when we observe the qualitative relationship between politics and the economy in that society, we see that taxes were extremely important. Therefore, I would like to say a little about the character of yearly taxes in Tokugawa Japan.[37]

Taxes in the Edo period were collected through the channel of the *kokudaka* system that was made possible by Toyotomi Hideyoshi's land survey edicts. They were not simply for the private consumption of the daimyo, however, but were also used for administrative expenses, which meant that a portion of the taxes returned to the people who bore the burden of payment. The lord had to conduct a variety of public works (*gofushinsho*)— including not only his own residences, but highways and riparian works, out of his own revenue. He also had to maintain the peace in his domain, prevent crime, and pay for punishments, all out of his own revenue base. Furthermore, he was charged with maintaining the stability of his domain through such measures as the granting of relief, and rewarding meritorious or virtuous conduct. Thus, while he was the lord of his domain, he was at the same time its chief administrator.

If he failed in his administration, he could be dismissed by the Shogun—as Ikeda Mitsumasa observed in the 1650s, "the Shogun receives his authority from heaven; the daimyo receives authority over the people as a trust from the Shogun"[38] and, consequently, "if we govern carelessly, so that there are people [in the domain] who are starving and cold, or so that parts of the province are depopulated, then we shall not escape confiscation of the domain by His Majesty" (Ishii et al. 1959: 265).

Thus the taxes the lord collected had the dual character of private rent and tax. When the Meiji government "revised" the land tax in the 1870s, it negated this dual character and made the relationship between the state and the taxpayer one-dimensional. The "rent" portion segregated as part of the relationship between the landowner and the tenant, which was clarified through the right to own land. The importance of the shift was in its qualitative meaning.

As Masaru Iwahashi shows in Chapter 2, Edo period taxes may superficially have been intended to expropriate the entire surplus from the producing classes, but the lords were never able to do so. In the first place, the *kokudaka* system was predicated on the assumption that the productivity of the land was unchanging over a long period of time, and in fact, for anyone working from a familiarity with agriculture in the preceding centuries, that assumption would not have seemed off the mark. Making certain assumptions—entirely reasonable to someone setting policy in the early seventeenth century—it was perfectly logical to conduct a baseline land survey land that established long-term productivity, and then set taxes on the basis of short-term changes in production through spot inspections. That "certain assumption" was that productivity was stable.

But in fact, the productivity of land (on an output/area basis) rose throughout the country, due to increases in the utilization rates for land, the use of fertilizers, deep plowing, and the increasingly intensive level of labor inputs. The problem was who would get to keep the increased portion. This was a quiet struggle, but it was the greatest struggle of the Edo period. Would the lords, the farmers who produced it, the merchants, or other farmers who were third parties to production, take the increase? Different answers could result in very different social structures. The ultimate result was that the lords entirely dropped out of the struggle, so that the increase reverted to the farmers and the merchants.

In order for the lords to win, they would have had to repeatedly perform land surveys, accurately grasp the increasing productivity of the land, and adjust the tax burden accordingly. But the social status order of the daimyo class was determined by the *kokudaka* system and so long as the maintenance of the original methods was seen as the primary condition for the survival of the *Pax Tokugawa*, continual reinspection of land was impossible. The tax rate was unable to keep up with the rise in productivity so that the portion received by the lords suffered a relative decline. The ratios of "50:50 between lord and people," or even "60:40 between lord and people," commonly heard phrases, were in the end, public fictions. Research shows that by the end of the Tokugawa period the tax burden had fallen, as Miyamoto will point out later in this volume, below one-third of the entire income of the peasants.[39]

It should be no surprise that the resulting structural problems meant that the finances of most daimyos were chronically in the red.[40] By the middle of the Edo period, the daimyo class had given up on expropriating the increases in production through the land tax, and turned to a periodic fixed payment system (*jômen*) in which taxes were set over a five-, ten-, or twenty-year-period. But even in this system, as long as no new land surveys were performed, the original *kokudaka* assessment remained unchanged, and if the tax rate remained the same, the tax burden remained unchanged.

It is difficult to understand why the shogunate would create a system that would bind it like this, and why the various domains would continue to employ it. One possible interpretation is that the existing methods for surveying and inspecting land made the costs of collecting taxes too high. It is also possible that this was to guard against any instability in the tax income. Occasionally it is said that the early eighteenth-century Kyôhô reforms that put the fixed payment system into place were a policy aimed at increasing tax collection. This is an interpretation of short-term effects, but it is not accurate with regard to the long-term effects. Rather, in the long term it appears to have been a trade-off between an increase in the yearly taxes for stable acquisition.

From the perspective of the taxpayers, the fixed-payment system may have meant an increase in the tax burden at first, but with the tax amount fixed, they could expect to keep any increases in production resulting from their own efforts. Therefore, the result was that the fixed-payment system became a positive stimulus to increase and improve productivity, and thus to increase earnings. It also led to the birth of a class whose *raison d'être* was to acquire this increased portion and use it to engage in economic activities. This was the very class whose appearance was necessary for the development of a market economy.

In sum, taxes in the Edo period were such that the amount to be borne by the producers was fixed and any production beyond that amount was theirs to keep, creating a sense of vested interest on the part of the peasantry. Peasant uprisings therefore were not so much about the levying of taxes, *per se*, but were more often about tax increases or new taxes that threatened their vested interests.[41] Furthermore, with certain limited exceptions, taxes were not regularly levied on commerce or industry, nor were there any taxes comparable to today's income and inheritance taxes. Therefore, we simply cannot say that the peasants were crushed by a burden of heavy taxes.

Taxes in Tokugawa Japan were based on the principle of establishing a fixed level of production and levying taxes on that. This system of taxation was not simply a matter of the lords' compassion, but also of the difficulty of increasing the amount collected.

Taxes could be levied on the peasants in two main ways. The lord could leave the peasants with a fixed amount and take the rest, or the lord could take a fixed amount as the yearly tax. While the lords would have preferred the former, in reality it was the latter method that prevailed. In a society with dispersed power, taxes could only be levied in such a manner. The former method was possible in a society in which taxes were easily collected because the rulers' power was invincible and the peasants had no room for resistance. But Tokugawa Japan was not that kind of society.

Even so, while the tax burden on producers was fixed, it did not lead directly to the accumulation of surplus. Its underlying potential was manifested when the tax system functioned as a stimulant to production, generating increased output; at that point, the question became who would get to keep the new surplus. The tax levy on newly opened fields was relatively low in order to encourage the development of new fields, both by keeping *kokudaka* assessment low at inspection time, and by taxing *shinden* at a lower rate. Moreover, since levying taxes on the non-agricultural activities of peasants would amount to official recognition of those activities, the peasants were not taxed on that portion of their income. Thus, the lords gave up on taxing new increases in production or income and settled for the expectation of stable tax income from the villages.

One can find in this a common thread between western Europe and Tokugawa Japan. In early feudal Europe, the tax rate was so high that it probably left no surplus for the peasants. In extreme cases, the ratio of sown seeds to harvested grain was as low as one to two, so that as much as one-third of the land had to be given over to the production of seed for the next year's planting.[42] However, weekly labor in the lord's fields was the centerpiece of the tax system, while the land tax was levied under principles agreed upon by both lord and peasant, at a fixed amount, or in special cases at a fixed rate. If given the opportunity, the peasants could increase production and make the fruit of that increase their own.

By focusing on these points of similarity, it may be possible to find a single phrase to describe the societies of both western Europe and Tokugawa Japan, but the overused and problematic "feudal" will not fill the bill. It would have to be a phrase that can encompass both European feudal society and the Tokugawa system in which authority and power were shared between the shogunate at the center and the hundreds of domains. If we were to give it a name now, "politically decentralized societies" might be our best bet.

Translated by Alan S. Christy.

Notes

1. The standard view is that the end came for the shogunate when Oda Nobunaga drove the last shogun, Ashikaga Yoshiaki, from Kyoto on July 19, 1573. For convenient introductions to this period, see the essays, Hall, et al. (1981, 1988–99: especially Vol. 4), and McMullin (1984).
2. On the initial Portuguese encounters in the 1540s, as well as the evolution of Japan's relations with Europe from then until the expulsion of the Iberians and suppression of Christianity, see Boxer (1951) and Sansom (1950).
3. The best study of the Ezochi/Hokkaido fishery and fertilizer industry is Howell (1995).
4. The lush forest covering much of Japan, both in the Edo period and in our own time, is not "natural," but the result of human management, a silviculture economy that emerged in the early and middle Edo period. For example, the cedar forest planted by the forestry enterprise in Owase in Kii Province (part of modern Mie prefecture) began at the latest in the 1750s (Hayami 1968: 169–215). For an important introduction to the emergence of forest management in the Edo period, see Totman (1989; repr. 1998), and id. (1995).
5. On literacy, see Ronald Dore (1965). On the publishing industry, see especially Kornicki (1998).
6. In fact, the Japanese state ceased minting its own coins after the middle of the tenth century, finding it simpler and more effective to acquire Chinese cash through trade with Song, Yuan, or Ming China. As noted below, it is only with the establishment of the early modern order that the economic, political, and social conditions were sufficient to sustain the issuance of a domestic Japanese currency.
7. Heilbroner was the first, to my knowledge, to use the concept of an "economic society" (Heilbroner 1970). But in light of the fact that he titled one section, "The Economic Society of the Middle Ages," it should be clear that I am not using the concept in the same way he did. For a more detailed explanation of how I view the concept, see Hayami (1973: 14–28).
8. For an excellent study of medieval traffic, see Tonomura (1992); see also, Toyoda (1977: 129–44) and Brown (1951). On commerce in the last quarter-century of the sixteenth century, see especially Fujiki (1981). Haruko Wakita distinguishes medieval cities, as having developed as "concentrations of merchant and artisan groups, whose appearance accompanied the development of a social division of labor," from ancient cities, which were "residences of the aristocracy" (Wakita 1981). In contrast to this portrayal is the stimulating work of Yoshihiko Amino who turns his attention even to the economic activities of

the transient peoples of the fishing and mountain villages. One example of this perspective may be found in his essay (Amino 1986: 56–98).

9. For an earlier presentation of Tashiro's views, see Tashiro (1976: 85–105). The most comprehensive English-language analysis of the economic impact of foreign trade in Tokugawa Japan is Innes (1980).

10. Luis de Camões (1950: 381). Canto X, Verse 131:

Yet greater stretch of land is hid from thee,/ Till the time come her mystery to show./ But do not shun the islands of the sea,/ For nature wills that hence her fame should grow,/ This that fronts China, though half-hid it be/ And first found out this little while ago,/ Is called Japan, whence comes the silver fine,/ It shall be lightened by the Law Devine.

11. Tashiro notes that, "silver in the Tokugawa period functioned both as a 'currency for domestic circulation' and as an 'international commodity.'" (Tashiro 1981: 340).

12. Recounted in the preface to Iwao (1966).

13. On the development of the domestic cotton industry in early modern Japan, see Hauser (1974).

14. Declining steadily from its peak of 64,523 in 1696, the population of Nagasaki dropped to 20,166 in 1838 (Sekiyama 1969: 236). Innes (1980), discusses the relationship between trade and population in Nagasaki.

15. The most famous example is from the case of Hiroshima domain where, on the occasion of the change from the old silver-based currency to the new in 1852, scrip with a face value of one *ryô* of gold became equivalent to 32 *kan* 500 *me* of silver, in other words it dropped to 1/500th the original market rate (Tsuchiya and Yamaguchi 1974: 280).

16. A century before San'yô, Muro Kyûsô had presented a memorial to the eighth shogun, Yoshimune, *Kenka-roku*, in which he wrote that Tokugawa Ieyasu, founder of the Tokugawa *bakufu*, "had established the lords in their provinces, and granted large provinces to [branches of the Tokugawa house]...creating a *hôken* system...just like the [ancient Chinese house of] Zhou," and thus ensured "the endurance of the line through time" (Takimoto 1928). However, Kyûsô's memorial was not published until well after the Meiji Restoration, and there is no certainty that San'yô had access to it.

17. See especially Masuda's introduction, where he discusses the theories of Otto Hinze.

18. This is the perspective of the so-called "Pirenne thesis" (Pirenne 1987).

19. In his conclusion, Pirenne states that, "la rupture de la tradition antique a eu pour instrument l'avance rapide et imprevue de l'Islam...L'Occident est embouteille et force de vivre sur lui-même, en vase clos." (1987: 131). This is, after all, merely to observe that feudal society that was premised upon self-sufficiency.

20. For example, the research of Takashi Uranagase, who has studied the conditions of currency flow in the latter half of the sixteenth century, shows that a shift from "the use of coins to the use of rice" as a means of payment can be seen "across a broad area of western Japan." In particular, he draws attention to the fact that this "came about almost entirely in the very short period from the latter half of the 1560s to the early 1570s." The reversal of this trend began

in the middle of the 1580s, when we once again see the use of silver (Uranagase 1985*a*, *b*).

21. Ueno-chô Kyôikukai (1941: 817), see the "Official Notifications."
22. This point has been eloquently made by Smith (1961); reprinted in Smith (1988*a*).
23. On the urban history of early modern Japan, see especially Rozman (1973), and McClain (1982). As McClain notes, by 1700, Japan was home to the world's largest city, Edo, and to five of the largest twenty.
24. The classic study of the alternate attendance system is Tsukahira (1966). More recently, see Vaporis (1994).
25. For recent studies on the history of Edo, see McClain, et al. (1994); on Edo-period Osaka, see McClain and Wakita (1999).
26. For example, the common theme at the fifty-fifth annual meeting of the Association of Social Economic History was "Urban Communities and Guilds." The reports at this meeting made clear that aristocratic rule was nearly universal in European cities. For a summary of the proceedings, see Shakai Keizaishi Gakkai (1987).
27. The link between the demand pull of the urban market, and the socioeconomic response of farming villages has been set forth in Thomas C. Smith's seminal *Agrarian Origins of Modern Japan* (1959).
28. For a brief but provocative view of the networks binding together Tokugawa Japan, see Moriya (1990: 97–123); also, Rozman (1973).
29. McEvedy and Jones (1978: 28, charts 1–10). Even more accurate figures are available for the period after 1700 (Anderson 1988). For a more detailed view of Edo period demographic history, and especially the relationship between regional and national population dynamics, see Hayami and Kurosu (2001: 295–321).
30. See the charts in McEvedy and Jones (1978: 167).
31. Livi-Bacci (1992: 61–7) offers an interesting comparison of Ireland and Japan.
32. Saitô (1985). As Saitô shows, real wages and employment opportunities directly governed the age at marriage and determined the size of the population in western Europe. That is, when real wages rose and employment opportunities increased, the age at marriage declined (112–15). In the case of Japan, earnings (living standards) mediated fertility and mortality rates and had an indirect relationship to population scale through the age at marriage and the mortality rate (224).
33. It was the Dutch agricultural historian, Slicher van Bath, who strongly argued this in relation to the population increase of the twelfth and thirteenth centuries. Slicher van Bath (1963: 77–97).
34. This process has been admirably sketched by Smith (1959).
35. Comparing a survey of the Nôbi region (modern Aichi and southern Gifu prefectures) in the 1670s, *Kanbun muramura oboegaki*, and another survey in the same area a century and a half later, *Owari junkôki*, I found that there was one cow or horse for every three or four households in the 1670s, while the figure declined to one cow or horse for every fifteen to twenty households in the later period (Hayami 1992: 23–38; Hayami 2001*b*).
36. Dore (1965) has estimated that school attendance rates (the rate of those getting some kind of school education) in 1868 were 43% for boys and 10% for

girls in the late Edo period. The estimate is based on school attendance rates from the Meiji period, and takes regional differences into account. The education of these young people was most likely a basic form of reading, writing and arithmetic. For a more recent view, see Platt (1998).

37. For a more detailed discussion of the Tokugawa period land tax, see Smith (1988*b*).
38. Quoted in Hall (1966: 403).
39. Shunsaku Nishikawa's economic analysis of the late Tokugawa text, *Bôchô fûdo chûshin'an*, compiled by the Chôshû, Nagato and Suwô Provinces, domain, shows that, "...[t]he total land tax revenue was 31,000 kan...The land tax was 33 per cent of production." According to Nishikawa, the calculation of the land tax, which was the basis of domain finances, was fixed while household earnings were an inflexible estimate, with a high possibility of being conservative (Nishikawa 1979: 29).
40. Craig (1960) has a detailed examination of the straitened finances of the Chôshû domain in the late Edo period, as well as a discussion of the ways that domain was able to restore itself to solvency.
41. There was something of a boom in the study of Edo-period peasant uprisings in late twentieth century English-language scholarship, after about thirty years of disinterest. The classic study is Borton 1968. The later wave of interest began with Scheiner's "Benevolent Lords and Honorable Peasants," 1973. It was followed by several monographs, particularly Sippell (1977), Anne Walthall (1986), Vlastos (1986), Bix (1986), and Kelly (1985). These studies take a variety of approaches, and generally focus on different periods or regions; consequently their understanding of the motivations for resistance are not necessarily in agreement with mine. There is also a small literature on urban unrest in the Edo period, including Najita (1970) and Anne Walthall (1994).
42. B. H. Slicher van Bath (1963).

1

Quantitative Aspects of Tokugawa Economy

MATAO MIYAMOTO

1. Quantitative Overview of the Tokugawa Economy

Akira Hayami lays out in the introduction to this volume the broad historical specifics of the socioeconomic system of Tokugawa Japan, in which he sees the emergence of an "economy-minded society." What kind of macroeconomic performance was produced in that process? We have only extremely limited data for macroeconomic figures of the Tokugawa period, so it is very difficult to get an accurate grasp of the details of Japan's economic development, but we are able to obtain a general picture from the fragmentary data. In this chapter, I will draw a rough sketch of the process of macroeconomic development in the Tokugawa era, through a discussion of real goods in the first section and monetary aspects in the second, focusing on the period from the founding of the Tokugawa shogunate to the latter half of the eighteenth century.

Let us begin with movements in the population. Early in the twentieth century, Tôgo Yoshida estimated the aggregate national population at the beginning of the early modern period at 18 million, and this figure was generally accepted for many years. However, Hayami's more rigorous analysis estimates that the figure was far lower, somewhere between 9.8 and 12.27 million, in 1600.[1] Hayami's estimate is based on an examination of the relationship between assessed productivity (*kokudaka*) and registered population, but because he extrapolates from the data of a single region to the entire nation, it is also founded on a bold hypothesis. In any case, it is now widely accepted that Hayami is on the right track, and that the national population at the beginning of the early modern era was certainly far lower than the previously accepted figure of 18 million. For that reason, I will take the national population at 1600 to have been 12 million, now the most widely accepted estimate.

Beginning in 1665, the shogunate required all local jurisdictions (villages, town wards, etc.), regardless of whether they were in shogunal or daimyo domains, to make annual, nominal registrations of their population. This survey was mandated as much to ensure that there were no

Christians about as to count the census, but the effect was a form of census registry.[2] Then in 1721, the shogunate ordered the domains to total these local censuses, and report their populations to Edo; the shogunate then used those figures to calculate both province-by-province, and aggregate national population. Thereafter, these investigations were carried out every six years until 1846. If regularly carried out at six-year intervals for that entire time, there would have been twenty-two national censuses.

Today, we have the national population figures for nineteen of those censuses, and a breakdown by province for twelve of them. Samurai and their families were excluded from these censuses as a matter of military security, and a considerable number of other people, as well, were left out of these censuses. We have no way of knowing precisely how many people were not counted, but the figure for 1846 was 4.5–5 million, constituting 17–19 per cent of the total (Sekiyama 1958: 112–18). There is no evidence that the ratio of the population left out of the censuses was consistent, but we know that newborn infants were not registered, and that in some jurisdictions, children were left unregistered beyond infancy, to the age of eight, in one domain, and as late as age fifteen, in another. But since there are no other figures, we will assume that the uncounted population was 20 per cent of the census figures. So, in gauging the changes in national population after 1721, we will increase the shogunate's figures by 20 per cent.[3]

Setting the 1600 population at 12 million and the 1721 population at 31.28 million (multiplying the shogunate's figure of 26.07 million by 1.2), how did the population fluctuate in the period in between? We have absolutely no national data for that period, so we will take both years as benchmarks and we will have to resign ourselves to estimates of the change during the interim. Using the method Akira Hayami applied to the fragmentary data of 1600 to estimate the population of the Suwa region in 1670,[4] I estimate the population growth in the period 1600–1720 as follows. First, I divide this into periods of forty years. During this time, the population grew 260 percent. I assume that the growth rate in the second forty years was twice that of the first and third periods. Based on this, we are able to calculate average annual growth rates within each period. Next, we combined these figures and calculated the population for each year from 1600 to 1650, and linked those figures to the population figures in the bakufu's 1721 survey, as corrected for the uncounted populations (i.e. the bakufu figures multiplied by 1.2, to take account of infants not yet registered, samurai, etc.), and the Meiji government's census of 1872. The results are shown on Table 1.1, column one.[5] Let us now examine the land as a factor of production. The data for arable land during the Tokugawa period are even poorer than the data for population. It is extremely difficult to obtain reliable quantitative series, so I shall give here one example of estimation.

First of all, we can estimate the area of arable land by working from the figure for total estimated yield (*kokudaka*) of approximately 18.5 million

Table 1.1. Fluctuations in economic variables for Edo period (actual numbers)

Period	(1) Population (N) (unit: 10,000)	(2) Arable land (R) (unit: 1,000 chô)	(3) Actual harvest (Y) (unit: 1,000 koku)	(4) R/N	(5) Y/N	(6) Y/R
1600	1,200	2,065	19,731	1.721	1.644	0.955
1650	1,718	2,354	23,133	1.370	1.346	0.983
1700	2,769	2,841	30,630	1.026	1.106	1.078
1720	3,128	2,927	32,034	0.936	1.024	1.094
1730	3,208	2,971	32,736	0.926	1.020	1.102
1750	3,110	2,991	34,140	0.962	1.098	1.141
1800	3,065	3,032	37,650	0.989	1.228	1.242
1850	3,228	3,170	41,160	0.982	1.275	1.298
1872	3,311	3,234	46,812	0.977	1.414	1.447

Annual growth rate(%)

Period	(1)	(2)	(3)	(4)	(5)	(6)
1600–50	0.72	0.26	0.32	−0.46	−0.40	0.06
1651–00	0.96	0.38	0.56	−0.58	−0.40	0.18
1701–20	0.61	0.15	0.22	−0.46	−0.39	0.07
1721–30	0.25	0.15	0.22	−0.10	−0.03	0.07
1731–50	−0.16	0.03	0.22	0.19	0.38	0.19
1751–1800	−0.03	0.03	0.22	0.06	0.25	0.19
1801–50	0.10	0.09	0.18	−0.01	0.08	0.09
1851–72	0.11	0.09	0.59	−0.02	0.47	0.49

Notes: (1) Population: The population figures for 1600, 1650, and 1700 are estimates. The population for 1720 is based upon the shogunate's 1721 statistics, multiplied by 1.2. The population for 1730 is calculated by taking the average of the shogunate's statistics for 1726 and 1732, multiplied by 1.2. The population for 1750 equals the shogunate's statistics for that year, multiplied by 1.2. The population for 1800 equals the shogunate's statistics for 1798, multiplied by 1.2. The population for 1850 equals the shogunate's statistics for 1846, multiplied by 1.2. The population figure for 1872 is from the Meiji government's population survey for that year. Figures for the shogunate's statistics and the Meiji government's population survey are taken from Sekiyama, (1958).
(2) Arable land area: The figure for the arable land area 1730 is taken from the data during Kyoho to Enkyo eras, in Ôkura-shô, *Dainippon sozeishi*, vols. 1 & 2, Chôyôkai, (1927); the figure for 1872 is taken from the Meiji government's 1873 investigation, "Kyûtanbetsu," (Meiji zaiseishi hensankai, ed., *Meiji zaiseishi*, vol. 5, (1954); all others are estimates.
(3) Actual harvest: Nakamura, (1968: 168–170). However, Nakamura's figures for 1600, 1645, 1700, 1830, and 1867 are estimates. In this chart, I have extended the trend for 1600–45 to 1650 to calculate the estimated value for 1730, 1750, 1800, and 1850. I have used Nakamura's 1867 figure for 1872 (because Nakamura's figure for 1867 was originally the average value of agricultural production from 1877–79).

koku derived from the land surveys of 1598 carried out under Hideyoshi's *Taikô kenchi* orders. In doing so, we use the following method. As we can see from periods in which total productivity and arable land area did not differ greatly, the total productivity for the Genroku era (1688–1704) was 25,788,332 *koku* while the arable area in the Kyôhô-Enkyô era (1716–1744) was only 2,970,780 *chô* (1 *chô* = 1 hectare). The productivity of 1 *chô* of land for both eras turns out to be 8.68 *koku*. When we divide the total productivity of the *Taikô kenchi* (Hideyoshi's land surveys at the end of the sixteenth century) by the volume of the standard "Kyoto measuring," we arrive at a figure for 1600 of 2,064,657 *chô* of land. This is a higher estimate for arable area at the beginning of the early modern era than the figure of 1,500,000 *chô*—for long widely accepted—but it may yet be too low (Doboku Gakkai 1936; Furushima 1949: 397). That is because the yield per *chô* used here is from the beginning of the eighteenth century, but there is no question that the yield was even lower at the beginning of the early modern era. For the middle of the Tokugawa period we use the Kyôho–Enkyô era figures of 2,970,780 *chô* for the arable area in 1730 and for the beginning of the Meiji period we use the figure of 3,234,000 *chô* from the investigation of productivity carried out by the Tax Agency at the time of the Land Tax Revision (1873).

Let us next estimate arable land by periods corresponding to population statistics. Table 1.2 shows the number of construction projects for rivers, reservoirs, canals, and new fields by era. According to this table, the seventeenth century (particularly the latter half), had an increased number of public works projects related to the development of arable land. The eighteenth century was a time of stagnation and the nineteenth century was a time of renewed activity. There are problems in interpreting the data, because they are unclear as to both coverage, and the scale of projects. But if we set that concern aside for the moment, we may interpret the data as having a close relation to the degree of progress in developing new fields. The net gain in new villages (so-called *shinden* villages), by region during the Tokugawa period, as shown by Table 1.3, also runs parallel to the data on public works projects; during the first and last periods, there was a great increase in the number of new villages while in the middle period the increase was extremely small.

According to Toshio Kikuchi's study of village size, a village in 1645 averaged 388 *koku* per village. This increased to 468 *koku* in 1697, but there were no great increases in average village size after that: 481 *koku* in 1830 and 453 *koku* in 1873 (Kikuchi 1958: 139). In sum, the period from the beginning of the seventeenth century to the early eighteenth was an era of tremendous increase in arable land. There was new village construction and village expansion—in other words, expansion of the internal frontier—but from the early eighteenth century well into the nineteenth, land development stagnated as a whole while village expansion was the major form of development. For the rest of the nineteenth century, however, land development picked up again and the number of villages also increased.

According to the above data on arable land—there were 2,064,657 *chô* at the beginning of the early modern era, 2,970,780 *chô* in the middle, and

Table 1.2. Engineering projects relating to arable land development

	Riparian construction	Reservoirs	Irrigations channel	New field development
Prior to 1550	25 (20.5)	46 (12.9)	24 (5.5)	
1551–1600	16 (13.1)	3 (0.8)	11 (2.5)	14 (1.4)
1601–50	31 (25.4)	66 (18.5)	55 (12.7)	122 (12.2)
1651–1700	13 (10.7)	93 (26.1)	121 (27.9)	220 (22.1)
1701–50	11 (9.0)	27 (7.6)	52 (12.0)	103 (10.3)
1751–1800	12 (9.8)	23 (6.4)	31 (7.2)	88 (8.8)
1801–68	14 (11.5)	99 (27.7)	139 (32.2)	450 (45.2)
Totals	122 (100.0)	357 (100.0)	433 (100.0)	997 (100.0)

Source: Doboku gakkai (1936).

Notes: Figures in parenthesis are the percentage of each column.

3,234,000 *chô* at the beginning of the Meiji era—there was an increase of 906,000 *chô* from the beginning through the middle, but a gain of only 263,000 *chô* from the middle through the early Meiji era. These figures are consistent with the number of construction projects and the state of creating new villages, discussed above. So, inferring that the total construction figures by period, as shown in Table 1.2, reflects the extent of arable land growth, we divided the early modern era into two periods, 1600–1730 and 1731–1873, and attempted an estimate of the area of arable land in each period.[6] The years for which we made estimates were matched with population statistics: 1650, 1700, 1720, 1750, 1800, and 1850. The results are shown in Table 1.1, column 2.

Even *estimating* production volumes accurately for the early modern era is virtually impossible. *Kokudaka* appears to be an acceptable index of production volumes, at least for agriculture. But since land survey revisions and productivity reevaluations were only rarely conducted, increases in newly opened land or rises in agricultural productivity created a gap between actual production and *kokudaka* (assessed productivity). In general, it is likely that the gap between real production and *kokudaka* widened over time. And in that case, we might ask, in what ways did actual production change? Satoru Nakamura has attempted to estimate the changes in actual production—using the survey results for 1645 as benchmarks, when the daimyo were likely to have an accurate grasp of actual production and the agricultural production recorded in 1877–79 ("Agricultural Tables")—assuming that agricultural production grew by the same pace as arable land did (data similar to that used to estimate cultivated land above was adopted) (Nakamura 1968: 173–4). The "actual agricultural production volume" of column 3, Table 1.1. is based on Nakamura's estimates (albeit with minor adjustments). Of course, the

Table 1.3. Increases in the number of villages

	1645–97		1697–1830		1830–73	
	Village increase	Rate%	Village increase	Rate%	Village increase	Rate%
Western Japan	2,029	7.8	170	0.6	2,699	9.6
Eastern Japan	5,506	18.7	418	1.2	3,465	9.8
National	7,535	13.6	588	0.9	6,164	9.7

Source: Kikuchi (1958).

"actual agricultural production volume" is only related to the production of primary-sector agricultural goods, so it excludes both income from agricultural by-employment and all forms of nonagricultural production. Moreover, although there are a variety of further problems, it is useful as a general guide to the changes in agricultural production in the Tokugawa period.

2. Seventeenth Century Economic Development: The Great Land Reclamation and the Population Explosion

Let us look again at Table 1.1. From the seventeenth to the early eighteenth century, the population expanded rapidly. An annual growth rate of 0.61–0.96 per cent is surprisingly high-paced for a premodern society. For example, the estimated world population grew at an annual rate of only 0.05 per cent from 1548 to 1650 and a mere 0.3 per cent from 1650 to 1750. During the 1750 years prior to the modern period, the world population increased less than threefold (Yasuba 1980: 12), while the population growth rate of modern Japan after the Meiji Restoration was around 1 per cent per year. In comparison, the population growth of the seventeenth century may fairly be called an extraordinary "population explosion."

The area of arable land also increased rapidly along with the population in the seventeenth century. The years from the Warring States period through the seventeenth century were an era of unprecedented land reclamation. As the oldest agricultural book in Japan, the *Seiryôki* (written in the middle of the seventeenth century and believed to depict the appearance of late sixteenth century agriculture and agricultural villages), puts it: "wealthy farmers live in houses backed by the mountains, faced by rice paddies, with rivers on their left and dry fields on their right and surrounded on all sides by much inherited land." In other words, in the medieval agricultural landscape there were houses backed by the

mountains that provided fuel, fertilizer, and other productive resources
and faced by a small belt of valley fields that used mountain streams or
springs for a water source.[7] Rice agriculture took place in natural
wetlands that were not engineered on a large scale.

But from the end of the Sengoku period onward, agricultural
development moved downstream, from the upper reaches of river systems to the lowlands, with first flood plains then alluvial plains being
transformed into arable sites. The main venues of agricultural production
thus moved from the mountains to the plains. According to the prevailing
theory, this development was made possible by the establishment of the
large, coherent territorial domains of the Sengoku and early modern
daimyos, and the development of irrigation and engineering technology;
what might be termed "engineering adaptation."[8] On the other hand,
Osamu Saitô argues that this development was due to farmers' "agricultural adaptation" in the introduction of new varieties, such as *akamai*
(Indica red rice), which were suitable for cultivation in the flatter terrain
of riparian lowlands (Saitô 1988*b*). In either case, there is no doubt that
the expansion of the frontiers of arable lands, the continual construction
of new villages and the stabilization of rice agriculture produced an environment conducive to the division and long-term settlement of small
farmers. This also had an influence on demographic variables, as both the
marriage and birth rates rose.

There is no question that total agricultural production expanded
tremendously. As we see in the column for "actual yield" in Table 1.1,
production rose 1.6 times from the beginning of the early modern era to
1720. When we convert this to an annual growth rate, it comes to at most
0.5 per cent. This appears to be very low, but it is more an indicator of
growth than of stagnation. In any case, the rapid growth in population and
arable land in the seventeenth century, accompanied by an increase in total
production, means that this was a period in which a series of major
economic transformations broke down the state of balance between nature
and the economy that had been maintained for centuries prior to the early
modern era.[9]

Let us further dissect this process of extensive growth in the seventeenth
century. Table 1.1 shows that from the beginning of the early modern
period until 1730, the ratio of arable land to population (per capita arable
land) continued to decline. By the eighteenth century, per capita arable
had fallen below 1 *tan*. In the beginning of the early modern era, it was
quite common for farming families to divide their inheritance between
the main house, and branches established from time to time. The portion
of agricultural land given to branch households was met, to a certain
extent, by new land development. But since the overall population and
the number of farming households both increased more rapidly than

the amount of arable land, the scale of agricultural operations (in terms of land) tended to shrink over time.[10] Farming households responded to this declining ratio of land to population by restructuring to a more labor-intensive form of agriculture.

The intensification of labor and the contraction of land led to the rising productivity of land. The changes in yield per *tan* laid out in Table 1.1 reveal this. But without corresponding advances in technology or increases in capital intensity, even if farmers had continued to make additional labor inputs per unit of land, the production per unit of labor would decline by the law of diminishing return and, if the labor time per person did not change, the production volume per person would also decline. In fact, according to Table 1.1, the actual yield per person did continue to decline until 1730. Simon Kuznets characterizes "modern economic growth" as a continuous, long-term increase in per capita income, accompanied by a continuous increase in population (Kuznets 1959). In that light, the seventeenth century in Japan was not an era of "modern economic growth."

But did seventeenth-century economic development really follow a pattern of increase in population and arable land with a decrease in production per person? Will the population of an entire society continue to increase over the long term even while production per person continues to decrease?

The population increase of this period had much to do with a rise in the birth rate and an increase in the average life span. But since this was an era without any marked improvement in either medicine or standards of hygiene, and was also characterized by the rapid growth of urban populations, where mortality was higher than in villages, the increase in birth rate and life span must have been based on an improvement in living standards. The natural conclusion is that there was an increase in production per person. In other words, the "actual yield" of Table 1.1 underestimates the growth rate.

How is it possible that the production per person could increase while the area of land per person decreased? As Akira Hayami has observed, Japanese agriculture in the seventeenth century saw a transition from the plow to the hoe, while the number of oxen and horses, which were nearly the sole capital stock for agriculture at the beginning of the early modern era, tended to decline in relation to both population and land. Thus, it is difficult to argue that there was an increase in the stock of capital equipment. In fact, the main causes for any increase in production were these: an increase in per capita labor time and the intensification of labor management, the development of land through improvements in land quality, intensification of land use with dry paddies and such, increasing use of fertilizers, the introduction of durable, multiple harvest strains such as *akamai*, and the stabilization of rice agriculture.[11]

To explain these changes, we may note that with the issue of working hours, in small-farm family operations, based on the labor of family members, each member of the family had an incentive to increase productivity since the gains would revert to the family itself. This led to an "industrious revolution" in which the family would input many hours of labor in its own lands.[12] The extension of working hours compensated for the reduction in production per person that derives from the decline in labor productivity. It is often said that land reclamation proceeds from the best land available, to progressively inferior land. But there is no reason to believe that land reclaimed from the Warring States period through the first half of the early modern era was necessarily inferior. That is, the valley land characteristic of agriculture in ancient and medieval Japan did not necessarily possess better conditions for cultivation. The land located in long, narrow valleys or at the foot of mountains is exposed to less sunlight; those wet paddies that use river or spring water are liable to experience water shortages; and labor efficiency is poor on sloped or terraced fields (Hayama 1983: 54).

In contrast, the land developed after the Warring States period was fertile land with stable access to a water supply, located, as it often was, along the lower reaches of rivers. This kind of land improvement would have the effect of reversing any decline in harvests. The shift from wetlands to dry lands had great significance for rice agriculture and double cropping. That is, a sufficient supply of nitrogen is indispensable to rice plants. Constructing irrigation channels and drying the fields during the winter had a great effect in this area. The shift to dry fields also brought about an intensification of land use as it made possible the cultivation of second crops on paddy land. Osamu Saitô also point out that the introduction of new strains of rice, like *akamai*, along with the great land reclamation of the beginning of the early modern era, had the effect of stabilizing rice cultivation (Saitô 1998*b*). Finally, the development of a market economy created incentives to increase the cultivation of appropriate crops on appropriate land, with a consequent increase in the productivity of land.

The kinds of progress in agriculture discussed above had the effect of stemming the decline in per capita production that came with declines in land per person and the use of capital equipment. But continuing this kind of agricultural progress over a long period would surely force the peasants to expend tremendous amounts of energy. There are limits to the extension of working hours, and even using all available natural fertilizers —such as cuttings, animal, and human manure—it would be difficult to continue increasing investment. Technological progress in improvements in land and seeds also cannot be continued indefinitely. It appears that the agricultural development that was achieved through the expansion of the agricultural frontier and the labor-intensive technological progress

of the seventeenth century finally reached its limit at around the beginning of the eighteenth century.

Books on agricultural technology and agricultural policy first
appeared in Japan during the Tokugawa period. At first, these books
tended to be translations of Chinese texts or treatises on agricultural
policy that included Confucian ideology on control of the peasants. But
around the Genroku era (1688–1703), agricultural technology manuals
and regional agricultural books began to appear that were based on the
empirical observations of writers from every region. *Jikata kikigaki* (1668),
Denhôki and *Hyakushô denki* (1682), *Aizu nôsho* (1687), *Renmin buikuhô*
(1688), *Jikata chikubashû* (1689), *Nôgyô zensho* (1697), *Kôka shunju* (1707),
and *Nôji isho* (1709) are a few examples. Not all of these are systematic
treatises like Miyazaki Yasusada's ten volume *Nôgyô zensho*, nor were all
of them published and widely available—many circulated as manuscript
copies. But they were practical guides to agricultural technology that
came into the hands of regional officials, village officials, and the
people who actually worked the land itself, making it possible for them
to fulfill an important role in communicating advanced technology to
these people.

It is worth observing that it was from the last quarter of the seventeenth
to the beginning of the eighteenth century that many of the important
agricultural and rural texts of the Tokugawa period were produced. In a
time when there was decreasing room for growth in arable land and fixed
capital stock, technological progress was indispensable to efforts to
increase production from a given volume of production investment factors.
The concentrated appearance of agricultural and rural texts came at a
time when the development of small farming methods practiced since
the beginning of the early modern period had temporarily hit a wall. It
also reveals the rising desire of peasants to acquire even better agricultural techniques.

3. The Middle of the Tokugawa Period:
   A "Stagnant Society"?

The extensive economic growth at the start of the early modern era, with
its explosive increase in population and arable land and its expansion of
the total volume of production, began to approach its limit around the
turn of the eighteenth century. From the 1730s until the beginning of the
nineteenth century there was almost no increase in the aggregate national
population, and the expansion of cultivated land slowed markedly. Did
these conditions mean that the eighteenth century was a time of economic
stagnation?

Table 1.1 shows that actual yields continued to rise over the period in question, albcit gradually. The ratio of arable land to population also pulled out of the decline of the 1730s and rose incrementally thereafter, and the productivity of land likewise showed improvement. As a result, the actual yield per capita took a turn upward after the 1730s. As I said above, the figures for actual yield do not include nonagricultural production. So if we take into account the rise in processing industry earnings—in the form of agricultural by-employments—and commercial income in urban markets, then we may surmise that per capita income increased even further than the data shows.[13] The eighteenth century, therefore, was a time in which the extensive economic development of the seventeenth century, in which population and agricultural land area both increased, took a different turn to what might be called intensive economic growth.

The growth in agricultural production per capita may have been due to any number of factors. Of course the increase in agricultural land per person that we saw above would be one factor. In addition, the shift to dry paddies that was limited to western Japan in the beginning of the early modern period expanded in the middle period to areas in Kinai, the Inland Sea, Shikoku, northern Kyûshû, and the Hokuriku region (Oka and Yamazaki 1983: 132–5) With the shift to dry paddy fields came such crop rotations as rice to wheat, rapeseed to cotton, or wheat or rapeseed to rice. New capital factors, such as the development of a variety of hoes and sickles with specific uses for different stages of the production process, beginning with the Genroku period, also contributed to the new rise in productivity.

The shift in equipment used to flood paddies from the labor-intensive water wheel to the use of treadmills, spread from Osaka in the latter half of the seventeenth century to the entire country in the eighteenth century. In the years between Genroku and Kyôho (1688–1736), the early two-pronged thresher was gradually displaced by such labor-saving tools as the multi-toothed threshing stand. Rice-hulling technology, similarly, moved from the early wooden mortars to the stone mortars that appeared in the Genroku era, while in winnowing the early bamboo baskets and sieves gave way to more efficient standing sieves known as *sengoku tôshi* and *mangoku tôshi* that came into use in the early eighteenth century. Thus, in contrast to the shift from animal power to manpower in the seventeenth century, which appeared to have caused the shallowing of capital, the rate of capital equipment use started to increase from the eighteenth century with the development by Japanese agronomists and artisans of a wide variety of new agricultural tools.

The focus of ordinary agricultural inputs also changed markedly between the early seventeenth and the early eighteenth centuries. The early seventeenth-century reliance on locally available fertilizers (compost; cured human and animal waste) shifted with the rising use of such purchased fertilizers as sardine meal and the residue from pressing rapeseed oil, as well as investment in products from nonagricultural sources, such as whale oil, which was used as a pest repellant. Farmers also worked to improve seed quality, especially seeds adapted to local conditions, to the degree that several hundred varieties of rice were developed in one region alone. In particular, the development of middle- and late-growing strains of rice not only brought about an increase in per-*tan* yield, but also contributed to the spread of double cropping.

At the same time, the variety of crops grown increased greatly. Apart from the major grains, there was significant production of such commercial crops as cotton, rapeseed, indigo, tea, mulberry, tobacco, sugar cane, paper mulberry, hemp, safflower, and vegetables. These crops were grown as second crops in double-cropping fields, as part of a cycle of crop rotation, or specifically as non-paddy field crops. The total area of agricultural land grew from the Kyôho–Enkyô period to the early Meiji period by 263,000 *chô*. But of that growth, only 61,000 *chô* were for rice paddies while the other 202,000 *chô* were non-paddy fields. While the main grains were grown mostly in paddy fields, non-paddy fields were developed for commercial crops.

In addition, regional specialization advanced rapidly, as farmers matched cash crops such as indigo, paper mulberry, and safflower to the soil and climate conditions in their localities. These commercial crops stimulated the development of village-level agricultural processing industries, such as cotton yarn, cotton textiles, raw silk, indigo balls, and paper. These agricultural developments were not independent of each other, of course; they were mutually related and reinforcing. For example, if one is trying to undertake double cropping in order to use agricultural land efficiently, one has to dry the rice paddies during the winter months. But that alone does not make double-cropping possible. The demand for labor during the agricultural peak seasons of spring and fall was tremendous, because often in double-cropping either the harvest time for the narrow strip of the secondary crop overlaps with the planting time for the main crop, or else the harvest time of the main crop overlaps with the preparation and planting time of the secondary crop.

If, for example, the main crop is rice and the secondary crop is wheat, the wheat is harvested in the middle of the fourth month, which is followed by the tasks of threshing, preparation, and binding. Meanwhile, from the middle of the fourth month to the middle of the fifth month, the fields from which the wheat has been harvested must have the ground broken up, the ridges firmed up, and the grasses weeded; the ground is then plowed and fertilized—the rice seedlings must also be grown and transplanted from seedbed to paddy—all in succession. The same kind of thing then happens in the fall. Therefore, in addition to the need to distribute labor-power among these overlapping tasks, it was essential to introduce strains of rice that have a later planting period. Middle and late rice met this need, with planting seasons starting from the fifth month and harvesting in the ninth and tenth months, as opposed to the earlier strains that were harvested in the eighth month. With that, the planting time for the secondary crops slipped into the wintertime. Thus the spring and fall peaks in labor demand were spread out so that the demand for labor was nearly even throughout the year. Dry paddies and double cropping brought about not only a more effective use of land, but also a more efficient use of labor and animal power.[14]

Of course, this is not to say that the labor demand had entirely lost its seasonal nature. The shortage of hands during the agricultural peaks of spring and fall continued unabated. It is here that the development of new labor-saving tools took on the greatest importance. In particular, the multi-toothed threshing stands (*sembakoki*) that removed the hulls from rice and wheat plants played a big role in reducing the necessary labor at harvest times. These tools even got the strange name of "widow-topplers" (*goke taoshi*) because they robbed widows and children, who had previously done the threshing, of employment opportunities.

Middle and late strains of rice had a longer growing season than their early-planting cousins and they also produced a greater number of ears. On the other hand, these varieties required greater amounts of fertilizer. They were planted deeper to protect against loss of fertilizer, but they also needed both a large amount of initial fertilizer, and supplementary fertilizers later in the growing season. The increased use of fertilizer was also required to maintain the quality of the soil for double cropping. But there was no way to acquire enough fertilizer from local sources such as the natural grasslands. It was commercially purchased fertilizer that broke this bottleneck. Purchased fertilizer cut back on the labor used to spread the cut-grass fertilizer used before, but it increased the labor needed for weeding. It also required deeper plowing to compensate for the acidification of the soil. The introduction of the *Bitchû* plow, used for tilling, and of the grass sickle, used for weeding, were due to the need for aid in raising the efficiency of these tasks.

Thus, from the middle of the Tokugawa period, Japanese agriculture responded to the growing limitation on the expansion of agricultural land with the efficient use of the existing land and family labor. In other words, it showed a tendency to develop in an inward direction. On the production side, this was the single greatest factor in the rise in per capita income and the standard of living. But in order to take up that argument, we must turn to a discussion of the population that is the denominator in our calculation of per capita income (total income/population).

There are a number of theories as to why national population growth stagnated in the middle of the Tokugawa era. The first explanation that comes to mind is that the eighteenth-century pause in economic development led to the stagnation of the population. Most popular texts make the point that having lost room for further economic expansion by the middle of the Tokugawa period, the peasants began to suffer under the heavy taxes levied on them by the daimyos, thus causing them to turn to customs of abortion and infanticide. The population is said to have further stagnated due to the effects of famines and epidemic diseases. Thomas R. Malthus stated that human populations normally tend to increase, but that the production of foodstuffs is ultimately unable to keep pace with the population increase, thus leading to a decline in the standard of living. When the standard of living reaches its lowest level, epidemics, famines, and abortions bring a halt to population increase. Over the long run, the population achieves a balance with the lowest standard of living, neither increasing nor decreasing. This state of equilibrium is known as the "Malthusian trap." The theory that the population stagnation was equivalent to an economic stagnation in the middle of the Tokugawa period views Japan of that era as caught in the Malthusian trap. It used to be a conventional view among Japanese Marxist historians.

But the phenomenon of national population "stagnation" in the mid-Tokugawa period cannot be explained so simply. First of all, if we dis-aggregate the mid-Tokugawa population in regional terms, we see there were regions with population growth and regions with population decline. The "stagnation" of the national population is nothing more than the aggregate of regional figures. Between 1721 and 1804, the population decreased in the Kinki, Kantô and Tôhoku regions, but it increased in the Tôsan, Hokuriku, San'yô, San'in, Shikoku, and Kyûshû areas. The Tôkai region remained approximately unchanged. Taken region by region, we see that the number of regions in which the population increased was greater (the San'in and Shikoku regions had a population increase of 15–20 per cent). This makes it easy to imagine that the social and economic conditions that surround populations differed from region to region.

The three great eighteenth-century famines, which struck in the Kyôhô, Hôreki, and Tenmei eras, were one factor in the population decline. The rate of loss was particularly high during these periods in Tôhoku, Kantô, Hokuriku, and Kinki. The Kyôhô famine was caused by insect damage, with western Japan suffering the most; the Hôreki and Tenmei famines, on the other hand, were the result of low summertime temperatures. The cooling of the climate in the eighteenth century was a global phenomenon. Eastern Japan, particularly the northeast, was hit by cold northeast winds descending on the islands from a summer high-pressure area over Okhotsk. With the northeast constituting the far northern limit for rice cultivation for the technology of the time, the damage to rice which was in its ripening period was tremendous and caused a crop failure. But the crop failure and its attendant famine was not the only effect of the climatological cooling.

Lacking sufficient nutrition, the people were hit with chronic epidemics, with many people losing their lives. In that sense, the northern periphery was temporarily hit with a Malthusian check. But even in these regions, excepting the northern Kantô region, the population growth rate was normally in the positive numbers once the region had recovered from the effects of those disasters. Moreover, the effects of these disasters were small in the Tôkai, Tôsan, and regions of southwestern Japan. In other times, the population grew at quite a high rate.[15]

Thus even in the middle of the Tokugawa era, villages in many regions had the potential for population increase. But it remains true that the middle and late Tokugawa rate of population increase was far lower than during the first hundred years of the Tokugawa period. From 1600 to 1721, the national population increased by a factor of 2.6. During a period of nearly equal length, from 1721 to 1846, the population increased by only 1.12 times, even when focusing on average years when the population had escaped the effects of natural disasters (Kitô 1983a: 80). Why was the rate of population increase only moderate? Did the relation between the population and the economy change in the middle of the Tokugawa period?

One variable that had an effect on population trends was urbanization. The regions that had the greatest population loss during the mid-Tokugawa period, excepting Tôhoku, were the Kantô and Kinki regions (the former lost 7 per cent and the latter lost 15 per cent), which were the most heavily urbanized parts of the country (Sekiyama 1958: 141). Even in normal years, the rate of population increase in both of these regions was very small. In the northern Kantô, the population decreased even in normal years. What these two areas had in common was that they were economically advanced regions with many cities, including the three largest, Edo, Osaka, and Kyoto. In contrast, regions with a low urban population, such as the San'in, San'yô, Shikoku, and Kyûshû, experienced a high population growth rate in normal years. This kind of phenomenon, which might be called "the negative feedback function by urbanization," can also be seen in preindustrialization-era Europe.

There are several reasons why urban population growth would be slow. In early modern Japanese cities, there was a gender imbalance with the male population being far greater than the female. In consequence, marriage rates were low, the age of marriage high, and the birth rate low. The high population density gave rise to poor living and hygiene conditions for most of the population, which raised the risk of mortality due to disasters and communicable diseases, thus raising the actual death rate. Developing cities draw in population from the surrounding agricultural villages, but for those people who came in from the countryside, life in the city was "hell." Even if the young men and women who came to the city to earn a living managed to escape the hell of the city and return to their villages, they married late, thus affecting the birth rate of their home villages (Hayami 1974, 1975; Hayami and Kitô: Chapter 7, this volume). Moreover, Osamu Saitô points out that systems of servitude (*hôkônin seido*), such as the apprenticeship system (*kogaisei*) and the internal promotion system (*naibu shôshinsei*), restricted the sphere of personnel development and marriage, thus raising the marriage age of employees/servants and lowering their fertility.[16] Thus, the economic development that came with urbanization in the Tokugawa period did not bring about a population increase. The kind of population control mechanisms outlined above also fulfilled the function of checking the decline in living standards that would have resulted from population pressures if those mechanisms had not been in place.

Of course, this could not be said to have been the result of conscious decisions. Could it not be that before they are caught in a "Malthusian trap" people consciously take action to put preventive checks on population ("preventive checks" by Malthus mean those to prevent the limitation of population by disease and famine which would result from the population rising beyond the scale at which it can sustain a balance with the lowest standard of living, while "positive checks" by Malthus mean those to control population-rising after the deterioration in the standard of living due to disease and famine). I believe such preventive checks were taken.

Figure 1.1 shows the correlation of arable land growth rates by region (the horizontal axis) between the Kyôhô-Enkyô (1716–48) eras and 1880, and population growth rates by region (the vertical axis) from 1721 to 1880. Clearly, population growth rates and arable land growth rates had a high positive correlation. The figure shows a cross-sectional analysis of thirteen regions from across the country. But an analysis of the sixty-eight provinces of Japan also shows a correlation between population growth rates and arable land growth rates of 0.625 (significant at 1 per cent level) (Miyamoto 1976: 37–9). The correlation of population and arable land is interactive, so it is hard to define the causal relation: whether land development regulates population, or whether it is the other way around. Development began early in northern and southern Kantô, and the Kinai and its immediate surroundings so that by the beginning of the eighteenth century the ratio of arable land to population was low, and therefore the population pressure was high in those regions. If we posit that the rate at which new arable land was developed thereafter was low, then the degree to which population rose depended greatly on the degree to which there was room for further development of arable land.

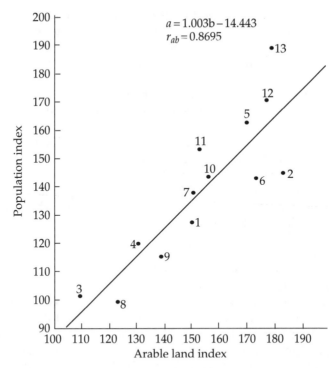

Fig. 1.1. Correlation of the population growth rate and the rate of increase in arable land. 1. Eastern Ôu, 2. Western Ôu, 3. Northern Kantô, 4. Southern Kantô, 5. Hokuriku, 6. Tôzan, 7. Tôkai, 8. Kinai, 9. Kinai Environs, 10. San'in, 11. San'yô, 12. Shikoku, 13. Kyûshû.

Source: Hayami (1975*b*).

Note: r_{ab} is the correlation coefficient of a and b.

One cannot leap to the conclusion that because the population growth rate was an increasing function of the arable land growth rate this means that the total production (which equals the total income) of each region was regulated by the size of arable land area or that accordingly the region's ability to maintain a population was also so constrained. If agricultural production constitutes an overwhelming portion of a society's total output—there is no change in the productivity of land, and such production investment factors as fertilizers are almost all obtained locally—then the size of that society's total production depends on the area of arable land. But as I mentioned above, mid-Tokugawa Japan did not fit this description. Nonagricultural industry that depended very little on local resources developed steadily in rural villages. Moreover, as we saw above, land productivity improved, with greater density of use due to technological innovations and an increase in investment in nonlocal resources such as the introduction of purchased fertilizers and the development of agricultural tools. Even though we may admit that the land remained the most important factor in production, its significance declined steadily. Then why did land nevertheless function as an important factor influencing the size of the population?

As I outlined above, the seventeenth century was an age of tremendous land reclamation and explosive population growth. But that road to growth began to narrow drastically at the turn of the eighteenth century. This was not just due to the fact that there was little land left that could be developed for cultivation. Limitations were also added on the potential use of two of the most important factors of agricultural production of the seventeenth century: water and grass.[17] Moreover, the technological progress that could overcome these problems also experienced a slow down. If, under these conditions, population continued to be added on the fixed area of arable land, for which there was little expectation of further increase, then per capita production would fall due to successively declining harvests. Thus, the tension between arable land and population heightened around the end of the seventeenth century and the signs of the approach of a Malthusian wall began to appear. In order to keep from hitting that wall, the decline ratio of arable land to population had to be stemmed.

One response of the ruling class to this social pressure can be found in the prohibitions against subdividing land below the scale of 1 *chô* or 10 *koku*, issued at the beginning of 1673 by the shogunate and various daimyo domains. At the village level, communal regulations were drafted to restrict rights to water and communal land to those families who already enjoyed such rights. These regulations led to the establishment of "regular membership of village" (*honbyakushô kabu*) and the fixing of official numbers of farm families in villages. At the level of individual families, inheritance patterns shifted from divided to undivided systems, while the *ie* (household) system of organization became firmly established. The *ie* system lowered the marriage rate, raised the age of marriage, and lowered the birth rate for male family members who were not the family head. In addition, with the average life span increasing from the seventeenth century, the age at which the heir received the transfer of agricultural land rose, as did his (or her) age at marriage.[18]

These social systems and customs contained mechanisms to fix the ratio of arable land to population and, as long as the area of arable land did not increase, they moved in the direction of suppressing population growth. They were first introduced for logical reasons to prevent Malthusian checks. However, these systems and customs were still maintained even in the late Tokugawa era when the economy managed to escape, to a certain extent, the limitations on the possibility of utilizing new land resources. The result was that even though there was economic growth, the expansion of the population was suppressed and per capita income and the standard of living rose. Why were population suppressing systems and customs maintained?

Perhaps it was because both the ruling class and the peasants of the Tokugawa period felt that land resources were the supreme factor in production. With production of the main grains as the core of Tokugawa agriculture, it was believed that the possibility of expanding agricultural land was the decisive factor in economic development. Writing on the demographic influence of late Tokugawa proto-industrialization (rural industry), Osamu Saitô argues that whereas proto-industrialization in Europe led to population growth by lowering the age of female marriage and raising the birth rate, the population increase among grain-producing farm families in Japan was even greater (Saitô 1985: chapters 8–10). The effect on population of an increase in income depended on whether it was from development in grain-producing agriculture or de-agriculturalization. In the background are the particular economic views of the people of the time on land and grain-producing agriculture.

It is also possible to interpret the establishment of population suppression devices as the choices of people seeking a higher standard of living. According to Carl Mosk and others, the rise in income levels in late Tokugawa Japan raised the natural fertility of women and lowered the infant mortality rate (Saitô 1985: 236–46; Mosk 1983). As I stated above, the move to cities and towns to earn a living raised the average age of marriage for peasants. These facts suggest that a rise in income levels and an increase in employment opportunities indirectly brought about a decrease in the birth rate. These were long-term demographic changes and may not have been consciously experienced by people. Whether one got married and had many children or sacrificed that for high income and employment opportunity is, of course, a decision made in each case by the parties involved—though individual decisions of course were shaped by ever-changing socio-cultural norms. Higher marriage age was not the only way that births were restricted. There were also many immoral means, such as abortion and infanticide. But these latter were more of the character of broadly defined birth control (preventive) measures meant to raise living standards than they were actions unavoidably taken in the face of poverty.

These mechanisms for adjusting population led to moderate growth of the national population after the mid-Tokugawa period, when the tempo of land development was slowed and income levels saw a steady rise. These conditions not only provided a quiet stimulus to the economy; they also brought the economic benefit of avoiding the degradation of standards of living that come from rapid population growth.

As we saw above, the mid-Tokugawa economy showed superficial signs of "stagnation" in a deceleration of both population growth and the development of arable land. But this was an economy with steady growth that achieved improvement in the living standard of commoners. Compared to the early Tokugawa era when, economic growth was supported by extensive expansion of resources, the mid-Tokugawa economy discovered a route to growth through the efficient use of given resources.

However, mid-Tokugawa economic development was not necessarily the beginning of "modern economic growth." That is, if we use Kuznets' definition that "modern economic growth" is characterized by a continual rise in per capita income along with long-term, high-rate population growth, then the economic growth of mid-Tokugawa was not consistent with this definition for the following reasons. The population growth of this era does not match the model. Moreover, the increase in per capita income was assisted by artificial population controls, occasionally through immoral means. When exceptional crop failures continued for a number of years, a number of regions immediately fell below a subsistence standard of living, and there was no system at the national level that could absorb the shock. And finally, the predominant social and economic ideology of the time laid tremendous emphasis on land and grain-producing agriculture, and deprecated commerce and nonagricultural industry. These phenomena make us hesitate to call this the beginning of modern economic growth.

4. The Nineteenth Century: The Beginning of Economic Growth

Economic development entered a new phase around the turn of the nineteenth century. As Table 1.1 shows, the national population clearly turned from decline to growth. Rates of increase in arable land area and actual yield also rose to higher levels than during the eighteenth century. Per capita yield and land productivity (actual yield/arable land area) also improved steadily. (The rates of increase for these latter variables were low for the period 1801–50, but this is likely due to the influence of the Tempô famine (1833–36). If we look at the entire period of 1801–72, the rates of increase were higher than those of the eighteenth century.) The fact that arable land acreage increased again probably means that the demand for agricultural products rose. The population increase was doubtless also closely related. But the greatest characteristic of the period was the further expansion of nonagricultural production.

Using what might be called the "Economic White Paper" of Tempô era (1830–44) Nagato and Suwô Provinces (the westernmost provinces of Honshû), the *Report on Conditions in these Two Provinces* (*Bôchô fûdo chûshin-an*), to make the "national economic accounting" of the domain, Shunsaku Nishikawa estimated that the ratio of agricultural to non-agricultural production out of the total production of the two provinces in the 1840s was 52–48, or 65–35 according to a value-added base.[19] De-agricultural-ization had proceeded to an unimagined extent. The nonagricultural production in the two provinces included paper and salt making, *saké* brewing and cotton textiles, and took the form of proto-industry carried out for the most part as farm family by-employment. In the final analy-sis, proto-industry is "rudimentary industry" prior to industrialization and was not necessarily directly linked to the modern factory-system. But we cannot ignore the fact that proto-industry became the archetype of "traditional industry" of the Meiji period, nor that the social economic changes attendant upon the appearance of proto-industry—for example, the penetration of the market economy into agricultural villages and the changes due to demographic variables—played the role of spurring the beginning of full-fledged industrialization.

5. Monetary Aspects of Tokugawa Period Economic Development

Tokugawa Japan depended on the development, to a certain degree, of a market economy and a money economy. Therefore, an examination of Tokugawa era economic changes must not only look at actual goods, but also pay attention to currency conditions. Of course, national economic accounting or modern economic statistics did not exist in the Tokugawa period, so our analysis in this area requires some contrivance. The history of prices—the examination of fluctuations in prices, for which there is a relatively large amount of quantitative data—is one method for investi-gating total fluctuations in the economy in a pre-statistical age. This field has a long tradition in studies of European history. In the area of Tokugawa-period economic history, Hiroshi Shimbo, Masaru Iwahashi, and Ryûzô Yamazaki have actively promoted this method over the past decades. In Chapter 5 of this volume I offer a detailed analysis of eco-nomic change, based on a price history approach. In the following overview, we will reduce the Tokugawa period to its early, middle, and late periods.

Figure 1.2 shows long-term changes in the price of rice in Hiroshima, the domain with the most continuous record of rice prices among the var-ious regions for which Masaru Iwahashi collected data. Beginning with the fluctuations of the seventeenth century (excepting the Kan'ei famine of the 1630s), the price of rice tended to rise from approximately 20 *monme* per *koku* in the 1620s to the 50 *monme* range of the early 1660s. The price remained at a plateau thereafter, until it rose suddenly in the last few years of the century. In fact, it appears that the early seventeenth century trend of rising rice prices had begun in the middle of the sixteenth century

Matao Miyamoto

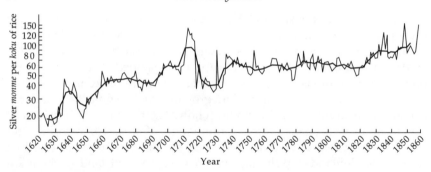

Fig. 1.2. Rice price fluctuations and trends in Hiroshima (moving eleven year median).

Source: Iwashashi (1981: 410–11).

(Iwahashi 1985: 25–7). The Tokugawa period opened in the midst of a secular trend of rising prices. Let us begin, therefore, by examining this aspect of early modern price history.

It is natural to see the rise in rice prices, from the beginning of the seventeenth century to just past its mid-point, as deriving from a rising demand for rice due to population increase (Iwahashi 1981). Throughout this period, the shogunate's rice price policy sought to keep the price of rice down, which took the concrete form of demand-suppressing policies such as limitations on *saké* brewing, restrictions on the rice market, and prohibitions against rice hoarding. This is evidence of demand pressures. Ryûzô Yamazaki argues that more than being a matter of the increase in national population, the price of rice was pushed up by an increase in the urban population, beginning with a price rise due to an imbalance between supply and demand in the central markets of Osaka and Edo, which then led to rising prices in castle town markets with close connections to the central markets—such as in Hiroshima and Nagoya. The leveling of the price of rice from the mid-1660s until just prior to the Genroku recoinage was due to the easing of the urban supply–demand stringency due to the establishment of rice shipping systems to Osaka and Edo (Yamazaki 1983). Yamazaki's hypothesis focuses on the late establishment of a distribution system for the population that had concentrated in the cities, and an advancing social division of labor, to explain the mechanism by which rice prices rose.

Even if a tightening of supply and demand for rice was the cause of the increases in the price of rice, it is incorrect to argue that there were limits to the ability to meet demand and that the entire rise in demand was absorbed in the price rise. If that were true, then actual per capita consumption would decline, which is hard to correlate with the decline in infant mortality—which is seen as a factor in the population growth of this period—and with the improvement in the standard of living, which

brought about an extension in the average life span. As we saw above, the
early part of the Tokugawa period was an age of widespread land reclamation and the development of techniques suited to small-scale agriculture.
That is, it also appears that supply capacity expanded. Therefore, even if
population pressure is taken as a causal factor in rice prices increases, the
rise in demand due to population growth would come first and the
expansion of supply capacity would follow. The rise in rice prices would
come about as a result of the continuation of this demand first and
supply second relation. Put another way, the rise in rice prices due to a
continuous demand–supply gap would have spurred land reclamation
and rice cultivation.

However, one cannot explain the long-term rise in rice prices, which
had continued since the previous century, with supply and demand
factors in real terms alone. Even if potential demand expanded as the
population grew, effective demand would not expand if the potential
demand did not take form in purchasing power with money expenditures. Moreover, as noted above, there was a tremendous expansion of the
scale of the economy in the seventeenth century. Other relevant developments in the market economy, such as the emergence of a market in the
tax rice collected by daimyo (*nengumai shijô*), were also seen. There is no
doubt that the transaction demand for money experienced a remarkable
increase. Under these conditions, an inadequate money supply would, in
fact, lead to falling prices.

As Masaru Iwahashi, in Chapter 2 in this volume, examines the
process by which the currency system of the Tokugawa period was established—at the very beginning of its reign, the Tokugawa shogunate
unified the currency system, producing both gold and silver coins. From
1636, the shogunate minted great quantities of copper coins known as
Kan'ei tsûhô for use by commoners. Japan on the eve of the Tokugawa
period had suffered from a shortage of the Chinese copper coins, which
were its basic currency. Moreover, smooth economic transaction was
hampered by the fact that the coins' utility as a standard of value was in
decline due to wear and tear, and consequent loss of specie content.
Therefore, the shogunate's establishment of a currency system and
issuance of a large volume of uniform coins played a crucial role in the
development of a money economy.

These policies were further supported by the large-scale production of
gold and silver due to the advance of mining and engineering technology
since the Warring States era. It is also important that the famous "Taikô's
windfall" (*taikô no kanekubari*), the gold and silver that had been accumulated by Toyotomi Hideyoshi, was appropriated by the Tokugawa with
the fall of Osaka castle and then released into circulation after being
reminted as the shogunate's currency.[20] Nevertheless, the volume of coins
available for domestic circulation was diminished by their use as export

goods for foreign trade, with an estimated 80 per cent of silver coins and 13 per cent of gold coins minted during the seventeenth century flowing out of the country, with that outflow at its highest in the first half of the century.[21] Overall, however, the money supply increased tremendously during the first half of the seventeenth century, when there was a plentiful volume of precious metals used for currency made available from mining. Shunsaku Nishikawa estimates that the volume of gold and silver currency in the domestic economy increased by a factor of four during the seventeenth century (Nishikawa 1985: 49–50).

The price of rice ceased rising after the 1660s, maintaining a plateau or falling into slight decline until the end of the century. This was due, in part, to an increase in the capacity of the agrarian sector to supply rice thanks to the developments in rice cultivation from the beginning of the early modern era outlined above. But what was more important were continuing difficulties in providing an additional supply of currency to meet the demands from economic activity. Many of the gold and silver mines that had increased production since the Warring States period, began to dry up, and the gold and silver stocks began to hit bottom. The volume of silver sent to the shogunate from the largest mines of the Tokugawa period on Sado Island showed a continual decline.

In the 1620s, during the reign of the third shogun Iemitsu, an average of 6,000 *kan* of silver per year was sent to Edo. That figure declined to 1,000 *kan* per year during the Kambun (1661–73) era under the fourth shogun, Ietsuna, and 800 *kan* per year during the Genroku era under the fifth shogun Tsunayoshi (Taya 1963). The flow of silver coins abroad through Nagasaki rose during the 1650s and reached a peak during the 1660s, but went into decline thereafter. But the outflow continued through Tsushima until the middle of the eighteenth century, as Kazui Tashiro shows in Chapter 3 in this volume. In 1668, the shogunate prohibited the export of silver through the Dutch trade in Nagasaki, and in 1685 it limited trade with China and the Dutch by adopting official limits on trade volume. The shogunate furthermore encouraged "substitute exchanges"—exporting copper instead of silver. All of these policies suggest that the shogunate had recognized that the shortage of silver for domestic currency had become increasingly desperate following nearly a century of extensive outflow.

Fukui domain is said to have pioneered domainal paper currency in 1661. According to Yôtarô Sakudô, forty-six domains had issued paper currency by the Hôei period (1704–11), thirty-five of which were located in Kinki or regions to the west (Sakudô 1958: 158, 206). There are many reasons why domains issued paper currencies, but if we recognize that many of the issuing domains were located in the silver-utilizing economic sphere, that is, in western Japan, then the shortage of silver coins seems a natural reason. The establishment of specialist financiers, such as money changers, came in the middle of the seventeenth century, as did the wide-spread use of a variety of exchange notes. For example, during the Kambun–Empô era, the Osaka merchant house of Kônoike Zen'emon began to offset remittances to Osaka of money from sales of its *saké* in Edo with exchanges of remittances to the Edo mansions of western daimyo; for the sales of their tax rice in Osaka (Sakudô 1961: 313–15; Kawakami 1970; Miyamoto 1978: 64–8). The 1691 decision of the shogunate to change from actual overland transport of currency acquired in the west to exchange remittances via the Echigoya (Mitsui) exchange house and others (known as the Osaka Treasury Exchange) (Nakai 1961: 189–95), suggest that this kind of exchange system had already taken shape to a certain extent. The development of credit instruments that had the effect of saving official currency, and the development of "near money" within the development of a money economy suggest the onset of a relative currency shortage.

It appears that the continuing difficulties with the currency supply that accompanied the development of a market economy brought the economy to a state of slow-down around the 1680s. I suggested in the previous section that the end of the seventeenth century began to see a narrowing of development on the real goods front as well. That may have been a consequence of the relative shrinkage of the currency described above.

The timing of the Genroku recoinage (1695) was clearly related to these factors. There is no denying that one of the major goals of the Genroku recoinage was the earning of recoinage profits by a shogunate that was directly facing budgetary troubles. The reasons (Ôkurasho, T922–25: Vol. 2, 568–69) given by the shogunate for the "recasting"—that "the stamps on the gold and silver coins had grown old" and that "the amount of silver and gold produced in the mines in recent years has not been great and the number of coins in use has been gradually declining"—were by no means simple prevarication. There were, indeed, many coins that had been lost or damaged and there was a general shortage of coins.

Under the Genroku recoinage, gold coins were debased from the Keichô gold-content levels of 84.29 per cent to the Genroku gold-content level of 57.36 per cent, while silver coins were debased from the Keichô *chôgin* level of 80 per cent to the Genroku level of 64 per cent. Silver coins were further debased to a silver-content level of 50 per cent in 1706, with the production of Hôei silver coins. It is estimated that the currency supply rose by 85 per cent between 1695 and 1710 under the recoinages of 1695 and 1706 (Iwahashi 1976: 258). In the exchange of Keichô gold for Genroku gold, the initial exchange was made at 101 *ryô* of Genroku gold for 100 *ryô* of Keichô gold, a premium of 1 per cent. Later that premium was increased to 20 per cent. Silver was originally exchanged at a premium of 2 per cent, but that was later adjusted to 25 per cent. Therefore, the nominal currency holdings among the population increased by no more than 20–25 per cent. Of the 85 per cent increase in currency from these recoinages, 55–60 points went to the shogunate as recoinage profits, which were then reminted and put back into circulation. In fact, the shogunate earned nearly 100,000 *kanme* in silver alone from the two recoinages (Taya 1963: 193).

On the other hand, the price of rice (the simple average of the rice price indexes in Osaka, Hiroshima, Edo, and Nagoya) rose only 15 per cent during this period. The goal of the recoinage—to earn recoinage profits and rescue shogunal finances—was achieved, but as I noted above, there appears to have been a considerable deflationary gap in the economy of the time. So the recoinage had the effect of raising real incomes without raising prices very much. Of course, had the good coins (the Keichô gold and silver) not been exchanged for the debased coins, but been hoarded instead, then prices would not have risen, nor would real incomes increase appreciably. However, the Genroku era prosperity of the cities and the flourishing of merchant culture could not have occurred in an economy with shrinking currency. One could argue that the Genroku recoinage had an exemplary reflationary effect.

The Genroku recoinage was the brainchild of the Finance Magistrate (*kanjô bugyô*), Ogiwara Shigehide. The shogunate also carried out recoinages in 1710 and 1711, perhaps because it was becoming accustomed to the taste of success. Silver coins were recast into the Eiji-gin (40 per cent fine), the Mitsuhô-gin (32 per cent fine), and the Yotsuhô-gin (20 per cent fine), while gold coins were restored to the gold-content levels of the Keichô era, albeit in half the volume of the Keichô and Genroku coins. As a result, the number of coins increased by 23 per cent from 1710 to 1714 (Iwahashi 1976: 258). During the same period, the price of rice rose by 81 per cent.

Compared to the period prior to the Genroku recoinage, the amount of currency had increased by 127 per cent and the price of rice had risen by 109 percent. The money supply had not expanded as much as it had under the Genroku and Hôei recoinages, but prices rose at a high rate. Why? There is a strong possibility that shogunal budgets, bloated by the enormous recoinage profits from silver alone, which rose to 176,000 *kan* (Taya 1963: 193), caused an inflation gap in an economy that had already reached a state of equilibrium with the Genroku recoinage. Judging by the real supply capacity of the economy at the time, an extension of the money supply by 2.3 times over a twenty-year period was excessive. As a result of the successive recoinages and inflation, cash wages also rose, albeit with a time lag. Ogiwara experienced one further misfortune that complicated his task: there were recurrent crop failures in western Japan between 1714 and 1716. When a supply shock was added to the above conditions, prices necessarily exploded. Accordingly, the Hôei recoinage was a currency policy with poor timing, and so was not as successful as the Genroku recoinage.

Ogiwara, harshly criticized by Arai Hakuseki for close relations with minters who had earned profits from the Genroku and Hôei recoinages, was forced to retire. According to Hakuseki's memorial, the shogunate had undertaken a recoinage (known as the Shôtoku–Kyôhô recoinage) that restored coins to their Keichô-era quality in 1714. As a result, the volume of coins fell by 33 per cent between 1714 and 1736 (Iwahashi 1980: 258). But the price of rice fell even more steeply, by 65 per cent. Compared to the period prior to the Genroku recoinage, the volume of currency had risen 51 per cent, but the price of rice had fallen by 26 per cent. Why did the price of rice fall even further than the contraction of currency? Or, why is it that even though the volume of currency was still higher than prior to the Genroku recoinage, the price of rice did not return to its old level? The answer may most likely be found in the development of the following process.

At the time of the Shôtoku–Kyôhô recoinage, the shogunate was undertaking a policy of drastic budgetary contraction, drastically cutting back on unnecessary expenditures. The shogunate was likely hit hard by recoinage losses from a currency appreciation policy. Both government expenditures and samurai class consumption were forced to contract. The contraction of the volume of currency, government expenditures, and samurai class consumption meant a reduction of demand for urban merchant and artisanal services, leading to a decline in townspeople's cash income. The Kyôhô era policy of increasing tax levies also forced peasant consumption to contract. This reduction in consumption led to a decline in prices, particularly that of rice (the income elasticity of rice demand was greater than it is today because rice was, at the time, a luxury item for most commoners). It was the samurai and the peasants who would suffer from a decline in the price of rice.

The price elasticity of the rice supply was slight, so that if the price fell the supply increased (sales from straitened circumstances). That is, the supply curve might have had a negative slope. This would have been particularly true for the daimyo and samurai class, which had no way to acquire cash other than by marketing their tax rice. Moreover, the economic stimulus from the Genroku and Hôei recoinages raised the productive power of agriculture. This caused the amount of tax rice shipped by the domains to the cities to rise. On the one hand, effective demand declined (a downward shift of the total demand curve), while on the other hand there was an increase in the supply seeking to acquire cash (a downward shift of the total supply curve). Therefore the deflationary gap widened, making the precipitous drop of prices, especially rice prices, unavoidable. There is no doubt that the economy was driven into extreme instability. If even the earnings of the Kônoike Zen'emon house, one of the greatest urban merchant houses of the time, suffered a setback, the impact on lesser merchant and artisanal establishments must have been even more severe (Yasuoka 1970a).

The shogunate naturally attempted a variety of measures in response to a situation in which "the price of rice is low although the prices of other commodities is high." These measures included supply restriction policies, such as the order to limit shipments of tax rice, and demand stimulus policies, such as orders to purchase rice, the encouragement of *saké* brewing and the recognition of a rice futures market.[22] But these policies, with their focus on the goods themselves, did not lead to a fundamental resolution of the problem. Thus, in 1736, the eighth shogun, Tokugawa Yoshimune, adopted a monetary policy that took a 180 degree turnabout from the policy he had adopted twenty years earlier. This was the Gembun recoinage.

The method used for exchanging the old coins for new under the Gembun recoinage was the "premium exchange method" (*mashibu kôkan hôshiki*). In other words, when old coins were exchanged for new, sixty-five additional *ryô* were issued for every hundred *ryô* of gold coins, and five *kanme* were issued for every ten *kanme* of silver. The Gembun *koban* (gold coin) was debased to 48 per cent of the purity of the Kyôho *koban*. The Gembun *chôgin* (silver coin) was cut to 57.5 per cent of the Kyôho *chôgin*. Therefore, the shogunate earned a profit even though it paid a premium on the old coins, although the Gembun earnings were lower than those from the Genroku and Hôei recoinages. When one includes recoinage expenses, it turns out that the shogunate earned almost nothing. According to Hiroshi Shimbo, "The policy taken by the shogunate at the time of the Gembun recoinage was to sacrifice recoinage profits in order to promote the circulation of the new currency" (Shimbo 1978: 56).

As a result, when the entire supply of old coins was exchanged for the new, the volume of gold coins increased by 65 per cent and the volume of silver coins increased by 50 per cent. The exchange did not happen all at once, but the potential volume of currency in the market rose in an instant. As a result, the price of rice in Osaka doubled from 1735 to 1738. General prices rose, but the exchange of rice mainly took place in the cities where the new currency began to circulate first, and where the cash income flexibility of demand was high, so its rate of rise was relatively high. The recoinage had the desired effect of raising the relative price of rice, but what about the goal of rising real income?

The Shôtoku–Kyôho recoinage gave rise to a condition of financial stringency. With the appearance of an expanded potential supply capacity, an increase in the money supply was like a merciful rain irrigating the economy. However, according to wage data for western Settsu Province, in the area around Osaka, cash wages clearly rose after the Gembun recoinage compared to their earlier levels (Saitô 1976a). This means that the total supply curve shifted upward, so that price levels rose even higher than they might otherwise have while suppressing the rise in real incomes, even while nominal income rose. But other evidence, such as the fact that after the Gembun recoinage the shogunal budget achieved a remarkable balance between revenue and expenditures, suggests that the economy was vibrant.

As we saw above, the half-century from Genroku to Gembun witnessed several recoinages, and recurrent and violent fluctuations in prices in response. However, recoinage not only affects price levels, but also influences people's preference with regard to investment, consumption, and savings, through the effects it has on government budgets and the money supply. Recoinage also affects the economy in real terms and, through all of this, alters both general price levels and the relative prices of various commodities. In other words, even if the volume of bullion in a society does not change, one can create effects in the real economy by changing the nominal volume of currency through recoinage. Thus, the shogunate had acquired a new tool of economic policy. But if the money economy or market economy had not fully permeated society, these policy measures would have had little effect. The economy of the middle of Tokugawa period had experienced sufficient development of a money and market economy for these kinds of monetary and financial policies to have adequate effects.

As Tashiro also points out, Keichô gold and silver coins were both domestic currency and an "export commodity." Given that dual character, shogunal recoinages could have only limited effects on domestic economic conditions. Changing the precious metal content of coins (while retaining the same face value or weight) meant changing the quality of the export commodity. This could cause trade friction (as Tashiro shows, the greatly debased Hôei silver coins were refused in Korea, forcing the special minting of a high quality silver coin for use in the ginseng trade) and would make the use of a gold-to-silver exchange rate, which was different from that in foreign markets, difficult in an open system. Moreover, if there were a domestic free market in precious metals, then the agency in charge of currency would be unable to set the relative value of gold to silver unilaterally. In order to give the shogunate a free hand in managing the quality and volume of currency, while using precious metal coins as the base currency, the domestic market in precious metals had to be separated from foreign markets, and the domestic market had to be controlled.

What made the recoinages from Genroku through Gembun possible was that the restrictions enacted on the export of gold and silver had obtained a measure of success. Seen from the other side, the frequent recoinages of the shogunate's currency had an effect on their acceptability as export goods, putting a halt to the dual character of the currency. The terms *ryô* and *monme*, which had originally designated weights of a fixed

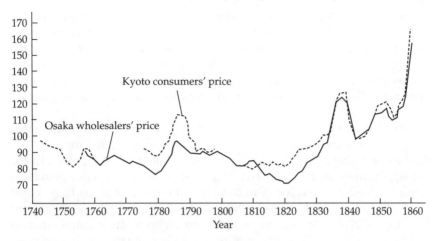

Fig. 1.3. General price trends (index: five-year average fluctuations).
Source: Shimbo (1978: 38).

quality of precious metals (gold and silver, respectively) now became the denominations for coins. For example, "silver *monme*" still designated a unit of weight, but no longer of a fixed purity. Thus, thanks to the recoinages from the Genroku to Gembun eras, the shogunate's currency lost its character as a commodity currency and embarked on the path of becoming a kind of fiat money. This acted as the forerunner of the *Nanryô nishugin* in the Tanuma era (1767–86).

The rapid rise in prices after the Gembun recoinage was a temporary phenomenon. From then until around 1820, excepting the period of the Tenmei crop failures, prices remained stable, or declined (see Figure 1.3). Hiroshi Shimbo points out that although there was an increase in currency during this period, with the minting of the *Nanryô nishugin* and other coins (in fact the volume of shogunal currency rose about 40 per cent from 1736 to 1818), the stability of prices can be explained by "the development of a market economy" and "the expansion of the volume of transactions."[23] Put another way, there was an appropriate money supply for this kind of economic development and a balance was maintained in the economy between its goods and monetary aspects.

The increase in demand for money must have been great. According to Shimbo and Hasegawa, in Chapter 5 in this volume, an examination of transshipment statistics in Osaka in 1714 shows that the city had a large import surplus. This was not a phenomenon of that year alone, but was the normal situation. And the same was true for Edo. As long as the advance of a money economy continued in agricultural villages, the supply of the necessary shogunal currency would have to come first of all through the scattered cities. The domainal trade surpluses with Osaka demonstrate the flow of currency from Osaka to the regional domains (of course, as Shimbo and Hasegawa point out this alone does not account for the import surplus in Osaka). As long as the domains continued to absorb currency, the shogunate was able to "pollute [the realm] with bad coins." In fact, "pollution" was necessary to support the advance of the money economy.

Why is it that the money supply continued to operate smoothly even though there were no major recoinages after Gembun? It turns out that the *Nanryô nishugin*, minted under Tanuma Okitsugu's rule, was a major innovation in the history of currency. The *Nanryô nishugin* was a gold face-value coin—with the value of two *shu* of gold stamped on its face—eight of which could be exchanged for one *ryô* of gold. Its weight was 2.7 *monme* and it was 97.75 per cent pure silver, so eight of these coins equaled 21.1 *monme* of pure silver. The quality of the Gembun *chôgin* circulating at the time was 46 per cent silver. Thus, with the shogunate's official gold to silver exchange rate at one *ryô* of gold for sixty *monme* of silver, 27.6 *monme* of Gembun *chôgin* silver was equal to one *ryô* of gold. The market price for gold at the time was one *ryô* for 30.8 *monme* of Gembun *chôgin* silver. In other words, while they were both silver coins, the silver in the *Nanryô nishugin* coins was valued higher than the silver in the weighted silver coins (the Gembun *chôgin*).

The contradiction of a single metal being valued in two ways was hidden by the representation that the "*Nanryô*" was composed of high-quality imported silver. Thus, for the same amount of silver, the *Nanryô nishugin* was minted in greater value, at face value, than was the *chôgin*. So in retrieving the *chôgin* and minting the *Nanryô nishugin*, the shogunate not only earned profits, it was also able to increase the amount of currency in circulation. The *Nanryô nishugin* was also a gold standard coin, so adjusting the proportions to the weighted silver coins resulted in an adjustment of the market price of gold. If a gold standard supplementary coin like the *Nanryô nishugin* had not been conceived, then the shogunate's means to supply currency would have been limited.

However, even with the *Nanryô nishugin*, the shogunal currency increased from 1736 to 1818 by only 40 per cent. This alone may have caused a currency shortage. In fact, prices fell from the end of the eighteenth century, according to Figure 1.3. The currency shortage was supplemented by the issuance of domainal notes and the expansion of a system for issuing credit notes by exchange houses. These financial developments completed the Tokugawa era currency system, which had seen no major reforms, excepting the issuing of the *Nanryô nishugin*, after the Gembun recoinage.

Studies of price history are able to begin taking into account the relative prices of various commodities from the eighteenth century. My other essay in this volume (Chapter 4) takes this up in detail. Nevertheless, considering the issues Hayami raised in the Introduction to this volume, we must take up the fluctuations in the relative prices of agricultural to industrial products. In an analysis of the relative prices of rice, cotton, rapeseed, and raw silk, Ryûzô Yamazaki has shown that from the middle of the Kyôhô era to the end of the Kansei era the price of rice fell to these other commodities. Yamazaki explains this by noting that the development of rice productivity throughout the seventeenth century caused the price of rice to fall from the mid-Kyôhô period. Based on those developments, commercial agriculture grew throughout the eighteenth century in such commodities as cotton and rapeseed. Yamazaki sees in this an overall growth of the eighteenth century agricultural economy (Yamazaki 1983; see also Yamazaki's statements in Harada and Miyamoto 1985, chapter 3).

Likewise, Shimbo notes that until 1780 the price of rice relative to other commodities, and the relative price of agricultural goods in general, remained at low levels, and that, furthermore, the prices of comestible agricultural products, such as rice, soy beans, and wheat, remained at a relatively low level compared to prices of industrial raw materials derived from agriculture, such as rapeseed and cotton. It is here that Shimbo finds the key to the growth of the agricultural processing sector (Shimbo 1978).

Indeed, the most important problem for the shogunate's price policy after the middle of the Kyôhô era was how to respond to the relative decline in the price of rice. The shogunate struggled to resolve this problem by ordering various restrictions on the issuance of rice voucher (*kome kitte*) issued by the Osaka warehouses of the various domains and by formulating a rice purchasing policy through forced loans beginning in 1760.

From all of this we can surmise that over the long term in the eighteenth century, the supply of agricultural products (particularly grains) did not decline to insufficiency, but rather tended toward overproduction. On the other hand, there was expansion of demand for commercial crops used in industry and for non-agricultural products, which stimulated the development of non-agricultural production and services in agricultural villages. In the eighteenth century fallow fields began appearing in the countryside, with an expansion of non-agricultural employment in the form of agricultural by-industry, and the growth of specialized production in every region. This may be seen as a change in the distribution of resources from agriculture to nonagricultural industries due to a change in the conditions of exchange between agriculture and industry. This occurred in conjunction with the changes in the economy in real goods that we saw in the previous section.

6. The Distribution Flow of the Tokugawa Economy

6.1. *The distributing flows among economic corporations*

It is often said that Tokugawa society was established on the foundation of a certain level of market economy. If that is the case, then how was this market economy constructed and how did it function?

Today's capitalist society is basically composed of three economic corporations; the household, enterprise, and government. The household contains the factors of production (labor, land, and capital). It supplies these to enterprises and receives in return wages, land rent, profit, and interest. With these forms of income, the household purchases consumption goods and services from enterprises. On the other hand, enterprises use the production factors they purchase from the household to carry out production and supply the family. These transactions between the household and enterprises take place in the product market and the production factors market.

Of course, enterprises purchase intermediate goods, such as raw materials, parts and such, from other enterprises. Those transactions take place in the intermediate goods market and the capital goods market. There is a relatively large number of instances in modern society where round-about production has reached a high level. Households and enterprises take information on prices established at the market (prices for goods and services, wages, land rent, and profits) and act in such a way as to maximize their own economic interests. The distribution of resources is determined by the aggregate of the activities of these countless economic actors. The government, in turn, takes taxes from households and enterprises and provides public goods and services. This is the non-market economy portion.

Thus, in capitalist society, enterprise and government carry out production of goods and services, while household and government undertake consumption and savings. Of course, family operated enterprises, such as farm families and family stores, are involved in both production/investment and consumption/savings, and enterprises also save. But in essence we may say that economic subjects divide up the functions of production/investment and consumption/saving.

What was the Tokugawa period like in comparison? Let us begin with the early period. Figure 1.4 is an attempt to illustrate the circular flows in the early Tokugawa era economy. The existence of three economic subjects is assumed: peasants, tradesmen (merchants and artisans), and the samurai class. Peasants and tradesmen were simultaneously households and enterprises. In the Tokugawa period, the stem family was the unit of daily life. Even though there were a variety of restrictions on consumption imposed by the ruling class, the peasants and the tradesmen were the subjects who determined consumption and savings. At the same time, they were the subjects who possessed and provided the production factors of labor, land, and capital. With regard to labor, there were various restrictions on movement and regulations for the monopolistic determination of occupation based on status. But the household was free to allocate its labor hours, and thus the peasants and tradesmen were the subjects who determined the labor supply. This makes Tokugawa society different from a slave or patriarchal extended family society in which a ruler determines these labor factors not related by blood.

With regard to the means of production, land had come to be owned de facto by the peasants and small farm families owned production tools. Of course, we should note that common lands, such as grasslands and water facilities, which held a far greater importance as means of production then than now, were not possessed by single households, but by communities. Thus, it is clear that the household was established as the unit of consumption and savings, and as the possessor and provider of production factors. On the other hand, the household was the subject that produced goods and services by using production factors and carried out investment. The small family farm operation, which was the main form of early Tokugawa agriculture, carried out production with household labor power, using the land and tools owned by the household.

Tradesmen also used their own capital and their families provided the core labor power. During the Tokugawa period, peasants and tradesmen were functionally both households and enterprises.[24] The flow of production factors from the household to the enterprise and the flow of income from enterprises to possessors of production factors both took place within the peasant or tradesman household. The flow of production factors within the blocs of the peasants and tradesmen, surrounded by a solid line in Figure 1.4 represents this process. Accordingly, there was no development of an exterior market for production factors (a labor and capital market), or, if there was one, it was very small. The fact that there are so few records on wages and interest rates for the early Tokugawa period is probably due to these conditions.

However, a product market and an intermediate and capital goods markets were necessary. The household was the site of production and consumption, but that does not mean that it was self-sufficient in all production resources or essential goods. Not only tradesmen, but also peasants had to purchase handicrafts, salt, agricultural tools, and those agricultural products they could not supply themselves. Households consumed goods and services produced by other households, as well as investing in them, and they also sold goods and services to other households. The bold line connecting the peasant and tradesmen blocks in Figure 1.4 shows this flow of goods and services. The flow of currency was in the opposite direction. How thick these flows would become—in other words, what the scale of the market would be—depended on the

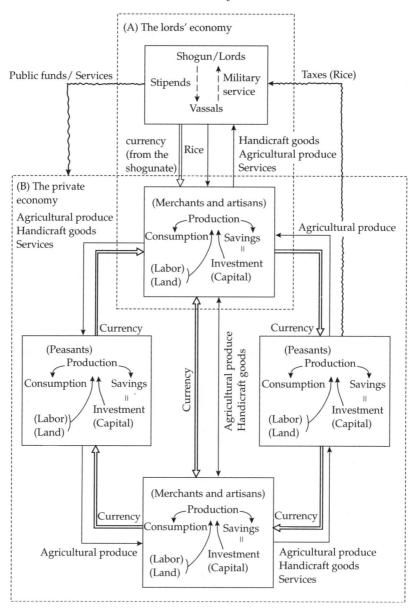

Fig. 1.4. The flows in the Tokugawa economy (1).

scale of self-supply and the development round-about production. What is certain is that it was not as great as it is in modern capitalist society. But it is a mistake to think that this pipeline was completely disconnected during the Tokugawa period.

The above is a description of Block B, the block surrounded by the dotted line in Figure 1.4, that is the private sector of the economy. What about Block A, the economy of the daimyo and samurai? We cannot equate the shogunate and the daimyo, including its vassals, with governments of modern times. But as noted by Hayami (Introduction, this volume), the annual rice taxes (*nengu*) of the Tokugawa period were the price of the administrative services of roads, irrigation, peacekeeping, maintenance of order in the market, and disaster relief. Tax revenues were not completely consumed by the daimyos' households, but served toward the provision of "public goods" as well. It is also important to note that they were returned to the circular flow of the economy as investment in social overhead capital. The flow of taxes and public goods and services was the non-market portion of the economy and is represented in Figure 1.4 by the wavy lines. The figure represents the costs of providing public goods and services as if they were wholly paid for by agricultural taxes. This is an oversimplification, but it is recognition of the fact that the system for taxing commerce was weak.

Rice was at the core of annual taxes, but the rice received by the samurai class was not simply a form of in-kind land rent applied to the daily consumption of the lords. Rather, it was the principal goods that were exchanged on the market for cash, which was then used to purchase other articles for consumption. This process was the foundation of the tax rice market and the market for handicrafts, services, and agricultural products other than rice. The lordly commodity market that developed around tax rice has often been seen to be independent of the reproduction of the private sector of the economy. But as we can see in the overlap between the two blocks surrounded by dotted lines (Blocks A and B), the lords' economy and the private economy were bound together through the mediation of the tradesmen.

As I discussed above, there was a necessary circulation of commodities among peasants, between peasants and artisans, and among artisans themselves. This circulation gave birth to commercial and merchant activity, which formed the prerequisite to the sale of tax rice, which in turn was the foundation of a ruling-class commodity economy for purchasing daily necessities. As I shall elaborate further below, the release onto the market of a stable supply of tax rice, which was the most important daily commodity for tradesmen living in the cities and castle towns, supported the flows in the private economy.

When turning to the supply of currency that supports a market economy, the almost sole source of currency in the early Tokugawa period when there was as yet an insufficient development of financial institutions (such as money exchange house) was a shogunate that possessed a monopoly on mines. The shogunate, which possessed a monopoly on the right to mint coins, deducted the costs of minting from the face value of the coins and kept that portion as seignieurage. This portion returned to the private economy after passing through the lordly commodity economy. Therefore, in the relations between the lordly economy and the private economy, the lordly economy had excess receipts of commodities and excess payments of currency. But this does not mean that the liquidity demanded by the private economy was appropriately provided for in this system. With the decline of the precious metal stocks used for coins, the shogunate lost its power to mint coins so that as the private money economy developed further it was faced with insufficient liquidity. As currency debasements occurred in succession, there was an excess of liquidity that caused inflation. As we saw in the earlier part of this chapter, the changes in the shogunate's currency policies in fact produced these economic results. This fact proves that the flows of the lordly and private economies, as depicted in Figure 1.4, worked.

Let us now turn to the diagram of late Tokugawa period economic flows in Figure 1.5. The division I am drawing here between early and late Tokugawa is not meant to designate a strict boundary, but aims at a relation of chronological order. The late Tokugawa period requires consideration of the development of financial institutions, so I have reclassified the "tradesmen" designation as "tradesmen/financiers." Peasants and tradesmen/financiers constituted both "households" and "enterprises," as in the earlier period. However, the specialization of production had progressed through a division of labor and the markets for products, intermediary products, and capital goods had expanded further due to the development of agricultural processing industries for such products as cotton and vegetable oils. But what was even more important was the development of the production factors market in such forms as: the movement of hired labor from the villages to urban sites or to the rural operations of wealthy farmers; loans of land from landlords to small cultivators (tenancy); loans of money from merchants, financiers, and landlords to handicraftsmen, merchants, and peasants;[25] loans from merchants and financiers to the ruling class; the formation of a joint venture made possible by the receipt of investments from relatives. These mean that transactions in production factors from the "household" portion of one household to the "production" portion of another household became nothing out of the ordinary. This made possible the appearance of income paid to production factors (wages, land rent, interest, profit). The broken lines in Figure 1.5 represent this income. This means that the separation of the subject of production and investment from the subject of consumption and savings had progressed to a certain extent.

Since the amount of annual tax rice the lords collected did not expand very much, the weight of the lords' purchases of daily necessities, using cash exchanged for tax rice, in the overall economy declined. But in the late Tokugawa period, many domains engaged in monopsony purchases of particular commodities produced within their boundaries, which they

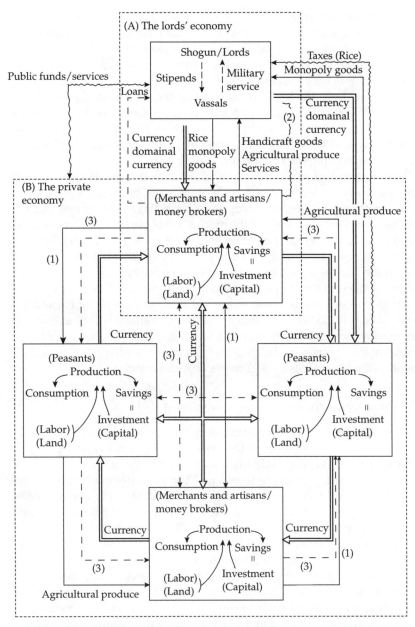

Fig. 1.5. The flows in the Tokugawa economy (2). 1. Agricultural produce, handicraft goods, monopoly goods, services. 2. Taxes on commercial and artisanal activity. 3. Factors of production.

had designated as "monopsony goods." They then established domainal product trade and finance bureaus (*kokusan kaisho*), and warehouses through which they engaged in monopoly sales of the goods in extra-domainal markets. Thus, this area of activity was added to the lords' economy. This is why the category of "special products" was added to the flow of assets from the lords' households to tradesmen in Figure 1.5. The official authorization of trade associations (*kabunakama*) made possible the levying of various taxes on tradesmen, such as forced contributions and loans and special taxes for the privilege of operating a trade and business such as *myôgakin* (offertory money).

Thus, the product market, the production factors market, and the lords' commodity market all expanded in absolute terms, but what was the corresponding change in the money supply? The coinage debasements starting with the Genroku recoinage and the production of stamped, face-value coins (the *Nanryô nishugin*) starting with the An'ei period (1772–81), were all means to increase the supply of money. Two more channels were added to these in the late Tokugawa period. One was the issuance of domainal notes and the other was the issuance of credit (in a variety of notes) by money exchange houses. The inclusion of both of these in the flow of currency, as shown in Figure 1.5, must be interpreted. Both domainal notes and money exchange house-credit instruments had limited circulation, but there is little doubt that they weakened the shogunate's supreme authority over currency, as well as the effects of the shogunate's financial policies.

6.2. *The structure of interregional circulation*

The circular flows among economic subjects that we saw above could be found in many domains. With the separation of samurai and peasants, and the separation of merchants and peasants, the samurai class and tradesmen lived in the castle towns and the peasants made the villages their place of residence and production. Accordingly, tax rice and other agricultural products made their way from the villages to the castle towns and handicraft goods flowed from the castle towns to the villages. Markets were established in the castle towns or in villages under the aegis of castle town merchants. But the circular flows within each domain was not self-sustaining. Artisans were concentrated in the castle towns, but their technological and productive levels were low. With village industry also as yet undeveloped in the early Tokugawa period, the samurai and commoner demands for handicraft goods, art, military goods, and agricultural processed goods could not be fulfilled within the domain alone. However, paddy-field rice cultivation was stabilized from the Warring States period to the beginning of the early modern era, thanks to land reclamation in alluvial plains and the introduction of new strains of rice.

This led to the settlement of an agricultural class centered on rice cultivation. Not only did they achieve self-sufficient production of the major grains, but also they were able to produce enough rice to exceed the demands from the samurai, merchants, and artisans. This necessitated a long distance trade in rice and other agricultural products for handicraft goods between the peripheral domains and the advanced central region. This pattern of a regional division of labor is one of the major characteristics of the circular flows in the early Tokugawa economy.

The Kinai region was the advanced central region I referred to above. In Chapter 5 in this volume, Shimbo and Hasegawa used Shigeyori Matsue's *haikai* collection, *Kefukigusa*, to examine the state of regional specialty production at the beginning of the early modern era. As their analysis clearly shows, the Kinai region overwhelmed other regions in the production of such handicraft items as clothing, household goods, industrial tools, arts and crafts, and arms. For example, cotton was grown in Ômi, Ise, Owari, Mino, Hida, and Tamba Provinces, but cotton textiles, and secondary goods such as *obi, tabi,* and *hakama*, were produced in Kyoto, Kawachi, Osaka, and Sakai. The same was true for silk and hemp textiles: mulberry was grown in the areas around the Kinki region, but silk and hemp textiles were manufactured mainly in Kyoto, Nara, and Sakai. Thus, during the early Tokugawa period, the Kinai region was in a position of absolute advantage over all other regions in the production of almost all assets, based on a high-level social division of labor. With other regions possessing a comparative advantage in agricultural, forestry, and maritime goods, as well as minerals and the raw materials for handicraft production, a regional distribution of production was established.

This regional distribution was not something that developed only with the advent of the Tokugawa period. Since ancient times, the Kinai region had been the center of politics. It also contained many groups of artisans who had originally been subordinate to *shôen* proprietors and the government workshops that had introduced advanced technology from the continent, but who later became independent due to improvement in their ability to meet rising demand. Thus the preeminence of the Kinai region was also due to such historical factors as its comparative advantage over other regions in the concentration and advancement of technology. With the restrictive foreign policy of the Tokugawa period, it became more difficult to acquire such handicraft goods as arms, high quality clothing, and arts and crafts through international trade. Thus, the regional distribution of production was stimulated by the high dependency of the regional domains on the cities of the Kinai region, the increasing demand of the lords for currency due to the system of alternate attendance and the increasing necessity of participating in the market.

The political division of labor between shogunal and daimyo domains (*bakuhan-sei*) was established on the foundation of the regional division of labor described above. For the lords who ruled regional domains that possessed a comparative advantage in agricultural products, particularly rice, their uniform acquisition of rice as taxes, the commodity in greatest demand in the advanced cities, was nearly their only way to make use of opportunities in the market. This also had the effect of taking that opportunity away from the peasants. It is possible to explain the establishment of the *kokudaka* system as a rice tax system from this perspective.

But the rice tax system had other meanings as well. As noted above, the large-scale rice market for the regional domains was in the distant Kinai region. The transportation of rice was carried out in a point-to-point mode of transport from each of the domains to Osaka. The routes that linked these points were primarily water routes, given that rice was a heavy bulky good, and given the conditions for transport during the Tokugawa period. But water transport does not become economical unless a large volume of goods is shipped all at once. The lord's unilateral acquisition of his domain's rice as taxes had the function of lowering the social costs of rice transport. The fact that with the tax reform of the Meiji era the payment of taxes in cash ended the obstruction to the smooth transport of rice, and the fact that the lords closest to the Kinai region did not ship rice to the market shows how important it was for the lords in distant regions to gain control of the process of shipment. If the rice tax system had not been adopted, and if rice had been shipped by individual mechanisms, there would have been greater difficulties for shipping rice across great distances, which would have acted as a brake on the development of a regional division of labor in the Tokugawa period.

We also cannot ignore the economic effects of the establishment of a regular, official rice market in the central city of Osaka where the tax rice accumulated. With a great ability to process transactions, Osaka rice market functioned as a national center of price formation for rice. Buyers and sellers of commodities incur transaction costs by their participation in a market economy. For example, the seller has transportation costs, sales mechanism construction costs, costs in finding and negotiating with transaction partners, and costs incurred in collecting payments. The seller is furthermore confronted with costs in procuring market information, such as on the conditions of prices and demand. The buyer is also faced with such transaction costs.

These costs are high when there is a new market with each transaction. But when they take place repeatedly in the same market, they become fixed costs. So, as transactions become regularized the average cost per transaction decreases. That is, economies of scale are at work in reducing transactions as well. Likewise, information on prices formed at a market with a large volume of transactions also becomes information on the macro demand for the commodity. The provision of appropriate means for communicating this information so that those engaged in trade can easily access it also contributes to the lowering of transaction costs. For bulk goods like rice, the problem of these transaction costs is quite large.

Let us now explain the circular flow of the early Tokugawa period interregional economy as it is depicted in Figure 1.6. The figure shows three idealized regional units: "peripheral domains," "Osaka and the Kinai," and "Edo." As I stated above, the regional domains had an advantage in the production of agricultural products, particularly rice, making them potentially self-sufficient in that regard. Osaka and the Kinai held an advantage in the production of handicraft goods. Edo was a city founded at the beginning of the Tokugawa period, so it was a consuming city without a supporting region that could supply it with agricultural or handicraft goods. But with the shogunate holding a monopoly on the right to issue currency, it was first of all the city from which the shogunate's official currency was circulated.

Under these conditions, many peripheral domains became involved in a trade of their agricultural goods for the handicraft goods of Osaka, with Osaka possessing a high industrial productivity and also shipping the goods produced in production sites in its surrounding hinterland. Balance of commodity trade shows Osaka to have had an unfavorable balance,

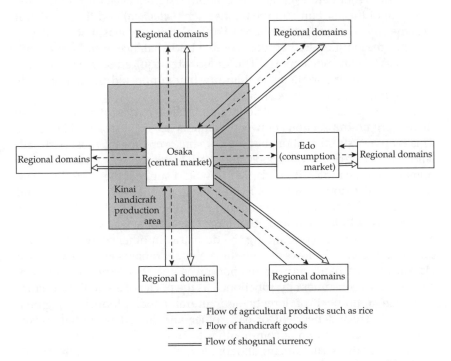

——— Flow of agricultural products such as rice
– – – – Flow of handicraft goods
===== Flow of shogunal currency

Fig. 1.6. The structure of flow in the interregional Tokugawa economy (1).

and the peripheral domains to have favorable balances. But the balances of currency transactions show the opposite. This is because the domains had to get their supply of currency—which was necessary for the development of a cash economy—from the central region. Domains that had this kind of trade relationship with Osaka included those in Kyûshû, Shikoku, Chûgoku, Kinki, Hokuriku, and along the Japan Sea coast of Tôhoku, as well as a portion of those in the Tôkai and Chûbu regions. Domains with this kind of relationship with Edo could be found in the Pacific Ocean coast of Tôhoku, the Kantô, Chûbu, and Tôkai regions. Figure 1.6 shows regional domains grouped in six blocks, five of which were linked with Osaka and one of which was linked with Edo. These figures alone do not reveal the relative scale of the Osaka and Edo economic regions, but there is no doubt that in the early Tokugawa period, the Osaka economic region was larger than that of Edo.

As I observed above, Edo did not possess a supporting production region, so it had to acquire its supply of both agricultural and handicraft goods from Osaka and the regional domains. These goods were then either consumed in Edo or re-exported to other regional domains. However, in the early Tokugawa period, Edo was not that large a distribution market, so it has been designated as a consumption city in Figure 1.6. What held even greater economic significance for Edo was the presence of the shogun and the bannermen (*hatamoto*) and the fact that it was the city where a large volume of official currency was first circulated. For that reason, Edo had an unfavorable trade balance with Osaka, with an excess of currency exports. The shogunate acquired seignieurage due to the fact that it supplied the liquidity that supported the nation-wide development of a money economy.

If we understand the interregional circular flow as described above, then there were no transactions between domains, as suggested by Figure 1.6. This is an oversimplification, but the domains were, for the most part, self-sufficient in agricultural goods and had little ability to supply other domains with handicraft goods, which would support the view that there was little inter-domainal trade. Even if we grant that there was trade and a division of labor among the regional domains, it took place through the mediation of Osaka, Edo, and other large cities. There was still little sign of a complex trade network among the domains. In other words, the structure of the economic flows among the regional domains was one in which Osaka, with its handicraft production areas and its distribution market, and Edo, as a consumer city, functioned as the nuclei of a satellite structure in which a number of largely agricultural goods-producing regional domains were independent of each other and linked by radial spokes through the distribution of commodities to and from the centers.

Because of this structure, the shogunate took direct control of the pivots of the long-distance distribution networks, such as Osaka, Edo, and

Kyoto, and the gateway to foreign trade at Nagasaki. By putting into operation its commercial policies at these points, and by maintaining a grip on the right to mint currency, the shogunate was able to manage the market economy and the distribution of commodities to a considerable extent. In the sense that a large number of regional domains existed independently, the shogunal–domainal system was a multistate structure. But this structure was inseparably linked to the "non-domainal" regions of Kinai, Osaka, and Edo.

Let us now turn to the structure of the late Tokugawa period as shown in Figure 1.7. Compared to the earlier period, the following changes took place. (1) While the regional domains remained, as before, as agricultural regions, there was regional specialization, with some regions focusing on rice, some regions leaning towards production of industrial raw materials such as rapeseed and cotton, and others putting their energy into the production of special products such as indigo, *tatami* straw, and safflower. There was also the appearance of regions that developed village industries such as cotton textiles, raw silk, paper, rapeseed oil, and soy sauce, with the diffusion of technology from the advanced regions of the Kinai. (2) The overwhelming superiority of the Kinai in the production of handicraft

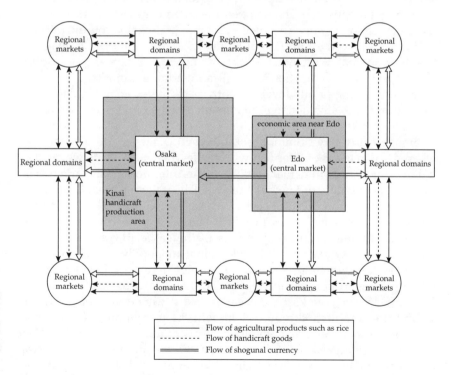

Fig. 1.7. The structure of flow in the interregional Tokugawa economy (2).

goods was shaken by the diffusion of advanced technology to other regions, so that there occurred a specialization in Kinai as well toward products that were still competitive. (3) The areas around Edo not only expanded their agricultural production, but also developed silk, cotton, and oil pressing industries. Thus development was not limited to Edo. Instead, a supply hinterland for the entire Kantô region—in other words, the Edo economic sphere—took shape.

These changes in the structure of interregional production naturally came along with changes in the structure of distribution. The net flow of assets was as before. In basic terms, rice and other agricultural goods flowed from the regional domains to Osaka and Edo while handicraft goods flowed from Osaka and Edo to the domains. But flows in the opposite direction also appeared. Figure 1.7 represents these flows with two-way arrows. The trade between Osaka and Edo was also as before, with agricultural and handicraft goods flowing from the former to the latter. But whatever the absolute numbers, the relative weight of "down goods" (*kudarimono*) among the goods flowing from Osaka and Kyoto area into Edo declined. This was due, in part, to the growth of the Edo economic sphere. It was also due to the expansion of the trade directly between Edo and the regional domains. Up until then, regional shippers and domainal monopoly bureaus had first shipped their goods to Osaka and then forwarded them on to Edo. The greater number of domains conducting such transactions directly with Edo in Figure 1.7 than in Figure 1.6 illustrates this development. With that, Edo exceeded its role as a great consumption market and came to function as a central distribution market.

One further important development was in inter-domainal trade due to agricultural specialization in each domain and the rapid rise of handicraft production. With that, core regional markets arose in such towns as Akamagaseki (today's Shimonoseki), Hyôgo, Nagoya, and Sakata. Even when these markets overlapped with castle town markets, however, they did not function as domainal markets, but as inter-domainal markets. This inter-domainal trade did not take place solely at these regional markets. It also took place through the central markets in Osaka, Edo, and Kyoto. There were not a few cases in which special regional products passed through middlemen and wholesalers in the castle towns to be sold to wholesalers in Osaka, or where domainal monopoly goods were sold through Osaka warehouses. In fact, in absolute terms, the development of inter-domainal trade probably expanded the scale of the central markets. As stated above, Osaka in the early Tokugawa period functioned as a handicraft production center, along with its surrounding Kinai region, as well as functioning as a commodity distribution center. In the latter half of the Tokugawa period (excepting the last decade), Osaka's craft production function went into decline. Its commodity distribution function, however, grew stronger, as did its role in the corollary field of finance. Thus, the existing central market changed in character and was woven into the interregional distribution network.

Whether the inter-domainal distribution of commodities passed through the mediation of the existing central markets or through the new regional markets depended on the differences in costs, defined broadly, between the two. For example, if regional shippers were in a weak position vis-à-vis the central market wholesalers and could be bought out cheaply, then their costs of selling through the central markets would be high. However, even when the sales price was low, if the central market wholesalers had a large capacity to absorb transactions while also possessing an informational function and providing advance credit to regional shippers, then the regional shippers would be likely to choose the central over the regional markets.

This competition between markets was a new condition. Thus, there was a change from the early Tokugawa radial, point-to-point distribution network between the domains and the central markets to the formation of a complex distribution network involving both inter-domainal routes and domainal–central routes. As a result, the position of the central markets suffered a relative decline. The shogunate's distribution policies, which had sought to control the market economy by directly controlling the major cities, had been effective in the point-to-point market economy. But it was unable to exert sufficient power over a developing market economy featuring the complex confluence of countless points.

Looking next at the flow of money, there was no change in the national mobility of the shogunate's currency. With the development of inner domainal and inter-domainal markets, the structure in which currency flowed from the central markets of Osaka and Edo to the regional domains continued as before. As I stated in the earlier part of this chapter, the currency debasements beginning with the Genroku period and the expansion of the currency supply with the issuing of the *Nanryô nishugin* fit well with the structure of this money flow, whatever the intentions of the shogunal officials involved.

However, there were financial developments in late Tokugawa whose effects on this structure cannot be ignored. These were the domainal notes and exchange house credit instruments. Domainal notes were issued as means of payment for transactions within the domains and the *azukari tegata* (exchangeable notes of deposit) and *furi tegata* (check-like notes) issued by the Osaka exchange houses were used as means of payment at least in Osaka. But since they were issued without provisions or deposits of equal amounts of the shogunate's currency, they brought about an increase in the money supply. The widespread use of exchange bills between Kyoto–Osaka and Edo had the effect of economizing on official currency by keeping currency in circulation that would otherwise have been taken out during the period in which it was transported between the two areas. The complex network of interregional economic relationships depicted in Figure 1.7 was supported by these financial developments. On the other hand, as I stated above, this also had the effect of weakening the shogunate's supreme rights over currency and made an impact on the effectiveness and receptivity of the shogunate's financial policies on economic flows in the system.

Figure 1.7 only depicts the flow of goods and currency. It does not show the flows of factors of production or factor income. Leaving aside land, there is no doubt that there was a great deal of movement of labor and capital (loans) across regions in the late Tokugawa period. It appears, in particular, that peasants labor migration for work in distant regions (*dekasegi*) became somewhat regularized. In that sense, it would be a good idea to show these flows as well. But the majority of these flows of production factors and factor income took place within the regional domains or within cities (including their immediate surroundings). Compared to the commodity market, we must conclude that a national production factor market developed late.

Translated by Alan S. Christy.

Notes

1. Yoshida (1910: 25–6); Hayami (1968: chapter 6); Shimbo et al. (1975). Yoshida's "estimate" simply took the common belief that 1 *koku* (180 L) of rice was required to sustain a person for a year. He extrapolated from the aggregate national assessed productivity (*kokudaka*) of 18 million *koku* computed by the land surveys of the late sixteenth and early seventeenth centuries, to arrive at a population of 18 million.
2. These annual village-by-village registers, though they bear a variety of titles in different regions and jurisdictions, are collectively known as *shûmon nimbetsu aratame-chô* or *shûmon aratame-chô*, "registers of population and sectarian affili- ation." For a discussion, see Hayami (2001: 25–37).
3. We know from the early Meiji census, for example, that approximately 7% of the population were samurai, and hence uncounted in the Edo-period enumerations.
4. Hayami believed that the growth process of the population of the Suwa region during 1600–70 drew a logistic curve. He therefore hypothesized that the annual growth rate for 1600–30 was 0.5%, 1630–50 was 1.0%, and 1650–70 was 1.4%. The actual population growth rates for the region after that, obtained from an analy- sis of temple registries, were 1.4% for 1670–90, 0.46% for 1690–1710, and 0.22% for the 1710s. In other words, the population grew quickly from the beginning of the seventeenth century to the 1720s, but that growth rate was not uniform throughout the period. It was slow at first, and then sped up until it began to slow down at the turn of the century. Hayami (1973: 23–4).
5. For more on the estimation process used here, see Miyamoto (1976).
6. For details on the process of estimation here, see Miyamoto (1976).

7. For a useful overview of changes in agricultural land sites from the medieval to early modern period, and the development of small scale agriculture that went along with them, see Hayama (1983).

8. For a lucid presentation of this view, see Yamamura (1981).

9. It should of course be noted that growth was not uniform throughout the seventeenth and early eighteenth centuries, for the early modern economy was subject to the same forces that make for cycles of expansion and contraction today, and was particularly more vulnerable to adverse natural conditions, such as long- and short-term climate change, epidemics, and agricultural pests. Japan was affected, for example, by the short-term cooling effects of the eruptions that occurred in east Asia around 1640 including those at Japan's Mt Komagatake, Indonesia's Mt Awu, and Philippine's Mt Parker, which lowered temperatures and depressed agricultural output throughout the northern hemisphere in the late 1630s and early 1640s. See Atwell (2001). Japan suffered from both famine and epidemic as a result, and almost certainly witnessed a short-term drop in population. That aggregate agricultural production increased 160%, and aggregate population more than doubled, in 120 years, despite these short-term phenomena, speaks of an overall economic and demographic vigor.

10. See Smith (1959) for the classic analysis in English.

11. Many of these changes are masterfully set forth by Thomas C. Smith (1959) in his *Agrarian Origins of Modern Japan*.

12. For the concept of "industrious revolution," see Hayami (Introduction, this volume).

13. In a study based on data from the Chôshû domain, Thomas C. Smith estimates that farming families there derived nearly half their income from by-employments, rather than direct agricultural work. Smith (1988*b*).

14. Hiroya Akimoto has given us an interesting analysis of the relations among double cropping, dry paddy fields and the introduction of late growing rice strains in the example of the Nagato and Suwo Provinces in the late Tokugawa period. Akimoto (1987: chapter 3). This essay owes much to his discussion.

15. See the following for regional comparisons of population fluctuations from the middle to late Tokugawa period: Hayami (1971*b*), Kitô (1983*a*: especially chapter 3), and Umemura (1965). Those readers interested in the data on which this chapter is based will want to read Hayami and Kitô (Chapter 7 this volume).

16. Saitô (1987, especially chapter 4). However, Saitô points out that the argument that the system of servitude suppressed fertility of the urban population is applicable to the cities of Kyoto and Osaka, but not to Edo where the population of miscellaneous workers increased in the late Tokugawa period.

17. Around the Genroku era, a number of Confucian scholars announced their opposition to further development of new agricultural lands, giving as their reason the fact that new fields caused water shortages for old fields and reduced available grasslands. See Kikuchi (1958).

18. In the *ie* system, although there were customary restrictions on women inheriting household headship, an adoptive heir (*muko yôshi*) could be brought in to marry a daughter, and inherit the headship. Absence of a male heir was the most common reason for such adoptions, but they also occurred in cases where there was a "natural" male heir. For Japanese "*ie*," see Nakane, (1990).

19. Nishikawa (1985: 106). Using the same materials, Hiroya Akimoto has calcu-
    lated the same ratios at fifty-eight to forty-two and seventy-two to twenty-
    eight. Akimoto (1987: 2).
20. At the fall of Osaka castle in 1615, those laying siege found up to 28,060 pieces
    of gold and 24,000 pieces of silver inside. The shogunate's minter Gotô
    Shôsaburô appropriated this bounty. Matsuyoshi (1964: 14).
21. Iwahashi (1976) and Yamawaki (1980). See Tashiro (Chapter 3 this volume) for
    a more detailed examination of the outflow of gold and silver through overseas
    trade.
22. For further information on the Kyôhô era decline in the price of rice and the
    recognition of the rice market, see Miyamoto (1988: 197–202).
23. Shimbo (1978: 57–8). However, even though the effect on prices of "the devel-
    opment of a market economy" and "the expansion of the volume of transac-
    tions" may be the same, their effects on actual income and interest rates differ.
    On this point, see Miyamoto (1988a: 147).
24. For a discussion of the identity of "household" and "enterprise" in the
    Tokugawa period, see Fruin (1983).
25. On the activities of one rural banker in supplying credit to rural enterprise, see
    Toby (1993: 55–90).

2

The Institutional Framework of the Tokugawa Economy

MASARU IWAHASHI

1. Introduction: Why an Institutional Framework?

The two centuries following the outbreak of the Ônin War (1467–77) were characterized by fundamental socioeconomic changes, sufficiently radical to be readily apparent.[1] The political and military conflicts among powerful senior officials within the Muromachi shogunate undermined the effectiveness of centralized power—which had existed since the ancient *ritsuryô* state—and forced changes in socioeconomic as well as cultural structures.

These two revolutionary centuries may be divided into two phases. The first phase corresponds to the Warring States period (1467–1568). The second phase extends from the era of Oda–Toyotomi hegemony (called the "Shokuhô" era, 1573–98, by Japanese historians) to the formative period of the Tokugawa shogunate.[2] The first phase witnessed an increase in agricultural productivity and a transformation of the agent of agricultural management, which exceeded the controls and framework of the *shôen* system and the provincial constable system (*shugo ryôgokusei*). This phase also saw a deepening division of labor in commerce and production and the emergence of politically and economically independent regional "countries" under powerful local lords (*sengoku daimyô*). In the second phase, the new hegemony thoroughly undermined the rule of local lords by more successfully acquiring the profits of agricultural growth. Moreover, the hegemony separated the warriors from the agrarian population, forced merchants and artisans into town residency and brought the productive power of the peasants (*nômin*) under their control through land and population surveys.

The Tokugawa economy has long since been reinterpreted, and seen as the foundation of the modern Japanese economy. In this chapter, therefore, I will not reexamine economic conditions—such as capital accumulation and production technology—that were direct preconditions for industrialization, an approach exemplified by studies of management and the family, many of which emphasize economic incentives and group-oriented management. Rather, the main focus of my reevaluation will be the continuity of social and cultural structures that contributed to Japanese industrialization, and which existed prior to the nineteenth century introduction of the Euro-American economic system and its technology.

Furthermore, this reevaluation has focused on the particularity of Tokugawa society in contrast to the modernization of China, which had also severed its relations with Western culture and was left behind by Western development. For example, it has been argued that in Japan the discrepancy in the distribution of wealth between the warrior class and the rest of the population was small, despite the existence of the so-called four-class status system (warriors, peasants, artisans, and merchants). In addition, a meritocratic value system is said to have developed. These developments are explained by characterizing shogunal authority as not based upon a despotic hereditary bureaucracy but as a system of dispersed power. Furthermore, the high degree of commercial development is seen as having given townspeople wealth and practical power. Finally, scholars have observed that there were no powerful structures that preserved tradition in Japanese society, such as the clan system or the examination system in China (Tominaga 1980: 836).

Taking the position that modernization means westernization, Tetsurô Watsuji once argued "if Japan had maintained contact with the West after the sixteenth and seventeenth centuries, Japan's modernization would have taken place earlier" (Watsuji 1950). The trend of *gekokujô* ("the low overthrow the high") which began in the Northern and Southern Courts period (1337–92) created a fluid social structure, and the activities of merchants based in such autonomous cities as Sakai, Hakata, and Hirano, attested to the rise of popular power. Therefore, internal conditions were ripe for modernization. Since merchants from the newly rising European powers, the Netherlands and England, were also coming to Japan, Watsuji saw the putative "national isolation" policy (*sakoku*) as the "tragedy of Japan."[3]

In effect, those who praise the heritage of medieval Japan and decry the implementation of the "national seclusion policy" support theories of Tokugawa society as a "feudal reaction" and "the reconstitution of feudalism." Traditionally, Tokugawa society has been understood according to the universal (i.e. Marxian) world historical concept of feudalism as a stage of development that necessarily precedes "modernity." In that paradigm, the emphasis has been on the pervasive coercion and the stagnation of economic activity arising from exploitation of the peasants by the shogunate and domainal powers. What, however, would be the position that views Tokugawa Japan as the foundation of modern Japan?

It goes without saying that one cannot gain any perspective on the fact of modern Japanese economic development through a scheme of late medieval socioeconomic development followed by early modern economic stagnation. Those who would find the various elements leading to the economic development of modern and contemporary Japan in Tokugawa society—the theory of "the Tokugawa heritage"—tend not to see the fifteenth to seventeenth centuries as constituting that great a transformation. Thus, there have as yet been almost no attempts to situate Tokugawa economic society in a continuous perspective running from the late medieval to modern eras.

The purpose of this chapter is to discuss the institutional framework that both supported and limited the Tokugawa economy. There are too many theories and arguments concerning the characteristics and historical stages of development of Tokugawa society to address in the space of this chapter. Therefore, I will confine my discussion primarily to those institutions related to the socioeconomic elements that were important in the development of a modern economy in Japan. While acknowledging connections to the "heritage" of the medieval social economy, I would like to offer a more encompassing examination of the institutional framework of the Tokugawa economy, in the following fashion. Tokugawa society has been characterized as a *"bakuhan* system" (shogunal–domainal) society as well as an "estimated yield system" (*kokudaka* system) society (Wakita 1975), which has easily led to the images of a society governed by a natural economy, and by absolute authority of lords over the merchants, artisans, and peasants. But in fact, the money economy that emerged from late medieval economic development was the pillar of Tokugawa society, around which was built an institutional and economic framework that formed the foundation for modern economic development.

In this chapter, I will discuss three conditions of Tokugawa society that support my argument: (1) social stability was maintained for over 200 years under a continuous governing authority and system; (2) as a result, a variety of systems were developed that were able to expand the scale of the market; and (3) a social environment was formed that was able to provide constant economic incentives to both townspeople and peasants.

2. *Pax Tokugawa:* Institutional Stability

The second siege of Osaka Castle that began in the fourth month 1615, concluded with the suicides of Toyotomi Hideyori, his mother Yodogimi, and others the following month. The struggle for hegemony that had begun with the death of Toyotomi Hideyoshi in 1598 ended two years later with Tokugawa Ieyasu's victory in the Battle of Sekigahara (1600). Since then, Ieyasu had been the *de facto* ruler of Japan. When he was named shogun by the emperor in 1603, Ieyasu was now ruler in reality as well; his victory at Osaka in 1615 eliminated the last remnants of opposition, and left him and his heirs unchallenged as the supreme political authority in Japan.

For about 250 years thereafter, until the Tokugawa Yoshinobu returned political rule to the imperial court in 1867, Japan was continuously governed under the same political system and the same family. The durability of the Tokugawa regime gave Japan the longest period of political stability in its premodern history.

It goes without saying that political and social stability are important conditions for the development of commerce and the growth of a money economy. Political stability is particularly indispensable to the unified monetary system that forms the basis of a money economy, and to maintaining the value of the shogunate's currency. What was it, then, that made this long-lasting stability possible?

The traditional approach to this question has been to look for the cause of that stability in the system of political rule in Tokugawa society. The prewar theory of "centralized feudalism" and the postwar theories of "the *bakuhan system*" and "the *bakuhan* State" fall into this category. The theory of "centralized feudalism" held that medieval society was a feudal society characterized by decentralized rule, and that political and social stability was finally achieved when the Tokugawa shogunate established a strong and durable central authority. Concretely, the national rule of the shogunate (or the Oda and Toyotomi regimes) during the Kamakura, Muromachi, and Shokuhô years was obstructed by powerful vassals (*gokenin*), provincial constables (*shugo daimyô*) or the five elders (*tairô*). In contrast to these periods and the anarchy of the Warring States period (1467–1568), the Tokugawa shogunate was skillfully able to centralize control over both the regional lords and the peasants.

There are numerous theories as to how the "*bakuhan system*" was applied to the social economic sphere, making it difficult to summarize them all. However, Tamotsu Fujino offers an explanation that is more comprehensive and internally coherent than the concept of "centralized feudalism" (Fujino 1983: 30–5).

First, according to Fujino, the "*bakuhan*" system was essentially feudal, but the separation of warriors and peasants and the *kokudaka* system were the two unique elements of Tokugawa administration that distinguished it from feudalism in Europe and elsewhere. The significance of the fact that the separation of warrior and peasant differs from the general concept of European feudalism is: (1) the old land-owning class, who had been the local rulers, were removed from the process of production and transformed into a feudal vassal band under the shogun or daimyo; (2) the power of the rulers in the "*bakuhan*" system was enhanced by separating warriors from peasants, both physically (the former in towns, the latter in villages) and by status, thereby creating a new status hierarchy (warrior, peasant, artisan, merchant); and (3) by concentrating warriors and the commercial classes in the towns and cities, city and village were not only separated physically but also socially, thus constituting the starting point for a division of labor.

The *kokudaka* system, which was one of the principles of social organization in the *"bakuhan"* system, also differed from Europe in two ways. One difference was that the estimated yield was both the standard for the assessment of military duty (*gun'yaku*) and the basis for the proprietary system and the structure of hierarchical relations between the shogunate and the domains, and between the domains and their vassals. One other difference was that as the measure of land tax expropriation between the lord and the peasants the estimated yield formed the basis of landholding.

How was it, then, that the Tokugawa shogunate was able to sustain its position as the highest power in Japan for such a long time? The usual explanation is that, first, the shogunate, as a territorial lord, directly controlled domains on a scale that exceeded that of all other lords. Scholars next point to the maintenance of the following three powers that were qualitatively different from those of other lords: (1) the acquisition of monopoly on the power to mint coinage, due to direct control of the major mines; (2) the acquisition of a monopoly of authority over the central market and foreign trade, through shogunal control of major roads and cities; and (3) the shogunate's authority to command the lords' military service, and to relocate or confiscate their fiefs. Fujino argues that this last set of powers were the decisive area of shogunal authority. After the Osaka Summer Campaign, in 1615, military duty was transformed into a combination of the alternate attendance system (*sankin-kôtai*), and the levying of construction service duty on the daimyo.[4] The shogun's authority to relocate or dispossess daimyo fiefs was predicated on the separation of warriors and peasants. Enforcement of those powers, along with the alternate attendance system, was unique to Japan and unseen in European feudalism. If we focus on these facts, then we will have trouble seeing Tokugawa society as fitting within the concept of "feudalism."

If we hold that the shogunate's absolute dominance over the various lords was what made possible the maintenance of 250 years of Tokugawa institutional stability, we are led to wonder why the shogunate did not push its power further to completely crush the outside lords (*tozama daimyô*) and construct an absolute monarchy. The standard definition of feudalism centers on a mutual contract system in which the lords provided protection to their vassals and peasants, and in return the vassals and peasants owed the lords loyalty and taxes. There are those who argue that, in contrast to feudalism as defined above, state power in Japan was established during the Tokugawa period. That is, the Tokugawa shogunate had the character of a monarchy, as it was based on a unidirectional sovereign–subject relation in which the shogunate levied heavy military obligations on the lords, while the lords had absolute authority over the entire families of their vassals. On that basis, the ultimate proprietorship over the land, including the land of the lords and their vassals, belonged to the Tokugawa shogun (Fujino 1983: 22–35). However, this perspective remains unpersuasive because it is unable to explain the fact that the shogunate was ultimately unable to transform the lords into bureaucrats within its own institutional framework.

Masahide Bitô argues that the ruler's will to power is not a sufficient factor in explaining why the separation of warriors from peasants (*heinô bunri*) proceeded without any real resistance, nor does it explain the durability of the long Tokugawa peace that stemmed from that separation. Instead, he emphasizes the importance of the "duties" (*yaku*) system, which was the organizing principle of early Tokugawa society. This concept of "duties" refers to both the functions of the individual in society and the responsibilities that accompanied those functions. In concrete terms, the warrior was obliged to provide himself with vassals, retainers and weapons and use these to serve his lord in time of war. They also fulfilled various administrative duties as "officials" (*yakunin*). Along with their obligation to pay taxes, middle and upper level peasants, known as *honbyakushô* ("original peasants"), had the obligation to provide corvée labor for such projects as castle construction. These peasants bore the burden of certain "duties" as formal members of the village. Townspeople also possessed "duties," paying taxes proportional to the size of their land, or lacking land, providing technical labor services in accordance with their profession, a portion of their products, or labor power in general.

These "duties" were not limited to the lords and the peasants. They also extended to the emperor and the shogun. In other words, the "duty" of the emperor was to be the sovereign of the state, and the "Laws Governing the Imperial Court and Nobility," promulgated by the shogunate, stipulated that the emperor be equipped with the education and cultural refinement appropriate to that role.[5] The shogun was expected to possess enough political and military power to maintain the domestic peace and defend the country from foreign enemies. That is why the shogun's authority weakened and disintegrated, regardless of whether the shogunate's weakness was revealed after the arrival of Perry in 1853 (Bitô 1981).

The "duty system," organized with the emperor and shogun at the pinnacle, was linked to the status system, providing that there were "duties" for each rank and profession in each status. To faithfully fulfill the "duty" appropriate to one's status was to live peacefully in accordance with one's ascribed status. Therefore, it is possible to see the durability of the Tokugawa polity as arising from the general accord between the will of the rulers in the early Tokugawa period and the demands of the population as a whole.

It appears that Bitô's theory, although he does not make it explicit, is in agreement on many points with the theory of social structure proposed by the social economist Ken'ichi Tominaga; that is to say that it maintains that economic behavior cannot be theorized apart from social structural factors, and argues that economic agents perform certain functions while being contained within a complex net of social relations. Since the performance of those functions is situated within social relations, they are inevitably confined to a set pattern. Society's expectations constrain agents. Agents, in turn, strive to fulfill the role expectations that others have. When multiple interrelated roles are integrated, an "institution" is formed. In other words, an institution is defined as "a complex of integrated roles." To borrow a Durkheimian expression, one can define an institution as the objectively established behavioral pattern that constrains individuals despite their own will (Tominaga 1980: 826–7).

Bitô's system of "duties" associated with every status and every rank, from emperor and shogun to townsfolk and peasant, is precisely the ethics of role expectations articulated by Tominaga. These institutionalized values and norms lasted until such a time as the members of society recognized that the ability of the social system to perform under the present social structure was insufficient to meet functional necessities. The dissatisfaction arising from that recognition made change inevitable. These key sociological concepts cannot fully explain the 250 years of continual institutional stability in the Tokugawa period. But they are more persuasive than the traditional perspective in Japanese history that tries to explain the stability using the centralized and coercive nature of the Tokugawa shogunate as its key concept.

The sources of institutional stability behind Tokugawa period economic development, especially the development of a money economy, have been sought in the social factors discussed above. But not only is this a bit too abstract and difficult to grasp; it is also possible to list any number of counter examples, depending upon how one sees them. However, Yoshihiko Amino's discussion of the nature of taxes in the medieval and early modern periods, with their deep connection to economic and social stability, provides a powerful support for the argument in this section. Peasants in the medieval *shôen* estates are generally regarded as having been in private servitude to local land proprietors. However, Amino argues that the payment of the annual levy by peasants, and the collection of that levy by *shôen* officials, was carried out on a contractual basis. In other words, it was a burden that peasants contracted to bear as free people. By absconding, or other such means, peasants stubbornly resisted attempts by military stewards (*jitô*) and *shôen* officials to enslave the peasants or carry out any other unlawful acts. On the other hand, they carried out their duty to pay annual taxes as prescribed in order to maintain their position as free people. Moreover, by the medieval era, there had appeared certain annual taxes that were put to public uses, acquiring the fundamental character of a public tax. Medieval peasants recognized such social necessities and paid taxes for such purposes as their duty. That is why there may have been uprisings calling for a reduction of annual levies, or in reaction against tax increases, but there were never any uprisings that called for the complete abolition of taxes, either in the medieval or the early modern eras (Amino 1986: 86–93).

Thus, if annual taxes were not based on the unilateral coercion of the proprietor/lords from at least the medieval era, but were rather paid in order to maintain the peasants' basic social status, then what Tominaga calls "role behavior" had already begun to emerge in the medieval era. However, the country plunged into Warring States era without having established an agent who served in the role of ruler of the country. The *"bakuhan"* system developed as an institution of "a complex of integrated roles" with the appearance of an agent who could fulfill such role expectations in the transition through the Momoyama and into the Tokugawa period. Bitô's theory of the system of "duties" may be seen as the critical factor that constituted the *"bakuhan"* system and integrated the role behavior of every subject, in this way assuring the institutional stability that supported Tokugawa economic development.

3. The Expansion of the Market

Although the *Pax Tokugawa* was a critical factor in Tokugawa economic development, the basic institutional framework for such development depended on a variety of policies aimed at expanding the market and encouraging the smooth circulation of commodities, beginning with Oda Nobunaga's 1567 Order for Free Markets and Open Guilds (*rakuichi rakuza rei*), issued in Kanô, in Mino Province (modern Gifu Prefecture) and continued by the Tokugawa shogunate.

Yet Nobunaga might not be in fact the first to put into practice measures intended to promote free trade by eliminating all market privileges and interventions, measures which also included the abolition of highway toll barriers (*sekisho*), waiver of land taxes (*jishi*), establishment of an official, standardized measure of volume (*masu*), and ban on selective acceptance of currency (*erizeni*). During the Warring States period, these measures had already been partially instituted at the local level by such powerful local lords as the Imagawa in Suruga, and Uesugi in Echigo. Oda's contribution was to promulgate these policies on a nationwide basis, and to build a foundation for efficient distribution by establishing links to expanding agricultural production. Without question, another important factor in the growth of markets was growth in population seen in the sixteenth and seventeenth centuries. However, this population growth might have slowed or even reversed had it not been for the various institutions first put in place by the Oda and Toyotomi regimes, and completed by the Tokugawa shogunate. The significance of these institutions, which promoted market expansion, will be discussed in the following section.

3.1. The unification of the country

The political unification of Japan, which followed the rivalry among regional powers and the unstable conditions of the Warring States period, contributed more than institutional stability to the economy. Kozo Yamamura points out the spatial impact of the creation of larger territories in facilitating increased investment efficiency, and the temporal effect of the consolidation of power in bringing greater security to long-term investment. Moreover, the rapid progress of political unification, along with increases in agricultural productivity, contributed to a sharp upswing in commerce (Yamamura 1978). On the other hand, D. C. North and R. P. Thomas state that the position of large-scale political power was enhanced by commercial expansion (North and Thomas 1973). Accordingly, political power on a grander scale was closely intertwined with advances made in commerce.

To indicate what is meant by scale, let us compare the scope of political power exercised by the highest political authorities of different periods in the areas under their direct governance. The Muromachi shogunate claimed national authority; and the shogun was even accorded the title "king of the country" within the international order established by the Chinese Ming empire. However, aristocrats, temples, and shrines were not under the complete control of the Muromachi shogunate. Moreover, provincial constables (*shugo daimyô*), who were direct vassals of the Ashikaga, maintained their own independent local power bases. Therefore, with the onset of the turbulent Warring States period, the Muromachi shogunate was only able to control Kyoto and the immediately surrounding areas. The contrast with Oda Nobunaga, who brought the Muromachi shogunate to an end, is striking. With the provinces of Owari, Mino, and Ômi as the core of his territorial power, Nobunaga, together with his vassals, came to exercise control over the greater part of the Kinai and Chûbu regions by the time of his assassination at Honnôji in 1582. Although there are no surviving records to provide numerical data for the territory under Nobunaga's direct control, it included areas held by his most important ally, Tokugawa Ieyasu, as well as the fiefs of such powerful vassals as Shibata Katsuie and Akechi Mitsuhide. We do have data on Toyotomi Hideyoshi's holdings from the "Inventory of Revenue for the Third Year of Keichô [1598]" (*Keichô sannen kuraosame mokuroku*), which gives us a figure of 2,200,000 *koku*, or about 12 per cent of the entire country's *kokudaka* as estimated in Hideyoshi's Land Surveys. At the beginning of the Tokugawa period, the *kokudaka* of the territories under the direct rule of the Tokugawa shogunate was roughly comparable to that of the

Toyotomi holdings: between 2,300,000 and 2,400,000 *koku*. Thereafter, the Tokugawa holdings grew, until they stabilized at around four million *koku* in the eighteenth century.

The location and distribution of the holdings of these leaders had an even greater influence on commercial expansion than did the scale of their territories. When Nobunaga established his hegemony, the cities under his direct governance, such as Sakai, Ôtsu, and Kusatsu, were limited to the Kinki and surrounding region. When Hideyoshi came to power, cities under his jurisdiction included not only Kyoto, Osaka, Nara, Sakai, and Ôtsu, but also Nagasaki and Hakata in Kyûshû. Hideyoshi also gained control over many mines—major financial assets—including the Sado gold mines and Iwami silver mines.

In addition, whenever Hideyoshi gave a conquered territory back to its previous lord or distributed it to a new lord, he had the lord reserve a fixed portion of the land to provide for military forces in the event of mobilization. With Hideyoshi's authority recognized from the province of Mutsu to the province of Higo—almost the entire country—conditions were now ripe for the beginning of commercial distribution on a national scale. As for the Tokugawa shogunate, it carried on and expanded the legacy of the Toyotomi regime.

Most major cities throughout the country were placed under shogunal jurisdiction, and shogunal officials were placed in each region for village administration.[6] Totaling twenty-one provinces in the 1670s and leveling off at thirty-eight in 1710, shogunal territories were located in every corner of the country, excepting a few of the very large domains held by outsider lords (*tozama*) in Tôhoku, Shikoku, and Kyûshû. The Tokugawa shogunate also claimed authority over certain important transportation sites even if they were outside of its official jurisdiction, entrusting their administration to a neighboring domainal lord. Finally, the need to transport rice taxes collected from shogunal territories spurred the development of the eastern and western sea routes, followed by the growth of nationwide commodity distribution networks.

Political unification did not necessarily demand that the Tokugawa shogunate extend its direct control to every corner of Japanese territory. So long as the shoguns held complete sovereignty in terms of external affairs, and established secure and recognized domestic legitimacy, a polity predicated on the coexistence of the *bakufu* and the daimyo domains was a sufficient system of governance. According to Ronald P. Toby, the *bakufu* in its early years sought direct trade with Ming China, and even showed a willingness to enter the "Chinese world order" as a tributary state. However, while direct trade might have assisted the *bakufu* in its search for domestic legitimacy, accepting tributary status would have damaged Japan's diplomatic autonomy. Therefore, the *bakufu* ultimately abandoned the hope of the trading profits that normalization with

Ming might have offered, instead manipulating its diplomatic relations with Korea and the Ryûkyûan kingdom to achieve the same effects. The shogunate, Toby argues, used the ceremonies and public pomp in its diplomatic reception of Korean and Ryûkyûan diplomatic missions to impress the Kyoto court, the *tozama* daimyos of western Japan, and the rest of political society with its immense authority (Toby 1977b, 1984).

The establishment of this system of governance made it possible for the state to establish a variety of systems affecting the relationship of the domestic and external economies. Before turning to these systems, however, let me say a few words about two forms of social and political segregation that were the starting point for the development of the market economy in Tokugawa Japan, the separation of warriors and peasants, and the separation of merchants and artisans from peasants.

3.2. The policies separating warriors and tradesmen from peasants

Official policy not only separated warriors from peasants, but equally as important, separated merchants and artisans from the peasantry. In this section, I will examine the impact of these policies on the expanding market economy of the Tokugawa period.

The official policy separating warriors from peasants, enacted in the transition period between the medieval and early modern eras, forced warriors to reside in castle towns, thus ending direct warrior control of the peasants. This strategy to maintain military and political stability depended on a certain degree of growth in agricultural production and circulation routes for the flow of goods between villages and castle towns. While this policy of separation contributed to the *Pax Tokugawa*, it also had a huge influence on investment in agriculture and expanding production.

The removal of commerce and manufacturing from rural villages effected under the policy of separating merchants and artisans from peasants was carried out in order to support the urbanization of the warrior class. That is, regular supplies of both military and daily necessities had to be secured in order to achieve the military goal of resettling the domainal lord and his vassals, along with their families, in the castle towns. Staples such as grain and horse feed could be obtained from villages in the form of annual taxes. However, higher grade items such as weapons, including muskets, swords, and spears, or the textiles and furnishings necessary to uphold the authority and prestige of the warrior class, had to be supplied by artisans in the local castle town or on order from one of the great cities. Without doubt, the urbanization of warriors pushed the social division of labor on both the domainal and national level far beyond the level seen during the Warring States period.

Nevertheless, in contrast to the strict enforcement of a division between warriors and peasants, the policy of separating merchants and artisans from peasants was not as strictly applied as had once been believed. The three-article edict regulating status that Hideyoshi issued in 1591 served as the prototype for this line of policy. While these articles prohibited peasants from abandoning agricultural cultivation altogether to concentrate on commerce or work for wages as an artisan, they did not forbid peasants to engage in such activities as sidelines. The legal codes compiled almost a century after the establishment of the Tokugawa shogunate prohibited peasant engagement in commercial activities in principle. However, the shogunate permitted peasants to trade in lumber and marine products in regions where they could not sustain themselves on agriculture alone, and permitted peasants who had been engaging in commercial activities over a long period to continue to do so, even in ordinary rural villages.

Thus, while the policies dividing warriors, merchants, and artisans from peasants provided an institutional foundation for the expansion of the market economy, at the same time, this expansion stimulated commercial development and paved the way for the subsequent development of manufacturing in rural villages.

3.3. The standardization of weights and measures

In the course of establishing its hegemony, the Tokugawa shogunate undertook the standardization of weights and measures. However, this project did not always proceed smoothly: various areas made use of their own independent systems of weights and measures throughout the early modern period. Nevertheless, the efforts of the shogunate to impose common standards on the heterogeneity of medieval weights and measures, which reflected the fragmentation of political power at the time, brought immeasurable benefits to commerce. First and foremost among these was a reduction in transaction costs. According to North and Thomas, production for the market encompasses both the production of commodities and the various transaction processes whereby the commodities reach the consumer. North and Thomas break down "transaction costs" into three components: the costs which accrue in the gathering of information regarding transaction opportunities (survey cost), the costs accruing in the course of negotiating a transaction (negotiation cost), and the costs which accrue in determining a procedure for executing the contract (execution cost) (North and Thomas 1973).

In the ancient period, there were attempts to bring uniformity to Japanese weights and measures by adopting standards used in China and Korea. The units for measuring length established in the ancient period remained relatively unchanged and widely used until the early modern period. However, even these units were not free from confusion. For example, serious trouble could arise between lord and peasant depending on the specific *kenzao* (a pole approximately 1.8 m in length) used for a land survey. Nevertheless, *kenzao* were based on the unit known as a *shaku* (approximately 30 cm), which was fairly uniform throughout the country. The *shaku* varied somewhat in different fields of application. In construction work, the carpenter's rule (*kanejaku*, sometimes also called *sashigane* or *kanezashi*), made of metal, was used throughout the country from before the Tokugawa period. For cloth, there were two options. The tailor's rule (*gofuku-jaku*) was 1.2 times the length of the *kanejaku*, and made of bamboo, wood, or bone, had been in use since ancient times, while the *kujirajaku* was 1.25 times the length of a *kanejaku* (37.9 cm), which was never officially sanctioned, first appeared halfway through the Tokugawa period. While the Tokugawa shogunate initially attempted to make the *kanejaku* the universal standard, over time it came to leave such matters to deeply rooted popular custom.[7]

Not surprising in light of its critical importance for tax collection and trade, the unit of volume known as the *masu* was in fact the primary focus of efforts, beginning in the mid-sixteenth century, to tidy up the disarray of the medieval era. The foundations for standardizing the *masu* were first laid by Nobunaga and Hideyoshi. When Nobunaga entered Kyoto in 1568, he ordered that the *jû-gô masu* (based on the ratio of ten *gô* to one *shô*, approximately 1.8 l) be used as the official unit of cubic measure, in line with what was already common practice in Kyoto and Nara. Hideyoshi followed suit by mandating the use of *jû-gô masu*, also known as *kyômasu* or *banmasu*, for calculations of land productivity in land surveys, thereby promoting the practice on a countrywide basis. The Tokugawa shogunate took an even more active stance regarding use of the *kyômasu* as the official standard, establishing *masu* guilds in Kyoto and Edo and protecting the guild monopoly on production of these measures. However, around the 1630s, the Kyoto *masu* guild began to produce a new *kyômasu* that was 3.7 per cent larger in volume, for widespread use centered in the Kinai region. The economic significance of Kyoto and Osaka to the domestic market eventually led the shogunate to order domains to switch to the new *kyômasu* as the official standard. In sum, the guilds not only possessed a monopoly on *masu* production, but also had the right to modify the dimensions of the official measure of volume.

Nevertheless, a number of large domains, such as Okayama and Himeji, on the Inland Sea, Tokushima (eastern Shikoku), and Takada (Echigo Province), relied on their own standards for measuring volume, taking the new *kyômasu* into account but diverging from *masu* guild specifications regarding dimensions or total volume. For example, the *gokokumasu*, 4.278 per cent larger than the shogunate's *masu*, served as the standard measure in Saga domain (northwestern Kyûshû). Cubic measures with different capacities at different transactional stages were also employed in some domains. Generally in such cases, even if merchants with close ties to national markets were permitted to use the shogunate's official *masu* (under the name *machimasu*), the domain would use *osamemasu* (larger than *machimasu*) to collect taxes from villages and *fuchimasu* (smaller than *machimasu*) to disburse rice stipends (*fuchimai*) to their vassals (Hôgetsu 1961: 389–481; Iwahashi 1981: 152–3).

In contrast to attempts to create standard measures for length and volume, the creation of a uniform system for measuring weight was far more successful. Standardizing weight measures was important not only for calculating the amount of a particular commodity required to satisfy the demands of a specific transaction, but also for the smooth circulation of currency. Silver ingots, for example, had to be weighed in order to determine their value. Reform efforts targeted both weights and scales. In the case of measuring weights (*fundô*), Gotô Tokujô, who also ran the gold mint, enjoyed official recognition for his production of measuring weights from both Toyotomi Hideyoshi and Tokugawa Ieyasu. His status was confirmed when in 1665 the Tokugawa shogunate gave the Gotô household monopoly rights over production of weights. Thereafter, measuring weights with the imprint (*gokuin*) of the Gotô household supplanted the various measuring weights that had previously been used throughout the country.

In the case of scales, Tokugawa Ieyasu granted monopoly rights to the Shuzui house even before his appointment as shogun, while the Jin household did business in Kyoto and the surrounding regions after it received monopoly rights in 1615. In 1653, the shogunate made official the regional division of monopoly rights between the Shuzui in the east and the Jin in the west. The Shuzui family then established the Edo scales guild (*Edo hakariza*), and the Jin family founded the Kyoto scales guild (*Kyô hakariza*). Together the two guilds imposed unified standards for the production of scales, enjoyed monopoly status in their respective spheres, and set standard prices (Hayashi 1973: 1–52).

4. The Establishment of Economic Incentives

Domestic peace, social stability, and the creation of an institutional environment conducive to the development of a market economy, however, could not alone give rise to the rapid economic expansion of the sixteenth and seventeenth centuries if economic actors had remained trapped within a traditional behavioral framework. The basic behavioral model for economic actors in ancient and medieval Japan was that the ruling class directly consumed crops collected as taxes in kind from peasants, while peasants engaged in agricultural production both to feed themselves and to pay their taxes. Therefore, markets, which depend on a division of labor and specialization in production, were very limited in scale. However, in the sixteenth and seventeenth centuries, as small farm household enterprises became the norm, peasants began to include production for trade among their objectives. As peasants increasingly came into contact with a cash economy, they encountered a variety of opportunities to augment their income with cash. Even independent peasants with little or no land were presented with economic opportunities (Hayami 1973b: 50, 57–8). According to Akira Hayami, the introduction of economic incentives in the sixteenth and seventeenth centuries was the driving force behind Tokugawa economic development. This insight provides an important key to understanding the establishment of the economic society of the sixteenth and seventeenth centuries. Accordingly, the remainder of this chapter will discuss the emergence of economic incentives for early modern peasants in terms of the taxation system and land rights.

4.1. The tax system and peasant incentives for production

As long as land remained the foundation of peasant production, peasants had no reason to switch to more labor-intensive forms of agricultural production without an institutional framework linking the acquisition of land to an improved economic outcome. In other words, economic incentives to improve peasant living standards required an institutional framework that assured that hard work and innovation would result in increased economic returns to the peasants themselves. Under a system in which the ruling class can appropriate peasant production at will, or to a degree that leaves only the bare minimum for peasant reproduction, there is nothing to encourage peasants to put extra effort into producing a "surplus" they would never themselves enjoy.

In order to understand the actual conditions of peasant production incentives in the Tokugawa period, it will be useful to examine the tax system of the time. In past studies of the tax relationship between domainal lords and peasants, debates have generally centered on the issue of taxation rates. There is in fact there is little data on how peasant production was divided between lords and peasants. Scholars have relied on the taxation rates recorded in official reports on tax payments (*nenguwaritsuke* or *menjô*) in order to estimate the apportionment between lord and peasant. They also had to assume that the average annual harvest was roughly equivalent to officially estimated yield (*kokudaka*) that served as the basis for calculating taxes. However, very few scholars today believe that the estimated yields or land parcel sizes recorded in land survey registers accurately reflected the actual yields or amount of land under cultivation. For example, from the beginning of the Tokugawa period, it was not unusual for differences to exist between the official amount of land under cultivation recorded in land registers as the basis for taxation (*honse*) and the actual area in use (*arise*) (Takeyasu 1966).

When land surveys were conducted, lords tacitly accepted the existence of *arise* (also called *nawanobi* [stretched surveyor's rope] or *yobu* [overage]) in addition to the official total or *honse*. This in turn gave rise to such illegal activities on the part of peasants as concealing cultivated fields (*onden*) and opening up new fields without telling the officials (*kirisoe*). Further, although it was officially forbidden to sell agricultural land, such transactions did take place, for example, in the form of foreclosure when a peasant was unable to redeem land used as collateral for his share of the village taxes. Such foreclosures and other sales of land contributed to the emergence of the landlord system. The fact that land transactions between peasants were conducted on the basis of *arise* rather than *honse* indicates discrepancies between the two. It is also clear that estimated yields did not correspond to actual yields, since the estimated yields recorded in land registers were seldom revised to reflect the increase in the productivity of land that resulted from a shift toward more labor intensive agricultural methods during the Tokugawa period.[8] In sum, it is nearly impossible to determine the actual proportion of the crop taken by the lord and left to the peasant from trends in tax rates, for taxes were laid on estimated yields and *honse*, which only constituted the official figures for production volume and land area under cultivation.[9]

The gap between *honse* and *arise*, and the relatively fixed figures for estimated yields motivated peasants to increase production. This was because, in addition to the tacitly accepted *nawanobi* and *yobu*, peasants secretly opened up and cultivated small fields that were completely tax-free, while unrevised yield estimates against which tax levied were calculated, allowed peasants to enjoy the fruits of their increased productivity. However, it was illegal to conceal newly cultivated lands, which became subject to taxation when discovered by the authorities. Meanwhile, domain lords responded to rising productivity by raising taxation rates. Following the initial land surveys conducted by the Tokugawa shogunate, certain domains tried to catch up with changing conditions by redoing the surveys in greater detail and on a more frequent basis, as well as by raising tax rates. For example, from the time Matsudaira Sadayuki was appointed domain lord in 1635, the official value assigned to Matsuyama domain in Iyo Province (northwestern Shikoku) remained 150,000 *koku*. Yet if we look at domainal tax rates in the Kikuma region (Ochi District, Matsuyama domain [modern Ehime Prefecture]) from the mid-Tokugawa period, we see that some villages were taxed at rates that exceeded 100 per cent. These curious circumstances were the result of the domainal administration frantically hiking tax rates to compensate for the differences between the official estimated yield and actual production. Even so, tax rates became stable again throughout the latter half of the Tokugawa period.[10]

In this manner, the official standards used in tax collection presented peasants with economic incentives. Yet the taxation system as it was practiced offered even more economic opportunities. The basic collection system used in shogunal territories at the beginning of the Tokugawa period was called *sebiki-kemi*. This was implemented on a general basis in the Kan'ei era (1624–43) as a tax law for the estimated yield system, and continued in use until the adoption of the *arige-kemi* system during the Kyôho reform period (1716–30). Practice under this tax law can be summarized as follows: sample surveys of the harvest were conducted annually, and when the actual crop was less than official expectations, the peasants were allowed deductions in accordance with the degree of shortfall, but when the crop was larger than expected, the amount of taxes owed remained the same. To be more specific, officials would use fixed tax rates (40 or 50 per cent) in their calculations of the standard amount of unhulled rice that could be expected to be harvested from one *tsubo* (3.3 m^2) for different grades of land (*kokumori*) recorded in the land registers. They then compared their figures with the actual amount of unhulled rice collected by sampling each grade of field (*tsubokari*). If the amount collected by sampling was greater than their estimates, the tax rates would remain at 40 or 50 per cent. If the amount collected was less, then the difference between test-yield and the estimate would be converted to a land area that represented the year's losses. These fields were not taxed (Ôishi 1969: 167–9). In fact, the term *sebiki* (which means "deducting area") derives from the custom of excluding the portion of land corresponding to shortfalls incurred during times of major crop failure.

In contrast to *sebiki-kemi*, in the *arige-kemi* system, tax officials dispensed with the official estimated yields and conducted crop surveys each year, applying predetermined tax rates to the harvest. Under this system, even if peasants might hope for inaccurate survey results, there was no strong economic incentive to drive peasants to increase production, since such increases would always be taxed at a fixed rate. However, surveying the entire crop each year was time-consuming and costly. This tax system was particularly unpopular in areas where double cropping was practiced, since the surveys delayed the planting of the second crop. The shogunate itself did not intend to stay with *arige-kemi* indefinitely, since the system discouraged increases in peasant productivity. In fact, *arige-kemi* was just a strategic move on the part of the shogunate to create advantageous conditions for the implementation of the *jômen* (fixed-rate) taxation system implemented in the Kyôho reform era (1720s). Under the *jômen* system, tax rates over a certain period in the past were averaged, and then applied to the estimated yield recorded in land registers, with deductions allowed only for exceptional losses. *Arige-kemi* appears to have been aimed at raising tax rates to their highest possible levels before calculating a fixed average rate. For peasants, even though the *jômen* taxation rates were pegged at a high level, this method also all but guaranteed that they would benefit from any production increases made after these rates had been set. Therefore, the *jômen* system also provided peasants with economic incentives.

Domainal taxation systems were diverse and not necessarily identical to that of the shogunal territories. However, according to the data on trends in tax collection available today, both taxation rates and the total amount collected tended toward stabilization. For example, T. C. Smith's analysis of trends from 1651 in annual tax rates for 424 villages of Kaga domain and trends over 150–200 years in annual tax rates and total taxes collected for eleven villages throughout the country offers numerical support for the above account of Tokugawa taxation systems (Smith 1958).

4.2. *Peasant land rights*

Without social assurances of peasant rights to use the economic "surplus" they had generated to acquire land, however, peasants would not have necessarily converted such gains into increased land holdings. At the very least, if peasants did not possess practical rights to conduct land transactions, then the ruling class could rob a peasant of what the land produced or entirely dispossess a peasant from the land he cultivated, which would make land acquisition an unlikely means for peasants to accumulate wealth. The actual conditions of peasant land rights will be my topic in this final section.

According to Shirô Ishii, medieval peasants (*hyakushô*) were independent self-cultivators, that is, managing contractors with the basic "freedom to stay or leave" in the land they worked. The status of such peasants was at its height in the Kamakura period: as long as peasants paid their annual taxes, military land stewards could not arbitrarily dispossess them of their land. Certainly, elite proprietors wanted to "restrain peasant mobility and freedom." Yet, at least in the case of the Imagawa territories along the central Pacific coast, even during the Warring States period peasants were understood to be contractors. It is generally accepted that, during the Tokugawa period, peasants were tied to the land and had only a very limited degree of freedom. As Ishii put it, transformations during the Tokugawa period marked the peak of "restraints on peasant mobility and freedom" (Ishii 1966: 148–51).

However, when we examine these "restraints on peasant mobility and freedom" more closely, we find that "feudal land proprietors" (in the European sense) did not govern peasants. That is, the peasants who cultivated the lands of the "Grundherr"—the archetype of land proprietors in medieval Europe—were generally unfree serfs, subject to the hereditary authority of the Herr. However, this was not the case for Tokugawa peasants, who did not have a personal relationship with their lords. For peasants, being under the control of lords simply meant fulfilling their assigned quota of annual taxes and corvée labor (*fueki*) (Ishii 1966: 201, 224–5). In other words, the authority exercised by the overlords regarding land and peasants only pertained to the land recorded in land registers, and to *naukenin*, the peasants listed as responsible for the annual taxes and corvée labor assessed on the land. The personal ties with peasants typically seen in the medieval western European system of resident lord were cut, while the creation of land registers confirmed peasant rights to the land they worked. From the very beginning of the Tokugawa period, lords recognized transfers of land between *naukenin* peasants, as long as they fulfilled their obligations for annual taxes and corvée labor. That is, a system was established in which peasant land transactions received institutional recognition.

Ryôsuke Ishii also maintains that Tokugawa peasants who owned land were able, despite certain limitations, to control their land permanently, or to dispose of it as they chose (Ishii 1964: 219). What Ishii means with regard to peasant ownership by the term "control" is the ability to profit from the land, while "disposition" refers to the ability to acquire or alienate land. Tokugawa peasants may appear on the surface to have had a low degree of freedom, according to Ishii, because there were various legal restrictions on peasant ownership of land. Such regulations were particularly strict with regard to the *taka-uke* land owned by villagers, since *taka-uke* land bore the burden of the annual taxes, which served as the primary source of revenue for the ruling class. These restrictions included a ban on permanent land transactions, limits on subdividing land, and limits on the kinds of crops and uses to which the land could be put.

However, various expedients undermined the effectiveness of these restrictions. Despite the ban on permanent land transactions, peasants could buy and sell land on a temporary basis. For example, in *nenki-uri* (fixed-term sales), a peasant could borrow money against a piece of land for a fixed period of time, using what remained of the harvest after paying taxes (*sakutoku*) to pay back the principal and interest within the time limit. In *honmono-gaeshi*, land could be sold on the condition that original owner would buy back the land after a fixed period of time by returning the principal. In theory, the land would eventually return to the original owner in both forms of transactions. However, the repeated renewal of *nenki-uri* was in effect a permanent sale, while in *honmono-gaeshi*, if the original owner could not pay back the principal, the creditor gained possession of the land (Takeuchi 1973: 405–6; Kitajima 1975: 77). In such ways, land transactions continued to take place among peasants in response to their need for currency.

Furthermore, it is well known that, under the status system that characterized Tokugawa society, a peasant could not freely choose or change his status regardless of how much land he had accumulated. Despite gains made in land ownership by some peasants, wealthy landowners of the peasant class could never become lords, since only members of the warrior class possessed the right to govern and collect taxes. It was not impossible, however, for peasants to purchase a town residence and transform themselves into tradesmen. In response, the ruling class strictly forbade the sale of town residences to peasants.

Even though these kinds of restrictions were placed on peasant land accumulation, peasant discontent with the status system was never on the point of explosion. This is demonstrated by the fact that participants in peasant rebellions (which were not infrequent during the Tokugawa period) generally sought to improve their economic position by requesting tax reductions or greater freedom to engage in commercial activities, but almost never demanded release from their peasant status (Aoki 1966). In other words, the status system of the Tokugawa period did not have much of a negative effect on peasant economic incentives.

Translated by Yoshikuni Igarashi.

Notes

1. For a full treatment of the Ônin War, see Varley (1967).
2. The political, legal, and economic changes of the Shokuhô and early Tokugawa eras are treated in detail in the essays collected in Hall et al. (1981).
3. Whether there was an explicit "*sakoku* policy" in the seventeenth and eighteenth centuries has been the focus of heated scholarly debate in the past two decades. Those who reject "*sakoku*" note, *inter alia*, that the term and notion are inventions of the early nineteenth century; and that Japanese trade increased for much of the seventeenth century. On the side of those who question the notion, see Tashiro (1981), Toby (1984), Arano (1988). For a contrary view, see Yamamoto (1995).
4. On the *sankin-kôtai* system, see Tsukahira (1966); on the national highway system, Vaporis (1994).
5. The first article of the "Laws Governing the Imperial Court and Nobility," issued by Tokugawa Ieyasu in 1615, specified the emperor's duty as mastering "the various arts, the first of which is scholarship."
6. A few large cities, such as Kanazawa (with population of c. 100,000 in 1700) and Nagoya (c. 50,000), developed under *daimyô* governance after 1600, but Tokugawa Ieyasu took direct control of all the other major towns and cities that were in existence in 1600.
7. Koizumi (1977: 18–41). In English, see Brown (1988).
8. On this process, see Thomas C. Smith's classic *Agrarian Origins of Modern Japan* (1959).
9. A fair analogy is the laying of taxes on real property in most jurisdictions in the United States, where the mill rate (tax rate) is applied to an assessed valuation that reflects, but it is far lower than, the market value of the property. Since assessed valuation may be as little as a quarter to a third of market value, the nominal tax rate appears to be three to four times higher than it actually is.
10. Kikuma-chô (1979). See also Smith (1958).

3

Foreign Trade in the Tokugawa Period—Particularly with Korea

KAZUI TASHIRO

1. Introduction

Though we are accustomed to thinking of the Edo period as one of "national seclusion" (*sakoku*), that did not mean, as the term would seem to imply, a complete rejection of international relations.[1] It is well known that throughout the Edo period the Tokugawa shogunate maintained limited relations with a handful of foreign entities. In the port of Nagasaki, the shogunate supervised trade between Japanese and Chinese merchants and the Dutch East India Company. In addition, the Sô clan of Tsushima (the island province between Korea and Kyûshû) and the Shimazu clan of Satsuma (the southernmost province of Kyûshû) served respectively as intermediaries for relations with Korea and the Ryûkyûs. The conditions under which such international relations took place were quite distinctive to the Edo period: trade with China was pursued in the absence of official diplomatic relations; trade with Korea was conducted through the development of a diplomatic relationship based on mutual equality; and interaction with the Ryûkyûs was shaped by the imposition of political control (Tashiro 1982: 288–90). However, recent scholarship has begun to reevaluate *sakoku* in terms of both the international and domestic concerns of the day, namely, the establishment of a Japanese world order in east Asia and securing the legitimacy of the Tokugawa regime (Toby 1984: 173). Such studies reveal that *sakoku* was an affirmative policy meant to shape and control international relations along lines desired by the Tokugawa shogunate, rather than an attempt to avoid or take a passive stance toward contact with foreign countries.[2]

This chapter is the basis for the translation of my chapter of "Japanese Silver in East Asian Trade during the Seventeenth and Eighteenth Centuries." It originally appeared as a section on "Trade in the Tokugawa Period." Takeshi Hamashita and Heita Kawakatsu, eds., *Ajia kôekiken to Nihon kôgyôka* (Fujiwara Shoten 2001).

Any discussion of the domestic economy of the Edo period, let alone trade under the *sakoku* regime, must take into account the production and circulation of precious metals, particularly silver. Japanese silver production grew rapidly from the late sixteenth to the early seventeenth century. As trade increased with China, which had the world's largest silver standard economy, Japan's economic position rose within the east Asian sphere. On the domestic front, the availability of more silver made the minting of high quality silver coins possible. One result was that the western Japanese economic region, where virtually all foreign trade was conducted, shifted to a silver standard, in contrast to the gold standard that remained in effect in eastern Japan. These changes all stemmed from the large, unprecedented supply of silver in Japan at this particular point in time.

However, the technological limitations of the mining industry in Japan eventually led to a gradual decline in output of silver and gold from the mid-seventeenth century. The shogunate, which had previously exported large amounts of silver in order to obtain Chinese products, was forced to adopt policies to restrain silver exports due to a rising demand for money in the domestic economy, which experienced exceptionally rapid urbanization and commercialization in the course of the seventeenth century. This shift became entrenched as official policy from the 1660s; first, by proscribing the export of silver by the Dutch from Nagasaki, and then by limiting the total volume of trade with the Chinese in the 1680s. Such measures imposed tight restrictions on the export of silver, one result being that the leading export commodity from Nagasaki switched to copper (Tashiro 1991: 81).

Nevertheless, it took a long time for the flow of silver from Japan to cease entirely, since the export of silver through Tsushima's trade with Korea and Satsuma's trade with the Ryûkyûs continued until the 1750s. Given that the final destination of the silver exported along both routes was China, the decline of domestic reserves of silver in Japan must be attributed to the continuing popularity of Chinese goods in the domestic market, goods which had to be purchased with silver (Tashiro 1989).

In this chapter, I explore the role played by Japanese silver in east Asian regional trade in the late seventeenth and the eighteenth centuries, when Japan tried to restrict exports of its silver supply. In particular, I will examine the outflow of silver through the Korean trade route, which expanded rapidly to replace Nagasaki as the predominant route for silver flowing from Japan to China. Finally, though space limitations do not allow me to discuss fully the shogunate's response to such domainal trading activities, I will note how this was related to the problem of domestic production of raw silk. That is, technological limitations in silk production were one reason that the export of silver through domain (i.e. Tsushima–Korea and Satsuma–Ryûkyû) trade routes could not be easily stopped.

2. Trends in Export Silver

Japanese trade in the 1630s, after the promulgation of the so-called *sakoku* policy, was conducted with the Chinese and Dutch in Nagasaki, with Korea through Tsushima, and the Ryûkyûs through Satsuma, and with the Ainu in the north, through Matsumae.[3] At first, Nagasaki was the main site for silver exports. Prior to *sakoku*, the currency used in foreign exchange was primarily "*haifuki* silver," which was refined at the Iwami mines and similar sites by the cupellation method.[4] However, in 1609, in order to preserve a dwindling supply of silver for minting coins, the shogunate prohibited the export of *haifuki* silver. As a result, thereafter silver coins in domestic circulation had to be used for export. Domestic silver coinage was a mixture of Keichô silver minted by the Tokugawa shogunate from 1601 and a number of local currencies of varying grades of purity produced in regional mints, all inferior to cupellated silver. As these coins were more difficult to use in trade, export merchants began smuggling large amounts of cupellated silver. In the end, it took about thirty years to complete the shift from cupellated to domestic silver coins in foreign trade. In other words, tightened control—through "*sakoku*"—over trade at Nagasaki to stamp out the rampant illegal traffic in cupellated silver, together with increased production of Keichô silver, gradually effected the switch to domestic silver coinage as the primary export commodity (Tashiro 1991: 78–80).

Keichô coins were 80 per cent pure silver, their quality guaranteed by the stamp of the shogunal mint (*ginza*). International trade would have benefited greatly had the export of silver coins not deviated from the standard of the Keichô silver coin. The 1660s marked the peak of Keichô coin export: Chinese ships alone carried off over 20,000 *kan* (1 *kan* = 3.75 kg) of silver each year. The Confucian scholar Arai Hakuseki later estimated that nearly 90 per cent of the total production of Keichô silver (1.2 million *kan*) was exported as a trade good. The uniform quality of these domestic coins made them tremendously popular as an international commodity throughout east Asia.

The decline in silver production noted above radically transformed the structure of Japan's foreign trade, based as it had been on the export of Keichô silver as the principal settlement medium. During the 1670s and 1680s, Nagasaki merchants felt the first effects in the form of tight restrictions on the export of silver. Trade with Korea and the Ryûkyûs also suffered from the remintings of the Genroku (1688–1703) and Hôei (1704–10) eras. That is, the 1695 decision of Ogiwara Shigehide, in charge of the shogunate's financial policy as Magistrate of Finance, to remint the silver coinage set in motion a steady decline in the purity of silver coins: Genroku coins were only 64 per cent silver; Hôei coins (1706), 50 per cent; Eiji coins (1710), 40 per cent; Mitsuhô coins (1710), 32 per cent; and Yotsuhô coins (1711), 20 per cent.[5]

This devaluation led foreign merchants across all Japan's trade routes to lose faith in Japanese silver; Japan was offering low-grade coins in exchange for commodities from foreign countries, although the specifics varied from one trade route to another. For example, 50 per cent of the Hôei minting was exported from Nagasaki in the China trade, where shogunate policy imposed restrictions on the volume of exported silver. Chinese merchants refused to accept coins from the Eiji and subsequent remintings. Even when they did accept debased coins in payment, they made sure to exchange them for copper or other products before returning to China. If they were unable to make the exchange in time for the trip home, the mint in Nagasaki would exchange the coins of lesser purity for Futatsuhô silver. Thus, the debased silver did not leave the country.

The standards for Korean and Ryûkyûan trade were even more exacting, with the 64 per cent Genroku issue constituting the limit of acceptability. The exchange of Genroku silver in the Korean trade posed particular difficulties. After two years of negotiations, Genroku coins were assigned an international value of 63 per cent and an exchange rate with Keichô coins of 1.27. Since Japanese silver was reexported to China from Korea, this exchange rate was the result of concern on the part of Korean officials and merchants that the debased silver was having a bad effect on their own trade with China. This reveals the importance of silver quality to trade between Japan and Korea, which had previously been grounded on faith in Keichô silver. Hôei coins were completely unacceptable on this particular trade route. The shogunate was accordingly asked to produce a special minting of high quality silver for trade on the Korean and Ryûkyûan routes. For trade with Korea, silver known as *"ninjindai-ôkogin"* (literally "ancient-style silver for ginseng") was minted at 80 per cent purity, while coins for trade with the Ryûkyûs were of the same quality as the Genroku minting. Such concessions made it possible for these trade routes to survive the era of rapid devaluation.

The shogunate's policies of restricting silver exports and devaluing its silver currency also had the effect of shifting the main point of the movement of Japanese silver into the east Asian market, from Nagasaki to the domains of Tsushima and Satsuma. As this trend became clear, the shogunate began to perceive the flow of silver out of Tsushima and Satsuma as a problem. Arai Hakuseki's distinctive views on trade and precious metals provided a strong stimulus for plans to protect the national economy by restricting silver exports from domainal ports, just as had been done at Nagasaki. However, unlike Nagasaki, which was under the direct jurisdiction of the shogunate, the domainal markets were located beyond shogunate direct control. Moreover, the Shôtoku–Kyôhô silver coins from Hakuseki's 1714 reminting marked a return to the standard of Keichô silver (80 per cent). In fact, Japanese currency made a comeback in the east Asian markets that lasted until the devaluation of 1736, when 46 per cent silver Gembun coins were issued. Conservative estimates of the amount of Shôtoku–Kyôhô silver that went abroad place it at over 30,000 *kan*, approximately 10 per cent of the total minting (Tashiro 1989: 104). International supply and demand, and not fluctuations in shogunate policy, drove the renewed Japanese response to China's ability to absorb silver in the eighteenth century.

3. Domestic Production and Importation of Silk

The difficulty of stanching this outflow of silver from Japan points to the persistence of high demand for Chinese products in the Japanese market, the most desired items in all trade routes being raw silk and silk textiles. Japan's ability to buy these Chinese products rose dramatically as silver production reached its peak. Although Japanese sericulture had dwindled into extinction in the late sixteenth century, raw silk, especially the highest quality raw silk, was indispensable for the silk weaving industry centered in the Nishijin district of Kyoto. Despite a gradual revival during the Edo period, Japanese sericulture could not achieve levels of quantity or quality comparable to Chinese raw silk by the early eighteenth century. As a result, raw silk imports during the years of peak demand ran to 300,000 *kin* (1 *kin* = 0.59 kg) annually. Imported raw materials were the lifeblood of the domestic silk weaving industry, without which production would come to a standstill, and the rapidly expanding demand of general consumers for silk products could not be met.[6]

However, the importation of raw silk at Nagasaki declined in the 1680s. In 1662 the Dutch lost their base on Taiwan, from which they had traded with China, and the shogunate's prohibition on silver exports forced a general retreat from the Chinese raw silk market. Limits imposed by the shogunate made it impossible for the greatly reduced number of Chinese ships to maintain the previous volume of trade. While import totals in the 1690s were generally in the range of 40,000 *kin*, they dropped in the 1710s to about 10,000 *kin*, and had virtually ceased by the 1770s (Yamawaki 1964: 229; Nagazumi 1987: 25). Restrictions on exporting silver from Nagasaki were clearly responsible for the sudden decline in raw silk imports, thus revealing the special relationship between Japanese silver and Chinese raw silk in the east Asian market.

The late seventeenth century trend toward declining imports of raw silk at Nagasaki is generally understood as having opened the door to the development of Japanese sericulture. According to this line of thought, domestic production benefited from the falling imports by rising to meet domestic demand with Japanese thread (*wa-ito*) (Shôji 1964: 20; Kudô 1983: 104–5). Yet this hypothesis is nothing more than a vague impression, unsupported by solid research. It is true that during the Tokugawa period the quality of Japanese thread improved and production increased to the degree that, when Japan was "opened" in the late 1850s, Japanese silk became the leading export item. There is no need to review here the role played by the development of the sericulture industry in the various fields of Japanese agriculture, manufacturing, and industry. The question is: when did domestic thread reach levels of quality and production sufficient to meet the needs of the Nishijin weavers? Is it true that the late seventeenth century drop in imports more or less coincided with the increase in production of domestic thread?

While no one has yet studied in detail the market shift from imported to domestic thread, but the following facts are generally known (Sasaki 1932: 168–70; Masui 1936: 2–6):

1. In 1713, the shogunate ordered Nishijin weavers, who were faced with a shortfall in materials, to use domestic thread.
2. In 1715, 200,000 *kin* of raw silk were sent to Kyoto, the totals climbing to 300,000 *kin* in the 1720s and 1730s.
3. There were only nine wholesalers in 1687 that supplied Nishijin with raw silk. Since the number of wholesalers grew to twenty-two by 1731, and a licensed cartel (*kabu nakama*) was formed among thirty-four wholesalers in 1735, we can surmise that the supply of silk to Kyoto had also increased.[7]
4. By the late 1730s, domestic thread of a quality roughly equivalent to imported goods was being produced in Ueda (Shinano Province), Kakogawa (Harima Province), and Yûki (Hitachi Province).

The chronology above reveals that the changeover made by Nishijin weavers from imported to domestic silk took some time, spanning the 1710s to the 1730s. In the 1710s, although domestic silk was being produced in the Kantô area, and in Ômi, Mino, and Echizen Provinces, the Japanese sericulture industry was still undeveloped, characterized by a significant number of waste and low quality cocoons. As a result, much of the thread produced at the time had defects such as knots and snags, making it unsuitable for weaving fine textiles. Known for his achievements in superior silkworm production, Kametarô Toyama offered the following assessment of the state of early eighteenth century sericulture in his *Sanshuron* (On Silkworms, 1909):

A large number of provinces—Mutsu, Nambu, Kôzuke, Shinano, Ômi, Echizen, Kaga, Tango, Yamashiro, Kai, Hida, Sagami, and elsewhere—were able to produce raw silk by the Shôtoku and Kyôhô eras (1710–1730). But silkworm-raising technology was still in its infancy, and only the most advanced silkworm-raising households used the barest of artificial heating techniques. According to Toyama, raw silk was produced in nearly every region of Japan during the first few decades of the eighteenth century. However, the importance and means of controlling the temperature of the room housing the silkworms—a fundamental aspect of high quality production—were not yet sufficiently understood. This example reveals the scope of the technological problems encountered in silkworm raising at the time.

It is hard to believe that the domestic silkworm industry could respond to the decline of raw silk imports via Nagasaki with immediate technological sophistication and large production volumes, given the virtual disappearance of the older form of sericulture at the end of the sixteenth century. A great number of technological problems had to be overcome before high quality silk could be produced in any volume; years were required to achieve a certain standard. A look at surviving guides to silkworm raising from all over Japan can give us a good sense of the gradual changes in technology which occurred in the course of the bitter struggles of people to produce superior cocoons. The oldest extant guide is the 1702 *Sanshi yôhôki* (Techniques for Raising Silkworms) by Nomoto Dôgen of Tsugaru domain. Although *Kogai yôhôki tekagomi* is rich in creative contrivances, the technological gap between Dôgen and Uegaki Morikuni's 1803 *Yôsan hiroku* (Secrets of Silkworm Culture, translated into French as *Yo-san-Fi-Rok*, L'art d'élever les vers a soie au Japon, translated by J. Hoffmann, and M. Bonafous, Paris and Turin, 1848 is undeniably wide. It was not until the 1840s, for example, that an instrument called a *santoukei* (a thermometer used to keep track of silkworms' condition) was invented. Applied to a silkworm to measure heat and cold, the *santoukei* greatly aided control of temperature and humidity, two critical factors in the production of quality cocoons. The technological revolution from the late eighteenth to the nineteenth century was truly remarkable (Inoue 1981: 443–71).

Thus it is clear that the increase in domestic silk production actually came some years after the decline in silk imports. Domestic technological development proceeded slowly and in response to different regional conditions. In the end, the shift from imported to domestic silk required some seventy to eighty years.

4. Kyoto and the Importation of Raw Silk during the 1710s

From the 1680s (when raw silk imports from Nagasaki declined) until the time the domestic industry was able to supply sufficient quantities of high quality product, the Japanese silk weaving industry faced extreme shortages. The very increase in the number of sumptuary regulations issued by the shogunate restricting the wearing of silk indicates just how difficult it was to enforce such laws. Despite the diminished stock of silk thread, general demand remained high; even commoners had an enormous appetite for silk.

During this period, the trade routes from Korea through Tsushima and from the Ryûkyûs through Satsuma grew in importance for supplying raw silk to Nishijin. Their direct relations with China placed Korea and the Ryûkyûs in a good position to obtain Chinese goods independently, in both official and private trade. Mediated trade with Korea represented the bulk of such transactions: Tsushima handled a total volume of 1.62 million *kin* of raw silk from 1684 to 1710. The 1690s, in particular, were marked by smooth trade conditions. Raw silk imports (shipped through from China) averaged about 78,000 *kin* each year, but at times reached as high as 140,000–150,000 *kin* (Tashiro 1981: 279–83). Although the details of Satsuma's trade with the Ryûkyûs are unclear, we do know that Satsuma was able to meet some of the domestic demand, in *bakufu*-sanctioned sales of raw silk and cloth through its authorized Ryûkyûan wholesaler in Kyoto.

The Kyoto market welcomed the supply of raw silk arriving through domainal trade routes, particularly that of Tsushima, which had surpassed Nagasaki in importance as a conduit. Raw silk and silk textiles entering Japan through Nagasaki were generally conveyed by land or sea to Kansai warehouses in Kyoto, Osaka or Sakai. These "Nagasaki warehouses" were under the control of specially licensed merchants dealing in raw silk (*itowappu*). The *itowappu* merchants then sold the silk to brokers, adding a transaction fee. In the case of raw silk, the purchaser usually represented one of the raw silk specialty houses in the "thread district" (Itoyamachi) located on Ômiya-dôri in Kyoto. In the case of silk textiles, then the purchaser was generally from one of the textile warehouses in the Muromachi district of Kyoto (Yamawaki 1960: 166).

An alternative arrangement emerged with Tsushima's purchase of a compound on Kyoto's Kawaramachi-dôri, in 1687, when it began to handle larger volumes of Chinese goods through its Korean trade. From this site, and three associated warehouses, Tsushima sold raw silk, silk textiles, and other import items. Like the "Nagasaki wholesalers" described above, Tsushima, as the "Korean wholesaler," provided goods to *wakeitoya* and *makimonoya* dealers, charging a fee for the transactions. Accordingly, Chinese raw silk was delivered to dealers via three separate distribution mechanisms—the Nagasaki wholesalers, the Korean wholesaler, and the aforementioned Ryûkyûan wholesaler.

Regardless of how it entered the country, imported raw silk was known as *karamono* ("Chinese goods"). While the name *karamono* obscured the fact that the goods arrived from a variety of production centers and over different distribution routes, the *karamono* were quite conscious of the differences among them. This sensitivity can be seen in the major shift that occurred from the late seventeenth to the eighteenth century, from reliance on the Nagasaki wholesalers to reliance on the Korean wholesaler for the bulk of the raw silk they handled. For example, a 1715 list of investors in the Korean trade includes the names of nine Itoyamachi silk retailers mixed in among those of the financial specialists one might expect. The silk merchants agreed to provide silver to Tsushima, and in return received a specified quantity of raw silk equal in value to the amount invested. In this way, these merchants were able to secure preferential access to a set amount of raw silk from the Korean wholesaler.[8] This credit relationship between the silk retailers and the domain of Tsushima indicates the degree to which the Kyoto market relied on the importation of raw silk from Korea.

Silk retailers were not the only ones taking advantage of the route via Korea for Chinese goods. For example, the Kyoto financier Fukaeya Jimbei provided Tsushima with a generous sum for its Korean trade, receiving import items as "security" (*skichimono*) for his money. Fukaeya was thus in a position to sell imported goods outside the distribution relationship between the Korean Wholesaler and silk and textile retailers. Fukaeya's largest client was the Kyoto headquarters of the dry goods store, Mitsui Echigoya. The Mitsui family eventually came to have complete financial control over Fukaeya, which meant that Mitsui funds had a hidden channel into the Korean trade.

The Mitsui house conducted its business on the principle of cash transactions, unusual at the time. The store gained a large clientele without the lure of credit purchase by reducing retail prices. Selling goods in stock, rather than taking special orders, to keep prices low, was the only way to realize this strategy of "reduced profit for high volume sales." However, this sales method ignited opposition among wholesalers and even Mitsui's competitors because of the way the store had circumvented one level of the brokerage business. So Mitsui had to be both flexible and discreet in maintaining its large stock, procuring goods from major wholesalers in a customary fashion, from wholesalers over which it had financial control, and from subsidiary stores.

Therefore, as far as Mitsui was concerned, Fukaeya was nothing more than a dummy front for Mitsui's "direct purchase" of Chinese goods in the Korean trade. Although the Mitsui family dealt more in silk textiles than in raw silk, house records show that they were generally able to undersell from the Kyoto market price for either commodity, by 10–20 per cent (*Shoyôdome*). This economic clout enabled Mitsui to obtain import items from Tsushima at profitable rates; meanwhile, Tsushima looked to Mitsui as an important source of export silver.

5. Japanese Silver in the Wakan Market

Tsushima injected large amounts of Japanese silver into the Korean trade as payment for Chinese products, above all, raw silk. Even in the early eighteenth century, when silver exports from Nagasaki had ceased, Tsushima was sending abroad approximately 1,000 *kan* of silver per year. Apart from the period of devaluation discussed above, domestically circulating silver coins could be used for overseas trade, so Tsushima was generally able to procure the silver it needed at its Kyoto office. The silver was then conveyed from Osaka to Tsushima, after which it was immediately shipped to the Pusan trading and diplomatic post known as the Wakan (*Waegwan*, in Korean).

The Wakan was originally established by the Korean government to receive and entertain embassies from Japan in the early fifteenth century, but over time the Wakan also took on the functions of a trading office (factory). Until the early seventeenth century, official trade in designated goods at set prices was the norm. But as large sums of Japanese silver came to circulate in private trade with Korean merchants, trade relations between Korea and China also received a small boost.

In 1721, the representative in charge of Tsushima's private trade, Korean translators, and Korean merchants drew up the following contract regarding transfers of Japanese silver at the Wakan (*Bunrui kiji taikô*):

1. Silver transfers at the Wakan shall take place when the *rekishikô* (calendar mission) and the *tôjishi* (winter solstice envoys) are dispatched.
2. Payment for raw silk must be made in silver. Raw silk paid for last year will be collected this year, and raw silk paid for this year will be collected next year.
3. Payment for ginseng will be made half in silver and half in cotton, iron, copper, or some other commodity.

The *rekijikô* referred to in Item 1 was sent in the eighth month of each year by Korea to the Qing court to receive the Chinese calendar, returning in the eleventh month. The *tôjikô* also journeyed each year to Beijing with a greater number of attendants to deliver New Year's greetings and perform other prescribed rituals, departing from Korea in the eleventh month, and returning in the fourth month of the following year. The coordination of silver payments at the Wakan with the dispatch of these embassies demonstrates that Tsushima's Korea trade was closely connected to Korean–Chinese exchanges. In addition, Items 2 and 3 of the agreement reveal that, while payment for the most important Korean commodity in the Korea–Japan trade, medicinal ginseng, could be made half in silver and half in cotton or iron, payment for raw silk had to be made entirely in silver and was, in actuality, prepayment for raw silk that would not be received until the following year. These facts speak to the primacy of raw silk as a commodity in the Wakan market.

The deliberate timing of Tsushima's silver transfers to coincide with the dispatch of tribute embassies from Korea to China largely determined the transport schedule for silver from Japan to the Wakan. Figure 3.1 charts Tsushima's silver shipments to the Wakan by month and ten-year intervals over a forty year period, from 1710 to 1750. This graph reveals that shipments of silver were concentrated in two periods, in the seventh and eighth months, and in the tenth and eleventh months. Silver sent in the seventh and eighth months was in preparation for the dispatch of the *rekijikô*, while silver sent in tenth and eleventh months was geared

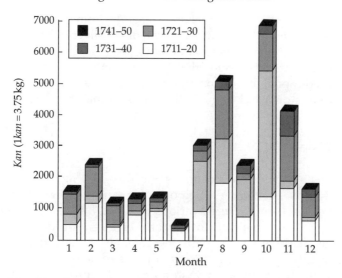

Fig. 3.1. Monthly silver exports to Korea: the seasonal cycle of silver transport.
Source: Mainikki (Diary of the Japanese Concession in Pusan), in the Sô family documents, National Diet Library.

toward the *tôjikô*. As one would expect, silver shipments were greater for the more impressive New Year's envoy. More detailed analysis shows that the seventh month shipment comprised 9.5 per cent of the total annual shipment; the eighth month, 15.8 per cent; the tenth month, 21.3 per cent; and eleventh month, 13.0 per cent. In sum, 60 per cent of the total annual shipments of silver were concentrated in these four months.

The seasonal nature of silver shipments was particularly strong during the years 1721–30. This period most faithfully reflects the directives for transferring silver in the 1721 contract. We might further note that, in comparison to other periods, September is high and November is low, indicating that the silver for the New Year's (in solar–lunar calender) envoy arrived a month early. This high concentration of silver shipment points to the smooth and regular nature of exchanges of Japanese silver for Chinese raw silk made at the Wakan. Transactions in other commodities besides silver and silk at the Wakan were also influenced by the regular dispatch of these embassies, since they were the means of conveying Japanese silver to China and Chinese products back to Korea.

Kyoto was both a starting and ending point for this trade route that extended through Tsushima, Pusan, and Seoul to Beijing. Tsushima's Kyoto office carried out the task of procuring silver for export. The transportation schedule for silver—called either "imperial calendar silver" (*kôrekigin*) or "winter solstice silver" (*tôjigin*)—from Kyoto was clearly calculated in terms of the eventual arrival of the silver in Korea. *Kôrekigin* had to be in Tsushima by the sixth month, while *tôjigin* had to arrive by the eighth. There is no question that Tsushima and many of the financiers who invested capital in the Korean trade kept a close eye on trade conditions between Korea and China in the course of their transactions.

6. Conclusion

This chapter provides an account of the way in which trade between Japan and Korea—centering on exports of Japanese silver and imports of Chinese raw silk—encountered various problems but sustained a moderate level of development up to the early eighteenth century. Although I have not discussed trade with the Ryûkyûs in any detail, smaller amounts of silver were sent to China by this route over an even longer period. Japanese silver played an important role, through the intermediaries of Korea and the Ryûkyûs, as an international commodity in early modern east Asian markets. Moreover, study of the circulation of Japanese silver must take into account the changing conditions of the Japanese sericulture industry.

As the output of Japanese silver mines fell even further, the shogunate adopted a policy of forbidding the export of even one single *monme* of silver. Previously, the shogunate had successfully used the edict of "national seclusion" to replace exports of cupellated silver with domestically circulating silver coins. However, the same policy also generated the conditions, which made it impossible for the shogunate to put a complete stop to the outflow of silver. Since Tsushima and Satsuma maintained contact with international markets beyond shogunate control, all they needed was for Japanese coins to maintain a quality level accepted by other east Asian countries. Such coins were very easy to acquire within Japan itself, after which the currency was boxed and loaded in ships heading abroad. Thus, despite the shogunate's injunction, Japan continued to serve as a supplier of silver in the east Asian region for more than ninety years after the prohibition of Dutch exports of silver.

The ultimate destination of this "Silver Road" was China. Although we usually think of ginseng as the primary object of trade between Japan and Korea, the real driving force was demand for raw silk and silk textiles. Silk products were the most highly valued commodities in the Japanese domestic market, as Tsushima knew well, having built itself on trade. The domain's finances were intimately tied to the large volumes of silver sent to the Wakan in order to purchase the Chinese products, particularly raw silk, brought back home to Korea by missions to China. The fact that raw silk had to be purchased through advance payments made solely in silver coins reveals more than the special relationship that developed between silver and silk. It also demonstrates the extremely high value placed on raw silk in the competitive east Asian specialty product trade. The premium price of Chinese raw silk was further sustained by high technological standards that other producing countries could not easily duplicate; moreover, the demand for raw silk was greater in Japan than in any other country. The Japanese sericulture industry struggled to overcome this technological gap, but was unable to do so until the end of the eighteenth century. For this reason, despite shogunal policy, Japan continued to act as a silver supplier to the rest of the east Asian economy.

To achieve, slowly but surely, the domestic production—import substitution—of hitherto imported goods was one of most fervent desires of shogunal officials, who sought to halt this flow of silver to foreign countries. Indeed, when this finally took place, the export of silver through trade between Japan and Korea came to an end. Diffusion of domestic products not inferior in quality to foreign imports lowered the market price of such profitable commodities as raw silk, silk textiles, and ginseng, disrupting previous patterns in the circulation of capital. By once again devaluing silver coins (Gembun silver, purity level of 46 per cent) in 1736, the shogunate adopted an even stricter stance toward the outflow of silver from Tsushima. Although, as before, the shogunate permitted the minting of high quality silver for export, it also set a very high rate for currency exchange with Tsushima. In this way, the shogunate brought the silver trade to a standstill. Silver exports to Korea from the late 1740s through the 1750s did not even amount to 500 *kan* per year, and eventually died out. Thus, for the first time, Japan was able to resolve the financial crisis generated by the drain of its currency reserves to Asia, as well as move away from reliance on imports by successfully transplanting Asian products to domestic soil.

Translated by Alan S. Christy and Noriko Aso.

Notes

1. Indeed, the consensus, built on my own work, as well as that of Naohiro Asao, Yasunori Arano, Fusaaki Maehira, Robert L. Innes, Ronald P. Toby, and others, that has emerged since the mid-1980s is that the term *sakoku*, which was coined only in the early nineteenth century, is both anachronistic and an inaccurate description of Japan's international situation in the seventeenth and eighteenth centuries.
2. Indeed, the term *sakoku*, which C. R. Boxer rendered "the closed country," did not even exist in the seventeenth century. It was a neologism coined in 1801, when Shizuki Tadao, a retired Nagasaki interpreter of Dutch, translated an essay by the late-sixteenth century German physician Engelbert Kaempfer. For details, see Kobori (1974); for a brief discussion in English, see Toby (1984).

3. Matsumae, a Japanese outpost in southern Ezo, was a center for trade with the indigenous Ainu population there, licensed to the daimyo in much the same way that Satsuma and Tsushima were authorized to trade with Ryûkyû and Korea, respectively. The Matsumae trade was significantly different from the Satsuma and Tsushima trade, owing largely to the profound differences in social, political, and economic organization of Ainu society and culture. Until quite recently, there was little study of the Matsumae–Ainu trade, but now we have several excellent studies, particularly Howell (1995), and Morris-Suzuki (1994).

4. Cupellation is a method of refining metals such as gold or silver by melting the metallic charge in a shallow, porous vessel, then exposing it to a blast of air, thereby oxidizing unwanted metals such as lead, copper, and tin, which either sink into the porous vessel or are swept away by the blast.

5. Taya (1963: 168–90). See also Innes (1980).

6. For a discussion of the impact of changing levels of imports on the population and economy of the Nishijin silk-weaving district, see Innes (1980).

7. The best discussion of *kabu nakama* in English is given in Hauser (1974).

8. The Sô family documents within *Kyoto–Osaka onshakugin nenpu oboegaki*, M.S., are located in the Tsushima Museum of Historical Ethnology collection in Nagasaki Prefecture.

4

Prices and Macroeconomic Dynamics

MATAO MIYAMOTO

1. Introduction

In this chapter, I will explore the macroeconomic dynamics of the late Edo period, and the process by which the structure of production changed, through an analysis of changes in prices. Statistical data on the macroeconomic trends of the Edo period are virtually non-existent, but the combination of a highly commercialized, money-based economy, and high rates of literacy, with an inveterate penchant for record-keeping, has produced an extensive legacy of excellent data on prices.

The goal of the discipline of price history is to understand short- and long-term macroeconomic trends, using prices as a barometer of economic activity. Of course, there are severe limitations to our ability to see the movements of the actual economy solely through the monetary phenomenon of price movements. In that sense, this chapter serves as a supplement to the remaining chapters in this volume, which take a more microeconomic perspective. The two perspectives combine to form an excellent picture of economic conditions and trends.

In the first part of this chapter, I will consider general trends in prices from the Kyôhô period (1716–1736) to the end of the shogunate in 1868. I will focus in this section on the following questions. What can long-term trends tell us about the point at which can we say that the Tokugawa economy began to display the "characteristics of modern economic growth"? What kinds of cycles can be found throughout these long-term trends? What was the relationship between price trends, cycles, on the one hand, and the movements of the real economy, on the other? In the second part, I will pursue the background to these macroeconomic movements—the changes in industrial structure that produced the macroeconomy—through an analysis of changes in the relative price structure of various commodities.

Since I understand "modern economic growth" to mean roughly the same thing as "industrialization," the beginnings of a shift from "agrarian society" to an "industrial society" are another major theme of this chapter. The second section of this chapter was written toward that end. Finally, I will review the observations made of the issues above and sketch late Edo economic development as seen through the history of prices.

PART ONE: PRICE TRENDS IN THE TOKUGAWA ERA

2. Trends in Early Tokugawa Rice Prices

The broad price trends of the early Tokugawa era were largely as outlined in Chapter 1 of this volume. To review in brief, the seventeenth century as a whole was a century of rising rice prices. However, compared to the rising trend of the period from the 1620s to the 1660s, from the 1660s to the end of the century, prices held more or less at the plateau reached by 1660. We may also note that there was a sudden spurt in prices from the end of the seventeenth century into the first years of the eighteenth.

As is noted in Chapter 1, the rapid rise of rice prices in the first half of the seventeenth century is explained by Masaru Iwahashi's "national population increase thesis" (Iwahashi 1981: 409–21) and Ryûzô Yamazaki's "urban population increase thesis" (Yamazaki 1983: 78–85; Harada and Miyamoto 1985: chapter 2). But these real economic factors alone are insufficient to explain the long-term inflation of the period. An increase in the money supply was another important factor, as I noted in Chapter 1 on the monetary system, above. On the other hand, I believe that growing difficulties in supplying money to the developing market economy were a basic factor in the high stability of rice prices from around 1660 to the middle of the 1690s.

Not much needs to be said about the way the repeated recoinages from the mid-1690s to about 1740 generated violent fluctuations in the price of rice. But what I would like to reaffirm here is that of all these recoinages, the Genroku recoinage was an appropriate fiscal policy response to the existing deflation gap caused by an insufficient money supply. The Hôei recoinage had a strong potential to overheat the economy by creating a money supply that was excessive for the latent real economic capacity of the time. In contrast, the monetary contraction of the Shôtoku–Kyôhô recoinage was a case of overkill. Of course, the shogunate searched for various policies to counteract the excesses of this "stop-and-go" policy, but none of their attempts had much effect. The macroeconomic solution came only with the Gembun recoinage of 1736.

The Gembun recoinage put a temporary stop to the violent price fluctuations of the Genroku to Kyôhô period that had followed the "century of inflation." The Gembun recoinage, which initiated a period of relative price stability in the eighteenth century, and transformed the Tokugawa monetary system from the Keichô system to a new system that lasted to the end of the shogunate, marked the boundary between the early and late Tokugawa economies.

In the following section, I will consider price trends in the latter half of the Tokugawa period, following the Gembun recoinage.

3. Drawing up a General Price Index

Several general price indexes have been proposed for the late Edo period, such as Hiroshi Shimbo's "An Index of Osaka Commodity Prices" (for the years 1725–26 and 1755–1867).[1] Nevertheless, the existing indexes were compiled on the basis of a relatively limited "market basket" of goods, so I believe it is necessary to calculate a new, more broadly based price index. In Figure 4.1, I offer a general index of prices for the Kyoto–Osaka region computed from the most broadly inclusive price data available. I have used data discovered since earlier indexes were developed, thus covering a larger number of goods and filling in time gaps in the existing indexes as much as possible.

However, if I had restricted myself to the Osaka region, as Shimbo did, I would not have been able to pick up data on such a wide range of goods. So I have treated Osaka and Kyoto as a single region composed of two linked areas, and used all the available data pertaining to both areas. When I have data from both areas for the same item, I have used the average of the two. I have included even those commodities for which data for many years are missing. Moreover, prices for silkworm cocoons, silk floss, raw silk, silk textiles, and other items related to silk are extremely important for viewing the movement of prices in late Edo, but there are not enough data on silk-related prices for the Kyoto area alone, so for these commodities, I have made an exception and used data from eastern Japan as well. The results, seen in the "Data at a Glance" section at the end of

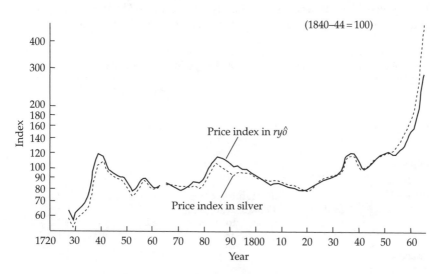

Fig. 4.1. The Osaka–Kyoto general price index (moving 5-years' averages).

this chapter, are a general price index composed of the forty-two most important commodities, twenty-two of them agricultural products, and twenty industrial products. The period for which this general price index was computed is the period from 1725 to 1867.

In composing the general price index, I used both Shimbo Hiroshi's method of weighting rice 30 per cent, and Osamu Saitô's method of giving all agricultural products (including, rice, forestry, and marine products) a weight of 57 per cent and the total of industrial production a weight of 43 per cent. I gave no particular weight to the individual items included in the categories of non-rice agricultural commodities and industrial production. All were weighted evenly. The standard years for the price index are 1840–44, following Shimbo's method, for which I have set the prices at the value of 100.

4. Cyclical Changes and Long-term Price Trends

In Figure 4.1, we can discern four major cycles in general price movements of the late Edo period. Plotting the peaks and troughs of these cycles on a five-year moving average reveals the first cycle beginning in a trough in 1729, peaking in 1739, and ending with a trough in 1770; the second cycle proceeds from a trough in 1770, through a peak in 1785, to a trough in 1820; the third cycle moves from a trough in 1820, to another trough in 1854, which includes the small cycle around two peaks in 1838 and 1851. The fourth cycle passes from a trough in 1854 to a rise that continues beyond the end of the period. Although beyond the scope of this study, this cycle ends with a trough in the middle of the 1870s. If we calculate the rates of periodic change for the passages from troughs to peaks and peaks

Table 4.1. Periodic and annual rates of change in general prices

	Period	Direction	Periodic rate of change (%)	Annual rate of change (%)
Phase 1	1729–39	Trough to peak	+105.3	+7.5
	1739–70	Peak to trough	−32.0	−1.2
Phase 2	1770–85	Trough to peak	+44.1	+2.5
	1785–1820	Peak to trough	−30.5	−1.0
Phase 3	1820–38	Trough to peak	+51.5	+2.3
	1838–42	Peak to trough	−17.1	−4.6
	1842–51	Trough to peak	+21.9	+2.2
	1851–54	Peak to trough	−4.3	−1.5
Phase 4	1854–65	Trough to peak	+146.5	+8.5

Note: Calculated on the moving five year averages of the general price index in *ryô*.

to troughs for each of these cycles and then calculate the rates of annual change, we produce the figures in Table 4.1. Excluding the initial and final phases, and the anomalous period immediately after the Tempô famine, the absolute value of the rates of price increase and decline were an annual average of 1–2 per cent. This may appear to be a leisurely pace of change, but from another perspective the data reveal that the Tokugawa economy was dynamic rather than static.

In this way, we can divide the price trends of late Edo period into four phases of cyclical change. Over the first and second phases, it appears that price levels were stable, or had a slight tendency to fall (if we draw our trends along the line from the Gembun recoinage in 1740 to 1820). In the second and third phases, prices show a consistent tendency to rise. Therefore, over the long-term, the Bunsei era (1818–30) was a major turning point. In the sections below, I will examine what brought about these long-term tendencies and cycles as well as what kind of macroeconomic changes this involved.

5. Prices and the Macroeconomy of the Mid-eighteenth Century

It goes without saying that the rapid forty-year rise in prices that began around 1730, during the first phase, was closely related to the Gembun recoinage of 1736. In the Gembun recoinage, old coins were exchanged for new at a premium (*mashibu kôkan hôshiki*). In other words, when old coins were exchanged for new, a sixty-five *ryô* premium was added for each hundred *ryô* of gold coins exchanged, and a five *kanme* premium for every ten *kanme* of silver coins. In the end, when all the old coins had been exchanged, the gold coinage in circulation increased by 65 per cent while silver coinage increased by 50 per cent. The exchanges did not occur all at once, but the potential volume of currency in the market did increase instantly. A rise in prices was inevitable. The Gembun recoinage was a response to the deflation brought on by the Shôtoku–Kyôhô recoinage, particularly the relative drop in the price of rice. At least in terms of price policy, the Gembun recoinage was a success.

But what about its effectiveness in making real incomes rise? Hiroshi Shimbo calls it "an effective currency policy" (Shimbo 1978: 303). Shunsaku Nishikawa is even more unequivocal that, "it may well be one of the few cases of a successful reflation policy" (Nishikawa 1985: 58). The expansionary benefits induced an increased money supply in an economy where potential capacity had been depressed by the high quality money policy of the Shôtoku–Kyôhô eras. Shigeo Akashi, who has attempted new estimates of the nominal money supply in the late Edo period, looks for movements in real income by dividing the nominal money supply by the Osaka rice price index to calculate the real money supply.[2] According to

his calculations, the real money supply declined just after the Gembun
recoinage, and then was held to a slow rise after 1740.[3] In other words,
Akashi does not see the reflationary effect of the Gembun recoinage as
being as strong as earlier scholars have thought.

I do not have sufficient materials at hand to definitively resolve this
problem, but I would like to note a bit of collateral evidence. According
to the chart of the movements in tax rates (*nenguritsu*) for the shogunate
and Kumamoto domain in Figure 4.2, the high tax rate that obtained in
Kumamoto from 1700 to 1720 dropped rapidly around 1720, falling to a
sharp v-shaped trough in the middle of the 1730s. The shogunate's rate
also fell sharply in the middle of the 1730s. But the shogunate's tax rate
took a turn up in the middle of the 1730s, continuing so until just beyond
1750. For Kumamoto, however, after the rise in the middle of the 1730s,
the tax rate dropped again at the end of the decade. Since the rate began
to rise in the early 1740s, the rise in the middle of the 1730s put an end to
the downward trend of the early 1700s, and was doubtlessly the starting
point of a change in direction. Of course, tax rates do not directly reveal
the movement of the actual economy. But it is likely that when real output rose, tax collections also increased, and that when output did not
increase, collections declined. On this point, I see the reversal of the
downward trend in tax rates in the early 1700s, to the rising trend after the
Gembun recoinage, as an expression of a change from a recessionary to an
expansionary economy.

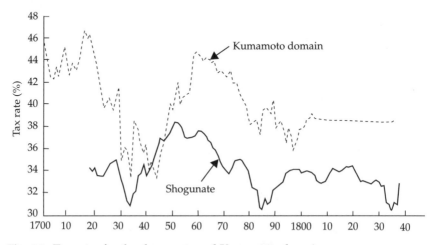

Fig. 4.2. Tax rates for the shogunate and Kumamoto domain.

Source: Tax rate for the shogunate: Edo sôsho kankô-kai (1917) and Tsuji et al. (1964). Tax
rate for Kumamoto domain: Hosokawa hansei-shi kenkyûkai (1974).

Figure 4.3(a) shows the annual revenues and expenditures of the shogunal treasury. After the Gembun recoinage, revenues and expenditures both increased significantly. That in itself was the result of inflation, but the tremendous surplus seems also to reflect a business boom. Moreover, according to data on wages in western Settsu (the Osaka area) agricultural villages collected by Osamu Saitô, carpenters' wages rose 113 per cent after the recoinage while agricultural day laborers' wages rose 59 per cent, when 1737 wages are compared to average wages for the 1731–35 period (Saitô 1976a: 4). During this same time general prices rose by 42 per cent, so real wages were rising. From these pieces of collateral evidence, it would seem that the Gembun recoinage had a reflationary effect.

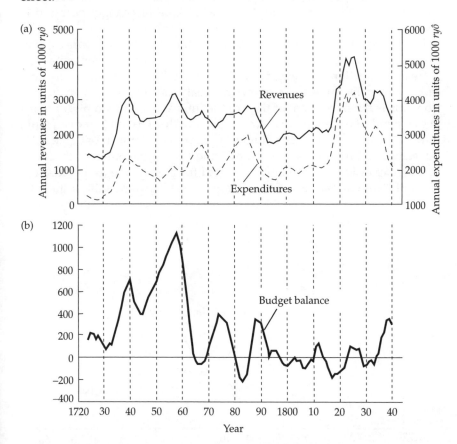

Fig. 4.3. (a) Annual revenues and expenditures of the shogunate and (b) budget balance of the shogunate (moving five-years' averages fluctuation).

Sources: Hiroshi Shimbo, *Kinsei no bukka to keizai hatten* [Early Modern Prices and Economic Development] (1978). Primary sources: *Seisai zakki* (Miscellany of Seisai) and *Kahei hiroku* (Secret Records of Currency).

The rise in prices induced by the Gembun recoinage ran its course in four or five years, and prices tended to fall from the early 1740s to the early 1770s. During this period of decline, prices rose briefly in the middle of the 1750s. But as we can see from the decline in the tax rate during that time (Figure 4.2), this rise was due to a poor harvest. So if we exclude this brief period, we have a long-term decline in prices continuing over about thirty years. What was the cause of this? First of all, if we look at Akashi's estimates of the volume of currency in circulation at this time (Figure 4.4), we see that there was a small increase until the middle of the 1740s, but after that there was a miniscule decrease. There is little doubt that the slow pace of the increase in the money supply suppressed prices. But during this period, general prices fell even further than the decline in the volume of the money supply. So, what kind of changes occurred in the real economy?

Following the equation $M = kPy$, since the decline in P (prices) was greater than the decline in M (volume of currency in circulation), either (1) y (real production) increased, or (2) Marshall's k (propensity to hold money) rose. Figure 4.4 also shows the real totals of currency in circulation; this is the movement of the product of k and y. Put simply, option 1 above would be due to "real economic growth." Option 2 above would imply "an increase in the volume of exchanges using money" due to "development of a market economy" and "a rise in commercialization" and an expansion of speculative demand for money due to the development of a capital market. Option 1 implies a downward shift of the total

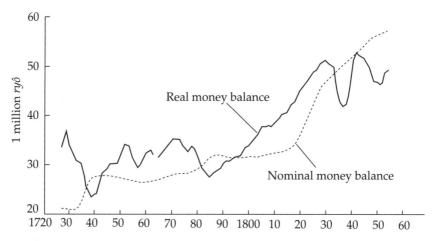

Fig. 4.4. Nominal and real money balance (moving five-years' average).

Source: The nominal money balance was compiled from Akashi (1989).

Note: The real money balance is calculated by dividing the nominal money balance by the general price index of this chapter.

supply curve, but option 2 signifies a downward shift of the total demand curve. Both of these could pull down prices, but in option 1 real production would rise with a decline in interest rates while in the case of option 2 there is a great possibility that real production would decline and interest rates rise. If both options took place, then the result would be the same since real production and interest rates would not change.

The tax rate in Figure 4.2 shows a period of slight decline in the middle of the 1750s, but in general the rate rose from the first half of the 1740s and was highly stable from the 1750s to the 1770s. The tax rate during the period of 1750–70 was within the 40–45 per cent range for Kumamoto and 35–39 per cent for the shogunate. The stability of the tax rate was due, in part, to the dissemination of the *jômen* (fixed tax rate) system. But if we understand that under the *jômen* system the tax rate was unresponsive to good harvests but responsive to poor harvests—in other words, it was inflexible toward the former and elastic toward the latter—this stability helps us recognize that agricultural production developed relatively smoothly. That is also supported by the fact that shogunal annual revenue during this period was at a very high level, as we can see in Figure 4.3.

Moreover, of Figure 4.5(c) below shows the changes in "year-end inventory of rice" (*etsunenmai-daka*) in Osaka. There is an increasing tendency from the 1740s until around 1780. The "year-end inventory of rice" is an approximate figure for the amount of rice actually in storage in Osaka warehouses. As such, its rises and declines may be seen as a reflection of supply and demand relations in the market. In that sense, the increase in year-end inventory of rice is a manifestation of a national rise in productivity in rice.

When we look at the movement of real wages in the case of carpenters' wages in rural villages in western Settsu, the average index of 80 for the period of 1740–44 was surpassed by the average index of 101 for 1770–74 (a 26 per cent rate of increase). The index for agricultural day labor rose from 64 to 96 (a 50 per cent rate of increase). (The above figures are computed by dividing the 1802–04 cash wage index, set at 100, by the rice price index.)[4] Since the gap between carpenters and agricultural day laborers decreased, we can see that there was real growth in the agricultural sector.

As for interest rates, we have data for the average interest rates on all loans made by the Kyoto headquarters of the Mitsui Exchange House. From 1728 to 1740, the interest rate often exceeded 5 per cent, but during the 1740s it dropped to the 4 per cent plateau. In the 1750s it dropped even further to the 3 per cent level. In the 1770s it fell just before breaking 3 per cent (Shimbo 1978: 234). In Osaka's Kônoike Exchange House, the average interest rates on loans of silver was 6–7 per cent during the 1740s, but fell to the 4 per cent level during the 1750s and 1760s (Yasuoka 1970a: 56–7). From the above we can see that it was highly likely that behind the phenomenon

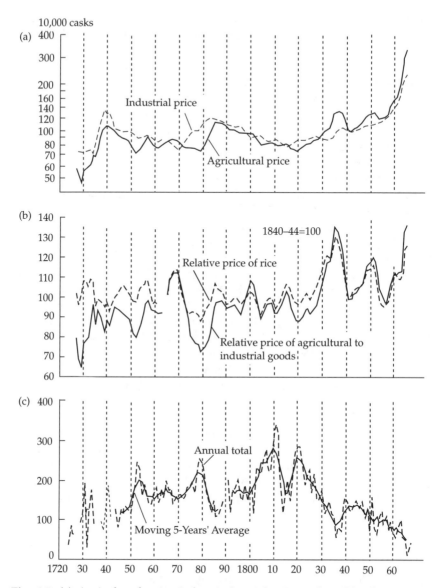

Fig. 4.5. (a) Agricultural price index, industrial price index, (b) relative price index of agricultural to industrial goods, (c) relative price of rice and balance of Osaka New Year's rice (moving five-years' average).

Sources: See the "Data Overview" at the end of Miyamoto (1989) for (a) and (b). Figure 4.5(c) was compiled from Kabushiki kaisha Dôjima beikoku torihikisho (ed.) (1913).

of a drop in prices that was even greater than the decline in the money supply was an increase in real production (namely, option 1 above).

However, it is also possible that the drop in prices was the result of "the development of a money economy and a market economy." One basis for this assumption can be found in the shogunate's execution of the forced loans (goyôkin) order and the order to purchase rice in Osaka in 1761. These orders were responses to the decline of rice prices at the time and led to the collection of 1.7 million *ryô* from Osaka merchants, two-thirds of which was then loaned out in Osaka to be used to purchase rice to be stored in warehouses. The reason the shogunate attempted this order is because it had believed that Osaka merchants had stored up idle capital. In fact, 700,000 *ryô* were collected through this order and as a result of purchasing the rice, its price rose quickly from fifty-four *momme* for one *koku* in the twelfth month of 1761 to sixty-eight *momme* for one *koku* in the first month 1762. So it appears that a good deal of cash that had not returned to market was released by the policy (on this point see Miyamoto 1987: 359–60).

To give a related matter, we may note that the copper cash market (the amount of silver *momme* equivalent to one *kamme* of pennies) rose during the period of around 1750–70. Explaining this rise, Shimbo states, "the rise in the relative value of copper pennies to gold and silver coins implies that the demand for copper cash, which was the means of payment for small transactions, was expanding." Also, "behind the trends in penny amounts, we must find lurking the development of a cash economy in the rural villages" (Shimbo 1978: 209–10). This explanation surely supports the view that the fall in prices during this period was due to "the development of a cash economy and a market economy." Of course, during the late Edo period, there developed a financial system in which exchange stores issued credit and notes were used for large transactions. Therefore, the possibility of a growing demand for currency causing financial stringency would be diminished by that alone. That is probably why the interest rate showed a tendency to fall during this period.

6. Prices and the Macroeconomy from the Late Eighteenth to the Early Nineteenth Century

As I stated above, the decline in prices hit bottom at the beginning of the 1770s and thereafter took a turn upward. There is little doubt that the sudden rise of prices in the middle of the 1780s can be attributed to the continuing crop failures of the Temmei era. The instability of agricultural production is vividly expressed in the large drops in the tax rate (see Figure 4.2).

But the crop failures alone were not responsible for the rapid rise in prices of the 1780s. The bottom line of the shogunal budget ceased recording the surplus it had shown since the 1730s and went into the red during the 1760s. Tanuma Okitsugu became a grand chamberlain of the shogunate in the middle of all this, in 1767, and became Senior Councilor in 1772, at which point he began a series of aggressive policies. The many chartered trade associations (*kabunakama*) of Osaka were officially sanctioned in 1770. And it was in 1772 that his central policy, the minting of the *Nanryô nishugin* coin, took effect. These aggressive policies were directly meant to bring in money to a declining shogunal treasury. But on the other hand, it was carried out in the midst of the objective condition of the stagnating development of the real economy that lacked an additional supply of money. Thanks to profits earned from the minting of the *Nanryô nishugin* coins and the distribution of tax income from the sanctioning of chartered trade associations, shogunal revenue rose from the beginning of the 1770s and the balance returned into the black. Because of this, the nominal balance of currency in circulation also increased from the end of the 1760s, as we can see in Figure 4.4. The extension of the money supply and the multiple effects of the budget aggravated the sudden rise of prices from the Temmei crop failures. From the 1770s to the middle of the 1780s real production naturally fell. The movement of the real balance of currency in circulation in Figure 4.4 was neither effected by nor unrelated to the movement of real production. Tanuma's aggressive policy may be judged an appropriate macroeconomic policy from the movements of the money economy over the previous decades. But his misfortune was to run into the Temmei crop failures.

After reaching a peak in 1785, prices fell continuously until about 1820. Figure 4.1 is a logarithmic graph, so rates of change are easy to compare. Therefore, we may note that the line denoting the drop in prices from 1740 to 1770 is nearly parallel to the line for the drop in prices from 1785 to 1820. In that case, the tendency of prices to decline from 1740 to 1770 may have been temporarily stopped by the "external shock" of the crop failures of the middle 1780s. But once the shock had passed, prices resumed their previous course. If we divide the nominal currency balance by general prices to get the real currency balance, we find the sharp growth curve from 1780 to 1830 seen in Figure 4.4. This is also on about the same angle as that from 1740 to 1770. This must mean that beneath the drop in prices there was the same real growth as occurred from 1740 to 1770.

However, when we examine the movement of real wages, we find that the periods 1740–70 and 1785–1820 are completely different. The rate at which real wages rose for carpenters over the approximately thirty years from 1786–90 to 1814–18 in western Settsu was 21 per cent and the rate of rise for real wages of agricultural day laborers was 32 per cent. Both of these were below the rates discussed above for the thirty-year period of 1740–70 (carpenters = 26 per cent, agricultural day laborers = 50 per cent) (Saitô 1976: 4–5). However, the figures for agricultural wages in villages in Harima Province collected by Seiji Uemura show a slightly higher rise than those for western Settsu (Uemura 1986: 168–90). Turning to an urban example, the data for wages at the Kyoto headquarters of the Mitsui Dry Goods store show that real wages for carpenters rose by only 16 per cent and for day laborers by only 13 per cent over the period of 1791–1820. The above data all show a tendency for real wages to rise from around 1790 to around 1820, implying that real production increased in the background. At the same time, however, the figures show that the rate of growth was less steep than during the first phase and that growth was higher in the nondeveloped regions than it was in the cities or the villages surrounding them.

There are other ways in which the periods 1740–70 and 1785–1820 differed. In the former period, shogunal and domainal tax rates were high, the shogunal treasury was full, and the balance was in the black. In the latter period, tax rates were low, the shogunal budget shrank, and the balance was in the red. As we shall see below, it appears that rice production increased during the period 1785–1820, particularly from the beginning of the nineteenth century. Therefore, the decline in the tax rate did not reflect a worsening of the actual economy (since, for example, with the establishment of the *jômen* [fixed rate] tax system the actual tax burden lightened). If the real economy experienced growth, then the distribution of earnings fell in favor of the agricultural villages. On the other hand, the merchants who depended heavily on cash expenditures by the *daimyô*; class—the shogunate and the domainal lords—took a relatively hard hit. In fact, the sales of one of the representative urban merchants of the Edo period, Mitsui Echigoya, declined from the 1770s to the 1820s (Kagawa 1985: 287–90). Indeed, Mitsui's total operating assets declined from the 1770s to the 1820s. There are no signs of growth in the family assets of the Kônoike Zen'emon family of Osaka until the 1810s either (for Mitsui see Togai 1961; for Kônoike see Yasuoka 1970a). Regarding the conditions of the Kansei to Bunka eras (1790–1820 approximately), Hiroshi Shimbo states:

The deflation caused by the shrinkage of the shogunal budget brought about a shrinkage of the effective demand that had a strong link to shogunal expenditures ... causing a stagnation of the central cities' markets. However, there was an expansion of regional markets due to the permeation of the cash economy into the villages and the development of regional industries... thus leading to an increase in effective demand in each domain. Therefore, this deflation did not have the same impact on every region and in every area of the economy. (Shimbo 1978: 316)

This means we must recognize that the economic growth in periods one and two of our periodization was different.

Nevertheless, as our discussion above shows, the real economic growth in the recovery from the Temmei crop failures was, macroeconomically speaking, part of a tendency toward growth that had been in place since the 1740s. If we view late Edo period economic growth as a long-term process, we will run into a problem with Shimbo's theory of "post-Bunsei era inflationary growth"—that is, that there was a refraction of growth in the Bunsei era. It is to that issue that we will turn next.

7. The Theory of "Post-Bunsei Era Inflationary Growth"

The prices that had been in decline since the middle of the 1780s began to rise again around 1820. In explaining this continuous rise, Hiroshi Shimbo focuses on the recoinages that occurred frequently during the Bunsei to Tempo eras (roughly 1818–44). But Shimbo believes that the route toward price increases from recoinage was different from the case of the Gembun recoinage. The Gembun recoinage followed a course from devaluation to exchange of old for new coins via the premium exchange method to an increase in the money supply to a rise of prices. But in the Bunsei–Tempô recoinages, the shogunate earned huge profits by exchanging old for new coins at equal face value. With the shogunate minting new coins in order to earn revenue, prices rose because of the investment in the market of increased budgetary expenditures. In other words, the links were from recoinage to an increase in shogunal financial income, to an increase in shogunal expenditures and an increase in the volume of currency issued, to an increase in effective demand to a rise of prices. Since the effects of an increase in expenditures manifested themselves continuously, the rise in prices during the Bunsei–Tempô era proceeded more steadily than did the rise after the Gembun recoinage (Shimbo 1978: 317–24). In other words, the total demand curve took an upswing and prices rose due to the multiple effects on real goods of an increase in budgetary expenditures and the asset effects of an increasing supply of money.

Shimbo does not see the Bunsei–Tempô recoinage and budget increases as bringing about only a rise of prices. In addition, he argues "economic development was stimulated by the expansion of effective demand," giving way to "inflationary growth." However, there is not necessarily sufficient data to back up the claims about the effect on real income. For that reason, there have been a number of debates about the merits of this "theory of inflationary growth." Let me introduce a few of these debates below.

Osamu Saitô argues against Shimbo, stating that, first of all, even if the shogunate earned huge profits from the recoinages, the portion of the "national income" occupied by the shogunal budget was not that large. Therefore, the multiplying effects of the increase in budgetary expenditures from the recoinage would not have been that great. Second, the budgetary expenditures were distributed among the three cities of Edo,

Osaka, and Kyoto. So exports from the countryside to these cities, whose "import dependency" was high, were stimulated, but Saitô expresses doubts as to how great the elasticity of supply was to the regions. In other words, since the total supply curve was close to vertical, would it not be the case that the increase in expenditures would create an inflation gap causing only prices to rise? Third, since the Bunsei–Tempô recoinage saw an increase in expenditures accompanied by an increase in the supply of currency, it is logical to expect that there would be an increase in investment due to a decline in the interest rate.

But Saitô wonders how much investment at the time was sensitive to the interest rate. Moreover, we cannot prove from existing data that the interest rate declined in fact. Fourth, even if the mechanism of a low interest rate leading to increased investment was not at work, there is a strong possibility that there was a change in investment figures due to a rise in anticipated interest rates based on continual inflation and such domainal economic policies as the issuance of domainal currency, the authorization of monopolies and the promotion of domainal production. We will have to wait for further research in order to understand just how great was this increase in production (Saitô 1980*b*).

While Mataji Umemura expresses basic agreement with Shimbo's thesis, he has sought to augment the "inflationary growth thesis" from other angles on the grounds that the multiplying effects of increasing government budgets lacked sufficient power to drive the engine of late Tokugawa economic development. Toward that end, Umemura first turns to the fact that during the period of continual price rises real wages fell dramatically. As a basis for this argument, he looks at carpenter's wages at the Mitsui Headquarters in Kyoto and carpenters' and agricultural laborers' wages in western Settsu and points out that at least the former remained nearly constant. If we remember that prices rose after 1820, then we can clearly see that real wages fell. Masaharu Uemura's data on agricultural wages in villages in Harima Province show the same kind of trend after the 1830s.

Umemura observes that this wage inflexibility, or its lagging rise, increased profit, the benefits of which went to those who employed laborers, mainly regional entrepreneurs. Since taxes were light on non-agricultural activities, taxes on agriculture were inflexible. This fact also contributed to the entrepreneurs' accumulation of profit and their reinvestment. Umemura argues that with the rise in prices and the expansion of profit, entrepreneurs' expectations of profits also rose and their will to invest was greatly stimulated. As evidence for this, Umemura cites the expansion of shipping volume and investment in the Japan Sea, increasing use of fertilizers from Matsumae (Hokkaido), "increased exports" of Niikawa cotton and Kaga silk textiles, and the extensive development of new agricultural fields.

Umemura also makes the important point that this kind of expanded popular investment was not seen uniformly throughout the country. Just as the population grew after the Bunsei era in San'in, San'yô, Hokuriku, and Shikoku, but stagnated or fell in Kinki and Kantô, the increase in industrial investment took place mainly in the peripheries. Umemura sums it up thus: "in the end, the late Tokugawa period saw a general decline of the center and development of the peripheries" (Umemura 1981).

But of course, real wages did not drop with the beginning of inflation after the Bunsei era. Excepting the case of the data for Mitsui carpenters, whose cash wages remained constant, real wages for servants in Harima Province villages showed a slight tendency to rise from 1820 to around 1834. Real wages for Osaka carpenters also rose from the 1830s to the middle of the 1840s. Umemura's decline in wages came after this period. In that sense, Umemura's "wage lag/interest inflation thesis" is useful for explaining how growth sparked by expanded government budgets and an increase in the volume of currency moves onto a more continuous path. It thus indeed enhances Shimbo's thesis.

In response to these criticisms, Shimbo has recognized that, of course, the expanded budgets of the late Tokugawa era alone could not function as the engine of the economic growth of the period. He affirmed the utility of Umemura's augmentation and added three further points. First, he proposed that the foundational and prerequisite conditions for late Edo economic growth and development were formed in the agricultural sector from the end of the eighteenth to the beginning of the nineteenth centuries. He then argued that the Bunsei recoinage functioned as the wake-up call that sparked this potential growth. Second, he stated that the multiplying effects of the increase in shogunal budgets that came from using the profits from recoinage were not short term or temporary, but made significant, continuous and long-term contributions to economic growth. Third, he pointed out that there was visible growth in agricultural handicraft and nonagricultural arenas after the Bunsei era. From these points, Shimbo asserts that the inflation after the Bunsei era doubtlessly accompanied real economic growth (Toshimaru Harada and Matao Miyamoto 1985: 109–46).

Ryûzô Yamazaki has also entered the debate on the "inflationary growth thesis." Yamazaki states that we can understand inflationary growth from the Bunsei era if we operate on the understanding that the post-Bunsei growth was due to growth in the agricultural sector during the Kansei to Bunka era that served as the prerequisite to the post-Bunsei growth in the nonagricultural sectors. But he expresses doubts that there was sufficient development of a class of agricultural managers that could hire large enough numbers of laborers so that Umemura's mechanism of investment stimulus from real wage decline and interest rise could be applied to this era (Toshimaru Harada and Matao Miyamoto 1985: 138–9).

Shimbo and Yamazaki's theses treat post-Bunsei era inflationary growth as an extension of the path of development from the end of the eighteenth century, with the main characteristic being that the sector leading the growth switched from the agricultural to the nonagricultural sector. To this extent, the originality of the "inflationary growth thesis"—which holds that the Bunsei and Tempô recoinages and growth of the governmental budget, accompanied by an increase in the money supply, was the engine of growth—is weakened somewhat. But as I stated above, I believe it is generally correct. Shigeo Akashi finds that there was a continuous rise in the volume of currency actually in circulation from the Great Temmei Famine to the end of the Tokugawa period. But he also argues that even if the Bunsei recoinage gave a temporary acceleration to economic growth, there is no evidence, which shows it brought about a dramatic change in economic development (we can check Akashi's thesis in Figure 4.4. The growth in the real currency balance continues along a nearly straight line from the middle of the 1780s until about 1830. The deflection in the Bunsei era is not clear).

However, if we reflect on whether the growth from the late eighteenth century could have continued without the Bunsei–Tempô recoinages, we must conclude in the negative. The nominal currency balance in Figure 4.4 is nearly unchanging from the middle of the 1780s until just before 1820. Had this condition continued beyond this point, the economy would sooner or later have slipped into a rapid decline. By the Bunka era, the shogunate responded to the decline in the price of rice by ordering the people of Osaka to buy rice in 1806 and 1810. At the same time, in order to accumulate capital to buy rice, the shogunate demanded forced loans from Osaka merchants in 1810 and 1813. In 1810, when the great exchange merchants functioned as the contractors for these loans, capital was accumulated relatively smoothly. But in 1813, when over 600 merchants were ordered to submit funds, there were difficulties gathering the funds and, in the end, only 50–60 per cent of the expected amount was collected.

There were mass runs on exchange houses in Osaka and the traders at the Dôjima Rice Market who issued bills of exchange experienced such a financial crunch that trading was stopped. In other words, the forced loans crowded out private funds and, as a result, the purchase of rice from the forced loan principal was unable to achieve much result (for more on this point, see Miyamoto 1987: 655–8). This state of affairs was different from what occurred during the forced loans of 1761. This suggests that there was a hidden crunch in financial conditions at the time. If such were the monetary conditions on the eve of the Bunsei recoinage, then the expansion of the government's budget and the increase in the volume of issued currency would have had a tremendous uplifting effect.

8. "A Price Revolution" after the Opening of the Ports

A simple glance at Figure 4.1 shows that after the opening of the ports in 1859 prices rose at a leap. Calculating over the period from 1854 (five years prior to the opening) to 1865, prices rose at an annual rate of 8.5 per cent (Table 4.1), truly a state of hyperinflation. Of course, part of this was a continuation of the trend for prices to rise since the 1820s. But it is clear that a new inflation set in under the different economic environment of the open ports.

The main cause of this hyperinflation, it need hardly be restated, was a recoinage which was necessary to bring the relative prices of gold and silver in Japan in line with the relative prices in international trade. After the Ansei-era *Nishugin*, which was issued in 1859 to correct the gap between the relative gold–silver prices in Japan and those in the international arena, failed due to foreign resistance, the shogunate carried out a recoinage in 1860 that dramatically changed the price of gold in a way that was different from the previous year's recoinage in which the shogunate raised the amount of pure silver per unit of currency (the *ryô*) in stamped silver coins. That is, the shogunate issued an order that the Tempô *koban* circulate at a value of three *ryô* one *bu* two *shu* and that the Tempô one *bu-ban* circulate at a value of three *bu* one *shu*. Moreover, they degraded all gold coins at this proportion in that year's recoinage. Through this augmented valuation and debasing of the coins, the nominal volume of currency increased from 53 million *ryô* to 130 million *ryô*. This sudden increase in the volume of currency brought about a sudden rise in prices (Shimbo 1978: 279–89).

As Shimbo points out, the impact that a recoinage will have on prices depends on the methods used to exchange the old coins for the new. That is, in the exchange of the old good coins for the new debased coins, the premium exchange method which places a premium on the old coins quickly increases the volume of currency in circulation in the market after the recoinage, also raising prices quickly. In the case of the face value exchange method, in which the old coins are exchanged at equal face value with the new and debased coins, the shogunate took the path of increasing its budget through the profits acquired in recoinage, gradually increasing the volume of currency thereby. Since the multiple effects of the increase in the government's budget also take effect slowly, the rise in prices proceeds gradually. Of the Edo period recoinages, only the Gembun recoinage was conducted on the premium exchange method. The Genroku, Hôei, Bunsei, and Tempô recoinages were all carried out on the equal face value exchange method. As we have already seen, prices rose at a leap after the Gembun recoinage while they rose steadily after all others.

In the 1860 (Man'en) recoinage, old coins were exchanged for new on the premium exchange method. In which case, if it followed the pattern of the Gembun recoinage, prices would rise quickly after the recoinage and then stabilize after that. But in fact, such was not the case. Prices continued to rise rapidly throughout the final years of the shogunate. Why was this so?

To proceed directly to my conclusion, the main players in the rapid rise of prices at the time of the Man'en recoinage were the *koban*, the one *bu-ban*, and the newly minted Man'en two *bu-kin*. While the Man'en two *bu-kin* was nominally a gold coin, it contained no more than 22 per cent gold. To complement the issuing of 667,000 *ryô* of the other two, 46.948 million *ryô* of the Man'en two *bu-kin* coin were issued, making it the basic coin of the late Tokugawa–early Meiji era (Yamamoto 1983). What was even more important is that most of the silver that composed 78 per cent of the material of the Man'en two *bu-kin* coin was acquired by melting down foreign silver coins.

According to Takehiko Ôkura, the shogunate acquired a huge volume of foreign silver through exchange with the one *bu-gin*. Since there was a trade surplus after the opening of the ports, the market for foreign silver fell. Because of that, the shogunate earned profits by exchanging foreign silver and the one *bu-gin*. They then melted that silver down to mint the one *bu-gin* (one *bu* silver) and the two *bu-kin* (one *bu* gold). The shogunate's profits from the recoinage of foreign silver were not brought about merely by the fall in the market for foreign silver. Instead, those profits became even larger by recoinage of that silver into the two *bu-kin* coin, which had a face value far higher than was its real value and which functioned as the supplementary currency to the standard *koban*. The profits earned by the shogunate through this recoinage of foreign silver (especially into the two *bu-kin*) were enormous, comprising nearly 53 per cent of the shogunate's expenditures for 1863 (Ôkura 1987). These recoinage profits naturally increased the shogunate's budget and the volume of the money supply, and this, in turn, spurred the sudden rise of prices even further. In other words, the sudden rise in prices after the opening of the ports occurred through a combination of the Gembun recoinage pattern of a simple increase in the nominal currency volume and the expansion of the government budget due to recoinage profits characteristic of the Bunsei–Tempô recoinages. From its violence and from the important international element, this was truly a "price revolution," as Shimbo has dubbed it.

It is difficult to describe the movements of the real economy as they occurred in the process of the price explosion of the last years of the shogunate. But one thing is clear: the Man'en recoinage took place in the midst of a long-term inflationary trend. It would be difficult to believe that the recoinage policy, carried out under foreign pressure, would directly lead to real economic expansion.

It may be that the effects of the late Tokugawa "price revolution" were greater in the structure of income distribution than they were in macroeconomic aspects. Umemura's proposal that there was a process of "wage lag and interest inflation" in late Tokugawa inflation is actually more appropriate to the period after the opening of the ports. One further thing that should be pointed out is that in the inflationary process, debtors and the holders of financial assets suffered losses, but those who owned the debt and possessed material assets had a high possibility of earning profits. The fact that the financial assets of the representatives of the urban merchant class, the Mitsui and Kônoike families, rose at a rate that was lower than the rise in prices, but the assets of the Tokushima indigo merchants, the Miki Yokichirô family, rose steadily throughout these years, which shows us how this manifested concretely in the last years of the shogunate. (For further information on the examples of the Mitsui and the Kônoike families, see Togai 1970 and Yasuoka 1970, for further information on the Miki Yokichirô family, see Amano 1986.) Further research is needed on this point, but when we remember that the entrepreneurial activity of the Edo period urban merchant class was in relative decline in the Meiji period and that entrepreneurs from peripheral areas were far more active, we may be forced to recognize that late Tokugawa inflation had an important impact on the accumulation of capital.

PART TWO: RELATIVE PRICES AND TRANSFORMATIONS IN THE INDUSTRIAL STRUCTURE

9. Relative Prices of Agriculture to Industry and Changes in the Relative Price for Each Commodity

Figure 4.5 is a graph showing the agricultural price index and the industrial price index (Figure 4.5(a)), the relative price index of agricultural to industrial goods (Figure 4.5(b)) (calculated by dividing the agricultural price index by the industrial price index), and the relative rice price (Figure 4.5(c)) (obtained by dividing the general price index by the rice price index). Table 4.2 shows a combination of the fluctuations in general prices and fluctuations in the relative agricultural–industrial prices to show both the periodic rate of change and the annual rate of change for agricultural prices, industrial prices, and the relative agricultural–industrial prices. Table 4.3 shows the rate of change for each period of the commodities used to compose the price index.

According to Figure 4.5, agricultural prices and industrial prices moved together over a long period of time. Admittedly, there were minor differences in this movement and it was these differences that account for the movements in the relative prices of agricultural to industrial goods. The relative agricultural–industrial price index is calculated with the price index for the period of 1840–44 set at 100. Over the long term, industrial

Table 4.2. Rate of change by period of agricultural prices, industrial prices, and relative prices of agricultural to industrial products

Phase	Period	Direction of change of general prices	Rate of change for the period			Annual rate of change		
			Agriculture	Industry	Agri./Indust.	Agriculture	Industry	Agri./Indust.
Phase 1	1729–39	Trough to peak	+128.1	+86.1	+28.3	+8.6	+6.4	+2.2
	1739–70	Peak to trough	−20.1	−44.4	+38.3	−0.7	−1.9	+1.1
	(1729–70)		+82.2	+3.5	+77.3	+1.5	+0.0	+1.5
Phase 2	1770–85	Trough to peak	+35.1	+57.6	−14.8	+2.0	+3.1	−1.1
	(1770–79)		−11.1	+39.0	−36.2	−1.3	+3.7	−5.0
	1785–1820	Peak to trough	−33.2	−27.1	−8.3	−1.1	−0.9	−0.2
	(1779–1800)		+30.0	−12.9	+50.4	+2.4	−1.2	+3.6
	(1800–20)		−21.9	−5.0	−18.5	−1.2	−0.3	−0.9
Phase 3	1820–38	Trough to peak	+76.3	+22.5	+43.9	+3.2	+1.1	+2.1
	(1820–38)		+71.5	+10.3	+54.1	+3.0	+0.5	+2.5
	1838–42	Peak to trough	−24.6	−4.3	−21.4	−6.8	−1.1	−5.7
	(1838–41)		−21.7	+7.7	−26.8	−4.0	+1.2	−5.2
	1842–51	Trough to peak	+31.5	+9.1	+20.6	+3.1	+1.0	+2.1
	(1841–51)		+30.2	+7.7	+20.9	+2.6	+0.7	+1.9
	1851–54	Peak to trough	−10.1	+4.8	−13.8	−3.5	+1.5	−5.0
	(1851–56)		−4.8	+16.3	−18.3	−1.0	+3.1	−4.1
Phase 4	1854–65	Trough to peak	+178.8	+102.8	+32.6	+9.8	+6.6	+3.3
	(1856–65)		+168.4	+82.3	+39.8	+11.6	+6.9	+4.7

Note: Calculated on the moving five years' average of the general price index in *ryô*. Years within parentheses are calculated on the fluctuations of the relative price of agricultural to industrial products.

Table 4.3. Rate of change of prices by period for each commodity

General price index	1729–39 TR→PK	1739–70 PK→TR	1770–85 TR→PK	1785–1820 PK→TR	1820–38 TR→PK	1838–42 PK→TR	1842–51 TR→PK	1851–54 PK→TR	1854–65 TR→PK
	+105.3	−32.0	+44.1	−30.5	+51.5	−17.1	+21.9	−4.3	+146.5
Rice	+98.1	−21.1	+39.8	−37.2	+88.6	−31.3	+42.5	−19.9	+235.2
Wheat				−39.3	+133.3	−38.1	+17.9	−8.0	+175.8
Barley						−63.2	+46.2	−24.9	+183.4
Soy beans			+21.4	−30.1	+89.2	−22.2	+22.6	−5.7	+132.7
Rapeseed	(+86.6)	(−17.9)	(+43.6)	(−38.1)	+86.8	−20.7	+7.5	−0.1	+161.9
Cotton	+283.1	−36.9	+64.5	−43.9	+123.4	−26.2	+4.0	−19.4	+228.8
Cocoon			(+23.4)	(−12.6)	+27.5	(−11.7)			
Silk floss			(+114.2)	(−34.5)	(−15.5)	(−30.9)	(+59.3)	(−3.4)	
Wax				−36.9	+136.6	−9.0	−9.7	−3.5	+146.1
Firewood				+11.2	+19.7	+4.8	+5.2	−4.3	+147.0
Coal				+7.6	+15.3	+8.6	−4.5	−4.1	+120.6
Rice bran						−19.6	+32.2	−8.9	+183.9
Shiitake						+19.0	−10.3	−0.1	+139.8
Tatami straw								−4.0	+107.0
Lumber						−20.7	+10.0	−3.6	+86.5
Bamboo						+15.8	+51.8	+109.6	+29.9
Bamboo brooms						+8.2	+26.9	+8.2	
Tobacco						+10.2	+8.6	−2.1	+97.7
Vegetables						+14.9	+24.9	+10.0	+57.7
Dried bonito						−2.0	+83.2	−8.2	+153.3
Dried squid						−4.0	+16.5	+4.9	+348.7
Fish fertilizer						−14.8	+4.7	+5.9	+185.2
Cotton fabrics			(+19.2)	+4.2	+34.5	+3.6	−7.2	−7.5	+128.7
Cotton yarn							−11.2	−9.5	+160.1
Silk fabrics				(−6.1)	+17.0	+7.5	−2.4	−5.1	+252.7
Raw silk	+111.9	(−43.4)	(+6.4)	−3.0	+23.2	+1.9	+2.9	−0.7	+290.8

Hemp thread	(+67.5)					−1.4	−17.1	+10.4	+130.8
Rapeseed oil	(+7.5)	(−19.2)	+31.6	+31.1	+53.1	−10.9	+11.5	−1.9	+98.8
Soy sauce		(+29.1)	(−11.2)	−11.8	+38.2	−16.5	+1.2	−7.2	+144.2
Miso	(+59.9)	(−47.6)	(+88.3)	−27.4	+42.4	−24.8	+22.1	−8.8	+204.6
Refined *saké*	(+101.4)				+64.4	−34.8	+33.8	−18.2	+156.9
Salt					+90.5	−27.5	+7.2	−15.6	+222.4
Sugar						−21.6	+17.5	−3.4	+124.1
Iron						+42.1	+8.0	−14.7	+264.0
Copper						+29.3	+5.3	−2.1	+131.3
Nails						+1.1	+17.1	+3.6	+30.2
Cooking pots						+4.9	+18.3	+8.3	+231.8
Tiles						+2.2	−5.3	+3.9	+160.3
Hand buckets						+3.2	+20.8	+3.6	+75.6
Lime						+4.1	+30.4	+93.4	+65.6
Korean ginseng				+10.1	+12.2	−20.2	−39.5	+7.4	−51.2
Sappanwood				−61.8	−2.5	+6.9	+75.3	+27.1	−77.0

Note: TR = Trough, PK = Peak. The rate of change is calculated on the moving five years' average. However, when the moving five years' average was not available, each year's value or the average of the preceding and following years, was used. Those cases are shown inside parentheses.

prices were relatively higher before 1790, compared to the base period; prices were approximately the same from 1790–1830 and agricultural prices were relatively higher after 1830. Therefore, we may say that over the 150 years of the late Tokugawa period represented in this figure, agricultural prices had a greater tendency to rise than industrial prices.

Next, the fluctuations in the relative price of rice were far smaller than the fluctuations in the relative price of agricultural to industrial goods. There were many times when rice prices changed in harmony with general prices. This is in part due to the fact that rice prices were given the high weight of 30 per cent in calculating the general price index. But it also reveals the foundational nature of rice prices among all prices in the Edo period. Nevertheless, there were fluctuations in the relative price of rice and those fluctuations resembled the fluctuations in the relative prices of agricultural to industrial goods.

When we turn to the fluctuations in the relative prices of agricultural to industrial goods, the undulations are not as clear as those found among general prices. But if we were to point out the waves, we could find four: the first being from a trough in 1729 to a peak in 1770 to another trough in 1779; the second being from the trough in 1779 to a peak in 1800 to another trough in 1820; the third being from the trough in 1820 to a peak in 1835 to another trough in 1856; and the fourth being the wave after 1856. Earlier, I pointed out that there were four long-term fluctuations in general prices. When we place these two sets of fluctuations on top of each other, we find a minor difference. In particular, the first wave of relative agricultural–industrial prices lags nine years behind the first phase of general prices (1728–70). This makes the second phase begin that much later. We may observe almost the same movement in relative rice prices.

Let us now examine each period separately. Prior to the first wave—that is, in the period leading up to the first trough in 1729—both relative prices of agricultural to industrial goods and relative rice prices dropped suddenly. This most likely reflects the well-known mid-Kyôhô period phenomenon of "cheap rice and rising prices for other commodities." Since there was a major crop failure in 1732, the upturn around 1730 in the relative prices of agricultural to industrial goods and the relative price of rice was not due to the stemming of the relatively low prices for rice and agricultural products. As we saw in the section above, the tax rate at the time was in decline and the lords' annual revenue was gradually shrinking, so the drop in relative prices of agricultural to industrial goods, and especially the decline in the relative price of rice, struck an even greater blow to domainal finances.

The 1736 (Gembun) recoinage carried out under the "Rice Shogun" Yoshimune was one response to the decline in rice prices. But relative prices of agricultural to industrial goods and relative rice prices both declined until about 1740 (according to Table 4.2, the relative prices of agricultural to industrial goods rose from 1729 to 1739, but if we take just the last half of the 1730s, then they fell). The commodity whose relative price rose at the highest rate, according to Table 4.3, was raw cotton, with raw silk placing second. This means that consumption of clothing materials, which had been suppressed by a currency shrinkage recession prior to this point, expanded rapidly. The relative prices of brewed goods such as soy sauce and refined *saké* declined, but this was because their price level around 1729 had been fairly high. The shogunate's goal of relatively raising the price of rice through the Gembun recoinage was not successful relative to the price of clothing materials, but it rose very quickly relative to the prices of such industrial products as various oils, soy sauce, and refined *saké*. It is interesting that the Gembun recoinage was relatively unfortunate for urban industrial type goods, but beneficial to rural village type production.

But the above phenomena were restricted to the period immediately after the Gembun recoinage. From 1740 to 1770, relative agricultural–industrial prices had a tendency to rise. Nearly the same was true for relative rice prices. Figure 4.5(c) shows the movement of year-end inventory of rice in Osaka. While the line for 1740–70 is a bit of a zigzag, there is a tendency to rise. As I stated above, year-end inventory of rice was a term used to describe the volume of rice actually in the warehouses. If we take the volume in warehouses to be a rough reflection of harvests, we see that relative prices of rice and other agricultural products rose along with a rise in production volumes from 1740 to 1770. It may be that the shogunate's monetary policy was taking effect in a time lag.

However, although the year-end inventory of rice went into decline from the late 1750s to the early 1760s (this began in the early 1750s), relative agricultural–industrial prices and relative rice prices declined. Although there was a decline in the year-end inventory of rice, the stocks from the bountiful harvests of the early 1750s were still much higher than those of the late 1740s. During this period, the shogunate struggled to stop the relative fall in the price of rice by issuing its 1761 restrictions against domainal sales of rice and carrying out the purchase of rice through forced loans. There was also a trough in the relative prices of agricultural to industrial goods and the relative rice price in the early 1750s. Thus, although this period showed a slight tendency for the relative agricultural–industrial price and the relative rice price to rise, it was not along a straight line and there were intermittent periods of decline. Therefore, the common explanations, which emphasize the "relative drop in rice prices" of the mid-eighteenth century, are not necessarily in contradiction on this point (e.g., see Nakai 1971: 36–7). The long-term tendency was for relative agricultural–industrial prices and relative rice prices to rise, so agricultural and rice production was stimulated. But cyclical overproduction occasionally brought about a slight declining phase in the relative prices of agricultural to industrial goods and relative rice prices.

For other commodities such as rapeseed, raw cotton, and rapeseed oil, there were very few showing relative rates of decline; instead relative prices rose. The commodity that had the greatest rise in relative price was soy sauce, while the commodity that had the greatest decline in relative price was salt. Relative prices for raw silk and refined *sake* also fell. As one can easily tell from a glance at Table 4.3, there is a tendency for commodities that suffered a decline in relative price in the previous period to rise in this period, while those commodities that had seen an increase in their relative price in the previous period saw a decline in this period. Some commodities responded quickly and some slowly to the effects of increased currency after the Gembun recoinage.

After that, the relative prices of agricultural to industrial goods and the relative rice price dropped dramatically during the period 1770–90. This we can see dramatically in Figure 4.6 and Table 4.2. The decline in the relative prices of agricultural to industrial goods signifies that the terms of trade had become more beneficial to industrial products. But whether this became an element leading to Tanuma Okitsugu's emphasis on mercantile and industrial policy, or whether the increase in currency due to the minting of the *Nanryô nishugin* and Tanuma's policy of promoting industry brought about a relative rise in the price of industrial products, is an interesting question. On the other hand, we can tell that the underlying tone of increased production was maintained because the year-end inventory of rice continued to rise until about 1780 and the shogunate continued to struggle with policies to control the excessive supply of rice. It may be that agriculture had more potentiality to expand production in response to the creation of demand arising from financial policies of the Tanuma era than industrial production did.

General prices reached bottom at the end of the 1770s, thereafter rising in the middle of the 1780s due to the influence of the great crop failure of the Temmei era. During this process, the relative price of agricultural to industrial products and the relative price of rice both naturally rose (the annual rate of rise of the relative price of agricultural to industrial goods was 3.6 per cent), but they reached their peaks later than the peak for general prices; the relative price of agricultural to industrial products peaked around 1800 while the relative price of rice reached a plateau from 1780 to 1800. This is due to the fact that while industrial prices rose explosively during the famine years, they also went into decline soon thereafter while agricultural and rice prices maintained a high level until around 1800. This condition reminds us of the French historian of prices, Labrousse, and his thesis. That is, the rise in the price of grains from poor harvests causes a decline in household expenditures on industrial products, thus also causing a decline in the relative price of industrial goods. In fact, we can see the suppression of consumption under the crop failures by noting the tremendous drop in the relative prices of soy sauce, raw silk, and cotton as shown in the movement of the relative prices of

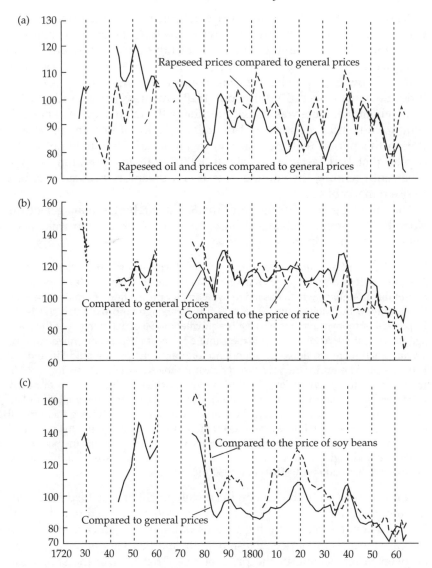

Fig. 4.6. Relative prices of agricultural processed goods. (a) rapeseed oil, (b) refined *saké*, and (c) soy sauce and their Raw Materials (Compared to general prices and prices of the raw materials: moving 5-years' average) (1840–44 = 100).

industrial goods from 1770 to 1785 in Table 4.3. Of course, the relative prices of not all industrial products fell; the decline in the relative price of rapeseed oil was slight while the relative price of refined *saké* rose. This is because the oil was a daily necessity, while the rise in the price of *saké* was due to a rise in rice prices, leading to increased costs in materials and labor.

As we saw above, the relative price of agricultural to industrial products experienced a tremendous wave from the Gembun recoinage to about 1800. At the beginning of the nineteenth century the relative price of agricultural to industrial goods and the relative price of rice fell. Although there was a slight zigzag pattern, thereafter, there was very little movement overall until about 1820. But if we measure from the Temmei famine, there was a slight decline in the relative price of agricultural to industrial products and the relative price of rice. In fact, it was during this period that the year-end inventory of rice pulled out of the depths that had lasted until about 1800. From the beginning of the nineteenth century, the volume of year-end inventory of rice continued to rise remarkably.

The following is a passage from the *Sanka zui*, by the manager of the Kônoike Zen'emon Exchange House, Kusama Naokata who was also a famous economist in those days.

Due to the recent plentiful harvests everywhere, the price of rice has fallen .... After 1788, the various domains opened a remarkable number of new fields on the coasts and in the mountains which has led to even greater production of grains than even the bounty of the Meiwa and An'ei eras fifty years ago (approximately 1764–81). 70 percent of today's average harvest is equivalent to 90 or 100 percent of the average harvest of 50 years ago. So, if the same degree of harvest continued for 3 or 5 years, then there would be an abundance of grains, the price would fall and the people would be hurt. This was already clear by the Kansei era (1789–1801).... In recent years, there have been plentiful harvests, which include rice from newly developed lands, and the price of rice has dropped. The lords have taken in less gold and silver as a result, putting them at a disadvantage and forcing them to sell all the rice in their storehouses. Now even more rice has flooded into the ports and the price of rice has fallen further. The country is going into decline; the people are exhausted and high and low alike are driven to extremes. Thus, even a drop in the price of rice has bad effects. (Kusama 1930: 195–6)

Naokata points out that due to the development of new fields and continuing good harvests, the price of rice had fallen. This led to a decrease in the currency received by the various domains, which caused them to increase the amount of rice they sold on the market. This, in turn, spurred an even faster decline in the price of rice. That is why the shogunate undertook the measures described above: Ordering the merchants to buy rice (and doing so themselves) and forcibly collecting loans from merchants in 1810 and 1813 for the purchase of rice. This reveals that the production of rice had pulled out of the period of instability at the beginning of the nineteenth century. This is also consistent with the theories discussed above; namely, the arguments of Shimbo and Yamazaki and the proposition that it was agriculture and agricultural villages, rather than industry and the city that was the driving force behind the economic development of this time.

Glancing at the relative prices of individual commodities on Table 4.3, we can immediately see the relative decline in the prices of rice; raw cotton, rapeseed and wheat, while a good number of industrial commodities, such as cotton fabrics, raw silk, silk textiles, and soy sauce experienced a relative rise. The good conditions for agriculture increased the demand for industrial goods, which then experienced a relative rise in price. We can observe the stimulus given to the proto-industrial textile industry. The rapid rise in price of energy sources, in the form of firewood and coal, may suggest the increasing demand for industrial uses. In any case, it is worth noting, as is the large rise in the price of cocoon relative to the price of cotton.

During the period of continuous inflation after 1820, both the relative price of agricultural to industrial goods and the relative price of rice clearly rose. As we can see in Table 4.3, the prices of almost all agricultural products rose tremendously while the prices of such industrial goods as silk fabrics, cotton fabrics, soy sauce, and *miso* paste were limited to a gentle increase. Not only did the poor showing of agriculture cause a rapid rise in the price of agricultural products; it also brought about stagnation in the demand for industrial goods. The drop in price for ginseng and sappan-wood was due to the same reason, and the decline in prices for energy sources may be explained through demand side. But if we examine this in the light of previous cases of recoinage, industrial prices rose most quickly immediately after recoinage, the relative price of agricultural to industrial goods temporarily declined, turning to a rise after several years.

In the case of the Bunsei recoinage, the price of industrial products rose immediately afterward (see the years after 1820 in of Figure 4.7(a)). However, that rise was limited to a few years while the relative price of agricultural to industrial products continued to rise from 1820 throughout the 1830s. We must take note of the way that in the midst of such an increase in the issuance of currency, the rise in the price of industrial goods was only slight, despite the fact that the price of the raw materials of industrial production also rose. What was likely behind this was a decline in costs due to an increase in productivity in industrial sector. According to Table 4.2, we can see that from 1785 until the opening of the ports, the rate of increase in the price of industrial goods was limited to 1 per cent per annum or less. This suggests that the strength of the industrial sector continued to increase to the extent that it was able to absorb such shocks as poor harvests and monetary conditions to a considerable extent.

After the great crop failures of the Tempô era, from the mid-1830s to the beginning of the 1840s, general prices fell, pulled down by such grains as rice, barley, wheat, and soy beans, and by such agricultural resources for industrial processing as rapeseed and raw cotton. The prices for industrial products using these, such as *miso*, refined *saké*, and rapeseed oil, also fell. On the other hand, many goods saw their prices rise during this period.

A few items, which experienced a marked rise, were iron, copper, bamboo, vegetables, tobacco, coal, and silk fabrics. If we extend this to relative prices, then we can add firewood, coal, dried bonito, cotton fabrics, raw silk, hemp cloth, nails, cooking pots, tile, and sappanwood to the list of goods that experienced a high rate of increase. In other words, during this period when prices in general were falling, prices for commodities which were sensitive to business conditions, such as investment and construction materials, daily necessities, clothing, supplementary foodstuffs, and energy sources, rose either absolutely or relatively, revealing a remarkable economic recovery. From the middle of the 1830s, due to a time lag, the destination of the additional currency supply, which had been absorbed in the rapid rise of agricultural prices, began to turn toward the above noted commodities. In that sense, we may be able to see the manifestation of the expansion of currency issuance and official finances of the Bunsei and Tempo eras only in the 1830s.

General prices rose from 1842 to 1851 led by the rise in prices for grains and the commodities processed from them, such as *miso* and refined *saké*. The prices for industrial goods such as cotton fabrics, cotton yarn, silk fabrics, raw silk, hemp cloth, soy sauce, iron, copper, and tiles, and agricultural resources for industrial processing such as rapeseed and raw cotton, fell either absolutely or relatively. It is believed that the rise in prices for grains was the cause of the decline in demand for these goods. But the degree to which the prices of grains rose was not as high as during the period of the Tempô famine, so we should not exaggerate its effects. What is interesting is its relation to the "theory of inflationary growth;" that is, whether it was the result of a worsening economy or declining costs due to the increased productivity of the industrial sector.

The eve of the opening of the ports, from 1851 to 1854, was a period of declining prices, particularly for rice, barley, raw cotton, refined *saké*, salt, *miso*, soy sauce, and iron. The relative prices of cotton fabrics, cotton yarn, silk fabrics, and such also declined slightly. On the other hand, the relative prices of vegetables, hemp cloth, nails, cooking pots, buckets, tiles, fish-based fertilizers, lime, ginseng, and sappanwood all rose. The particularly high rise in prices for fish fertilizers and lime hints at the expansion of agriculture.

Around 1854, the tendency for prices to fall took a turn toward a tendency to rise, beginning a slide toward the unprecedented price explosion of the late Tokugawa and early Meiji period. Thus, while there was inflation in late Tokugawa Japan prior to the opening of the ports, the causes of the fluctuations in prices before and after the opening were different. We may therefore surmise that the changes in the relative price structure before and after the opening of the ports was also different. So in order to clarify the difference between price rises before and after the opening, we took 1858 as a dividing line between two periods and we calculated the rates of increase in each period for each commodity. Table 4.4 is the result of those calculations, ranked in order from highest rate of increase. According to our calculations, the commodities with a high rate of price increase prior to the opening of the ports were lime, sappanwood, ginseng, lumber, bamboo, rice, barley, silk fabrics, dried sardines, and salt, while those with a low rate of increase included cotton yarn, tiles, and refined *saké*. Raw silk, cotton fabrics, copper, rapeseed oil, soy sauce, nails, *miso*, sugar, *tatami* straw, hemp cloth, soy beans, beeswax, rapeseed, and dried bonito all declined. Compared to the prices for rice and salt, the decline in the prices of traditional industrial goods, including refined *saké* is noteworthy. On the other hand, the rise in prices of traditional import items, such as ginseng and sappanwood was steep.

The situation after the opening of the ports (1858–67) was remarkably different. First of all, the leading export item, raw silk, leapt to the top in terms of rate of price increase. Wax also became an important export item, and its price also rose sharply. The rates of price movement for raw silk, wax, and copper (which also became an important export item) had all been in the minus prior to the opening of the ports, so this represents a huge change. The prices of traditional import items such as ginseng and sappanwood dropped dramatically as did prices for nails, and rapeseed oil thought to be in competition with petroleum. The relative price of iron also fell. However, the prices for goods put into competition against foreign imports, such as raw cotton, sugar, cotton yarn, and cotton fabrics did not drop during the period under observation. Thus, the rise in prices of export items preceded the decline in prices of import items and those domestic products placed in competition with them, as Shimbo has pointed out. He has also observed that the decline of the latter came after 1867 (Shimbo 1978: 289–97). But there is no doubt that the relative price structure changed dramatically after the opening of the ports. This is one reason why the price phenomena of this period are known as the "price revolution."

10. Processed Agricultural Goods and the Relative Prices of their Raw Materials: The De-agriculturalization of the Late Edo Period

The late Edo period was an era in which a shift from agriculture to non-agricultural production began. This did not mean the arrival of a so-called genuine industrialization with factory system industry as its core. Rather, it was a proto-industrialization centered on village industry such as agri-cultural by-employment and household industry. But it was an economic change that might well be called the initial movement toward modern growth. In what ways can we recognize this change in industrial structure

Table 4.4. Rate of price increase before and after the opening of ports

Rank	According to moving five years' average: 1854–65	According to the 1854–58 figures		According to the 1858–67 figures	
		General prices	+19.3	General prices	+134.5
		Agricultural products	+18.3	Agricultural products	+158.7
		Industrial products	+20.8	Industrial products	+101.3
1	Dried squid	Lime	+124.5	Raw silk	+361.7
2	Raw silk	Sappanwood	+69.6	Wheat	+306.1
3	Iron	Korean ginseng	+66.7	Rice bran	+301.2
4	Silk fabrics	Lumber	+42.9	Miso	+296.0
5	Rice	Bamboo	+33.5	Cooking pots	+285.4
6	Cooking pots	Rice	+29.8	Barley	+283.6
7	Raw cotton	Barley	+28.4	Soy sauce	+276.9
8	Salt	Silk fabrics	+25.6	Wax	+261.8
9	Miso	Dried squid	+23.4	Salt	+257.1
10	Fish fertilizer	Salt	+18.8	Shiitake	+247.0
11	Rice bran	Silk floss	+17.5	Soy beans	+245.3
12	Barley	Raw cotton	+16.3	Fish fertilizer	+240.9
13	Wheat	Tobacco	+13.1	Raw cotton	+236.6
14	Rapeseed	Coal	+12.7	Refined sake	+231.4
15	Tiles	Iron	+10.7	Sugar	+222.7
16	Cotton yarn	Vegetables	+9.8	Cotton yarn	+215.1
17	Refined sake	Cooking Pots	+7.0	Rapeseed	+220.6
18	Dried bonito	Hand buckets	+6.7	Dried squid	+176.5
19	Firewood	Firewood	+4.9	Firewood	+172.5
20	Wax	Cotton yarn	+4.7	Rice bran	+169.0
21	Soy sauce	Wheat	+4.5	Cotton fabrics	+164.5
22	Shiitake	Bamboo brooms	+4.4	Hemp cloth	+148.1
23	Soy beans	Tiles	+2.2	Silk fabrics	+146.4

24	Copper	Refined *sake*	+0.5	Tile	+145.8
25	Hemp cloth	Fish fertilizer	+0.3	Iron	+134.2
26	Cotton fabrics	Rice bran	−1.1	Rapeseed oil	+128.3
27	Sugar	Raw silk	−1.5	Dried bonito	+123.1
28	Coal	Cotton fabrics	−2.0	Lumber	+119.1
29	*Tatami* straw	Copper	−2.3	Copper	+117.6
30	Rapeseed oil	Rapeseed oil	−5.0	Coal	+97.5
31	Tobacco	Soy sauce	−5.6	*Tatami* straw	+94.1
32	Lumber	Nails	−5.9	Tobacco	+94.0
33	Hand buckets	*Miso*	−7.4	Hand buckets	+79.7
34	Lime	Sugar	−7.6	Vegetables	+10.6
35	Vegetables	*Tatami* straw	−8.5	Bamboo	−8.5
36	Bamboo	Hemp cloth	−11.7	Nails	−21.1
37	Nails	Soy beans	−12.3	Lime	−35.6
38	Korean ginseng	Wax	−13.3	Korean ginseng	−76.1
39	Sappanwood	*Shiitake*	−14.6	Sappanwood	−90.6
40		Rapeseed oil	−18.0		
41		Dried bonito	−19.0		
Uncertain	Cocoon	Cocoon		Cocoon	
	Silk floss			Silk floss	
	Bamboo brooms			Bamboo booms	

Matao Miyamoto

in the history of prices? In this section I would like to pursue this question by considering the changes in the relative prices of the typical commodities processed from agricultural goods of the Edo period—rapeseed oil, refined *saké*, and soy sauce—while also examining the relative prices of the agricultural goods that were the raw materials for these commodities.

Figure 4.7 shows the relative prices compared to general prices for rapeseed oil and rapeseed (Figure 4.7(a)), refined *saké* and rice (Figure 4.7(b)), and soy sauce and soy beans (Figure 4.7(c)) in the form of the commodity price index/the general price index.

Let us begin with rapeseed oil and rapeseed. As Figure 4.7(a) shows, the relative price of rapeseed oil passed across small peaks and troughs from the middle of the eighteenth century until around 1830. In general, however, one can see a tendency to decline. During this time, the relative price of rapeseed tended to remain nearly horizontal until the beginning of the nineteenth century. The production and distribution of rapeseed oil was centered on Osaka in the early Edo period. By the middle of the Edo period, however, agricultural villages of Settsu-Izumi were using waterwheels to press the seeds at a much higher level of productivity than was achieved via the hand-pressing method used in Osaka. By the latter half of the eighteenth century, the Kantô region, which had traditionally received its supply of rapeseed oil from the Kansai region, began to see the production of oil in the villages surrounding Edo and comprising its economic region. The dispersal of rapeseed oil production regions and the interregional competition that arose thereby, as well as the technological revolution in the shift from manpower to waterwheel pressing, account for the long-term decline in the relative price of rapeseed oil.

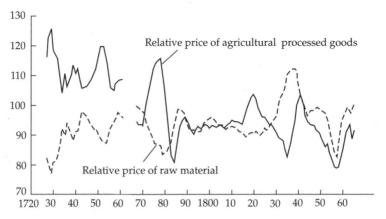

Fig. 4.7. Relative price of agricultural processed goods and their raw materials (compared to general prices: moving five-years' average).

From the beginning of the nineteenth century until around 1820, the relative price of rapeseed fell along with that of rapeseed oil. In particular, the line in Figure 4.6(a) for the relative price of rapeseed intersects with that for the relative price of rapeseed oil as it passes below the latter, right around 1820, describing a major drop in the price of rapeseed. This drop in the price of rapeseed led to great dissatisfaction in the villages producing rapeseed in Settsu-Izumi from around 1790, reaching a peak in two large-scale suits submitted to the shogunate in 1805 and 1823. The lawsuits concerned the fact that certified merchants of Osaka asserted their monopolistic rights and bought up the villagers' rapeseed and then raised the price of rapeseed oil. The villagers' request was that they be allowed to freely sell their rapeseed (in other words, to anyone besides the Osaka wholesalers). The final decision of the 1823 suit was not to recognize the free sale of rapeseed, but by 1832 the villagers' desire had become reality. But what is interesting is that even after their demands became a reality and rapeseed was sold freely, the relative prices of rapeseed and rapeseed oil took an even sharper downward turn from the early 1840s. Whether or not the Osaka wholesalers bought up all the rapeseed, what was behind the decline in the relative prices of rapeseed and rapeseed oil in the late Edo period was the long-term increase in production of rapeseed and rapeseed oil.

Taking up the relative price of refined *saké* vis-à-vis general prices in Figure 4.6(b), we can see that there was hardly any movement over the long period from 1740 to around 1830. The fluctuations can be accounted as follows: during periods of price rises, particularly when the price of grains rose, the relative price of *saké* declined, and when prices fell, the relative price of *saké* rose (see the Temmei and Tempô famine periods for the most marked shifts). Therefore, the relative price of *saké* depended greatly on the expansion or contraction of demand. But over the long term, the relative price of *saké* was synchronized with the trends in general prices. In this connection, when we calculate the relative price of refined *saké* vis-à-vis the price of rice, (the dotted line of in Figure 4.6(b)), we find a nearly continuous tendency to fall from 1780 to the end of the shogunate. The price of the product fell compared to the price of its raw material, meaning that the supply curve shifted downward over the long term. So the fact that the price of the product maintained a parallel movement to that of general prices means that the demand curve shifted upward over the long term. That is, both the production of and demand for *saké* expanded. Having said that, however, it is not clear at present whether the sharp decline in the relative price of *saké* after the middle of the 1830s was due to a downward shift of the supply curve or to a decline in the demand for *saké* in the period of confusion at the end of the Tokugawa period. According to Manabu Yunoki, the volume of *saké* shipped to Edo from the twelve districts of Settsu-Izumi was over 830,000 casks in 1803, more than 1,060,000 casks in 1832, and under 950,000 in 1856. The Tempô period was

thus the peak, and it was never surpassed in the final years of the shogunate (Yunoki 1988: 83–85). It appears that there was stagnation in demand.
At the same time, however, these figures do not show such a big decline
in demand. In which case, we may have to conclude that there was development in the production of refined *saké* as well.

Let us finally turn to an examination of the price of soy sauce. According
to Figure 4.6(c), the relative price of soy sauce rose sharply during the period
of 1740–50. According to Chapter 5 in this volume by Hiroshi Shimbo and
Akira Hasegawa, the relative price of soy sauce to rice rose in Kyoto in
the middle of the eighteenth century thus becoming the occasion for the
introduction of Tatsuno soy sauce into the Kyoto market. Their explanation
conforms to the observations made in this chapter. The relative price of soy
sauce dropped dramatically during the period of the Temmei crop failures
of the 1780s. But this reveals that soy sauce was a luxury item during the Edo
period. However, the decline in the relative price of soy sauce made a turn
around by 1820 and began to rise, although the levels prior to the Temmei
crop failures were not restored. After the price of soy sauce relative to the
price of soy beans (see the dotted line in Figure 4.6(c)) also fell off sharply in
the 1780s, it returned to a rise in 1820. But again past levels were not
achieved. It appears that the causes of the decline in the supply price of soy
sauce during this period may be found in conditions of production.
Moreover, the price of soy sauce relative to general prices and relative to the
price of rice fell off dramatically from the 1820s (or the 1840s) until the end
of the shogunate. As with the case of refined *saké*, we cannot tell at present
whether this was due to conditions on the demand side or the supply side.

We have examined above the movements in the relative prices of commodities processed from agricultural products. When we combine these
insights with an examination of textile products, excluding silk, the price of
industrial products relative to general prices and relative to the products that were their raw materials clearly fell from the eighteenth to the
nineteenth century (particularly after the 1780s). If we calculate an average
relative price index vis-à-vis general prices with cotton fabrics, cotton yarn,
soy sauce, *miso*, refined *saké*, rapeseed oil, raw silk, and silk fabrics designated in a lump as "agricultural processed goods" and raw cotton, rapeseed,
rice, wheat, cocoon, and soy beans designated as "industrial raw materials,"
we can produce the graph in Figure 4.6. That the relative prices of agricultural processed goods and industrial raw materials move over the short
term in a negative correlation suggests that in times of poor harvests the
demand for industrial goods stagnated while in times of plenty demand
increased. Along with these fluctuations, however, we can clearly see a long-
term trend for the relative price of agricultural processed goods to decline.

During periods of poor harvest, the relative prices of agricultural
processed goods were depressed while the process of recovery afterward
never restored the earlier levels, which in turn was due to the inflexibility

of the prices of agricultural processed goods. During this same period, the relative prices of the raw materials stayed even over the long term, even showing a slight tendency to rise. This gave birth to the decline of prices for products processed from agricultural goods relative to the prices of the raw materials. We can also imagine that in the area of agricultural processing, productivity rose and costs declined. It is here that we can confirm the development of a nonagricultural arena in the late Edo period.

11. Conclusion

In sum, I would like to review the main points we observed above.

1. To simply summarize the long-term trends in prices over the 250-plus years of the Tokugawa economy, we can draw an outline of the following: the rise of the seventeenth century and the stagnation at the end of the seventeenth century; the sharp rises and falls from the late seventeenth century to the early eighteenth century; the rise in price level brought about by the Gembun recoinage in 1736 to the slow decline until around 1780; the sudden temporary rise at the time of the Temmei crop failures to the decline and stabilization around 1820; the expansion after 1820 of the continual rise on the occasion of the Bunsei recoinage and the Tempô recoinage and crop failures; and finally the hyperinflation after the opening of the ports.

2. In these long-term fluctuations, the pivot that turned the decline or stabilization of prices to a rise was, in almost all cases, a recoinage carried out by the shogunate. The Genroku recoinage, the Gembun recoinage, the issuing of the *Nanryô nishugin*, and the Bunsei recoinage all functioned in this way. We may judge these recoinages as successful macroeconomic policies in that they were carried out under conditions in which there was a stagnation of prices and the insufficient supply of currency was limiting real economic growth. While the Gembun recoinage immediately brought about a quick rise in prices, within ten years or so the increased currency was absorbed by the development of the economy in real goods, or the market economy, and so wound up with a decline in prices. The issuing of the *Nanryô nishugin* was quickly followed by the Temmei crop failures so that prices leapt up. But once that period had passed, prices again fell. The Bunsei and Tempô recoinages exacerbated the supply shock of the Tempô crop failures, thus leading to a surge in prices. But after that, the rise in prices had fallen off a notch by the opening of the ports. Looked at in this way, the shogunate's increase of the money supply through the debasement of the currency and the expansion of the ceiling of the money economy worked in the direction of drawing out the growth power of the real economy over the long term. Phenomenologically, this is just like the way

a child, having been given oversized clothes, grows until, before he knows it, the clothes fit perfectly. The Tokugawa economy possessed this kind of potential growing power over the long term.

However, since the method of recoinage was undertaken by a shogunate which was, in essence, trying to restore the finances of what was, after all, a daimyo household, there was no guarantee that the real macroeconomy and the monetary economy could be equilibrated. Therefore, there was no way to avoid excessive or insufficient supplies of currency in the recoinage. (The Gembun recoinage may not have been carried out for reasons related to the shogunate's finances, but since its aim was to rescue the *hatamoto* [bannermen], *gokenin* [vassals], and daimyo classes by raising the price of rice, it was strongly marked by the character of a household economy.) The Shôtoku and Kyôhô recoinages are examples of recoinages that produced insufficient money supplies. The Hôei and Tempô recoinages, on the other hand, are examples of recoinages where attempts to stem excessive supply were not effective. Both of these latter recoinages added fuel to the fires of inflation begun by the Genroku and Bunsei recoinages. Moreover, when all is said and done, the Edo period economy in real goods was based on agriculture, which has many features, which are controlled by natural conditions. Therefore, even if it appears that currency is available in an appropriate supply, such supply shocks as a crop failure can cause the money supply to become excessive. The Hôei recoinage, the issuing of the *Nanryô nishugin*, and the Tempô recoinage were all cases in which a crop failure occurred either during or immediately after the recoinage.

Compared to the above recoinages, the Man'en recoinage, carried out in the face of the opening of the ports, was neither carried out in a time of declining prices nor in an attempt to revive shogunal finances. Instead it was carried out in order to make a currency system which had existed in a closed system conform to the new open system. Achieving equilibrium with the outside was emphasized more than achieving a domestic equilibrium. The previous increases and contractions of the money supply may have been carried out according to the determinations of the shogunate, but as we saw above, in the long term (and in conclusive terms), they did little to upset the balance between the economy in real goods and the economy in money. In contrast, the Man'en recoinage was able to give little consideration to the domestic equilibrium, so the major upheaval in prices that resulted could well be called a "price revolution."

3. As to the question of what kind of movement of the economy in goods was reflected in the movement in prices, we may posit that there was an expansion in real production as well as (or perhaps) a development in the market economy from the Gembun recoinage until around 1770. From the crop failures of the 1780s until around 1820 there was growth in agriculture and the regions and a consequent increase in demand for industrial production, accompanied by a relative dulling of urban growth.

The "theory of inflationary growth"—in which the recoinages that increased currency supplies and expanded official budgets from the Bunsei era brought about both inflation and growth—does not mean that the start of real economic growth was cut off only by the recoinages of the Bunsei and Tempô eras. If there had not been the continuation of economic development in which agriculture had played the leading role since the end of the eighteenth century, nor had there been increases in currency and the expansion of official budgets, the economy, which might otherwise have dropped off rapidly, would have been buoyed up by the inflation. The theory may be supported in that sense. However, when it comes to whether or not this inflationary growth was able to continue all the way to the last years of the shogunate, the theory of "wage lag and profit inflation" explains this continuation, but in the fluctuations we are unable to confirm whether or not there was real growth from the end of the 1840s until the eve of the opening of the ports. Furthermore, the inflation after the opening of the ports may have been unprecedented, but its effects were greater in the areas of industrial structure and the distribution of earnings than they were on the macroeconomic levels.

4. As for the changes in the relative price structure of various products, prices for agricultural products had a greater tendency to rise than did prices for industrial products from several years after the Gembun recoinage until around 1770. However, we also observed an intermittent "relative decline in the price of rice" during that period. From the 1770s to the 1780s the relative price of agricultural to industrial goods experienced a major turn from decline to rise. But after that, from the end of the eighteenth century to around 1820, the relative price of agricultural to industrial products showed a tendency to stabilize or even decline. During the inflationary growth after 1820, it turned back up. The turn in the relative price of agricultural to industrial products around 1820 implies a change in economic structure from agricultural leadership to an expansion of the relative weight of nonagricultural production.

5. When we look at individual commodities, the prices of such agricultural processed goods as rapeseed oil, refined *saké*, and soy sauce went into decline relative to general prices, as early as the middle of the eighteenth century for some and as late as the beginning of the nineteenth century for others. During this same period, the prices of the raw materials for these products, such as rapeseed and soy beans, as well as the raw cotton which was the raw material for cotton fabrics, maintained a movement that was parallel to that of general prices, if not showing a slight tendency to decline. Compared to rice, however, these raw materials all experienced a clear decline. We surmised that this decline came about because of the late Edo introduction of these crops into new lands that led to the rise of competition with the areas that traditionally

produced them and a decline in supply prices. On the other hand, since the relative prices of agricultural processed goods fell even further, the price of the commodity relative to its raw material fell over the long term. This appeared to be a phenomenon born along with the increasing demand for agricultural processed goods. It was this that allowed us to recognize the development of the agriculture processing arena and its increasing productivity in late Edo.

6. As for after the opening of the ports, prices had been in decline prior to the opening, but afterwards the relative prices of such export items as raw silk, wax, and copper saw a rapid rise. On the other hand, the relative prices of import items and those commodities forced into competition such as rapeseed oil, nails, iron, ginseng, and sappanwood, declined. While the relative prices of such import items as raw cotton, sugar, cotton yarn, and cotton fabrics showed no significant decline until the Meiji period, as a whole the relative price structure of various commodities undoubtedly began to undergo a major transformation. To the extent that the opening of the ports began a process in which the price system of a closed system was forced to the level of the world price system, the tremendous rise in prices after the opening of the ports could truly be called a "price revolution."

Translated by Alan S. Christy.

Notes

* Regarding an appendix table "An Overview of Data Relating to the Price Index for the Kyoto–Osaka Region (1725–1867)", please see Miyamoto (1989: 122–3).
1. Shimbo (1978: 30–7). Other late Edo price indices include Shimbo's "Kyoto Consumers' Price Index: 1725–1867," and "Late Tokugawa-Early Meiji Period Osaka Price Index," both of which are found in Shimbo (1978); Osamu Saitô, "*Osaka Commodity Price Index: 1757–1915*," in Saitô (1980); Miyamoto Matao, "Kyoto Commodity Price Index," in Miyamoto (1981).
2. In these calculations, $M/P = ky$, where k is assumed to be fixed, M/P (real money supply) is taken as a proxy for real GDP. M is nominal money supply, P prices, k Marshall's constant, and y real income.
3. Akashi (1989). See Fig. 4.4, although note that in Fig. 4.4 M is divided by the general price index.
4. Saitô (1976: 4–5). However, these calculations are based upon the real wage series composed by Hiroshi Shimbo using Saitô's data.

5

The Dynamics of Market
Economy and Production

HIROSHI SHIMBO AND AKIRA HASEGAWA

1. Introduction

Scholars today agree that the Japanese economy was basically expanding throughout the Tokugawa period. However, this economic growth was not uniform in either pace or pattern. From the beginning of the seventeenth to the early eighteenth century, population size rose, new fields were opened up for cultivation, and rice production increased. Urban centers and urban populations also showed marked growth. From 1650 to 1750, the population doubled in Edo, Osaka, and Kyoto, the three largest cities of Japan. Meanwhile, eight regional centers (including Nagoya, Sendai, Kanazawa, and Fukuoka) grew by 60 per cent (Seiji Saitô 1984: 61–3, appended table 5.2.) However, the foundations for this economic expansion began to shift at the end of the seventeenth century.

Closer examination of the population figures reveals that by the 1730s Japan had actually entered a period of stagnation. While regional differences existed, the population of the country as a whole remained relatively stable for the next century. In addition, the high rate at which new fields were opened for cultivation in the seventeenth century began to slow down into the mid-nineteenth century (Miyamoto 1976: 26, table 5). Gradually, the arable land to population ratio began to improve.

On the other hand, agricultural productivity continued to grow steadily during the latter half of the Tokugawa period. The low rate of population growth coupled with rising agricultural productivity inevitably led to increased production of crops other than the staple grains. In turn, cultivation of cash crops, particularly industrial raw materials, facilitated the development of manufacturing. However, rural, not urban, industries were the primary beneficiaries. There were also major changes in the pattern of urban growth. From 1750 to 1850, Edo, Osaka, and Kyoto, and the large regional towns actually lost 10 per cent of their population, while small and medium-sized towns experienced a surge of growth (Smith 1977: 154–5; Saitô 1987: 23, table 1–2). This is quite different from the way in which urban development had taken place in the previous century. Economic expansion in the latter half of the Tokugawa period was thus characterized by increased commercial agricultural production; growth in the nonagricultural sector, particularly village industry; and stagnation in the three major metropolitan areas and regional capitals in contrast to growth in small and medium-sized regional cities and market towns.

The basic foundation for Tokugawa economic growth was closely linked to the increase of commodity production and the social division of labor, that is, to the spread of a market economy. Accordingly, close attention to these trends will allow us to track overall shifts in economic development. Our goals in this chapter, then, are twofold. First, we would like to clarify the developmental dynamics of commodity production and the division of labor in relation to the various conditions that fuelled economic expansion during the first half of the Tokugawa period. Second, we would like to explore, in light of the early to mid-eighteenth century shift in the character of economic growth, the dynamics of further developments in commodity production and the division in labors in the latter half of the Tokugawa period.

2. Production and Distribution under the *Bakuhan* System

2.1. *The framework of the* bakuhan *system*

Historians commonly refer to the political structure of the Tokugawa period, which began in 1603, as the *bakuhan* system, that is, a polity built upon the central authority of the shogun's government, or *bakufu*, and the local authority of territorial daimyo, whose domains are called *han*. This system can be summed up in terms of the following six characteristics:

1. Annual taxes levied by domainal lords were calculated for all arable lands in terms of standard crop yields in rice (*kokudaka*). Even if certain land parcels were not used for rice cultivation but, for example, for housing, annual taxes were still based on the principle of payment of a fixed percentage of the parcel's potential productivity in rice. Under this system, taxes were not levied on an individual basis, but rather upon each village as a whole.

2. In order to accomplish what is known as the separation of the military and agricultural classes (*heinô bunri*), status distinctions between *samurai* (warriors) and *nômin* (peasants) were strengthened, peasants were forbidden to possess weapons, and warriors were uprooted from rural villages and concentrated in castle towns. At the same time, a similar division of peasants from merchants and artisans was carried out. With the

exception of such craftsmen as smiths and carpenters, who were necessary for agricultural reproduction, artisans and merchants were required by law to reside in castle towns or other urban areas.

3. Under the *Bakuhan* system, each domainal lord served as a retainer to the shogun yet governed his own domain in an independent manner. The shogunate itself was no more than the equal of other domainal administrations in relation to its own directly held lands. Nevertheless, the shogunate did not take the lord–retainer relationship lightly. In 1634, as one means of maintaining a carefully crafted *Pax Tokugawa*, the shogunate established an alternate attendance system. Under this policy, not only was each domainal lord obligated to reside every other year in Edo, but also had to leave his family behind in Edo as virtual hostages whenever he returned to his domain. In fact, Edo owed its transformation from a backwater to a bustling metropolis to the great concentration of warriors resulting from this alternate attendance system.

4. The Kinai region, which included the cities of Kyoto, Nara, and Osaka, had already been the most advanced economic area since the medieval period. In the sixteenth century as well, Kinai overwhelmingly dominated the production of manufactured goods and served as a center for trade between territories. The shogunate complicated the structure of governance in this wealthy region by breaking it up into units administered by minor domainal lords, distant domains, and the shogunate itself, rather than allowing it to come under the control of major domainal lords. Kyoto, Osaka, and other prominent cities were also placed under direct shogunal management. Accordingly, governance of the Kinai region was organized in a complicated checkerboard fashion rather than in strictly territorial terms.

5. Another way in which the shogunate's authority as "overlord" (*taikun*) was clearly exercised was the monopolies it established over the minting of currency and international diplomacy. Although certain domainal lords minted coins for use in their own territories, only the shogunate could issue the three official currencies of the Tokugawa period. Japan's main gold and silver mines, which supplied the raw materials for minting coins, were also under the control of the shogunate. Therefore, the shogunate could determine the volume of currency to be made available for circulation.

6. From 1633 to 1639, the shogunate issued five decrees that formed the basis of the system of "national seclusion." As a result, the shogunate took complete control of the international trade conducted in Nagasaki. Trade also continued with Korea via Tsushima, as did trade with China via the Ryûkyûs. Although these two trade routes were not directly under the shogunate's control, such exchanges were conducted with shogunal approval and subject to regulation when deemed necessary. Since politics and economics were closely intertwined in Tokugawa trading relations,

the shogunate's administration and regulation of foreign trade can be seen as an exercise of its rights over foreign diplomacy.

These six characteristics described above intertwined to form a single system that provided the institutional framework for economic growth in the Tokugawa period.

2.2. Advancing urbanization and the composition of the rice markets

As we can see from above, the *Bakuhan* system was based on the precondition of increased circulation of goods and money, that is, on a growing market economy. At the same time, the *Bakuhan* system was instrumental in promoting further production and distribution of goods along with urbanization. As warriors became concentrated in castle towns, merchants, artisans, and other nonagricultural workers who provided necessary goods and services joined them. Indeed, the population of a castle town was often equally divided between warriors on the one hand and merchants, artisans, and the like on the other.

Castle towns varied in scale, roughly corresponding to the size of the domain in which the castle of the domainal lord was located. The population of a castle town in the mid-seventeenth century generally ranged from 10,000 to 30,000; at the high end, from 40,000 to 50,000. Nagoya and Kanazawa, however, tipped the scale at 90,000–110,000. Added all together, the total castle town population was approximately 1,400,000 (Seiji Saitô 1984). Meanwhile, Edo was growing into one of the world's largest cities through the expansion of the shogunal bureaucracy and entrenchment of the alternate attendance system. The total population of Edo—composed of roughly equal numbers of warrior and commoners— had already reached about 430,000 by the mid-seventeenth century; one hundred years later, Edo surpassed the population mark of one million.

The prosperity of Edo and the castle towns was closely linked to the founding of the *Bakuhan* system. However, long-established cities in the leading economic region of Kinai, such as Kyoto, Nara, Fushimi, and Sakai, were also growing at a healthy pace. Add in the denizens of the great financial center of Osaka, and their combined population reached nearly 800,000 by 1650. Thus, the urban population of Japan topped 2,500,000— more than 15 per cent of the country's inhabitants (Seiji Saitô 1984).

The domainal lords and their retainers living in Edo and the castle towns were dependent on annual taxes on rice crop yields paid in kind for their income. In order to obtain the currency necessary to meet their daily and administrative needs, they had to sell this rice on the market. The taxation system was thus clearly based on the prior existence of a rice market. Demand was driven by the following: (1) warriors, Shinto priests, Buddhist priests, merchants, artisans, and other nonagricultural workers who needed rice for consumption; (2) residents of mountain and fishing villages who also needed rice for consumption; (3) farmers who purchased supplemental amounts when they did not produce enough for their own needs; (4) industries, such as *saké* brewing, which required rice as a raw material for their production processes. Category (1) was by far and away the greatest source of demand, and as the urban population continued to grow, so did the need for rice. However, a significant portion of the annual tax rice had to be sold on the rice markets outside of the territory in which it was produced. First, the supply of rice generally exceeded demand in territories outside of the Kinai area. Therefore, it was impossible to sell all of the locally produced rice in nearby markets. Second, a considerable portion of the currency gained by selling domainal tax rice had to be sent to Edo in order to cover the domainal lord's needs when in residence. A variety of historical documents confirm that the costs associated with living in Edo constituted a large percentage of the domainal budget (Tsuchiya 1927: 83–5; Nishikawa 1985: 27).

The large, central rice markets were located in such Kinai cities as Osaka and Kyoto and in the great metropolis of Edo. The various domains of southwestern and central Japan sent their tax rice (*kuramai*) to Osaka, while domains in the northeast sent their rice to Edo. By the end of the seventeenth century, sixty-five domains were sending to Osaka approximately 1–1.4 million *koku* each year, representing 28–34 per cent of their total income from rice taxes (Miyamoto 1988: 138–43, tables 2–3). In addition, approximately one quarter of the tax rice was sold on consignment in Osaka (*nayamai*) rather than directly handled by the domainal warehouses. Thus the Osaka market received roughly 1.3–1.8 million *koku* of rice each year. We must also keep in mind that rice was not the only commodity for which there was great demand; markets for other daily necessities existed alongside those for rice.

2.3. The growth of the three central cities

The continued growth of Osaka, Kyoto, and Edo throughout the seventeenth century spurred further production of commodities and their market transactions. In particular, the expanding populations of these cities required huge quantities of rice, vegetables, and other foods. Yet each city had its own distinctive character as a central market, giving rise to different ways of handling commodity production and exchange. First and foremost, in contrast to the consumption-oriented market of Edo, both Osaka and Kyoto were major centers for industry.

However, before proceeding to explore this broad distinction, it is important to note that, while both were key sites for commodity production, Osaka and Kyoto differed from one another as well as from Edo. Osaka concentrated on the production of goods necessary for daily life, while Kyoto was renowned for the production of traditional handicrafts.

From well before the Tokugawa period, Kyoto was the premiere production site in Japan for textiles, gold and silver work, and weaponry, both in terms of quality and quantity. However, demand on the part of Kyoto's handicraft industry for raw materials (including raw silk, gold, silver, and iron) did not stimulate growth in the villages of the Kinai region to meet such needs, as the Kyoto producers looked beyond the immediate environs for their supplies.

In contrast to Kyoto, Osaka was known more for the production of daily necessities. Its representative industries were generally involved in processing agricultural products, such as rapeseed and cotton. By the mid-seventeenth century, Osaka had supplanted Ôyamazaki and Oriono as a center for the extraction of oil from rapeseed; from around the 1610s, oil wholesalers representing demand in Kyoto and Edo were setting up shop in Osaka. The cotton processing industry also came to be centered on Osaka, with numerous wholesalers establishing themselves in the area by the mid-seventeenth century. Since oil for lamps and cotton goods were near universal necessities, production output and attendant demand for raw materials naturally increased. Rapeseed for oil and cotton were already widely cultivated in Kinai villages; the concentration of oil extraction and cotton industries in Osaka provided a further stimulus to these efforts, particularly in the villages of Settsu, Kawachi, and Izumi. From the 1630s, there was a growing trend toward setting lands aside for cotton cultivation. The spread of this practice accordingly reduced the amount of land devoted to rice production and soon led to the appearance of peasants who purchased, not produced, rice. Indeed, cotton production became so entrenched in some places that a division of labor in the Kinai region emerged between areas specializing in the production of rice and areas specializing in cotton.

It was previously noted that 1.3–1.8 million *koku* of rice were sent to Osaka each year. If we add in the rice that went to Ôtsu and Hyôgo, the total volume of rice entering the Kinai region never dipped below 2 million *koku*. This generous supply far surpassed the available demand from the urban population of the cities and castle towns. The remaining amount went to satisfy demand arising in villages in the Kinai that specialized in growing cash crops and market towns where the first level of commodity exchange with the villages and early stages of processing took place. At the beginning of the Tokugawa period, only the Kinai region could boast of this sophisticated network of relations. Thus, the economically advanced Kinai region can be seen to have spearheaded the expansion of commodity production and circulation.

In contrast, Edo, whose population reached one million in the eighteenth century, emerged as a great consumer metropolis under the *Bakuhan* system. Edo was dependent on outside supplies for nearly all of its daily needs, the majority being provided by Osaka. Table 5.1 is based on data

Table 5.1. Average quantity and values of transported goods from Osaka to Edo by ships, 1724–30

Items	Quantity (A)	Unit price in 1726 (B)	Values (A × B)
		monme (silver)	*kan (silver)*
Lint	890,357 *tan*	22.2	19,766
Cotton (white)	1,310,957 *tan*	4.4	5,768
Seed-oil	25,047 *koku*	203.0	5,085
Soy sauce	54,611 *koku*	65.0	3,550
Sake	83,185 *koku*	105.0	8,734
Rice	7,687 *koku*	49.8	383

Sources: (A) Osaka-shi sanjikai (1911: 650–1). (B) Shimbo (1978: 334–5 and 346–7).

from a survey conducted by the shogunate regarding the volume of eleven commodities (rice, *miso* (bean paste), coal, firewood, *saké* (rice wine), soy sauce, oil, fish oil, salt, cotton cloth, and ginned cotton) shipped from Osaka to Edo from 1724 to 1730.

Table 5.1 shows the volumes of rice and the next five commodities sent in greatest quantity to Edo. Even excluding rice, these five commodities represent extremely large shipments, with ginned cotton clearly outstripping the rest. Cotton cloth, oil, soy sauce, and *saké* are all finished products; Edo's character as a consumer center is revealed in its complete dependence on Osaka for these goods. However, the prominent place occupied by the semi-processed product of ginned cotton in the Osaka–Edo trade indicates a healthy demand for materials arising from industries located in Edo and its environs. Edo was thus not simply a site of consumption, but also a site of production. Growth in Edo's industrial sector eventually led to a lessening of the city's dependence on Osaka for daily necessities, but this did not emerge as a clear trend until the latter half of the Tokugawa period. Regardless of such developments, the major trade route established between Osaka and Edo facilitated their tightly knit economic interdependence.

2.4. Regional markets

Let us turn now to a discussion of the production and distribution of commodities outside of the Kinai region. As previously mentioned, shogunal policy divided warriors, merchants, and artisans from peasants and decreed that the former live in castle towns. Accordingly, castle towns provided a major source of demand in their respective domains, particularly drawing on nearby villages for food and other agricultural products. At the same time, however, castle towns were also a source for items the villagers could not produce for themselves, supplied by town-dwelling artisans and other nonagricultural workers involved in the manufacture of common implements, arms, dyed cloth, construction, and the like. Although the Kinai region, particularly Kyoto and Osaka, maintained a monopoly on the production of high-end crafts, castle towns throughout Japan constituted smaller centers for the production of more mundane goods. A division of labor emerged in which the castle town supplied finished goods, and surrounding villages provided food and agricultural materials. Even as a castle town acted as a central coordinating point for exchange within the territory, it also served as a key site for trade with the major metropolitan centers. Thus castle towns represented critical nodes for trade both within and across domains.

It should be noted, however, that the castle towns generally did not interact directly with surrounding villages; rather, market towns (*zaimachi*) served as intermediary sites. By the sixteenth century, these towns were already offering regular markets, which stimulated commodity production and circulation among rural villagers. Upon the establishment of the *bakuhan* system, various domains reorganized these market towns, which then drew merchants, artisans, and similar nonagricultural laborers from the villages. Scattered throughout the territory at fixed intervals (Takeuchi 1969: 140–6; Matsumoto 1983: 62–8), these towns offered, in addition to their regular market days, the services of a resident population of general store operators (*yorozuya*) and small numbers of artisans. The market towns accordingly became places where peasants from the surrounding area could sell their produce and purchase goods necessary for reproduction of their daily lives (Matsumoto 1983: 127). In this way, territorial trade networks were formed that linked villages to market towns to a castle town at the center. In turn, castle and port towns functioned as nodes joining these networks to trade between territories. Expanding commodity production in the first half of the Tokugawa period was premised on the existence of this web of trading relations.

2.5. Moving toward a "closed system"

Finally, we must turn our attention to foreign trade, or more precisely, the problem of "national seclusion" (*sakoku*) as a condition affecting the production and circulation of commodities during the Tokugawa period. Since the next chapter in this volume will provide a detailed discussion of "national seclusion," we will limit ourselves here to points essential for our overall argument.

Japan's foreign trade had reached new heights early in the seventeenth century. Japan's main export at the time was silver, the availability of which profoundly influenced the scale of foreign trade. From 1596 to 1623, annual silver exports averaged from 40,000 to 50,000 *kan* (131–165 tons, pure silver base) (Iwao 1966: 222–3). This translates to approximately two million *koku* in terms of the contemporary value of rice, or about 10 per cent of the total agricultural output. Since the exported silver brought in a large volume of imported goods, this trade was of considerable importance to the Japanese economy as a whole. Nevertheless, we should note that these imports were, with the exception of weaponry, primarily luxury consumer goods such as silk thread. While imports of silk thread greatly contributed to the development of Kyoto's high-quality textile industry, the foreign imports of this period did not possess a deep connection to the reproduction of commodities used in everyday life.

Japanese silver production reached its peak in the late sixteenth and early seventeenth century, after which it steadily declined. Silver exports, and therefore foreign imports, decreased in response. In response, the shogunate promulgated a "national seclusion" policy in the 1630s, but, as discussed elsewhere in this volume, this did not mean that the Japanese economy had become a completely "closed system." Foreign trade continued at Nagasaki under shogunal management, while exchange relations with Korea and China were maintained through Tsushima and the Ryûkyûs. Nevertheless, the scale of foreign trade as well as the types of commodities circulated changed greatly over time.

First, in terms of the scale of Japanese foreign trade, we can see from Table 5.2 (indicating trends in the volume of imports brought by Dutch ships to Nagasaki) that foreign imports to Nagasaki steadily declined, particularly in the eighteenth century. Moreover, trade with Korea via Tsushima dropped gradually from the end of the seventeenth century. Since the Japanese economy itself was expanding, the relative importance of foreign trade was greatly reduced. By the early nineteenth century, conditions near to those of a closed economy had been established. Over the

Table 5.2. Annual average number of arrivals of Dutch ships and imports

Period	Ships	Imports (silver *kan*)
1622–48	7.85	4,579.878
1649–68	7.55	3,786.570
1669–88	4.65	2,991.456
1689–1708	4.25	1,945.909
1709–28	2.47	1,545.695
1729–48	2.05	1,477.757
1749–68	1.90	1,041.912
1769–88	1.68	746.363
1789–1808	1.24	593.859

Source: Numata (1964: 51, table 2.1; 63, table 2.2).

course of a hundred years, Japan shifted, little by little, from an open to a closed economic system.

Second, let us examine trends in the kinds of commodities exchanged in Japan's foreign trade. Japan continued to rely heavily on the export of precious metals, although the specific type shifted from silver to copper. Meanwhile, by the early eighteenth century, sugar had replaced silk thread as the focus of import activity. While 130,000 *kin* of Chinese silk thread entered Japan in 1614, import limitations instituted from the end of the seventeenth and into the early eighteenth centuries drastically reduced shipments. During the Kyôho period (1716–35) silk thread imports did not even reach the level of 10,000 *kin* (Yamawaki 1960: 110).

One would expect that such a dramatic drop in silk thread imports would have dealt a serious blow to high-class silk textile industries such as that of Kyoto, which had hitherto been dependent on foreign trade for obtaining their materials. However, the silk merchants of Kyoto actively searched out sources of supply other than Nagasaki in order to survive this early eighteenth century crisis. In fact, the limits imposed on silk thread imports provided an excellent stimulus to domestic seri-culture and silk reeling, with import substitution becoming possible by the latter half of the eighteenth century. It could also be argued that the successful imposition of limits on imports of raw silk was dependent on a combination of factors, such as the previous domestication of sericul-ture and silk reeling, which made it possible to substitute domestic for foreign silk.

The gap left by silk was filled when refined white sugar import vol-umes quickly jumped at the end of the seventeenth century. By the mid-eighteenth century, sugar imports reached three million *kin* per year (Yamawaki 1976: 130, table 2). Yet a trend toward import substitution in the case of sugar, just as with silk, became discernible from the end of the eighteenth century. By the early nineteenth century, the low prices and large quantities of domestic white sugar—largely produced in Shikoku, especially the provinces of Sanuki and Awa—were driving imported sugar from the market. Import substitution was complete when domestic production of white sugar surpassed ten million *kin* in the 1830s (Tôgyô kyôkai 1976: 23–9). And this time, no commodity emerged to take the place of sugar as a major import item. The Japanese economy had become a "closed system," not just in name but also in actuality.

Due to such factors as the expanding production base that made import substitution possible, the Japanese economy gradually changed over time from an "open system" to a "closed system." On the other hand, in the intellectual world of the day there were also various attempts to challenge the boundaries of this "closed system," expressed as interest in European culture. From the late eighteenth century, "Dutch Studies" increasingly inspired excitement and attracted adherents. This, too, must be kept in mind when examining reactions to the "shock from the West" which accompanied the end of "national seclusion" in the mid-nineteenth century.

3. Early Tokugawa Market Economy

3.1. *The early seventeenth century regional division of labor*

In this section, we will clarify the structure of commodity production and distribution across Japan, that is, the regional division of labor as it took shape in the early Tokugawa period. In addition, we will note the changes that took place in such production and trade patterns from the early seventeenth century to the mid-eighteenth century. Previous scholarship has generally relied on such historical sources as Volume IV of the 1637 poetic work *Kefukigusa* for its list of notable products from various regions, the 1714 goods and their prices transported into Osaka from other regions in Japan and the 1736 goods and their prices transported into Osaka from other regions in Japan. Although we will also be making reference to these texts, we will examine them from a new perspective.

Volume IV of the *Kefukigusa* offers a table of 1807 "Notable Products from Various Regions."[1] Though far from comprehensive, these lists provide a useful overview of regional specialization across Japan in the early seventeenth century. The craft items listed in the *Kefukigusa* are concentrated in the section on the Kinai region, especially Kyoto, Osaka, and Nara. However, these items tend to be high-end specialty crafts rather than daily necessities for the general population. Table 5.3 shows the regional distribution of twenty products in wide use, which allows us to make the following points:

1. The relative importance of the Kinki region cut across all product categories. This was true not only for high-end crafts, but for manufactured items related to daily life.
2. Textile-related industry tended to be concentrated east of the Kinki region. San'yô, San'in, Shikoku, and Kyûshû did not appear at the time to have any involvement with the production of silk thread and silk fabrics, although Kyûshû did provide cloth and cotton.
3. During the Edo period, production sites for paper, a commodity in great demand, were widely distributed throughout the country, except for the Kinki region.
4. The lumber industry was mainly concentrated in the west of Japan. Of course, this does not mean that lumber was not produced elsewhere. This simply indicates that lumber sold as a regional specialty at extra-territorial markets generally came from western locales.

Table 5.3. Regional distribution of leading special products in *Kefukigusa* (number of Provinces)

Products	Tōhoku	Kantō	Tōkai	Tōzan	Hokuriku	Kinki	San'yō	San'in	Shikoku	Kyūshū
Yarn (raw silk)	1			1	2	6				
Pongee		2	2	1		1				
Silk		2		1	2	2				
Ramie	1	1		1	2	1				
Clothes		1		2	2	2			1	3
Raw cotton		1	2	2		4				
Cotton (textiles)		1	2	1		3				5
Safflower	1		1							1
Indigo		2	1	1		1				
Lumber				2	1	2		2	2	2
Wax	2		1	1	1	1		1		1
Paper	2		1	2	1		3		2	1
Tea			1			4				1
Saké			2			5	2	1	1	3
Seed oil						2				
Pottery			1	1			2			2
Gold	2				1	1				
Silver	1			1	1	2	1	1		
Copper		1		1			1			
Iron								2		

Source: Takenouchi (1943).

5. Aside from the Tôkai region, the *saké* industry was concentrated west of Kinki. However, the same qualification raised with respect to lumber also applies to *saké*.
6. Based as it is on data from the 1637 *Kefukigusa*, this table is not able to indicate the emergence of various sites which became known by the mid-Tokugawa period for the production of certain specialty products, such as indigo from Awa and cotton cloth from the coastal region of the Inland Sea.

We can see from the above that the Kinai area also held a comparatively dominant position in the production of goods used in everyday life. At the same time, however, areas throughout Japan were producing regional specialties for sale at extraterritorial markets, and, by the 1630s, production of commodities for daily life had spread widely.

3.2. The early eighteenth century regional division of labor

In what ways did the above regional division of labor for production change in the early eighteenth century? We can approach this question by examining the 1714 lists of goods sent to and from Osaka and the 1736 list of goods sent to Osaka. However, we should keep in mind the fact that goods produced in eastern Japan, such as cotton-related items, were directly sent to the markets of Edo, not Osaka, and therefore would not be reflected in these particular texts. This point is particularly salient when comparing these works with the *Kefukigusa*.

Table 5.4 illustrates the price structure of goods entering Osaka in 1714 by commodity. As we can see from the table, food, agricultural products, and maritime produce comprised 60 per cent of the goods entering Osaka, while items sent from Osaka were predominantly manufactured goods. Moreover, most were geared toward use in everyday life. Thus, as in the early seventeenth century, the Kinai region, centered on Osaka, maintained a relatively dominant position even with regard to the production of everyday commodities.

Table 5.5 (using the same method as Table 5.3) illustrates the regional distribution of production sites for commodities imported to Osaka in 1736. According to this table, production sites for all commodities tended to be located in Kinki and to western provinces. However, as noted above, this is a result of the particular bias of our historical data. There would be no reason for texts specifically focused on conditions in Osaka to include information regarding commodity production for all of Japan. Keeping this in mind, we can make the following points based on Table 5.5:

1. Production sites for commodities including rice and other grains, tobacco, hemp, lumber, wax, paper, marine products, and copper were

Table 5.4. Goods transported to and from Osaka in 1714

	Imported in		Exported out		
Items	Number of items	Composition in value (%)	Items	Number of items	Composition in value (%)
Foodstuffs	15	19.5	Seed oil and candle	5	36.4
Materials of seed oil	4	12.9	Rapeseed cake	1	3.4
Tea and tobacco	2	2.8	Processed food	8	6.1
Fertilizer	2	6.4	Cloth	6	25.2
Forest products	11	5.9	Dresses and ornaments	16	5.8
Marine products	10	20.2	Furnitures and carpets	9	0.5
Mining products	9	7.5	Lacquerwares and pottery	2	4.6
Tatami and mats	6	2.0	Instruments	19	7.5
Cloth	14	15.4	Arms	10	0.5
Kyoto handicrafts	6	0.9	Goods of arts and crafts	5	0.4
Others	27	2.4	Others	12	2.4
Importing goods	13	4.1	Exporting goods	2	7.3
Total	119	100.0	Total	95	100.0
	silver	*kan*		silver	*kan*
Value		286,561	Value		95,800

Source: Oishi (1975: 241).

Table 5.5. The distribution of goods transported to Osaka in 1736 by district (number of provinces)

Items	Tōhoku	Kantō	Tōkai	Tōzan	Hokuriku	Kinki	San'yō	San'in	Shikoku	Kyūshū
Rice	2		5	1	5	6	6	2	4	7
Cereals	2	5	1	1	1	5	4	2	3	8
Tea			2	1		6				1
Tobacco	1	4		1		5	4			1
Seed weed						6	4	2	2	9
Raw cotton						4	5		3	2
Sesame						2	3		3	6
Ramie	1	2		1	2	1	2	2		1
Cotton						6	1		1	
Lint						6	3	1		1
Indigo						1			1	
Lumber	2		1			6	1		3	4
Miscellaneous wood						4			3	3
Coal						3	2		4	2
Paper	1	1		1		5	5	1	4	3
Salt						1			1	
Raw fish						5	5		4	2
Salt or dry fish	1	3			2	8	5	2	4	7
Dried sardines		5				1	3		4	6

Table 5.5. *Continued*

Items	Tōhoku	Kantō	Tōkai	Tōzan	Hokuriku	Kinki	San'yō	San'in	Shikoku	Kyūshū
Oil cake	2				1	2	5		2	4
Wax	2	1		1	3	2	2	2	1	5
Floss					3	5			2	
Silk		2		1	2	2				
Pongee		4		1		1				
Clothes					4	3	1			
Cotton yarn						4				1
White cotton						7	2		2	2
Striped cotton						4				
Second-hand clothes						7	4			
Pottery			1			4	1		2	
Iron						1	5	3	1	
Copper	2					2	1	1	1	1

Source: Osaka-shi sanjikai (1911: 770–9).

distributed throughout the country. While in the 1630s the Kinki region did not appear to have been producing paper, 100 years later, all five provinces of Kinki were sending paper to the Osaka markets.

2. Just as in the 1630s, the production of silk-related goods was concentrated east of Kinki, particularly in the Kantô region. The reason that raw silk does not appear in Table 5.5 is that it was all shipped to Kyoto.

3. In contrast, we can see marked changes with regard to cotton-related goods. In the early seventeenth century, cotton goods tended to be produced in the areas east of Kinki, but a hundred years later the areas west of Kinki took over as suppliers to Osaka. Since the production sites in the Tôkai and Kantô regions listed in the *Kefukigusa* were doubtless shipping to Nagoya and Edo, they did not make an appearance in our commodity lists for Osaka. Our data does show, however, that, unlike their entries in the *Kefukigusa*, the San'yô and Shikoku regions had become heavily involved in the cotton industry. In the course of a century, the cotton industry had spread rapidly throughout the Inland Sea area.

4. Another notable change is the emergence of Awa as a production site for indigo.

5. Although dried sardines were not even mentioned in the *Kefukigusa*, they were ranked fourth among goods transported to Osaka in 1736. In addition, residuum from the processing of rapeseed into oil was shipped both to and from Osaka. Thus we see that use of commercial fertilizers such as the above had greatly increased around the Kinai region from the seventeenth through the early eighteenth century, indicating that agricultural production had moved in the direction of growing reliance on fertilizer and labor-intensive methods.

We can clearly see from the above that various important changes had taken place, such as the entrance of the Inland Sea area into the cotton industry, the emergence of Awa as a production site for indigo, and the increased volume of trade in dried sardines and rapeseed oil cake as fertilizer. Yet it would be difficult to argue that the general conditions and regional division of labor across Japan for the production of commodities were drastically different from the picture provided by the *Kefukigusa*. As mentioned previously, the Kinai region exercised relative dominance in both high-end crafts and in the manufacture of goods for daily life. This is clearly demonstrated by Table 5.6, which shows trading volumes and prices for the top fifteen commodities shipped in and out of Osaka in 1714. A glance at this table shows that goods related to daily life comprise the majority of commodities moving in and out of Osaka. Moreover, many were bound in a paired relationship in which raw materials were brought in to Osaka and finished materials were shipped out, as, for example, in rice to be processed for *saké*, rapeseed for rapeseed oil, iron for iron implements, copper to be sent on to Nagasaki, cotton for ginned cotton and

Table 5.6. Top fifteen goods transported to and from Osaka in 1714

Items		Quantity (unit)	value (silver *kan*)	Percentage
Transported from Osaka				
1	Rapeseed oil	33,272 *koku*	26,005	27.1
2	Striped cotton	698,747 *tan*	7,066	7.4
3	Copper to Nagasaki	5,000,000 *kin*	6,587	6.9
4	White cotton	739,938 *tan*	6,264	6.5
5	Cotton seed oil	7,900 *koku*	6,116	6.4
6	Second-hand clothes	409,838 *ko*	6,004	6.3
7	Lint	108,640 *kan*	4,209	4.4
8	Soy sauce	32,206 *koku*	3,898	4.1
9	Iron fabrics	—	3,750	3.9
10	Rape oil cake	1,596,560 *kan*	3,267	3.4
11	Lacquar wares	—	2,839	3.0
12	Notions	—	2,838	3.0
13	Sesame oil	2055 *koku*	2,088	2.2
14	Pottery	—	1,574	1.6
15	*Saké*	5909 *koku*	1,200	1.2
	Subtotal		83,705	87.4
	Other 30 items		12,094	12.6
	Total		95,799	100.0
Transported to Osaka				
1	Rice	282,792 *koku*	40,813	14.2
2	Seed weed	151,225 *koku*	28,048	9.8
3	Lumber	—	25,751	9.0
4	Dried sardines	—	17,760	6.2
5	White cotton	2,061,473 *tan*	15,749	5.5
6	Paper	148,464 *maru*	14,464	5.0
7	Iron	1,878,168 *kan*	11,803	4.1
8	Micellaneous wood	31,092,394 *kan*	9,125	3.2
9	Copper	5,429,220 *kin*	7,171	2.5
10	Cotton	1,722,781 *kin*	6,704	2.3
11	Tobacco	3,631,562 *kin*	6,495	2.3
12	Sugar	1,992,192 *kin*	5,614	2.0
13	Soy beans	49,930 *koku*	5,320	1.9
14	Salt	358,436 *koku*	5,230	1.8
15	Wheat	39,977 *koku*	4,586	1.6
	Subtotal		204,633	71.4
	Other 104 items		81,928	28.6
	Total		286,561	100.0

Source: Oishi (1975: 143-67).

various textiles, and soy beans, wheat and salt to make soy sauce. In sum, Osaka brought in raw and semi-processed materials to produce finished goods to send out, serving as a major center for the manufacture of items necessary in daily life. Given the existence of a division of labor such that the Kinai region provided finished goods and outlying territories supplied raw and semi-processed agricultural materials, did this mean that the regional territories were completely dependent on Kinai for finished goods?

Rapeseed oil, an essential item in daily life, constituted 27 per cent of the total volume of goods sent from Osaka, topping a list of 119 commodities. Meanwhile, rapeseed as a raw material was second among goods entering Osaka, approximately 10 per cent of the total volume. However, although this does not appear in Table 5.6, 310,000 *tan* of rapeseed oil cake, worth 527 *kan* in currency, were also sent to Osaka. Moreover, in 1736, the eight provinces of Settsu, Bizen, Bitchu, Bingo, Sanuki, Buzen, Bungo, and Chikuzen were producing rapeseed oil cake as well as rapeseed to ship to Osaka. These areas had developed the capacity to process rapeseed into oil to the point of being able to send the cake to markets beyond territorial borders. The same was true in the case of certain other processed goods. For example, a trade volume of two million *tan* and a 5.5 per cent share of the total value of goods entering Osaka placed plain white cotton cloth (representing a low level of processing) among the top five commodities. Such trade volumes were possible because thirteen provinces in the San'yô, Shikoku, and Kyûshû regions had become involved in both growing and processing cotton. These examples indicate that territories outside of the Kinai region had become widely engaged in the production of processed goods necessary in daily life. Even if this production did not reach output levels high enough to send the commodity to other territories or to central markets, output was often sufficient to meet local demand. Accordingly, with regard to daily necessities, Osaka should be thought of as a production and distribution site primarily geared toward the Kinai region, particularly the areas surrounding Osaka, and toward the great consumption metropolis of Edo.

3.3. *The structure of Osaka's trade in 1714*

However, in 1714, the total volume of goods shipped from Osaka came to 95,799 *kan* in silver. In contrast, the total volume of goods entering Osaka reached 286,561 *kan* in silver; if we add to this approximately 170,000 *kan* in silver for tax rice and other grains, the total exceeds 450,000 *kan* in silver. The ratio of goods shipped from and to Osaka then becomes a strikingly lop-sided one to five. This trade imbalance has attracted the interest of many scholars, who offer a range of explanations and interpretations. However, any discussion of this imbalance must take the following points into consideration.

First, we can assume that the average annual shipment to Edo in 1714 was roughly comparable to the figures for the years 1727–30 given in Table 5.1. If this amount were included as part of the recorded volume of goods sent to "various regions," then only a small portion would be left over after shipments to Edo for distribution to other areas, including the Kinai region. This clearly does not make sense. There was probably a separate set of records of shipments to Edo, since the volume of goods sent from Osaka to "various regions" in 1714 generally corresponded to the volume received from the same. Moreover, if we calculate the value of the eleven goods bound for Edo represented in Table 5.1 in the units of the 1714 accounts of goods transported to and from Osaka, we come up with 80,000 *kan* in silver. Adding in the value of other goods sent to Edo, the total approximates the value of goods sent from Osaka to other areas. Given that demand from the Kinai and the surrounding areas, in terms of population size, was roughly equivalent to demand from Edo and its environs, shipments from Osaka must have been directed toward Kinai and nearby areas rather than to the regional territories that supplied Osaka with raw-and semi-processed materials. This point confirms that Osaka served as a provider of daily necessities primarily for the Kinai and surrounding regions and Edo and its environs.

If we think of goods sent to "various regions" and goods shipped to Edo as separate categories, adding the two together will give us a total that does not exceed 180,000–200,000 *kan* in silver. This is still far from reaching the previous total of 450,000 *kan* in silver for goods entering Osaka (including 170,000 *kan* of tax rice and other items).

And so we arrive at our second point: wholesaler commissions and shipping charges need to be factored into our calculations. We need to understand that the value assigned to goods entering Osaka included shipping charges and other expenses (the CIF or Cost, Insurance, Freight value), while the value assigned to goods leaving did not (the FOB or Free On Board value). We also need to deduct fees paid to Osaka wholesalers for storage and interest on prepayments made by the wholesalers for commodities entering Osaka. For example, in the case of indigo from Awa, the sum total of these fees and interest payments came to nearly 10 per cent of the cost of the indigo (Amano 1986: 19). As for transportation, since there was greater use of Osaka ships than local ships[2], Osaka again stood in a position to profit. It seems that even when sending goods from Osaka, shipping and other expenses generally remained "in-house."

Wholesaler commissions, interest accruing to prepayments, shipping, and other expenses can be roughly estimated to have come to 15 per cent of the value of goods entering Osaka and 10 per cent of the value of goods leaving Osaka. If these were accounts receivable by Osaka, then about 100,000 *kan* reduces Osaka's payment totals. Nevertheless, the trade imbalance still has not been erased.

Finally, we must take into consideration payments of interest on loans to domainal lords. Indeed, in 1714, the Kônoike family (one of the great Osaka money-lending enterprises) enjoyed an income of over 2,000 *kan* in silver primarily derived from interest payments (Yasuoka 1970: 90). There is no question that the amount of interest paid by various domains to Osaka merchants came to a considerable sum.

Although this goes some way toward addressing the trade imbalance, it does not in the end reverse the situation in which Osaka was paying out more than it was receiving. As long as domainal lords were not forced to run up huge expenses in service to the shogunate, currency (and not just the official coin of the realm) flowed outward from Osaka to regional territories. The economy was expanding and trade in commodities was growing apace in regional territories; a shortage of currency was inevitable, since the shogunate had a monopoly on the minting of coins. Thus it was in the interest of regional territories to sell more goods to Osaka than they purchased, as a means of overcoming the currency shortage. In other words, currency itself was an important commodity for the regional territories.

Based upon the above analysis, the following points can be made. High-end crafts aside, regional territories did not depend heavily on Osaka or the greater Kinai region for processed goods necessary for daily life. These areas sent food, raw materials, and semi-processed goods to the Kinai region, particularly Osaka, in considerable volume. In turn, they received goods in which the Kinai region had an overwhelming edge in production, goods otherwise difficult to produce under local conditions, and currency to supplement their shortfall. On the other hand, Osaka met the daily consumer needs of Osaka and its environs by bringing in food, raw materials and the like from regional territories. Osaka also acted as a supplier of goods such as oil, *saké*, soy sauce, cotton goods, and various implements to Kinai and nearby areas, as well as to Edo and its environs. However, even though Edo relied on the Kinai region, particularly Osaka, to supply it with manufactured goods necessary for everyday life, over time it was also increasingly able to turn to its more immediate surroundings for such items. This structure of commodity production and trade characteristic of the early eighteenth century underwent great changes over the course of the next century.

4. The Eighteenth Century as a Period of Change

4.1. *Changes in the economic structure*

Throughout the eighteenth century, the economy continued to grow and its structure underwent the following changes:

1. After peaking in the 1730s, the population of Japan alternated between stagnation and decline. However, there was considerable variation among different regions. While the Kinki, Kantô, and Tôhoku regions registered declines, Kyûshû, Tôzan, and Tôkai grew at a moderate pace,

and Shikoku, San'yô, and San'in actually experienced large increases. As a result, from the 1720s to the 1840s, we see a shift of the center of gravity of population from east to west (Shakai Kôgaku Kenkyûsho 1974: 125).

2. From the 1720s, the urban population declined both in absolute numbers and relative proportion. Once again, however, we need to keep in mind variation in accordance with the size and particular character of the city. Most striking was the decline in the major metropolitan areas of Edo, Osaka, and Kyoto, followed by that of such large regional centers as Nagoya, Kanazawa, and Sendai. On the other hand, small and medium sized regional cities hovered between stagnation and slight growth, while market towns, hitherto never topping 3,000, swelled.

3. The pace for opening up new agricultural fields slowed down. During 130 years spanning 1600–1730, arable land area increased by 44 per cent, but during the next 120 years from 1730 to 1850, arable land area actually declined by 11 per cent (Miyamoto 1976: 26, table 5). However, since population growth had leveled off, the ratio of land to population improved.

Against this backdrop of structural change, we see new developments in the production and circulation of goods: commodity production became further entrenched and the regional division of labor underwent reorganization. Throughout the latter half of the Tokugawa period, both the agricultural and nonagricultural sectors experienced continuous growth as commodity production flourished.

Turning first to the agricultural sector, according to the estimates of Satoru Nakamura, agricultural output was 30,630,000 *koku* (100.0) in 1697, had grown to 39,770,000 *koku* (129.8) by 1830, and reached 46,810,000 *koku* (152.8) in 1867. Agricultural output had grown 58 per cent over the course of a century and a half (Nakamura 1968: 170). Since the pace for opening up new lands for cultivation had slowed down, this increase in agricultural output was clearly due to climbing levels of productivity.

Rice was the heart of Tokugawa period agriculture, and a variety of factors contributed toward increases in rice crop yield per land parcel: increased double-cropping and dry field farming; improved varieties and greater use of mid- and late-seasonal types of rice; improvement and diversification of agricultural implements (such as forked rakes and rice threshes with teeth made of bamboo); and superior methods of fertilization and greater use of such commercial fertilizers as dried sardines and rapeseed oil residuum. For example, from the mid-eighteenth century to the early nineteenth century, the rice crop yield per parcel rose by 50–60 per cent in Settsu, and exceeded two *koku* per parcel in Settsu, Kawachi, Aki, and other provinces (Imai and Yagi 1955: 105).

However, since population growth had leveled off, demand for rice did not grow at a similar pace. Rising levels of productivity in rice production inevitably led to more land being turned to growing crops other than rice, particularly to commercial production of raw materials for manufacture.

Accordingly, commercial agricultural production contributed greatly to the growth in agricultural output seen in the latter half of the Tokugawa period. The expansion of commercial agricultural production in regional territories was particularly striking. By such measures as importing technology and techniques from leading economical regions and selecting cash crops suitable for local, natural, and geographical conditions, regions throughout Japan became increasingly involved in the production of specialty items for markets outside of the territory.

4.2. The emergence of regional specialty products

Both agricultural and nonagricultural specialty products made their way to central markets by trade routes established in the early Tokugawa period for the transport of foods, particularly rice, and raw and semi-processed materials. Competition between rival production sites emerged as a result, giving rise to a reorganization of the regional division of labor.

In a classic example from the agricultural sector, the Kinai region retreated from cotton production as the Inland Sea and Tôkai regions expanded their involvement and the San'in and the Kantô regions came to dominate the cotton sector. This trend toward specialization continued to the point where local self-sufficiency in rice decreased in some areas, and others made rice production their specialty. Rice markets flourished as a division of labor emerged between regions that produced rice and regions, which produced cash crops. For example, as Awa began to specialize in the production of indigo, it grew dependent on other regions to supply it with rice, about 70,000 *koku* each year by the early nineteenth century (Naruto-shi shi henshû iinkai 1976: 1423). Even within Awa, there existed a regional division of labor in which different zones specialized in rice, indigo, or sugar cane production. This kind of division of labor was seen among the villages of Kinai in the first half of the Tokugawa period and spread to the rest of Japan after the latter half of the eighteenth century.

Turning our attention to the manufacturing sector, a diffusion of industry from major cities such as Kyoto and Osaka to villages and outlying territories also contributed to the restructuring of regional relations. This trend had already begun in the Kinai region, particularly in the areas surrounding Osaka, by the late seventeenth and early eighteenth centuries. Typical cases of this kind of diffusion include production in western Settsu of Osaka-style *saké* and oil extracted by water wheel. Not only did these industries provide stiff competition to their big city counterparts, but also they came to dominate the markets in the latter half of the eighteenth century.

Similar rivalries were established throughout the country during this time period. New centers for the production of cotton textiles emerged in the Kantô, Hokuriku, Tôkai, San'yô, San'in, and Shikoku regions, while silk textiles began to be produced at Kiryû and other sites throughout the Kantô region. Meanwhile, soy sauce production expanded rapidly at Noda and Chôshi in the Kantô region, and Tatsuno in the Kansai region. Metal work from Miki (Harima Province), Kurayoshi (Hôki Province), Takefu (Echizen Province), and Sanjô (Echigo Province) began to make headway in markets throughout the country. Even lacquerware from places with a long tradition in this craft, such as Wajima, Noto Province, and Aizu, Mutsu Province, was only produced as a commodity for markets throughout Japan from the latter half of the eighteenth century (Watanabe 1965: 247–8).

4.3. *The emergence of an Edo regional economic sphere (market area near Edo)*

Next, we must consider the formation of an "Edo regional economic sphere" as part of the general reorganization of a regional division of labor. The production of such goods as ginned cotton, cotton textiles, oil, soy sauce, and silk textiles in the Kantô region grew rapidly from the last half of the eighteenth and into the nineteenth century. As a result, Edo markets became considerably less dependent upon goods shipped in from Osaka and Kyoto (Hayashi 1969: 229–38). Moreover, if we look at the regional structure of Japanese production output in 1874 as calculated by Kanji Ishii, the contribution of Kantô, even in the manufacturing sector, was close to that of the Kinki region (Ishii 1986: 10–11, table 2). It is true that sericulture, which expanded rapidly upon the opening of treaty ports at the end of the Tokugawa period, became Kantô's primary industry. But even before this, the Kantô region was well able to compete with the Kinki region as a production zone. This economic development in Edo and its surrounding areas was part and parcel of the general efflorescence of regional specialty production from the latter half of the eighteenth century. Since, however, the Kantô region had come to possess undeniable importance for the Edo markets as a source for daily necessities by the early eighteenth century, an "Edo regional economic sphere" was already in existence by the latter half of the Tokugawa period.

Nevertheless, the reduced dependence on goods sent from Osaka and Kyoto resulting from growth in the Edo regional economy did not mean that its cash crops and manufactures necessarily held a comparative advantage over specialty items from other regions. According to Hiroshi Shimbo's work in comparing Edo and Osaka commodity prices from 1830 to 1857, there was little difference between the Edo and Osaka prices for major crops such as rice, barley, and soy beans. However, in other cases, Edo prices were considerably higher than those of Osaka. For example, Edo prices for ginned cotton were on average 17 per cent higher; for wax, 15 per cent higher; for soy sauce and rapeseed oil,

12 per cent higher; and for refined *saké*, 30 per cent higher (Shimbo 1986: 13–14). The addition of shipping and other charges to Osaka prices for these commodities generally brought them up to the level of Edo prices, with the exception of refined *saké*. Accordingly, commodities produced in the Edo region were able to hold their own against goods shipped in from outside. But they were not priced competitively enough to penetrate the Kinai and Shikoku markets. This was true in general, not just in the case of the Edo regional economy: major improvements in transportation would have had an inevitable impact on the reconfiguration of the regional division of labor.

4.4. The entrance of small farm families into the market economy

As commodity production continued to expand, the relationship of small farm families to the market economy underwent drastic changes. Inevitably, the trade networks connecting castle towns, market towns, and villages were reconfigured. In the seventeenth century, nonagricultural workers did not generally live in the villages, while villagers conducted market transactions at the fairs regularly held in market towns. Yet, increasing involvement with the market economy resulted in gradually growing numbers of villagers pursuing nonagricultural sidelines, while market transactions in the village became common. For example, in Hanakuma village (Yatabe District, Settsu Province), only a handful of the residents were engaged in nonagricultural economic activities in the seventeenth century. But by 1767, thirty-one of a total of seventy-eight agricultural households had members involved in nonagricultural activities as either a primary or secondary source of income (Shimbo 1967: 115–17). Similarly, in Yokone village (Saku District, Shinano Province), the number of nonagricultural households gradually increased from the 1770s until they constituted more than one-third of all households by the end of the Tokugawa period (Sekiguchi 1983: 13–14). Incorporation of market transactions into daily village life undermined the *raison d'être* of the regular fairs held in market towns, some of which were indefinitely suspended as a result. However, many market towns were reborn as collection and shipping centers in regions boasting vigorous village industries. In the case of Kantô silks, wholesalers laid in their supplies at markets held six times each month at twenty-five such towns in Musashi Province and twenty-one in Kôzuke Province. Clearly, relations between the castle towns, market towns, and villages had undergone dramatic changes.

As the backbone of commercial agricultural production and village industry, small farm families thus became increasingly tied into the changing and expanding market economy. Entry into the market economy inevitably meant that these small farm families also had to face fierce competition, not only between different regional production sites, but also between different households within a given region. In response, small farm families had to learn to behave as economic actors in a market economy. Their fates were governed by whether or not they could make appropriate decisions in response to market conditions. As a result, economic competition stimulated class differentiation and local capital accumulation.

There were various ways in which small farm families came to particip-ate in the market economy, and therefore to compete as economic actors. As it spread in the latter half of the Tokugawa period, village industry generally took the form of small farm families performing nonagricultural side jobs within the household, as we see in the case of the spinning indus-try. Agriculture and industry became inextricably intertwined in house-hold management, although the specific balance struck between the two could vary considerably. In some cases, nonagricultural activities were pursued as sideline jobs carried out between agricultural duties, generally by the women of the family. In other cases, light industry became the pri-mary source of household income, with work in the fields confined to that necessary to produce food for the household's own consumption. Over time, the relative proportion of households centered on industry grew, particularly in newly established centers for the production of specialty items. Moreover, as regional village industry became geared toward the central and extra-territorial markets, industry increasingly came to have the upper hand in its relationship with agriculture in the lives of many villagers. Indeed, Settsu, Kawachi, and other provinces boasting advanced cotton textile industries were forced to retreat in the face of the stiff com-petition provided by the new production sites springing up throughout Japan from the end of the eighteenth century (Saitô 1985: 191–2).

It is important to note that these families did not always participate in the market as independent actors. Although it became fairly common by the end of the Tokugawa period to substitute currency for rice when paying annual taxes, villagers still usually provided their portion of the annual tax to the village headman in kind. The village headman would then sell the collected rice and pay the taxes due, to the domainal lord with currency obtained at market (Shimbo 1967: 288–91). This payment method is, of course, rooted in the system by which villages were held responsible for taxes as a collective, but we may note how it helped continue to separate ordinary villagers from the rice markets. Similar methods were also at times adopted when selling commercial agricultural produce. To return to the previously mentioned example of Hanakuma village, from 1818 to 1830, villagers did not sell their rapeseed crop as individuals; rather, the village as a unit sold its rapeseed to a wholesaler. This practice appears to have been widespread among the rapeseed villages of Settsu, Kawachi, and Izumi Province (Lee 1980: 111–15). Moreover, small farm families involved in the production of commodities were not able to act as completely independent economic agents within the domainal monopoly system that emerged from the end of the eighteenth and into the nineteenth century. Of course, this is not to say that small farm families never participated in the market economy as economic actors during the latter half of the Tokugawa period. At the same time, however, independence as economic actors became a major issue for small farm families in the process of modernization.

5. Production and Distribution of Local Specialties and Central Markets

5.1. Various patterns in the production and distribution of regional specialty products

From the latter half of the eighteenth century, production of specialty items, particularly in the industrial sector, to send to central and extraterritorial markets rapidly increased in regional territories and villages. However, increased commodity production for regional or local markets preceded the inroads later made in central and extraterritorial markets. The transition from commodity production for local markets to production for markets outside the territory took place in a variety of ways. For example, in the case of the silk textile industry, wholesalers from the major metropolitan areas actively sought goods from regional production sites, thereby encouraging the establishment of new industrial locales. In the case of the soy sauce industry, regional producers energetically campaigned to break into the central markets. The "domainal monopoly system" provided yet another stimulus for commodity production aimed at markets throughout Japan, examples of this including paper from Nagato and various areas in Shikoku; wax from Aizu, Uwajima (Iyo Province), Fukuoka (Chikuzen Province), and Kumamoto (Higo Province); indigo from Awa; raw silk from Gujô (Mino Province); silk textiles from Hikone (Ômi Province); cotton textiles from Kameoka (Tamba Province) and Himeji (Harima Province); *tatami*-mat facing from Fukuoka; and sugar from Takamatsu (Sanuki Province) and Kagoshima (Satsuma Province). In some cases, under this "domainal monopoly system" goods such as cotton from Himeji, brown sugar from Kagoshima, and refined sugar from Takamatsu were collected like rice taxes at domainal warehouses to be converted to currency at the central markets, or, as in the case of indigo from Awa, the domain extended protection and provided oversight for local merchants shipping regional specialties to the central and extraterritorial markets.

Production of regional specialties also took place in a variety of ways. Spinning (mainly cotton and silk) and brewing (refined *saké*, soy sauce, and the like) were two particularly prominent industries of the era, but they were structured in strikingly different ways. In the brewing industry, production took place at a central facility, while in the spinning industry, small farm family households often carried out production as a sideline. Even within the spinning industry, there were several options. On the one hand, in a kind "putting out" system, a local wholesale merchant might advance raw materials and spinning machinery to small farm family household, returning later to collect the processed goods. On the other, a household able to afford the raw materials and requisite machinery might produce goods to sell to the local wholesale merchant.

Next, we would like to turn to the traditional industry of soy sauce brewing, which has hitherto received little scholarly attention despite the importance of soy sauce as a widely used commodity. In order to illumin-ate the structure of the production and distribution of soy sauce, we would like to examine the specific case of Tatsuno soy sauce as a regional specialty of Harima Province that enjoyed increasing success from the mid-eighteenth century.

5.2. *The entry of Tatsuno soy sauce into the central markets*

The use of soy sauce as a seasoning first spread among commoners dur-ing the Tokugawa period. However, the only specialty items mentioned in the *Kefukigusa* that have any relation to soy sauce are Maruyama Hishio (a kind of bean paste) from Yamashiro Province and *Tamari* (a kind of soy sauce) from Izumi Province. It seems, then, that soy sauce production had not yet spread outward from the metropolitan core of the Kinai region in the early seventeenth century. As previously mentioned, in 1726 approximately 10,000 barrels of soy sauce were sent from Osaka to the Edo markets, but this soy sauce was most likely produced in or around Kyoto and Osaka. This is supported by the fact that materials necessary to produce soy sauce, including soy beans, wheat, and salt, figured promi-nently among the commodities shipped to Osaka in 1714.

However, early in the eighteenth century, production sites for soy sauce, as in the case of other commodities, gradually became established outside of the Kinai area. Favorable production conditions allowed regional soy sauce brewers to enjoy a relative advantage as they began to make inroads on the central markets. At the beginning of the eighteenth century, soy sauce from other regions had not yet made an appearance in the Kyoto markets. But Bizen soy sauce blazed a path in the latter half of the 1720s, soon followed by soy sauce from Harima and Ômi in the 1750s. The local soy sauce industry found itself hard-pressed by its new rivals.

Let us turn now to a concrete look at the process by which Tatsuno soy sauce entered the Kyoto market. It is said that soy sauce production in Tatsuno began as a sideline to the refined *saké* brewing industry already in existence in the area, but it is difficult to identify exactly when this took place. However, local documents from 1684 reveal that soy sauce was subject to domainal taxes. Therefore, Tatsuno was already producing soy sauce as a commodity by the latter half of the seventeenth century (Hasegawa 1993: 26–8). At the time, this locally produced soy sauce was distributed to the domainal castle town and environs. Tatsuno domain was particularly fortunate in terms of soy sauce production for a variety of reasons: wheat was already grown within the area, adjoining regions could supply soy beans and high quality "Akô" salt, and expertise based on *saké*-brewing was readily at hand. Moreover, the Ibo River, which cut across Tatsuno, not only offered high quality water for brewing, but also a means of transportation for raw materials and the finished product. This happy combination of factors made it possible for Tatsuno soy sauce to begin to make headway in the central markets by the early 1730s. One of the oldest breweries in Tatsuno, the Maruo family enterprise, boasted the highest output throughout the latter half of the Tokugawa period. According to family records, the Maruo brewery was sending modest quantities of soy sauce on consignment to wholesalers in Kyoto, Osaka, and Edo by 1731. Then, in 1746, the Maruo family staked out its own place in the Kyoto markets by establishing a store in the city for selling soy sauce both at the store itself and to brokers (Hasegawa 1993: 32–3).

Price was another factor contributing to the success of Tatsuno soy sauce in the Kyoto markets. Table 5.7 shows mid- to late-eighteenth century price trends for Kyoto rice and soy sauce and Tatsuno soy sauce. Rice prices in Kyoto peaked in Period IV, after which they declined. In contrast, prices for Kyoto soy sauce bottomed out in Period III, after which they rose in Period IV. The result, illustrated in Figure 5.1, was that the relative cost for Kyoto soy sauce in comparison to rice was at its lowest in Period III, after which it rose until Period X. Rising levels of per capita income as well as other factors contributed to an explosion of demand for soy sauce in Kyoto from the mid-eighteenth century, sending prices upward. However, while the prices of Kyoto soy sauce were skyrocketing, the cost level of Tatsuno soy sauce remained around 50 *monme*. Accordingly, as shown in Figure 5.1, the relative price of Tatsuno soy sauce in comparison with Kyoto soy sauce plummeted. It was not surprising, then, that Tatsuno soy sauce was able to make such inroads in the Kyoto markets, where demand for this commodity only continued to grow.

There were also important institutional factors, shogunal policy in particular, shaping the way in which regional specialty products came to be sold in the central markets. In fact, the shogunate initially refused to allow products from other regions, such as soy sauce from Bizen, into the Kyoto markets. The protectionist stance adopted by the shogunate gave priority to local soy sauce brewers from Kyoto and its environs. However, under pressure from the increased demand for soy sauce, the shogunate

Table 5.7. Prices of rice in Kyoto, and soy sauce in Kyoto and Tatsuno (price = silver *monme*)

Term	Year	(A) Rice in Kyoto (koku)	(B) Soy sauce in Kyoto (koku)	(C) Soy sauce in Tatsuno (koku)	(B)/(A) × 100	(C)/(B) × 100
I	1726–30	55.0	65.0	35.6	118.2	54.8
II	1731–35	60.3	64.2	39.0	106.5	60.7
III	1736–40	70.0	62.5	63.0	89.3	100.8
IV	1741–45	82.3	79.8	63.8	97.0	79.9
V	1746–50	80.0	89.5	56.0	111.8	62.6
VI	1751–55	63.2	93.3	50.0	147.6	53.6
VII	1756–60	77.4	93.7	55.0	121.1	58.7
VIII	1761–65	56.5	90.5	48.2	160.2	53.3
IX	1766–70	—	—	53.0	—	—
X	1771–75	58.0	100.0	48.0	172.4	48.0
XI	1776–80	64.4	94.3	44.0	146.4	46.7
XII	1781–85	74.7	80.0	47.5	107.1	59.4

Source: Hasegawa (1975: 161–2).

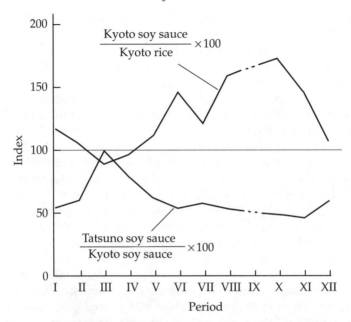

Fig. 5.1. Trends of relative price in soy sauce.
Source: Tables 5.7.

eventually found it could no longer continue to deny entry to soy sauce producers from other regions seeking access to the Kyoto markets.

In 1761, the shogunate finally permitted the establishment of a whole-saler association for the soy sauces of other regions. This organization, built around Bizen soy sauce, was the first to receive authorization for transactions in Kyoto. In 1780, another organization involving twenty-one wholesalers for soy sauces from other regions also received official authorization, adding soy sauces from Harima, including Tatsuno soy sauce, and Settsu to that of Bizen. However, official regulations stipu-lated that regional soy sauce wholesaler associations be absorbed within "parent share"-holding Kyoto soy sauce wholesaler associations. The case of the regional soy sauce wholesalers in Kyoto is a classic example of the economic policy during the Tanuma years (1767–86) to incorporate prominent regional merchants by expanding the associate system. This establishment of a mechanism to distribute regional soy sauces to the Kyoto markets provided an important opportunity for the expansion of Tatsuno soy sauce. The output of the Tatsuno soy sauce industry increased steadily, and the percentage sent on to the Kyoto markets rose even more briskly.

In the face of the growing market share held by regional soy sauces, such as that of Tatsuno, the local soy sauce industry around Kyoto began to retreat. Meanwhile, competition between regional soy sauce producers heated up. By the beginning of the nineteenth century, Tatsuno had replaced Bizen at the head of regional soy sauces sold in Kyoto. In 1816, the Kyoto market received more than 75,000 barrels of soy sauce from other regions, 45 per cent of which came from Tatsuno, 35 per cent from Bizen (Hasegawa 1993: 62–3).

The Tatsuno soy sauce industry as a whole achieved growth by moving from local sales to sales outside of the region, but not all local soy sauce breweries made shipments to the Kyoto markets. Table 5.8 indicates the structure of the Tatsuno soy sauce industry in 1830 in terms of scale of output. We can see from this table that 90 per cent of the total Tatsuno soy sauce output was shipped outside of the territory, while the remaining 10 per cent was sold locally. Breweries serving the local markets comprised 60 per cent of a total of twenty-five Tatsuno soy sauce producers, and generally produced less than fifty *koku*, with the exception of three breweries that produced fifty to one hundred *koku*. In contrast, breweries producing more than one hundred *koku* were always involved in shipping to Kyoto. In other words, small-scale breweries met local demand, while those of larger capacities handled sales outside the region. So long as the enterprise was geared only toward local or regional markets, there was no hope of major expansion. However, sales to markets outside the immediate territory or to the central markets made a new, larger scale of enterprise possible. In sum, growth in regional commodity production and competitive participation in the central markets led to market expansion. This in turn promoted further development of regional industry and large-scale enterprises. Of course, this pattern was not unique to Tatsuno soy sauce. For example, the Chôshi and Noda soy sauce industries, located in the Kantô area, which produced twice as much soy sauce as Tatsuno and had completely conquered the Edo markets by the end of the Tokugawa period, basically followed the same path (Arai 1959; Hayashi 1990).

In this way, the production of specialty items became entrenched in every region throughout Japan from the mid- to late-eighteenth century.

Table 5.8. Composition of soy sauce manufacturing in Tatsuno (1830)

Production size	No. of operation	(Kyoto exporter)	Production *koku*	Percentage
Under 50 *koku*	12	1	251.5	5.4
50–100 *koku*	5	2	320.0	7.0
100–500 *koku*	5	5	1,466.0	32.0
Over 500 *koku*	3	3	2,550.0	55.6
Total	25	11	4,587.5	100.0

Source: "Bunsei 13 toradoshi sangatsu yasumikabu tsukurikabu torishirabechô." in Tamura ed. (1959: 9–12).

Although the timing and other specifics varied by region, the relative advantages enjoyed by such specialty products made it possible for them to advance into the central markets and establish a place for themselves.

Translated by Noriko Aso.

Notes

1. For other works which have drawn on the *Kefukigusa*, see Asao (1961), Wakita (1963), and Nakabe (1967).
2. In general, Kaga Domain relied upon Osaka's ships to transport its rice to Osaka. In 1691, the ratio of Osaka ships to local ships used for this purpose was seven to three. See Wakabayashi (1957: 37).

6

The Finances of the Tokugawa Shogunate

YÛJIRÔ ÔGUCHI

1. Introduction

The history of the financial policies of the Tokugawa shogunate begins first with the household accounting of the Tokugawa family of the Warring States period, when they were just one of a number of warlords (*daimyô*), and proceeds to the point when household accounts became the treasury (*kanjôkata*) of the ruling shogunal family which, as the government (*kôgi*), financed the expenses of the state. Based on these considerations, we may point to the following three as the particular characteristics of shogunal finances.

Let us begin with those dimensions where the character of a warlord's household accounts remained. In the basic structure of the shogunate's finances, annual revenue was primarily acquired from the annual rice tax collected from the villages under direct Tokugawa control. Annual expenditures were divided into three areas: (1) rice stipends (*hôrokumai* and *fuchimai*) provided to the bannermen (*hatamoto*) and vassals (*gokenin*) who were the family's direct vassals; (2) expenses for Edo castle, which was a Tokugawa family asset; (3) expenses for the various government offices which carried out the business of the state.

Second, once the Tokugawa family took control of the realm, its direct holdings expanded quantitatively and qualitatively. As the state, the Tokugawa family also came to deal with other warlords' domains. In terms of the former, the Tokugawa family secured command of the national distribution of commodities and foreign trade through its domainal control of the three main cities of Edo, Osaka, and Kyoto and the port of Nagasaki. It is also significant that it had a monopoly on the right to mint currency and that it possessed the major mines, guaranteeing a supply of the raw materials for minting coins. In terms of the latter, the services (*fushin'yaku*) provided to the shogun by the warlords came to have a huge financial significance.

Third, in managing its budget, the Tokugawa shogunate adopted a basic policy of budgetary balance (*zaisei kinkô shugi*), taking seriously a balance between income and expenses and following the principle of "measure one's income and then make payments" (from the Confucian text *Record of Rites*). The laws of 1634 listed one of the duties of the senior councilor (*rôjû*) as "overseeing the collection of gold and silver and managing its general expenditure." Therefore, at least around this time, it appears that a system was in place for proposing plans for expenditures that might simply be called a kind of budget system.

Taking the essential features of the shogunate's finances along these lines, I will examine in this chapter the structure of public finances from the eighteenth century to the early nineteenth century (prior to the opening of the ports). In particular, using account books surviving from 1730 and 1843, I will illuminate the special characteristics of the financial structure as it related to the various policies of the famous shogunal reforms of the Kyôhô and Tempô eras. I will also consider the changes and the problems of public finance during this period.

State finances are endowed with the function of redistributing social wealth. From that perspective, I would also like to pay attention to the following points. One issue has to do with how the warlord class would absorb the wealth (surplus) that had formed and accumulated with the development of agricultural productive power from the eighteenth century. Likewise, how would the warlord class mediate (or not mediate) the production relations and distribution systems that had formed in relation to that wealth? I will explore these issues through an examination of the structure of income and expenditure, and financial policy.

Next, I would like to look at how the shogunate attempted to absorb the wealth of the domains. Originally, the shogun required military service (*gun'yaku*) from the warlords in time of war. In peacetime, this military service was converted to a form of service known as *fushin'yaku*, directed toward the construction of the city of Edo and the shogun's castle. However, from the eighteenth century, a method was conceived whereby the portion of expenses that had come from shogunal income would henceforth be born by the people of other warlords' and vassals' domains. On the other hand, we also see cases where the shogunate provided aid to particular domains that had fallen into a state of poverty. Thus, I would like to examine a number of problems that arose from the absorption within the shogunal budget of the lordship of daimyo that had previously been seen as outside affairs.

There has been a tendency to lump together shogunal and domainal finances and treat them as a set; that is, as "lord finances." But this chapter will treat these two as different in essential points. There is no space here to sufficiently examine domainal finances, but when it is necessary, I hope to compare the two and make clear their differences.

2. The Accounts Structure in 1730 and the Kyôhô Reforms

The *Osame-harai kanjôchô* (The Income and Expense Account Book, 1730), which has survived in the family of the Kyôhô-era senior councilor (*rôjû*), Matsudaira Nobutoki, is the only remaining record that tells of the accounts of shogunal finances from the early eighteenth century (Ôno 1971: 42–64). I would like to use this account book to take a concrete look at the particularities of shogunal finances (Ôguchi 1969: 15–75).

Since the form of tax submissions at the time was divided into rice submissions and gold submissions, shogunal budgets were also divided into rice and cash (gold and silver) portions. According to Table 6.1, the rice portion showed a total income of 854,000 *koku*, which contained a breakdown of 500,000 *koku* of annual rice taxes (*nengu*, collected the year before) and 281,000 *koku* of purchased rice. The purchased rice was a shogunal policy adopted that year in response to the decline in the price of rice. In normal years, the annual rice tax occupied close to 90 per cent of the rice income. Expenditures totaled 592,000 *koku*, which included a breakdown of 312,000 *koku* for various forms of rice stipends (*kirimai, yakuryô, gôrikimai*, and so on) for bannermen and vassals, and 203,000 *koku* of sold rice. Thus, over half of the rice collected as rice tax from Tokugawa domain villages went to support the bannermen and vassals.

What about the cash portion of the budget? First, as I stated above, the basic structure of domainal finances was that annual taxes were collected from villages in the domain and these were then used to pay stipends to

Table 6.1. Rice accounts in the shogunal finances for 1730

Item	Kokudaka	Percentage
Income		
Tax rice	500,019	58.5
Agemai	72,661	8.5
Other rice submissions	234	0.0
Purchased rice	281,326	32.9
Total	854,240	100.0
Expences		
Stipends	151,264	25.5
Wages	161,077	27.1
Household expenses	11,277	1.9
Bureaus	12,933	2.2
Local officials	8,356	1.4
Sell off	203,323	34.2
Others	44,768	7.6
Total	592,998	100.0

Table 6.2. Monetary accounts in the shogunal finances for 1730

Item	(1,000 *ryô*)	percentage
Income		
Annual tax (gold)	509.0	63.7
Kuniyaku	24.9	3.1
Kofushin	26.9	3.4
Yakusho Osame	55.0	6.9
Rice sales	112.9	14.1
Agemai	29.0	3.6
Loan repayments	20.8	2.6
Others	9.8	1.2
Reminting profits	10.4	1.3
Total	798.8	100.0
Expences		
Stipends	297.3	40.7
Household expenses	60.4	8.3
Administrative costs	149.5	20.4
Reconstruction/repair	68.5	9.4
Purchased rice	103.5	14.2
Aid	12.1	1.7
Loans	34.9	4.8
Others	5.2	0.7
Total	731.2	100.0

direct retainers, cover the private expenses of the lord, and cover administrative costs. Looking at Table 6.2 on this basis, tax income was 509,000 *ryô* and stipends, private expenses, and administrative costs were nearly equal, at a total of 506,000 *ryô*. Taken together, annual expenses maintained a high ratio of three to two in relation to income. Thus, the shogunal budget in this period still retained a deeply traditional character. Let us look next at the main expense items.

Local officials throughout the country in the villages under their jurisdiction, where its quality was ascertained, first inspected annual tax rice. The total value was then submitted in grain and cash (gold and silver). In 1730, the territory that composed the shogunate's domains was spread throughout the country and was divided between territory directly controlled by shogunal officials and territory whose administration was entrusted to fourteen warlords. The total value of these lands, expressed in terms of rice productivity, was 4,446,000 *koku*. The taxes collected that year included 701,000 *koku* of rice, 337,000 *ryô* of gold, and 10,000 *kan* of silver. A portion of these taxes was returned to the villages where it was produced by the local official (*daikan*) in the form of waterway construction costs, tax transport costs, and loan to the village (*fûjiki tanekashi haishakukin*). The remainder was transported

Table 6.3. The numbers of daimyo and bannermen and their *kokudaka*

	Persons	*Kokudaka*
Daimyo	264	17,550,100
Bannermen (fief-holding)	2,670	2,637,530
Bannermen (with stipends and wages)	19,839	557,780
Official salaries	1,058	54,835
Nijo, Osaka, and Suruga posts	Unfixed	75,700
Various kinds of rice		13,350

Source: Ôkurashô (1924, Vol. 9).

to the shogunate's warehouses in Edo by ship or horseback at the responsibility of the villagers themselves. A portion of these shipped taxes was then sent to shogunal rice warehouses in Osaka, Nijô (in Kyoto), Ôtsu, Sumpu, and Kôfu.

The largest item among that year's expenditures was the payment of stipends to house vassals. Table 6.3 shows the composition of the vassals of the shogun in 1722. Among these vassals were some lords with their own domains and upper and middle-level bannermen who ran their households on taxes they drew from fiefs they had been granted by the Shogun. These people may therefore be considered as residing outside the finances of the shogunate. Those within the finances of the shogunate included the lower level bannermen and house vassals who received periodic stipends (*kirimai*) and rations (*fuchimai*) from the shogunate's warehouses. These groups received 40 per cent of the value of their fiefs, with payments in rice or gold received in spring, summer, and winter at a ratio of 1:2. The rate at which they were paid, and the exchange rate, known as the "posted price" (*harigami nedan*), used were calculated by the treasury of the shogunate upon consideration of the market price for rice and the amount of rice in shogunal warehouses. Salaries for warriors who held government office were paid with an additional hereditary stipend (*karoku*). Rations were the method used to pay the lowest level house vassals and were calculated in per person units (at a proportion of five *gô* of rice per day, totaling one *koku* and eight *to* per year). Payments known as *gôrikimai* and *gôrikikin* were also made to the officials at the shogunate's warehouses in Osaka, Nijô, and elsewhere. The proportion of these payments to vassals out of the shogunate's total expenses was high. They also increased over time. Many domains were unable to keep up with these payments and so resorted to cuts in payments, known as fief reductions (*genchi*) and fief loans (*shakuchi*), over an extended period of time. The shogunate was able to avoid taking such measures until the end of its rule.

"Interior expenses" referred to the private expenses of the shogun's family within Edo castle, including the daily expenses of the shogun, his wife, concubines, and children. This portion of the shogunate's expenses was deeply imbued with the flavor of family expenses.

Administrative expenses included payments to offices that managed the daily reproduction of life within Edo castle, such as the kitchen office, the construction office, and the clothes office. They also included payments to state administration office, such as the city hall of Edo and the treasury. Finally, expenses related to regional administration, such as payments to local offices (*daikanjo*) and expenses related to land reclamation, came under this category.

The Accounts Book from 1730 allows us to see the details above as constituting the basic characteristics of the shogunate's finances. Shogun Tokugawa Yoshimune had earlier led a reform of the shogunate in which there had been several important reforms attempted in the area of finances. Let us now turn to a brief examination of the value and results of his reforms.

Taking the opportunity of the previous year's worsening financial condition due to crop failures from poor weather, the shogunate in the fifth month of 1722 asked its various offices to reduce costs, warned the bannermen to prepare for cuts in their periodic stipends, and set out on a radical reform program.

Looking toward a long-term reform, the shogunate explored avenues for increasing tax revenues. The first step was to expand the territory of the shogunal domains through land reclamation. In the eighth month of the year, the shogunate posted an edict board by the side of Nihombashi in Edo encouraging urban merchants to invest their capital in the development of new arable land. The following month the shogunate revealed its aggressive desire for land development by declaring that the shogunate possessed rights over all new fields situated along the border of Tokugawa and other lords' lands.

The second step was to institute the fixed tax system (*jômensei*). Earlier, in 1718, the finance magistrate had informed the local officials of Musashi Province to begin preparations for instituting a fixed tax over a period of several years. There were debates within the shogunal treasury at the time over whether or not a fixed tax system was desirable, so a decision had been made to experiment with the system in a limited region. But in 1722, when there had not as yet been sufficient time to judge the results, the shogunate ordered its execution over a wide area (Furushima 1978: 333). In areas where the capacity of agricultural production had stabilized, the adoption of the fixed tax system assured the receipt of a steady volume of rice each year, not taking into account its quality. When the fixed tax was up for review at the end of its term, there was the expectation that the tax volume would increase. Peasants, on the other hand, saw the system as a method that should be welcomed for its linkage of increased productivity with their own accumulation.

These agricultural reforms did contribute to the long-term increase of revenue. But it took years for that result to be realized and thus was ineffective in resolving the financial difficulties of the moment. Based on discussions with the lords of Mito and Owari, Shogun Yoshimune hit upon a bright idea to secure revenues for the present: the *agemai* system. According to this system, the lords of the land were ordered to submit rice to the shogunate's storehouses at a rate of one hundred *koku* for every 10,000 *koku* of estimated value of their domains. In exchange, the lords were allowed to shorten their alternate attendance stays in Edo from one year to half a year. According to the Confucian scholar, Muro Kyûso, who was questioned about the financial problems of the time, a plan to secure revenue through coinage reminting profits was rejected due to the experience of the failure of the previous Shogun Tsunayoshi's inflationary Genroku coins. A plan to rely on loans from urban merchants was also rejected due to Yoshimune's personal opposition. The *agemai* system was approved under these conditions. A 1730 shogunal Accounts Book records that revenue for that year from the *agemai* system amounted to 72,000 *koku* of rice and 29,000 *ryô* of gold. When we compare this to the figures for stipends and official salaries for that same year, we see that the revenue of *agemai* rice amounted to 48 per cent of the stipend rice while *agemai* gold came to 12 per cent of the stipend gold. Thus, the *agemai* system turned out to be a reform that brought immediate results to a financial situation in which the shogunate faced difficulties with its stipend payments.

3. The Limits of Rice Tax Collection and the Taxation of Commerce and Industry

In this section, we will be examining the changes in tax collection volumes. We will check the results of the tax increase policies beginning with the Kyôhô reforms and we will consider the significance of the fact that these increases eventually hit a ceiling. We will also examine how, beginning with the Tanuma era, there was a shift away from increasing annual taxes and toward the development of a system for collecting "offerings" (*myôgakin*) out of the processes of commodity production and distribution.

The particular characteristics of the process of levying rice taxes in the Edo period were that (1) they were based on an estimated yield (*kokudaka*) that had been determined in a land survey; (2) they were based on the results of an annual evaluation of the quality of the harvest; (3) they were levied on the village unit (the *murauke-sei*, or village contract system); and

Table 6.4. Tax rates in shogunal territory (total annual levies/total estimated yield), 1716–88

Year	Rates	Year	Rates	Year	Rates
1716	34.0	1741	34.2	1766	35.1
1717	33.3	1742	30.8	1767	36.4
1718	35.5	1743	35.4	1768	35.3
1719	34.4	1744	38.9	1769	36.4
1720	34.4	1745	36.2	1770	33.6
1721	32.1	1746	38.1	1771	30.9
1722	35.0	1747	35.1	1772	34.9
1723	31.7	1748	36.0	1773	34.4
1724	34.8	1749	38.0	1774	34.9
1725	33.6	1750	38.6	1775	34.7
1726	34.8	1751	38.8	1776	35.8
1727	36.7	1752	38.9	1777	35.4
1728	33.2	1753	38.1	1778	34.7
1729	36.2	1754	37.4	1779	34.9
1730	34.6	1755	37.2	1780	32.6
1731	30.1	1756	37.4	1781	33.7
1732	30.8	1757	35.1	1782	33.7
1733	32.2	1758	37.3	1783	28.0
1734	29.6	1759	38.0	1784	34.2
1735	32.2	1760	37.8	1785	32.4
1736	29.2	1761	37.6	1786	24.9
1737	36.6	1762	37.6	1787	33.1
1738	33.5	1763	37.6	1788	32.7
1739	36.4	1764	37.4		
1740	32.6	1765	36.3		

Source: Seisai zakki.

(4) they were apportioned within the village on the principle of the ratio of yield held by each family in the village.

Table 6.4 shows the changes in the tax rate (the total annual tax levy/the total estimated yield of the shogunate's domains) for the villages under the direct control of the shogunate. As the table shows, the tax rate remained at the 33–34 per cent level for a while from the 1710s. It then shot up suddenly to 38 per cent and then maintained an average of 37 per cent for the next twenty-two years. These tax increases were usually not the result of a land survey (the negation of Item 1 above), but the result of an examination of the actual harvest (*arige kemihô*). The reform of the tax system to respond to developments in agricultural productivity succeeded in raising the amount of annual tax that was collected. The saying attributed to the finance magistrate who adopted the harvest investigations, Kan'o Haruhide, "peasants are like sesame seeds; the more you squeeze them, the more they produce," represents the agricultural policy perspective of the time (Mori 1993: 135–60).

But the high tax rate did not continue for long. It began to decline from the 1760s and continued to decline into the crop failures of the 1780s. It remained stuck at the 33–34 per cent level until the 1830s, the period for which we have records. Why was it that a high tax rate could not be maintained despite the intentions of the shogunate? It appears that changes in village structure made the tax collection system obsolete. With the penetration of a cash economy into the villages, a division opened up in the villages between wealthy landlords and a majority of small-scale peasants. To continue withdrawing taxes through a system in which taxes were apportioned uniformly on the basis of the estimated yield each family possessed meant that villages faced the danger of small peasants being unable to bear up under a heavy tax burden (thus reaching an impasse in Item 4 above). Increasing taxes meant acquiring the wealth of rich peasants. But since the ruling class depended heavily on the wealthy farmers to maintain village order in the midst of these changes, there was no choice but to continue the old system that had favored them.

It was also difficult to absorb the new surpluses formed with the development of the village handicraft industry simply by increasing the main rice taxes. That is why the system of offerings was introduced. From the early Edo period, a tax known as *komononari* was levied on villages against profits from the use of rivers and forests. But new taxes were levied on village production of handicraft goods and transport from the eighteenth century. These taxes were of two types: taxes levied on the village unit and levies born by merchants.

At the end of the eighteenth century the treasurer of the shogunate ordered the local officials of shogunal domains to undertake investigations of *saké*, soy sauce, and vinegar brewing, oil pressing, waterwheel operations, and riverbank sales of firewood for levying "offerings" taxes. In order to force payments of "offerings" on *saké* brewing and waterwheels in every village, the shogunate had to grasp the details of village handicraft production. But the actual revenue received was insubstantial. For example, offerings collected by the local officials in Suruga and Shinnanô were only 0.1 per cent of the annual tax totals. There were grave limitations on the ability to tax village handicraft production through the village contract system in the same way that dry field crops were taxed.

Let us examine the cases where merchants were the vehicles for the collection of offerings. In 1770, the silkworm merchants of Kôzuke and Shimotsuke set up quality check stations in the Shindatsu region of Mutsu Province. Their plan to pay 180 *ryô* in offerings to the shogunate in return for the right to charge one silver *bu* for each silkworm egg card checked was approved by the shogunate. At first, the producers saw the merit in having their egg cards given an official seal of approval. But sales eventually declined due to the high prices of the seals. In 1783, the system was abolished on appeal from local producers (Shôji 1958: 43–73). Later, there were requests to organize a cotton chartered trade association in Settsu-Kawachi in return for an annual fee of 150 *ryô* paid to the town magistrate of Osaka (Yagi 1962: 233–5; Nakai 1971: 118–24), and a request to establish a textile–silver inspection post (*aratame-dokoro*) where inspection fees could be collected on silk thread and silk cloth produced in Kôzuke and Musashi (Hayashi 1967: 149). But neither of these plans was realized due to intense opposition from locals. A kind of tax contracting system was introduced during the Tanuma era (1769–86) in which particular merchants were authorized to collect such inspection fees on the distribution of special products in exchange for payment of a portion of those fees to the shogunate as "offerings." But all of these ended in failure due to the opposition of local producers.

Whether through a village contract method or a merchant contract method, the shogunate did not succeed in sufficiently capturing the results of village handicraft production. The wealth produced by handicraft production and distribution in the villages remained in the hands of wealthy peasants in the countryside.

4. Investment Capital in the Villages: Townsmen's Capital and Public Loans

What kind of funding efforts were made in the villages that were the largest base of shogunal financial income? In this section, we will first examine capital-investment related to land reclamation aiming at expanding productivity. Following that, we will examine the provision of aid for the poor who were suffering from famines and such.

I discussed earlier the shogunate's promotion of new land reclamation as a link in the Kyôhô reform policy of increasing tax revenues. The first such projects were the reclamations of grasslands in Musashino Shinden and Shimôsa Tôgane. These were called "official-directed reclamations" (*daikan mitate shinden*) because local officials chose the land to be developed and then had the peasants perform the labor. The Edo town magistrate Ôoka Tadasuke specially assembled the team that carried this out (Ôtomo 1978: 2–3). The new fields of Musashino were grasslands that were divided among the peasants in 1724 that turned out to be not so easy to reclaim at first. In 1728, a small amount of money was provided to the peasants who had moved to the area, under the labels "housebuilding funds" and "farm tool costs." Both of these were recorded as one item in the 1730 Accounts Book as "housebuilding funds for new fields in Musashino and Shimôsa: 2,445 *ryô*." But, in fact, it took until the 1740s, about twenty years after reclamation began, for the reclaimed land to become stable and begin to link up to increased tax revenue. In the case of the Shimôsa Tôgane land reclamation, the project was contracted to officials under the town magistrate and, like the Musashino efforts, required the payment of house-building funds to the new residents in 1729. Its main difference from the Musashino project was in the introduction of Edo townsmen's capital. On the opening of the Tsukazaki new fields in Tôgane in 1735, land fees on the scale of 1,500 *ryô* were provided by two merchants of Edo: Iseya Denzaburô and Katokuya Jiroemon. In return, the sale of 240 *chô* of forest and grassland was recognized.

Other large-scale land reclamation projects carried out by the shogunate included the draining of marshlands in Shimôsa Iinuma and Echigo Shiunji. There was no way to make the new residents of these areas or the members of the local villages bear the burden of the costs of construction in these projects, so in many cases, funds from urban merchants were used to pay for development. In 1772, the shogunate issued a new proclamation in order to make the entry of outside funds easier. Until that time, the petitions of local people had taken precedence over the development petitions of urban dwellers. After the shogunate's proclamation, however, preference was given to those petitions that arrived first. This signaled an aggressive intent to use capital from outside the domain.

In the final analysis, did new field reclamation contracted to urban merchants produce economic profits for the townsmen? There are no documents for new field developments contracted out by the shogunate. So we will examine the case of new field development in Gôdo, along the Ise Bay, carried out by Gôdoya Bunzaemon, a merchant under contract to the Owari domain (Kikuchi 1958: 324–7). The new fields of Gôdo had already been drained in 1708, but had since been damaged by high tides. From 1723 Gôdoya invested 5,000 *ryô* to drain the fields. Gôdoya's first estimate was that the cost of draining the fields would be 5,000 *ryô* and that the period of tax relief would be eleven years. At an annual interest rate of 8 per cent, he calculated that he would be able to write off the investment in those eleven years. But, in fact, the amount of rice harvested was lower than anticipated and the price of rice was low, so in the end Gôdoya was unable to amortize his investment in the expected eleven years. He petitioned for an extension of the fields' tax exemption, and overall it took about twenty-nine years to recoup his investment. Once he started paying taxes on the field, the rice left after taxes converted to 200–300 *ryô* per year. With a profit rate stuck at 4–6 per cent on his initial investment of 5,000 *ryô*, he was unable to expect much merit in the land reclamation project. Despite these conditions, the Gôdoya family continued drainage operations along Ise Bay until the end of the shogunate. That they did so may well have been due to the fact that, through their main business as lumber merchants, they possessed a close relationship with the Owari domain and thus received its protection. New land reclamation did not pay as an economic investment. But when viewed as a form of forced loan, the investors anticipated returns for their main businesses and hoped simply to recoup their investments.

Conditions were even worse for merchants when reclamation was undertaken under the aegis of the shogunate. The period of tax exemption was only three years. Taxes, even just a few, had to be paid from the fourth year and the investors could not expect protection from the shogunate. For example, in the case of the draining of the Inba marsh in Shimôsa, the investors went bankrupt in the middle of the project, but received no compensation from the shogunate whatsoever.

Thus, new field development was not yet an economically secure endeavor, but retained a deeply speculative side. Nevertheless, the shogunate aggressively sought to introduce outside funds to the task. We may therefore view the investment of urban merchant funds in agriculture as having been important.

Let us now turn to an examination of loans from the shogunate to agricultural villages. In our 1730 Accounts Book, we have an entry for loans for aid to villages that had suffered disasters under the item of "2963 *ryô* for *fujiki tanekashi haishaku*." At a stage when general financial organizations were still immature, loans of shogunal funds held great significance. Many of these loans were made to aid pioneering families as they opened new fields. For example, Uesaka, the official who opened the new fields in Musashino, received a zero interest loan of 1300 *ryô* simply as a land reclamation fee. Uesaka used this as principal in loans to powerful peasants and then used their interest payments to provide starting funds for new field peasants (Ôtomo 1978: 21). By using a mediatory when making loans, the lender could avoid taking a loss on the loan. This method was thereafter frequently used in loans of public funds.

However, there were many cases in which borrowers had trouble paying back these loans. In 1734, the shogunate diminished the loan framework by deciding not to permit any more loans, barring due consideration for "special disasters," such as major crop failures or loss of housing and property due to fire. Moreover, in 1775, the shogunate recognized that the interest on official loans was causing many villages to go bankrupt, so it ordered that no more loans be approved to villages in shogunal domains. After that, the main recipients of shogunal loans were limited to domainal lords and bannermen. When bannermen borrowed public funds from the shogunate, they put up the future taxes of the villages in their fiefs as collateral. There were many cases in which the leaders of the village signed loan agreements. Bannermen suffering from

straitened family circumstances would borrow money from the shogunate's public funds to meet temporary needs, thereby forcing the peasants
in their fiefs to struggle for a long time to repay the debt. This led to the
financial ruin of many villages.

In the middle of the eighteenth century, villages in shogunal domains
lost access to "benevolent loans" even as the shogunate strengthened its
appropriation of taxes and as it significantly decreased its investment of
capital in the villages. High interest loans from elsewhere, nominally for
temples and shrines, made up for this lost capital. But they also eroded
the villages, which wound up tremendously weakened. The disasters of
the 1780s (the Tenmei Famine) hit in the middle of these conditions,
delivering a terrible blow to villages. The shogunal reforms begun by
Matsudaira Sadanobu placed an emphasis on the restoration of villages
that were exhausted by these disasters. This was done through policies
that supported the financial side of villages, such as by mitigating the
conditions of emergency loans (*fujiki tanekashi*), or by extending the repayment periods of existing loans, or even extending new loans. In short, the
shogunate took measures to aggressively extend aid to villages that had,
until then, been left alone. In 1817, the shogunate unified the public
loans offices that had been run by local officials in every district into
the Bakurochô Loan Bureau. At the same time, the shogunate obtained
interest on loans to villages in private domains and then turned those
interest payments around to use in its own villages as aid funds (Takeuchi
1965: 214–24).

5. Relations with Daimyo Domains

The finances of the shogunate had been based from the start on the annual
taxes drawn from the villages directly under its rule. As the entire country
came under its rule, however, it began to develop policies that took the
lord's domains into view. How the shogunate's finances came to encompass the warlords' domains is the subject of this section. From that
perspective, the adoption of the *agemai* system, in which the alternate
attendance requirements were cut in half in exchange for the submission
of rice from the lords to the shogunate, was an epoch-making decision. For
the lords to submit rice to the shogun in the place of military service meant
that the lords' domains were woven into the shogunate's financial
resources. Of course, the alleviation of the attendance–service system was
subjected to strong criticism within the shogunate's cabinet. And when the
financial circumstances of the shogunate recovered in 1730, the alternate
attendance system was reinstated and the *agemai* system was terminated.

In addition to the *agemai* levies, the shogunate also collected service
fees (*kuniyakukin*) from the lords' domains. These fees were meant for

the limited purpose of river way construction and they were levied in units of provinces, which exceeded the districts controlled by most lords (Kasaya 1976). When repairs were made to the Daiya and Takegahana rivers in Nikkô in 1720, the shogunate bore the cost of only 20 per cent of the repairs. The remaining 80 per cent was levied on the villages throughout Shimotsuke province at a rate of the yield. This method had also been used in distant shogunal domains, such as in the Kinai and Mino, at the beginning of the Tokugawa period. But until the construction in 1720, it was rare that the *kuniyaku* method had been introduced in cases in Kanto where such operations were carried out by the shogunate. In 1722, in order to meet the increased costs of river repair work, the shogunate decided to regularize the *kuniyaku* system. In the following year, the shogunate decreased its burden in such projects to one-tenth the cost and declared the system valid for the entire country, including all of Kantô and Kinai. Not only did *kuniyaku* construction reduce the costs to the shogunate, it also served as an alternative to the lords' other construction fees (*otetsudai fushin*, as a form of military service to the shogun, the lords contracted other kinds of construction projects). The lords undertook no *otetsudai* construction projects from 1722 to 1730, during the period in which the *agemai* system was in use. So *kuniyaku* construction made up for the loss (Yoshizumi 1968). We know the details of part of the costs of *kuniyaku* construction during this period. These are shown in Table 6.5. According to the table, some tens of thousands of *ryô* in *kuniyaku* fees were passed to villages and peasants in regions related to the projects, regardless of whether they were in shogunal or private domains, at a ratio proportional to the estimated yield of the village. These fees were collected along with the annual taxes.

Kuniyaku fees were applied to the costs of river repair projects throughout the islands for the next ten years, until they were terminated in 1732. The reason given for their termination was that due to the increase in the financial burden of emergency aid and loans the shogunate could no

Table 6.5. *Kuniyaku* for river construction

Year	Region	Total costs	Out of domainal funds (*ryô*)
1720	Shimotsuke (River Daiya and Takegahana)	2,700	0
1724	Kantô, Tôkaido, and Shinano province	46,000	37,000
1729	Kantô and Tôkaidô	49,000	23,000
1730	Kantô and Tôkaidô	10,500	4,600

Source: Ôkurashô (ed.) (1922–25: Vol. 4, 829).

longer bear its 10 per cent share. But the real reason may have been that with the termination of the *agemai* system, the warlords were once again able to undertake their *otetsudai* obligations. Thereafter, major river construction projects were turned over to the *otetsudai* obligations of outsider lords (*tozama daimyô*). For example, eleven domains, including the Chôshû and Okayama domains, were mobilized for the floods of the Tone River in Kanto in 1742. Satsuma domain was given responsibility for irrigation construction in the Nôbi-Wajû region in 1753, which it successfully completed after long efforts and many sacrifices. By 1758, the limitations of making one domain alone responsible for construction projects were revealed by the example of Satsuma domain. So the *kuniyaku* system was revived. Thereafter, *kuniyaku* construction, *otetsudai* construction and shogunal construction were all employed, with the specific method for any given project being determined by the shogunate's treasurer (Ôguchi 1984: 226–8). In that sense, we may say that the lords' private domains continued to be encompassed within the finances of the shogunate. In the nineteenth century, a portion of the costs of transportation and entertainment for the Korean envoys was levied on the provinces along the travel route in the form of *kuniyaku* fees.

Having seen how the shogunate incorporated the lords' domains into its financial resources, we shall now turn to the shogunate's loans as benevolent measures for the lords. In the early Tokugawa period, the lords could not expect benevolent aid from shogunate, even though they had rendered services, such as castle construction, to the Shogun as an expression of their loyalty. The first large-scale benevolent loans were made in the first month of 1657 after the great Meireki fire in Edo. Loans to those lords whose homes had burned were distributed in nine ranks from 100 *kanme* in silver to those lords with income over 10,000 *koku* to 300 *kanme* in silver to those lords with incomes up to 100,000 *koku*. Lords with incomes over 100,000 *koku* were left out of this loan program because it was probably felt that, as lords of a domain, they should make their recovery themselves.

When famine broke out in western Japan in 1732, the shogunate authorized loans to the domains affected. According to the proclamation at the time, those domains unable to collect up to half of their annual taxes would be able to receive loans upon petitioning the treasury. The loans were interest-free and allowed for repayment between two and five years later. A list of the lords receiving these loans includes large-scale domains possessing over 300,000 *koku*, such as Satsuma, Kumamoto, and Hiroshima, regardless of status as outsider or vassal (*fudai*) lord. Instead, the loans were granted for the perspective of aiding victims.

But if we examine the twenty-one loans granted in 1786, in the midst of the Tenmei famine, we find them to be of a very different character from the loans of 1732. Of the twenty-one loans, two were granted to Tokugawa branch lords, one to an outsider and the rest to vassals. Moreover, an examination of the vassal recipients shows them to have been employed in the important posts of the shogunate, such as senior councilor, junior councilor, Kyoto magistrate, Osaka castle manager and so on. The senior councilor Tanuma Okitsugu fell from power, in the year 1786, leaving the political world in turmoil. So the distribution of funds was made with preference given to those who had performed good services for the shogunate. This was clearly different from the principle of preference to disaster relief in 1732.

When Matsudaira Sadanobu's political reforms began the year after Tanuma's fall, the self-serving pattern of loan-making disappeared. Thereafter, the shogunate's loans were concentrated on the three collateral houses (*gosanke*) and the three aristocratic houses (*gosankyô*) as well as those lords related to the descendants of the shogun. In other words, loans were nominally made as household aid. Rather than functioning as public service, shogunal loans came to play the role of prolonging the operation of shogun family household enterprises.

6. The Tempô Reforms and the Structure of Finances in 1843

When we compare the shogunate's Tempô reforms to the Tempô reforms of the big southwest domains, we find similarities in that both got their start in a consciousness of crisis arising from famine, uprisings and riots. But the shogunate's reforms were behind the times and were more reactionary. We will consider the causes of this difference from the perspective of finances. Domainal finances suffered from a condition in which income could not keep pace with the expansion of annual expenditures, and the lords were constantly concerned with savings and developing new financial resources. These were the issues through which domainal reforms were developed. While the shogunate fell into the same financial straits, it took advantage of the fact that it possessed the right to mint coins. From the 1820s, the shogunate earned large profits by reminting large quantities of good coins into poor quality coins, enabling it to keep pace with the expansion of annual expenditures. For that reason, the crisis consciousness of traditionalists such as Tokugawa Nariaki and Mizuno Tadakuni became the leading ideological response in the shogunate's debate over economic policy, taking precedence over mercantilists who were concerned with economic effectivity. In the end, the intent and results of the financial and economic policies of the Tempô reforms, begun in 1841 under Mizuno Tadakuni, were mutually contradictory. In the following discussion, we will look at the particular characteristics of the tax methods, price policies, and shogunate–domainal relations in the midst of this trial and error (Ôguchi 1988*b*: 1099–116).

First, the reform of tax collection methods took the form of the enterprise known as *otorika kaisei* (field tax reform) that was put into practice
in all shogunal lands throughout the country in 1843. The goal of this
reform was to raise taxes by fixing the borders of paddy fields and opening undeveloped land. It may be praised as the first national inspection
of arable land since the beginning of the early modern period. But there
was no sign in the shogunate's reforms of the attempts by many
domains to promote industrial growth and thereby acquire new revenue
through handicraft goods and commodity crops. Even though some
domains and agricultural economists devised policies that took into
account the reality of village divisions, the shogunate's reforms had no
such vision.

Second, in the area of price policy, scholars have focused on the
attempts to force down market prices and the dissolution of the chartered
trade associations. Both of these policies came out of a traditional disdain
for commerce and ignored economic principles. The economic bureaucrats
of the shogunate did not necessarily agree with these policies. For example, the Osaka town magistrate, Abe Shôzô, saw the decline of goods
shipped to Osaka wholesalers as the main cause of the sudden rise of
prices. Abe criticized the domains' trading bureaus and the regional shippers who interfered with the Osaka wholesalers, and proposed a policy of
centralizing the national circulation of goods through the Osaka wholesaler associations. But this idea was snuffed out by the shogunate's order
to dissolve the chartered trade associations. Moreover, since the dissolution stripped the wholesalers of their function, the previous distribution
mechanisms suffered a mortal blow and the shogunate was decisively
delayed from taking control of the national market.

Third, this period saw the development of a new relationship between
the shogunate and the lords of the various domains. The shogunate's 1811
plan to switch the lords of Kawagoe, Tsuruoka, and Nagaoka domains
ended in failure due to Tsuruoka's petition in opposition. The shogunate's
attempt in 1843 to consolidate its lands in an order to a number of lords
to turn their fiefs over to the shogunate also failed due to the opposition
of affected lords. The shogun originally had the authority to freely dispose of other lords' domains. But the feelings of unity between lord and
domain that had grown over long years of domainal rule made it difficult
to switch domains around. These failures brought an end to the rule of
Mizuno Tadakuni. The failures also forecast the budding of a new relationship between the shogunate and the lords that could not be fully
established under the original order.

The shogunate's political reforms quietened down a bit when Mizuno
Tadakuni retired due to the failure of his 1843 fief consolidation order.
Mizuno's successor, Doi Toshitsura, submitted a financial reform plan at
the end of 1843. After firing many of the economic bureaucrats of the

Table 6.6. Rice accounts in the shogunal finances for 1844

Item	*Kokudaka*	Percentage
Income		
Tax rice	595,045	97.1
Other rice submissions	11,072	1.8
Purchased rice	7,416	1.2
Total	613,535	100.0
Expences		
Stipends	304,192	46.4
Wages	229,863	35.1
Household expenses	6,964	1.1
Bureaus	27,108	4.1
Local officials	41,233	6.3
Sell off	19,881	3.0
Others	26,125	4.0
Total	655,371	100.0

reform group, Doi followed the ultra-retrenchment line of Torii Yôzô, a former shogunate inspector and town magistrate, and sought to cut expenses all the way back to the levels of the 1790–1810 era. I have used the Accounts Book from this reform period, 1843–44, available for study today, to compose Tables 6.6 and 6.7. We will now investigate the character of late Tokugawa finances through a comparison of the 1843–44 Accounts Book with the 1730 Accounts Book we examined above (Ôguchi 1969: 27–47).

First, we see in Table 6.6 that the payment of rice stipends to vassals expanded significantly. We also see that it was somehow paid for with an increase in tax rice. In Table 6.7, we see that the shogunate had already reached the point where gold stipend payments were not met by tax gold receipts. Despite repeated orders to be frugal, the basic expenses (stipends, household expenses, and administrative costs) in 1843 had expanded by 60 per cent over the same costs in 1730. A strict order to reduce expenses in 1843 stipulated a reduction of household expenses by 33 per cent and of bureaucratic costs by 50 per cent. But the following year, those costs had only been reduced by 3 and 14 per cent, respectively. Vassals' stipends had already been subject to major reductions in the domains. But the shogunate became concerned with protecting the lifestyles of its house vassals (*gokenin*), so there was no plan for the reduction of fiefs. Instead, the shogunate provided several tens of thousands of *ryô* to loan institutions for bannermen and vassals in 1843, thus increasing its financial burden. Furthermore, in an attempt to strengthen the authority of the shogun in connection to these reforms, the shogunate planned the first shogunal visit to Nikkô in decades (the trip involved the

Table 6.7. Monetary accounts in the shogunal finances of 1843–44

Item	1,000 *ryô* (percentage)	
	1843	1844
Income		
Annual tax	603.7 (39.1)	646.8 (25.1)
Kuniyaku	20.2 (1.3)	7.2 (0.3)
Kofushin	22.4 (1.5)	23.3 (0.9)
Yakusho osame	45.9 (3.0)	71.3 (2.8)
Rice sales	45.7 (3.0)	32.1 (1.2)
Forced loans	158.0 (10.2)	706.4 (27.4)
Loan repayments	208.8 (13.5)	165.7 (6.4)
Others	43.8 (2.8)	66.3 (2.6)
Reminting profits	394.4 (25.6)	856.4 (33.3)
Total	1,543.0 (100.0)	2,575.5 (100.0)
Expenses		
Stipends/salaries	405.0 (28.0)	428.3 (20.1)
Households	91.9 (6.4)	89.0 (4.2)
Bureaus	337.0 (23.3)	288.8 (13.6)
Reconstruction/repair	73.0 (5.1)	68.0 (3.2)
Purchased rice	96.8 (6.7)	95.0 (4.5)
Aid	146.5 (10.1)	183.7 (8.6)
Loans	127.7 (8.8)	80.8 (3.8)
Nikko costs	101.0 (7.0)	2.0 (0.1)
Main keep reconstruction		836.1 (39.3)
Others	66.5 (4.6)	57.5 (2.7)
Total	1445.4 (100.0)	2129.1 (100.0)

formation of a procession of lords accompanying the twelfth shogun, Ieyoshi, to report his accession to the post of shogun at the mausoleum of Tokugawa Ieyasu). The shogunate spent 100,000 *ryô* in this political demonstration.

Whenever there had been this kind of expansion of costs, the shogunate had covered the costs with the profits from a debasement of the currency. However, according to traditional monetary theory, the debasement of the quality of coins was not desirable. Some as a major cause of the rise in prices particularly criticized this tendency. Within the shogunal cabinet, Torii Yôzô and his supporters pushed for an end to remintings. The treasurer had no choice but to accede to their pressure and terminate the Bunsei reminting of 1843. But from the treasurer's perspective, a certain amount of funds was necessary to carry out reforms. So in place of reminting profits, the treasury determined to demand large-scale forced loans from wealthy Osaka merchants. After long negotiations, the shogunate received 1.1 million *ryô* at an annual interest rate of 12.5 per cent over twenty years. This introduction of Osaka merchant funds into the shogunate's treasury was terribly significant.

In the midst of this financial retrenchment, the main keep of Edo castle burned down in the fifth month of 1844. The shogunate struggled to respond to this development, but the Doi cabinet decided to make the reconstruction of the main keep its top priority. In doing so, the Doi cabinet decided to rely on construction offerings from the lords and bannermen to pay the costs. But the lords were opposed to this heavy burden and the shogunate was forced to extend the period for submitting the offerings and refine the reconstruction plans. Above all, it was difficult to unilaterally impose on the lords for construction costs. In the end, the only other source of funds was in the profits available from a reminting. So the reminting that had been terminated just ten months earlier was revived. Table 6.7 shows shogunal finances being supported by the earnings from reminting in 1843 and 1844. But it was the above conditions that were hidden behind this.

Finally, we may take the following points as characteristic of the shogunate's finances in the 1840s. First, even though the basic structure of tax revenues and annual expenditures—in stipends, Tokugawa household expenses and administrative costs—was barely maintained through contracting budgets, the total scale of the shogunate's finances was two to three times as large as those of the 1720s, at a level of 1.5–2.0 million *ryô*. Second, the bloating of the budget—through aid to bannermen and vassal lords, through costs of an official trip to Nikkô and through costs for the reconstruction of the main keep of Edo castle—was due to temporary expenditures adopted for political reasons related to the overall shogunal reforms. Third, revenue needed to balance the budget was acquired through such temporary means as reminting profits; taxes levied on lords and forced loans from merchants.

The expansion of the scale of the budget provided the shogunate with the ability to withstand increased costs for the late Tokugawa maritime defense policies. We know the outline of maritime costs in shogunal finances in the 1850s. These costs included such temporary expenditures as the construction of batteries, cannons, and other weapons, and the construction of ships. Even these costs were no more than around 2 million *ryô*. Revenues were somehow obtained through taxes on lords and merchants and through reminting profits. The Abe cabinet's passive response to these problems, represented by its attempt to pass the costs of maritime defense along to the various lords, was born of financial considerations. In other words, the shogunate was able to respond to conditions around the time of the opening of the ports because of measures it had taken with regard to the scale of its budgets in the 1840s.

However, with the beginning of trade with various foreign countries in the 1860s and the increasing domestic political chaos, the shogunate was faced with a series of huge expenses—in the purchase of ships from abroad, in the payment of indemnities to foreign powers and in the trips to and from Kyoto undertaken by the shogun. In addition, with the new economic conditions arising from such factors as the massive influx of Mexican silver dollars, the shogunate's finances underwent a tremendous change. An examination of these changes will have to await another examination (Ôguchi 1981: 31–62, 1988*a*: 159–80).

Translated by Alan S. Christy.

7

Demography and Living Standards

AKIRA HAYAMI AND HIROSHI KITÔ

1. Population and Society

In order to fully grasp the conditions of a society or country, it is important to examine the scale, structure, and trends of its population. Through such analyses of the behavior and organization of individual men and women, married couples, and households, we can arrive at a more accurate understanding of the lives of ordinary people than if we were to look only at institutional and governing structures.

In a narrow sense, a population is defined as the number of people in a given society. Yet humans are characterized by the primary attributes of sex and age, as well as by the secondary attributes of position in family and household, occupation, religion, social status, class, nationality, ethnicity, and physical condition. In addition to such static attributes, humans possess a dynamic dimension. All people must experience birth and death, and the majority of adult men and women marry, build a family, has children, and move around. Our existence is the result of these activities for tens of thousands of generations, since the beginning of humankind.

Demography as an area of research encompasses this broad range of human attributes in order to gain a comprehensive understanding of human groupings, differing slightly in terms of focus from the narrower field known as population studies. Maintaining a strict distinction between these two approaches may in actuality is difficult and not even necessary, but we want to make it clear at the outset that in this chapter we have approached the problem of population from a demographic perspective.

The relationship a population has with its surrounding environment is one of mutual influence. Particularly in situations where there is an additional feedback effect, this relationship cannot be schematized in a simple manner. The ways in which this influence occurs may even be reversed depending on the era and region. T. Robert Malthus hypothesized that a population grows in a geometric series, but resources only increase arithmetically, so over time the balance between resources and population will be destroyed, with catastrophic results. This view has been held as generally valid for preindustrial societies. However, a new formulation has gained force in the postwar period—that of Ester Boserup, who argued that moderate population growth stimulates an increase in production, promoting technological advances and acting as an important catalyst for human development (Boserup 1965).

No final conclusion has been reached with regard to which of these completely opposed views on population growth is correct. While both may be valid under certain conditions, we cannot recognize either as universal. Through the application of modern scientific technology, particularly in the fields of medicine and public health, declining mortality rates have led to a population explosion in developing countries. This rapid growth has constituted a serious obstacle to economic progress, as predicted by Malthus, and spawned a host of other social problems. On the other hand, advanced industrialized nations are currently confronted with problems related to their transformation into aging societies due to low birth rates. Yet just before the onset of true industrialization, these countries all experienced a population growth that stimulated the expansion of national markets and paved the way for industrialization. Although population growth has not always facilitated industrialization, an increase in population growth may be a prerequisite for the spread of industrialization.

In addition, if we divide the population in terms of residence into an urban sector and a rural sector, generally speaking, the former is involved in commerce and industry, governmental administration, and education, while the latter is exclusively devoted to agricultural production. Accordingly, if we imagine a closed society, a high proportion of urban dwellers would seem to indicate a high level of agricultural productivity able to provide the surplus necessary to support a nonagricultural population. However, this scenario presents us with two problems.

The first is the character of the urban population. If an urban population is supported by heavy taxes on the output of agricultural villages together with commercial taxes, both exacted through the coercion of a highly centralized government, even a large urban population would not stimulate the market economy. In this scenario, even if a market economy existed, it would not spread to the surrounding region but would remain confined to the city. However, if an urban metropolis stood at the center of a network of small-to medium-sized cities, the metropolitan and rural areas would be linked by a market economy. Commodities, labor, capital, and information would circulate throughout the network, demonstrating the establishment of a regional market economy.

Second, cities in pre-industrialized societies were not able to defend themselves against illness, famine, war, and natural disasters. When such a crisis occurred, large numbers of residents died or left the city. In other words, urban populations were unstable. Accordingly, even as a market economy developed and the proportion of the urban population increased, crises would give rise to large numbers of victims and the population of the region, including the city, would not climb. This kind of decline—seen in pre-industrial Europe—has been called a negative feedback function or the "urban graveyard effect" in regional economic development and population trends. In the case of Tokugawa Japan, this phenomenon has been called the "urban ant lion sand trap" (*toshi ari jigoku setsu*), in reference to the insect known as an ant lion, which lies hidden in a pit it has dug in the sand, which functions as a trap to snare its prey (regarding the situation of Europe, see Wrigley 1969). However, in recent years, it has become clear that theories solely based on mortality rates are unable to explain the low reproduction rates within urban populations in the preindustrial era. In both Japan and Europe, many scholars have come to recognize the need to broaden their outlook by examining urban marriage and family organization, ratios of men to women, and rates of movement in and out of cities (Saitô 1989b: 239–62).

Taking the long view, there is no question that the population has grown overall. However, such growth has not necessarily progressed in a straight line or even a two-dimensional curve. At times, the population has stagnated, declined, or sharply risen over a sustained period. Population trends marked by such changes have simultaneously influenced and been influenced by surrounding conditions. Moreover, even as one can analyze population trends on a macro level in terms of country or region, one can also pursue a more detailed examination of the actions of towns and villages, households and married couples, and individual men and women, so long as documentary records exist. Such research and analysis will illuminate the everyday behavior of ordinary people, hitherto taken lightly or ignored in Japanese scholarship. New horizons will emerge.

This perspective informs the following examination of population structure and changes during the Tokugawa period.

2. The Population of Tokugawa Japan

2.1. Population growth in the seventeenth century

Following the compilation of the ancient registries of the *ritsuryô* state, there is a gap of approximately 700 years in our surviving records of regional, let alone national, population. However, with the emergence of exclusivist regional sovereignty at the end of the sixteenth century, territorial lords made efforts to ascertain the population figures for their respective regions. The primary purpose was to measure how much labor could be requisitioned within the region. At first, the focus of the surveys was how many "households" could provide compulsory labor, and distinctions were not drawn between households and individuals. On occasion, these population surveys were held concurrently with land surveys, which were also conducted with great energy during this era (Hayami 1958: 1–59). However, the population surveys became independent over time and shifted from counting households to individuals, thereby taking on the character of a population census.

The clearest example is that of the domainal lord Hosokawa. While lord of Kokura, Buzen Province, daimyo Hosokawa ordered a survey of population and livestock (*jinchiku aratame*) in his territory. One section of the surviving records gave the totals village by village, while another section provided nominative data (population register type) with the names and ages of each individual in the villages. Then, in 1633, immediately after Hosokawa was moved to Higo Kumamoto, he ordered the compilation of the *Higo Register of People and Livestock*, a detailed survey of not only the human population but of their buildings, property, and livestock (*Higokoku jinrchiku aratamechô*. 5 Vols, 1955; *Kokura-han jinrchiku aratamechô*, 5 Vols, 1956–58).

Similar surveys (*nimbetsu aratame*) followed in areas under direct Tokugawa shogunal control as well as several other domainal territories, yielding much useful information for researchers today. General administrative surveys of the domainal territories were carried out in the latter half of the seventeenth century, providing us figures regarding the residents, houses, and estimated rice yields for each village.

However, because the purpose of these registers, particularly the early ones, was to locate labor to requisition, the census takers focused on young, able-bodied men. Meanwhile, the subjects of the census sought to evade such demands on the same. These tensions make the age records somewhat problematic. As statistical demographic records, then, the population registers from the initial period are not entirely reliable.

Nevertheless, the appearance of such demographic records (regardless of their flaws) at the beginning of the early modern period is highly significant. After the initial period of consolidation of *ritsuryô* political power, the 700-year documentary blank in population statistics finally came to an end. Governmental interest in population figures revived, even as conditions grew ripe for the undertaking of such surveys.

While these records contain various errors and were not conducted for the "nation" as a whole, as an experiment, we can still use this micro-data from the early Tokugawa period to estimate the total population of Japan at that time (for specifics, see Hayami 1968: chapter 6). Fortunately, we have as a national statistic the estimated rice yield for each province in 1598 as a result of the Taikô land survey. This estimated yield was the tax value of land, not the quantity of production. However, in the years when land surveys were enforced, it is not unreasonable to surmise that these figures were close to the quantity of production.

In searching for records rich in information on and around the year 1600 so as to provide us with as accurate as possible a ratio between population and crop yields, we found that the registers of Kokura domain on people and livestock for the Keichô-Genna period (1596–1624) met our requirements. However, we cannot simply use the numbers listed in the registers as they are. Figures for the ages of young children and the number of girls are extremely scarce, and if we calculate the number of boys to every hundred girls on the basis of these statistics, we arrive at 136. Therefore, we must first correct these gaps in the population figures. We begin with a total of 5,262 for the number of entries recorded for the ages of the residents of the seventy-one villages of the Hayami District of Bungo Province (now the area surrounding the city of Beppu). We then turn to historical records from which we can derive an accurate understanding of the population structure in terms of age in the latter half of the seventeenth century. Assuming the figures for individuals over thirty-one are reliable, if we make corrections by applying the ratios based on the above age structure, we arrive at a total of 8,210, which is 1.56 times more than the population officially noted in the Hayami district records.

The 1622 Kokura domainal registers provide us with the population and estimated yield for the 462 villages of the provinces of Buzen and Bungo Provinces. The ratios of estimated yield to population directly taken from those records vary in terms of region, ranging from one *koku* per 0.28 people for a flatland area, to one *koku* per 0.95 people in mountainous areas. However, we should treat the latter figure as exceptional, since the mountainous regions from which the data derives were few in number. Therefore, for the majority of villages, about 94 per cent, the coefficient is between 0.28 and 0.44, with a high mutual coefficient.

By multiplying these ratios of crop yield to population by the national total of 18 million *koku* derived from the Taikô land survey, we come up with 5.18 to 8.14 million as an estimate for the nation's population. This result is unusually low compared with the generally accepted figure of 18 million advocated by Tôgo Yoshida. Yoshida applied the one to one ratio derived from the Tempo period correspondence between a national yield of 30 million *koku* to 30 million people to the beginning of the early modern period; he even declared as much at a talk (Yoshida 1910: 25–6). Yoshida's purpose is understandable, but the fact that scholars thereafter accepted this figure without raising any questions is disturbing. Certainly, our figures derived from yield to population ratios based on historical records from the early modern period lead us to a conclusion vastly different from that of Yoshida.

However, our new estimate also relies on a number of hypothetical extrapolations. Can the ratios of yield to population taken from one area in Kyûshû be applied across the nation? How do we factor in the regional differences, which appeared in the ratios we derived from the Bungo surveys? Such problems are difficult to resolve. We also need to include figures for urban and nonagricultural populations, which were not recorded in terms of crop yield estimates. By thus expanding the scope of this estimate, the national population of the early modern period comes to 10 million plus or minus 2 million, which still falls short of Yoshida's 18 million.

Our estimate indicates that the population increase of the early modern period was considerably larger than previously thought. According to first of the national population surveys initiated by the shogunate in 1721, the population of Japan was approximately 26 million. This figure is lower than the one we arrive at later in this chapter. However, the shogunate's calculations omitted 5 million who should have been included, so in the end the total of 26 million is fairly reliable.

If this is the case, then after 1600 the population of Japan increased by at least 2.6 times, if not 3.9 times over a 120-year period. The question arises as to whether it was possible to maintain this growth, between 0.8 and 1.3 per cent annually, for over a hundred years. We believe that this sustained population increase is plausible. To support our hypothesis, we discuss below a number of background factors that contributed to this growth.

First, we must look at the advance of urbanization during this period. Beginning with Edo, over 200 castle towns appeared throughout the nation within an extremely short period of time. The proportion of the population living in cities shifted from an unusually low level to an unusually high level for a pre-industrialized society. People migrating from rural villages swelled this urban population.

Yet, even in rural areas, unprecedented changes were taking place. Before 1600, there were two types of agricultural households: those based on the labor power of subordinates (*nago* or indentured servants, *fudai* or hereditary servants, and *genin* or menial servants) and relatively small-scale conjugal family households composed of the direct relatives of a particular couple. Over time, the latter model came to overshadow the former, resulting in a major change in the agricultural household structure. In the type of household that relied on subordinate labor, the majority of these subordinates spent their entire lives unmarried. Since both partnering and birth rates were low, the reproductive rate at this social level was negative. The children of the main central family who were not in line for succession supplied labor power.

This was the primary reason why population growth was extremely sluggish during the 800 years following the Nara period. That is, before the seventeenth century, those who were able to marry, have children and constitute households were limited in number. Numerous others, both men and women, never formed a family, remaining unmarried for the entirety of what were expected to be short lives.

However, from the sixteenth century in the Kinai region, and from the early seventeenth century in the rest of Japan, the pace of population growth picked up. Diverse factors, such as urbanization and the expansion of cultivated land, drastically altered the structure of agricultural households, resulting in rapidly growing population figures. In short, it became possible for all agricultural workers, so long as they reached adulthood, to marry and establish families. Much of the resulting population growth was absorbed by the new cities and the increased land opened up for cultivation. Therefore, throughout the seventeenth century, population controls were unnecessary and growth continued to the very brink of what resources could support.

There are number of historical materials we can look to for confirmation. For example, one text described the conditions of late seventeenth century rural villages in the Aizu region of northeastern Japan as follows: "Nowadays the vigorousness of the people is like the tide" (see the quotation from the Aizu domain samurai in Fujita 1952: 50). In Aizu during this period, agricultural households that relied on subordinated labor vanished, giving way to stem family households. This, together with the increase in population, inspired the above exclamation by a domainal official.

In a case study made by the authors, we have ascertained that during the final thirty years of the seventeenth century, the population in Suwa, Shinano Province, grew at an annual rate exceeding 1.4 per cent, that this upward trend began in the 1620s with the formation of Suwa domain, and that during the same period the norm for agricultural households in this region became that of stem family households (Hayami 1969). Despite a high infant mortality rate, the number of children for each complete family (couples where marriage continued at least until the wife reached the age of fifty) was 5.9 in cases where the wife married at age twenty. If we add in the number of deceased children not listed in the historical records, the corrected overall birth rate was about eight children. This demonstrates that couples did not impose limitations on births. Such limits were in fact unnecessary, since most of the children not in line for succession in the main household formed separate homes and new households upon reaching adulthood (Hayami with Uchida 1972: 473–516).

In the Nôbi region as well, wetland reclamation and the development of new rice fields on the coasts and in downstream river areas protected by embankments contributed to striking population increases during the seventeenth century. Not only in the Nôbi region, but all throughout Japan, agricultural production in the flatlands was made possible through the irrigation projects of the shogunate and domainal administrations.

This development of agriculture in highly productive areas together with the population growth in rural villages in turn supported the sharp growth in urban populations.

2.2. Population trends after the eighteenth century

This rapid population growth during the seventeenth century could not continue forever. Although there were many regional differences, in many places the tide of population growth had subsided by the first half of the eighteenth century. One reason was that urban populations had reached their limits. For castle town and city populations, the most important factor in determining urban consumption was the quantity of annual taxes collected by the regional lord. However, even if growth in urban populations ceased, since cities still had to absorb migrants from rural villages, they continued to contribute as before to rural population increases (this section draws upon Hayami 1971b: 247–63).

The nationwide census taking, first conducted in 1721 and held every six years between 1726 and 1846, was a groundbreaking undertaking for a premodern society. Fortunately, statistics for each province survive twelve, while we can even determine the sex ratio of the population from the six surveys (see the shogunate's population survey by province in Hayami 1993: 135–64). However, these surveys were different from their modern counterparts in that the surveys were not conducted uniformly nor simultaneously throughout the nation, and the surveyers received no special training for their task. Rather, pre-modern surveyers simply followed established methods in preparing and submitting a report to the domainal lord or officials. These methods for creating population registers varied considerably among the territorial lords: for example, while reports made to the shogunate consistently excluded the warrior population, some domains did not record children under the age of eight, while others did not even record those who were under the age of fifteen. The basic figures on the population of each village and town derived from either the *shûmon aratame-cho* or the *nimbetsu aratame-cho*, which were produced on different principles.

First, on the principle of "primary residence," individuals, excepting those who married or were adopted out of the area, were registered in terms of their birthplace. This can be thought of as a record of the population *de jure*. According to this principle, people who moved away to another area to work as servants were, even in their old age, recorded as if they still lived where they had been born. When this registration method was employed in places where it was common for people to leave the area to work as servants, the registered population differed markedly from the actual figures.

In contrast, the principle of "current residence" can be thought of as recording the population *de facto*. Those absent due to work as servants away from home were excluded from the census, so these surveys were a more accurate reflection of actual conditions in a given area. However, these surveys also omitted infants who were born and died between censuses, so the information on infants is incomplete.

Nevertheless, regardless of such shortcomings, these surveys provide vital region-by-region information not available from any other source on population trends. Most Tokugawa period historical materials that deal with the nation as a whole were only concerned with estimated crop yields or the size of land parcels, so the aforementioned population surveys, being national in scope, rich in data, and fairly reliable, are invaluable. Based on these materials, Table 7.1 illustrates national population trends by region from 1721–1846. Regional variation is immediately apparent: the populations of Ôu, Kantô, and Kinki were on the decline; the populations of Tôkai, Tôzan, and the regions surrounding Kinki were stagnant; and, although they vary slightly, the populations of Hokuriku, San'yô, Shikoku, Northern Kyûshû, and Southern Kyûshû were overall on the rise.

The total population of Japan during this period remained fairly stable around 26.02 million to 26.9 million, 1828 representing the high end with 27.18 million, 1792 representing the low end with 24.89 million, and

Table 7.1. Population growth by region (1721–1846)

Region	Growth rates (%)			Index of temperature	Rate of urban population (%)
	Total	Crisis	Normal		
1 East Ôu	−18.1	−28.0	9.9	86.4	9.0
2 West Ôu	4.0	−18.4	22.4	88.6	14.5
3 North Kantô	−27.9	−19.3	−8.6	103.2	6.1
4 South Kantô	−5.2	−8.2	3.0	117.2	27.9
5 Hokuriku	17.6	−12.0	29.6	105.8	15.9
6 Tôzan	13.2	−6.5	19.7	95.8	5.2
7 Tôkai	10.5	−6.0	16.5	122.4	10.3
8 Kinai	−11.2	−17.6	6.4	122.3	32.7
9 Kinai environs	−5.1	−12.9	7.8	117.0	10.4
10 San'in	23.6	−4.3	27.9	114.2	9.7
11 San'yô	20.2	−2.9	23.1	120.4	8.8
12 Shikoku	26.8	2.0	24.8	126.1	8.6
13 North Kyûshû	6.8	−3.2	10.0	129.5	9.2
14 South Kyûshû	23.6	11.9	11.7	135.0	8.2
Total	3.0	−9.8	12.8	114.1	13.3

Source: Kito (1985: table 2).

Notes: (1) Growth rates: Hayami (1971*b*). Total = 1846−21. Crisis = (1750−1721)+
  (1792−1750)+(1840−1834) Normal = Total−Crisis.
  (2) Index of tempeature: Calculated from fifty cities average temperature
  (1941−70) in each region.
  (3) Rate of urban population from: Rikugun sanbôbu (1976).

changes averaging plus or minus 5 per cent. However, we must keep in mind that the label "stagnation" only applies to the national population figures. When we take a closer look at each region, considerable differences become readily apparent.

For example, let us compare the population of the San'yô region in western Japan (excluding Mimasaka), which demonstrated the greatest increase, with the population of the northern Kantô region in eastern Japan. When the first survey was held in 1721, both had populations of around 1.8 million. However, according to the final census of 1846, the population of the San'yô region had increased to 2.3 million, while the northern Kantô region had declined to 1.3 million. If we add the two regional totals together, their combined population remains 3.6 million. On the surface, the population of Japan looks as if it had come to a standstill, but this was just a coincidence. In other words, there was no mysterious force at work to maintain the Japanese national population at a certain level. Therefore, we need to track population trends region by region.

The population decline in northeastern Japan, especially in northern Kantô and the Pacific Ocean side of Ôu, was the result of climatological changes for the worse that took place in the eighteenth century. In particular, a series of unusually cool summers dealt a severe blow to the production of rice in these areas, resulting in the Hôreki Famine of 1753–56 and the Tenmei famine of 1783–86. In addition, the Asama volcanic eruption of 1783 not only inflicted direct damage but also had a long-term impact on agricultural production in the northern Kantô region due to soil acidification from fallen ashes. Based on the highly reliable records of the Yonezawa and Aizu domains, Figure 7.1 illustrates the drastic nature of such population decreases during the eighteenth century. Without question, this decline was most dramatic in the domains of Tsugaru, Nambu, Sendai, and Sôma, where the population figures did not begin to recover until the beginning of the nineteenth century (Hayami 1982: 70–92).

It would seem quite straightforward if the economic development in southern Kantô, which included Edo, had led to population growth. However, the actual case was the reverse: the population declined. Although it is difficult to obtain accurate figures for the population of Edo, a population of one million appears to be a fair estimate, divided into 500,000 *samurai* and 500,000 commoners. The question we are confronted with is why the population never surpassed one million. In a pre-industrial society, an urban population of one million would require large quantities of food, clothing, fuel, and building materials, as well as attention to such issues as waste disposal. These demands act as a check on potential urban population growth. At the very least, such limitations existed for the population of Edo under the municipal administration. Even when expansion took place, it took the form of urbanization in the surrounding areas outside of the city's jurisdiction.

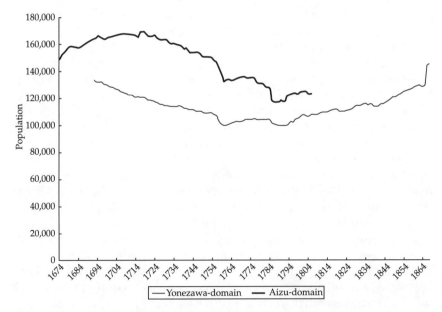

Fig. 7.1. Population trends of two northeast domains.

The population growth in southwest Japan, which continued at an annual rate of 0.2–0.3 per cent, presents us with a marked contrast to northern and eastern Japan. While this rate is not high by modern standards, it is not low for a pre-industrial society, and certainly a far cry from "stagnancy." Why did the population continue to climb in this region? The answer is that in a society like early modern Japan where the basic unit of production was the stem family (since multiple generation households were the norm in Japan, the term "stem family" is more appropriate than "nuclear family"), marriages rates were high. Therefore, population growth was only to be expected. The real question when examining population trends in Tokugawa Japan is what forces were at work in places where decline was apparent.

On the one hand, southwest Japan was an economically developed region marked by advances in opening new rice fields and the production of regional specialties and non-agricultural commodities. On the other hand, this region lacked large cities like Edo, Kyoto, and Osaka with populations of 500,000 or more, which meant that the negative feedback function of economic development and urban populations was not at work. For these reasons, this region saw sustained population growth over a long period. It might even be said that these factors facilitated efficient use of regional resources by the growing population. Is it a mere coincidence that, without exception, the regions that produced the individuals who

served as the driving force of the Meiji Restoration all experienced population increases during the period preceding the Restoration? While
directly linking population growth and political revolution is risky, an
explanation may be possible by providing a series of intermediary steps.

A rich variety of different trends can be seen in central Japan, located
between the two regions discussed above. The population of the central
Kinai area declined while that of the surrounding area leveled off, the
growth rate in the Hokuriku region was positive, and the Tôkai and
Toyama regions experienced incremental increases. The central Kinai area
with its two large urban centers, Kyoto and Osaka, is generally understood as having been the most economically advanced region in early
modern Japan. The contrast of the population fluctuations in the Kinai
region to the stability of the population of the surrounding areas presents
us with a wonderful illustration of the urban graveyard effect.

In any case, this urban population performed the function of absorbing
large numbers of people from surrounding areas. Up until 1910, the growth
rate of urban populations in Japanese cities had been negative (Itô 1990:
227–69). As a result, the movement of large numbers of people from villages
to cities in regions with high urban population ratios led to population stagnation or even decline throughout the entire region. While it is difficult to
ascertain the urban population ratio of each region in early modern Japan,
according to early Meiji statistics (according to Rikugun sanbôbu, ed.
(reprint) 1976, this figure is the ratio of the population of more than
5,000 people living in "a convergent area"), this ratio was over 30 per cent in
the central area of the Kinai region, which included Kyoto and Osaka, and
20 per cent in the southern Kantô region, which included Edo. These percentages were unusually high for a pre-industrialized society; indeed, they
corresponded to the most highly urbanized regions in western Europe.

These conditions explain why population increases were not seen in the
economically developed and urbanized southern Kantô region, central
Kinai, and its surrounding areas. In contrast, southwest Japan with its low
urban population ratio continued to grow.

However, Ôu and Hokuriku constituted exceptions to the above. On
the one hand, while the Ôu region had a low urban population ratio,
deterioration of the natural environment led to a decline in population. On
the other, the urban population ratio in the Hokuriku region was above
15 per cent, so it is not clear why the population continued to increase in a
marked manner. As yet unexplained factors appear to have been at work.

National population trends had entered a valley at the end of the eighteenth century, but shifted toward growth at the beginning of the nineteenth century. That is, the populations of northern and eastern Japan,
which had declined throughout the eighteenth century, began to turn
around. However, there were frequent interruptions to this growth. First,
between 1836 and 1837, the entire country was hit by an epidemic, with

urban populations sustaining particular damage. During this two-year period, the population of Osaka declined by 11 per cent, while a quarter of the adult population of a town in Owase, Kii Province, died. Breaking out during what came to be called the Tempô famine, this epidemic led to insufficient labor power and the stagnation of agricultural production and transportation. Yet it is important to note that the root cause of the Tempô famine was not a poor harvest, as had been the case in the Tenmei famine in which the aged and very young died in great numbers. In contrast, during the Tempô crisis, the mortality rate of adults was particularly high. According to current research, the communicable disease that led to this epidemic is thought to have been an illness affecting the digestive system, complicated by measles (Jannetta 1987).

The second crisis followed directly after the mid-nineteenth century "opening of Japan." The opening of the ports brought Japan many things, one of which was an epidemic of cholera that resulted in many deaths. Unfortunately, cholera was spreading throughout the world at the very time when the Japanese policy of "national seclusion" came to an end, and Japanese with weak immune systems were hit hard. Although the exact number of deaths cannot be ascertained, based on the 1886 population census that recorded the population structure by age of each prefecture, we can conclude that the epidemic wreaked the most damage in central Honshû (Naimushô sômukyoku kosekika (1992); the entry in *Kokusei chôsa izen, Nihon jinkô tôkei shûsei 2*, records the population by spouse and by sex in every age bracket and every prefecture at that time).

While such crises, which occurred every few decades, caused temporary population decreases, they did not substantially alter the long-term trend toward growth. By the end of the Tokugawa period, *samurai* influence was on the wane, as was their power to collect land taxes. As a result, castle towns and the metropolitan centers of Edo and Osaka experienced declining populations and consumer demand. This meant that the causes of population stagnation and decline had lost their force, to the detriment of large cities and castle towns. Rural areas saw population increases, creating conditions for social instability.

While the quarter of a century spanning 1846, the final year of the shogunate's national population survey, to 1870, when the Meiji government conducted its first national census, is a blank in the history of population statistics, marked population increases were seen in villages and regional cities, particularly in eastern Japan, during this period.

2.3. Births, death, marriage, and migration

For detailed information on the population of Japan during the early modern period, we can turn to records used in the investigation of religious sects (*shûmon aratame chô*, hereinafter "SAC") and population registers (*nimbetsu aratame chô*, hereinafter "NAC"). The SAC is a product of the Tokugawa shogunate's prohibition of Christianity, codified in 1638 along with the shogunate's national seclusion policy, and enforced in areas under direct shogunal control. In 1671, a law was passed requiring all domainal lords to create these records. The SAC was an instrument of religious interrogation, forcing all Japanese to receive stamps from the temples to which they belonged as proof that they were Buddhist, not Christian. Nevertheless, since village and town officials, not temples, generated these records they were administrative in nature (Cornell and Hayami 1986).

The basic goal of the SAC was to list all members of a household, to record their religious affiliation, and to offer proof that they were not Christians. Indeed, throughout the Edo period, some of these record collections only covered these three items. However, in many areas, the information included in these surveys expanded to include notes on items outside of the original purpose of the SAC, such as age, status within the household, recent changes in situation, income, and even the number of livestock owned by a household. This shift indicates that Christians no longer posed a discernable social threat, and that the SAC was transformed into a register of the commoner population, or a kind of survey of national trends.

As mentioned above, like other records from this period, the SAC did not have a uniform name or format, and could be conducted as surveys of either "primary residence" or "current residence." The contents of these records were also uneven in terms of depth or lack of detail. Some domains only held these surveys once every six years, and certain domains are thought to not have conducted any SAC at all. Moreover, even the most detailed SAC did not record children who were born but did not survive between population surveys.

Despite such defects in the SAC, nowhere else in the world can we find such detailed and relatively reliable demographic records of commoners gathered by a pre-modern society. Let us suppose there exists for some town or village a richly detailed SAC that relied on the principle of "current residence" and was regularly conducted over a long period of time. With such records it would be easy to derive statistics on both static and dynamic aspects of the general population. Moreover, they would allow us to trace specific households, married couples and individual men and women as subjects for active analysis, that is, event history analysis.

As successors to the people and livestock registers of the late sixteenth century, the NAC possessed a different origin from the SAC. However, over time, the NAC and SAC drew increasingly closer in content and even came to be called *shûmon nimbetsu aratame chô*, a name which incorporated elements from both. Although there were places, like the domain of Nihonmatsu, Mutsu Province, which gathered detailed information for a

NAC every year up to the Meiji Restoration (for research using these materials, see Narimatsu 1985, 1992), most domains conducted a "primary residence"-type SAC on an annual basis, supplementing it with a NAC from time to time. Since it is not necessary to distinguish between these two types of historical records for our purposes, we will treat both of them as SAC.

We do not at present have complete records for the entire country, since the discovery and publication of SACs has proceeded at different rates in different regions. A fair number of cases to research have been found in the rural villages of central Honshû, Shinano Province, the Nôbi region, and Kinai. Additional potential case studies have been discovered in rural villages in Kantô and the southern Ôu region. Yet considerable regional variations in the demographics of the time are believed to exist, so it is a bit premature to construct an overview of the national population based on these individual cases. Particularly since we have little or no information on conditions in the northern regions of Ôu, the Hokuriku region, western Japan, and urban centers, we need to continue the search for and study of such historical records.

Drawing on our research on the Suwa region, the Nôbi region, and cities in Kinai, we will now turn to a discussion of the demographic topics of birth, death, marriage, and migration.

3. Demographic Indices

3.1. Fertility

The main drawback in using the SAC for research is their inexact figures for childbirth. Irene Taeuber, who has written the most comprehensive study on the population of Japan, observes that the birth and death rates she was able to obtain from the work of various scholars of the Edo period were so low that they were difficult to accept (Taeuber 1958: 29). This no doubt reflects the results of past research, which based its calculations on the assumption that the SAC were accurate records of births and deaths. Currently, scholars have begun to revise their understanding of the birth figures in the SAC, looking for numbers that take into account all births. In general, birth rate figures are known in demographic terms as the "crude birth rate" or "CBR." The CBR is derived by dividing the annual number of births by the population of that year and is expressed as the number of births per each one thousand of the general population.

Depending on the time period and region, we see considerable variation in CBRs. During periods of population growth, a CBR exceeding 40 per thousand was not unusual, while roughly 35 per thousand was fairly standard. However, during periods of population stagnation, the

CBR dropped below 30 per thousand to hover around 25 per thousand. Urban CBRs were even lower at 20 per thousand.

The CBR is easy to calculate so long as the population figures and number of births are available. However, since various other factors need to be taken into account, it is difficult for the CBR to function as an accurate index of fertility. For example, the ratio of men to women, marriage rates, and age of marriage all had an impact on birth rates and should be factored into the calculations. Therefore, as more accurate indicators of births, we need to examine birth rates by age and the total marital fertility rate (TMFR). Birth rate by age is, as the name suggests, the rate of births in terms of the age of the mother, measuring how many births occurred during a year within a certain age bracket. The TMFR measures the fertility of a mother between the ages of 15 and 49 on the basis of birth rate by age, and TFR includes births outside of marriage.

Broadly speaking, the standard birth rate by age allows us to add in infant deaths that did not appear in the SAC. Even with this revision, however, birth rates were quite low compared with western Europe. There is debate as to whether the natural birth rate was low because of spacing between births due to comparatively long periods of breast-feeding. This point has caught the attention of international scholars, who are currently publishing important research in this area.

Susan B. Hanley and Kozo Yamamura found that the number of births recorded in the SAC of Okayama domain in western Honshû was extremely low. They argue that this figure was the result of "rational" population limits imposed by the villagers, indicating their aspirations to maintain and improve their living standard. Needless to say, before the introduction of modern birth control, abortion and infanticide were the primary means to limit population size. Although abortion and infanticide should not be thought of as the same, and misery accompanied the practice and even terminology for both these measures for limiting the population were seen at the time as "rational" and free of moralistic condemnation (Hanley and Yamamura 1977).

Making use of historical materials from a village in central Honshû, Thomas C. Smith analyzed the agricultural management practices and demographic behavior of the villagers. Smith also found that the birth rate derived by family reconstitution was low compared with case studies of various European countries. He advanced the hypothesis that sex-selective infanticide had been practiced, which he verified with the SAC. While Smith proved his hypothesis in the case of this particular village, questions regarding sample size and the nature of the historical materials make it doubtful that this theory can be applied to other villages and regions. Setting aside the issue of birth rate, the significance of Smith's work lies in his indication of quantitative changes in the family cycle and land ownership (Smith 1977*a*).

Incidentally, the total marriage fertility rate, or the number of times a woman gave birth during marriage, is the total of the aforementioned birth rates by age, with the same characteristics. In the Suwa district, Shinano Province, during the seventeenth century, young women who married at age fifteen bore nine children throughout their lifetimes, but from the latter half of the eighteenth century, this figure declined to five children.

In actuality, marriages could end for various reasons, and possibilities for remarriage were not the same throughout Japan. Since mortality rates for married women and births outside of marriage should also be factored in, birth rates by age and total extraordinary birth rates are not sufficient by themselves as birth indices. Nevertheless, the limited observations above can explain broad population trends in a satisfactory manner, even if mortality rates have not yet been figured into these numbers.

3.2. Mortality

Information obtained from the SAC regarding deaths has the same flaws as information on births. In other words, one cannot obtain figures on infant deaths that occurred between the creations of SACs. As a result, there have been attempts at using historical materials other than SAC, such as Buddhist temple death registers (*jiin kakochô*) and pregnancy documents, in order to obtain accurate infant mortality figures (for research using these materials, see Suda 1987; for materials that use the pregnancy documents, see Kitô 1976). However, numerous problems arise even in using these documents. For example, the temple registers were limited only to the parishioners of specific temples, and the boundaries of villages and temples differed. In addition, there is still room for doubt as to whether or not they recorded all children who were born. Furthermore, because they are private documents, there are restrictions on their use. The only extant pregnancy documents are from the southernmost Ôu region and part of the northern Kantô region and do not contain information that would be applicable on a national level.

However, because deaths were recorded in the majority of SACs starting from age two, these statistics may be used as indicators of all deaths, excepting those of infants. Like the birth rates, the mortality rate is usually expressed as the crude death rate (CDR); in other words, the number of deaths during a one-year period divided by the annual population. Like the CBR, the CDR is simple to calculate but is incomplete as an indicator of deaths. For an exact figure, one must find high-level indicators such as the age distribution of deaths, the death rate by age and life span. Such indicators can be derived from SACs, which record ages and focus on current residents.

In the majority of cases, the range of fluctuation is wide, aided by the fact that the CDR obviously deals with a small number of people. In years

of mortality crisis, the CDR, unlike the CBR reached levels that far surpassed the number of deaths in an average year. Although there were no
large wars in early modern Japan, many people lost their lives due to epidemics and famines. Thus, although there is not much sense in presenting
the average CDR, we will in any case note that the standards of average
years were at least 25–30 per thousand. However, one must not overlook
the fact that differences in the age structure of the population and differences in urban and rural living environments are directly reflected in the
levels of the CDR.

When we look at the distribution of deaths by age in rural villages, the
mortality rate remains high throughout the years of infancy, decreases in
childhood and adolescence, begins to increase again after the age of fifty
or so, and then decreases at its peak at age seventy. If the residents of rural
villages survived the dangerous period of infancy, they were able to live
comparatively long lives. This revises the mistaken belief that people of
the Edo period had short lives and warns us that studies of inheritance
and succession in agricultural families must give sufficient consideration
to demographic conditions. In other words, the age at which peasants
passed on the family headship to their successors and the age at which
they died were very late.

The high death rate of infants was the same in the cities, but the death
rate does not change from adolescence to old age. To put it in extreme
terms, deaths were not surprising in urban environments. This difference
between large cities and rural villages probably influenced the perceptions of death held by their respective residents. If we consider that many
early modern works of literature and philosophy were created in cities, it
is possible that these perceptions of death are reflected there as well.

If we were to draw a diagram of the age distribution for deaths in cities,
our figure would show a broad lower end followed by a straight rise that
finally narrows to a point, taking on the shape of a space shuttle. In contrast, the same diagram for villages has a broad lower end then, after a
brief narrowing, there is a grouping near the tip, giving our diagram the
shape of a mushroom cloud (Hayami 1990: 170, figure 5).

The death rate by age had a same pattern both for villages and cities: a
high death rate during infancy, followed by a decline in adolescence and
early adulthood, with a second rise in old age. It goes without saying that
the mortality rates above the age of ten were higher in cities.

In order to compose a life expectancy with the same accuracy as is possible with modern population statistics, one must be able to determine
mortality rates by age to the degree of weekly units for three months after
birth and then to monthly units after that. With few examples of death,
one cannot derive a life expectancy for a population where the death rate
by age is zero. If we must construct a life expectancy under such restrictions, we can only hypothesize the death pattern at birth from maturity.

To take the example of just one village, Nishijo village (in Ampachi district, Mino Province), there were about 360 deaths, male and female, between 1773 and 1869. Assuming that the pattern of death in infancy was the same as the present, the average life expectancy at birth was 36.8 years for males and 36.7 years for females (Hayami 1992: 249–50, Charts 9–24). These figures are probably not far from the national standard. Examples from past research, do not clearly record the methods of measurement and, because they do not consider death just after birth, the figures are high. The danger is that these results may be taken as indexes that reveal the living standards of people of the Edo period.

It is uncertain whether or not there was a lengthening of the average life expectancy during the Edo period. To take one example: in a village in the Suwa region, the life expectancy for both men and women in the early Edo period was just under thirty, but due to a decline in the infant mortality rate life expectancy had passed forty at the end of the Edo period. However, this calculation was not corrected for infant deaths and so cannot be taken as an absolute figure.

3.3. Nuptiality

Commoner society did not have legal arrangements for marriage. Therefore, we can only assume marriages existed when they were recorded in the SAC. From these records, it is possible to derive indicators of age at marriage, the length of marriage, the age when marriage ended, and the marriage rate. However, it would be premature to attempt a bird's-eye view of the entire country based on existing research. In general, the average age of marriage in eastern Japan was early while that in western Japan was late. Calculating backward using statistics from early Meiji, we see that the regional division of marriage ages during the Tokugawa period maps along the *fossa magna* of the earth's crust that cuts vertically down the center of Honshû (Hayami 1987).

At the end of the Tokugawa period, the average age of marriage for women in eastern Japan (especially in the Ôu region), where the population stagnated and even declined, was low: around age 15–18. In western Japan, which experienced population growth, the age of marriage was quite high: at 22–25. From the calculations of birth rates by age, the difference in numbers of births between regions was 2 or 3. If marriage age is the primary factor determining the number of births, this observation is maladjusted. We must find our explanation for this difference in the possibilities that, in eastern Japan, this condition emerged from naturally low fertility or an unusually high infant death rate or birth restrictions. It is likely that the second and third causes played a major role.

Marriage ended at divorce or at the death of the husband or wife. The majority lasted under five years, with only one-fourth of the marriages continuing over twenty-five years. However, remarriage after the death of one's spouse was usual and most men under fifty and women under thirty-five remarried.

3.4. Migration

Until recently, villagers of the Edo Period were seen as tied to the soil, denied the freedom of migration, under the restraints of feudal law. However, if we follow the lives of villagers who appear in the SAC, it becomes clear that many moved around between the cities and other villages. Of course, some migration was due to marriage or adoption into a family, and public servants also moved substantial distances. Among the children born in a village in Mino Province, 50 per cent of the boys and 62 per cent of the girls lived past age ten, but when we look at percentages of those who left the village and went to work in the cities, towns, or other villages, we see that half of the boys and one-third of the girls left, mainly for cities or towns. The size of the population of this village did not change in the final one hundred years of the Edo period, but the birth rate far surpassed the death rate. The difference was found in the net figure of those who had moved to the cities (Hayami 1985).

This migration had usually been seen as resulting from the poverty of villagers, as represented in the phrase *kuchi-berashi*: decreasing the number of mouths in a family. To be sure, even if we cannot deny those factors, servitude was not simply a way to decrease the number of mouths in a family. Although the likelihood was small, migrating to the cities offered a chance for success. In reality, most people who moved from villages to cities had the choice, after working for decades as apprentices to merchants, of returning to their villages or remaining in cities. However, among those who chose the latter, there were some people who worked as clerks or managers until they owned their own shops. Others married into landlord families and yet others attained lifestyles that would have been impossible had they remained in the villages. If we combine this fact with the high mortality rates in cities, migration to cities, holding the possibility of both success and early death, could be called a trade-off with the rural lifestyle where there was little change but a better chance for a longer life.

According to urban SACs, one characteristic of the lifestyle of urbanites was the extremely short period of residence at a fixed location. Changing of residence, which was rare between villages, was an everyday occurrence in the cities. In Kikuya-chô in Osaka, setting aside the homeowner class, 12 per cent of families of the tenant class changed residence during the periods between SACs. The average period of residence was four years, but 60 per cent of all families moved at one-year intervals. In this way, residents of large cities moved frequently within the city. The formation of communities that included the tenant class in such conditions was different from villages and must have been remarkably difficult.

4. Living Standards

4.1. Income and household budgets

Simon Kuznets saw the period of 1884–97 at the beginning of Japan's modern economic growth and estimated the GNP during this period at $74 per person (expressed in 1965 US dollars) (Kuznets 1971). Even the poorest countries in Western Europe, which had begun to industrialize earlier, had a GNP of about $200. So the early Japanese standards were quite low. This highlights the speed of Japanese modern economic growth as well as creating an image of Edo period economic development as extremely weak.

The wages of cotton-spinning factory workers in Japan in the latter part of the nineteenth century, an era that showed rapid growth in the cotton industry, were even lower than wages in India. A comparison of the exchange market at the time confirms this. But, does this mean that Japanese living standards at that time were tragically low? Research that compares the labor power of the cotton-spinning industries in both Japan and India suggests that care should be taken in drawing such conclusions (Saxonhouse and Kiyokawa 1986). That is because it is inappropriate to simply compare female factory workers' wages independent of such factors as differences in the composition of, and form of wage payment to, male and female labor, the brevity of periods of employment and the work-away-from-home character of employment.

The real wages of late Edo-period village servants in general rose from the beginning of the eighteenth century through the beginning of the nineteenth century. At the same time, wages for day labor in villages of the Kinki region closed the gaps with wages for the skilled labor of carpenters and urban daily wages. Real wages for daily agricultural labor stagnated early in the Kinai region, but continued to rise until quite late in regional villages. As a result, the wage differentials between the Kinai and regional villages, and perhaps the gaps between individual incomes, were reduced (Saitô 1979). After the continual price increases of 1820, real wages began a steady fall until the Meiji era due to the standardization of nominal wages and the slowing down of these price increases (Saitô 1993). Of course, since other price elements, such as interest rates, declined at the same time, the village entrepreneurs who would hire laborers could expect higher profits. This invited increased investment activity, priming the pump for economic development in the last years of the Edo period (Umemura 1981).

The household incomes of agricultural families differed greatly according to the scale of operations and social strata (land owners, independent farmers, and tenant farmers). But what is common among many examples is that if the area of operations was sufficiently large, if adult labor was ensured, if cash crops were grown, and if the family engaged in economic activities apart from agriculture, and then the conditions were in place to support a comfortable household budget. The tax rate was also a decisive element in the reproduction of operations. The formation of small-scale families from stem families and the deterioration of the ratio of population to cultivated land caused a reduction in the scale of average operations. However, one cannot deny that peasants engaging in proto-industrialization found advantages in the latter half of the Edo period as a result of improvements in land productivity (which differs from traditional theories), the stabilization of annual taxes at low levels, taxes entirely focusing on agriculture, and the absence of effective levies on nonagricultural production (Smith 1965).

Table 7.2 shows individual consumption in Chôshû (Nagato and Suwô Provinces) domain around 1840 and throughout Japan from 1874 to 1883. The proportion of food costs among total consumption in Chôshû—in other words the Engel's coefficient—is higher than the 65 per cent for all Japanese at the beginning of the Meiji period. However, because there were "savings" that were not accounted for in consumption, an examination of the compositional ratio of food costs in disposable income shows that the portion of food costs in regions with the lowest disposable incomes was 79 per cent in the Maeyamashiro region, and down to 60 per cent in the Ôshima region. In calculating the expenditures for rice in the

Table 7.2. Consumption expenditure per capita (%)

Item	Nagato Province (c.1840)		National (1874–83)
	Oshima saiban	Maeyamashiro saiban	
Food	82.8	82.1	65.2
Meal expences	74.7	79.1	—
Others	8.1	2.9	—
Clothes	9.6	13.7	7.6
Houses	1.7	2.9	8.4
Light and heat	4.6	1.4	5.9
Others	1.3	0.0	12.9
Hygiene	—	—	3.8
Transportation	—	—	0.2
Communication	—	—	0.1
Social expenses	—	—	4.9
Others	—	—	3.9
Total	100.0	100.0	100.0
monme in notes	94.0	83.7	

Chôshû domain as a whole, if we use 72 *monme* (3.6 *gô* per person with the price of one *koku* of rice at 55 *monme*) as the cost of food per person, and 120 *monme* as the average consumption costs for six regions, then the food cost ratio is 60 per cent. Even if we include food expenses outside of main meals, the Engel's coefficient does not far exceed 65 per cent (Nishikawa 1979).

4.2. *Peasant uprisings*

The latter half of the Edo period was the age of uprisings. Peasant uprisings erupted frequently throughout the country while "house smashings" (*uchikowashi*) aimed at wealthy merchants broke out one after another in the city. It would appear that popular economic troubles were behind these events, so their frequency has been taken as a sign of deterioration in the standard of living. But the truth was rather different. Toshio Yokoyama has compared uprisings by province by composing a "peasant uprising outbreak coefficient," which weights various uprisings by their form. According to Yokoyama, regions with a low per capita estimated yield (*kokudaka*) and with low agricultural productivity, such as Rikuchû (a part of Mutsu Province), Shinano, and Hida Provinces, were indeed areas with frequent peasant uprisings. But the reason for a high outbreak coefficient in these areas was not because they were located in mountainous areas where they were subject to such problems as transportation difficulties and frost. Rather, we should look for the cause of uprisings in the fact that they were engaged in production of commodity crops other than rice, or in nonagricultural activities, and were, in fact, in frequent contact with other regions and domains. "In no way could these uprisings be seen as a kind of brutal lashing out arising from crushing poverty." Instead, it appears that behind the uprisings were struggles to ensure and maintain rights against attempts by the lords to control and appropriate wealth from their core economic activities (Yokoyama 1977). Household budgets were enriched by nonagricultural activities and those activities became the targets of governmental policy.

5. Quality of Life

5.1. *Food and nutrition: the system of staple foods*

The Edo period was a time when a staple foods system on the pattern of rice and various grains formed. The estimated yield system (*kokudaka-sei*) and the rise in the commodity value of rice encouraged farmers to consume grains other than rice. With the development of agricultural technology, a variety of grains were grown in the rice paddies in large volume as secondary crops, thus increasing the role of these other grains as a staple food, along with rice. The addition of sweet potatoes to the staple diet from the middle of the Edo period signaled the beginnings of a transformation to the next stage of diversification (Koyama and Gotô 1985).

Table 7.3 shows the quantity of the staple foods available in Japan, the Chôshû domain, Yamaguchi Prefecture and Hida Province during the nineteenth century. In 1874, there was a supply of 527 g of staple foods (of all kinds) per individual per day in Japan. Of that figure, 60 per cent was rice, 17 per cent was wheat, 4 per cent miscellaneous grains, 5 per cent beans, and 14 per cent potatoes. From this we can see that, just prior to the beginning of industrialization in Japan, the staple foods system took the pattern of rice as the core, supplemented by wheat, miscellaneous grains, and potatoes. There are those who say that the peasants of the Edo period may have grown rice, but they were unable to eat their fill of it. But on the whole, it would appear more accurate to say that the Japanese were able to eat a surprising amount of rice.

However, the pattern of staple foods consumption differed depending on the region. In Yamaguchi Prefecture in 1887, the ratio of rice consumed was low while that of wheat and potatoes was high. In Hida Province, the supply of rice was relatively high due to its importation. But unlike Yamaguchi Prefecture, there was little wheat while miscellaneous grains, especially Japanese millet, were widely used. In Chôshû domain and Yamaguchi Prefecture, the supply of all staple foods increased over a

Table 7.3. Estimation of staple foods intake in 1840–87 (grams, per day, per head)

Item	National (1874)			Chôshû-han/Yamaguchi Prefecture		Hida Province
	Production	Food	Meal	c. 1840	1887	1874
Rice	368.8	318.4	264.1	279		284.9
Wheat	23.1	18.5	14.4			46.8
Barley	49.0	35.0	29.7	142	169	32.0
Rye	42.1	34.6	30.7			
Millet	17.4	10.9	8.8		5.0	
Broomcorn	1.6	1.0	0.8	7	5	0.3
Indian millet	1.7	1.0	0.8			—
Japanese millet	5.5	3.4	2.8	6	1	104.9
Buckwheat	7.1	4.4	3.6	17	11	4.5
Corn	0.4	0.2	0.2	—	—	—
Soybean	23.9	20.3	1.5	14	13	19.4
Red bean	5.1	4.7	2.2	5	5	—
Sweet potato	95.3	73.3	70.3	60	134	—
Potato	2.3	1.4	1.4	—	—	6.5
Total	643.3	527.1	431.3	530	650	504.9

Source: Kaitô (1989).

forty-year period but due to the rapid spread of sweet potatoes the use of wheat held steady and the ratio of rice consumption decreased. The changes during this period may in part be a result of differences in investigations, but they are consistent with the basic trends toward a diversification of staple foods.

According to an 1880 government survey of staple foods (*Jinmin joshoku shurui hirei*), the national averages for the structure of staple foods consumption were: rice 53 per cent, wheat 27 per cent, miscellaneous grains (foxtail millet, Japanese millet, miscellaneous grains) 14 per cent, other (sweet potatoes, taro root, vegetables, fruits and nuts, and seaweed) 6 per cent (Umemura et al. 1983). Compared with the structure of staple foods supply derived from agricultural production statistics, the percentage for rice consumption was low, while the percentage for wheat and other grains was high. Underreporting of dry field production statistics, discrepancies in the concept of normal eating, the subjective views of survey respondents, and the large quantity of indirect consumption of rice in processed goods can explain these.

With rice consumption rates of 91 per cent in Hida and 6 per cent in the Ryûkyûs, we can see that there were vast regional differences. Rice was consumed at a high ratio as the normal stable in the Japan Sea side of Tôhoku, Hokuriku, Kinki, the eastern part of the Chûgoku region, and Northern Kyûshû. Regions that consumed high ratios of staples other than rice included the Pacific Ocean side of the Tôhoku region, from western Kantô to the Tôkai and Nôbi regions, and Shikoku and southern Kyûshû. One characteristic of pre-modern Japanese diets, as pointed out by Tsuneichi Miyamoto, is that although many believe that the Japanese have always eaten only rice, the diet was actually diverse and in many cases consumption centerd around regionally produced products. Therefore, staple foods varied depending on the region (Kitô 1986).

If we estimate the potential supply of rice using figures for land productivity and the area of rice paddies, the figure for the 1830s reaches nearly the same level as that of the 1870s (0.8 or 0.9 *koku* per person per year) (Kitô 1983*b*). In the 1730s, a survey report (*Shokoku bussanchô*, A Record of Production in each Province) was compiled that recorded in detail the agricultural and natural goods produced in each domain (Morinaga and Yasuda 1977–85; Yasuda 1987). Counting the product types for staple foods (rice, barley, wheat, a variety of millets, corn, buckwheat, and potatoes) in the thirty-one provinces and thirty-five regions for which materials from these surveys survive today, we find a ratio of 46 per cent for rice, 19 per cent for wheat, and 35 per cent for other grains, with potatoes under 1 per cent (Kitô 1989). If we view this as a representative index of the staple food structure, we find that the staple food structure of the early eighteenth century was heavily weighted toward the miscellaneous grains, compared to the late nineteenth century. The figures for sweet potatoes, meanwhile, can almost be ignored. Since sweet potatoes were just beginning to spread throughout Japan at this time, the small ratio is not surprising. Nevertheless, we can say that the composition of staple foods in each region closely resembled the staple food structure of the 1870s. In other words, a staple food system on the pattern of rice, wheat, and miscellaneous cereals was formed in the early eighteenth century.

5.2. Quantity of food consumption

According to most estimates of food consumption during the early part of the Meiji period, the daily per capita energy intake did not reach 2,000 kcal. According to Yûjirô Hayami and Saburô Yamada, the overall per capita energy consumption between 1874 and 1877 (excluding from production volumes seeds, materials, crops processed for noncombustible goods and losses) was 1,758 kcal (Yûjirô Hayami 1973). In Yamaguchi prefecture in 1887, the energy derived from consumption of grains and sweet potatoes was 1,902 kcal. However, the figure for the consumption of staple foods for the same region (Chôshû domain) in 1840 was only 1,664 cal.

We also should not forget that there was widespread use of wild animals and plants that do not appear in the usual agricultural statistics from the Edo period. Foods consumed in Hida Province in the 1870s, included nuts (Japanese horse chestnuts, acorns, and chestnuts), starches (*katakuri*, arrowroot, and bracken) other wild grasses, shellfish, birds, and animals. Of the 168 products listed in the product survey of 1874, over half (94 goods) were wild food products (Koyama and Gotô 1985). Energy derived from these wild animal and plant products was 3.3 per cent of the total energy consumption of 1,850 kcal. If we take this into account, then total food consumption in the late Edo period did not drop below 1,800 kcal.

Compared with contemporary Japanese who consume 2,500 kcal per day, the 1,800 kcal of the Edo period is a modest figure, and yet this is equal to the standard consumption of the Philippines in the 1950s. If we also consider the fact that the physical builds of people of the Edo period were smaller than those of contemporary Japanese, their calorie intake may not have been high, but it was not below the level of starvation. Let us explore this point more simply. According to information based on excavated remains, the height of Edo period commoners was estimated at 157 cm for an adult male and 146 for an adult female (Suzuki 1971, 1983). The military conscription examinations from 1883 to 1892 also show that the average height for men was 156.5 cm. The standard weight for a height of 157 cm was 50 kg. At that time, the lowest basic metabolic quantity necessary for existence was 2,000 kcal. The United Nations Food and

Agriculture Organization (FAO) designates the limit of malnutrition (the lowest sufficient level of absorption) as 1.2 times the basic metabolic rate, and therefore an Edo period adult male of standard build would require 2,400 kcal to avoid malnutrition. However, the 1,800 kcal/day for a person in the mid-nineteenth century was the average for all people from infants to senior citizens. Converting to the consumption units required by men in their twenties, the figure settles to just above 2,300 kcal. Because 10 per cent below the standard body weight (in this case, 45 kg) is still within the zone of safety (for standard body weight), if an Edo period adult male's weight was near this leanness, he had cleared the boundary of malnutrition. Therefore, at the national level, the lowest necessary amount of energy was met.

5.3. *Quantity of nutrition supply*

Ninety-five per cent of the 1,758 kcal energy absorption that Hayami and Yamada estimated per person was derived from the staple foods: grains, potatoes, and beans. It was a grain-based diet. Proteins, consumed at levels of less than 50 g were also derived from these staple foods. According to calculations of the state of nutritional supply in the Hida region, based on regional product surveys during that time, the diet barely met requirements for energy and consumption of the three main food groups. Intake of animal proteins, vitamins A and C, and calcium was grossly insufficient. It is clear that the nutritional deficiencies of the Hida-pattern rice-and-grains diet were linked to the high infant mortality rate, the frequent occurrence of postnatal deaths and that of the delivery, and the weak resistance to infectious diseases (Fujino 1982). Despite their exclusion of foodstuffs other than the staples, the 1878 agricultural production statistics ("Meiji Ten Year National Agricultural Production Table") show that the consumption of sweet potatoes as one of the main staple foods of the coastal areas of western Japan resulted in a situation in which the supply and structure of nutritional elements in the region closely resembled the case of Hida, overlooking the increased absorption of vitamin C from the potatoes (Koyama and Gotô 1985).

In May 1887, the first impression that the British traveler Isabella Bird had upon arriving in Yokohama was that there were no beggars. However, what she saw throughout the streets were "small, ugly, kindly looking, shriveled, bandy-legged, round-shouldered, concave-chested poor-looking beings" (Bird 1984: 8). Women were "so very small and tottering in their walk," while men were "so lean, so yellow, so ugly yet so pleasant-looking." Although they are "lack(ing) of complexion, and do not have clearly prominent curves," Japanese clothing concealed the women's "defects of their figures" and made them seem bigger. Consumption of few proteins over a long time may have been responsible for their small-boned figures.

5.4. Education, culture, leisure

People of the Edo period possessed different abilities, feelings, and ideas from people of earlier periods. Examples of such differences include the spread and improvement of literacy, the deepening of interest in arithmetic and use of the abacus, the development of temporal perception with the establishment of time bells, and the development map-making skills and spatial perception through the use of maps. All these changes stimulated the formation of an economy-minded society and made it possible for the market economy to function smoothly.

These abilities were not naturally acquired. Children's education included not only physical memorization through on-site labor training, but also took place in a variety of educational facilities such as private schools, home schools, domain schools, and temple schools. The number of Terakoya (temple schools), which provided education to commoner children, increased remarkably from the end of the eighteenth century, experiencing a particular explosion from the 1820s. According to an 1883 Ministry of Education survey, 15,530 temple schools were opened throughout Japan by 1875. There was one school for every 200 children in the age group of 10–14 years old.

Table 7.4. The year of establishment of *terakoya*, private schools, and *Han* schools

Years	Terakoya	Years	Private schools	Years	Han schools
1469–1623	17				
1624–80	38			1661–87	4
1681–1715	39			1688–1715	6
1716–50	47	Before 1750	20	1716–50	18
1751–80	93	1751–80	21	1751–88	50
1781–88	101		61		
1789–1800	165	1781–1803			
1801–03	58			1789–1829	87
1804–17	387				
1818–29	676	1804–29	166		
1830–43	1,984	1830–43	223		
1844–53	2,398				
1854–67	4,293	1844–67	579	1830–67	50
1868–75	1,035	After 1868	181	1868–71	36
Uncertain	n.a.	Uncertain	187	Uncertain	4
Total	11,331+x	total	1,438	total	255

Source: Ishikawa (1978: 23, 29, 147).

School enrollment rates for children aged 6–13 in 1875 are reported as 54 per cent for boys and 19 per cent for girls. Based on these figures, Dore estimated that the school enrollment rate in 1868 for boys was 43 per cent and 10 per cent for girls (Dore 1965). The average age of enrollment was seven or eight, and attendance lasted for just a few years. Seventy per cent of the educational content at the temple schools involved reading and literacy while 25 per cent was focused on arithmetic. The remaining 5 per cent was devoted to advanced studies, such as in the classics of Japanese and Chinese literature, and practical and academic skills. However, we should appreciate the contributions these schools made in training children in the mathematics and reading skills necessary for business and in making it possible for them to enjoy reading.

In fact, in the Edo period, reading was no longer monopolized by a handful of scholars. Reading came to occupy a significant position in the everyday life of commoners both as a method for acquiring practical knowledge and as a form of entertainment. Publications covered a wide array of subjects: Japanese and Chinese textbooks, literature, picture books for children, practical books such as temple school copy books, pictures of famous places, travel guides, military books, famine relief books, and agricultural and industrial technology manuals, and so on. Interest in discovering information through publications increased widely and exceeded the bounds of mere hobbyism. Reading was even "an improvement of the lives of citizens and a link to military defence" (Konta 1977). The number of publications in the three cities of Edo, Osaka, and Kyoto did not reach the 400 levels between 1727 and 1731, but in the period from 1750 to 1754 it neared 600. The price of reading materials, however, was not accessible to most people. Many readers gained access to books by borrowing them from rental bookstores or walking book lenders. Konta estimates that with 656 rental bookshops in 1808 Edo, the number of readers of rental books reached over 100,000 households.

Townsend Harris, who was in Japan at the end of the Edo period to negotiate the Treaty of Amity and Trade, noted, "This country is the most difficult country in the world in which to acquire information. There are neither statistics nor publications that deal with industrial relations issues. There is not anyone who engages in experiments to improve their own tools nor is there anyone who attempts to measure the increasing yield of their own land by new farming methods" (Harris 1959). However, it is clear that this impression has no factual basis. A diverse array of agricultural texts was produced in every region of Japan and skilled farmers were devoted to the improvement of products and farming techniques. Farmers made note of seed quantities and crops, and kept records of the costs of fertilizer and payment of wages in accounts books. Travelers made surprisingly diligent notes of their expenditures, while merchants produced their own unique account-keeping forms, different from those of European multiple-entry accounts books. People had a great interest in quantitative matters and their behavior was based on economic calculations, taking pains to understand accurately the daily flections in the market economy.

Agricultural development in the Edo period was supported by labor ethics that promoted diligence in improving land productivity. Did this "Industrious Revolution" inevitably result in oppressive daily lives filled with continual hard labor? In fact, this was not the case. In this period of continued rapid agricultural expansion, it probably was not possible to find time to enjoy life. However, after the mid-eighteenth century, the demand for leisure time increased even in agricultural society. "Recreation days," when people took a day off from agricultural labor, at first ranged from around twenty to thirty days per year, but increased steadily thereafter. In Okkoto village, Shinano Province, there were twenty-four "recreation days" per year during the eighteenth century. But by the mid-nineteenth century the number had increased to thirty-nine. As far as we know at present, the highest number of "recreation days" was in Mutsu Province in Sendai domain where villagers had over eighty "recreation days" in 1805 (Furukawa 1988).

Changes did not stop at the increase of holidays. The character of leisure time also changed. Holidays were originally used for praying to the gods for excellent crops in farming. At first the increase in days off came as an increase in days to be used for sacred ceremonies. But over time the number of days off for physical rest increased. In addition to the regular days off taken by the entire village, there was also a rise in temporary days off taken at request.

The expansion of leisure was even more remarkable in cities. A "culture of behavior" (*kôdô bunka*) composed of such arts as plays, storytellers, and *sumo*, flourished among the urban populations from the middle of the Edo period (Nishiyama 1975). Many city dwellers participated in such artistic and leisurely activities as visits to temples and shrines, trips to famous places, bathing at hot springs, sightseeing, evening walks, flower-viewing, attending neighborhood festivals, festivals for the dead, temple festivals, exhibitions, sideshows, tea ceremony, flower arranging, dancing, and singing. These cultural activities flourished in the latter part of the Edo period, especially after the 1810–1820s.

The travel boom among commoners occurred as a result of the economic development of the Edo period. This travel boom was neither forced by the government nor was it an economic activity, such as migrating to another region for work (*dekasegi*). This was travel for leisure, and frequently took the form of pilgrimages to such sacred places as Ise, Kumano, and Zenkôji temple. Faith-based organizations known as "*kô*" were formed for these journeys and, like today's package tours, served the purpose of securing funds for group travel. The pilgrimage to Ise Shrine was the largest of these pilgrimages, with 400,000 people a year making the journey to Ise toward the end of the Edo period (Nishigaki 1983). It is even said that upward of 1 million people made the trip to Ise during particular years in which group pilgrimages known as *okagemairi* or *nukemairi* were formed. However, travel at this time had significance beyond just leisure. Travel played a major role in enabling people to get to know the world at large and experience different cultures, in effecting cultural exchange between different regions, and in introducing new kinds of crops, production techniques, and products between and among regions. Many travel guides, guides to famous places, and maps were published and travelers were provided with travel goods and conveniences. One may even call all these activities an industry.

Isabella Bird, who traveled in the Tôhoku region in the early Meiji period, was disturbed in her sleep by mosquitoes, fleas, and flies in the same way that the *haiku* poet Matsuo Bashô had been 200 years earlier. Despite all of this, Bird wrote with conviction that "throughout the world, there is no other place where a woman could travel as safely, without fear of danger or contrivances, as Japan" (Bird 1984: 8). In addition to the increase in leisure, the rise of travel was also supported by the maintenance of public peace, the upkeep of roads and post towns, the arrangement of checkpoints and the development of a money economy.

6. Conclusion: The Edo Period Civilization System

Since the "raising of the curtain" 10,000 years ago in the Jômon period, the history of the population of the Japanese islands can be taken as a repeated layering of four big waves of alternate growth and stagnation (Kitô 1983). The long-term waves of the population each began with growth that corresponded to the development of a unique civilization system, followed by stagnation as the system matured. The population growth of the seventeenth century and the stagnation of the eighteenth century parallel the formation of the Tokugawa civilization system and its maturation.

Although it is uncertain when and how seventeenth century population growth began, we may probably look to the fourteenth or fifteenth centuries as the beginning point of change. Naitô Konan points to the fifteenth century Ônin war as an epoch-making historical event, for thereafter, the common people played an important part in cultural history (Naitô 1976). Masuda Yoshio also shows that the modern Japanese cultural system was formed in the fifteenth and sixteenth centuries (Masuda 1967). It was during this period that the various elements of Tokugawa civilization formed a cultural system on a fixed pattern. Such elements, which came to form the basis of the traditional culture of contemporary Japan, include: cotton textiles; *kosode*, the basic form of the contemporary Japanese kimono; the *shoin* style of traditional Japanese residential architecture; the practice of eating three meals per day; Japanese foods such as *miso*, soy sauce, *soba* noodles, and *tempura*; the Ogasawara-ryû style of etiquette; the family system; tea ceremony; flower arrangement; *noh*, *kyôgen*, and *kabuki* theatre; dialects; and currency.

This civilization achieved internal development in the area of social structure with the polity, the family system, and the village system. However, material culture was formed through the absorption of Chinese civilization of the Song, Yuan, and Ming dynasties, and European civilization brought by the sailors Japanese called *"nanbanjin"* (southern barbarians). The elements with the most direct influence on population change were the construction of buildings with stone foundations, *tatami* flooring, cotton for keeping warm and absorbing moisture, bedding, the custom of bathing, and medical herbs. As for developments in agriculture that increased the industry's ability to support population growth, one cannot emphasize enough the increase of arable land, development of new strains of rice and sweet potatoes, product improvement, and the remarkable developments in cultivation techniques. A comprehensive examination of population change during the Tokugawa period would show that it was accompanied by these developments in the civilization system.

None of these new behaviors, customs, or goods was an isolated development. The introduction of cotton, for example, was not simply a matter of adding another material that could be used for clothing, contributing to the improvement of health, and supporting the agricultural economy with an important new commodity. Instead, we should see that the influence of cotton also had an impact on people's manners and their sense of aesthetics, permeating to the depths of society. The introduction of the sweet potato was also linked with the large-scale use of marine products that made up for deficiencies in protein intake. Agricultural developments aimed at the improvement of land productivity were linked with changes in the family structure and the formation of an ideal of hard work.

Edo period Japan was an agricultural society relying on the produce of the land for the majority of the energy and raw materials used in daily life. In light of the fact that the shogun and daimyo administrated the territory that produced these resources, it was also unmistakably a pre-modern society. However, through the development of a market economy, people pursued economic values and chose actions that prioritized economic rationality. Every region became linked through the market and, since the free movement of resources and labor power was restricted by the policy of national isolation (*sakoku*), the society formed an "expanded closed system" that provided its own domestic supply of resources and energy (Uchida 1982). In the words of E A. Wrigley, we could call this an "advanced organic energy based economy," (Wrigley 1988). Excluding Hokkaido, which had a population density of forty people per square kilometer in 1600, the population density of Honshû, Kyûshû, and Shikoku exceeded one hundred persons per square kilometer in the early eighteenth century. Even by today's standards, this is not a small number. In addition to population growth, the rise in living standards directly and indirectly caused an increase in the demand for bio-energy sources, and was linked to the energetic use of farm and mountain land. The eighteenth century saw continued destruction of forests and loss of topsoil, on top of occasional climatological deterioration, which caused a number of disasters (Chiba 1973; Andô 1992). Environmental destruction did not reach a state of desperation because, compared to Europe, the climate was relatively warm and moist and because ecological balance was narrowly achieved through population adjustment.

During the eighteenth century, the mortality rates for newborns and infants are estimated to have greatly improved (Hayami 1973a). The decrease in the death rate and the lengthening of life span are seen as direct indicators of the improvement of living standards. If management of childbirth, in what was a land-based agricultural society, had not been realized by the control of birth periods—by marriage later in life and longer lactation periods, as well as through abortion and infanticide—sooner or later, the balance of population and resources would have been destroyed and society as a whole would have inevitably fallen into poverty. As Susan Hanley argues, it is not possible to judge whether the living standards of the Japanese at the end of the nineteenth century were higher than those of contemporary western Europe or western Europe at the beginning of its industrialization (Hanley 1983). Nevertheless, it is a fact that elements measuring the quality of life such as health and life expectancy, material culture, and lifestyles improved from the sixteenth century through the nineteenth century.

Eighteenth-century Edo society was the period of maturation for Tokugawa civilization as well as the period that saw the first movements of a new civilization system. The development of a heightened curiosity about the outside world, especially Europe and the United States, was a sign of this new civilization. A group of people with modern ideas and behavior patterns emerged from these conditions. The emergence of a popular society of large-scale production, consumption, and communication became apparent during the 1810s and 1820s (Kawazoe 1979). The population growth that began again in the nineteenth century was the first step in departing from the ecological balance that was achieved in the eighteenth century.

Translated by Kim Kono.

Note

On the demography of pre-industrial Japan, see Akira Hayami (2001*a*).

8

Domains and Their Economic Policies

SHUNSAKU NISHIKAWA AND MASATOSHI AMANO

1. Introduction

It was customary in the Tokugawa period to speak of the "three-hundred lords (daimyo)," but the number of holders of domains rated at greater than 10,000 *koku* (approximately 50,000 bushels), which was the precise definition of the daimyo status, was a little more than 260. These domains—the territory the lords ruled—produced more than 74 per cent of the country's assessed product of about 30 million *koku* (Fukuzawa, 1959: 294–5). A "*koku*" is a unit of measure for grains and liquor equal to about five US bushels. However, in the *kokudaka* (putative rice yield) system of the Tokugawa economy, a *koku* invariably referred to rice. A *kokudaka* of 200,000 *koku*, for example, would signify the estimated yield of the domain when converted into rice, 40 per cent (80,000 *koku*) of which would, as a rule, be the share of the lord and his vassals. This imputed yield was the estimated amount of the total rice harvest within the territory, but this did not necessarily correspond to the actual amount of rice harvested. *Kokudaka* assessments—albeit the adopted average yields per unit of land being lower than those for wet paddies—were also levied on dry fields where rice cultivation was impossible. If 80 per cent of a 200,000 *koku* assessed productivity is assumed to have been wet-paddy rice agriculture, a rice tax of 80,000 *koku* would have come to 50 per cent of the amount of rice actually harvested in the domain.

Rice production rose in the seventeenth century due to an extensive expansion of paddy fields, and in the eighteenth century due to advances in productivity brought about by intensive agricultural methods. The seventeenth-century increases were, by and large, the result of domains' land reclamation projects to increase their annual tax base in response to being forced to expend at least half or more of their annual revenue under the alternate attendance system (*sankin kôtai*). To a certain extent, the fruits of the seventeenth-century land reclamation effort were later added to the imputed rice yield (*kokudaka*) through a reappraisal of the land. In contrast, it is difficult to make precise estimates of productivity gains in the eighteenth century, for the rise in the imputed rice yield itself generally was lower than the actual harvested yield. For this reason, it was not uncommon for effective tax rates to fall to less than 40 per cent of the actual harvested yield. Furthermore, increases in rice production caused a drop in rice prices relative to other prices, as well as making it possible to turn to other crops, especially the so-called cash crops such as rapeseed, safflower, indigo, salt, and cotton, most of which were served as "industrial materials."

As a result, cash values of agricultural products rose well above rice earnings (rice price × production volumes). The above types of cash crops as well as the processed goods made from them—such as lamp oil, paper, and cotton cloth—were generally regarded as domainal specialties (*kokusanhin*). Intent on increasing production of these goods, selling them at the national markets centered in Osaka and Edo, and adding these profits to domainal coffers, domains were already establishing domain monopolies (*senbaisei*) throughout the country in the mid-seventeenth century. But, as we will see below, their numbers rapidly increased from the eighteenth to the nineteenth century. In previous research these were regarded as domainal mercantilist policies. However, (1) most previous research tends to be limited to individual domains or individual goods; (2) it has also largely ignored the fact that such mercantilist domains had to face the competitive situations in Osaka, which was the central market for the aforesaid commodities; (3) research has been inattentive to the fact that in order to plan production increases in domainal specialties many domains printed domainal notes and made it easy to finance domainal production and business transactions on-the-spot. However, Yasuzô Horie's 1933 work is an exception to points (1) and (3).

This present chapter begins in Section 2 with a review of Horie's pioneering research, followed by a summation and classification of domains' monopolies and their institutional arrangements in the form of trading bureaus (*kokusan kaisho*), and of cases of note printing and circulation which have been brought to light by later research. We outline, via quantitative data, periodic trends and the distribution of eastwest variations and domainal size differences. In Section 3 we shift to individual case studies of the promotion of exportable commodities in wider markets from the late eighteenth to the early nineteenth century in Tokushima and four other domains. In Section 4 we conclude by touching on the thought of Kaiho Seiryô, who strongly promoted export-oriented domainal economic policy.

2. Monopolies, Trading Bureaus, and Domainal Notes

2.1. *Monopoly or monopsony?*

The first comprehensive research on domainal monopolies was Horie's "List of domainal monopolies" (Horie 1933: 268–76). However, written almost seventy years ago, its list of examples is limited to seventy-eight items. Even so, it is an analytical list, noteworthy for classifying each example by both purchasing (or production) and selling (or distribution) methods.

Table 8.1 is a cross-tabulation derived from Horie's tables. The numerical values indicate the number of monopolies in terms of a single product scheme. Accordingly, if one domain put into operation multiple monopolies each monopoly could add to the aggregate. In addition, there are three cases in which the form of trading deviated because the operational guidelines for one monopoly were changed along the way: the wax of Chôshû (a domain of 369,000 *koku*), the iron of Matsue (186,000 *koku*), and the paper of Tosa (240,000 *koku*). In Table 8.1. these are each counted as 0.5 before and after the change, making a total of 1. Among the seventy-five total monopolies, 38.5 are unspecified with respect to purchasing and 25.5 are unspecified with respect to selling. If we throw out the 22.5 unspecified with respect to both purchasing and selling, the total number of monopolies that we are talking about is no more than about fifty. Nevertheless, we can see the following.

From the above table we see that among the systems designated a "domainal monopoly" a scant twelve were intra-domainal monopolies (row 5, column 1) and most (34.5) were intra-domainal monopsonies (rows 1–3, column 6). When we take into consideration the competitive nature of the central markets for commodities that were exported monopolistically, this fact becomes all the more clear. According to Akira Yoshinaga, more than thirty domains (in the case of paper) and close to twenty (in the case of wax) were selling outside of their domains via domainal monopolies or through trading bureaus (Yoshinaga 1973: 231–33). Of course, since there were differences in quality and prices among these we cannot say that all were equally competitive goods. But,

Table 8.1. Distribution of frequency of monopolies by their types

Purchasing	Selling					
	Distribution in the domain	Export out of domain	Both of the left	Resemblance to export	No entry	Total
Production	0	0	2	0	0	2
Direct purchase	6	9	4	8.5[1]	2	29.5
Indirect	1	3	0	0	1	38.5
No entry	5	11	0	0	22.5[1]	75[2]
Total	12	23	6	8.5	25.5	

Source: Nishikawa and Ishibe (1985: table 3 originally, Horie (1933)).

Notes: (1) About a fraction of 0.5, see the text.
(2) Although the original data have three "Shimeuri," we have removed them.

on the other hand, since we also cannot consider them completely exclusive, we would have to say that there were competitive goods in every commodity market. Accordingly, it did not always mean that whichever domain supplied these goods, was able to demonstrate strong monopolistic power. However, in the following discussion, we have decided to respect the customary inclusive concept of monopoly and refer to cases of domains attempting to monopolize exports outside their domains as "domainal monopolies" or simply "monopolies."

2.2. Monopolies and the trading bureaus

Yoshinaga's "List of *kokusan kaisho*" (1973: 234–340) is more than a one-page table—it actually fills up a small book. It is an all-inclusive list arranged chronologically and classified nationwide by domain, covering such things as the implementation of monopolies and various forms of trading bureaus, changes in operations (including suspensions and reopening), and terminations. Looking at this source we see that forty years after Horie's list, clear historical evidence has increased phenomenally, due especially to the development of socioeconomic history and regional historical research in the postwar period.

Let us take a look at the example of Chôshû domain. Horie listed four items—paper, wax, indigo, and imported foreign cloths, to which added in the Yoshinaga table was rapeseed. But only their inaugural year (1791) is recorded and it is unclear whether they were suspended or terminated. In addition, ten agencies in all were established as trading and finance bureaus, beginning with the Bureau of Welfare (*Buiku-kyoku*) in 1763 up until the Paper Trading Bureau in 1857. Among these, cotton, salt, rice, maritime products, paper, and others were handled by such offices established for specific items, but both *Kokusan-kata* and *Sanbutsu kaisho* were trading and finance bureaus that did not specify the item they handled. Moreover, bureaus established in the Inland Sea port towns of Shimonoseki and Kaminoseki were branch offices of the Bureau of Welfare and served as financial intermediaries for cargo exchange with merchant ships that docked there. Thus we must take heed of the fact that in the first instance the functions of the *kaisho* also included financial services, and extended even to protectionist agencies, as with the Indigo Trading Bureau in the domainal indigo industry.

It was also natural that domains engaged in trade with each other for mutual profit. Thus, for example, we see from Yoshinaga's data on Chôshû that in 1834 the domain had planned to trade its locally-produced salt for coal from northern Kyûshû, and actually implemented trade with the Satsuma domain in southwestern Kyûshû in 1859. Chôshû's trade with domains such as nearby Gôtô, Kokura and Tsushima, as well as distant domains such as Aizu, more than 800 km. to the northeast.

It should be noted that domestic merchants participated in domain-run trade and the trade organizations of wholesalers were substantially included among them. In the case of the Salt Trading Bureau of Nakanoseki (present-day Hôfu), the domainal retainer in charge only collected export taxes, hardly participating at all in the actual management of the bureau. Even in those cases of monopolies in which retainers were more deeply engaged in management, there is no reason to ignore the fact that merchants also participated in trading and financing operations.

Table 8.2, based in part on Yoshinaga's table, is the result of adding up the number of domains that enacted monopoly and/or *kaisho* policies by period. This periodization is crude and merely commonsensical. Given

Table 8.2. The numbers of *Han*: monopoly and *Kaisho* carried out

Period	1601–87	1688–1735	1736–88	1789–1829	1830–59	1860–71
Total of Sorts						
(1)	26	28	37	69	70	39
(2)	1	1	6	29	56	82
(3)	1	1	4	18	28	15
(4)	26	28	39	80	98	106
Large *Han* (over 100,000 *koku*)						
(1)	20	19	26	31	26	15
(2)	1	1	6	18	26	36
(3)	1	1	4	12	17	9
(4)	20	19	28	37	35	42
Small *Han* (under 100,000 *koku*)						
(1)	6	9	11	38	44	24
(2)	0	0	0	11	30	46
(3)	0	0	0	6	11	6
(4)	6	9	11	43	63	64
Eastern Japan						
(1)	12	10	10	23	23	10
(2)	0	0	3	11	29	35
(3)	0	0	1	5	12	2
(4)	12	10	12	29	40	43
Western Japan						
(1)	14	18	27	46	47	29
(2)	1	1	3	18	27	47
(3)	1	1	3	13	16	13
(4)	14	18	27	51	58	63

Source: Nishikawa and Ishibe (1985: tables 1 and 2). The original is Yoshinaga (1973).

Note: (1) Monopoly to the single commodity
(2) *Kaisho*
(3) Overlapping
(4) Is given by, (1) + (2) − (3).

the circumstances of the entries in the original table, even dividing it more finely would probably not obtain meaningful figures. Further divisions can be deemed impossible because there are too many cases in which the duration of the monopoly cannot be confirmed, or else the constant reorganizations and renaming of trading bureaus revealed by historical materials and research have been too exhaustively documented. In calculating the number of domains, we counted as one a domain that had attempted even one monopoly or trading bureau (*kaisho*) respectively in a particular time period, and we decided not to be particular about it even when a domain ceased recording them or completely terminated their operation the following year. As a result, domains that put into operation a monopoly (row 1) and a *kaisho* (row 2) together at the same time would be counted in duplicate. Since rows (1) and (2) differ only in name while the degree of domainal participation varied, and since authorizing the establishment of a *kaisho* meant, in any case, that the domain enacted a policy of increasing domainal commodities, it is necessary to exclude from the gross total cases (row 3) where (1) and (2) are duplicated. The result obtained in row (4) turns out to be the number of domains that had initiated or enacted at least one or the other of a monopoly or *kaisho*.

If we look again at the case of Chôshû, this domain is calculated as one straight through to the Meiji period. This is due to the adoption of an unusual tax system for the poor mountainous region where short of wet paddies, paper was collected as annual tribute instead of rice. Moreover, this took the form of the domain buying up the paper. This purchase was a fictive transaction. One may regard this as a peripheral system, but since "purchased" paper was exported to Osaka by the authorities, this should be seen as a genuine domainal monopoly. It was indeed an early example of it. Since the larger the domain the more it had as export goods, there were many that, like Chôshû, were included in our calculations from beginning to end, implying that the table cannot measure the efforts by these domains to increase commodity production from the eighteenth century (salt and other commodities that became the target of *kaisho* scheme in the case of Chôshû). However, because even the large domains of Tsu, Hikone, Tottori (300,000 *koku* each), Kurume (210,000 *koku*) and others were not tabulated until the first quarter of the eighteenth century, and because there were various domains of 100,000 *koku* possessing neither monopolies nor *kaisho* and still others that did not even try to, the totals for the domains for each period make it at least possible to see trends and distributions by period, domain size (*kokudaka*), and location (eastern or western Japan). Accordingly:

1. The number of domains that put monopolies or *kaisho* into operation increased. The increase of *kaisho* schemes is especially striking.
2. The increase was remarkable from the late eighteenth to the early nineteenth century, with the number of domains doubling from thirty-nine

to eighty. In Table 8.2 the figures for size of *kokudaka* and east–west clas-
sifications are abridged, but Nishikawa and Ishibe (1985: tables 1 and
2) have recorded the following trends.

3. In the size analysis, large domains (above 100,000 *koku*) took precedent
in the seventeenth and the first half of the eighteenth centuries, while
small domains (under 100,000 *koku*) caught up from the eighteenth century on.

4. There is no notable discrepancy in the east–west comparison, except
for the total number for western Japan in general being consistently
large and occupying over one-half to two-thirds of the national total.

5. During the ten years from the year after the opening of the ports (1859)
until the abolition of the domains (1871), 106 domains attempted
monopoly or *kaisho* operations, but among these were country products such as raw silk and tea which were destined for export overseas.

2.3. Domainal commodities and note issues

Taking up the relation between monopolies and domainal notes, Horie
indicated that there were connections in the eight domains listed in Table
8.3. Horie's study examined forty-eight domains, so this amounted to
nearly 20 per cent. He made a provisional distinction according to
whether a monopoly or domainal note was adopted first, but since this
leads to the same results more attention should be paid to the fact that
both were linked on many occasions.

Incidentally, Horie did not count Chôshû domain among these.
However, this must be deemed a slip-up because Chôshû's issuing of
notes goes back to the late seventeenth century (Nishikawa and Tanimura

Table 8.3. Cases of monopoly and domainal notes

Han (Kokudaka)	Aims	Commodity	Year[1]	Domainal notes
(koku)				
Himeji (150,000)	Monopoly	Cotton	1821	1820–21
Gujô (40,000)	Monopoly	Raw silk	1860	1854–60
Kanô (32,000)	Monopoly	Umbrella	1860	1859
Akita (286,000)	Domainal notes	Rice	1754	1755–56
Funai (21,000)	Domainal notes	Mat	1832	Horeki Notes?
Matsue (186,000)	For issued notes[2]	Iron[3]	1687	1675
Uwajima (100,000)	For issued notes[2]	Paper[3]	1804–18	Horeki notes?
Kameoka (50,000)[4]	For issued notes[2]	Cotton[3]	Uncertain	Kansei notes?

Source: Horie (1933: chapter 4). Year relied upon Nihon ginkô (1975).

Notes: (1) Year of introducing monopoly or issuing of domainal notes.
(2) Utilizing to the already issued domainal notes.
(3) Commodities for utilizing the domainal notes.
(4) Also called Kameyama-han, Tamba Province.

1980). Moreover, since it is safe to say that all the other domains in Horie's sample also were looking into the use of domainal notes, it is best to consider the relations between monopolies and note issues as rather close. In fact, according to Miki, who conducted a detailed investigation of the issuing of notes by Awa domain (Miki 1964–65: Vol. 37, 321–41, Vol. 38, 126–42 & 227–49), the opinion statements of *samurai* officials in the domain clearly reveal recognition of the Paper Money Bureau—along with the Indigo Office and Bill Finance Office—as an authority in charge of domainal financial affairs.

Table 8.4 shows the number of note-issuing domains so far known, by period, that Shimbo (1980) compiled from "The List of Paper Money in the Tokugawa era" in *Currency of Japan*, Vol. 6. (Nihon ginkô chôsakyoku 1975.)

The periodization differs slightly from Table 8.2, but that does not really become an obstacle to verifying the parallel trend toward the increase in both monopolies and domainal notes from the eighteenth century on. The correlation between the upper row (monopoly and/or *kaisho*) and the lower row (domainal notes) can be clearly seen. The drop in the number of note-issuing domains for the period 1736–71 compared to the previous period is likely due to the 1707 ban by the *bakufu* on note use. This ban was lifted twenty-three years later, but as is widely known permission to re-issue was restricted in most cases to domains that had already issued paper currency before (Nihon ginkô chôsakyoku 1974). Consequently, it is not unusual that such a ban was used as a temporary check on re-issues and illegal issues.

According to Yamaguchi's calculations, the regional distribution of note-issuing domains was most dense in Kyûshû and Shikoku (nearly 100 per cent), followed by Chûgoku, Kinki, and Chûbu (70–75 per cent),

Table 8.4. Monopoly, *kaisho,* and the issuing of domainal notes

Periods	1601–87	1688–1735	1736–88	1789–1829	1830–59	1860–71	Uncertain
Number of *han* introducing monopoly and *kaisho*	26	28	39	80	98	106	—
	1601–1735	1736–71	1772–1817	1818–29	1830–59	1860–71	Uncertain
Number of *han* issuing the domainal notes	67	47	44	48	91	59	27

Source: Upper section: Table 8.2. Lower section: Shimbo (1980).

with Kantô and Tôhoku (40 per cent) at the lowest level (Yamaguchi 1983: 113–42). The gap between the 70–100 per cent rate for western Japan and the 40 per cent rate for eastern Japan is substantial, and it is likely that it indicates differences in financial development.

3. Case Studies

In this section we will examine several individual cases to shed light on the historical significance of domainal commodity promotion policies. In the last half of the seventeenth century, under the reigns of Tokugawa Ietsuna and Tokugawa Tsunayoshi, the renewing, shifting, and transferring of fiefs among lords diminished and lords (daimyo) of the latter half of the eighteenth century strengthened the stability of domains. Faced at that time with the impending bankruptcy of domainal finances, lords moved away from relying on the imposition of extra taxes and domainal debt and began to cope with the situation by depending increasingly on the production and distribution of market-oriented goods. Thus, regulations concerning commodity trading were strengthened, and with the promotion and monopoly of exportable commodities as an objective, paper currency began to be issued in a conscious linkage with commodity promotion policies. In this section, taking up the cases of five domains, Tokushima of Awa, Himeji of Harima, Kaga, Takamatsu of Sanuki, and Wakayama of Kii, we would like to point out the fact that domainal commodity promotion policies show signs of a continual strengthening from the latter half of the eighteenth century to the end of the Tokugawa period.

3.1. Tokushima domain: the late eighteenth century

In order to see the developmental process of domainal commodity promotion policies in the late eighteenth century we will first take up the case of Tokushima domain (258,000 *koku*). Under the Meiwa and Kansei-era Reforms in the late eighteenth century, the domainal government planned the promotion of an important specialty commodity, indigo. Let us now examine the circumstances of its promotion (Amano 1986: 11–46).

The origins of Awa indigo go back to the early fifteenth century, but its development as a specialty product is seen from the mid-Tokugawa period. Awa indigo did not appear in the *Kefukigusa*, a well-used source from which one can learn a great deal about the national scope of commodity production in the early seventeenth century, but it did appear in the early eighteenth century *Wakan Sansai Zue*. However, the appraisal of Awa indigo in the *Zue* was still lower than that of Settsu indigo and Yamashiro indigo. In terms of cultivated area, Awa indigo was still produced in the hundreds of *chô* (1 *chô* = 0.992 ha) around the mid-seventeenth century. However, at the beginning of the eighteenth century it had over swept the coastal villages of the River Yoshino. According to a 1740 survey, 237 of 331 villages (approximately 70 per cent) in the seven districts along the river cultivated up to 3000 *chô*. Indigo production then again intensified through the last half of the eighteenth century and totaled 6,500 *chô* of cultivated area in 1800. This doubling of cultivated area during the sixty-year period from 1740 to 1800 reveals the extent of the growth of Awa indigo in the eighteenth century.

Tokushima domain had occasion to strengthen regulations concerning the production and distribution of Awa indigo in the early eighteenth century, but they had to be lifted due to the opposition from leaf producing farmers. Consequently, the growth of indigo production in the eighteenth century brought about a buyer's market at the important Osaka market, giving rise to a kind of rivalry among urban wholesalers on the one hand and regional merchants and producers on the other. The aim of the Meiwa-era domainal reforms carried out by the tenth lord of Tokushima domain, Hachisuka Shigeyoshi, was to resolve such crises and to enact specific measures against domainal bankruptcy.

The Meiwa Reforms that related directly to Awa indigo were carried out in accordance with the 1766 proposal of Ogawa Yasozaemon, headman of Takabatake Village in Myôzai District, which constituted the consensus opinion of indigo interests within the domain. Ogawa's proposal made clear what kinds of problems Tokushima's indigo industry was facing in the late eighteenth century and what kind of reform was needed, and submitted a new scheme to this end. Awa indigo of the eighteenth century, supported by the financial strength of the Osaka market, was growing, even while dependent on its distribution and financial controls. But such controls eventually became fetters. Ogawa's proposal, taking the eighteenth-century development of the indigo industry as its basis, called for the establishment of an indigo-ball trading bureau which the domainal government would control in Tokushima and keep separate from the distribution and financial controls of Osaka wholesalers. It next proposed opening indigo markets and soliciting purchases in Tokushima from Osaka brokers, conducting transactions in competition with the Osaka market. In order for this trading bureau, which would eventually materialize as the government indigo office, to conduct business smoothly, this same proposal also called for the Tokushima government to function as a commercial credit provider in place of the Osaka merchant houses. According to the proposal, the bureau would pay exchange loans of up to three months and compute reductions in interest rates for rural shippers while on the other hand it would also provide credit of up to sixty days for the Osaka brokers who came to Tokushima. It can be said that the establishment of an indigo-ball trading bureau in Tokushima was something that would threaten and attempt to take the place of the Osaka wholesalers, who occupied the top ring of the national commodity distribution network. Tokushima domain, which decided to follow Ogawa's proposal once it recognized the proposal's significance, moved in the direction of acting as an advocate for a regional economy formed by the growth of industry and local capital.

However, it was during the Tanuma period (1758–86) when the reorganization of the national commodity distribution system was advancing in the form of central city leadership. Tanuma's trade association policy, which was aimed at Osaka, was conducted in an effort to reorganize the national commodity distribution system centered on the Osaka market by organizing as chartered trade associations the new national distribution network that had grown in the eighteenth century. In this period, economic policies were consequently developed in both center and periphery, in an antagonistic relation, reflecting their respective interests. The shogunate, taking the side of the Osaka wholesalers and brokers in their opposition against Tokushima's Meiwa scheme, ordered its termination. But Tokushima took further efforts to see it through. Finally, in 1769, the shogunate ordered the retirement and house arrest of the 32-year-old lord Hachisuka Shigeyoshi and annulled the scheme by government fiat. The antagonism in this period between center and periphery due to the industrial development of the eighteenth century thus came to an end in the form of the collapse of the Meiwa scheme and the reversion back to the old state of affairs. However, despite this collapse, the problems it raised were inherited and their resolution was sought from 1790 on by the Kansei-era Reforms of Hachisuka Haruaki, the legitimate heir to Shigeyoshi as Tokushima's eleventh lord. Under the Kansei Reforms, the institutional framework related to the production and distribution of indigo was structurally overhauled and markets were formed through the systemization of Awa indigo merchants and producers. Tokushima managed to sustain the expansion of the indigo market by implementing the Meiwa and Kansei-era Reforms following the eighteenth-century growth of Awa indigo production.

3.2. *Himeji and Kaga domains: the early nineteenth century*

Next we will take up the early nineteenth-century cases of Himeji (150,000 *koku*) Harima Province and Kaga (1,023,000 *koku*). By the early seventeenth century, Harima had already become one of Japan's principal cotton-producing regions, ranking with Kawachi, Izumi, Settsu, and Bingo. At the onset of the eighteenth century, cotton cultivation expanded and cotton cloth production grew into a rural industry. Then in the late eighteenth century, an antagonistic relationship with the distribution controls of the urban wholesale merchants in the Osaka market developed as Harima became known for its white cotton cloth. We can say that Himeji's trade monopoly was an attempt to resolve such difficulties and at the same time to take measures against the bankruptcy of domainal finances. Here we will first examine Himeji's trade monopoly, mainly following the work of Hozumi (1970: 84–254).

In Himeji, domainal government reforms were carried out at the beginning of the nineteenth century under the direction of chief retainer Sun'ô Kawai in order to resolve the bankruptcy of domainal finances. This marked the appearance of aggressive development in domainal commodity promotion policy. A cotton monopoly was implemented as its main link. To overcome the Osaka wholesale merchants' distribution controls—one of the main difficulties facing Himeji cotton cloth at the time— Himeji planned a shipment of cotton cloth to Edo in 1810. It took about ten years of preparation and testing before Himeji's cotton cloth monopoly could be realized in 1821. An examination of the scheme of this cotton cloth monopoly reveals that it took the form of opening trading bureaus in Himeji's cotton districts, licensing thirty cotton cloth wholesalers for Edo shipment, collecting the cotton cloth from weavers via brokers exclusively through the licensed wholesalers and turning the cloth into finished product via bleaching processors commissioned in the domain. But what one must be aware of in this instance is that this method required prepaying 70 per cent of the cloth's value per cargo booking with paper money called *momen kitte* (literally cotton cloth notes) that the *kokusan kaisho* issued. Consciously weaving in the measure of issuing domainal notes as regional currency, Himeji's cotton cloth monopoly was able to realize a certain success. Shimbo and Hasegawa (1988: 264–7) note that this can be seen as one innovation that appeared in the nineteenth century. Shipments of Himeji cotton cloth to Edo expanded greatly once the system of direct shipments was established. According to data on Edo wholesalers published by Hayashi (1967: 252) the volume of shipments received in Edo showed phenomenal increases: 370,000 *tan* (1 *tan* approximately equals 10 yards) in 1824; 620,000 *tan* in 1837; and 870,000 *tan* in 1838–40. Thus, in response to chief retainer Sun'ô Kawai having seized upon this cotton cloth monopoly as the means to build up domainal wealth, Abe Masakura, Magistrate of Osaka West District and shogunate supporter, recognized the gravity of the situation and vigorously demanded the monopoly's suspension in 1842. We may justly conclude that, as the nineteenth century progressed, the structure of commodity production and distribution within the shogunal–domainal structure was clearly changing.

Kaga domain provides another example of a domain putting into practice the direct shipment of domainal products to Edo. According to Tanaka (1986: 77–243), Kaga's domainal commodity promotion policy began in earnest from the late eighteenth century and was put into operation intermittently until the end of the Tokugawa period. The late eighteenth century production policy was implemented after the domain suffered the effects of the failed Hôreki Reforms, which had attempted to conquer the poverty of domainal finances at the time. Along with the provision of low-rate loans for production districts centered in Etchû and Noto, surveys of the volume of the domain's commodity production and consumption were carried out, and then, as the nineteenth century began, these product surveys turned toward a quantitative grasp of the trade structure. These surveys became the basis for production policy spanning a nearly twenty-year period from 1818 to 1837. This production policy was in effect for a long time, and had such a conspicuous influence on the domainal economy that it cannot be ignored. We should note, as well, the details of this policy development. Direct delivery of Kaga's products to Edo was achieved in 1828 in the process of developing this production policy.

Kaga's specialty products, such as Komatsu silk and Jôhana silk (together known simply as Kaga silk), competed in the Kyoto market with local silk, such as Tango silk which had attained rapid growth under the aggressive promotion of Miyazu domain at the time. Kaga silk had gradually stagnated as a result of such competition between production areas. It is likely, therefore, that the policy of direct delivery to Edo of Kaga commodities broke through the stagnation of Kaga silk and was a newly instituted marketing strategy based on steady domainal industrial development centered in Etchû. Further investigation is necessary concerning the value of this policy, but its significance is not inconsiderable judging from the following: (1) the implementation of direct Edo delivery for not only Kaga silk but also for a wide range of domainal commodities such as cotton and other cloths, metal products, and paper; (2) the attempts to acquire manufacturing technology expected to add still more value to finished goods over unfinished ones in order to further independence in the current markets; (3) the development of the idea of providing credit by product categories or shipping; and also (4) the promotion of ship construction in order to better secure means of transport. Incidentally, this policy of direct delivery to Edo of Kaga's domainal products appears to have been implemented again even in the production policies of the 1840s.

Through the cases of Himeji and Kaga, one might go so far as to say that early nineteenth-century development policies took even deeper root over those of the late eighteenth century in two ways: in policy measure terms with the conscious use of domainal notes as regional currency and also in marketing strategy terms with the direct shipment of domainal commodities to Edo. We will now turn to a consideration of the kinds of developments we might see in domainal commodity promotion policies in the course of the nineteenth century.

3.3. *Takamatsu and Wakayama domains: the mid-nineteenth century*

The cases of Takamatsu (120,000 *koku*) and Wakayama (555,000 *koku*) will provide us with a look at the process of developing domainal commodity promotion policies in the mid-nineteenth century. At the beginning of the nineteenth century Takamatsu first adopted an aggressive policy known as the Kyôwa new policy (*Kyôwa no shimpô*), and in the 1830s, put into operation a systematic domainal commodity promotion policy targeting sugar as a strategic industry, reaping the success of what is called the sugar exchange scheme (*satô kawase shihô*). Based on this expansion of the sugar industry, the scheme was extended to the operation of inter-domainal trade with Wakayama, which tied together Sanuki, Kii, and Kantô. Here we will mainly relate the particulars of this operation following the works of Kihara (1978: 82, 88) and Einenkai (1932).

The new policy was enacted in accordance with the proposals of Tamai Saburoemon who became chief retainer at the start of the nineteenth century when the reign of the eighth Takamatsu lord Matsudaira Yorinori began. The new policy was a wide-ranging domainal commodity promotion policy that utilized domainal notes. Through the enforcement of the new policy, the domain reclaimed the frontage of Higashihamachô in Takamatsu, built Shinminatomachi, and, forming a wholesale district, prepared a distribution organization there. In conjunction with this, it enacted a domainal commodity promotion policy in order to encourage import substitution of the goods that flowed in from Osaka area and various domains and to check the outflow of domainal gold and silver. It dispensed loans of production capital with domainal notes, targeting for domainal commodity promotion a wide variety of goods not previously produced in the domain, such as: pots, pottery, paper, brushes, ink, silk and cotton textiles, medicines, tea, cabinets, chests, umbrellas, lacquer, wax, slaked lime, and *tatami* facing. Developments in sugar manufacturing methods were made after Japanese sugar production was pioneered in the mid-eighteenth century by the fifth lord Matsudaira Yoritaka, who supposedly enjoyed the study of medicinal herbs. It seems that with Sakiyama Shûkei's success in manufacturing fifty *koku* of refined sugar in 1790 in Sanbonmatsu Village of Ôuchi District, the improvement and dissemination of technology for sugar cane cultivation and sugar manufacturing methods were promoted in the domain in the beginning of the nineteenth century. Sakiyama himself served as "*seihô denjuyaku*" (manufacturing method instructor). The area of sugar cane cultivation increased from the end of the eighteenth century to the first half of the nineteenth century, reaching 1,000 *chô* in the 1830s. The Kyôwa scheme is thought to have performed a definite role in this enlargement in the area of sugar cane cultivation.

Yet, the Kyôwa policy package also included loans to regional merchants and wealthy farmers as well as to retainers impoverished with consumer debts. In doing so, the aggressive measures of the policy package soon tended toward recklessness and lacked regularity in their execution. This ceased in 1807. Although the Kyôwa package performed a certain role as a development policy during several years at the start of the nineteenth century, it lacked scrupulous discipline and failed when it came to the supervision of currency flow in the region. As it entered the nineteenth century, Takamatsu fell into a chronic financial crisis and made efforts to offset this through the financial power of the Osaka market, but it is difficult to say if even this had any results. Finally, Takamatsu was driven into the corner of issuing additional domainal notes, which resulted in the value of its notes plummeting.

Having suffered this failure, Takamatsu domain, under the ninth lord, Matsudaira Yorihiro, undertook the Tempô Reforms from the 1820s to the 1830s, with the management of Kimura Wataru, Kakei Masanori (who later changed his name to Kakei Hayami) and others. These reforms vigilantly regulated paper money and effected drastic fiscal reform. In 1828 Takamatsu took the measure of allowing long-term tax exemption for the fields of wealthy farmer-merchants (*gônôshô*) who paid the domainal government a lump sum in domainal notes corresponding to the long-term share of tax rice for their land holdings. Along with this measure, Takamatsu also sought the withdrawal of circulating notes with profits gained through the sale of government forests and land from 1828 to 1830. By such measures, a total of more than 40,000 *kan* (1 *kan* = 8.27 pounds) worth of silver notes were withdrawn from circulation. Then in 1832, Takamatsu took action on fiscal reform. In conjunction with halting the repayment of loans due to creditors in Edo and Kyoto for three years, Takamatsu levied a government rice fund of 10,000 *koku* rice and 50,000 *ryô* gold on the domainal population. By halting the repayment of loans, they cancelled Osaka-bound rice shipments and sold them within the domain. By shipping the rice to Hyôgo and selling it to the *saké* brewers of Ikeda, Itami, and elsewhere, they endeavored to amass hard currency to increase its specie reserve.

On these premises Takamatsu discontinued the circulation of Hôreki-era notes in the third month of 1833 and issued new Tempô notes. On this occasion, by taking a specie reserve into account, they set the exchange of ten *monme* of the new notes at one hundred *monme* of the old notes and sixty *monme* of the new notes at one *ryô* of gold. By exchanging the devalued old notes for the new notes by government fiat and resolutely enforcing the regulation of old notes, Takamatsu sought a revival of note circulation. They then contrived a plan known as the sugar exchange scheme in which the domainal economy would be rebuilt based on the issuance of Tempô notes and a systematic promotion of the sugar industry. This scheme was conceived and presented by Note Bureau Comptroller Kusaka Gizaemon while searching for a way to repay the domain's Edo and Osaka debts after the repayment suspension period ended in 1835. Kakei Masanori, who was in charge of domain accounts, had recommended Kusaka as someone knowledgeable in finance.

The domain, which had decided to adopt Kusaka's recommendations, concurrently posted him to the "*Osumashikata*" (Settlement of Accounts Office) that was created as an independent agency in charge of debt repayment operations under the jurisdiction of the Accounts Magistrate in the twelfth month of 1835. Once they had amassed the rice and specie that had until then been lent out for debt repayment in the *Osumashikata*, they turned it into a specie reserve and issued paper currency at the Note Office. Through the government sugar office and the *kaisho* offices in the districts, they extended sugar exchange fund loans to sugar producers and shippers. Producers and shippers who received sugar-related credit, after having shipped and sold the sugar to the Osaka sugar trading bureau set up by Takamatsu domain's Osaka storehouse, returned its hard currency to the domainal *kaisho*, thus repaying the sugar exchange fund. Along with amassing specie and applying it to the repayment of debts and funds destined for expenses in Edo, the domain amassed surplus money at the Takamatsu Note Office.

The sugar exchange fund was intended for Osaka-bound sugar from the very beginning. Loans from the fund, made in notes, covered 70 per cent of the costs prior to shipment and were focused on the shippers' exchange (*senchû-kawase*) where accounts were settled with hard currency at the Osaka sugar trading office. However, the types of exchange funds also increased, leading to systematic sugar industry financing. Thus the operation of the sugar exchange scheme, which encompassed various stages from production to distribution, began to offer considerable convenience to sugar interests. Two to three years after initiating the project, the amount loaned for the shippers' exchange climbed annually from 80,000–90,000 *ryô* to 100,000 *ryô*. It was later said to have extended from 140,000–150,000 *ryô* to 200,000 *ryô*.

Through the operation of the scheme, the volume of notes in circulation in the domain increased a second time. There were some who had misgivings about this, but their fears were never realized. Having failed once at currency management at the start of the nineteenth century, Takamatsu domain had learned many lessons. We can conclude that upon entering the 1830s they had acquired and established practical knowledge of currency management, and had created a harmonious supply system of stable currency necessary for industrial development in the domain. The rebuilding of the domainal economy was accomplished in the 1840s through the smooth operation of the sugar exchange scheme, with the concurrent payoff of even further growth of the sugar industry in the domain. The area of sugar cane cultivation in Takamatsu, which had reached 1,000 *chô* in the 1830s, steadily enlarged afterward, surpassing 2,000 *chô* at the end of the 1840s and attaining 3,000 *chô* by the mid-1850s.

Japanese sugar production in Sanuki also exhibited phenomenal growth throughout the nineteenth century, but this brought about big changes in existing investment–production relations and gave rise to the problems of fertilizer procurement and the opening of markets. In the 1840s an inter-domainal trade plan tying together Sanuki, Kii, and Kantô was conceived and implemented in part. The trade plan, which was proposed by Yatoji Ôta of Kamihogunji Village in Uta District of Takamatsu domain, was a large-scale effort that involved both Takamatsu and Wakayama domains (Fujita 1975: 1–11). Premised on the enforcement of the shogunate's trade association dissolution order in the Tempô period, Ôta's petition called for setting up a trading bureau (*kaisho*) at Kada Bay— a strategic point for Kantô sea traffic in the Ama District of Kii—and bypassing the Osaka market. Exactly, it envisioned trade in which sugar and salt from Sanuki and Awa would be received at the Kada Bay trading bureau, where under the label of Wakayama domainal products it would be shipped directly to the Kantô area. In concert with this, it was anticipated that dried sardine fertilizer from Bôshû and Jôshû would be shipped back from the Kantô. This movement for the establishment of a *kaisho* at Kada Bay, which was promoted by Sanuki and Awa sugar producers and shippers, came to include Wakayama domain in 1845. And, in collaboration with Wakayama's Edo Warehousing Office (*Edo Shiirekata Yakusho*) it was decided to go operational in the form of inter-domainal trade tying together Sanuki, Kii, and Kantô.

It should be observed that in the background of Wakayama's decision to accept and participate in this trade plan there were changes in the domain's socioeconomic conditions. According to Fujita (1966: 134–84), the character of the "*Oshiirekata*" scheme—Wakayama's domainal commodity promotion policy—changed in the late Tokugawa period from a scheme that advocated "*osukui*" (relief) to one that pursued "*kokueki*" (literally prosperity of the country). As can also be realized from the fact that it was named "*Osukuikata*" (relief office), early Tokugawa-period "*Oshiirekata*" (Warehousing Office) sought mainly to assist the revitalization of production for residents in the coastal and mountainous areas of outer and inner Kumano, Ise, and elsewhere. But, in the nineteenth century under the reign of the tenth lord, Tokugawa Harutomi, "*Oshiirekata*" was also established in Osaka, Kyoto, Edo, and elsewhere as centers for a national commodity trade network and for regional development zones. Through the trade of domainal products they were predisposed toward the pursuit of domainal prosperity. In this sense it must be said that the joint Takamatsu–Wakayama trade plan was conceived and executed on top of changes in the economic foundations of both domains from the late eighteenth century to the nineteenth century.

According to Uchida (1985: 23–31), the shogunate, which had been observing the changing situation with great concern, announced in 1846 the termination of the trade plan's implementation and added further restraints so that the joint Takamatsu–Wakayama trade plan ceased without at all progressing as expected. However, we should note that even the partial implementation of the plan gives a picture of the times in the mid-nineteenth century. The partly realized movement for the establishment of a domainal commodity trading bureau in Kada Bay, involving as it did the *kamon* (Tokugawa-collateral daimoyo) domain of Takamatsu and the *go-sanke* (Tokugawa-related) domain of Wakayama, predated the well-known trade of the Satsuma and Chôshû domains in the late Tokugawa period. Even though it was just one early incident, the Takamatsu–Wakayama plan still has inherent historical significance for inter-domainal trade. With the development of industry and the growth of local capital in the late Tokugawa period, many domains became advocates of regional economy and began moving in the direction of functioning as unifiers of regional will. It is safe to say that the mid-nineteenth century was a period when such domains began to search together for ways to form trade networks that built upon industrial development.

As we can see in the above case studies, domain's trade promotion policies were being implemented with great breadth and depth from the late eighteenth century to the end of the shogunate. Being more than merely financial supplementation measures, these policies were progressive developments. Through the implementation of such promotion policies, domains from the late eighteenth century on prepared the institutional framework necessary to support domainal industrial development. And by attending to its systematic maintenance, these policies actually guided nineteenth century economic development.

However, when we examine the implementation of these trade and industry promotion policies, we see that they were processes of trial-and-error; in certain cases they succeeded and in others they failed. By experiencing these successes and failures, the domains were gradually able to formulate policies that were flexible and appropriate to actually attain their goals. In this sense the period from the late eighteenth century on can be regarded as one in which results could differ widely depending on the skill of policy management. We must also pay attention to the fact that people who could be called on as specialists in devising and implementing such policies were emerging in the domains. The appearance of a group of such finance officials, which could be discerned in various domainal reforms, points to this fact. Moreover, this period's characteristic feature may be that policy development tended on the whole toward progressive measures and was occasionally taken up by domain's bureaucrats knowledgeable in developmental economics. The success of Takamatsu's sugar scheme was likely a product of such conditions.

4. Political Economy in the Late Tokugawa Period

The contemporary who most clearly recognized the inevitability of domains' involvement in commerce and interregional trade was Kaiho Seiryô. He was born in Edo as the eldest son of a councilor of Meats domain (70,000 *koku*). When Seiryô was an infant his father was made a masterless samurai and became a Confucian scholar. Before long, the son too became a Confucian scholar. However, the son preferred traveling and giving lectures as service to a particular lord, and honed his own doctrine based on observations gained by his regional travels. According to Watanabe's calculation (1985: 22), the number of people who made a living the way Seiryô and his father did increased rapidly from the onset of the eighteenth century. Seiryô's dictum "the way the lord and the retainer are bound is nothing but the way of the market"—meaning that the retainer provides service to the domainal lord and receives a salary as his remuneration—was a declaration that theirs was not a feudal relationship founded on loyalty and duty (see, for example, his last work, *Keiko-dan* [Talk on Public Practice], 1813). When seen from this angle, the various domains' policies of increasing the production of exportable commodities and increasing their revenues were truly in accord with the times. Seiryô was an admirer of Masuya Koemon (1748–1821), known as Masuko—his pen name was Yamagata Bantô—who, as the head clerk of the Masuya rice merchant of Osaka, had come up with the idea of rice notes for Sendai domain (622,000 *koku*) and reaped a tidy profit for himself (Najita 1987: chapter 6). Seiryô dedicated a work to him entitled *Masuko-dan* [(Talks on Masuya Koemon]). While lamenting the dearth of substantiating evidence, Tessa Morris-Suzuki (1989: 34) surmises that by relating his doctrine in a simple fashion to "samurai officials" of various domains, Seiryô served as a catalyst for "the profound changes in economic and political structure (namely the Meiji Restoration), which were to take place half a century after his death."

Clear, direct evidence is rather meager, but it is not entirely lacking. According to Kuranami (1990: 182–9), Seiryô devoted a rather detailed passage to Chôshû's country commodities in one of his works, *Taigo dan* ([Talks on an Excellent Economist] 1813), a work that was subsequently heavily quoted in an essay written by an anonymous Chôshû retainer. Furthermore, Murata Seifu, the director of the Tempô Reforms in Chôshû, possessed a number of Seiryô's works in his library, and a memo in which Seifu recommended a careful reading of *Taigo-dan* to Sufu Masanosuke, who became the central figure in domainal policies after the Tempô Reforms, was recently discovered.

Indirect evidence and witnesses are plentiful as well. Fujita (1984, 1988) has pointed out that there are no small number of memoirs and proposals by anonymous or pseudonymous *samurai* officials. Of great interest among these is the *Kokusan-ben* [On domainal commodities] penned, by an anonymous retainer of Akita domain. Its interest lies in the author's focus on exportable commodities other than rice, such as lumber. This shows us that rice was a potent product for the domains in the northeast due to trends in rice cultivation from the middle ages and due to the necessity and profitability of supplying rice to Edo (see Table 8.3 for Akita). For that reason as well, it reveals to us that the northeastern domains turned toward Seiryô's recommended domain-run trade a little later than the domains in the west.

It is not known whether or not such financial officials as Ogawa of Tokushima or Kusaka and Ôta of Takamatsu, or others knew of Seiryô's ideas. But it is believed that their management of domainal notes and trade with Wakayama more than met with Seiryô's dictates—indeed, they outdid them. Moreover, the important point is that Ogawa and Ôta were of the farming class. It is important to realize that if they were knowledgeable in commerce and industry, despite their being peasant farmers, they did submit proposals on economic policy to domainal governments and also directly took part in realizing them. Morris-Suzuki presumes that Seiryô influenced "samurai officials" as well as "middle-ranking" samurai, but it would be more accurate to say that those in charge of domainal economic policy included "lower-ranking" samurai, merchants, and "upper-ranking" farmers.

After the Meiji Restoration, similar commodity promotion plans appeared in response to government calls, including many proposals submitted by commoners—former farmers, merchants, and doctors (Fujita 1993: 391–419). Thus, in terms of intellectual climate, Morris-Suzuki's thesis is correct. However, to tie the political economy represented by Seiryô directly to the Meiji Restoration itself and to the industrial policy that followed risks the danger of short-circuiting. This is because Seiryô's ideas, which rebelled against Confucian and Mencian doctrines, could not sweepingly disavow the Tokugawa political economic order altogether. Moreover, in the indigenous political economy, domainal commodities— being no more than one domain's products—were in the final analysis "provincial" even if they were in the national interest (*kokueki*). They did not obtain a truly "national" reach. For this reason, even in the *ancien régime*, one can see the shogunate prohibiting the domainal commodity promotion plans of various domains. Fujita (1993) has pointed out that proposals that invoked western political economy first began to appear in the middle of the 1870s. But even so, it was also natural that the central government of Meiji Japan, as a national body, did not give a full hearing to proposals tinted by motley, provincial remnants. This was because for the Meiji leaders the most urgent of all economic policy issues were: first, the introduction and development of manufacturing and mining based on modern technology, and second the maintenance of a balance of trade under the "rules of the game" of international currency. We have no objection to adding Seiryô's doctrines—especially his recommendations for domainal trade and commerce—to the Tokugawa legacy. But we end by noting that the practice of using domainal notes and the know-how concerning their management were equally an important legacy in helping Meiji Japan to weather the stormy period from the 1870s to the mid-1880s (Nishikawa and Saito 1985: 175–91).

[Nishikawa wrote Sections 1, 2 and 4, and Amano Section 3.]

Translated by Gerald Figal.

9

The Transformation of Traditional Industries

OSAMU SAITÔ AND MASAYUKI TANIMOTO

1. Introduction

The period from the beginning of the nineteenth century to the early 1880s, the deflationary period occasioned by Finance Minister Matsukata's policy package, can be seen as an age of rural development. One of the driving forces behind this development was cottage industry. The present chapter discusses how such traditional industries were affected and forced to restructure after 1859, when the opening of Japan's ports to overseas trade altered the domestic market and distribution systems. In discussing this issue, we consider external factors such as overseas trade that commenced with the opening of the treaty ports, as well as domestic factors such as how agrarian economies were affected by macrolevel fluctuations in business conditions and by the central government's fiscal policies. This becomes particularly critical with respect to the transition from the inflationary period of the late 1870s to the ensuing period of deflation.

As for development of the domestic market, we would like to draw attention not only to the expansion of market size at the macrolevel but also to (1) geographical shifts in marketing, (2) change from production for self-consumption to consumption of purchased goods, and (3) changes in the structure of distribution of those goods. Among the traditional industries existing in 1874, cotton and silk were of particular interest. They were leading industries of the day. According to Miyohei Shinohara's estimates of manufacturing output based on an early survey report of products (Shinohara 1972), the cotton and silk industries, together with the brewing industry that included *saké* brewing and the fermentation of *miso* and soy sauce, comprised 33 per cent of all manufacturing. Moreover, it was these two textile industries that were affected by the opening of trade and underwent a major transformation. The present chapter therefore concentrates on these two areas, using them as case studies of traditional industries transformed.

Section 2 examines sericulture and silk reeling, which by the latter half of the Tokugawa era had begun to develop as separate trades from the weaving sector. In this section we focus on the way the opening of the Treaty ports affected growth, and we further consider the implications of this industry's regional concentration in eastern Japan. Section 3 constitutes the core of this chapter. The opening of the ports had a dramatic impact on the cotton textile industry by allowing imported goods to flow into the marketplace, and foreign trade exerted an especially complex effect on this industry, raising the question of why certain regions flourished while others underwent a decline. We address this question from the perspective of the points noted above, and from an analysis of the formation of particular weaving districts. Then we will touch very briefly on the brewing industry (particularly *saké* brewing) in the conclusion.

2. Sericulture and Silk-reeling

2.1. Output growth

In 1864, exactly five years after the Tokugawa shogunate commenced foreign trade by opening the treaty ports at Kanagawa, Nagasaki, and Hakodate, the Edo silk wholesalers estimated in a report to the city magistrate that "before the opening of the ports, the average annual production levels" of "raw silk in the various provinces" amounted to "approximately twenty thousand bales." Calculating that one bale equals nine *kan* or 0.8 picul, then it meant 180,000 *kan* or 16,000 piculs. By 1862–63 the yearly output doubled to "approximately forty thousand bales," reaching approximately 360,000 *kan*, or 32,000 piculs. Average yearly export levels in 1862 and 1863 were "approximately thirty thousand bales," which comprised 75 per cent of domestic output. These figures attest to the tremendous stimulus to those regions producing raw silk provided by the opening of the treaty ports.[1]

This stimulus was a composite of two factors: an increase in price and an expansion in demand. Figure 9.1 is a semilogarithmic graph indicating the changes in the price of raw silk during the years between 1859 and the Meiji Restoration of 1868. Specifically, with the opening of the ports, domestic silk prices jumped 60 per cent and continued to increase at a rate of 10 per cent annually until 1865, a very high rate of price appreciation. The levels of 1865–66 represent a fourfold increase over the 1856–57 levels. It is true that there was a sudden surge of inflation during this period. But estimated price indices reveal only a threefold rate of increase over the same period, thereby indicating that raw silk increased more than other products (Shimbo 1978). Conditions at this time were indeed favorable for domestic producers of raw silk.

It may well be that the majority of the profit derived from this price increase fell into the hands of merchants rather than producers. In fact,

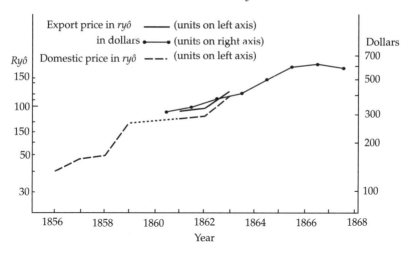

Fig. 9.1. Fluctuations in the price of raw silk, 1856–68 (per *kôri*; vertical axis indicates logarithmic units).

Source: Yokohama Shiyakusho (1961).

Note: For details about historical sources and calculation methods in this figure or those below, refer to Saitô and Tanimoto (1989).

Figure 9.1 reveals a gap of ten *ryô* for each bale (0.8 piculs) between the export price and domestic price (compare the solid lines and broken lines for the years 1861–63). Even during the 1880s, a consistent price differential was reported between the Yokohama market and regional markets, indicating that "regional wholesale merchants functioning as brokers were positioned to acquire speculative profits" (Yokohama Shiyakusho 1961: 505–6). On the other hand, it is important to remember that there also existed a set of factors allowing rural producers to derive substantial profits. As we saw above, the price differential was not merely a product of geographical or systemic conditions but should also be attributed to a "price revolution" that emerged as part of the dynamic adjustment process when an open system suddenly replaced a closed economic regime. In other words, the true reason for the price increase was that the emergence of a new overseas market led to a significant change in the demand curve, which in turn caused a sharp rise in the demand for exports as well as an increase in prices.

   As we have already seen, the level of exports in 1862–63 was extremely high, and it is reported that approximately half of all raw silk produced for the domestic market was sent to Yokohama. Such an extreme export drive did not last long, since it was achieved at the sacrifice of the supply to domestic weaving centers such as Nishijin in Kyoto. This was thus followed by a drop in output volumes and stagnant export prices caused by the shogunate's restrictive trade policy for raw silk, a panic in 1866, and the reduction in Japan's international competitiveness due to the deteriorating quality resulting from hasty mass production of inferior goods. After the Meiji Restoration, however, a recovery took place. Beginning in the early 1870s output started increasing at a high rate, averaging 8 per cent annually, and by the early 1890s had reached the level of more than 60,000 bales (51,500 piculs). (Even had demand remained stable at 20,000 bales, this signifies more than a quadruple increase in output during this thirty 40 year period that commenced just before the treaty ports were opened in 1859.) This represents a truly remarkable change.

2.2. Changing rural economy

These changes created enormous profits, not so much for foreign traders, but for Japanese merchants. Especially, profits grew to enormous sums for local merchants who acted as consignors to export merchants in Yokohama. A perfect example of such a figure is Kôshû-ya Chûemon, whose success story is found in the *History of Yokohama*. Chûemon was born into the Shinohara family of Higashi-Aburakawa Village, Yatsushiro District in the Province of Kai. His family had been a producer of both silkworm eggs and raw silk. But Chûemon purchased those products from neighboring villages, and together with his own products he sent this to a merchant in Yokohama. With this trade the family amassed a pure profit in excess of 266 *ryô* in 1867. Only eight years before this year, when the ports were opened to international trade, the household's total income was a mere twenty-three *ryô*. Even taking into account the three-fold increase in the cost of goods during this time, it is clear that their trading profits were enormous. Having said this, however, one must note that immediately afterward, Chûemon's business failed and his family was forced to reduce their trade in cocoons. The large profit of 266 *ryô* may therefore have been a somewhat extreme example, but it does seem likely that very few successful farmers and entrepreneurs were blessed with profits on the order of fifty to sixty *ryô*.

Yet it was not only those entrepreneurs from wealthy farm families who could enjoy large trading profits. Many farmers who purchased cocoons and silkworm eggs from families such as the Shinohara (see above) were from the village official class of large landholders, but this group also included other farmers who could be classified as small holders. Profits from trade undoubtedly reached peasant farmers as well. Consider a couple of village cases. The village of Kirihara in the Province of Kôzuke was a silk-producing village with no rice paddies, and carried out the entire process from raising silkworms to reeling yarn and weaving. A survey taken in 1887 reveals which activity the farm household was engaged in, sericulture or reeling, for sixty-seven out of the ninety households in the village. Of the sixty-seven households, forty-nine (73 per cent) were engaged in sericulture and fifty (75 per cent) in reeling, which means that at least three-fourths of the village was involved in one or the other aspect of silk production. When broken down by class, we find that of the thirty-six households having a dry-field farm larger than five *tan* (of these, only one household farmed more than fifteen *tan*), thirty-four were engaged in both sericulture and reeling, and the remaining two households were involved in one or the other. In contrast, among the twelve households farming three to five *tan*, three-fourths (nine households) were engaged in reeling (with eight engaged in sericulture); and of the eighteen households farming less then three *tan*, only five were involved, leaving 72 per cent of these households engaged in neither sericulture nor reeling. It is apparent that as the landholding class decreased, so too did the percentage of households involved in sericulture and reeling. The reason for this is not necessarily clear, however. It has been argued that class differences were related to the size of family labor, access to capital needed to purchase mulberry leaves, and the ability or willingness to assume financial risks. Yet we cannot ignore the fact that about a half of the small-holder households reaped profits when overseas trade started (Furushima 1963: 286–7).

The above is an example of an old silkworm-producing region where sericulture and reeling were not yet separated, but one can also cite the example of the four villages of Yatsushiro District, Kai Province. These villages were located along the southeastern shore of the Fuefuki River, an area specialized in sericulture, in contrast to villages on the other side of the river being specialized in reeling. An analysis of microdata for a pilot census conducted in 1879 shows that more than 80 per cent of the total households in all four villages were farmers, and that 80 per cent of these farm households were engaged in sericulture. Women provided sericultural labor, with 78 per cent of married women in sericulture. In this district, 83 per cent of women from owner–cultivator households, 83 per cent from part-owner or part-tenant households, and 72.5 per cent from tenant farmer households were sericulturalists. As with Kirihara village above, the higher the landholding class, the higher the ratio of farm households engaged in sericulture, but with the increasing specialization seen in the Yatsushiro region, the gap between the upper and middle classes had disappeared, and it is significant that only one-fourth of the tenant farm households were not engaged in sericulture (Saitô 1986: 411–14). In other words, the more sericulture developed, the more it appears to have benefited lower-class farm households. Having surveying detailed case studies, Yamazaki Ryûzô concluded that the expansion of sericulture following the opening of the treaty ports enabled tenant farmers to buy back their land and hence to stay on as independent farmers, a conclusion that is consistent with the findings discussed above (Yamazaki 1977: 149–50).

One may ask how much profit the small and medium-sized farm households actually made. Unfortunately, few documents exist that enable us to address this question, although we can learn from the data for the Machida family, a wealthy farm family running a business of buying cocoons and raw silk in Yamada village, Azuma District, in Kôzuke Province (Fujii et al. 1962: 34–5). A close look at documents for the years 1859 and 1863 reveals that the volume of raw silk supplied to the Machida family from fourteen farm families engaged in sericulture in a village next to Yamada increased from 80.1 to 147.55 *kan*. The average supply in 1863 was 10.54 *kan* per household, which is comparable to the average of 9 *kan* for the Yatsushiro villages in 1879. The rate of increase from 1859 to 1863 was 84 per cent with the increment of 4.8 *kan* per household or 14.3 *ryô* in value. In contrast, farm households engaged in silk reeling show slightly different data. Of the thirteen village households that supplied raw silk to the Machida family (most of which were contract producers), the total volume increased from 9.825 to 11.12 *kan*, representing a 13 per cent increase. It was a mere 0.1 *kan* increase or 6.7 *ryô* in value, which does not approach the gain enjoyed by those sericulturalist households. The volume of per-household supply in 1863 was 0.855 *kan*, which is substantially lower than the output level of 1.73 *kan* per household for Kirihara village in Jôshû Province. Yet one must exercise caution when making such comparisons, for it is recorded that not a few of those sericulturalist farmers who had previously been under financial control of the Machida family through advance payment arrangements managed to cut off the tie with the family, presumably initiating business with buyers other than the Machidas. If this is indeed the case, the actual extent of output growth in both sericulture and silk reeling may have been somewhat greater than that indicated above. In any case, it is likely that since the average number of workers per farm household must have been approximately five, the gain per worker engaged in sericulture would be three *ryô*; similarly the gain in silk reeling would be approximately 1.5 *ryô*.

These numbers offer a glimpse into how the profits from the raw silk trade in farming villages trickled down to peasant farmers of lower rank, especially in those villages engaged in sericulture. Indeed, urban merchants and government officials of late Tokugawa did witness that "it was not unusual for poor villagers in remote regions such as Kai, Shinano, Ôu, and Yashû to become rich from raw silk and to achieve extraordinary wealth."[2] Other contemporaries asserted that "after the opening of the ports, mountainous regions involved in sericulture, silk reeling and related processes showed threefold to fivefold price increases depending on the product, and such regions became wealthy."[3] Such claims were not necessarily exaggerations, at least for provinces of eastern Japan, especially Kai, Shinano, Mutsu, Dewa, Kôzuke, and (although it was not mentioned) Musashi, where "unexpected wealth" was brought to those once impoverished people of hill regions. The silk trade had a longer history than did the cotton industry, but the location of the silk industry had undergone a major shift since medieval times, especially during the 250 years of Tokugawa rule. By the time the treaty ports were opened, sericulture and silk reeling had already moved to the "barren lands amongst the mountains" commonly found in central and eastern Japan, and the industry came to be concentrated in such regions (Saitô 1983). Chapter 11 of this volume will examine the reasons for and significance of this shift. It must be noted that these industries did not penetrate all of eastern Japan's agricultural regions. For example, there was little penetration of Hitachi or Shimotsuke. It is nevertheless significant that in the late Tokugawa period the production centers were found in agriculturally disadvantaged areas of the east. The opening of export trade did not make the rich farming villages richer; instead, in the words of the Kanagawa magistrate, it brought wealth to "the poor peoples of remote territories."

2.3. Patterns of regional specialization

It is well known that the silk reeling industry achieved phenomenal growth after the Meiji Restoration. This process involved shedding many characteristics as a traditional industry. Or to quote Nakamura Takafusa, an old, traditional industry underwent a transformation and became a "neo-traditional" industry by "incorporating borrowed technologies and foreign materials" (Nakamura 1985). Viewed from a regional level, this change entailed increased production in newly emerged districts—many of which were in Nagano Prefecture—and was accompanied by a regional shift in industrial districts. As can be seen from Table 9.1, in the year 1877 Nagano Prefecture was second only to Gunma Prefecture, exceeding the national annual growth rate by more than four points and expanding at an annual rate of 13 per cent. By 1889, Nagano was in first place with 18 per cent of national production. Furthermore, when examining Suwa District (the new production center that came to lead the nation's silk reeling industry with its "Suwa-type" machines of appropriate technology), we find that in 1881 its output was 7,000 kan, which amounted to a mere 7 per cent of Nagano's total output and only 1 per cent of the nation's total; yet by 1889 it had reached 136,000 kan, or 40 per cent of Nagano's output and 15 per cent of the nation's total. Consequently, the growth of the silk reeling industry during Meiji signifies the emergence of mechanized reeling in lieu of a handicraft industry—the advent of a factory system in place of traditional reeling conducted as a household industry with a domestic, sedentary reeling method.

Table 9.1. Regional characteristics and changes in output of raw silk

Rank	Region	Average for years 1876–78 Output (in 1,000 kin)	Component ratio (%)	Change	Rank	Region	Average for years 1880–90 Output (in 1,000 kin)	Component ratio (%)	Annual average growth rate (%)
1	Kōzuke	333	16.0		1	Shinano	1,036	18.5	13.0
2	Shinano	239	11.4		2	Kōzuke	975	17.4	9.4
3	Musashi	209	10.0		3	Musashi	487	8.7	7.3
4	Kai	171	8.2		4	Iwashiro	389	6.9	7.2
5	Iwashiro	168	8.0		5	Kai	348	6.2	6.1
6	Uzen	111	5.3		6	Ōmi	276	4.9	10.8
7	Ōmi	81	3.9		7	Uzen	221	3.9	5.9
8	Mino	73	3.5		8	Iwaki	204	3.6	10.6
9	Kaga	72	3.5		9	Mino	176	3.1	7.6
10	Echigo	72	3.4		10	Sagami	138	2.5	13.9
	Top five provinces	1,118	53.7			Top five provinces	3,236	57.7	9.3
	Bottom five provinces	410	19.7			Bottom five provinces	1,015	18.1	7.8
	Top ten provinces	1,527	73.3			Top ten provinces	4,250	75.8	8.9
	Nationwide total	2,083	100			Nationwide total	5,610	100	8.6

Some might assume that the more the production came to be concentrated in certain regions, and the more the factory production replaced silk reeling as a side-line activity of the farm household, the less the industry enriched "the poor people of remote territories." Table 9.1 appears to support this conclusion. We wish, however, to draw attention to several points.

First, we must consider the meaning of such a surprisingly high rate of total growth. Setting aside the twofold increase in those years immediately following the opening of the ports, it is difficult to claim that the continuation of an annual growth rate of roughly 8 per cent for a decade had a limited effect. During this time, even though production was increasingly concentrated in the Suwa region, other regions no doubt experienced gains as well.

Second, while the share of those top five regions did expand from 54 to 58 per cent, when compared with the case of the white cotton cloth trade discussed below (Table 9.4), it is clear that the extent of regional concentration was by no means extreme in the silk industry. In fact, when compared with the white cotton textile industry, where the leading five provinces suddenly jumped from a share of under 50 to 85 per cent, the increased share of a few points experienced by the leading silk reeling regions might even be considered a miniscule change. The silk reeling industry was lopsidedly concentrated in eastern Japan, but it must be recognized that even in the mid-Meiji period the industry remained comparatively dispersed within that region.

Third, the industry's impact on the agricultural side should also be taken into account. Its impact on sericulture was considerable. Whereas the cotton textile industry was under pressure to switch from domestic to imported raw cotton in its production process, the increased foreign demand for raw silk provided stimulus to Japan's indigenous trade of cocoons. As Table 9.2 indicates, there was a slight variation in the pattern of regional specialization within the sericulture sector. Unlike the case with raw silk, the share dropped slightly for those principal sericulture provinces such as Shinano and Kôzuke, while other regions saw significant expansion in the volume of cocoons harvested. The point here is that small- and medium-sized districts achieved higher rates of increase. In the old sericulture regions such as Mutsu and the Shindatsu (the latter comprising the Shinobu and Date Districts in present-day Fukushima Prefecture), sericulture and silk reeling were not yet separated as production processes, and this trend continued even after the ports were opened (Shôji 1964), but the trend from the final years of the shogunate was toward a division of these processes and toward regional specialization. In the silk reeling industry this led to a concentration in certain regions while, by comparison, sericulture underwent a comparative dispersal across regions.

Table 9.2. Regional characteristics and changes in output of cocoons

Rank	Region	Average for years 1876–78		Change	Rank	Region	Average for years 1876–78		Annual average growth rate (%)
		Output (in 1,000 kin)	Component ratio (%)				Output (in 1,000 kin)	Component ratio (%)	
1	Shinano	3,133	20.0		1	Shinano	11,705	15.9	11.6
2	Kōzuke	1,912	12.4		2	Kōzuke	8,939	12.1	13.7
3	Musashi	1,411	9.0		3	Musashi	7,699	10.4	15.2
4	Iwashiro	1,293	8.3		4	Iwashiro	5,224	7.1	12.3
5	Kai	925	5.9		5	Ōmi	3,688	5.0	13.2
6	Ōmi	826	5.3		6	Mino	3,612	4.9	14.4
7	Mino	721	4.6		7	Uzen	3,557	4.8	16.2
8	Uzen	587	3.8		8	Kai	3,336	4.5	11.3
9	Hida	517	3.3		9	Iwaki	2,981	4.0	15.7
10	Iwaki	517	3.3		10	Sagami	2,250	3.1	18.4
	Top five provinces	8,675	55.5			Top five provinces	37,237	50.5	12.9
	Bottom five provinces	3,169	20.3			Bottom five provinces	15,736	21.4	14.3
	Top ten provinces	11,844	75.7			Top ten provinces	52,972	71.9	13.3
	Nationwide total	15,638	100			Nationwide total	73,717	100	13.8

Source: Nōmushō kannō kyoku (1978–79) and Nōshōmushō for each year.

2.4. The impact on rural consumer markets

The above facts suggest that the export of raw silk significantly stimulated consumer activity in rural areas from the late Tokugawa through the early Meiji period. Particularly, sericultural growth was instrumental in spreading the gains from export trade both horizontally across regions and vertically as it extended to the lower classes of the agrarian population. In his book *Tôjin ôrai* (or Foreign intercourse; written amid the cry of "expel unwelcome foreigners" in the mid-1860s and circulated only in manuscript), the famous thinker of the time, Fukuzawa Yukichi, remarked on the emerging conditions where "people started reeling silk from cocoons one after another," adding that "as their incomes have improved, they are building houses and buying *kimono*." While Fukuzawa's description is probably accurate with respect to the building of houses, the change with respect to clothing was not simply that people started purchasing *kimono* more often than before, but rather that those who could previously afford only used *kimono* were now able to purchase new ones. With respect to food as well, it would seem to indicate an increase not only in the quantity consumed but also in quality: for example, being able to buy refined *saké* instead of drinking the home-brewed, unrefined type.

Of course, it is neither accurate nor necessary to attribute the expansion of rural consumer markets solely to the impact of silk exports. It is generally agreed that farmers profited from inflation, and this must have been especially true when inflation served to lower the actual tax amount to be paid in cash. Such a case occurred after the land tax reform of 1873. Cash payment of land taxes were linked to legally established, fixed land values, which effectively served to decrease their tax payments as agricultural prices increased. The direct positive effects of the silk trade may indeed have been limited to the regions from central to northeastern Japan, but inflation distributed those effects throughout the nation. In the following section, we wish to examine the impact of such changes on the traditional cotton textile industry.

3. The Cotton-weaving Industry

By the end of the Tokugawa period, markets for cotton textiles had already grown substantially with weaving districts emerging in various regions. Further growth during the quarter century of economic fluctuations between 1859 and the mid-1880s enabled this traditional industry to occupy an unmistakable place in the nation's industrial base. At the same time, the period saw cotton weaving undergoing significant changes within the industry. The reasons can be traced to the external factors of the influx of foreign-made cotton yarn and cloth, but local responses to such challenges varied significantly from one area to another, depending on the actual conditions of the given district. Below, by categorizing the major trends in weaving districts we will explore regional aspects of the transformation process of the industry.

3.1. *Changing domestic markets for cotton cloth*

Let us begin with the chronology of quantitative change over the period in question.[4] Figure 9.2 shows how graphs of imports and domestic demand and supply behaved (note that the vertical axis is logarithmic so that the slope can indicate a rate of change, but caution is needed when examining the absolute level). According to this chart, imports increased at an extremely high rate from the opening of the ports until the early 1870s. When imports reached their peak, imported goods represented 34 per cent of the domestic demand (C over A in Figure 9.2). The graph for domestic demand showed a strong increase between 1875 and 1880, followed by a sharp, temporary drop in the deflation period of the early

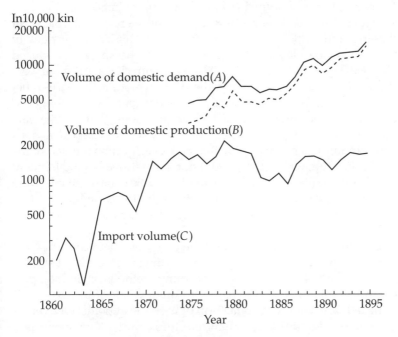

Fig. 9.2. Changes in demand for domestic cotton (vertical axis indicates logarithmic units).

Source: Nakamura (1968); calculations are from the attached tables.

Note: $A = B + C -$ export volume; calculation in terms of units of ginned cotton.

1880s; it resumed this increasing trend, and by 1895 it reached a level in excess of three times that of the 1875 level. Although the magnitude of growth is not comparable to that of raw silk, the upward trend is clear.

This increase in demand for cotton cloth derives from an increase in the volume purchased by traditional buyers as well as the emergence of new buyers. Consider Table 9.3. During the 1830s, we know that in villages of Chôshû's Maeyamashiro region (part of present-day Yamaguchi Prefecture), there were three ways to procure clothing, all of which were practiced at the time: purchasing used clothing, weaving cotton for home use, and purchasing cloth. Especially noteworthy is the high ratio of clothing procured by the first two methods, accounting for as much as 75 per cent of the total clothing expenditure. Only upper and middle groups who represented 23 per cent of the village population purchased cotton cloth; the others are thought to have made do outside the cloth market. Turning to another region, Akita, trade statistics indicate that the volume of cotton cloth brought into the region over the period 1808–10 was 174,397 *tan*. This implies that only 40 per cent of its population of 450,000 made a purchase during this three-year-period if the import figure corresponded roughly to the amount of cotton cloth purchased by that region and if the average volume of consumption is assumed to have been approximately one *tan* per person. Of the materials brought into the region were 117,101 pieces of used clothing and 6,400 *maru* of ginned cotton (166 kg, equivalent of 180,000 *tan* of cotton cloth), while 105,161 *kin* of hemp was produced domestically (63 kg, equivalent of 84,000 *tan* of hemp cloth). All these were the methods of procuring clothing in the Akita region of the early nineteenth century. Both the Maeyamashiro and Akita regions are thought to have been economically backward, which indicates that in the late Tokugawa period, most people in commercially less developed regions were in the economy of home production. However, even in the part of the Yamaguchi Prefecture within the Chôshû domain, an area having frequent contact with the market economies of the Inland Sea coast, people were engaged in home production of cotton cloth in the 1830s, suggesting that lower-class peasants did not have frequent contact with the market even in advanced regions of the day.

Moving on to the late nineteenth and the early twentieth centuries, we find that the situation had changed little. According to an oral history survey conducted around the year 1900 concerning methods of clothing procurement, rolls of cloth were purchased in roughly half of the cases (171 of 346), but 260 cases involved some form of weaving at home. Of twenty-seven cases in the Aomori and Akita Prefectures, thirteen were engaged in the cultivation of hemp, and seventeen purchased used clothing. This evidence suggests that in the rural districts, while the practice of purchasing rolls of cloth increased, home production of hemp and cotton cloth continued, as did the purchase of used clothing, which attests to a

Table 9.3. Maeyamashiro Saiban—breakdown of annual clothing expenditures by class (1830s–40s)

	Class population	Upper class 864 (8.3%)	Middle class 1517 (14.9%)	Lower class 7815 (76.8%)	Total 10,178 (100%)
Clothing expenditure					
Cotton cloth	Consuming volume price (A)	1,692 tan (54.4)	1,417 tan (45.6)		3,109 tan (100.0)
		23.04 kan (55.9)	18.165 kan (44.1)		41.205 kan (100.0)
	Number of Tan consumed per person	2 tan	0.9 tan		
	Expenditure (B)	27.2 monme	12.8 monme		
Used cloth	Consuming pieces price (C)		1,417 mai	6,018 mai	75.857 kan (100.0)
			13.252 kan (17.5)	62.605 kan (82.5)	
	Number of tan consumed per person		0.9 mai	0.77 mai	
	Expenditure (D)		9.4 monme	8.0 monme	
Cotton	Purchased price (E)	4.23 kan (8.3)	7.585 kan (14.9)	39.075 kan (76.8)	50.89 kan (100.0)
	per person (F)	5 monme	5 monme	5 monme	
	(A) + (C) + (E)	27.27 kan (16.2)	39.002 kan (23.2)	101.68 kan (23.2)	167.952 kan (100.0)
	(B) + (D) + (F)	32.2 monme	27.2 monme	13.0 monme	

Source: Yamaguchi kenritsu toshokan (ed.) (1960–64).

Table 9.4. Regional characteristics and changes in white cotton yield

Rank	Region	1874 Yield (in 1,000 *tan*)	1874 Component ratio (%)	Change	Rank	Region	1894 Yield (in 1,000 *tan*)	1894 Component ratio (%)	Annual average growth rate (%)
1	Tōyama (Niikawa)	1,627	13.9		1	Aichi	12,800	44.4	—
2	Osaka (Osaka–Sakai)	1,502	12.8		2	Ehime	4,337	15.1	—
3	Aichi	945	8.1		3	Osaka	3,097	10.8	—
4	Hiroshima	834	7.1		4	Nara	2,187	7.6	—
5	Hyōgo (Shikama)	599	5.1		5	Saitama	1,962	6.8	—
6	Saitama (Saitama – Kumagaya)	517	4.4		6	Hyōgo	563	2.0	—
7	Ehime	509	4.4		7	Wakayama	548	1.9	—
8	Yamaguchi	408	3.5		8	Hiroshima	545	1.9	—
9	Shimane	340	2.9		9	Yamaguchi	345	1.2	—
10	Niigata	285	2.4		10	Niigata	338	1.2	—
	Top five provinces	5,507	47.1			Top five provinces	24,382	84.7	7.7
	Bottom five provinces	2,059	17.6			Bottom five provinces	2,339	8.1	0.5
	Top ten provinces	7,566	64.7			Top ten provinces	26,721	92.8	6.5
	Nationwide total (estimates)	11,695	100			Nationwide total	28,801	100	—

Source: 1874: 'Meiji 7 nen fuken bussanhyo'.
1894: 'Dai Iiji noshomu tokeihyo'.

transitional situation from an old pattern. By 1908, according to a district survey of Tsugaru, Aomori Prefecture, expenditures for the purchase of cotton were declining relative to overall clothing expenditures, and hemp production was also disappearing. The annual clothing expenditure per person, when converted to units of white cotton, was slightly less than three *tan*. The myriad methods of clothing procurement seen at the end of Tokugawa rule underwent a transition during the Meiji period, and eventually the purchasing of woven fabrics was established as the dominant method, although this transition took several decades. In other words, the development of the cotton market in the late nineteenth century accompanied a shift in rural consumers' clothing procurement choice. The other evidence indicates that the 1870s and 1880s can be seen as a critical stage in this transitional process. According to an 1883 survey, "the people living in the north have become extravagant, and those who formerly wore used clothes are now wearing new clothes woven from imported cotton cloth"; and an account of the Izawa District of Iwate Prefecture, c. 1888 noted that "before the Meiji Restoration, farm households were supplied with hemp textiles for clothing, but since that time farm families have been wearing cotton". Documents such as these are thought to portray the general situation in rural Tôhoku, and it is this region where the growth of demand for cotton cloth was higher than the national average if assumption is made that the growth rate in the amount of cotton textiles brought into the region was not much different from that of the region's demand for cotton cloth. In such a remote region, a rural market was for the first time created for marketed cotton cloth.

Our next task is to consider the factors behind the market expansion in early Meiji. In general, two factors come to mind in explaining this expansion: rising standards of income and a drop in the price of cotton cloth. While it is difficult to know the extent to which farm household incomes changed during this period, we have noted that strong foreign demand for silk stimulated sericultural growth, which resulted in income growth of peasant farmers in the silk-producing provinces, and also that the inflationary period of the late 1870s led an increase in farmers' after-tax earnings, and it is undeniable that farmers benefited from the rising level of rice price. Growing income raised the level of consumption by farm households, increasing expenditures on clothing. In fact, an April 25 1881 newspaper article noted that "originally, in this prefecture [Iwate] peasant families from the middling group and below all wore used hemp clothing …nowadays, this is no longer seen since they have reached the point where they wear used cotton clothing." This article suggests that the rise in farm family income changed the pattern of clothing consumption, enabling them to participate as consumers in the market for cotton cloth. If we look at the trends in cotton cloth prices as represented in Figure 9.3, the relative price of cotton cloth vis-á-vis rice in Sendai (one of Tôhoku's

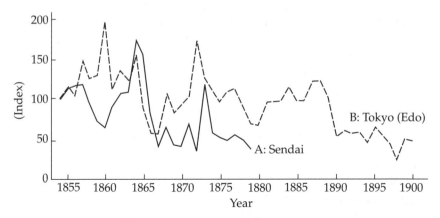

Fig. 9.3. Fluctuations in the relative price of cotton cloth vis-á-vis rice (the year 1854 = 100).

Sources: A—survey conducted in 1880 by Miyagi Prefectural Chamber of Commerce. B—Kin'yû kenkyûkai (1937).

main cities) reached two peaks, in 1864–65 and again in 1873, the first resulting from a sudden rise in the price of materials for ginned cotton exports and the second due to the sudden drop in the price of rice. In 1879 the price of cotton relative to that of rice was half of the level obtained in 1856. If we examine the prices in Tokyo during the late 1880s after the recovery from the Matsukata deflationary policies, the relative price of cotton stabilized at an even lower level. With respect to both supply and demand, conditions were ripe for an expansion of the cotton textile market in rural villages.

This meeting between rural demand and supply from cotton weaving districts could not have occurred without an appropriate distribution system, which took shape in the period of late Tokugawa and early Meiji. Among the established textile wholesalers of Tokyo and Osaka as existing in 1898, most of the leading companies got started between the 1850s and 1870s, with some having begun as early as the first part of the nineteenth century. These merchants served as wholesale distributors in the newly formed trading centers, and established nationwide distribution routes for textiles during the late Tokugawa era and early years of Meiji. Consider, for example, Tokyo's "Chôgin" (Kobayashi Gin'emon), born in Ômi, in the 1830s, he was working as a travelling salesman and expanded his sales route beyond the framework of the original distribution network for Edo *kimono* wholesalers. By the early years of Meiji, he had extended his principal sales route to include Tôhoku and Hokkaidô. Similarly, another Ômi merchant named Benichû (Itô Chûbei) extended his sales region to include the Inland Sea area, and the islands of Shikoku and Kyûshû by 1879. In the process of forging sales routes in rural markets, both men appear to have expanded the scope of their business. There also emerged merchants in the rural markets who forged ties with these new wholesalers. For example, in the mid-1860s the house of Kurimori Kichiemon in Ôdate, Akita Prefecture, began small-scale textile sales. Around 1870, he began stocking goods from Chôgin and others, establishing his position as a small retailer in the region. It thus appears that the connection between local merchants and those wholesalers operating in the new trading centers led to the formation of new textile distribution networks. The growing latent demand in rural areas was linked through the emerging distribution system to sales expansion in cotton producing districts.

3.2. Changing geographical patterns of weaving districts

The earliest nationwide data on cotton textile production is contained in the 1874 survey of products, which gives output data by prefecture. This survey is distinguished for its ability to provide a clear picture of the production of different cotton types. Subsequently, there was no statistical data about production volumes by cotton type until the appearance of the 1894 report of the Ministry of Agriculture and Commerce. Tables 9.4 and 9.5 list production volumes by prefecture for the years 1874 and 1894, comparing white cotton (unbleached cotton and *sarashi* cotton) with other types.[5] While the prefectural names and regions listed in the above two source books do not always correspond, it is possible to make a rough comparison by considering adjustments to prefectural areas and by examining the regional distribution of weaving districts.

What is especially notable about white cotton is that production was concentrated in specific prefectures. The degree of concentration in the top five prefectures increased from 47 per cent in 1874 to nearly 85 per cent in 1894, and a clear gap existed between the output levels in the top five and the other prefectures. In most of the remaining prefectures, the output level remained stagnant. The overall increase during this period can therefore be seen as borne by the top five prefectures' output growth. On the other hand, other types of cotton showed a different pattern. Output rose in all prefectures, which was accompanied by a diversification of weaving districts. The trend was for the degree of concentration to decrease and for the differentials between prefectures to gradually close. With this in mind, we trace the general trends back to the late eighteenth century by focusing on fifteen weaving districts for which we have information.

Ups and downs of these districts are summarized in Table 9.6. One feature to be seen here is that the picture is substantially different from that evident in the post-1874 statistics. Many white cotton districts showed a declining trend, since the nature of the product made it so difficult for the districts to differentiate from each other that regional competition

Table 9.5. Regional characteristics and changes in non-white cotton yarn

Rank	Region	1874		Change	Rank	Region	1894		Annual average growth rate (%)
		Yield (in 1,000 *tan*)	Component ratio (%)				Yield (in 1,000 *tan*)	Component ratio (%)	
1	Saitama (Saitama – Kumagaya)	1,422	16.9		1	Aichi	2,193	10.5	—
2	Tochigi	742	8.8		2	Saitama	2,185	10.5	—
3	Nara	685	8.1		3	Tokushima	1,416	6.8	—
4	Ehime	679	8.1		4	Ehime	1,349	6.5	—
5	Niigata	571	6.8		5	Wakayama	1,240	6.0	—
6	Aichi	551	6.6		6	Tochigi	1,063	5.1	—
7	Gifu	438	5.2		7	Niigata	974	4.7	—
8	Kanagawa	389	4.6		8	Nara	919	4.4	—
9	Osaka (Osaka – Sakai)	365	4.3		9	Yamaguchi	862	4.2	—
10	Hiroshima	280	3.3		10	Kanagawa	820	3.9	—
	Top five provinces	4,100	48.6			Top five provinces	8,383	40.3	3.6
	Bottom five provinces	2,023	24.0			Bottom five provinces	4,638	22.3	4.2
	Top ten provinces	6,123	72.6			Top ten provinces	13,022	62.6	3.8
	Nationwide total (estimates)	8,434	100			Nationwide total (estimates)	20,794	100	—

Source: For 1874, Kangyōryō (ed.) (N.A); for 1894, Nōshōmushō (1959–63).

became tough. With the post-1874 trends taken into account, the white cotton districts may be divided into three types: (1) those that declined from the early years of Meiji; (2) those that managed to maintain their output level and retained their relative position within the industry until about 1880 but subsequently declined; (3) those that grew during the 1870s and, after a lull in the deflationary period, established themselves as leading districts in the 1890s. The traditional production which from the late eighteenth century onward produced a volume in excess of 1,000,000 *tan* are all included in Types 1 and 2, with the exception of Sennan (the southern part of Izumi Province). The regional concentration that took place in the early Meiji period was accompanied by the rise of newcomers and by the fall of a majority of those old centers.

Information for districts producing cotton textiles other than white cotton is shown in Table 9.7. They are more numerous and the scale of production in each district was comparatively small. For the century-long period, one cannot find a single district producing 1,000,000 *tan*, with the majority producing around 500,000 *tan*. This is thought to reflect the variety of cotton being produced in each area. Another notable feature is that with a few exceptions none experienced a salient drop in output levels. Those making a variety of cotton textiles were more or less able to avoid competition by product differentiation, leading to an increase in the number of weaving districts. In the 1870s, they increased output and from the late 1880s they firmly established themselves.

All this implies the transformation of the traditional cotton weaving industry was a composite of the decline of principal weaving districts that had flourished before the Meiji Restoration, and the development of newly risen districts that became apparent after the mid-1880s.

3.3. *Factors of expansion*

What were the primary factors behind the above-mentioned changes in the cotton textile industry? The period from the 1860s through the 1880s saw a massive influx of imported cotton yarn and cloth, during which the domestic market for cotton textiles was expanding. We should examine the connection between this changing economic environment and the cotton textile industry.

As noted above, those regions producing non-white cotton did not experience a discernable stagnation in production during the 1870s. According to Figure 9.2, the volume of imported cotton cloth rose suddenly in 1870–71, and by 1875 it occupied over 30 per cent of the domestic demand for cotton textiles. Yet this large volume of imported goods did not exert a direct impact on areas producing nonwhite cotton textiles. Rather, the effect is most visible when examining the spinning sector. As Table 9.7 indicates, most districts producing textiles other than white

Table 9.6 Trends in white cotton producing districts

Current Prefecture	District	Type	Production trend (in units of 10,000 *tan*)			
			Nineteenth century	1874	Inflation (late 1870s)	1894
Tochigi/ Ibaragi	Môka (Makabe)	1	1810–1840s	38 Tochigi/ Ibaragi/ Saitama/	7	Tochigi/ Ibaragi
Saitama	Musashi	3				
Aichi	Mikawa	3			52 } 1881 (first) 95 } half (1878)	76 }
	Chita	3	1850	55–61 } Aichi		135
Toyama	Niikawa	2	1860s	155–200 } Niikawa	163 1879	100
Osaka	Kawachi	2	1830s	300 } Osaka/	150	300 }
	Izumi	3	1860s	240 } Sakai		510
Nara	Yamato	3			20	
Wakayama	Kishû	1	(peak period)	100	4	120
Hyôgo	Himeji	2	1980s–30s	100–200	60 1879	
Tottori	Inaba/Hôki	1	c. 1830	100	26	
Shimane	Izumo	2	c. 1830 (sold to other region)	50	34 1878	48
	Aki	2	c. 1870	100	83	
	Suwô	2	c. 1840	55	41	150–200
	Imabari	3	c. 1870	40	51 1877	40

Source: Abe (1983, 1988); Takamura (1987); Hayashi (1974); *Aichiken Kyôdoshiryô kankôkai* (1974); Kikuura (1972); *Mitsuke shiyakusho* (ed.) (1981, 1983); Niwa (1982, 1983); Yunoki (1982); Fukui (1984); and Kasai (1928).

Table 9.6 *Continued*

Year of import of machine-spun thread	Existence of monopoly	Three stage	Cotton stage	*Watagae*	Cotton thread	Placework
21 1877–86		○	○			
196 1872/73 (late 1870s, patterned machine-spun thread)	○	○	○	○	○	
1280 (c. 1881–82, patterned machine-spun thread)	○		○	○		
4		○	○	○		
310			○	○	○	○
219						
55	○	○	○			
56			○	○		
12	○○	○○	○	○		
19	○○	○○	○			
55	○○○	○○	○○○	○		
35						
434	○○○	○○	○○○		○	

Production system structure (mainly Pre–Meiji era)

Table 9.7. Trends in non-white cotton producing districts

				Production trends (unit: 10,000 tan per year)				Production system (mainly in Meiji Restoration period)				
Current	District	Main types of cotton textile	Epoch of development	Nineteenth century	1874	Inflation period	1894	Period of introduction of imported machine-spun thread	Existence monoply system	Overproduction of low quality products (late 1870 to early 80s)	Distribution of cotton thread	Piece-work
Niigata	Kameda	*Shima* (striped)	1830s	c. 1870 15–16	57	1878 24–25	97				○	○
	Kamo	*Shima* (striped)	1877									○
	Mitsuke	*Shima* (striped)	1830–40s	1873 18							○	
Gunma	Ora	*Kasuri, Nakamo-Kasuri*	1850s	1850s			21	1850s, 1860s		○	○	○
Tochigi	Sano	*Shima, Chijimi* (white cotton)	1820–30s	1850s / 1872	74		106	1865–68		○	○	○
Saitama	Kita-Saitama	*Ao-shima*	1800–20s					c. 1877				
	Kita-Adachi	*Shima, Soushi*	1861–64		142		219	1861–64		○	○	
	Iruma	*Kasuri, Shima*	1850s	1850s–1860s 30				1861–64			○	
Kanagawa	Tama	*Kasuri, Shima*	1850s		39		82	c. 1885		○	○	
Aichi	Higashi-Mikawa	*Shima*	1879, 80	1872	55	1878 12	219	(1874–76, patterned machine-spun thread)			○	
	Bisai	*Yūki-shima, Santome-shima, Yūki-shima*	1800–1820s			1878 52		1861–64	○	○	○	○
Gifu	Mino	*Santome-shima, Yūki-shima*	Late 18th c.	1872 62	44	1879 171	159	1861–64		○	○	○
Mie	Matsuzaka	*Shima*	Second half of 18th c.	1861–64 30	10	1881(1st half) 8	51	1850s, 1860s		○	○	○
Osaka	Kawachi	*Unsai, Asshi, Shima*	1850–68		37	(peak at 1877–79)	23	1865–68		○		
	Tarui	*Monba*	1820–30s	1830–44 17		1877 23		c. 1875		○		
Wakayama	Kishū	*Flannel*	c. 1870	1850s–60s 30	11	1879 12	124	1870		○	○	○
Nara	Yamato	*Shima, Kasuri*	Second half of 17th c.		69		92	c. 1875		○	○	
Hyōgo	Banshū	*Shima*	1830–50	Boom in 1870s	8	(increasing)	43	c. 1880			○	
Okayama	Kojima	*Kokura*	1770s–1820s		6		38	1850s, 1860s	○	○	○	○ ○
					14 (*hon*)	38	28 (*hon*)					
Hiroshima	Ajina	*Kasuri*	1850–60	1870s 10		1880 12		1850s, 1860s				○
	Numakuma	*Shima, Kasuri*	1804–30	(Fukuyama-shima) 28		(Demand Expanded)		c. 1870				
	Kannabe	*Shima*	1850s									

				(Late Tokugawa) 20–30						1873, 1874		
Yamaguchi	Iwakuni	*Chijimi*	1818–44		21 ⎫			86	1873, 1874		○
	Yanai	*Chijimi*	1860								○
Tottori	Kurayoshi	*Kasuri*	1853		25	1878	11	19			○
Ehime	Matsuyama	*Shima, Kasuri*	1818–30	1818–30	68 2	1877	80	135			○
Tokushima	Awa	*Shima*	1818–30		15	1879–80	120–130	142			
Fukuoka	Kurume	*Kasuri*	1860–64		5	1881	18	74	c. 1877		○

Source: Same as for the Table 9.6.

Note: hon, Unit of cloth used to make *obi.*

cotton employed imported machine-spun yarn. It should be noted that the imported yarn had been introduced in the 1860s, which suggests that the substitution of foreign-made for domestic yarn was a response by those producers to changes created by the opening of the ports. Imported yarn being cheaper, at the same time, it made possible the emergence of new producers in newly emerged weaving districts, which in turn brought about an expansion of the domestic market. Another factor for its success is concerned with the question of sales routes, we know that striped cotton of the Iruma District in Musashi found new consumers in remote regions such as Tôhoku and Kyûshû through Hachiôji, a traditional marketplace, where local merchants could extend dealings with newly emerged wholesalers such as Chôgin and Itô-chû (Tanimoto 1986). Similar cases can be seen for Banshû cotton (Hyôgo Prefecture), which c. 1870 made its way primarily in "the five provinces of Rikuzen, Rikuchû, Mutsu, Uzen, and Ugo." For Kurume (Fukuoka Prefecture), where c. 1863 Ômi merchants came in contact with local producers, for Ashina (Hiroshima Prefecture) where, c. 1870, 200 *tan* was sold to Osaka's Itô-chû, leading to the expansion of sales routes to the Tôhoku, Hokuriku, and Kyûshû regions. For Mitsuke (Niigata Prefecture), whose sales developed around 1878 in Hokkaido, Aomori, Yamagata, Miyagi, and Akita (see Hattori and Shinobu 1937: 221; Kakimoto 1982: 25).

But circumstances were different for districts producing white cotton. As noted earlier, the years 1870–71 served as a turning point when large quantities of foreign-made cotton goods flowed into Japan. Roughly 70–80 per cent of those imported in this period were gray shirting—in other words, thin white cotton cloth (Kawakatsu 1976). During the same period, districts producing white cotton (Type 1 according to the above classification) were undergoing a decline and their output decreased substantially. Apparently, imported cotton had a direct impact on producers of white cotton, which is supported by the body of existing literature (Takamura 1987). However, how much pressure imports actually generated on white cotton producers of Types 2 and 3 needs to be examined. Type 2 districts maintained an output roughly comparable to earlier levels, even though production stagnated or decreased temporarily in the 1870s, so that one cannot view them as a "failure pattern." There were even cases, such as Himeji, which experienced a mild recovery during the last half of the 1870s. We must ask why, despite the large influx of imports, these producers did not show a substantial drop in production levels. Given the fact that the size of the domestic demand for cotton cloth grew over this period, those weaving districts too adapted themselves to market situations in the rural areas. These areas constituted an important sales route for imported cotton cloth. It was the gray shirting of inexpensive, low, and medium quality that flowed into rural regions, thereby changing the image of imported shirting from being a "high-quality good" to "a product in demand among people of lower rank." For example, in the Hienuki District of Iwate Prefecture, the influx of shirting into villages, where the villagers had previously worn hemp, created "a demand for the inexpensive cloth in every farming household." Even used clothing made from the imported cotton cloth began to appear. This reflects a process in which the methods for clothing procurement in the villages shifted from hemp cloth and used clothing to the purchase of imported shirting. The influx of such inexpensive, imported cotton textiles must be also seen as a response to the emerging rural demand for cotton cloth and not necessarily as just an incursion into the existing cotton cloth market. Furthermore, the quality difference between the traditional and the imported shirting—between thick and thin—was one factor that limited the shift in demand among Japanese consumers, whose taste remained with the former. Supported by this tenacious demand for the traditional type, the domestic market seems to have been able to leave room for the producers of traditional white cotton cloth. Type 3 districts producing white cotton cloth benefited from the emergence of this kind of market. With the exception of Imabari of Ehime Prefecture, which followed its own distinct pattern, these weaving districts all introduced the new types of yarn either imported or produced with the *garabô* device, an improvement on the traditional hand-spinning technique. In the cases of Musashi and Yamato, the introduction of foreign-made yarn is thought to have provided them the opportunity to develop into full-fledged weaving districts. "Those who had until this time worn used apparel were now donning new clothes made from cotton cloth and imported yarn." As this description indicates, such cotton textiles responded to the emerging demand in rural areas, and by releasing this latent demand they succeeded in increasing output.

In the early 1880s, however, as Figure 9.2 indicates, the domestic demand for cotton cloth began to drop off and Type 2 producers entered a decline. The reduction in demand during the Matsukata years of deflation is commonly thought to have prevented these producers from staying afloat. At the same time, however, the volume of imported cotton cloth started declining after reaching a peak in 1879. In the 1890s, imported cloth occupied only a small percentage of the domestic demand. Given the supposition that both domestic and imported cotton cloth had been advancing into rural markets until this time, this would seem to indicate that, faced with a shrinking market, producers entered into a more competitive relationship from which imported cotton textiles emerged the loser.

The reason for this must be sought in terms of both the quality and price of the cotton textiles themselves. An 1887 Commercial Report by the British Consulate noted that once farmers and lower-class city dwellers began using imported shirting, problems of quality and durability led them to shift to domestic cotton cloth.[6] It is not hard to imagine manual laborers finding the type of thin, imported cotton textiles to be unsuitable. Sennan near Osaka was one of leading Type 3 producers of white cotton cloth that used imported machine-spun yarn, where already in 1879 it was reported that "owing to the wide use of imported thread in weaving cotton cloth," there were signs that low-grade shirting were being outsold "in the provinces." The price of Sennan's cloth, higher than that of imported shirting in the beginning of the 1880s, had fallen to the same level by 1884–85. The price of Senshû cotton known as "*maru-kara momen*," which used imported thread for both the warp and the woof, had dropped below that of imported cloth (Osaka Daigaku kindai bukkashi kenkyûkai 1982). From early on, the development of cotton textile production that used imported thread as raw material served to reduce the price difference between domestic and foreign cotton textiles. The rural market absorbed the pressure from imports during the period of expansion, and when that market shrunk it rejected imported cotton. Thus, in contrast with Type 1 and 2 districts, Type 3 producers of white cotton cloth and producers of cloth other than white cotton exhibited a temporal pattern delineated above over the 1870s and 1880s. One factor shared by these latter districts was their introduction of foreign-made yarn or domestic, *garabô*-made yarn, or both. Indeed, contemporary documents describing the situation surrounding the distribution of imported yarn to major cotton cloth producers in Tokyo and Osaka in the years 1878–79 recorded notable differences in distributed volume depending on the area, with high concentrations in Type 3 weaving districts of white cotton and in those of non-white cotton cloth (Shibusawa eiichi denkishiryô kankôkai 1957: 246, 267; Nihon keieishi kenkyû 1972: 252–3). A second point to be noted is that among those districts, not a few made an aggressive attempt to develop marketing opportunities. An important difference between the two groups, Types 1 and 2 versus Type 3 and producers of non-white cloth, appears to lie in their response to new markets and technological conditions. In order to shed light on factors affecting these differences, we would like to have a look at the internal structure of the weaving district.

3.4. The internal structure of weaving districts

For many white cloth producing districts, especially Type 1 and 2 areas, cotton cultivation, spinning, and weaving were carried out within the same farm household (Table 9.6). This form of manufacturing seems to have been a development in cotton growing areas, although homegrown raw and ginned cotton were marketed within the region, and sometimes "exported" to other areas. For example, in Aki (present-day Hiroshima Prefecture) and *Suô* (present-day Yamaguchi Prefecture), both cotton-growing provinces, the supply of raw cotton was sometimes insufficient, making it necessary to bring in from other areas. Non-cotton growing regions such as Niikawa (present-day Tôyama Prefecture) were completely dependent on sources outside the region for raw material. Yet even in those cases, the two processes of spinning and weaving appear to have been conducted within a single farm household. *Watagae* was one arrangement found in those, especially Type 1 and 2 weaving districts. Under this *Kaufsystem*-like system, a farm household was supplied with raw cotton from a cotton merchant, spinning and weaving were carried out within the household, and the finished product was then handed to the merchant. The three-process production was also found among Type 3 districts. Mikawa was a well-known case. The *watagae* practice was observed in Chita. However, a different arrangement developed in other Type 3 areas. In the Sennan district many farm households were engaged only in hand spinning, with the finished product handled by cotton merchants, which suggests that from early on, a division of labor between the spinning and weaving processes had developed. Such a tendency was even more pronounced in districts producing nonwhite goods such as striped and slashed. As Table 9.7 shows, hand-spun cotton was traded widely. Brand-names such as Kishû-*kase* and Awaji-*kase* were well-known (products from present-day Wakayama Prefecture and Awaji Island, respectively). Compared with Type 1 and 2 producers, these weaving districts differed in the degree to which the production processes were separated.

This issue may be discussed in relation to the introduction of imported yarn. It is likely that the farm household engaged in all the three processes was one whose major concern was the manufacture of clothing for home use. The goods marketed were nothing but a surplus. Even with the *watagae* system there were such cases, as attested to in the following document: "*chakuryô* (clothing for home use) is known as *watagae*. If a farm household purchases ten *tan* worth of cotton, they produce seven *tan* for cash and three *tan* for their own clothing."[7] For farm households such as these, the coming of imported yarn changed the status of cotton production within the household economy. For market-oriented weaver–farmers, too, the coming of foreign-made yarn meant the loss of their cotton cultivation and hand spinning businesses, and hence jeopardized the basis of their own livelihoods. Naturally, they were repulsed by the introduction of imported thread. On the other hand, the consequences were different for the cases in which cotton growing, spinning, and weaving had already been separately established. Whereas the influx of imported yarn must have been a life-and-death matter for the suppliers of hand-spun yarn, little impact was felt on the employment question in the weaving districts. Thus, whether the introduction of imported machine-spun yarn had a beneficial or detrimental effect depended largely on one's position within the industry, and this appears to account for the differential responses among the districts.

Similarly, different sections of the distribution industry were differently affected by the imported yarn. The separation of the hand spinning process had already given birth to local dealers of yarn, and it seems likely that they were able to make a relatively smooth transition from dealing in hand-spun to imported machine-spun goods. In cases such as the *watagae* system, however, where the spinning process was not yet separated from other production processes, cotton merchants handled the raw material for textiles. For those merchants, the change that entailed the abandonment of traditional distribution routes was never palatable—especially when they were involved in some form of monopsony under the old *han* government. There too must have been losers as well as gainers depending on where the merchant was in the whole distribution process, and in what type of weaving district his customers belonged to.

Yet we must also consider the possibility that a fresh class of merchants emerged, as can be seen in the case of newly arising weaving districts. We must also examine who made their rise possible since machine-made yarn, foreign to any domestic weaving district, should be brought in directly from the treaty port, or through the distribution centers of Tokyo and Osaka (Tanimoto 1992*b*). Those who took this initiative could have been merchants already in business, but could also have been newcomers. Imported yarn was purchased by brokers at the treaty port, with whom, in the cases of Bisai (present-day Aichi Prefecture) and Iruma, district merchants conducted the direct transactions (on Bisai and Iruma, see Shiozawa and Kondô 1985: 112–13; Tanimoto 1992*b*). To undertake the introduction of foreign-made yarn required a sense of how it could be used profitably, which in turn required an intimate familiarity with not only the material itself but with production conditions in the given district. The district merchants, being located near the producers, were likely to have been well versed in local production conditions. Furthermore, if they themselves went directly to the treaty ports or had the opportunity to meet merchants from the distribution centers, and if they also had access to sources of information, then it is likely that they were cognizant of the potential profit to be made by introducing imported thread. Imported thread was introduced early in Bisai and Iruma (see Table 9.7), which seem to indicate that the local merchants played a key role in this process.

Situations in Types 1 and 2 districts producing white cotton were different. Foreign machine-made yarn did not make any headway. This calls attention to institutional legacies from the Tokugawa period since, according to Table 9.6, some form of monopsony was in operation in those Type 1 and 2 areas with the exceptions of Môka (present-day Tochigi and Ibaragi Prefectures) and Kawachi (near Osaka). In Himeji and Tottori domains, it is demonstrated, such a system functioned and was a compelling force (Oka 1963; Yamanaka 1965; Yunoki 1982). On the other hand, there are few cases of the monopsony system having existed in the

Type 3 districts and in those producing non-white cotton. It seems that the system was at work in Chita (present-day Aichi Prefecture), but only for a limited time. If we look at how this mercantile system worked in Himeji domain, we find that brokers who formed a gild collected the finished cotton, which was passed on to the particular wholesaler with which they were affiliated, then sent to the shipping agent bound for Edo. Under this type of system, the shipping agents were the sole window for outside distribution centers or consumer markets, so that local merchants could have few opportunities for contact with merchants in Edo and Osaka. Being cut off from the nationwide distribution networks, the locals were limited in their ability to gather information and to market their own goods beyond their immediate realm. This must have been one reason for their inability to respond effectively to the new economic environment, to find new markets for their goods opened up, and to establish new sales channels to reach the markets during the crucial period from the 1860s to the 1880s. The *han* monopsony system served to create a distribution structure by establishing channels through which goods produced by small-scale producers were marketed in large volumes and in a wider trading world. It was under this mercantile system that the major weaving districts of white cotton were able to establish themselves in the late Tokugawa period. With the abolition of the *han* the system broke down as a formal system, but an examination of trends in those weaving districts during the 1870s suggests that it did not lead to an immediate decline. The distribution practices established under the old system seem to have continued to function for the time being. But monopsony did seem to leave a negative legacy by preventing local merchants to create a more flexible response to the abrupt changes in market and production conditions occasioned by the opening of overseas trade.

Finally, we wish to touch on the mode of production in cotton weaving of this period. Virtually in all Type 1 and 2 cases, production was carried out as a side-line activity by female members of the farm household. Output of a given household was miniscule, and their woven products were collected by buyers. The *watagae* system linked the supply of raw material with the collection of manufactured product, but there appeared to be little difference as far as the mode of production is concerned. On the other hand, by the late Tokugawa period, areas producing non-white cotton—Kameda and Mitsuke in Niigata, Kita-adachi (present-day Saitama Prefecture), Bisai, Mino (present-day Gifu Prefecture), Banshû (present-day Hyôgo Prefecture), Tarui (present-day Osaka Prefecture), and Bizen (present-day Okayama Prefecture)—were already engaged in the putting-out or *debata* system. Together with this system, a manufactory (*uchibata*) was also found in Mitsuke and Bisai. There is research that even in Type 3 districts such as Izumi, a manufactory-type existed (Tsuda 1960; Nakamura 1990; for a critical reassessment of this view, see Tanimoto

1992*a*). One may speculate that differences in the mode of production had something to do with each district's subsequent rise or decline. But Mikawa and Chita (both in present-day Aichi Prefecture), both Type 3 districts, showed no significant differences in this respect from Types 1 and 2 producers until the *garabô*-technique was introduced. In the case of Izumi as well, the manufactory system coexisted with widespread instances of *Kaufsystem*-like practices. In both Musashi of white cotton and Iruma of striped cotton, the incorporation of imported machine-spun yarn provided the opportunity for development, and growth was achieved by engaging more farm households in by-employment. In the Iruma case, putting-out was not fully established until the late 1870s.

Scholars have argued that both manufactory and putting-out emerged as the social division of labor advanced and thereby production processes became separated with each other in early stages of industrial history. It is not likely, however, that neither manufactory nor putting-out system was the prime type found in weaving districts in this period of market expansion. The choice of the mode of production had little direct impact on output trends in those weaving districts. Instead, it was the switch to imported machine-spun yarn and the establishment of new marketing channels that were decisively important as far as the period up to the beginning of the 1880s is concerned. However, market conditions of the deflationary 1880s altered the whole configuration of the industry. Indeed, there is evidence that putting-out came into existence in great many weaving districts after this deflationary period. The depressed market intensified competition among the districts and led to the flood of slipshod products being manufactured. The weaving districts were faced with the need to lower production costs as well as to sustain and control product quality and standards. While the establishment of craft and trade organizations is thought to have addressed this need, the organization of producers into the putting-out arrangement was another way to remain competitive. It was at this time that the mode of production appears to have first acquired the important implication for productivity of the weaving trade.

4. Conclusion

One salient feature of the economic history from the 1860s through the 1880s was that consumer markets emerged in rural areas, particularly in commercially less developed provinces. The impetus came from sericulture and silk reeling, which grew with the support of strong overseas demand, while macroeconomic fluctuations determined alternating phases of the development process. To all this, traditional industries responded differently. One decisive factor explaining the differences is whether or not the industry in question was export-oriented, while competition with imports, the degree to which the new product was preferred as a replacement for home-produced ones, and the flexibility of demand in the face of changes in income and price were other important determinants.

In the case of *saké* brewers, especially of local brewers who represented the vast share of the trade of the day, little change took place. Because the demand for refined *saké* rose and fell sharply with changes in both income and price levels, and because refined *saké* proved a comparatively easy alternative to home-brewed *saké*, this industry did not need to undergo a major transformation despite fluctuating output in response to shifting market conditions (Saitô and Tanimoto 1989; especially chapter 3).

The silk industry experienced precisely the opposite. As an export trade, silk reeling consistently maintained a high growth rate, and in terms of both production technology and organization it gradually shed its identity as a traditional industry. On the other hand, sericulture, which provided raw materials for silk production and remained as a by-employment for farm households, developed at the same tempo (or even faster), serving as a compelling force of the expanding rural consumer market. Yet what is most intriguing and of greatest significance in the context of the present chapter is the case of cotton textiles, which were subjected to pressure from the influx of imports to the domestic market. In particular, the white cotton trade, which was forced to compete with imported gray shirting with considerable price elasticity, came under strong pressure to transform the existing industrial setup.

Two additional points are to be made in relation to the cotton trade. First, the transformation took place not only within the intraregional structure but also on the interregional landscape. During the quarter century since the opening of the ports, many long-established weaving districts declined while new districts emerged. In other words, the opening of the ports accelerated a shake-up in the district rankings. Second—and this applies to non-white cotton as well—the opening of overseas trade not only put pressure on the traditional cotton industry but also afforded it opportunities to develop. As we have argued in this chapter, districts that were able to grow during this period were those that did so by switching from domestic hand-spun to imported machine-made yarn. While the whole industry was shaken up by the opening-up of overseas trade, it led to the creation of a new market for a new type of raw material; that is, imported machine-made yarn, allowing capable producers to respond to this challenge, to recover from the shock, then to achieve further growth. One consequence of the changing landscape in the cotton weaving industry was to accelerate the transformation within the individual production areas. It was local merchants who played a principal role in organizing these localities into coherent industrial districts during this period. The fact that the putting-out system did not emerge as a dominant form of industrial organization in the weaving district until the end of the deflationary period of the 1880s should be seen in this context.

The industrial history of cotton weaving after the opening of the treaty ports was substantially different from those of raw silk and *saké* brewing. What we have suggested in the present chapter is that the differential history of traditional industries of the 1860s through the 1880s was accounted for largely by differences in the market environment at local, national, and overseas levels.

Translated by Michael S. Molasky.

Notes

1. Unless otherwise noted, all data in this chapter concerning sericulture, raw silk production, and silk exports are drawn from the following sources: Yokohama shiyakusho (1959, 1960, 1961, 1980), Ishii (1972, 1984), and Sugiyama (1988).
2. June 1865, Kanagawa Magistrate, quoted from Ishii (1944: 395).
3. September 1864, a merchant from Fukagawa, Edo; quoted in Yokohama shiyakusho (1960: 187).
4. Descriptions in this section are drawn from Tanimoto (1987).
5. For information on special characteristics of various types of cotton, refer to Uchida (1988).
6. "Reports on the Native Cotton Manufactures of Japan" in "Foreign Office Miscellaneous Series," No.49, in British Parliamentary Papers, 1877, LXXXII: 12.
7. *Bocho-fudo-chushin-an*, vol. 12, p. 219.

10

Country Bankers in Proto-industrial Japan: The Transformation of Credit

RONALD P. TOBY

1. Introduction

Well before the opening of Japan's ports to unlimited foreign trade, and the advent of the Meiji industrialization, Japan had entered an "age of proto-industrialization" in the late eighteenth and early nineteenth centuries.[1] A money economy was so far advanced that in some regions even rural households derived half or more of their income from wage labor, cottage industry, and other nonagricultural pursuits.[2] Indeed, a money-and-market orientation had progressively altered rural economic and social structure, promoting a differentiation of primarily agricultural villages from increasingly industrial ones. The latter relied on the market for ever larger proportions of their income, for a growing portion of the raw materials for production, and for their consumption needs in food, fuel, and fiber. These changes favored smaller farm and household size, increased use of purchased materials and labor, and cash-crop outputs. As employment opportunities in the villages grew more numerous and attractive, urban centers began to lose population to the proto-industrializing countryside (Smith 1973).

By the early nineteenth century advancing rural industrial production and long-distance trade, brokered by rural merchants and destined for distant urban markets, demanded concentrated accumulations of capital to which nascent entrepreneurs might turn to finance their enterprises. Yet the place of credit and credit institutions in the age of proto-industrialization has yet to be studied, in either Japan or the West.[3] In this chapter, I examine the operations of rural credit and creditors in southern Mino Province (the southern part of modern Gifu Prefecture) in central Japan in the years 1828–44 to see how creditor organization and behavior changed in the proto-industrializing heartland.[4] I also suggest, from a meta-analysis of other studies of credit institutions in the later Tokugawa period that the same transformation was occurring across the country, a quiet financial revolution that helped fuel Japan's proto-industrialization.

My discussion is based on an examination of the banking ledgers of the Nishimatsu house, hereditary headmen of Nishijô. Nishijô is a peasant village, part of Niremata, in the polders of the Mino lowlands, some dozen kilometers southeast of Ôgaki, the nearest castle town, and 30 km west of Nagoya, the city on which the economic structure of the Nôbi region was focused.[5]

The examination will show that in the 1830s and 1840s, the Nishimatsu credit enterprise was dramatically transformed. Although the family had been lending on a modest scale locally since at least 1764—and almost certainly for many decades before that—they seem to have relied almost entirely on their own funds for loan capital until 1837. Loan capital was thus limited to personal surpluses; the returns from land rents, interest from previous loans, and the profits from other enterprises in which the family may have engaged.

Beginning in 1837, however, the Nishimatsu family relied increasingly for their loan capital on borrowing from a network of other local rural creditors like themselves. Where, as far as we can tell from the ledgers, virtually all their loan capital prior to 1837 was internally generated, borrowed capital thereafter accounted for an increasingly large proportion of total lending, rising from 10 per cent in 1837 to as high as 77 per cent in 1841, and seems to have remained at 60 per cent or more from then on.

The Nishimatsu ledgers show that this change reflected broader developments among rural credit institutions—principally moneylending headmen like the Nishimatsu—in the Mino lowlands as a whole. More and more, local lenders relied on the growing network of interbank wholesale credit to finance their own local, retail lending. Whereas the Nishimatsu and their peers had up to then lent but not borrowed, they now became both borrowers and lenders. By doing so, each participant in the network had access to larger pools of capital than he would have on his own. Consequently, local borrowers had more efficient access to credit, at lower interest rates, than might have been the case had lenders been forced to continue relying on internally generated capital.

These changes represent developments of signal importance in Japanese economic history. The emergence of rural interbank networks in the proto-industrial countryside substantially increased the efficiency, mobility, and liquidity of the money supply in their regions, which in turn kept capital costs low and thus promoted rising investment in the secondary sector.[6] The significance of these developments lies principally in two areas, economic history and business history. Economically, as has been suggested here, the emergence of wholesale interbank credit networks helps explain how the proto-industrialization was financed, how Japan was able to generate sufficient capital to proto-industrialize in the early nineteenth century and to industrialize later without resort to foreign borrowing.[7] There is little doubt that the rural sector held substantial potential for capital accumulation, for rural savings rates in some parts of the country approached 7 per cent (Nishikawa 1987), but it is unclear whether these accumulations were available for entrepreneurial investment and, if so, how they were made accessible to entrepreneurs.

From this perspective, the economic importance of the emergence of interbank networks is paralleled by their significance as a new mode of business organization and operation in the countryside, and by the willingness of credit entrepreneurs to undertake higher risks in pursuit of new banking opportunities and more rapid growth. For it will be seen below that by entering into a regional interbank network of credit merchants, the Nishimatsus were able to effect a fourfold increase in the size of their lending operations within a decade. Moreover, they transformed their business from a simple moneylending operation into something better characterized as a deposit bank, while also freeing sufficient capital to take up new forms of enterprise as well. Further, the Nishimatsus' experience suggests the high degree to which, during the Tempo era (1830–44), entrepreneurial activity, theirs and their customers' as well, was dependent on borrowed capital.

2. Late Edo-Period Credit and Creditors

Students of preindustrial Japan often see the local creditor as an exploitative usurer, reducing rather than enhancing peasant liquidity and economic opportunity. Village lenders, they say, charged "high," "outrageously high," or even "usurious" rates of interest on loans to desperate peasants. Many scholars too readily accept E. Herbert Norman's assertion that borrowing was no more than the last resort of the peasant who "turn[ed] in desperation to the usurer," while credit relations were a prime mechanism for the expropriation of land, and the ultimate reduction of the peasantry to "desperat[ion] in the face of 'conditions of life often below the subsistence level.' "[8]

Many who borrowed were, to be sure, the desperate poor; but others borrowed as well. How else could peasant entrepreneurs gain access to capital accumulated as savings? In order for petty savings to be available to finance entrepreneurial activities, they must be packaged through institutions such as banks and made accessible to borrowers. Some of these functions were already performed on a small scale in early nineteenth century Japan by voluntary mutual-aid associations called *mujinkô*, in which peasants pooled savings and rotated use of the pool among their members.[9] Another and larger source of credit was peasant moneylenders of the sort to be examined here, who lent their own savings, their surplus land rents, or accumulated profits from their other enterprises.[10]

Yet neither the *mujinkô* nor the village moneylender appears to add greatly to liquidity or to increase the efficiency or velocity of the money supply in the rural economy. The former concentrated and assigned to one the funds of all, while the latter accumulated his own profits from land, lending, and other enterprises, and lent them at interest. Neither was capable of increasing its lending at a rate that exceeded its own (or the group's) profits. If credit was to grow faster than the ambient profit margins of preexisting enterprises, thus adding to the net liquidity of the economy, reducing costs of capital, and promoting new investment and growth, lenders—*entrepreneurial lenders*—had to find new ways to increase their lending beyond their personal capital and accumulated profits. Somewhere there had to emerge an institution capable of having a multiplier effect on the local money supply, something analogous to banks, which bulk the petty savings of others, or otherwise direct capital through loans to the investments of the entrepreneur.

In the towns nascent bankers "were accepting deposits [as well as] making loans in the 1640s and probably considerably earlier," and in Osaka, Kyoto, and Edo, according to E. S. Crawcour, "moneychangers were well on their way to becoming bankers by the 1680s."[11] Some of these urban moneylenders, such as the Kônoike of Osaka, operated on a massive scale toward the late Edo period, lending sums exceeding the annual revenues of major daimyos.[12] But the rural moneylender in most of the historiography was a pure creditor, who lent but did not borrow, who had capital at hand to lend in the form of accumulated profits from his land rents, other enterprises, and earlier loans-at-interest, but neither held deposits nor borrowed from others.[13] The rural creditor portrayed in the historiography of the pre-Meiji countryside was a "landowning usurer" (Norman's term) in his counting house, but not yet a banker—nor even on his way to becoming one. Histories of credit institutions, money-lending, and money-changing in the Edo period abound; histories of "banking" invariably begin with the Meiji Restoration.

This essay distinguishes between the simple "moneylender" or "moneychanger," on the one hand, and the "banker" on the other. The former relies exclusively—or nearly so—on personal wealth and surplus revenues either from prior lending or from other entrepreneurial activities. Since he "has only his profits to reinvest...[he] is unable to...create a system of moneylending greater than his ordinary source of capital." Bankers, by contrast, "borrow from some in order to lend to others, and this process is regular and ordinary" (Melton 1986). By relying extensively on other people's money, which they borrow or accept on deposit, at interest, and relending it at higher rates of interest, bankers are indeed able to "create a system of moneylending greater than [their] ordinary source of capital." This transformation, as we have noted, has both organizational and socioeconomic implications.

The changes in rural credit examined here are important not only in understanding economic change in proto-industrial Japan, therefore, but in the broader proto-industrialization model itself. For although the role of credit has occupied the attention of both theoreticians and historians of economic change, it has been remarkably absent from the proto-industrialization debate itself. Schumpeter argues that credit is the essential catalyst enabling entrepreneurs to create "new combinations" of production and to "outbid" owners of older forms or "combinations" for the "required means of productions" (Schumpeter 1934: 71). Geoffrey Parker has even questioned "whether Europe would have known an 'Industrial Revolution' had not a 'Financial Revolution' preceded it," (Parker 1973) while Alexander Gerschenkron, although questioning the significance of banks in Britain's industrialization, nonetheless argues that elsewhere the role of finance may have been crucial in the industrialization of "backward" countries, including even continental Europe (Gerschenkron 1962).

Yet students of proto-industrialization largely ignore the role of credit and finance in their analyses. Mendels, as noted above, did not include credit in his model. Hans Medick, with whom Mendels collaborated at times, sees credit as a positive hindrance to capital accumulation, investment, and economic advancement, and, as if borrowing indeed "dulled the edge of husbandry," says that it "functioned as an impediment to the productive use of potential income in the form of investment capital."[14]

Recent students of the late Tokugawa economy, beginning with Hiroshi Shimbo, have proposed a Keynesian argument, that the *bakufu's* recoinage policies of the Bunsei era (1816–30) were in effect an expansionary monetary policy that served as a major stimulus to proto-industrial growth in the mid-nineteenth century. This new money entered the economy as *bakufu* expenditures, stimulating the economy at large. Entrepreneurial propensity to invest in new or expanded ventures, they argue, was stimulated by the resulting growth in the money supply and the slow secular inflation trend it initiated. The inflationary expectations of the age—Shunsaku Nishikawa labels it the "inflationary half-century"—made investment in proto-industrial activity attractive, they conclude.[15]

This monetary-expansion/slow-inflation model of the late Tokugawa economy does not rely on credit behavior for its explanatory power, yet inflationary expectations should also stimulate demand for credit. Similarly, as Hideo Hayashi has shown,[16] the *shima-momen* (stripe-woven cotton cloth) industry, whose development is central to the characterization of the Nôbi region as proto-industrial in the late eighteenth and early nineteenth centuries, depended heavily on various forms of credit. Thus a finding of local or regional networks of interbank credit that kept credit readily available and capital relatively cheap would enhance the power of the Shimbo–Umemura thesis to explain the proto-industrial age in Japan.

3. Gombei, Nishijo, and the Mino Polders

Nishijo was a moderate-size farming village[17] in the polder region of the
lower Kiso-Nagara-Ibi watershed in Mino Province, bounded on two
sides by rivers dyked to heights that loomed above the housetops, and on
two sides by the fields of neighboring villages (see Maps 10.1 and 10.2).[18]

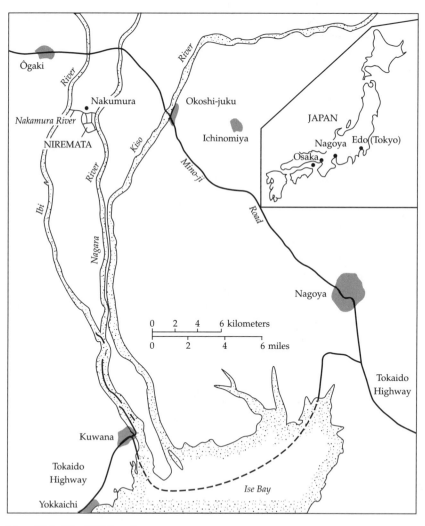

Map 10.1. The Nôbi region.

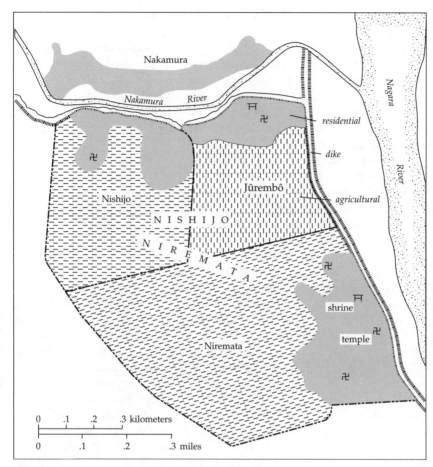

Map 10.2. Nishijo Village.

A ferry connected Nishijo with Nakamura to the north across the Nakamura River. Villagers raised several varieties of rice, wheat, barley, coarse grains, and beans, as well as rapeseed and cotton, which were cash crops. There was no oil press in the village, so rapeseed had to be sold as raw material or shipped out for pressing—in either case further enmeshing the village in market relations and the money economy. By the 1830s there was a *saké* brewery in the village as well, using 100 *koku* of rice a year as raw material, equal to nearly one-third of the Nishijo's assessed annual production. Because Nishijo was a polder village, fuel and lumber were scarce locally, and had to be purchased from mountain villages up-river; some commercial fertilizers, bought with cash, were also used. Neighboring villages in the same polder housed carpenters, blacksmiths, sawyers, coopers, masons, oil pressers, and a physician.[19]

The *mura meisai-chô* (village reports) for the 1840s record weaving as a common occupation for Nishijo women, but are silent as to whether this was subsistence weaving for home use, or participation in the *shima-momen* industry. But Nishijo was situated almost exactly on the border between a major area of *shima-momen* cotton cloth production to the east across the Nagara River, and a principally agricultural area to the west. Several of the people with whom the Nishimatsu bankers maintained credit relations, as borrowers, lenders, and depositors, were in the area that produced *shima-momen*.[20]

Nishijo's population in the period 1820–50 fluctuated widely between 277 and 330 persons, and 66–76 households, partly owing to the migration and mortality crisis of the Tempo famine, 1837–39.[21] The village was a *tenryô* (shogunal fisc) village administered for Edo by Ôgaki domain, and was about a half-day's walk from the castle-town of Ôgaki; it was about a day's walk from the larger towns of Nagoya (population, 100,000±), Gifu, and the port of Kuwana, where it delivered its tax rice to shogunal warehouses. Lacking its own sources of fuel, fertilizer, and construction materials, Nishijo was early enmeshed in the market and money economy.[22] For some administrative purposes, Nishijo was joined with its neighbor to the south, Niremata, although each had its own headman (*shôya*). Further, the eastern half of Nishijo had its own toponym, Jûrembô, which appears in maps and other local records. Jûrembô and the western half of Nishijo each had its own Buddhist temple, of the True Pure Land (*Jôdo Shinshû*) sect, and comprised separate, geographically coherent parishes, while the few villagers who were adherents of other sects of Buddhism—Zen and Pure Land—were parishioners of temples elsewhere in the polder.[23]

The heads of the Nishimatsu house, all of whom in the last century of the Tokugawa era took the name "Gombei" on succeeding to house headship, were hereditary headmen of Nishijo and its wealthiest residents from at least the 1770s, and most likely from the late sixteenth century. Likewise, extant ledgers show that they had been engaged in moneylending from the mid-eighteenth century, and there is no doubt that they were lending at interest long before that. Their ancestors had been village officers and major landholders since the early seventeenth century, and appear to have descended from local samurai who were resident in Nishijo by 1588.[24] Socially, economically, and politically apart from most Nishijo households to begin with, the Nishimatsu main and branch houses were affiliated with a Rinzai Zen temple a few kilometers south of Nishijo, where the Nishimatsu family graves were also located.[25]

The recent history of the headship of both the village and the Nishimatsu house is relevant to an understanding of Gombei's behavior as local creditor during the period under examination. Gombei I had succeeded his father as head of both house and village in 1804, governing the village, overseeing his tenants, and managing his moneylending and other business operations. Especially in the decade beginning in 1811 there had been a rapid turnover in land titles in Nishijo, leaving Gombei I and one of the village's two Buddhist priests with much larger land-holdings than just a few years earlier. The priest, who previously had held no registered land, appeared on the books with 26 *koku* in 1811, and 29 in 1814; while Gombei's holdings rose from 49 *koku* in 1773 to 86 in 1801, and 120 *koku* by 1825.[26] As Nishimatsu landholdings more than doubled, their share of total village arable rose from less than one-sixth to more than one-third (38 per cent). By 1833 the main and branch Nishimatsu houses held nearly half the village arable, though they comprised only one-twentieth of the households.[27] Yet after 1833, Nishimatsu landholdings did not rise significantly for the rest of the Tokugawa period.

The rapid concentration of village arable in the hands of the headman and priest may merely reflect changes in the way landholding was registered; the number of former *mizunomi* (landless) listed with holdings for the first time increased markedly—but their individual holdings were miniscule.[28] But the accumulation of land by headman and priest likely represents the results of foreclosures on bad loans. At least, it was resentment against Gombei I for abusing his position as headman and principal source of credit that provoked a village protest—led by the second-largest landholder—that forced him to retire from office in 1818. Although he retained the name Gombei, headship of the Nishimatsu house, and management of its land and business interests until his death in 1837, the village headship was transferred to Gombei's 18-year-old son, Kitasuke, under the supervision of a headman from a neighboring village.[29] Gombei I may have been chastened in his greed by this experience. But the most significant changes in the organization of the Nishimatsu credit operation appear quite abruptly from 1837, immediately after Gombei I died; they probably reflect an infusion of new ideas and practices introduced by a new generation of leadership when Kitasuke succeeded to household headship as Gombei II and began to manage the family enterprises.

The principal sources for this chapter are the Nishimatsu moneylending and banking ledgers (*Kingin taishaku-chô* [M.S.], 161 vols, Nishimatsu-ke Monjo, Rikkyô University Library), which form a nearly complete annual series from 1764 to 1925, lacking only a few years in the 1850s and 1860s. With rare exceptions, the Nishimatsu archives do not include individual loan contracts, which are not part of the ledgers, and this makes certain kinds of tests (such as types of collateral, default penalties, etc.) impossible.[30] These are strictly enterprise records, distinct from records of landholding and tenancy, or other family businesses, on the one hand, and from personal or household operations, on the other.

4. The Nishimatsu Credit Operation

The Nishimatsu credit operation changed rapidly in scale, nature, and complexity in the years under review. As credit demand increased, both Gombei I and Gombei II responded to the new environment by entering into new kinds of transactions that enabled them to keep pace with a growing volume of lending. What we witness, therefore, is not just a moneylending operation that is growing in scale and scope, but an operation that is being *transformed* into a new, more intricate, and highly ramified credit enterprise. Moreover, the relationship between Nishimatsu finance operations, their landholdings, and other entrepreneurial activities, may signal a new stage in their development as rural entrepreneurs. Nishimatsu credit operations, that is, metamorphosed in the Tempô period from "moneylender" or "moneychanger" to "banker," in the terms defined at the outset, to someone whose lending capital is principally other people's money, either borrowed at wholesale interest rates, or held on deposit, and is relent at higher rates of interest. The Nishimatsus entered the Tempô era as moneylenders; they emerged as deposit bankers.

In order to understand these transformations, which are by no means unique to the Nishimatsus, we will look at such indicators as the changing volume of credit business, at interest rates, and at the kinds of credit transactions in which Gombei I and Gombei II engaged.

Nishimatsu credit operations both within and beyond Nishijô expanded markedly in the years of the Tempô era (see Figure 10.1 and Appendix I). Indeed, the ledgers show that Nishimatsu credit operations

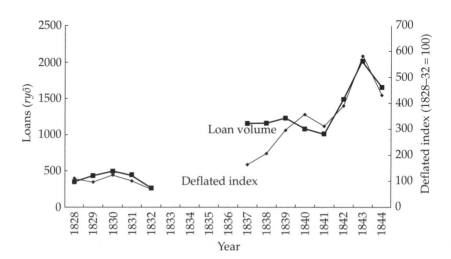

Fig. 10.1. Gombei's lending volume, 1828–44.

grew more rapidly in the Tempô years than at any other time in the last century of the Tokugawa period, 1764–1868. Where Gombei I booked 138 loans in 1833, by 1837—locally, the worst year of the Tempô famine—he had 217 borrowers, a 57 per cent increase in transactions. Total lending volume likewise skyrocketed: The year-end balance of loans outstanding rose from an average of 396 *ryô* in the years 1829–32, to an average of 1547 *ryô* for the years 1837–42, an increase of 391 per cent.[31]

The Nishimatsu accounts strongly suggest that local demand for credit in lowland Mino and Owari (Nishimatsu borrowers included residents of other villages and towns, both nearby and, increasingly, distant ones) grew rapidly in the mid-Tempô years. The credit climate was sufficiently attractive that, when Gombei II took over in 1837, he was willing—even eager—to capitalize on the expansion of credit, and prepared to rely ever more extensively on borrowed capital to finance his lending. The volume of Nishimatsu lending, as measured by year-end balances, increased nearly fourfold from the late 1820s to the mid-1840s. The ability to meet this rising demand and expand operations in this fashion—without a con-comitant rise in interest rates, by the way—was almost entirely depend-ent on the availability of outside sources of loan capital: wholesale credit that could be borrowed at what I shall call "interbank" rates, and relent at higher rates of interest.[32]

In 1837, the year Gombei II took over management of family enter-prises, only 10.5 per cent of his lending was financed by borrowed cap-ital, but in the following year the proportion had doubled to more than 20 per cent. The next year, it doubled once more to nearly 42 per cent; and

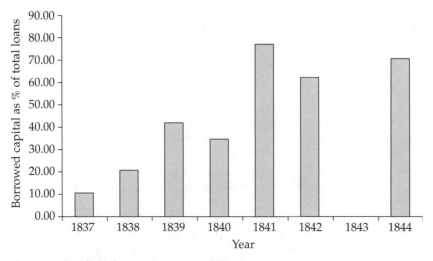

Fig. 10.2. Gombei's leveraging rates, 1837–44.

by 1841, more than three-quarters of his lending was financed by borrowed capital (see Figure 10.2 and Appendix II).

This pattern of increasingly highly leveraged lending is remarkable. It indicates a willingness to take significant new financial risks in pursuit of expanded enterprise and greater profit. With all, or nearly all his loan capital internally generated, Gombei I could survive a fairly high level of default or a decline in land (collateral) values. Even Gombei II, initially financing only one-tenth of his lending with borrowed capital, was fairly safe. But when he was borrowing three-fifths to three-quarters of the capital for his loans, his own financial survival could be endangered by even a small increase in the default rate.

Still more important, perhaps, this pattern of increased reliance on borrowed capital indicates fundamental transformations in the nature and behavior of rural credit institutions in Nôbi lowlands—and likely far beyond. First, as will be noted below, Gombei II worked with a network of like-minded wholesale or interbank creditor who were, like him, local financiers in the Mino polders; they were his counterparts as lenders, entrepreneurs, and headmen in nearby villages. They also appear in Gombei's ledgers from time to time as his debtors, borrowing from him at wholesale just as he borrowed from them. Several of them also appear in his books as depositors.

Gombei II, that is, had turned to what appears to have been preexisting network of cross-transactions among local financiers, rather than himself being the inventor of a new form of financial behavior. It is here that he made the transition from moneylender to banker. One can readily imagine—especially if one has participated in a family enterprise—that the young Kitasuke, seeing other local creditors expanding their business through the exploitation of this network of wholesale credit, was eager to join it to expand the Nishimatsu moneylending operation in the same fashion, and impatient with his father's unwillingness to take advantage of the opportunity of the times. In the regional interbank market, when one member was temporarily short of loan capital, he turned to another; a few months later, the situation might well be reversed. In effect, interbank or wholesale credit was short-term money, while retail credit was longer term. Thus, for example, while in 1837 Gombei II had retail loans turning over at an average rate of 1.68 times per year (average term, 7.2 months), his wholesale borrowings turned over 2.61 times (average term, 4.6 months). It was not unusual for Gombei II to be both creditor and debtor vis-à-vis the same person simultaneously, or to hold deposits to the account of a borrower.

The implications of this point are quite substantial. Gombei II was taking out loans to finance a banking enterprise that was, by 1841–43, lending an average of 3.6 times its capital (not correcting for deposit liabilities; see Figure 10.3 and Appendix). If lenders were willing to supply him with

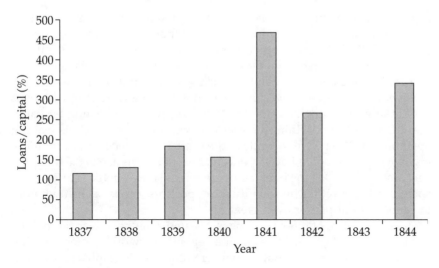

Fig. 10.3. Gombei's loans as multiple of banking capital.

short-term capital for that purpose, as he was happy to supply them, there must have been a high level of confidence in the soundness of these local financial institutions and the general stability of the financial climate. Lenders had to be confident of repayment from retail borrowers, both their own and, in this case, Gombei's, to justify carrying the risks entailed in lending other people's money, and in being overexposed to risk by a factor of three or four times their own capital. This suggests a highly developed network of faith in the institutions of finance, which is at root what "credit" means, as well as implying a hitherto unnoticed level of confidence in the stability of the broader economic outlook—in the currency, and in political institutions.

Several factors may account for this advancement of "faith" credit, but the arguments of Naomi Lamoreaux about the importance of kinship networks to the development of banking in early New England are highly suggestive. There, she argues, "the operation of . . . banks was shaped primarily by kinship networks—alliances. . . cemented by ties of marriage and consanguinity," which enhanced stability and flexibility, enabling credit merchants to raise considerable capital while reducing risks (Lamoreaux 1986). And indeed, among Gombei's clients as borrowers, lenders, and depositors were several of his affinal and collateral relatives both within Nishijo and among the elite of nearby villages.

Beyond the institutional points just noted, moreover, what we have found here has important implications for the broader sweep of Japanese economic development in the last decades of the Tokugawa era. Gombei I had acted primarily as a simple moneylender, mostly lending his own capital, supplementing it—as the Kondô family of Harima Province apparently did also—with profits from other Nishimatsu enterprises (Uemura 1986: 221). Using other people's capital, however, Gombei II was able to change the nature, and vastly increase the scale of his operations as a credit merchant, even while reducing the amount of his own capital involved. At the end of 1837, total loans outstanding were only 1.12 times his banking capital, which stood at 1030.5 *ryô* (before adjusting for liabilities to depositors). Within five years he was able to expand his lending operation by 28.5 per cent, while at the same time *reducing* the amount of his own capital involved by 45 per cent: he lent an average of 3.6 times the "net asset value"[33] of the banking operation as shown in his year-end balances. If we correct for his liability for depositors' funds (as he does not), the deposit multiplier is even greater.

The significance of this cannot be overstated. Gombei II was not unique in his behavior, but participated in a regional network of cross-lending among bankers of substantial proportions, both in geographic spread and financial scale. He went regularly to a half-dozen others in his own and nearby districts for loans at wholesale, interbank rates of interest, and they came to him in the same fashion. Thus they were able to move capital more efficiently from those who held it to those who needed it at retail, while keeping the retail risks local. When Gombei was short of loan capital, he borrowed it from others at short-term, wholesale interest rates (see section on, "Interest Rates,") to meet local retail demand; when others were short of loan capital they came to him. They did not demand repayment of Gombei's interbank debts to them before they were due, nor did they withdraw their deposits with him (*azukari*, see below). Rather, Gombei and his peers were simultaneously borrowers from, lenders to, and depositors with each other.

By joining and exploiting this network of wholesale credit, Gombei II and his peers were able to effectively increase the efficiency of the money supply and the velocity of money in the local economy. This increased efficiency almost certainly worked to keep the cost of credit relatively low (see section on, "Interest Rates"), encouraging the establishment of petty local enterprises and facilitating the operation of enterprises already in existence, thus further accelerating the proto-industrial transformation of the regional—and beyond the region, national—economy. This institutional reorganization of rural credit in the Nôbi lowlands, transforming moneylenders into bankers operating at deposit multipliers of three- and four-to-one, increased the efficiency of the use of money in the local and regional economy. The pattern found here can also be inferred for the Kinai region around Osaka as well, from Sakudô's data on the Kônoike. If this pattern is characteristic not only of the Nôbi and Kinai, but more broadly elsewhere, it increases the power of the Shimbo–Umemura thesis that recoinage and increased *bakufu* spending sparked a growth in the money supply and a slow, long-term secular inflation, to explain the advance of proto-industrialization that reversed the historic flow of population into towns, a relative and sometimes absolute decline in castle-town populations, and a rural revival.[34]

5. Interest Rates

Interest rates varied widely in the late Edo period, from interest-free loans sometimes provided as relief measures by the shogun or daimyos in times of crisis (Henderson 1975), and even between private creditors and borrowers,[35] to commercial retail rates that ranged as high as 30 per cent or more.[36] These have been variously described in the literature as "high," "outrageously high," or "usurious" (Honjô 1935; Walthall 1986: 7). But in order to judge whether these characterizations are warranted we need to know what interest rates actually were, and consider whether they existed in the context of a local, regional, or national credit market that constrained lenders' behavior. It would also be useful to make comparisons with interest rates in other pre- or proto-industrial societies. Ideally we would like to make calculations of such variables as default rates, collateral, anticipated effects of inflation (or deflation), enforceability of debtors' obligations and creditors' claims, and so on.

In the early modern Ottoman Empire, where the Koran's proscriptions on usury ought to have eliminated lending-at-interest, "an interest rate of 20 per cent per year was accepted by the entire religious community as in accordance with *sharia* [religious law]" (Jennings 1973). Interest rates in early modern Antwerp ran even higher—sometimes as high as 25 per cent. In England in the 1570s rates of 10 per cent were common; even after the passage of the usury laws of 1571, lenders used surcharges and other devices to keep effective rates well into double digits (Parker 1973: 17; Clay 1984). All such rates would have been "outrageous" by comparison to the rates on public debt in Britain around 1800, which averaged just over 5 per cent.[37]

Indeed, it is even open to question whether the rates cited by Takekoshi, or those in those in Henderson's loan contracts, were usual in Tokugawa Japan. Sakudô's classic study of the banking activities of the Kônoike house in Osaka reports that it charged interest of 10–20 per cent in the 1670s, but that rates fell below 10 per cent in 1685, and never again rose above that figure for loans to daimyos. Even loans to peasants were at single-digit rates in Sakudô's small sample of fifteen cases from the 1860s where the interest rates were recorded. The highest rate (and the most common, ten of the fifteen cases) was 8.5 per cent.[38]

Yasuzawa Mine examined a sample of forty loans, using records from a village west of Edo (and now part of metropolitan Tokyo) between 1791 and 1868. Principal amounts in her sample ranged from 1 to 32 *ryô*, and

Ronald P. Toby

loan periods from five months to ten years (with three open-term loans to *kô* [mutual-aid societies], three with term unspecified, and one "on demand"). Rates on the interest-bearing loans ranged from 10 (three cases) to 20 per cent (three cases), with the rate unrecorded in seven cases, and one loan at "market" rate. Yet even here, the most common rate was only 12 per cent (twelve cases), and in fully 75 per cent (twenty-one of twenty-eight) of the loans where the rate was both fixed and recorded, interest rates fell ranged between 12 and 12.8 per cent. The average rate for all loans was 12.92 per cent. In two other retail loan samples from the same village, average interest rates were slightly higher, but with one out-lier exception (21.7 per cent), the range was the same (Yasuzawa 1980: 266–73).

In the Fukuoka domain in northeastern Kyûshû, Arne Kalland found "normal" interest rates on loans made from domain-sponsored credit funds ranged from 10 to 15 per cent in the late Tokugawa period (Kalland "Rural Credit Institutions,"[M.S.] 5; Kalland 1984: 13). He calls there "very low interest rate[s]," that would be attractive to merchants who could bor-row from the fund, while relending funds at "15 to 30 per cent per annum." Kalland admits great difficulty in determining the level of inter-est rates in private lending agreements, noting that, "the interest varied according to the social relationship between the creditor and the debtor, the risk involve, the type of contract . . . etc." Still, he concludes, "nonethe-less it seems safe to say that short-term loans to farmers carried the high-est interest, usually 20 or 30 per cent in Fukuoka." Fukuoka domain had authorized interest rates of 25–30 per cent in 1771, and these limits still stood in the mid-nineteenth century.[39]

By these standards, Gombei appears to have lent at more or less normal market rates. Furthermore, he does not seem to have taken exceptional advantage of rural distress during the Tempô famine to extract greater profits by raising interest charges. I examined in detail the interest rates he charged his retail customers, and those he paid his depositors and his wholesale credit suppliers, for three separate years, 1829, 1833, and 1837, for all loans where the interest rate was recorded or could be calculated from data in his ledgers. Because Gombei himself made such a distinction, I differentiated between loans to fellow-residents of Nishijo, residents of Jûrembô, residents of Nakamura, and all others.[40] The results are summa-rized in Tables 10.1 and 10.2.

Gombei charged his borrowers interest rates varying from a low of 5 per cent to a high of 17 per cent.[41] Loans extended to borrowers outside Nishijô at rates lower than 10 per cent seem to have been to agents (*tori-tsugi*) relending for Gombei, or wholesale loans to other country bankers in the retail burgeoning interbank network. As in Yasuzawa's sample, the "normal" interest rate fell between 12 and 15 per cent. The rates were fairly stable over the years under study, more stable than pawnshop rates

Table 10.1. Interest rates charged by Gombei in 1829, 1833, and 1837, by borrower's residence

Interest rate per annum (%)	Nishijô		Nakamura		Loans to borrowers in Jurembô		Other villages		All lending	
	Number	% of total	Number	% of total	Number	% of total	Number	% of total	Number	% of total
1829 (Bunsei 12)										
0.00–9.99	7	21.88	9	30.00	0	0.00	1	9.09	17	22.67
10.00–14.99	13	40.63	5	16.67	0	0.00	5	45.45	23	30.67
15.00	10	31.25	14	46.67	2	100.00	4	36.36	30	40.00
15.01–17.00	2	6.25	2	6.67	0	0.00	1	9.09	5	6.67
Total cases	32	100.00	30	100.00	2	100.00	11	100.00	75	100.00
Mean a.p.r.	12.12%		12.30%		15.00%					
1833 (Tempô 4)										
0.00–9.99	11	22.92	5	27.78	1	25.00	0	0.00	17	22.37
10.00–14.99	14	29.17	7	38.89	0	0.00	1	16.67	22	28.95
15.00	20	41.67	5	27.78	3	75.00	3	50.00	31	40.79
15.01–17.00	3	6.25	1	5.56	0	0.00	2	33.33	6	7.89
Total cases	48	100.00	18	100.00	4	100.00	6	100.00	76	100.00
Mean a.p.r.	12.36%		11.84%							
1837 (Tempô 8)										
0.00–9.99	8	16.00	7	17.95	0	0.00	2	22.22	17	17.00
10.00–14.99	27	54.00	9	23.08	0	0.00	4	44.44	40	40.00
15.00	15	30.00	20	51.28	2	100.00	2	22.22	39	39.00
15.01–17.00	0	0.00	3	7.69	0	0.00	0	0.00	3	3.00
30.00	0	0.00	0	0.00	0	0.00	1	11.11	1	1.00
Total cases	50	100.00	39	100.00	2	100.00	9	100.00	100	100.00
Mean a.p.r.	12.86%		12.30%							

Table 10.2. Interest rates paid by Gombei on borrowed capital

% Rate	1829	1833	1837	1841
2.25	—	—	—	1
2.50	—	—	—	2
3.30	—	—	—	1
3.75	1	—	1	—
4.50	—	—	—	1
5.00	1	—	—	—
5.80	—	—	—	2
6.00	—	—	1	1
6.30	—	—	—	1
6.37	—	—	1	—
6.40	—	—	1	—
6.70	—	—	1	—
7.00	1	—	—	—
7.76	—	—	1	—
8.00	3	2	—	—
8.30	—	—	—	1
9.00	2	1	—	1
10.00	4	4	4	—
Mean rate	8.15%	9.29%	8.37%	5.11%

in Osaka, but like the latter, Gombei II's rates on retail loans, interbank borrowing, and deposits, were lower in 1841 than they had been at any time in the previous dozen years.[42]

It is also clear that Gombei differentiated among his customers by place of residence. He charged slightly lower interest on loans to his immediate neighbors, whom he administered and who were his main source of tenant labor. The average rates charged "outsiders" were marginally higher, and the modal rate for outsiders was also higher. Yasuzawa also found differences in the nature of loans made locally and those made to borrowers outside the lender's village, noting that the former tended to be for smaller amounts than loans where borrower and lender lived in different villages (Yasuzawa 1977, 1980). Still, she did not find the sort of interest rate differential seen in Nishijo.

Just why Gombei offered more favorable rates on local loans is unclear, for we are working from ledgers, rather than a statement of banking philosophy. The differential may reflect his greater enforcement power over peasants under his own jurisdiction, where his ability to calculate risk and enforce collection was more direct. Also, if a loan to a local borrower was secured, no other headman could block Gombei's access to the collateral. He may also have been constrained by a sense of obligation to his Nishijo neighbors, for he sometimes forgave interest when borrowers were in distress and, as noted above, appears to have ceased using loan foreclosures as a means of acquiring new land from about the time of the Tempô famine. Indeed, after 1833, the Nishimatsus stopped expanding their landholdings at all. Further, memory of the premature transfer of village headship in response to local protest may well have encouraged Gombei I and II to moderate the rates they charged when dealing with close neighbors.

Nishimatsu interest rates are generally consistent with rates in the local, regional, and national money markets. In a ledger from another village for the year 1840, interest rates on wholesale loans to other Mino villages in the bakufu fisc ranged from the rare interest-free loan to the more common rate of 10 per cent (Gifu Ken 1965–73: Vol. 3, 295–315). According to Table 10.2, this was at the high end of the range that Gombei II paid on borrowed funds, or charged for his own interbank loans.

Moreover, the markup between the interest Gombei paid to depositors (*azukari*) and wholesale-market creditors (*kari*), and the rates he charged retail customers on their loans (*kashi*) is not particularly high. Certainly, his rates are in line with the contemporary national market, judging from comparison with the data that Sakudô, Yasuzawa, Kalland, and others have found. If the lender has to recover through interest his anticipated losses owing to defaults, and offset the effects of the secular inflationary trends of the day,[43] these will be reflected in higher interest rates; this is independent of the moral judgment as to whether such recovery is "fair" or "exploitative."[44] Gombei I paid an average of 8.15 per cent on borrowed funds in 1829, and charged an average of about 12.5 per cent on his retail loans. For the four years tested, the rate differentials—markups— are shown in Table 10.3.

The Nishimatsus were charging markups of between 3.12 and 4.58 percentage points (15–54 per cent markups) over wholesale on their retail loans. Whether these interest rates are "normal" or "outrageous" depends on the factors noted above, many of which are impossible to compute from the available data. But in a decade when commodity prices and the relative values of specie were unstable, comparison with interest rates elsewhere in the country suggests that they were at least consistent with the contemporary market—and that a national credit market was in play.

Table 10.3. Differential between interest charged and interest paid

Year	Interest charged to borrowers (%)	Interest paid to creditors (%)	Interest paid to depositors (%)	Interest rate markup (% points)
1829	12.330	8.150	n.d.	4.180
1833	12.410	9.290	n.d.	3.120
1837	12.950	8.370	8.300	4.580
1841	10.410	5.113	7.040	5.297

6. Who Borrowed?

The Nishimatsu house's immediate environment was populated mostly by farmers, so, naturally, most of their borrowers were farmers—but some were not. Other than local farmers, and farmers and rural entrepreneurs in nearby towns and villages, they also extended loans to urban merchants and rural Buddhist temples. In 1837, for example, during the Tempo famine, they lent five *ryô* to a nearby Zen temple. But Nishimatsu lending was not entirely local; it was regional and even interregional. Indeed, Gombei I and Gombei II extended loans to merchants in Ôgaki and Nagoya, the latter more than 25 km to the southeast, and to a small-town *miso* (bean-paste) entrepreneur in Okoshi-juku, a post-town in the heart of the *shima-momen* region; occasional loans were made to borrowers as distant as Sakai, a commercial town south of Osaka more than 150 km to the west. The provision of these loans far beyond the confines of village and polder, across province and domain boundaries, and even to the commercial heartland of Osaka, further suggest how deeply the Nishimatsus and Nishijo had become enmeshed in a regional, and even national, credit market, and how truly national that market had become. In the last three decades of the Tokugawa period, Gombei II and III began "lending" (loans never repaid) to the office of the bakufu representative in Ôgaki. This may have been the price of Nishimatsu elevation to samurai status in 1861—or recovery of their pre-Tokugawa status.

But most Nishimatsu borrowers—more than 90 per cent in 1829, with the percentage rising through the Tempô era—were local peasants from Nishijo, Jûrembô, or neighboring Nakamura to the north. These were neither daimyos nor merchants in distant towns, whose credit needs provided Gombei with lending opportunities that tempted him, as has been widely suggested of headman-creditors, to exploit his peasant charges. He was not lured into "taking all surplus from the peasants... extracting taxes from [his] subordinates and neighbors, [while keeping] enough for himself to initiate" (Walthall 1986: 7) loans "to daimyo, villages, [or] irrigation districts..." (Smith 1959: 168). This is by no means to suggest that Gombei did not extract "surpluses from the peasants," but whether he did or not, peasants were his principal customers for credit.

Although Nishijo and Nakamura peasants formed the great bulk of borrowers, residents of many other villages also turned to Gombei for loans; in addition (though not visible in Gombei's ledgers) some local peasants went outside the village for credit, or even to others within the village, such as the priest noted above whose landholdings grew rapidly in the 1810s.[45] Some of their borrowers were fellow members of the local elite, members of the Nishijô governing council, as well as headmen from nearby villages. A regular customer throughout the Tempô years was a village headman a few kilometers to the west in the Fukutsuka polder; he happened to be Gombei I's father-in-law—or his successor.

Still, it is unlikely that, at least after the mid-1830s, Gombei was lending actively to the poorest or most "desperate" peasants. For example, his average loan was 7.4 *ryô* in 1833, 8 *ryô* in 1837, and 13.7 *ryô* in 1841.[46] These were considerable sums in a decade when a carpenter could be hired for an annual wage of 2.5 *ryô* in Kazusa province, north of Edo; when the average annual wage of a maidservant in one Harima village was between 1.6 *ryô* on one-year contract, or 2.08 *ryô* on short-term contract, and the annualized wage of planting-season agricultural labor at day rates in the Osaka area—where wages were relatively high—would come to 6.29 *ryô*, assuming (unrealistically) a 300-day work year (Henderson 1975: 7 (Kazusa); Saitô 1976a: 457 (Osaka); Uemura 1986: 182 (Harima)).

We have seen that the Nishimatsu lending operation encompassed a wide geographic and social reach, from Gombei's immediate neighbors in Nishijo and the Fukutsuka polder, to Ôgaki, Okoshi, Nagoya, and even Sakai; and we find Gombei himself entering the *saké*-brewing business by 1838. The increasing size of Gombei's average loan strongly suggests that most of his borrowers were not desperate members of the peasantry, the sort envisioned by Medick as borrowing merely to sustain themselves in the struggle for survival. Rather, they seem to have been middling peasants seeking capital to participate in the economic expansion that, Shimbo, Umemura, and Nishikawa argue, characterized these decades. The pattern is consistent with Nakayama's findings in Bingo Province, where the lender he studied altered his business activities so that, "after the Tempo era, peasant producers and the Fuchû [castle town] lower classes were excluded as the object of loans, which were increasingly limited to commercial capitalists in all areas [of endeavor]" (Nakayama 1986: 18).

To be sure, poorer peasants, too, must have borrowed from somewhere, for then as now the poor often fell into "a vicious circle of permanently having to live on credit" (Medick 1981: 49). But neither Gombei, nor the Nobuto family that Nakayama studied, was interested in this low-volume, high-risk market. What we witness, rather, is a market segmentation and specialization of creditors, with houses like the Nishimatsu and the Nobuto concentrating on the lower-risk, lower-interest premium market that included most rural entrepreneurs, leaving the riskier low-end market to others.

7. Types of Transactions

The rapid growth of the Nishimatsu credit operation under Gombei II, and his dramatic transformation from moneylender to banker in the late

Tempô era, came about through entrepreneurial initiative, to be sure, and especially because he was willing to engage in an ever more varied range of transactions. We will now examine that range of transactions as they appear in the Nishimatsu ledgers, looking first at where the Nishimatsu placed their loans, and then at the sources of their lending capital.

7.1. Uses of funds

Secured retail loans at interest comprised the bulk of Nishimatsu lending activity and consumed most of their available loan capital. But, as noted above, foreclosure on mortgaged land seems to have ceased after about 1833. At least, the Nishimatsu landholdings did not grow after that date, although they may have been selling foreclosed land for cash, selling mortgages to a second market, or accumulating land beyond Nishijo, though there is no indication of that. Unsecured loans at interest were a smaller part of the business. These loans were smaller, and carried higher rates of interest (as best as can be seen in the ledgers) because of higher risk.

Gombei II seems to have engaged in two distinct types of interbank lending:

First, loans placed wholesale through agents (*toritsugi*) in other villages, who lent the funds at retail, but on the Nishimatsu's account. In these cases, the *toritsugi* appear not to have been at risk to Gombei, but were paid a handling fee. In villages where Gombei had few direct local contacts, these agency loans offered better assurances than if he dealt directly with unknown retail customers.

The second form of wholesale lending comprised substantial sums Gombei lent wholesale to other rural bankers like himself, who in turn lent the money locally on their own account. These were mirror images of the wholesale interbank borrowing that Gombei himself engaged in from time to time, and his customers were often his creditors at the same time.

7.2. Sources of funds

Accumulated profits: Like other rural bankers, Gombei II surely used personal capital, that is, accumulated profits from land rents and other enterprises, including his moneylending, as sources of new loan capital. These however, are only implicit, and not immediately evident from the ledgers; hence they are not quantifiable from the data in hand. Yet until Gombei II began heavy wholesale borrowing, land rents and lending profits were probably his major source of loan capital. Most scholarship, however, sees this as the only source of loan capital for village moneylenders in the Edo period (e.g. Uemura 1986: 221).

Borrowed funds (kari): Funds borrowed at interbank rates from other rural capitalists in nearby villages, only a minor source of loan capital prior to 1837, became increasingly important until, by 1841, they were by an overwhelming margin Gombei's principal source of banking capital. It is worth reiterating that many of the same men from whom Gombei II borrowed were also people to whom he simultaneously lent large sums. These were other country bankers like himself who comprised the emerging interbank wholesale credit network that Gombei II had joined. They had formed this network perhaps to spread their risks, as well as to be able to respond more flexibly to local retail demand for loans. Moreover, the appearance of Gombei II's wholesale suppliers of credit simultaneously as his own wholesale credit customers suggests that, at least in the Nôbi lowlands, Gombei II was neither unique nor anomalous, but representative of an emerging class of village bankers who participated in an informal, but sophisticated regional network of interbank cross-credit arrangements. While most probably informal—if there were formal, codified procedures and rules, they do not appear in the Nishimatsu papers—the network was surely *routinized*, however, and almost certainly replicated elsewhere around the country.

Funds held on deposit (azukari): Gombei II's heavy reliance on borrowing from this interbank network for loan capital was augmented by his acceptance of deposits at interest, both fixed-term and on-demand, from individuals and institutions, who placed with him savings they wished to protect and increase—in an atmosphere of mild inflationary expectation—without the risks attendant on engaging directly in moneylending or other entrepreneurial activity. Depositors' funds (*azukari*) are clearly differentiated from borrowed funds (*kari*) in the ledgers; "deposits," "borrowings," and "loans" are separately labeled and separately recorded. By 1837, total deposits were nearly one hundred *ryô*, while deposits and borrowed capital together accounted for more than 21 per cent of Gombei's loan capital. In 1838, the largest single depositor was the headman of a nearby village, a maternal kinsman of Gombei II, to whom he also lent funds at the same time.[47] Other borrowers included a local widow who was an affinal relative of Gombei II, and a group of local parishioners (*kô*) at a nearby Zen temple.[48] Interest rates on deposits were, of course, lower than rates charged on retail loans, and a standard notation on new deposits was that the deposit was "received on [such-and-such date], but interest accrues only from the first of the following month." See Table 10.3.

Agency funds (toritsugi): Gombei also accepted funds in the capacity of agent (*toritsugi*) for other, nearby village bankers, to be lent on their account. Details are unclear from the Nishimatsu ledgers, and so we do not know just how Gombei himself profited from these transactions— he probably received a handling fee—but these *toritsugi* funds mirror monies that Gombei placed with others as agent for his account.

Agency placements were a minor source of funds, and it is not certain whether they should be counted as part of Gombei's loan capital at all, since they were not on his account.

Saké brewing: Another set of transactions appearing in the ledgers is a major non-lending use of funds in the later Tempô years, not noted directly in the banking ledgers as an account, but which may help to explain the rapid increase in reliance on borrowed capital over the second half of the Tempô era. This was Gombei's takeover—or, less likely, founding—of a *saké* brewery in Nishijo, which had been operated illegally by another local peasant until it was officially licensed in 1835 (*Goyô nikki* [M.S.], [1835], in Nishimatsu-ke Monjo, Rikkyô University Library). The bootlegger was head of an old elite house in Jûrembô, a long-time member of the Nishijo governing council, who had a history of declining landholdings and growing indebtedness to Gombei. It was he who had organized the protest against Gombei I in 1818. After 1835, he disappears from the rolls of the council, after more than sixty years of nearly continuous membership by himself and earlier heads of his house (*Goyô nikki; Kingin; SAC*). The brewery is noted in the official inventory of village economic activity by at least 1838 ("Meisai-chô," in Wanouchichô-shi Hensan Iinkai 1981: 869), and by 1841 was clearly in Gombei's hands; his ledgers note that the brewery was generating revenues of 130 *ryô* by that year; by 1844 brewing revenues had more than tripled, to 464 *ryô*. When brewing revenues were first noted in Gombei's ledgers (simply as an addendum at year's end, not as part of the banking business), they were equal to 38 per cent of the asset value of his banking business, and by 1844, 72 per cent.[49] There is no indication, however, that revenues from the *saké* brewery were redeployed in the banking business.

It had puzzled me why the rapid growth in lending activity, the transformation from moneylender to banker, and the move into what appears to have been a highly profitable brewing enterprise, were not reflected in an increase in Gombei's landholdings. The Nishimatsu landholdings, which had grown by 75 per cent between 1801 and 1833, did not rise significantly thereafter. But Gombei was no longer principally interested in land. What we are witnessing is not merely the transformation of a village moneylender into a country banker, but also that of a landlord into a general rural entrepreneur.

By the 1870s the Nishimatsu augmented their farming, banking, and their pawnshop[50] and brewing activities, with knitting mills, and the textile operations became the mainstay of the family's considerable wealth from the Meiji period (1868–1912) until the end of the Pacific War.[51] But it is important to note that it is in the 1830s that Gombei began to make a rudimentary year-end balance sheet, and to calculate the net equity value of his banking operations—the beginnings of what we might call a "capital account."

For many years Gombei had recorded total loans outstanding at year end, but in 1837, for the first time, Gombei II recorded his total borrowings, as well as total loans, outstanding. Although he did not use such terms as *shihon* (capital) or *shisan* (assets), from 1837 on, he closed the books at the end of each year's ledger by recording loans owed him, and his debts to others, and calculating the difference between them— which he simply termed *hiite* ("subtracting")—creating in crude form a calculation of the net worth of his banking business.[52]

At this stage, Gombei II was not treating deposits as a liability for purposes of his year-end accounting, as he did for his debts to fellow bankers, so he was understating the net worth of the business; yet we can see this as a primitive form of capital account. It remained a permanent feature of Gombei's accounting and bookkeeping practices, reflecting a new stage of entrepreneurial consciousness in transition to capitalism.[53] In this, Gombei was not alone, but part of a growing national trend, for as Noboru Nishikawa has recently shown, entrepreneurs around the country were also making year-end calculations of both net profit and capital (net worth; asset value) (Nishikawa 1995: 197–232).

Furthermore, it was precisely at this time that Gombei II ceased accumulating additional landholdings. This was not the case for the Tanahashi family in Niremata, who continued to invest in land until the very end of the Tokugawa period, adding 104 *koku* to their holdings within Niremata (they also held land in Nishijo) between 1853 and 1868, a 49 per cent increase. Yet Gombei II was not alone in shifting his interests from land to other forms of investments. Jinnoemon, an official in nearby Toyobami Shinden, another village in the Fukutsuka polder, nearly doubled his holdings between 1769 and 1844, from 108 to 211 *koku*, but then added only 20 *koku* more in the following nineteen years.[54] Clearly not all members of the local elite were disillusioned with land as an attractive investment for the future. Yet also plainly, Gombei II was not alone in reducing the importance of land within his broader portfolio of assets.

8. Conclusions

The Nishimatsu were wealthy, powerful, and well-connected peasants long before the 1830s, and their situation did not change with the crises of the time. Their banking operations, and those of other rural financiers like them, both in the Nôbi region and—drawing inferences from studies of other areas—in other regions as well, had already been evolving to meet the pressures and prospects of an increasingly monetized, commercialized, and proto-industrial economic environment in the countryside. However, in the Tempô era, growth in the money supply and a long-term secular trend of low but steady inflation, combined with other

long-term social and economic forces, to accelerate the proto-industrial
transition in Japan. This coincided with a generational transition in the
management of the Nishimatsu enterprises, and was the occasion for a
major shift in the way Gombei II deployed his considerable assets, a shift
that addresses the complex nature of moneylending and banking in a late
preindustrial society.

The pressures and opportunities of the Tempô era forced rural bankers
such as the Nishimatsus to make strategic decisions about the organization
of their resources in land and money, decisions both conditioned upon
and constrained by the need to adapt to the long-term trends noted above.
The changes Gombei II implemented starting in 1837 were to transform
him from moneylender to banker, and from village landlord to general
entrepreneur. The beginning of an "inflationary half-century" around
1820, we have noted, is credited with catalyzing a favorable investment climate and an accelerated proto-industrial trend. By the time
Gombei II took over management of the Nishimatsu enterprises in 1837,
well-established inflationary expectations would have increased people's
inclination to borrow for investment purposes—even borrow when they
had savings they might have used. Similarly, the expansion in proto-
industrial entrepreneurship, increasingly requiring a market orientation
in traditional production, as well as newer forms of production—
what Schumpeter called "new combinations" of production—generated
capital-hungry small entrepreneurs, some of whom turned to Gombei
for funds.

Taking over the family moneylending business in a time of apparently
rising demand for credit, Gombei II made a series of strategic and organizational decisions that enabled him both to expand the scale of his operations, and to alter their nature. These changes tell us a great deal about the
changing nature of rural credit in proto-industrial Japan. First, as we have
seen, Gombei II began to participate regularly, and more heavily, in a
regional network of interbank cross-lending, increasingly relying on borrowed capital to finance his own lending. As with many of the changes in
the operation of the various Nishimatsu enterprises, the records shed no
light on whether cross-lending was Gombei II's own idea, or originated
with others. As early as the later 1820s, Gombei I had occasionally borrowed small amounts, and the rapidity with which Gombei II made
the transition from personal to borrowed capital as the basis of his banking activities makes it highly likely that the network of interbank cross-
lending was operating well before 1837. He probably joined as a regular
participant that very year and, by the early 1840s, was borrowing nearly
four-fifths of his loan capital through the network.

One can imagine Gombei II: though nearly forty years of age, he had
been excluded from management of family enterprises. But with almost
twenty years' experience as village headman, and highly respected by his

peers, he had watched his fellow headmen, many of them also rural financiers, expanding their credit business through the creation and expansion of an interbank, wholesale credit network. He was impatient at his father's old-fashioned unwillingness to dive in and take greater advantage of it. Gombei II already had working relationships with most of the moneylenders/bankers in the area who were, like him, also headmen. As a newcomer to the network, he moved cautiously at first, going to the network for only about 10 or 20 per cent of his loan capital. But by 1840, he was relying on borrowed money for more than half his loan capital, and soon after was so heavily involved that he was borrowing sums equal to four-fifths of his outstanding loans.

Thus the Nishimatsu credit operation moved rapidly from simple moneylending to deposit banking, developing a primitive capital account as well, while diversifying assets from land and lending to a more complex array of enterprises. It is difficult to be certain whether these changes were as rapid as they appear from the record, or products of long evolution catalyzed into visibility by recent events. But the appearance in the Nishimatsu records of so many other local rural capitalists who participated with Gombei II in the regional banking network strongly suggests the latter case. Similarly, if the inference drawn above of lender reliance on borrowed capital in Fukuoka, and later in the Osaka region (Kalland, "Rural Credit Institutions" [M.S.]; Sakudô 1971; Kalland 1984), is correct, then further research should find patterns of debt-financed lending to be characteristic not simply of the Nôbi lowlands, but more generally of the proto-industrial transition around the country.

The reverse of this coin is a picture of entrepreneurship built more heavily on borrowed capital than has yet been generally recognized. The Nishimatsu ledgers do not reveal how individual borrowers used the money they borrowed from Gombei, and so this must remain speculative. But it is clear from the ledgers that substantial numbers of rural entrepreneurs, including the Nishimatsus, were supplementing their own capital by borrowing. It is equally clear that this sort of debt financing enabled the Nishimatsus to expand their scale of operations in one area—banking—while reducing the amount of their own capital in the credit enterprise, thus freeing capital for deployment in other projects.

The interbank network that Gombei II joined was situated in the proto-industrial heartland of Japan, straddling the boundary between the *shima-momen* producing industrial region east of the Nagara, and the more farming-oriented area west of the river. With the advance of regional specialization and industrial production for the national market becoming more central to the economy and society of the manufacturing subregion, the subregions became increasingly interdependent. Mendels's original model proposes not merely the industrialization of farming villages but the emergence of just this sort of organically interdependent subregions of primarily industrializing and primarily agricultural production. As noted above, since Mendels, the proto-industrialization model has been articulated without concern for the role of credit, but this is an oversight that will have to be corrected.

Study of the Nishimatsu banking operations reveals an increasingly active network of interbank wholesale credit, straddling both primarily agricultural and more heavily manufacturing-oriented subregions of the Nôbi lowlands, while the same sort of interbank cross-lending can be inferred for many other areas of proto-industrial Japan by meta-analysis of existing monographic research. These findings support Mendels's initial formulation, and offer a new way to elaborate the model still further, advancing our understanding of the place of credit in proto-industrialization, and of the proto-industrial age in Japan. For it is clear that Japan's proto-industrial transition relied heavily on institutional innovation in banking, and an expanded and far more efficient credit market.

Notes

1. The notion of "proto-industrialization" was articulated by Franklin Mendels (1972: 241–61) who proposed a model characterized by "the rapid growth of traditionally organized, but market-oriented, principally rural industry," whose production destined for distant markets, as opposed to local sale and consumption, mediated by merchants and long-distance trade. The fully articulated "proto-industrialization" model also entails sociodemographic changes of the sort adumbrated in the work of Smith (1959, 1973: 127–60, 1988:, reprinted as chapter 1). As Osamu Saitô notes in his essay reviewing Smith's œuvre from *Agrarian Origins* through *Native Sources*, while "Smith never used the term [proto-industrialization]" he may be credited with "the discovery of proto-industrialization," Saitô (1989b: 992–9). Following Saitô (1985), I take "proto-industrialization" here to characterize an era, rather than seeking some particular industry organized in the "proto-industrial" manner.
2. Smith (1969), reprinted as chapter 3 in Smith (1988), estimated that 55% of farm family incomes in one Chôshû county in the 1840s derived from nonagricultural pursuits. Using a broader data set covering all of Chôshû Province, Nishikawa (1987: 335), arrived at a slightly lower figure, but his definitions are different from Smith's, so their conclusions may not be precisely commensurable.
3. Remarkably, neither credit nor credit institutions are part of Mendels's model or the general discussion of proto-industrialization, despite their importance to earlier models of industrialization, especially Schumpeter (1934).
4. On the economic geography of the nineteenth-century Nôbi region, see Hayami (2002) and Iwahashi (1989). Of particular importance in characterizing the Nôbi region as "proto-industrial" in the late eighteenth and early nineteenth centuries is expanding production of striped cotton cloth, an industry that depended on long-distance trade for both raw materials and final markets. See especially Hayashi (1960) and Niwa (1982). For a regional-system analysis

focused on the Ina Valley, a mountain region northeast of the Nôbi Plain, see Wigen (1995). On the cotton industry itself, see Hauser (1974), which, however does not deal specifically with the Nôbi region.

5. For an introduction to the social ecology of the Mino polders in the Edo period, see Smith (1977a), Hayami (2002: especially chapter 3). Smith's "Nakahara" is a few kilometers west across the Ibi River from Nishijo. The notion of "village" is contested, denoting both administrative units imposed by the state, and self-identified solidary communities. Nishijo was both an administrative sub-village within Niremata—a still larger administrative village—and a semi-autonomous administrative unit itself, comprising two hamlets, or self-identified solidary communities, "Nishijo" and "Jûrembô." I have a manuscript in preparation discussing these nested levels of community in Niremata, Nishijo, and Jûrembô.

6. I have seen no other study proposing interbank wholesale credit networks in either urban or rural pre-Meiji Japan. There are examples of large urban *ryô-gae* ("moneychangers") such as the Kônoike of Osaka, engaged in the packaging of funds from several lenders, for the specific purpose of *daimyô-gashi* (lending to daimyos). In such cases, however, the Kônoike appear to have acted simply as the pooling agent, while the risk was shared, as in a joint investment: the Kônoike were not at risk to their fellow-creditors, but commonly at risk with them. I am not aware of any instances in the English or Japanese literature arguing the existence of the sort of wholesale interbank network of moneylenders-as-borrowers proposed here, where creditors used other people's money, capital borrowed at interest, to finance the operation and expansion of credit-supplying activities. A meta-analysis of Sakudô's data suggest that the Kônoike also lent to village lenders near Osaka, however who in turn relent those funds, while Kalland suggests in passing that by the late eighteenth century Fukuoka merchants were borrowing from public relief funds to relend at higher rates, but neither pursues the implications of this point. (Sakudô 1971; Kalland 1984).

7. This is the suggestion of Beasley (1988).

8. Norman (1940). A more recent historian in this tradition is Bix (1986: 10), "under such circumstances [as 'tribute exploitation' by fiefs and 'a rigid status system'], the increased exposure by the poor to merchant moneylenders accelerated a debt cycle in villages and defaults on land, hence social poverty." See also Walthall (1986: 7 ff.) and Vlastos (1986: 87), but Chambliss (1965: 36–8) takes the opposite view, that without credit and commercialization, "the degree of wealth and standard of living in Chiaraijima would have been much closer to a subsistence level," but later, on page 50, reverses himself to suggest that it was the "hard pressed peasant" who turned to credit.

9. For a brief analysis of *mujinkô*, also termed *tanomoshikô*, see Fukuyama (1975) or Sakurai (1962). For a fuller treatment, the classic study is Yui (1935). See also Kalland's, "Rural Credit Institutions," 11–14. Such institutions continue to function today in Japan and Korea—where they are called *kye*—and among Japanese and Korean–American communities in the United States. In English, see Najita (1988: 13–18).

10. Most scholars see these as the principal sources of loan capital. Representative is Uemura (1986), who finds, working from loan contracts, that the village

lender he studied in Harima (modern Hyôgo Prefecture) used exactly these sorts of loan capital.

11. Crawcour (1961: 348–49). Crawcour is not explicit about the distinction between "moneychangers" and "bankers." See Rosovsky (1961).

12. Sakudô (1971: 520 ff.) for example, finds the Kônoike making loans to peasant capitalists averaging more than 2,500 *kan* (and totaling more than 37,000 *kan*) of silver in the 1870s.

13. For this nearly universal view, see Fujita (1977: 118–44), Nagano (1986), Nakayama (1986: 1–20), and Yasuzawa (1977: 63–76).

14. Medick (1981). Medick takes a grim view of peasant borrowers, suggesting that their borrowing only dulled the edge of husbandry, as they wasted borrowed capital so that less was invested in production, capital formation was hindered, and the peasant family was driven into a "vicious circle" of reliance on credit that prevented them from taking new occupational opportunities. I do not suggest for a moment that no Japanese peasants borrowed in desperation; many did, and many fled their bankruptcy—even in Nishijo. However, then as now, those who borrowed from desperation formed a different market segment and generally went to different lenders. The issue of segmentation in nineteenth century Japanese credit markets is complex, however, and must be left to a separate discussion. Suffice to say here that the banking records examined here point to precisely such a segmentation.

15. Shimbo (1978: 58, 74) calculates a 57% growth in coinage in circulation, for 1818–32, and 8.4% growth for 1831–36, or an annual average of slightly under 3%, and credits this growth in what I term the formal money supply with catalyzing what Shunsaku Nishikawa has called the "inflationary half-century, 1820–70" (*infure no han-seiki*, 1820–70), in Nishikawa (1979). See also Umemura (1981: 1–30) and Yamamura (1974).

16. Hayashi (1960), finds that merchants at all stages in the product chain, from raw materials to final market, *shima-momen* industry were plagued by collection difficulties, and that much of the industry operated on consignment or other forms of credit transactions. He also finds the industry dependent on long-distance trade for raw materials and markets, and capital relations were increasingly interregional. For example, the Owari (modern Aichi Prefecture) peasant-entrepreneur who bought raw materials (dyed cotton yarn) produced in Kii (modern Wakayama Prefecture) from a Kyoto merchant, had them processed in Owari and sold the finished goods to a merchant in Matsuzaka. Such complex multi-stage interregional transactions were common to many industries, perhaps most strikingly the Ezochi (modern Hokkaidô) herring fishery discussed by Howell (1995).

17. The term "village," like the corresponding Japanese term *mura*, is flexible: Nishijo-*mura* was wholly contained within the larger Niremata-*mura*, and in some of its own documents referred to itself as "Nishijo-*mura* within Niremata-*mura*." Jûrembô, so far as I can tell, was never described as a *mura*.

18. The best discussions of life in late Tokugawa-era Nishijo are Hayami (2002) and Narimatsu (2000).

19. Wanouchichô-shi Hensan Iinkai (1981), contains *meisai-chô* from the 1830s for several villages in the polder. For the 100-*koku* production of the brewery, see *Goyô nikki* (M.S.) (1835), in Nishimatsu-ke Monjo, Rikkyô University Library, Tokyo. It is not certain that the rice used in the brewery was produced in

Nishijo; in any case, the "assessed production" of the village included other products besides rice (though calculated in their rice-equivalent value), so the brewery may have consumed the equivalent of half or more of the rice produced in Nishijo.

20. Niwa (1982) maps the principal *shima-momen* production areas of Mino, which is essentially east of the Nagara. Only three villages in Ampachi-*gun*, which includes Nishijo, are shown as producing *shima-momen*, and Nishijo is not among them. In 1888, this region produced 98.5% of Gifu Prefecture's *shima-momen*, and Ampachi-gun, almost none.

21. *Mino-no-kuni Niremata no uchi Nishijo-mura shûmon nimbetsu on-aratame-chô*, 97 Vols. (M.S.), (Rikkyo University Library). Precise titles varied slightly from one year to the next.

22. As early as 1620, for example, Nishijo's taxes were due partly in cash, though calculated in kind. Wanouchichô-shi Hensan Iinkai, (1981: 806).

23. I am preparing a separate manuscript on the nested communities of Niremata/Nishijo/Jûrembô.

24. *SAC* (1773, 1774); Wanouchichô-shi Hensan Iinkai (1981: 805); *Nayosechô* (1660), (M.S.), Nishimatsu-ke Monjo, Ôgaki Municipal Library; "Chigyô mokuroku" (Tenshô 16 [1588]), in Ichihashi-ke Monjo, Historiographical Institute, Tokyo University, reproduced in Wanouchichô-shi Hensan Iinkai, (1981: 785).

25. Shingan'in, in Shimo-Ôgure village, still maintains the Nishimatsu graves.

26. *SAC*. The landholding figures in the *SAC* do not match those in the *Menwarichô* (tax registers), but are an adequate proxy to show changing patterns of land registration.

27. Nishimatsu diaries, lawsuit documents, and other sources, show that they held land in other villages as well, and the *SAC* shows both *irisaku* (outsiders holding land in Nishijo) and *desaku* (locals holding land elsewhere). The Nishimatsus, though juridical peasants (*nômin*) were not farmers themselves, but purely landlords, entrepreneurs, and administrators. All their land was tenanted.

28. Most of these new holders (*takamochi*) were listed with tiny parcels that were probably house lots, reflecting a new degree of independence (perhaps more properly, self-dependence and precariousness) of the sort documented by T. C. Smith in *Agrarian Origins*; they do not signify a trend toward more even distribution of arable land.

29. Such headmen-in-receivership were apparently common in the Fukutsuka polder, especially in cases of disputed succession, village protest, or a young, inexperienced new headman. Here, two of these three conditions obtained. Cases of each sort are found in the *SAC* and other Nishimatsu papers. Kitasuke (Gombei II after 1837) became a talented headman mentor, and was often called upon to serve as such from the 1830s through the 1850s. The name "Gombei" went with household headship and dated from at least the mid-eighteenth century; it is unclear how many previous generations used the name "Gombei"; here we deal with only two, whom we call "Gombei I" and "Gombei II" for convenience.

30. On the other hand, the nearly universal practice in earlier studies of money-lending and credit in the early modern period is to rely exclusively on loan contracts in lenders' archives. Since completed loan contracts (*shakkin shômon*) were returned to the borrower on full repayment, contracts tend to bias studies

toward foreclosed loans. Ledgers are the only form of records preserving both foreclosed and repaid loans, and therefore give a broader and more balanced picture of the credit behavior of both borrowers and lenders.

31. The *ryô* is both a gold coin minted by the bakufu, and a unit of account. It was replaced as currency by the yen in 1871. See Yamamoto (1994) for the best analysis of the transition.

32. This finding differs significantly from the pattern Uemura found in Harima province (modern Hyôgo prefecture), where, he argues, the lender's principal source of loan capital was profits from prior lending and from his other enterprises. Even were the lender Uemura studied having recourse to borrowed capital, the loan contracts that were his core data would have masked such behavior. See *supra*, note 36.

33. Gombei's term is simply *hiite*, "subtracting," or the difference between total loans outstanding and total borrowings due others. Given the rapid rise in Gombei's reliance on borrowed capital it is unlikely that one could find a meaningful modal leverage rate (dependence on borrowed capital) among the participants in this interbank network. Even a half century later under modern Japanese laws, capitalization rates varied widely from bank to bank. See Teranishi (1982: 54).

34. Smith, "Premodern Economic Growth," shows that such rural industry drew population away from urban centers in the last decades of the Tokugawa period. It was employment opportunities created by petty industrial operations such as Gombei's, and those that operated on the credit he supplied, that were responsible for this population shift, which was visible in Nishijo as well after mid-Tempo.

35. Gifu Ken (1965–73: 3, 295–315), *Gifu kenshi shiryô hen*, 20 Vols.

36. Henderson (1975: document 21, 110–11) and Takekoshi (1930). Interest rates continued to vary widely long into the Meiji period as well. See, for example, Asakura (1961).

37. Presnell (1956). The 5% limit on interest rates in nineteenth century British usury laws was honored largely in the breach (Presnell 1956: 285).

38. Sakudô (1971: 457, 517, 520–1). The Kônoike appear in these cases to have been wholesalers, lending to retail re-lenders in the villages, who were themselves wealthy farmers like Gombei. Thus, although Sakudô does not comment on it, it would appear that the Kônoike were major suppliers of credit to a network of retail bankers in the Kinai region much like the interbank network the Nishimatsus enjoyed in the Nôbi region.

39. Kalland, "Rural Credit Institutions," (10 ff.). If Fukuoka merchants were using borrowed capital to finance their moneylending, as Kalland implies, they, like Gombei and his peers in Mino, were effecting a transition to banking. There is a contradiction between the difficulty Kalland has finding the interest rates governing private retail loans, and yet considering it "safe to say" that farmers were paying "the highest interest [of] 20 or 30%."

40. *Kingin taishaku-chô*, 1829–44. Gombei noted "Jûrembô" next to a few loan entries; in later years, he began segregating his ledgers by borrower's residence.

41. One exceptional loan appears, by calculating back from the interest payment, to have carried an interest rate of 30%, but that is probably payment of two years' interest at once.

42. Saitô (1976: 281–97). Saitô finds that the interest rates of Osaka pawnshops varied inversely with inflation, particularly after 1860, but the inverse correlation is less striking in the Tempô era.
43. See note 16.
44. Besides inflation and profit, the margin between wholesale and retail rates will reflect such factors as term, imputed risk, collateral, and the relatively higher unit transaction costs on smaller loans. The Mitsui house likewise had a sliding scale of interest rates varying with the amount of principal in the funds it lent its branch shops. In the early 1700s, rates varied from 7% per half-year for loans over 1,000 *ryô*, to 10 per cent for loans under 500 *ryô* (Fujita 1977: 131). More informally, a series of telephone calls to local banks in central Illinois in 1988 found that they were operating with almost exactly the same rate spread between wholesale and retail funds as Gombei did. If Kalland's Fukuoka merchants were indeed borrowing at 15% to relend at 25–30%, as he speculates, they were operating at margin levels undocumented elsewhere in Japan.
45. The moneylending ledgers of the Tanahashi house, hereditary headmen of Niremata, show regular loans in the mid-Tempô period to peasants in both Jûrembô and Nishijo. *Yorozu oboegchô*, M.S. (1834, 1838, 1839), Tanahashi-ke Monjo, Gifu Kenritsu Shiryôkan.
46. *Kingin*. Since many people borrowed more than once during the same year, the averages per borrower are somewhat higher: 11.2 *ryô* (1833), 16 *ryô* (1837), and 24.9 *ryô* (1841). This merely underscores the fact that Gombei was lending to prime credit customers, rather than to distressed peasants.
47. Depositors, that is, at times found it advantageous to maintain their "savings accounts" intact, while simultaneously taking out loans, rather than invading savings principal to avoid borrowing—just as, in the twenty-first century, it is not uncommon to take out a loan to purchase a home, auto, or other capital item—or start a small business—rather than to dip into savings. Depositor—that is to say, individual—economic behavior is beyond the scope of this chapter, but the Nishimatsu ledgers suggest that it is a fruitful avenue for future research.
48. It cannot be determined from the ledgers whether this *kô* was simply the temple's parishioners setting aside joint funds for a common purpose—say, rebuilding a temple structure or purchasing a new set of scriptures—or a revolving-loan group of the *tanomoshi-kô/mujin-kô* type.
49. As noted, one management and accounting advance Gombei II introduced was a year-end balancing of the books, and a rudimentary calculation of the net worth of the banking business.
50. The Nishimatsu pawnshop and the Nishimatsu banking operation were almost certainly separate operations, for the goods pawned—primarily clothing, though occasionally more valuable items such as gilded folding screens—would not be enough to secure most of the loans Gombei recorded in his *Kingin taishaku-chô* banking ledgers. For a catalog of goods accepted in pawn in 1828 and 1829, see Narimatsu (2000: 135, table 4-1).
51. Interviews with Nishimatsu descendants in Nishijo and Gifu-Hashima, and with others in Wanouchi-chô, October 1984; April and August 1985.
52. It was this year that Gombei died. Gombei I took over the banking operation, and entered with gusto into the interbank network; it may well be that his

peers, his fellow headmen-bankers, were already using just such a capital account, but this is a matter for future study.

53. Immanuel Wallerstein would deny the possibility of a capitalist consciousness prior to "incorporation" into the Atlantic-centered "modern world system"— indeed, specifically rejected the description of Gombei's behavior as "capital-ist" at an Association for Asian Studies panel on his world-systems work a decade ago. Wallerstein has restated his vision in several works since first adumbrating it in Wallerstein (1974).

54. Wanouchichô-shi Hensan Iinkai, (1981: 146, 148). Landholding data for the Tanahashi and Jinnoemon are available only for isolated years, so these data must be used with care.

Appendix 1. Total volume of lending (in *ryô* of gold) for selected years

Year	Volume Lent Index		Price Index	
	(A)	(1828 − 31 = 100)	(note ID)	Lending volume
1828 G	349	91	80.9	112
1829 G	432.5	109	112.7	97
1830 G	491	124	101.1	123
1831 G	442.75	108	105.3	103
1832 G	260	66	93.2	71
1833				
1834				
1835				
1836				
1837 G	1,152.75	292	178.9	163
B	121			
N	1,030.5			
1838 G	1,157	293	141.3	207
B	234.5			
N	881			
1839 G	1,218	308	114.4	296
B	509			
N	709			
1840 G	1,074	272	76.2	357
B	375			
N	698			
1841 G	1,007.75	255	82.0	311
G′	118.75			
B	776.25			
B′	8.75			
N	231.5			
1840 G	1,481	375	96.4	389
B	9,189.25			
N	563			
1843	*	*521	*91.5	*581
1844 G	1,639.5	415	96.4	430
B	1,162			
N	477.5			

Key:
A: volume excludes minute amounts recorded in silver monetary units.
B: gross sum borrowed (excludes sums held for depositors' accounts).
B′: another category of borrowed funds, unexplained in the ledgers.
G: gross lending volume
G′: appears to be loans written off as uncollectable (jigoku, or "hell")
ID: price index computed on basis of arithmetic average of spring, summer, and autumn Osaka wholesale rice prices as per Yamamura (1974, p. 52), with average for 1828–1834 equalling 100. "Deflated loan volume' is nominal volume deflated by this price index.
N: net asset value of loans (G−B) as calculated & recorded by Gonbei.
*: amounts recorded in private code; G, B both appear to exceed 2,000 *ryô*, with B under 2,100 *ryô*; index curve computed as G = 2,100. Assume G = 2,100, since we know that B was not less than 1 and not more than 2,100.
Totals for 1833–1836 are not recorded.

Appendix 2. Gombei's Leverage, 1837–1844

Year	Borrowings as % of Lending volume	Gross lending as % of asset value (i.e., Gonbei's personal loan capital)
1837	10.50	112
1838	20.27	125
1839	41.79	179
1840	34.92	154
1841	77.03	472
1842	61.99	263
1843	n.a.	n.a.
1844	70.88	343
1837	112	
1838	125	
1839	179	
1840	154	
1841	472	
1842	263	
1843	n.a.	
1844	343	

11

The Economy on the Eve of Industrialization

HIROSHI SHIMBO AND OSAMU SAITÔ

1. Introduction

The signs of a new era began well before the Meiji Restoration. They may
be traced back to the late-eighteenth century, especially to the years when
Tanuma Okitsugu wielded political supremacy, that is, a thirty-year
period from the 1750s to the 1780s. As early as 1912, in testimony to the
significance of this period, Zennosuke Tsuji remarked:

The Tanuma era was a period of confusion. On the other hand, it was also a time
when a new force was about to emerge, an era in which we can recognize the
budding light of a new civilization.... The seeds for the end of shogunate and the
opening of the country were planted during this time. Meiji culture traces its
initial moments to this period (Tsuji 1980: 328).

While this claim differs from the conventional chronology, the "new-
ness" alluded to here refer mostly to phenomena in the spheres of culture
and thought. Tanuma himself was said to like things Western, and the
period from the late eighteenth to the beginning of the following century
is a period that saw the emergence of Dutch learning in the country under
seclusion policy. It is in this context, therefore, Donald Keene, writing on
Honda Toshiaki, noted: "A page from any one of his writings suffices to
show that with him one has entered a new age, that of modern Japan"
(Keene: 1952).

In the historiography of the history of economic thoughts, similar
claims have been made with regard to the role that the Tanuma era played
in the evolution of a new thinking in economic policy. For example, a
vision of a uniform political structure emerged hand in hand with new
conceptualizations centered on goods, exchange, and currency policy.
However, when we shift our analysis to the actual economy, what do we
find? How did the various economic variables change over the Tanuma
years and beyond? What changes can be found in land, population,
production, and commerce in this period? The nineteenth century has
been characterized as an age of change, but were their discernable

changes taking place during the eighteenth century as well? Broad comparisons between the two centuries will thus be provided in the following section (Section 2) while Section 3 will examine the longer-run trends and their mechanisms that took place in the fundamentals. Shifting our attention to economic policy, Section 4 will look at the monetary aspects of economic management by the shogunate and the various domains, while Section 5 will turn to circulation mechanisms and market structure in relation to the real economy. Finally, brief sketches will be made with respect to fundamental changes taking place at various levels of society at large. Through these issues, we would like to clarify the nature of the roots of the new age.

2. The Eighteenth Century and the Nineteenth

The nineteenth century, especially the period from the 1820s to the opening of the ports in 1859, was a time in which things started to change; in comparison, the eighteenth century was a time of quiescence. This contrast is apparent in Table 11.1, which provides some key (macroeconomic) indicators as we know them today.

All the indicators show that the rate of change was low during the eighteenth century and high during the nineteenth century. Note that all values are computed by decade rather than by year, so it should be evident that any change during the eighteenth century was negligible. Of course, there is no clear demarcation point between the eighteenth and nineteenth centuries. With regard to population, growth during the nineteenth century did not occur suddenly; rather, the rise in population was slow during the early part of the century and accelerated after mid-century. Changes in prices and currency circulation had not started before the turn of the century, but occurred after the 1818 debasement. With these caveats in mind, the eighteenth century appears to be a time of little change.

On the face of it, all this seems to suggest that there was little economic growth during the eighteenth century. However, it is not easy to draw such a conclusion since Table 11.1 does not include information about production. Upon closer examination of Table 11.1, moreover, we discover two interesting facts that bear upon this question. The first concerns agriculture. It is clear from the table that there was little expansion of cultivated lands during the latter half of the Tokugawa period, especially during the eighteenth century. This is in sharp contrast with the previous century, when arable land expanded at 2.8 per cent per decade from 1600 to 1730. However, agricultural progress cannot be gauged solely by the measures of cultivated land area. The number of construction projects shown in the second column of Table 11.1 provides us a clue. The number, per decade, stood at seventy-two in the seventeenth century, and is fewer

Table 11.1. Differences in the growth rates of arable land, population, prices, and money circulation between the eighteenth and nineteenth centuries

	Arable land (1) %	Civil engineering works (2) %	Population (3) %	Osaka wholesale price (4) %	Money circulation (5) %
Eighteenth century	0.3	35	−0.3	0.4	5.4
Nineteenth century	0.9	103	2.3	12.0	15.7

Sources: (1) and (2) Chapter 1, this volume.
  (3) Chapter 1, this volume and Saitô (1988: 34).
  (4) Shimbo (1978: 30–7).
  (5) Akashi (1989: 51).

Notes: (1) 1730–1800 and 1800–72.
  (2) 1701–1800 and 1801–68.
  (3) 1721–98 and 1798–1881. The latter is the weighted average of 1798–1846 (1.1%) and 1846–81(4.0%).
  (4) 1725–26 to 1816–20 and 1816–20 to 1852–56.
  (5) 1725–29 to 1816–20 and 1816–20 to 1852–56.

than that of the nineteenth century. With the figure for the eighteenth century, thirty-five, it is evident that the relationship between such projects and land expansion had changed during the Tokugawa period. Indeed, there was considerable change in the nature of the projects. That is, since most projects in the seventeenth century were land reclamation projects, they led to growth in arable land. The number of such reclamation works declined sharply in the eighteenth and nineteenth centuries, and in their place there was a rise in projects involving riverbanks, irrigation channels, and irrigation ponds. These projects do not necessarily lead to an increase in arable land but affected the productivity of the fields. As documented in many studies of agricultural history, most of such land improvement projects made the transition from marshy paddies to drainable fields possible, which affected the choice of seed varieties, encouraged the greater use of fertilizer, and the introduction of commercial fertilizer, and thereby increased the proportion of double cropping. All this led to the growth, however gradual, in productivity. Contrary to the conventional supposition, therefore, eighteenth-century agriculture exhibited a steady progress (Kikuchi 1958; Yagi 1983: chapter 3; Akimoto 1987: chapters 2–4).

The second matter of interest is the volume of currency in circulation. For the period after 1810, the 12 per cent decadal inflation rate is associated with the 15.7 per cent increase in currency circulation volume. This was not the case in the eighteenth century, however. That is, fluctuations in prices were negligible but there was a noted increase in the volume of currency in circulation. Much of this increase can be attributed to the

Gembun debasement in 1736 and the issue of new silver coins by the Tanuma administration (*keisû ginka*, that is, silver coins denominated in gold), and it does not necessarily imply a steady and stable expansion of money supply during this century. However, it does seem likely that the increase did not lead to inflation and was rather absorbed by the rising demand for money. Indeed, the fact that the government placed a premium on the newly issued currency and, hence, made little profit from the debasement in the Gembun era, suggests that the chief reason why the government took a debasement policy at that time was to increase money supply to meet the growing market demand for currency, not to increase revenues to make up budget deficits (Shimbo 1978: 54–6; Nishikawa 1985: 54–8). In other words, market transactions increased during this period, which in turn suggests a growth of output.

Given the paucity of quantitative data, this conclusion should remain tentative. By taking a different approach, however, it is not impossible to document the changes that are supposed to have taken place from the eighteenth century on, to which we will turn.

3. The Age of Rural Development

The economy from the eighteenth to the nineteenth century is characterized by two changes. One is agricultural growth in the central region, Kinai, that is, economically advanced areas around Kyoto and Osaka. The other is the development of industry and commerce in the rural regions. Central to the first change was productivity growth in rice cultivation and the proliferation of industrial crops, which was most significant during the period up to the third quarter of the eighteenth century. On the other hand, the second change was associated with geographical expansion of handicraft industries, such as textiles, paper, and their related products, eyeing interregional markets. This became visible in the late eighteenth century in the form of trade promotion measures by domainal governments—indigo from the Tokushima domain is one good example—and grew rapidly in the nineteenth century, especially in the 1830s and 1840s, as noted in Chapter 7 of this volume.

These two movements were not simultaneous, but they were related and the agricultural progress in the central region is assumed to have been a critical precondition for the industrial development in the provinces (for this theory, see Shimbo and Saitô 1989: 18–24). Improvements in agricultural methods and growth in productivity, which is supposed to have begun from 1700 on, not only gave birth to wealthy farmers but also raised the standard of living for all peasant families. This led, on the one hand, to increases in demand for various products such as textiles, and, on the other hand, to an increase in labor costs within the central economy. This meant the emergence of a high wage economy. This change created a disadvantage for handicraft industries located in Kinai, but on the other hand, it produced an advantageous situation for competitors in the provinces. This is how the industry location shifted to rural regions with low wages. The price increase that began with the 1818 debasement also propelled this shift.

Rural industry that developed rapidly in the provinces differed from modern industry in that, technologically, it was a handicraft industry while, organizationally, it was based on household production, which often took the form of putting-out. To the extent that industrial development had begun prior to the industrial revolution and factory-based industrialization, this type of industry may be called "proto-industry" (Saitô 1983, 1985: chapters 7–8). In the following section, we will examine the process of proto-industrialization.

3.1. Proto-industrialization

Macroeconomic figures for the volume of shipments to the central market, that is, Osaka, and for the urban population nationwide, provide keys to understanding the extent of the development of rural industry at the peripheries during this period. The figures for shipping are summarized in Table 11.7 below. According to these figures, shipments passing through the Osaka market (known as "the kitchen of the realm") fell sharply from 1820 onward. This drop suggests a growing number of transactions taking place directly among the regional markets.

However, Osaka was not the only urban center to drop in stature. The same could be said about urban centers throughout Japan. Using population figures from thirty-seven castle towns, Thomas Smith argues that a process of de-urbanization took place during this period (Smith 1988a: 20–8). Urban population figures from sixty-four locations, including Edo, Osaka, and Kyoto, confirm this trend. According to these figures, the urban population dropped by 6 per cent during the one hundred years beginning in 1750. Clearly, we see a diminishing urban sector. However, if we look at Edo, Osaka, Kyoto, and castle towns with a population of more than 40,000 as of 1868 (such as Sendai, Fukui, Kanazawa, Toyama, Nagoya, Sakai, Fukuoka, and Kumamoto), we find that the cumulative total for these cities in 1750 was 4,473,000, while in 1850 it was 4,008,000. In contrast, for the numerous smaller castle towns located in the peripheries, there was an increase, however minimal, from 984,000 to 1,020,000. Population does not necessarily reflect fluctuations in industry and commerce, but the contrast between the larger and the smaller urban centers suggests development at the peripheries (Saitô 1987: 23).

Furthermore, we can determine the weight of nonagricultural production for several domains within their domainal economies during the

342 Hiroshi Shimbo and Osamu Saitô

nineteenth century, and such figures can provide direct evidence for the expansion of nonagricultural production during this period. Table 11.2 compares the domainal economies of Chôshû, Hiroshima, Kaga, and Suwa through nonagricultural output and chief product yields, expressed in terms of *kokudaka* (rice yields). The figures for the domain of Chôshû derive from what economists call an "input–output table". Therefore, the nonagricultural category encompasses a wide range of sectors including the service sector (Nishikawa and Akimoto 1977: 101–25; Nishikawa 1985: chapter 3; Akimoto 1987: chapters 5–6, 11; Nishikawa 1987: 323–37). For the other three domains, the totals reflect the major domestic products. Setting the domain's rice yield figures at 100, non-agricultural production levels compute to a relative weight 73 for Chôshû, 112 for Hiroshima, 44 for Kaga, and 26 for Suwa. Even in Hiroshima's case, where the total for seven products was greater than the total rice yield, was exceptional, we can see that the handicraft industry occupied a great weight within the domainal economy.

In the case of Chôshû, 80 per cent of all commoners were farmers. However, the percentage of agricultural production within the total production figures reaches 52 per cent ($= 64 \div 122 \times 100$) and within domestic income occupies 60 per cent ($= 57 \div 95 \times 100$). Thus, we can surmise that a significant proportion of the agricultural population was involved in farm family by-employment, such as the handicraft industry or commercial activities. The *Hanseiroku* (A History of Domainal Government, 1868) indicates that agricultural households (*hyakushô*) comprised on the average 78 per cent for the fifteen domains with verifiable records. The highest figure was 94 per cent and the lowest figure was 68 per cent (Tsuchiya 1931: 149–60). Thus, we can conclude that farmers engaged in by-employment carried out much of the nonagricultural activities, noted in Table 11.2.

Farm family by-employment during the Tokugawa period included a wide array of activities. The first type was household trade as by-employment, and included *saké* breweries and second-hand shops operated by wealthy farmers as a form of by-employment. The second type was the part-time work done within the household as by-employment, the prime example of which was women's cotton weaving. In addition, other activities such as sericulture and drying persimmons, normally considered examples of commercial agriculture, may also be considered by-employment. These comprised the third type of by-employment. The fourth was labor-for-hire, and included farmhands who sought outside work during the off-season. In short, all economic activities by farmers not included within the calculations for the rice yields were deemed farm family by-employment (Saitô 1986: 405–11). The five chief domestic products of the Chôshû domain included rice, paper, wax, salt, and cotton, all of which, with the exception of rice, were considered products of farm family by-employment. The manufacture of salt was accomplished by

Table 11.2. The weight of nonagricultural production in the nineteenth century *Han* economy

	Kokudaka (1)	Products (2)		Value added	
	1,000 *koku*	At market prices 1,000 *kan/ryô*	Kokudaka-equivalent 1,000 *koku*	At market prices 1,000 *kan/ryô*	Kokudaka-equivalent 1,000 *koku*
(3) Chôshû-*han* (1840s)	988.0				
On-agricultural sector		58	725	38	475
Agricultural sector		64	800	57	712
Total		122	1,525	95	1,187
(4) Hiroshima-*han* (1820s)	487.6				
Sake/iron/salt		24.8	412.9	—	—
Cotton/paper/hemp thread/*tatami*-straw		8.1	135.0	—	—
Total		32.9	547.9	—	—
(5) Kaga-*han* (1830s)	1,353.4				
6 Staple products		31.5	601.1		—
(Of which Shinkawa cotton)		(15.0)	(286.3)		
(6) Suwa-*han* (1820s)	45.9				
Raw silk		8.5	11.8		—

Sources: (1) Kokudaka at the Beginning of Meiji era, Kodama and Kitajima (eds.) (1977: p. 425ff).
(2) Products.
(1) Chôshû-*han*: Nishikawa (1985: 95). By paper money (80% of hard currency). 1 *koku* = 80 *monme*.
(2) Tanimura (1981: 79). 1 *koku* = 60 *monme*.
(3) Takase (1979: 392) and Takase (1980: 319–61).
(4) Saitô (1982: 400), in which the rice-equivalent was estimated at Edo's price. However, we take here from the price in Ina, Shinano Province, since the rice prices in these two are different. Iwahashi (1981: 214). The average of rice price between 1821 and 1825. Prices are in 1000 *ryô*.

seasonal workers, called *hamako*, and supplementary laborers (including women and children); wax production belonged to the third type outlined above, while paper and cotton production were based on the second type. Local wholesalers who oversaw the shipment of these goods, with the exception of rice and paper, belonged to the first type. While not included in the five products, the first type who in turn hired the fourth type— seasonal laborers—produced *saké*. We may further group these into industry categories supported by the pairing of by-employment types. Combinations of types one and four supported certain kinds of industries, while pairings of by-employment types two and three supported others.

As Table 11.2 indicates, the first pair was more prevalent in the case of the domain of Hiroshima while the opposite was true for the Kaga domain. The Niikawa cotton of Kaga constituted half the weight of the domain's major products and the remaining five goods belonged to either the second or third type of industry. The same was true in the Suwa domain where silk—one of the goods to carry the brunt of the Japanese economy after the opening of the ports—and cotton weaving were the major products. However, brewing industries, such as for *saké*, existed in all of the domains at a scale that cannot be ignored.

In general, the brewing industry claimed a significant percentage in overall production figures, and the second pairing played a notable role in the development of regional industries from the eighteenth to the nineteenth century. With the exception of certain regions where production was aimed at urban markets, such as soy sauce in Tatsu and *saké* in Nada, the first set of industries were mostly intended for small scale markets. The second set, in contrast, produced goods shipped outside the region of production, especially outside the domain. Table 11.3 notes the dependency on exports for each industry in the Chôshû and Kaga domains. The Chôshû figures include the portion consumed within the household, although it is not clear if such is the case for the Kaga numbers. Even including the amount consumed within the region, we may be better served by assuming that the numbers for consumption at home are unclear. In either case, the 40–50 per cent figures for export dependency must be considered fairly high. Examining individual industries, we may note that cotton exhibited little export dependency, given that the people themselves used it for clothing. However, as a whole, there was a sharp contrast between the high export level of textile products and the low level of non-domainal market dependency for *saké*. In many cases, female laborers from farming households supported the growth of export-oriented rural industries.

3.2. From west to east

We will examine this type of rural industry by taking up the examples of cotton textiles and raw silk. Through the Tokugawa period, cotton

Table 11.3. The dependence on "exports" in the local industry

	Paper	Cotton	Salt	*Saké*		Total
Chôshû-*han* (1840s)						
Output (1,000 *kan*)	3.9	7.9	6.8	6.4		25.0
"Export" (1,000 *kan*)	2.5	2.1	5.9	0.3		10.8
Dependency (%)	64	27	87	5		43
	Pongee silk	Flax(1)	Cotton	Sedge hat	Tobacco	Total(2)
Kaga-*han* (1830s)						
Output (1,000 *kan*)	4	7	15	4	1.5	31.5
"Export" (1,000 *kan*)	3	6	3.6	4	A little	16.6
Dependency (%)	75	86	24	100	—	53

Sources: Chôshû-*han*: Nishikawa and Akimoto (1977: 106–7).
    Kaga-*han*: see Table 11.2.
Notes: (1) Including hemp thread.
    (2) Total calculated from export of tobacco is minimal.

replaced the linen of the medieval era and raw silk replaced silk imported from China. In the process, production for both goods increased. We do not have figures for cotton, but in regard to silk, Narita Jubei writes in *Kogai kinu burui taisei* [Encyclopedia on Raising Silkworms and Sericulture] that, "In the one hundred years from the Keichô-Genna era (1596–1624) to the Shôtoku Kyôhô era (1711–36), silk production doubled; from Kyôhô (1716–36) to Bunka (1804–18), it quadrupled. Thus, the price of silk remains unchanged through good years and bad years" (Yamada et al. 1981: 321). Quadrupling in a century computes to a 15 per cent increase per decade. Silk must have been a remarkable industry in an eighteenth century otherwise noted for its lack of change. These two industries were to eventually lead the traditional sector into a growth path in the Meiji period.

These two goods differed, first, in the kind of agricultural landscape required for their raw materials, and second, in the nature of their consumers. Cotton was planted in the relatively fertile areas in western Japan (as an alternate to rice) while sericulture took root in mountainous areas. Producers made cotton for their own use, but cotton was also a product with widespread demand at the market as the commoners' choice for clothing. As a luxury item, silk, on the other hand, found its demand within a different social class. These differences notwithstanding, there was a common trend for these two goods. This common trend was the shift of the center of production from western to eastern Japan.

This trend is obvious for the cases of sericulture and silk spinning. The main silk weaving areas, based on shipment figures to Kyoto in 1756, were Kôzuke, Musashi, Kai, Kaga, Echizen, and Tango. According to the *Encyclopedia on Raising Silkworms and Sericulture* (completed in 1814) the main areas for sericulture were the Tôzandô provinces (Mutsu, Dewa, Shimotsuke, Kôzuke, Shinano, Hida, Mino, Ômi), Musashi, Kai, Kaga, Echizen, Wakasa, Tango, Tamba, and Tajima. But the main producers after the opening of the ports, according to shipment figures in Yokohama, were, in order of value, Shinano, Kôzuke, Iwashiro, Musashi, and Kai. This clearly constitutes a shift towards the east (Yamada et al. 1981: 321; Saitô 1985: 190, graph 8–2). For instance, the first recorded case of a shipment of silk to Kyoto from Suwa—which was to lead the spinning industry in the Meiji era—was in 1794, and the domain undertook free distribution of silkworms to promote the industry in 1824. Sericulture was already so widespread in the Suwa region by this time that there was a shortage of silkworms. The domain even went so far as to "purchase 2,000 *ryô* of silkworms from elsewhere" (Hirano-mura 1932: vol. 2, 12–21). This indicates a geographic division of labor between sericulture and spinning. Villages in Shinshû and Jôshû even began specializing in the production of silk cards.

These trends towards specialization were more pronounced in the case of cotton. The geographical expansion of cotton textiles during this period occurred with the establishment of cotton production in eastern Japan. Cotton was not grown in most of these places because of climatological or topographical considerations, but because of a dependency on purchases of cotton textiles from other areas. For example, in the Etchû-Niikawa area in the Kaga domain, cotton was produced for domestic use for sometime. However, in the 1820s, after a sales route from Shinshû Matsumoto was established, production reached 15,000 *kan*. This expansion was achieved by including cotton spinning not only from the traditional source in Sakai, but also from Osaka, Bizen, and Bingo (Takase 1979: 390–428). Môka and Sano in Shimotsuke were also to flourish as production sites during this period. Among the twenty production centers researched by Takeshi Abe, fourteen began to produce commercially in the late eighteenth to early nineteenth century. Of these, eight were located in eastern Japan and three quarters of those were in the Hokuriku or Kanto area. Six were in western Japan, including the Kinai area, but this number includes regions along the Sea of Japan, such as Inaba, Hôki, and Izumo (Abe 1988: 75). Clearly, there was a shift from the cotton producing areas of the Inland Sea and the Kinai to the peripheries, especially eastern Japan.

The export-oriented marketing and the local form of production (most of which were under either a *Kaufsystem* or a putting-out system) evident in this shift reveals that the shift in production was of a kind with that in western Europe. This means that we may call this proto-industrialization. However, Japanese historiography has been dominated by an urban–rural dichotomy. Tokugawa Japan, as noted earlier, exhibits a phenomenon of de-urbanization, and thus, such a dichotomy is not insignificant. Yet, a center–periphery dichotomy would provide a more meaningful framework. "Center" in this instance refers not only to the urban commercial center of Osaka but also to its surrounding rural areas. In turn, "peri-phery" refers both to domains as units and to larger rural regions as a whole. This period was, in this sense, the age of rural development, and during these years, there was a shift from the west to the east. Population figures during this period show a shifting weight to the east, first with Hokuriku and later the Tôzan and Kanto areas witnessing greater population gains (Saitô 1988). While there may be no direct causal relations, these shifts must have had some connection with the changes taking place among various industries.

4. Central and Domainal Governments and their Money Policies

During the Tokugawa period, there was a nationwide currency issued by the shogunate. In addition, there was what can be called local currencies, namely, notes issued by individual domains. Domainal notes grew in importance over the years, and by the nineteenth century, in response to numerous remintings by the shogunate, the number of domains issuing notes, and their total worth, increased rapidly. Shogunal reminting and domainal issuance of notes were important political measures in the economic policies of the shogunate and the domains. In this section, we will explore the nature of currency reminting and domainal notes as political tools. We will also inquire about the relation between shogunal currency and domainal notes.

4.1. Reminting during the eighteenth and nineteenth centuries

Following the failures of remintings in 1695, 1706, and 1714–16, Shogun Yoshimune's reminting of gold and silver coins in 1736 continued the currency system of the earlier remintings by not changing the types of gold and silver currencies and by debasing gold and silver coins without changing their relative values (see Table 11.4). In the end, the 1736 reminting was able to achieve a stable currency system. As noted in other chapters of this book, the 1736 reminting was not so much a budget policy aimed at raising funds, but a financial policy seeking to raise prices, especially that of rice, by increasing the currency in circulation. The circulation of newly issued gold and silver coins in the market and the collection of old coins proceeded without a problem, thereby firmly establishing the new currency system (Taya 1963: 289–90).

Table 11.4. Trends of gold/silver ratio

Period	To silver coins circulated by weight	To silver coins denominated in gold unit
1609–94	1 : 9.8	
1695–1709	1 : 11.0	
1710–13	1 : 14.0 (Futatsuhô silver)	
	1 : 5.6 (Yo'tsuhô silver)	
1714–35	1 : 11.5	
1736–71	1 : 11.5	
1772–1817	1 : 11.5	1 : 8.8
1818–36	1 : 10.2	1 : 7.2
1837–55	1 : 8.4	1 : 4.5
1856–59	1 : 5.0	1 : 5.1

Source: Kobata et al. (1966: 802–5).

For the next eighty-two years, until 1818, there were no comprehensive remintings of either gold or silver, and the volume of currency in circulation did not experience any major change, as we can see in Table 11.1. However, during the Tanuma era a new coin was minted that was to change the nature of the currency system. This coin was known as the *nanryô nishugin* (literally, sterling 2 *shu* silver coins; 16 *shu* were equivalent to 1 *ryô*). With the appearance of a silver coin based on the gold coin standard (*ryô*) and inferior in material quality to the extant silver coins, the silver currency system, which had previously been independent of the gold currency, became incorporated into the latter. Stamped silver coins began to function as a supplement to the gold currency, thus bringing into existence a de facto "*ryô*" standard (Mikami 1989: 70). Under this *ryô*-based currency system, the gold–silver exchange ratio established with the new silver coins gave greater value to silver than the prevailing ratio between gold and silver coins which had been circulated by weight. According to Table 11.4, the gold–silver ratio with respect to the extant silver coins was 1 to 11.5 while the ratio to the new coins was 1 to 8.77. This dual structure of gold–silver exchange continued to exist until the opening of the ports at the end of the Tokugawa period and was a significant feature of the late Tokugawa currency system. This structure was able to continue because, first, a free market for bullion did not exist in the domestic economy, and second, with foreign trade tightly restricted, free trade for both bullion and coins was not possible.

How did the minting of stamped coins fit within the context of Tanuma Okitsugu's policies as a whole? There was no one single policy that dominated the twenty-eight years of Tanuma's tenure from 1758 in the shogunal cabinet. The first half was characterized by a policy of retrenchment while the second half saw a turn to a policy of expansion

(Nakai 1971: 33–43). However, two goals define Tanuma's rule: first, expansion of a tax base beyond the rice tax, and second, reorganization and consolidation of the national market. The appearance of the *nanryô nishugin* was related to these two aims.

The tax collection system centered on rice collection in terms of expected yields (*kokudaka*) became an arrangement in which the lords were unable to absorb increases in agricultural productivity. Moreover, the lords essentially gave up on taxing nonagricultural (commercial and craft) production. Therefore, despite the fact that the shogunate had sought since the 1720s to increase tax collection, the shogunal treasury faced increasing difficulties from the late-eighteenth century. Fundamental reform of shogunal finances was impossible without incorporating gains from developments in commercial agriculture and nonagricultural activities into the tax base. Policies that responded to developments in the market economy such as the establishment of monopolistic trade associations (*kabunakama*) of merchants and craftsmen who paid operating fees, loans of public funds created from special taxes, and the establishment of guilds wielding monopoly privileges in ginseng, bronze, iron, and brass were all introduced during the Tanuma era as means to increase tax income. The minting of gold-denominated silver coins was in line with these policies. *Nanryô nishugin* were supposed to be produced from high quality silver imported from China (hence the name *nanryô*), but in reality, they were often remade from melted *chôgin* (silver coins known for their flat, irregular oval shape) or *mameitagin* (bean-shaped silver coins. Both with a value defined by weight) (Taya 1963: 313). There was a 28 per cent profit from the production of these coins, apart from the costs of production. But in this case, the shogunate did not adopt the system in which merchants were paid a premium for exchanging the old coins for the new *nanryô* coins, as had been done during the 1736 reminting. Thus, the profits fell to the shogunate. However, because the volume of *nanryô* silver coins minted during the Tanuma era was not so great, the income to the treasury from the minting of *nanryô nishugin* was held to a minimum and there was no significant increase in the volume of currency in circulation.

While the minting of these new silver coins was not meant to invalidate the existing silver coins, the intention was for a gold standard currency to become the universal medium of exchange even in areas like Osaka where silver was dominant. In other words, the aim was to consolidate the currency around a gold-based standard. In the next section, We will explain the nature of Tanuma's attempt to reorganize and consolidate a national market. Nevertheless, we can note here that the appearance of the *nanryô* silver coins was an integral element of this policy. While Matsudaira Sadanobu, who reconsidered many of Tanuma's policies, temporarily suspended the *nanryô* coins, they became widely accepted in place of the existing coins, even in areas dominated by silver. The volume in circulation increased steadily year after year, and by the beginning of the nineteenth century, the *nanryô* silver coins claimed over 20 per cent of the entire volume of currency in circulation.

The introduction of the new silver coins into the market temporarily destabilized currency exchange rates, but by the end of eighteenth century, when the new coins began to circulate without hindrance, the exchange rates began to stabilize (Shimbo 1978: 312). Price data show this to have been the most stable era of the Tokugawa period. But the complete reminting of gold and silver coins in 1818 marked the end of this era of tranquility and the beginning of an era of turbulent monetary conditions.

The aim of the Bunsei era (1818–30) reminting was to acquire profit from the debasing of coins and was thus more a policy intended to increase revenue rather than a financial policy. As noted earlier, the tax collection system based on expected rice yields made increases in tax income virtually impossible and was lacking an effective collection mechanism that could take advantage of the growth in commercial production and nonagricultural sectors. Moreover, Tanuma's plans to increase treasury income, such as the collection of operating fees from chartered trade associations and the system of making loans with public funds, failed to generate adequate income. On the other hand, shogunal spending saw a temporary decline during Matsudaira Sadanobu's retrenchment policy following Tanuma's ouster, but the shogunate's spending grew rapidly at the end of the eighteenth century. This growth was attributable not only to the extravagance of Ienari, the eleventh shogun, and his cohorts, but also to increased costs in the functions of a central government. In the end, the budget balance deteriorated rapidly (see Chapter 6, this volume). The shogunate, unable to find a way to increase income, elected to choose reminting as a means to raise revenue.

Because profit was the motive, the Bunsei reminting caused a significant drop in the quality of gold and silver coins. This decline was especially apparent in the case of the *nanryô nishugin*. The gold-denominated silver coins, whose appearance only half a century earlier had been groundbreaking, became more strongly characterized as a supplementary currency and the principal means for profiting from reminting. The Bunsei exchange of old currency for the new also eschewed a premium-paying operation, as had the case of *Nanryô nishugin*. Thus, the profits for the shogunate were significantly large and the balance of the budget temporarily witnessed a drastic improvement. However, the shogunate undertook the new minting of *nishukin* (2 *shu* gold), *isshukin* (1 *shu* gold), and *isshugin* (1 *shu* silver) coins from 1828 to 1832, to once again profit from the exchange. In all likelihood, the shogunate guessed that the growth of the market economy in rural areas would create a demand for smaller currency and that therefore a large-scale degradation of smaller currency, which had begun to function as supplementary currency, would not adversely affect its circulation. Through these remintings, the shogunate was able to earn a profit of some 5.5 million *ryô* (Taya 1963: 396–7). But in the same time span, the volume of currency in circulation increased 46 per cent (Shimbo 1978: 64). It was only natural that inflation was the result. And as noted, this series of events led to a new phase in the development of the Tokugawa era economy.

The minting of the smaller coins devastated the balance of the currency system, and with the exception of the *nishugin*, these small coins failed to circulate properly (Shimbo 1974: 1–7). Under these circumstances, the shogunate forged ahead with the 1837 reminting of the 5 *ryô ban* (5 *ryô* coin), the *koban* (1 *ryô* coin), the 1 *bu han* (1 *bu* coin; 4 *bu* equaled 1 *ryô*), the 1 *bu* silver, the *chô* silver, and the *mameita* silver. With this move, the smaller coins that appeared in 1828–32 were discontinued and all gold and silver coins smaller than 1 *bu* disappeared. In response to the shortage of smaller coins, the shogunate had already minted the Tempô 100 *mon* coins, equivalent to roughly 1 *monme* of silver. In any case, the abandonment of smaller currencies lower than 1 *bu* implied that the shogunate was willing to depend for smaller currencies upon the domain issued notes, especially the small denominations (ranging from 5 *fun* to 5 *monme*), which were in wide use as local currency. The national currency of the shogunate and the local currencies of the domains were clearly in an antagonistic relationship. But at the same time, domainal notes also functioned to supplement the shogunate's coins. Yet, clearly, these two sets of currencies were issued by different political entities and there were significant gaps in the unity and flexibility of supplies. Such deficiencies in the Tokugawa era currencies were exposed with the opening of the ports in 1859, which also uncovered a major discrepancy in gold–silver exchanges values between the domestic and foreign markets. As noted in Table 11.4, which illustrates the movements of the ratio between gold and silver, each reminting since the appearance of the *nanryô nishugin* caused the value of gold to drop in relation to silver. This illustrates that degradation of gold coins was greater than that of coins used by weight, and that the degradation of the gold-denominated silver coins was even greater. The shogunate was able to gain vast profits from these remintings, but simultaneously, the Japanese economy was to pay the cost in the form of an enormous flow of gold abroad upon the opening of the ports.

4.2. Domainal notes as local currency

The nineteenth century was an era of reminting, but it was also an era of domain-issued currency. Table 11.5 illustrates the number of domains

Table 11.5. Trend of the numbers of domains issuing the *notes*

		Period					
		1661–1735	1736–71	1772–1817	1818–59	1860–67	Uncertain
Eastern Japan	Gold	3	0	1	3	2	4
	Silver	9	8	7	17	13	2
	Copper	4	0	1	6	11	2
Western Japan	Gold	1	1	1	1	2	3
	Silver	52	37	27	55	27	8
	Copper	2	2	9	31	12	15
Total	Gold	4	1	2	4	4	7
	Silver	61	45	34	72	40	10
	Copper	6	2	10	37	23	17

Source: Nihon Ginkô Chôsakyoku (1975: 9–80).

issuing notes (gold notes, silver notes, and penny notes) by time and region. As this table reveals, the number of domains issuing silver and penny notes increased dramatically after 1818. Because the shogunate retained a monopoly over the minting of coins, the domains could counter shogunal reminting only by issuing notes. Through the numerous minting after 1818, the shogunate was able to greatly increase the amount of currency and in response, the volume of domainal notes, especially originating from domains in western Japan, grew at an accelerated pace. Unfortunately, we cannot accurately measure the volume of domainal notes during this era. A shogunate survey of 1842 reports fifty-two domains issuing notes worth 87,000 *kan* (equal to 1,450,000 gold *ryô*) (Yamaguchi 1966: 8), but these numbers underestimate the actual figures, especially the volume of domainal notes. Moreover, because domainal notes were issued in ever-larger volumes from the mid-1830s through the end of the Tokugawa era, we can assume that the figures greatly exceed those reported in the 1842 survey. According to Shimbo's estimate, the volume of domainal notes in 1867 amounted to about 1.9–2.8 million *ryô* and was equivalent to 15–22 per cent of the volume of shogunal currency (Shimbo 1980: 116–17). The nineteenth century was thus indeed the era of domainal notes.

But of course, domainal notes did not originate in the nineteenth century. Their history dates back to the notes issued in 1661 by Fukui domain. As we can see in Table 11.5, many domains, especially in western Japan, issued gold, silver, and copper (penny) notes. Of these, silver notes were the most prevalent. Domainal notes were issued predominantly in "silver-using" economic regions for several reasons. First, the market economy of western Japan, which was "silver-using," was more advanced than that of "gold-centered" eastern Japan. Second, with the exception of the period from 1710 through 1736, the percentage of silver currency by weight to the total currencies issued was exceptionally low and there was a general shortage of silver currency. Third, it was difficult to divide weighted silver currency into smaller denominations, and when transactions involved smaller amounts, it was inconvenient to use currency by weight as means of payment. The domainal silver notes that were actually issued were predominantly for amounts of less than 1 *monme*, and in addition to relieving the shortage of silver coins, their main aim was to act as means of payment for smaller transactions. However, domainal notes were issued not simply to relieve the shortage of silver coins or to merely act as a means of payment for smaller transactions. As domain-issued notes, they were also an instrument used to enlarge the treasury of the domains themselves. In fact, domainal notes were often issued in order to improve the domain's budget balance. Therefore, domainal notes were both a part of currency and financial policy, and budget policy. And these two policies were often the opposite sides of the same coin. This was the case throughout the history of domainal notes during the Tokugawa era, and the nineteenth century was no exception.

However, it would be incorrect to assume that domainal notes before and after the nineteenth century were similar on all counts. The shogunate's reminting policy changed drastically during the years from 1818 to 1830. Between the eighteenth and nineteenth centuries, there were not only quantitative changes in domainal notes, marked by a rapid rise in both number of domains issuing notes and their volume, but also a qualitative turn in terms of the types of domainal notes and the ways in which these notes related to domainal economies. We will trace the chief characteristics of these changes in the nineteenth century by examining Table 11.5.

First, the predominant domainal notes were silver notes in both silver- and gold-using economic regions, and this feature did not change from the eighteenth century. We have already noted that the shogunate sought to consolidate the array of currencies through the minting of silver coins valued on the gold standard and that those coins took the place of currency by weight even in silver-using regions as the main means of payment. While domainal notes were issued under the assumption that, as local currency, they would become the chief means of payment in daily transactions, gold notes based on the gold standard were minimal in quantity. Consolidation of local currencies on the gold standard was never achieved and an opposition developed between central and local forms of currencies. However, most silver notes that were issued were of smaller value, such as of the range from 5 *fun* to 5 *monme*, and these notes supplemented the shortage of smaller currencies within the shogunate's currency system. As a local currency, domainal notes existed in competition with the shogunate's nationwide currency while also supplementing its function.

Second, the number of domains that issued notes increased dramatically in eastern Japan. Prior to the Bunsei era (1818–30), domainal notes were issued primarily in western Japan with its silver-oriented economy. But in the nineteenth century, the number of domains that issued notes in eastern Japan increased considerably. The growth of a market economy in eastern Japan, centered in rural areas, contributed to this rise. The fact that smaller silver notes, used as payment in smaller transactions, made up most of the domainal notes despite the fact that eastern Japan was gold-using underscores this causal relationship.

The third characteristic was the rapid growth in penny notes. Penny notes were increasingly issued from the late eighteenth century, but from 1818, their volume quadrupled over that of previous periods. After the late eighteenth century, there was a remarkable growth of a market economy in rural villages, and with the coming of the nineteenth century, the development of rural craft industry fuelled the growth of a market economy. As a result, the shortage of smaller notes, especially small coins, became apparent and led to a drastic increase in the issuance of penny notes.

Lastly, and most significantly, in the nineteenth century the issuance of notes became a part of many domains' policy towards industry. In the nineteenth century, many domains sought to promote domestic industries, especially in the production of nonagricultural commodities directed at interregional markets, through a policy of domainal monopoly over certain goods. Of course, the aim was to expand income through this policy in order to overcome the obstacles of a taxation system based on the *kokudaka*. However, this kind of policy required large sums of investment capital. The method of creating this capital by issuing domainal notes appeared during this period, and many domains utilized this approach. In this method, the issuance of domainal notes became a critical feature of industrial policy.

Both domainal notes and domainal monopolies had existed since the seventeenth century, but a mechanism to connect the two was not a reality until the nineteenth century. For example, Fukui domain, which was the first to issue domainal notes, operated a monopoly over paper from a fairly early date and established a paper guild in 1699. However, only in the nineteenth century did it link its monopoly system with the issuing of domainal notes (Kobata 1956: 280–1). Another example of this linkage was the Himeji domain and its monopoly on cotton. It too established this mechanism only in 1821. To that extent, the issuing of notes as part of a domainal monopoly system was an innovation that appeared for the first time in the nineteenth century.

The single most critical issue facing the domains in issuing notes was how to ensure the stable circulation of their notes. If they did not circulate within the domain, it would be meaningless as either a budget or financial policy to issue the notes. The circulation of domainal notes was effected by enforced usage by domainal authorities and guarantees of exchange for actual currency. As for the latter, the larger the reserve, the greater the trust placed on domainal notes and the greater their usage in circulation. However, a high level of reserve of gold and silver currency would defeat the purpose of issuing domainal notes. In order to minimize the reserve and, at the same time, to encourage circulation, domainal notes had to be issued in response to demands for currency within the domain. Domains attempted a variety of schemes towards this end. Such schemes included issuing notes through merchants who had a demand for capital and who acted as the notes' issuers, or issuing notes in the form of loans to merchants (Shimbo 1972: 20–6).

However, as long as there were demands for new revenue on the part of the domains, there was always the possibility of a domain issuing excessive notes. In those cases, because domainal notes and shogunal currencies circulated in the market simultaneously, the demand for exchanges of the latter naturally rose and the circulation of domainal notes dropped. The silver notes of Amagasaki domain were widely accepted as a means of payment for smaller transactions, during the 1820s and 1830s, in areas such as Hanakuma village, a shogunal fief. However, when exchange was discontinued in 1834, primarily as a result of excessive volume (Nishinomiya Shiyakusho 1963: 778, 788), Amagasaki notes immediately disappeared from circulation in Hanakuma village (Shimbo 1974: 1–7). Since the domains were prohibited from resorting to reminting in order to raise revenue, one of their chief concern was to find a way to raise revenue to its maximum potential while at the same time ensuring the circulation of their domainal notes. Linking domainal notes to domainal monopoly operations was one way to respond to this concern.

As we will observe later, domains that had monopoly operations sought to escape the market control of wholesale merchants from larger cities, especially those from Osaka. Instead, they sought to create their own channels of circulation separate from the established system of circulation. In these situations, trading bureaus, which carried out domainal monopoly sales, were required to raise large amounts of operating funds. Thus, issuing domainal notes became a means to raise the necessary operating funds. A portion of shogunal currency, gained through exporting domainal goods to outside markets, was set aside as security for domainal notes, thereby ensuring their circulation. The cotton monopoly of the Himeji domain paid cotton producers in advance in the form of cotton stamps (domainal notes) through which the domainal trading association collected exportable goods. In the case of Fukui, the domain forwarded 50,000 *ryô* worth of domainal notes to a domainal trading bureau." With additional investment coming from local merchants, the capital was used to finance the domainal monopoly system (Kobata 1956: 406). While the shogunate had gained enormous sums of money through the reminting process, the gains were not used as operating funds for new industries. On the other hand, at the domain level, domainal notes became a tool to develop domainal industry by supplying capital. This can be characterized as supplying growth funds in the form of high-powered money. Domainal notes as a form of local currency had outgrown their supplementary function to the shogunal currency. Paper money tied to domainal monopoly practices were clearly an innovation. And this mechanism became a model for industrial policy in the early Meiji period.

5. Distribution and Market Structures

The driving force for a critical transformation in Tokugawa economic development was the diffusion of market-oriented industrial production to rural regions. At the same time, this change was accompanied by a transformation in distribution structures. For example, domainal monopoly operations which played a role in the development of local industries were intrinsically linked, first, to a break from established structures of commerce in Osaka and other metropolitan merchants and, second, to the emergence of a new structure of distribution in its place. These transformations required the diffusion to regional cities of commercial and financial functions, which had been concentrated in large metropolitan areas. The growth of rural industries implied the decline of the center and the rise of the rural economy in terms of commodity production aimed for interregional markets. This can be said for distribution as well. In this section, we will describe changes that took place in the structure of commerce and market organization from the late eighteenth century onwards.

5.1. Reorganization of the structure of distribution

Changes in the structure of the interregional division of labor—that is, the development of both rural industries and the hinterland of Edo sphere—spurred the expansion of direct transactions between regional domains and Edo and among the domains themselves. This growth also led to a relative drop in transactions between those domains and Osaka. Such changes signaled the weakening of Osaka wholesale merchants' control over the market. Moreover, this trend was accelerated by an emergence of new distribution channels established in Osaka and its outlying areas by those who were outside the circle of chartered trade associations. The growth of transactions not involving Osaka, and particularly the emergence of transactions in Osaka by outsiders to the chartered trade associations, greatly destabilized the Osaka wholesale merchants' capacity to maintain control over distribution (Miyamoto 1987b: 319). Naturally, these developments called for a fundamental reorganization of the structure of interregional trade including the role of Osaka wholesale merchants. Tanuma's policy toward chartered trade associations sought to address precisely the reorganization of the existing structure of interregional trade.

Tanuma's policy toward chartered trade associations sanctioned many such groups in the 1760s to 1770s, and most of these groups were located in Osaka and its environs, with just a few in Edo (Hayashi 1969: 23–7). This fact illustrates clearly how Tanuma's policy brought about Osaka's relative decline in interregional circulation and a weakening of Osaka wholesale merchants' control of the market. Newly established chartered trade associations recognized the commercial activities of merchants previously regarded as outsiders and allowed their participation as "insiders." For example, *saké* breweries and oil presses in the three hamlets of Nada in the western areas of Settsu had emerged and become established as a rural industry in the beginning of the eighteenth century. Growing rapidly to become "outside" competitors to the traditional *saké* breweries and oil presses in the Osaka, Ikeda, and Itami areas, these producers independently shipped to Edo before joining the distribution organization around Osaka in the 1770s to 1780s. *Saké* breweries in Nada joined an independent shipping alliance known as the "Twelve Edo-bound Sessen Districts" with those of Ikeda and Itami, but the control of this group was in the hands of Osaka *saké* wholesalers (Yunoki 1965: 23–7). Likewise, the oil pressing industries of western Settsu were required to sell their products to Osaka oil wholesale merchants in exchange for gaining recognition as chartered trade association members (Osaka-shi Sanjikai 1911b: 772). The Tatsuno soy sauce industry was able to enter the Kyoto market, in addition to the Osaka market, and become recognized as a member of the trade association during Tanuma's era. In exchange, the Kyoto soy sauce wholesalers held the controlling stock in the group (Hasegawa 1972: 62).

This reorganization of chartered trade associations' integrated distribution networks, previously existing outside the established system centered in Osaka, and as a result, Osaka wholesale merchants' influence over the market declined. At the same time, an orderly distribution system assuring a stable environment for transactions was restored and maintained. Structural reorganization and maintenance of interregional trade minimized price fluctuations and regional differences, and allowed for the expansion of goods passing through Osaka (see Table 11.7 below). On the other hand, as indicated in Table 11.6, interest rates in Osaka

Table 11.6. Trends of the interest rate in Mitsui and Kônoike Exchange Houses

Period	Mitsui Exchange House received interest to loans (%)	Kônoike Exchange House	
		Received interest to loans (%)	Contract interest with daimyo (%)
1721–40	4.9	6.3	12.45
1741–60	4.1	5.5	13.04
1761–80	3.4	4.9	11.31
1781–1800	1.7	3.8	9.28
1801–20	1.8	2.2	9.31
1821–40	1.9	3.4	8.28
1841–60	—	3.3	8.70

Source: Mitsui: Tanaka (1969) and Kagawa (1974). Kônoike: Yasuoka (1970*a*) and Saitô (1976*b*). Originally, Miyamoto (1963: 348–65).

declined, implying a lower profitability for Osaka merchants. Through the establishment of commercial and financial functions in the regional cities, the tendency toward diminishing returns (Hicks 1969: 45) worked to reduce the profitability of Osaka merchants.

With the coming of the nineteenth century, domainal monopoly operations experienced substantial growth and there were increases in direct transactions between regional merchants and production and consumption sites. Moreover, distribution routes that did not pass through the Osaka wholesale merchants appeared with the entry of outsiders into the Osaka market. It is well known that an 1842 report surveying the Osaka market submitted to the shogunate by Abe Tôtômi-no-kami Shôzô, an Osaka city magistrate, attributed the decline in the volume of commodities passing through the Osaka market to direct transactions between domainal monopoly operations and regional merchants (Osaka-shi Sanjikai 1910: 639–85). Osaka wholesale merchants' control over the market diminished yet again and the capacity of chartered trade associations dominated by Osaka merchants to maintain order in distribution was significantly challenged. These conditions appeared in no small part due to the growing financial autonomy of regional merchants and producers vis-à-vis Osaka wholesale merchants.

In the interregional distribution of commodities centered on Osaka, Osaka wholesale merchants paid advance loans to local commercial agents (local merchants and producers) while also giving extension loans (payment on sale) to middlemen and local merchants who bought from the Osaka merchants. Osaka wholesale merchants issued and mediated a series of advance loans and extension loans. However, circumstances changed rapidly on the turn to the nineteenth century. In the transactions between local commercial agents and Osaka wholesale merchants, local commercial agents began to receive advance loans in anticipation of an exchange of goods not from the Osaka wholesalers but from third parties (most commonly financiers known as exchange agents, but also "local wealthy farmers with connections in Osaka"). This transaction method was not premised on advance loans from wholesaler to local agents but was rather characterized by local agents holding control over the settlement of accounts for the payment of the transaction (Shimbo 1967b: 29–46).

Extension loans were still prevalent in the transactions between Osaka wholesalers and merchants located in consumer areas like Edo, although significant changes appeared in the method of settlement. The method of settling payments for goods shipped from Osaka to Edo changed from reverse remittance, with Osaka wholesale merchants assuming control over settlement, to a form of exchange remittance in which Edo wholesale merchants held control (Shimbo 1968: 1–17). Taking the example of *saké*, an important commodity shipped from Osaka to Edo, payment for the *saké* was made in the form of either reverse remittance or shipment of actual currency. From the beginning of the nineteenth century, exchange remittance became the primary form of settlement, due to the strong demand of the Edo wholesale merchants, and control of the settlement of accounts for the *saké* transferred to the Edo wholesale merchants. As a result, there were increasing cases of payment deadline extensions and payments-on-sale (Yunoki 1965: 305–14). These trends became common for other goods as well (Osaka-shi Sanjikai 1910: 679).

The decline of the Osaka wholesale merchants' control over the market can also be corroborated by the famous disputes over rapeseed and cotton that occurred in the first two decades of the nineteenth century. Farmers from Settsu, Kawachi, and Izumi formed an alliance transcending domainal boundaries and demanded the right to conduct business with merchants other than those from the priviledged trade associations. They made two large-scale petitions to the Osaka city magistrate for rights over rapeseed and cotton, and the petitions were accepted for consideration. Edo period custom dictated that conflicts among people were resolved among the involved parties with no intervention by the shogunate. Therefore, the very fact that the Osaka city magistrate accepted the petitions for a hearing implied a decline in the control over the market by Osaka wholesale merchants and the capacity of chartered trade associations to maintain authority over the distribution system. The judgments cast by the Osaka city magistrate, that is the shogunate, differed in the two cases: the farmers' petition was granted in the case of cotton and denied in that of rapeseed (Kobayashi 1963: 241–50). However, in the latter case, on the occasion of the 1832 reform of oil extraction technology, the farmers' demands were granted de facto (Osaka-shi Sanjikai 1912: 1016–25). The decline of market control by the Osaka wholesale merchants became increasingly apparent.

Under such circumstances, reorganization of the structure of the Osaka-centered, interregional distribution of commodities inevitably became a key concern for shogunal policy. The Tempô reforms, headed by Mizuno Tadakuni in the 1840s, disbanded the chartered trade associations and severely restricted domainal monopoly sales. However, these policies were anachronistic and only compounded the confusion in the structure of interregional trade. In 1851, the shogunate attempted to restructure the interregional circulation of commodities by resurrecting the chartered trade associations. However, there was no hope for the formation of a stable circulation structure and its status remained unpredictable and in flux. With the opening of the ports in 1859, a new variable would be introduced into the structure of interregional commodity circulation.

In this manner, the decline of the Osaka wholesale merchants' control of the market and the relative drop in status of Osaka proceeded apace. From the perspective of a center versus peripheries framework, it is clear that the countryside prospered at the cost of the center's decline. However, such change does not imply a faltering or reduction of interregional commodity circulation. The growth of a market economy in the nineteenth century is quite evident; intraregional and interregional trade expanded steadily, and the interregional division of labor became firmly established.

5.2. Market structure in the nineteenth century

Having drawn a model of the Tokugawa era market economy through an analysis of the rice market, Miyamoto Matao makes the following points about the national network of the rice market. First, by as late as the beginning of the eighteenth century, a unified rice market had come into existence in western Japan. Second, the market in eastern Japan was relatively independent from that of western Japan and yet had not emerged as an integrated market in its own right. Third, the areas of Kinai, the Inland Sea, Tôkai, and northeastern Japan had their own market centers, and these had strong ties to Osaka. Moreover, Miyamoto argues that the national network of these rice markets laid the groundwork for the establishment of a full-fledged national market in the 1890s (Miyamoto 1988b: 435–6).

In the Tokugawa period, most of the rice that was sold as a commodity was rice that had been collected as taxes. Apart from a portion that was sold within the domain's own castle town, much of the rice was shipped to central markets in Osaka or Edo. There was no actual circulation of rice between Edo and Osaka. Nevertheless, the Osaka rice market was consistently the price leader, and there are indications of strong ties between the price of rice in Osaka and the price in other areas. Despite the absence of a completely integrated national market, a national market was taking shape in the form of the strong ties between local rice markets and the Osaka rice market. Moreover, this national network came into being in the beginning of the eighteenth century, and its fundamental features did not change during the course of the Tokugawa period. However, markets for other forms of agricultural and foodstuff commodities did not necessarily have the same structure and history as the rice market. In the case of markets for industrial crops and handicraft goods, a national network was in place at the beginning of the eighteenth century. But unlike the rice market, these markets were structured around nexus between Osaka and Edo. There was also a vast transformation in response to the changes in the interregional division of labor, from the beginning of the eighteenth century through the middle of the nineteenth century.

In the beginning of the eighteenth century, Osaka and the Kinai region functioned as production centers to supply basic goods to Edo and its surroundings, and there was a strong tie between Osaka and Edo. Local domains exported foodstuff and industrial crops to the central markets and imported specialized and finely crafted goods. Meanwhile, the domains were not dependent on Osaka or the Kinai for daily necessities, choosing instead to produce these on their own. With the exception of rice, there clearly existed some form of interregional network developing out of the axis of the distribution links between Osaka and Edo. From the eighteenth to the nineteenth century, these interregional networks came to exhibit alternative features. In the peripheral domains, commodity production of industrial crops and handicraft goods aimed at interregional markets took root and expanded. In turn, the Kinai region lost its comparative advantage in the production of these goods and was forced to specialize in certain specific industrial crops and handicraft goods. As a result, the relative share of general handicraft goods expanded in the trade between Osaka and local domains in addition to industrial crops and intermediary goods. At the same time, interregional trade became more important within the domainal economy. However, direct ties between domains and Edo was not yet large, excepting those domains within Edo's economic sphere, and ties of mutual transactions among local domains had not become the rule. Therefore, interregional commodity circulation and trade between Osaka and local domains exhibited an enormous growth with the development of a market economy. Table 11.7 illustrates this trend through changes in the volume of goods circulating through Osaka between 1736 and 1840.

According to this figure, in 1736 rice collected as tax occupied by far the largest percentage of goods passing through Osaka. The shares for other goods were not very large, and cotton textiles, which accounted for the

Table 11.7. The comparison of commodities arriving at Osaka

Items	Quantity				Value in silver (*kan*)		
	1736 (in 10,000 units)		1804–29	1840	1736	1804–29	1840
Rice	120	*koku*	150	108.5	46,800	88,000	74,000
Salt	49	*koku*	120	98.7	—	3,300	3,260
Coal	69	*hyou*	250	181.8	1,520	10,000	9,450
Cotton fabrics	121	*tan*	800	300	5,320	48,000	27,000
Seed cotton	16	*kan*	150	97.7	370	1,500	1,760
Lint	4.8	*kan*	200	134.3	1,200	40,000	33,580
Wax	0.7	*maru*	10	6	30	200	180
Paper			13 10,000 *maru*	8.3	—	16,900	17,430
Pottery			1 10,000 *maru*	0.3	—	70	30
Iron			2 10,000 *saku*	0.84	—	1,000	840
Indigo	2.12	*koku*	4	4.22	550	8,000	22,630
Copper			100 10,000 *kin*	49	—	2,230	2,200

Source: Yasuoka (1970: 62). Originally, Osaka-shi Sanjikai (1910: 639–86, 1911: 679–779).

greatest share in terms of value (measured in silver), fell short of 12 per cent of rice. Even the total figures for cotton-related goods, which included raw cotton and yarn in addition to cotton textiles, did not exceed a fifth of those for rice. It is clear that regional specialization of industrial crops and general handicraft goods was uneven, and the scale of inter-regional trade was also limited. However, from 1736 to 1804–29, the volume of goods passing through Osaka rose significantly for each type of commodity. If we look at the growth rate for each commodity, rice shows the least growth and the figures for other goods exceed those for rice by a large margin. In particular, the growth rate for commodities linked to cotton, such as raw cotton, cotton textiles, and yarn, exhibit phenomenal increases, and the total for the three goods came to nearly match the total for rice. Regional specialization, including in the Kinai, continued for cotton-related goods during the eighteenth century, and it is only natural that interregional trade for these goods increased significantly. Moreover, because most cases of interregional trade were aimed at the central market, goods passing through Osaka, which functioned as a distribution hub, increased considerably.

From 1804–29 to the 1840s, change occurred in the reverse direction. With the exception of indigo, the volume passing through Osaka decreased for all commodities. While rice was no exception, its rate of decline was lower than those of other goods. In contrast, the rate of decline for cotton-related goods was particularly high. This change does not imply that interregional commodity circulation retreated significantly. Instead, interregional distribution of commodities continued to grow and to take root, and this trend is particularly apparent after the 1820s. The decline in the volume of goods passing through Osaka can be traced to the growth in transactions taking place directly between local domains and Edo and among the domains themselves, leading to the subsequent decline of Osaka's stature as a major distribution hub. In contrast, rice continued to flow through Osaka—just as the volume had not grown significantly during the period of 1736 to 1804–29—because the rice flowing through Osaka was essentially intended to answer demands in Osaka and its outlying areas. On the supply side as well, most of this rice was still tax rice. In other words, there was no fundamental change in the structure of the rice market. However, in regard to other commodities, ties between local domains and Edo, as well as domain-to-domain links, came to coexist with those between peripheral domains and Osaka. The formation of a complex and close knit interregional network was the result.

Table 11.8 provides some interesting observations in this regard. The table compares the average prices of individual commodities in Osaka and Edo between 1830 and 1858. According to the table, the price differential between Edo and Osaka was under 5 per cent for rice, wheat, and beans, and prices for these goods became standardized. In the cases of cotton yarn, wax, rapeseed oil, brown sugar, and soy sauce, the price in Edo was roughly 15 per cent higher. Price differences for *miso* and refined *saké* exceeded 20 per cent, with the price of *saké* in Edo reaching over 30 per cent of that of *saké* in Osaka. These price differentials reflect the market structure for each of these commodities and, in particular, the nature of the interregional network.

Regional specialization in the form of a commercialization of foodstuffs, such as rice, wheat and beans, did not emerge. However, as noted earlier, a nationwide network of rice markets did exist. Thus, there is no

Table 11.8. Relative prices of Osaka to Edo (1830–57 average)

	(Edo = 100)
Rice	95.8
Barley	100.1
Soybean	95.1
Ginned cotton	82.4
Wax	85.2
Seed oil	88.2
Raw sugar	85.0
Miso	124.5
Soy sauce	87.3
Refined *saké*	68.0

Source: Shimbo (1986: 1–20).

reason to wonder at the existence of a uniform price for rice between Osaka and Edo. Even in the unstable years of 1830–58, the fact that the price of rice remained uniform implies the continued effective operation of a nationwide network for the rice market. Uniform prices for wheat and beans, despite the separation of the Osaka and Edo markets, imply the existence of a nationwide network similar to that for rice.

The price differentials of cotton yarn, wax, oils, brown sugar, and soy sauce between Edo and Osaka remained within a narrow range. Moreover, the range of the price differential was not much larger than could be accounted for by shipping costs, which included transportation rates and the insurance costs appropriate to the risks. These goods achieved a fairly advanced level of regional specialization bound for interregional market production. For example, the soy sauce bound for Osaka and Edo were of different types (thick and plain sauce) and sources (Chôshi and Noda in the east, and Tatsuno, Kojima, Yuasa, and Shôdoshima in the west). The other four commodities can be divided into those which derived from specific sources in western Japan for both the Osaka and Edo markets, as in brown sugar and wax, and those which were supplied to Edo from both the Kinai and regions proximate to Edo, as in the case of cotton yarn and oils. With the exception of soy sauce, there is no reason not to expect that price differences between Edo and Osaka would not converge at a certain level through the growth of inter-regional trade. It is plausible to hold that prices for various regions became "linked" once the market's interregional network became established. There is a possibility that the price differential of soy sauce was held at 15 per cent by accident and it may be better to view it separately from the other four goods.

Lastly, *miso* never showed a tendency toward regional specialization aimed for an interregional market, nor was refined *saké* produced for interregional markets. However, Nada *saké*, produced for the central market, reached almost 100 per cent regional specialization. To that extent, both commodities can be characterized as non-competitive goods, albeit for different reasons. Therefore, the price differential between Edo and Osaka for these commodities became fairly large. As we can see, the production of industrial crops and handicraft goods was more concentrated in specialized districts, and with the establishment of interregional networks between local markets, the prices in various regions became linked. On the other hand, there was no regional specialization for rice. But a market network emerged in the beginning of the eighteenth century through the distribution of tax rice and there were strong links between the prices in various regions, anchored by the price in Osaka. Foodstuffs like wheat and beans possessed a market network similar to that for rice. Therefore, there was an interregional division of labor in regard to industrial crops and handicraft goods, but no regional division of labor between the main grains and industrial crops. Such was the form of the nineteenth century market structure. This is consistent with what Saitô Osamu said about Japan's proto-industrialization processes (Saitô 1985: 197–8).

The same structure can be observed in intraregional markets as well. As noted for the Greater Nôbi region, industrial crops and handicraft goods—in particular, the latter—exhibited regional specialization within the region. However, the demand and supply for the main grains were fairly uniform within each of the individual markets, and the circulation of the main grains between markets was not very high (Iwahashi 1989: 260–2). This fact is deeply related to the development of interregional market-bound handicraft production in the form of agricultural by-employment. This structure remained intact in the Meiji period.

6. Towards a New Era

Finally, in anticipation of what follows in the Meiji era, we would like to touch upon structural changes that took place in various social strata in response to the striking developments taking place in the market economy in the latter part of the Tokugawa period.

Tokugawa society is often characterized as a status society comprised of four categories—samurai, peasant, artisan, and merchant. However, the four categories were not based strictly on a vertical hierarchy but provided a form of division of labor and specialization. Samurai carried out military, police, and administrative responsibilities, while peasants practised agriculture, and the artisans and merchants fulfilled various functions within the city. Through the Tokugawa period, peasants were increasingly participated in market activities and commercial agriculture and nonagricultural production, in the form of farm family by-employment, expanded. However, the Tokugawa peasantry did not exhibit any tendency towards polarization and disintegration. While the penetration of a cash economy into the peasant society undeniably had a disturbing effect, it also functioned to keep the peasantry from disintegrating itself by having a levelling effect on the social strata in the village. Rural industrialization tended to keep peasant families on the land. In particular, sericulture and spinning, often found in agriculturally disadvantaged areas, had a marked class-levelling effect. Changes in the market economy during the late Tokugawa period did not make the poor poorer. The trade in raw silk that began with the opening of the ports in 1859 brought prosperity to lower class farmers as well and enabled domestic markets to expand.

Let us now turn to the situation in the urban areas. The samurai class had been removed from the lands and given a stipend as adminis-trators over budgetary, agricultural, and civil engineering matters. The bureaucratic nature of their position increased steadily throughout the Tokugawa period. In economic matters, there emerged the financial specialists, such as Murata Seifu of Chôshû domain and Kusaka Gizaemon of Takamatsu domain, who oversaw reforms in the domains and acquired know-how in the management of trade and currency. Bureaucratic pragmatism was one, albeit not the only, principle that supported the economic management of the post-Meiji Restoration era, and its roots can be found in this period. On the face of it, there is an enormous gap between the Tokugawa and Meiji eras in terms of the ruling sector. However, not only was there a considerable continuity of personnel among the initial Meiji financial bureaucrats, but there was also a substantial legacy in terms of skills for economic management left behind by financial specialists within the shogunal–domainal system. As Tetsuo Najita notes, the influence of the bureaucratic order from the Tokugawa period extended not only to the static structures found in politics but also to the "attitudes, modes of perception, and patterns of action" of the people involved in politics (Najita 1974: 13–14).

The shift towards bureaucratization was not limited to the ruling sector, but can also be found in the private sector, in particular in the large commercial houses of Osaka and Kyoto (Saitô 1987, chapter 3). Most large commercial storefronts in Edo were branch offices for merchant families in Osaka or Kyoto. Many Osaka and Kyoto merchants, such as Mitsui, Kônoike, and Daimaru (run by the Shimomura family), possessed numerous branch offices and were centrally organized bodies managing the complex tasks of both the central and branch offices. Daimaru possessed fourteen stores including the central office. Mitsui counted nine storefronts for its clothing outlets alone. It is easy to imagine the complex nature and enormous amount of exchanges in terms of capital, commodities, and information among these offices. Moreover, they had to manage over 1,000 workers, leading to a personnel system in which apprentices were first employed at the main store and later transferred to appropriate offices. This implies that the main store required specialists to manage the personnel system. By the beginning of the eighteenth century, there were already thirteen departments in Mitsui's headquarters in Kyoto, three of which were management departments and four assigned to oversee specific branch offices.

Within these main stores, we can find the formation of an internal labor market. An internal labor market is a system, in which each department acquires the necessary labor not from an outside labor market but following rules governing the organization, and chooses and transfers workers who had been employed within the store from a young age. This system is generally seen as the root of the corporate economies of contemporary Japan (e.g. see Odaka 1988). Contemporary characteristics of company organization can be found in the Edo period in the cases of Mitsui and

Daimaru. The management of a merchant family in the Tokugawa period inevitably had an appearance, in accordance with the ideology centered on the family (*ie*). However, shifting our attention to other areas, we can categorize the know-how regarding financial and personnel management that the merchant houses accumulated as a form of bureaucratization. Merchant house management during the Tokugawa period is generally discussed as a cultural issue, namely as a matter of the continuity of firm-family ideology. But its historicity becomes clear when we look at it as a problem of organizational principle. This may also be considered a legacy of the Tokugawa period.

Alongside the shift towards an internal labor market, there was another trend toward the use of temporary laborers (Saitô 1987: chapters 2–3). Temporary laborer is a broad category referring to day laborers and peddlers, known as *botefuri*, who did not possess a standing storefront. From the eighteenth to the nineteenth century, this class of laborers increased throughout Edo and other large cities, and their existence complemented the trend to replace live-in laborers and apprentices with seasonal hands and commuting laborers as well as day laborers. To borrow an expression from Mitamura Engyo, employers became "calculating" while those given work possessed considerable independent spirit, boasting that they "did not have a steady master, for all the white walls of Edo were their boss" (Mitamura 1933: 151). In other words, both employer and employee possessed a mentality devoid of organizational principles, and the urban labor market began to function literally according to market mechanisms.

The urban economy in the late Tokugawa period displayed these two opposing trends—toward an internal labor market and toward temporary labor—but in terms of quantity (although there is little data), the former was limited to large commercial houses, which were few in number, while the latter can be said to better represent the period as a whole.

Moreover, these trends were not limited to urban economies. The same could be found in the national economy as well. As noted above, merchants and producers in the countryside sustained economic development during this era. Local merchants were considerably smaller in scale in comparison to the Osaka wholesale merchants, and they did not require such sophisticated management systems for their organizational purposes. On the production side, there was a growth of putting out system, in which local dealers lent peasants the necessary tools or resources, or both, to produce goods. However, this system was intended to take advantage of cheap labor and to minimize production management. In terms of both commerce and production, it only took advantage of market forces rather than relying on any organizational system.

The age of rural development unfolded in this manner by taking full advantage of the market mechanism. But this did not mean that different trends did not exist. As local merchants began to engage in marketing intended for outside markets, they also began to import management styles found in the large commercial houses in Osaka. For example, as they began to advance into other areas and their scale of transactions grew, indigo merchants in Awa, as well as soy sauce producers in Noda and Chôshi, began to establish centralized management styles (e.g. Fruin 1983: 36–47; Amano 1986: 119–24). However, these trends never became part of the mainstream during this period. A shift to a factory system and other modes of discipline did not occur during this era. It took another one hundred years before the factory was to become a dominant element of the national economy.

Translated by Takahiko Hayashi.

APPENDIX[1]

The Administration of Tokugawa Japan (1603–1868)

Officially, the Imperial Family was the highest authority in Japan, but in actuality, the emperor was virtually powerless and the Tokugawa shogun generalissimos held the real power. The Tokugawa shogunate government was based in Edo (present-day Tokyo), after which this period is named the Edo period, and approximately a quarter of the entire country was under its direct jurisdiction (*tenryo*). *Daikan* magistrates administered the *tenryo*. The remaining areas of Japan were domains of daimyo, or territorial lords, who had pledged their loyalty to the shogun; *hatamoto*[2] (vassals to the shogun); and Buddhist temples or Shinto shrines. This system was different from the feudal system in Europe in that the daimyo might be ordered by shogun to change territories. The daimyo also had to leave their wives and children in Edo in a sort of hostage arrangement, and the daimyo themselves had to live in Edo every other year.

There was a strict division of the warrior class and farming class in both the *tenryo* and almost all the daimyo territories. Samurai warriors lived in castle towns and were rarely present in rural villages. The samurai may have been called to the villages during times of trouble, but the actual administration of the villages was left to local influential leaders. There were approximately 70,000 villages throughout Japan during the Edo period, and some villages had several lords. Compared with other countries, Japanese villages were small and had much community character.

The densely populated settlements were called "*machi*," which is sometimes translated as "town" or "city." However, the *machi* were different from Western cities, except for their function.

The local level above "*machi*" and village was the "*gun*." Although several times the term "*gun*" is translated into the English term "county," the "*gun*" was totally different from a "county." It is neither a unit of administration nor jurisdiction. In this book, we translate "*gun*" as "district." The "*gun*" was used simply as an expression to indicate a geographical area in the Edo period.

The next highest geographical level was the province (*kuni*). There were sixty-eight provinces in Japan during the Edo period. Among the daimyo (whose administrative units or domains were also referred to as "*han*"), there were great daimyos who had territories covering an entire province or even the whole of several provinces. On the contrary, some provinces had several lords, eventually the province was an aggregate of the domains of different lords.

One thing that is indispensable in our understanding of the administration of this time is the system of measuring the value of land, or *kokudaka*. This system was begun by Toyotomi Hideyoshi (1537–98), the man who unified Japan before the time of Tokugawa shogunate. He sent officers to the territories he controlled to undertake a cadastral survey of the land (both farming and residential land). The system of survey was called *kenchi*, and after Hideyoshi received the title of *Taikô*, the system became known as *taikô-kenchi*. For the *kenchi*, the boundary of each village was fixed, each section of each village was measured, and the type and class of the land were investigated. Then an amount of land value represented by *koku* was determined for each land type and class. At the bottom of each survey of land on the cadastre, the names of peasants were also recorded for each piece of land. The reason why the names of persons were recorded is still in question; some scholars regard it as a record of landholding; others as just the name of someone who had a relation to the land. *Koku* represented, in principle, an amount of rice (1 *koku* = 5.1 US bushels). The *koku* was multiplied by the land area to determine a total for each village (*muradaka*). The *muradaka* is the most important element in understanding the *kenchi* survey system. Totals were calculated for each province, and finally the *kokudaka* (the number of *koku*) for Japan as a whole could be measured. This cadastral survey was completed just prior to the death of Hideyoshi in 1598, and it showed a *kokudaka* of 18.5 million *koku* for the entire country. The Tokugawa shogun who succeeded him used the *kokudaka* to express the value of land given to the daimyo and retainers who had pledged their loyalty. The shogun and daimyo had lists of the *kokudaka* of each village in the territories they controlled, and territories were assigned to retainers based on the *kokudaka*.

The *kokudaka* system was also used within the villages during this time. The amount of land held by a farming household was expressed in *koku*, and land taxes and other levies were calculated based on it (*mochidaka* = the amount of land held by the household). However, in many cases, the *mochidaka* of a household was determined by the *kenchi* performed at the beginning of the Edo period or by the *taiko-kenchi*, and over time a gap widened between the estimated value and the actual yield of the land. For example, a farmer owing land valued at five *koku* did not necessarily produce five *koku* of rice. Rather, the farmer had an amount of land equivalent to a standard productivity yield of five *koku* when converted to a quantity of rice based on the *kenchi* that the territorial lord recognized as being valid.

The Calendar in the Edo Period and Era Names

A noble family in Kyoto in compliance with the wishes of the shogunate created the calendar used during the Tokugawa period. The calendar was basically a solar–lunar calendar originating in China; one month started with the new moon and lasted twenty-nine or thirty days, and one year had, in principle, twelve months. With this method, a year had 354–5 days, so the seasons would quickly fall out of alignment with the dates. Therefore, a "leap month" was added every two or three years to adjust their calendar to the solar calendar. In this book, we use the month without its peculiar name, but the order; for example, the fourth month to replace April, the tenth month to replace October. The leap month could be set for any interval between months during the year.

The leap third month, therefore, refers to a leap month following the third month of the year. Years that included a leap month had 383–5 days, making them nearly 8 per cent longer than an average year.

To convert Japanese year to the Western Gregorian calendar year, we express simply the Western year at the first day of Japanese year. This brings a mismatch in the twelfth month of the Japanese year, which is actually the next year in the Western calendar. As for the year with the leap month, the leap month could fall even on the eleventh month of the Japanese calendar.

In Japan, a system of era names has been used. Era names are used for a specific period of time regardless of intervals of month and date. The names consist of two Chinese characters that can be found in Chinese classics and that are considered to represent good luck. These era names have nothing to do with the changes of historical periods before 1868. But

Era name and year by AD

Era name	AD	Era name	AD
An'ei	1772–81	Kan'en	1748–51
Ansei	1854–60	Kansei	1789–1801
Bunka	1804–18	Keian	1648–52
Bunkyû	1861–64	Keichô	1596–1615
Bunroku	1592–96	Keiô	1865–68
Bunsei	1818–30	Kôka	1844–48
Empô	1673–81	Kyôhô	1716–36
Enkyô	1744–48	Kyôwa	1801–04
Gembun	1736–41	Man'en	1860–61
Genji	1864–65	Manji	1658–61
Gen'na	1615–24	Meiji	1868–1912
Genroku	1688–1704	Meireki	1655–58
Hôei	1704–11	Meiwa	1764–72
Hôreki	1751–64	Shôhô	1644–48
Jôkyô	1684–88	Shôtoku	1711–16
Jouô	1652–55	Tempô	1830–44
Kaei	1848–54	Tenmei	1781–89
Kampô	1741–44	Tenna	1681–84
Kanbun	1661–73	Tenshô	1573–93
Kan'ei	1624–44		

for the Japanese, era names are much familiar and in this book, we use, for example, the Genroku era (1688–1704), Bunka-Bunsei era (1804–30). Most of them are shown in the Western year as well.

Apart from these, people in this period followed the sexagenary cycle for years. This is composed of twelve animals and ten elements; actually five elements with an elder and younger. The animals are: rat, cattle, tiger, rabbit, dragon, snake, horse, sheep, monkey, hen, dog, and wild boar. The elements are: wood, fire, soil, minerals, and water. As their lowest common multiple is sixty, at sixty, one reaches the end of one's first round of life. Each year has its particular combination of animal and element, such as fire-horse, etc.

The Money in the Edo Period

The money circulated in the Edo period is somewhat complicated. The Tokugawa government minted the gold and silver standard money, and copper coins. The government decided the official exchange rate: Gold 1 *ryô* = Silver 50 *monme* = Copper 4 *kan*. But in reality, they came to have their own value, that is, the exchange rate fluctuated everyday. The rate fluctuated by 1 Gold *ryô* = 60 ± 10 Silver *monme* = 5.5 ± 1.5 Copper *kan*.

The gold money was minted as a face fixed coin, 10 *ryô oban* (large oval), 1 *ryô koban* (small oval), 2 *bu-kin*, and 2 *shukin*, in *Kinza*, Edo (2 *bu-kin* and 2 *shukin* had a rectangle shape). Gold money had quartering scale, 1 *ryô* = 4 *bu*, 1 *bu* = 4 *shu*. Ten *ryô oban* was not actually minted much and not used for the commerce. The name "*ryô*" came from the unit of apothecaries' weight; 1 *ryô* was 4 *monme*. The first 1 *ryô koban* minted in 1600 by the shogunate had 4.76 *monme* weight, including 3.8 *monme* gold.

The silver was minted as a weighing money. Fifty to sixty *monme* bullion or a few *monme* ball were minted, in Ginza, Edo. In its use, the bullion or ball was weighed by scales, and if necessary, the bullion was cut into pieces.

We can label the gold and silver moneys as the standard money in the Edo period. Eventually, there was a double standard of money system. However, as we can see in the text, after 1750s, the money was made of silver, but had gold face value. Therefore, it is obvious that the single gold standard money system had begun.

At first, the Tokugawa shogunate minted both gold and silver money with good quality. The money had 80 per cent purity and the silver bullion could be exported as a commodity. But after the last decade of the seventeenth century, the quality of the minted money became worse, for example the worst quality silver money had only 20 per cent purity. This was a consequence of the shortage of materials and there for cover the deficit of the finance of *bakufu*.

The copper coin began to be minted in 1636 in several places. A single copper coin was equivalent to 1 *mon*, with the exception of the 4 *mon* coin minted in the latter half of the Edo period. In 1836, the shogunate began to mint 100 *mon* copper coins in *Kinza*.

The copper coins were fundamentally made of copper. Since the copper coins minted in the early years were of good quality, they were exported to China or southeast Asia. But in the latter half of the Edo period, when access to copper became difficult, iron or brass was even used as the material.

The confusion that prevailed in the money system of this time owes to the issue of paper money by the local daimyo. The daimyo did not have to mint the money, but could issue the paper money with the shogunate permission. This has already been discussed in the text. We call this kind of paper money, *hansatsu*. The characteristics of *hansatsu* are as follows. They are valid only within the territory of the daimyo who issued them. They have of course their face value, in gold, silver, or copper, but in reality, they were used with some reduction in rate. In spite of these shortcomings, many daimyo issued *hansatsu* for making amends for the deficits in their finance. When daimyo decided to issue *hansatsu*, they ordered the circulation of gold or silver to be stopped in the territory, and to replace them with the paper money. Daimyo could obtain gold or silver money without much ado. In addition to this, the residents in the territory could enjoy the circulation of *hansatsu*, as gold and silver monies were much higher than their daily use, and the 1 *mon* coins were much lower. But often the *hansatsu* got the most adequate face value for their use; it was convenient at any rate.

Consequently, in the latter half of the Edo period, people in Japan had very low quality metal monies and paper money. This is a great change in contrast to the beginning of the period. People got to use money without paying attention to the value of materials. This attitude affected the Meiji Restoration. When the Meiji government was established, they had no reserves of precious metals. But the government had to issue money, made of paper. If the people had not known such kind of money, and not trusted if the government would have had to face a very difficult problem. The experience of using money made of poor metal or paper money helped the Meiji government and the Restoration.

Weighs and Measures

As is shown in the text, almost all kinds of weighs and measures were unified by Toyotomi Hideyoshi. Following is the conversion table of items using in the Edo period and in contemporary world. (Japanese traditional = Japanese next digit (if necessary) = metric system = yard–pound system.)

1. Linear measure
    1 *ri* = 36 *chô* = 3.75 kilometers = 2.44 miles
    1 *chô* = 60 *ken* = 109 meters = 109.4 yards

    1 *ken* = 6 *shaku* = 1.82 meters = 1.82 yards
    1 *shaku* = 10 *sun* = 30.3 centimeters = 0.99 feet

2. Square measure
    1 *chô* (*bu*) = 10 *tan* = 0.9917 hectare = 2.45 acres
    1 *tan* = 300 *bu* = 991.7 sq. meters = 0.245 acres
    1 *bu* (*tsubo*) = 3.306 sq. meters = 4.80 sq. yards

3. Dry measure
    1 *koku* = 10 *tô* = 180 litres = 5.108 bushels (US) = 4.95 bushels (UK)

4. Liquid measure
    1 *koku* = 10 *to* = 180 liters = 0.476 gallons (US) = 0.397 gallons (UK)

5. Weight measure
    1 *kan* = 1000 *monme* = 3759 grams = 8.27 pounds
    1 *monme* = 3.759 grams = 0.132 ounces

6. Other measures
    1 *tan* (for cloth rolls) = 13.1 meters = 12 yards

Notes

1. Mostly based on the Appendix, Akira Hayami, The Historical Demography of Japan. University of Tokyo Press, 2001; 179–82.
2. Lords whose territory were less than 10,000 *koku*.

REFERENCES

Abe, Takeshi (1983), "*Meiji zenki ni okeru Nihon no zairai sangyô: men'orimonogyô no baai* [Traditional Japanese Industries in Early Meiji: The Case of Cotton Textiles]," Umemura Mataji and Nakamura Takafusa (eds.), *Matsukata zaisei to shokusan kôgyô seisaku* [Matsukata Financial Policy and the Industrial Growth Policy], Tokyo: Kokusai Rengô Daigaku and Tokyo Daigaku Shuppankai.

——(1988), "*Kinsei Nihon ni okeru orimono seisandaka* [Silk Textile Production Volumes in Early Modern Japan]," Odaka Kônosuke and Yamamoto Yûzô (eds.), *Bakumatsu-Meiji no Nihon keizai, Sûryô keizaishi ronshû 4* [Essays in Quantitative Economic History, Vol. 4], Tokyo: Nihon Keizai Shimbunsha.

Aichi-ken kyôdo shiryô kankô kai (eds.) (1974), *Mikawa zasshô (zen)*, Nagoya: Aichi-ken kyôdo shiryô kankô kai.

Akashi, Shigeo (1989), "*Kinsei kôki ni okeru kahei, bukka, seichô: 1825–1856* [Currency, Prices and Growth in the Late Early Modern Period]," *Keizai kenkyû*, Vol. 40, No. 1.

Akimoto, Hiroya (1987), *Zenkôgyôka jidai no keizai: Bôchô fudo chûshin'an ni yoru sûryô-teki sekkin* [The Economy in the Age Prior to Industrialization: Quantitative Approximation in the 'Report on Conditions in Bôchô'], Kyoto: Mineruva Shobô.

Amano, Masatoshi (1986), *Awa ai keizaishi kenkyû: kindai ikôki no sangyô to keizai hatten* [Studies in the Economic History of Awa Indigo: Industry and Economic Development in the Transitional Era of the Late Early Modern Era], Tokyo: Yoshikawa Kôbunkan.

Amino, Yoshihiko (1986), "*Chûsei minshû seikatsu no yôsô*," Amino, Yoshihiko (ed.), *Chûsei saikô: rettô no chiiki to shakai*. Tokyo: Nihon Editâ Sukûru Shuppanbu.

——(1986), "*Chûsei no futan taikei—nengu ni tsuite* [The Medieval Levy System: On Nengu]," Nagahara Keiji et al. (eds.), *Chûsei kinsei no kokka to shakai* [State and Society in the Medieval and Early Modern Periods], Tokyo: Tokyo Daigaku Shuppankai.

Anderson, Michael (1988), *Population Change in Northwestern Europe, 1750–1850*, London: Macmillan Education Ltd.

Andô, Seiichi (1992), *Kinsei kôgaishi no kenkyû* [A History of Early Modern Pollution], Tokyo: Yoshikawa Kôbunkan.

Aoki, Kôji (1966), *Hyakushô ikki no nenjiteki kenkyû* [Annual Report on Research in Peasant Rebellions], Tokyo: Shinseisha.

Arai, Eiji (1959), "*Chôsi, noda no shôyu jôzô* [Soy Sauce Brewing in Choshi and Noda]," Chihôshi kenkyû kyôgikai (ed.) *Nihon sangyôshi taikei 4: kantô chihô-hen* [The History of Japanese Industry, 4: The Kanto Region], Tokyo: Tokyo Daigaku Shuppankai.

Arano, Yasunori (1988), *Kinsei Nihon to higashi Ajia*, Tokyo Daigaku Shuppankai.

Asakura, Kôkichi (1961), *Meiji zenki Nihon kin'yû kôzô-shi*, Tokyo: Iwanami Shoten.

Atwell, William S. (1977), "Notes on Silver, Foreign Trade and the Late Ming Economy," *Ch'ing-shin wen-ti*, Vol. 3, No. 8(December): 1–33.

Atwell, William S. (2001), "Volcanism and Short-term Climate Change in East Asian and World History, c. 1200–1699," *Journal of World History*, Vol. 12, No. 1 (Spring).

Beasley, W. G. (1988), "Foreword," Sugiyama, Shin'ya (ed.), *Japan's Industrialization in the World Economy, 1859–1899*, London: Athlone Press.

Bird, Isabella (1885), *Unbeaten Tracks in Japan*, London: John Murray.

Bitô, Masahide (1981), "Tokugawa jidai no shakai to seiji shisô no tokushitsu" [The Characteristics of Political Thought in Tokugawa Society] *Shisô* [Ideas], No. 685.

Bix, Herbert P. (1986), *Peasant Protest in Japan, 1590–1884*, New Haven: Yale University Press.

Borton, Hugh (1968), *Peasant Uprisings in Japan of the Tokugawa Period*, New York: Paragon Book Reprint Corp.

Boserup, Ester (1965), *The Conditions of Agricultural Growth*, London: G. Allen & Unwin.

Boxer, C. R. (1951), *The Christian Century in Japan, 1549–1640*, Berkeley: University of California Press.

Brett L. Walker (2001), *The Conquest of Ainu Lands: Ecology and Culture in Japanese Expansion, 1590–1800*, Berkeley: University of California Press.

Brown, Delmer (1951), *Money Economy in Medieval Japan: A Study in the Use of Coins*, New Haven: Yale University Press.

Brown, Philip C. (1988), "Practical Constraints on Early Tokugawa Land Taxation: Annual Versus Fixed Assessments in Kaga Domain," *The Journal of Japanese Studies*, Vol. 14, No. 2 (Summer).

Chambliss, William Jones (1965), *Chiaraijima Village: Land Tenure, Taxation, and Local Trade, 1818–1884*, Tucson: University of Arizona Press.

Chiba, Tokuji (1973), *Hageyama no bunka*, Gakuseisha.

Clay, C. G. A. (1984), *Economic Expansion and Social Change in England 1500–1700*, Cambridge: Cambridge University Press.

Cornell, L. L. and Hayami, Akira (1986), "The Shumon Aratame Chô: Japan's Population Registers," *Journal of Family History*, Vol. 11, No. 4.

Craig, Albert (1960), *Chôshû in the Meiji Restoration*, Cambridge, MA: Harvard University Press.

Crawcour, E. S. (1961), "The Development of a Credit System in Seventeenth-Century Japan," *Journal of Economic History*, Vol. 21, No. 3: 348–9.

de Camões, Luis (1950), *Os Lusiadas*, Leonard Bacon (trans.) New York: The Hispanic Society of America, Canto X, Verse 131.

de Vries, Jan (1984), *European Urbanization, 1500–1800*, London: Mathuen and Co. Ltd.

Doboku Gakkai (ed.) (1936), *Meiji izen dobokushi*, Tokyo: Iwanami Shoten.

Dore, Ronald P. (1965), *Education in Tokugawa Japan*, Berkeley: University of California Press.

Edo sôsho kankô kai (ed.) (1917), Otorika tsuji Kakitsuke in *Seisai Zakki Edo Sôsho*, Vol. 8.

Einenkai (ed.) (1932), *Zôho Takamatsu-hanki* [History of the Takamatsu Domain], Enlarged edition, Einenkai.

Fei, John, et al. (1986), "*Keizai hatten no rekishiteki perspective: Nihon, Kankoku, Taiwan* [Economic Development in Historical Perspective: Japan, Korea, Taiwan]," Ôkawa Kazushi (ed.), *Nihon no hatten to tojôkoku* [Japanese Development and Developing Countries], Tokyo: Keisô Shobô.

Fruin, W. M. (1983), *Kikkôman: Company, Clan, and Community*, Cambridge, MA: Harvard University Press.

Fujii, Mitsuo, Fujii, Harue, and Ikeda, Masataka (1962), *"Bakumatsu kaikô zengo ni okeru hokumô sanshigyô no tenkai* (2) [The Development of the Northern Kozuke-Shimotsuke Province Sericulture Industry Around the Time of the Opening of the Ports, 2]," *Shakai keizaishigaku* [Socio Economic History], Vol. 27, No. 5.

Fujiki, Hisashi (1981), "The Commercial Policies of Oda Nobunaga," Hall, Nagahara and Yamamura (eds.), *Japan before Tokugawa: Political Consolidation and Economic Growth, 1500–1650*, Princeton: Princeton University Press.

Fujino, Tamotsu (1983), *Nihon hôkensei to Bakuhan taisei* [Japanese Feudalism and the Baku-han System], Tokyo: Hanawa Shobô.

Fujino, Yoshiko (1982), *"Meiji shoki ni okeru sanson no shokuji to eiyô: 'Hida-gô-fudoki' no bunseki wo tsûjite"* [Meals and Nutrition in Early Meiji Mountain Villages: An Analysis of the Hida-gô-fudoki], *Kokuritsu minzokugaku hakubutsukan kenkyû hôkoku*, Vol. 7, No. 3.

Fujita, Gorô (1952), *Kinsei nôsei shi-ron* [Agrarian History of Early Modern Japan], Tokyo: Nihon hyôronsha.

Fujita, Teiichirô (1966), *Kinsei keizai shisô no kenkyû* [Studies in the Economic Thought of Early Modern Japan], Tokyo: Yoshikawa Kôbunkan.

—— (1975), *"Bakuhansei teki shijô kôzô no hôkai* [The Decline of Market Structure in the Shogunal–Domainal System]," *Wakayama kenshi kenkyû* 3.

—— (1977), *"Shôka no shihon chikuseki,"* Nakagawa, Keiichirô (ed.), *Edo jidai no kigyôka katsudô*, Tokyo: Yoshikawa Kôbunkan: 118–44.

—— (1984), *"Akita-han ni okeru keizai shisô"* [Political Economy in the Akita Domain], *Keizaishi keieishi ronshû*, Osaka: Osaka Keizai Daigaku.

—— (1988), *"Tokugawa keizai shisô no tassei to genkai"* [Achievements and Limitations in Tokugawa Era Economic Thought], Sakasai Takahito kyôju kanreki kinenkai (ed.), *Nihon kindaika no shisô to tenkai* [The Thought and Development of Japanese Modernization], Tokyo: Bunken Shuppan.

—— (1993), "Meiji zenki 'kokueki' shisô tsuiseki" [The Concept of the "National Interest" in Early Meiji Japan], *Dôshisha shôgaku*, Vol. 45.

Fukui, Sadako (1984), *Momen kuden*, Tokyo: Hôsei Daigaku Shuppankyoku.

Fukuyama, Akira (1975), *Kinsei nôson no kin'yû kôzô*, Tokyo: Yûzankaku.

Fukuzawa, Yukichi (1959), *"Bunken-ron* [Discourse on Local Government]," Keiô gijuku (ed.), *Fukuzawa Yukichi zenshû* 4 [The Collected Works of Fukuzawa Yukichi, Vol. 4], Tokyo: Iwanami Shoten.

Furushima, Toshio (1949), *Nihon nôgyô gijutsushi*, Tokyo: Jichôsha.

—— (1963), *Shihonsei seisan no hatten to jinushisei* [The Landlord System and the Capitalist System of Production], Tokyo: Ochanomizu Shobô.

—— (1978), *Kinsei keizaishi no kiso katei* [The Fundamental Processes of Early Modern Economic History], Tokyo: Iwanami Shoten.

Gerschenkron, Alexander (1962), *Economic Backwardness in Historical Perspective*, Cambridge, MA: Belknap Press of Harvard University Press.

Gifu ken (ed.) (1965–73), *Gifu-ken-shi shiryô hen*, 20 Vols, Gifu ken.

Gutmann, Myron P. (1986), "The Dynamics of Urban Decline in the Late Middle Ages and Early Modern Times: Economic Response and Social Effects [General Report]," *Debates and Controversies: The Ninth International Economic History Congress, Bern* (Zurich, 1986), 21–56.

Hall, John W. (1949), "Notes on the Early Ch'ing Copper Trade with Japan," *Harvard Journal of Asiatic Studies*, Vol. XII, Nos. 3 and 4: 444–61.

Hall, John W. (1966), *Government and Local Power in Japan, 500–1700*, Princeton University Press.

——Nagahara Keiji, and Yamamura, Kozo (eds.) (1981), *Japan Before Tokugawa: Political Consolidation and Economic Growth*, Princeton: Princeton University Press.

——et al. (eds.) (1988–99), *The Cambridge History of Japan*, 6 Vols., Cambridge: Cambridge University Press.

Hanley, Susan B. (1983), "A High Standard of Living in Nineteenth Century Japan: Fact or Fantasy?," *Journal of Economic History*, Vol. XLIII, No. 1.

——(1987), "How Well Did the Japanese Live in the Tokugawa Period?," *Economic Studies Quarterly*, Vol. 38, No. 4.

——and Yamamura, Kozo (1977), *Economic and Demographic Change in Preindustrial Japan, 1600–1868*, Princeton: Princeton University Press.

Hara, Shôgo (1970), "*Bakufuhô ni okeru kuniyaku fushinsei ni tsuite*" [On the Kuniyaku/Fushin Tax System in Shogunal Law], *Gifu shigaku*, Vol. 57.

Harada, Toshimaru and Miyamoto, Matao (eds.) (1985), *Rekishi no naka no bukka*, Tokyo: Dôbunkan Shuppan.

Harris, Townsend (1959), *The Complete Journal of Townsend Harris*, Rutland, Vt.: Charles E. Tuttle, Co.

Hasegawa, Akira (1972), "*Kinsei ni okeru tokusambutsu no seiritsu to chûô shijô: Tatsuno shôyu no Kyôto shinshutsu katei ni tsuite* [The Establishment of Special Regional Products and the Central Market in the Early Modern Era: On the Entry of Tatsuno Soy Sauce into Kyôto]," *Shakai keizaishigaku*, Vol. 38, No. 4.

——(1975), "*Kinsei chûki bukka no chiiki hikaku ni tsite no ichi kôsatsu—tokusambutsu no seiritsu to kanren shite*," *Keizaikeiei ronshû*, Vol. 17, No. 2 (September).

——(1993), *Kinsei tokusambutsu ryûtsûshi-ron* [The Circulation of Specialty Products in the Early Modern Period], Tokyo: Kashiwa Shobô.

Hattori, Shisô and Shinobu, Seizaburô (1978), *Nihon manyufakuchuashi-ron* [On the History of Japanese Manufacturing], Tokyo: Ikuseisha.

Hauser, William B. (1974), *Economic Institutional Change in Tokugawa Japan: Osaka and the Kinai Cotton Trade*, Cambridge: Cambridge University Press.

Hayama, Teisaku (1983), "*Shônô nôhô no seiritsu to shônô gijutsu no tenkai*," Sasaki, Junnosuke (ed.), *Gijutsu no shakaishi*, Vol. 2, Tokyo: Yûhikaku.

Hayami, Akira (1958), "Kinsei shoki no iesû ninzû aratame to yakuya ni tsuite," *Keiô Gijuku Keizaigaku nempô*, Vol. 1: 1–59.

——(1968), *Nihon keizai-shi e no shikaku* [A Perspective on the Economic History of Japan], Tokyo: Tôyô Keizai Shimpôsha.

——(1969), "*Aspects démographiqes d'un village japonais, 1671–1871*," *Annales: E.S.C*, Vol. 24, No. 3.

——(1971a), "*Mouvements de longue durée et structures japonaises de la population a l'époque de Tokugawa*," *Annales de Démographie Historique*, 247–63.

——(1971b), "*Tokugawa kôki jinkô hendô no chiikiteki tokusei*," *Mita gakkai zasshi*, Vol. 64, No. 8.

——(1973a), *Kinsei nôson no rekishi jinkôgaku-teki kenkyû* [Historical Demographic Studies of Early Modern Villages], Tokyo: Tôyô Keizai Shimpôsha.

——(1973b), *Nihon ni okeru keizai shakai no tenkai* [The Development of Economic Society in Japan], Tokyo: Keiô Tsûshin.

——(1974), "*Kinsei kôki chiiki-betsu jinkô hendô to toshi jinkô hiritsu no kanren*," *Tokugawa Rinseishi Kenkyûjo kenkyû kiyô*.

——(1975), *"Edo jidai no jinkô sûsei,"* Shimbo, Hiroshi, Hayami, Akira, Nishikawa, Shunsaku (eds.), *Sunyô keizaishi nyûmon* [Introduction to the Quantitative Economic History], Tokyo: Nihon Hyôronsha.

——(1982), *"Kinsei Ôu chihô jinkô no shiteki kenkyû joron,"* Mita gakkai zasshi, Vol. 75, No. 3: 70–92.

——(1985), "Rural Migration and Fertility in Tokugawa Japan," Susan B. Hanley and Arthur P. Wolf (eds.), *Family and Population in East Asian History*, Stanford, CA: Stanford University Press, 110–32.

——(1987), "Another Fossa Magna: Proportion Marrying and Age at Marriage in Late Nineteenth Century Japan," *Journal of Family History*, Vol. 12, 1–2: 57–72.

——(1988), *Edo no nômin seikatsu-shi: shûmon aratame-chô ni miru Nôbi no ichi nôson*, Tokyo: NHK Bukkusu.

——(1990), *"Kinsei toshi no rekishi jinkôgakuteki kansatsu—Nara higashimuki kita-machi: Kansei 5 nen-Meiji 5 nen,"* Mita gakkaishi (Special issue).

——(1992), *Kinsei Nôbi chihô no jinkô*, Tokyo: Sôbunsha.

——(1993), *"Meiji zenki jinkô tôkeishi nempyô,"* Nihon kenkyû, Vol. 9: 135–64.

——(2001a), *The Historical Demography of Pre-modern Japan*, Tokyo: University of Tokyo Press.

——(2001b), "Industrial Revolution versus Industrious Revolution," *Journal of Japanese Trade and Industry*, Vol. 20, No. 6: 48–52.

——(2002), *Edo nômin no kurashi to jinsei*, Kashiwa: Reitakudaigaku Shuppankai.

——and Kurosu, Satomi (2001), "Regional Diversity in Demographic and Family Patterns in Preindustrial Japan," *Journal of Japanese Studies*, Vol. 27, No. 2: 295–321.

——and Miyamoto, Matao (eds.) (1988), "Emergence of Economic Society—17 and 18th Centuries, Nihon keizaishi," *The Economic History of Japan*, Vol. 1, Tokyo: Iwanami Shoten.

——and Uchida, Nobuko (1972), "Size of Households in a Japanese County throughout the Tokugawa Era," Peter Laslett (ed.), *Household and Family in Past Time*, Cambridge: Cambridge University Press, 473–516.

Hayami, Yûjirô (1973), *Nihon nôgyô no seichô katei* [The Growth Process of Japanese Agriculture], Tokyo: Sôbunsha.

Hayashi, Hideo (1960), *Kinsei nôson kôgyô-shi no kiso katei*, Tokyo: Aoki Shoten.

——(1973), *Hakari-za* [Measuring Scale Guilds], Tokyo: Yoshikawa Kôbunkan.

Hayashi, Reiko (1967), *Edo ton'ya nakama no kenkyû* [Studies of the Edo Wholesaler Associations], Tokyo: Ochanomizu Shobô.

——(1969), *"Kinsei chû-kôki no shôgyô"* [Commerce in the Middle and Latter Early Modern Period], Toyoda, Takeshi and Kodama, Kôta (eds.), *Ryûtsûshi II*, Tokyo: Yamakawa Shuppansha.

——(1974), *"Shimodate men-orimonogyô to kin'yû,"* Yamaguchi, Kazuo (ed.), *Nihon sangyô kinyû-shi kenkyû—orimono kin'yû-shi hen*, Tokyo: Tokyo Daigaku Shuppankai, 753–68.

——(ed.) (1990), *Shôyu jôzôgyôshi no kenkyû* [Research in the History of the Soy Sauce Brewing Industry], Tokyo: Yoshikawa Kôbunkan.

Heilbroner, Robert L. (1970), *The Making of Economic Society*, Prentice-Hall, Inc.

Henderson, Dan Fenno (1975), *Village "Contracts" in Tokugawa Japan: Fifty Specimens with English Translations and Comments*, Seattle: University of Washington Press.

Hicks, J. R. (1969), *A Theory of Economic History*, Oxford: Oxford University Press.

Hirano-mura (ed.) (1932), *Hiranosonshi*, 2 Vols., Nagano-ken, Hirano-mura.

Hôgetsu, Keigo (1961), *Chûsei ryôseishi no kenkyû* [Studies in the History of the Medieval System of Weights and Measures], Tokyo: Yoshikawa Kôbunkan.

Honjô, Eijirô (1935), *The Social and Economic History of Japan*: Kyoto: Institute for Research in Economic History of Japan.

Horie, Yasuzô (1933), *Wagakuni kinsei no senbai seido* [Domainal Monopoly in Early Modern Japan], Nihon Hyôronsha.

Hosokawa hansei-shi kenkyûkai (ed.) (1974), *Kumamoto han nenpyô kô*, Kumamoto: Hosokawa hansei-shi kenkyûkai.

Howell, David L. (1995), *Capitalism from Within: Economy, Society, and the State in a Japanese Fishery*: California: University of California Press.

Hozumi, Katsujirô (1970), *Himeji-han mengyô keizaishi no kenkyû* [Studies in the Economic History of the Himeji Domainal Cotton Industry], Private edition.

Imai, Rintarô and Yagi, Akihiro (1955), *Hoken shakai no nôson kôzô* [Village Structure in Feudal Society], Tokyo: Yûhikaku.

Innes, Robert Leroy (1980), "The Door Ajar: Japan's Foreign Trade in the Seventeenth Century," Unpublished Ph.D. thesis, University of Michigan.

Inoue, Zenjirô (1981), "*Yôsan gijutsu no tenkai to sansho* [Silkworm Texts and the Development of Sericulture Technology]," *Nihon Nôsho zenshû* [Japanese Agricultural Encyclopedia], Vol. 35, Tokyo: Nôsan Gyoson Bunkakyôkai.

Ishii, Kenji (1972), *Nihon sanshigyôshi bunseki* [An Analysis of the History of the Japanese Sericulture Industry], Tokyo: Tokyo Daigaku Shuppankai.

——(1984), *Kindai Nihon to igirisu shihon—Jardine Matheson shôkai wo chûshin ni*, Tokyo: Tokyo Daigaku Shuppankai.

——(1986), "*Kokunai shijô no keisei to hatten* [The Formation and Development of Domestic Markets]," Yamaguchi, Kazuo and Ishii, Kanji (eds.), *Kindai Nihon no shôhin ryûtsû* [Commodity Circulation in Modern Japan], Tokyo: Tokyo Daigaku Shuppankai.

Ishii, Ryôsuke (1964), *Hôseishi* [A History of the Legal System], Tokyo: Yamakawa Shuppansha.

——et al. (comps.) (1959), *Hampô-shû* 1 Okayama han 1, Tokyo: Sôbunsha.

Ishii, Shirô (1966), *Kenryoku to tochi shoyû* [Power and Land Ownership], Tokyo: Tokyo Daigaku Shuppankai.

——(1986), *Nihonjin no kokka seikatsu* [The State Lifestyle of Japanese], Tokyo: Tokyo Daigaku Shuppankai.

Ishii, Takashi (1944), *Bakumatsu bôekishi no kenkyû* [The History of Late Tokugawa Trade], Tokyo: Nihon Hyôronsha.

Ishikawa, Matsutarô (1978), *Hankô to terakoya* [Domainal Schools and Temple Schools], Tokyo: Kyôikusha.

Itô, Shigemi (1990), "*Jinkô zôka, toshika, shûgyô kôzô*," Nishikawa, Shunsaku and Yamamoto, Yûzô (eds.), *Nihon keizaishi 5, Sangyôka no jidai ge*, Tokyo: Iwanami Shoten.

Iwahashi, Masaru (1976), "*Tokugawa jidai no kahei sûryô*," Umemura Mataji, Shimbo Hiroshi, Hayami Akira, and Nishikawa Shunsaku (eds.), *Nihon keizai no hatten* [The Development of Japanese Economy], Tokyo: Nihon keizai Shimbun Sha.

——(1981), *Kinsei Nihon bukkashi no kenkyû: kinsei beika no kôzô to hendô* [Studies on Commodity Prices in Early Modern Japan: The Structure and Transformation of Early Modern Rice Prices], Tokyo: Ôhara Shinseisha.

——(1985), *"Edo zenki (17 seiki) no beika dôkô to keizai,"* Harada Toshimaru and Miyamoto Matao (eds.), *Rekishi no naka no bukka* [Prices in History], Tokyo: Dôbunkan.

——(1989), *"Chihô keizai no chirigaku: 'kôiki Nôbi chihô-ken' no bunseki* [Geographical Studies of the Structure of Regional Economies: An Analysis of the Greater Nobi Region]," Shimbo Hiroshi and Saitô Osamu (eds.), *Kindai seichô no taidô* [The Initial Movement to Modern Growth], Tokyo: Iwanami Shoten, 219–66.

Iwao, Seiichi (1966/71/74), *"Sakoku* [National Seclusion]," *Nihon no rekishi 14*, Tokyo: Chûô Kôronsha.

Jannetta, Ann B. (1987), *Epidemics and Mortality in Early Modern Japan*, Princeton: Princeton University Press.

Jennings, Ronald C. (1973), "Loans and Credit in the Early 17th Century Ottoman Judicial Records: The Sharia Court of the Anatolian Kayseri," *Journal of Economic and Social History of the Orient*, Vol. 16, Nos. 2–3.

Kagawa, Takayuki (1974), *Mitsui ryôgaeten no keiei to chikuseki* [The Savings and Management of the Mitsui Exchange House], *Mitsui bunko ronsô*, Vol. 8.

——(1985), *Kinsei mitsui keieishi no kenkyû*, Tokyo: Yoshikawa Kôbunkan.

Kaiho, Seiryô (1976*a*), *"Keiko-dan* [Talks on Public Practice]," Kuranami, Shôji (ed.), *Kaiho Seiryô zenshû* [The Collected Works of Kaiho Seiryô], Tokyo: Yachiyo Shuppan.

——(1976*b*), *"Masuko-dan"* [Talks on Masuya Koemon], Kuranami, Shôji (ed.), *Kaiho Seiryô zenshû* [The Collected Works of Kaiho Seiryô], Tokyo: Yachiyo Shuppan.

——(1976*c*), *"Taigo-dan"* [Talks on an Excellent Economist], Kuranami, Shôji (ed.), *Kaiho Seiryô zenshû* [The Collected Works of Kaiho Seiryô], Tokyo: Yachiyo Shuppan.

Kakimoto, Hiroki (1982), *"Senzen no Banshûori* [Prewar Textiles from Banshû]," Kaneko, Seiji (ed.), *Jiba sangyô no kenkyû* [Studies of Local Industry], Tokyo: Hôritsu Bunkasha.

Kalland, Arne (1984), "A Credit Institution in Tokugawa Japan: The Ura-tamegin of Chikuzen Province," Gordon, Daniels (ed.), *Europe Interprets Japan*, Tenterden, Kent: P. Norbury: 2–12, 245–51.

——(unpublished MS). "Rural Credit Institutions," *Mino shima chitai ni okeru jisshô-teki bunseki.*

Kangyôryô (ed.) (N.A.). *Meiji 7 nen fuken bussan hyô: fu3 ken60*, Tokyo: Meiji bunken shiryô kankokai.

Kasai, Ransui (1928), *Kyôdô kenkyû Tokushima-ken-shi*, Tokushima: Tokushima ken Kyôdokai.

Kasaya, Kazuhiko (1976), *"Kinsei kuniyaku fushin no seijishiteki ichi* [The Political Historical Position of the Early Modern Kuniyaku/Fushin]," *Shirin*, Vol. 59, No. 4.

Kawakami, Masaru (1970), *"Kanbun empôki kônoike shihon no undô keitai,"* Miyamoto, Mataji et al. (eds.), *Osaka no kenkyû*, Vol. 5, Tokyo: Seibundô.

Kawakatsu, Heita (1976), *"Meiji zenki ni okeru naigai menpu no kakaku"* [Domestic and Foreign Prices for Cloth Textiles in Early Meiji], *Seiji keizaigaku zasshi* (Journal of Political Economics), Vols. 244 and 245, Tokyo: Waseda Daigaku.

——(1977), *"Meiji zenki ni okeru naigai men kankeihin no hinshitsu"* [The Quality of Domestic and Foreign Cotton-related Products in Early Meiji], *Seiji keizaigaku zasshi* [Journal of Political Economics], Vols. 250 and 251, Tokyo: Waseda Daigaku.

Kawazoe, Noboru (1979), *Tokyo no genfûkei* [The Primal Landscape of Tokyo], Tokyo: Nihon Hôsô Shuppan Kyôkai.

Keene, Donald (1952), *The Japanese Discovery of Europe, 1720–1830*, Stanford, CA: Stanford University Press.

Kelly, William W. (1985), *Deference and Defiance in Nineteenth Century Japan*, Princeton: Princeton University Press.

Kihara, Hiroyuki (1978), *"Sanuki Takamatsu-han ni okeru satô ryûtsû tôsei"* [The Control of Distribution of Sugar in Takamatsu Domain, Sanuki Province], *Kagawa daigaku kyôiku gakubu kenkyû hôkoku*, Vol. 44, No. 1.

—— (1982), *"Sanuki Takamatsu-han ni okeru satô kawase kin"* [The Exchange of Sugar in Takamatsu Domain, Sanuki Province], Watanabe, Norifumi (ed.), *Sangyô no hattatsu to chiiki shakai: Setouchi sangyô shi no kenkyû* [Regional Society and the Development of Industry], Hiroshima: Keisuisha.

—— (1988), *"Sanuki Takamatsu-han Marugame-han ni okeru hansatsu to kokusan tôsei"* [Domainal Currency and the Control of Domainal Commodities in Takamatsu Domain and Marugame Domain, Sanuki Province]," *Nihon ginkô kin'yû kenkyûsho itaku kenkyû*, Vol. 60, No. 2.

Kikuchi, Toshio (1958), *Shinden kaihatsu* [New Land Reclamation], Vol. 1, Tokyo: Kokon Shoin.

Kikuma-chô (ed.) (1979), *Kikuma-chô shi* [Kikuma Records], Ehime: Ehime-ken Kikuma-chô.

Kikuura, Shigeo (1972), *"Bakumatsu meiji ki no mensaku/men-orimono no dôkô (2),"* *Keizaikeieironshû* (Tôyô Daigaku), No. 66.

Kin'yû Kenkyûkai (ed.) (1937), *Wagakuni shôhin sôba tôkeihyô*, Tokyo: Kin'yû Kenkyû-kai.

Kitajima, Masamoto (ed.) (1975), *Tochi seido shi* [A History of the [Japanese] Land System], Vol. II, Tokyo: Yamakawa Shuppansha.

Kitô, Hiroshi (1976), *"Tokugawa jidai nôson no nyûji shibô—Kainin kakiagechô no tôkeiteki kenkyû,"* *Mita keizaigakkai zasshi*, Vol. 69, No. 7: 88–95.

—— (1983a), *Nihon nisennen no jinkôshi* [The Two Thousand Year History of the Japanese Population], Tokyo: PHP Kenkyûjo.

—— (1983b), *"Edo jidai no beishoku"* [Edo Period Rice Consumption], *Rekishi hyôron*, Vol. 89.

—— (1985), *"Zen kôgyô-ka jidai no keizai to shakai,"* Amino, Yoshihiko et al. (eds.), *Nihon rekishi no saihakken*, Tokyo: Nansôsha.

—— (1986), *"Meiji zenki no shushoku kôsei to sono chiikiteki pataan"* [The Composition of Early Meiji Staple Foods and its Regional Patterns], *Jôchi keizai ronshû*, Vol. 31, No. 2.

—— (1989), *"Kinsei Nihon no shushoku taikei to jinkô henka"* [Population Change and the System of Staple Foods in Early Modern Japan], Hayami, Akira, et al. (eds.), *Tokugawa shakai kara no tembô: hatten, kôzô, kokusai kankei* [The Perspective from Tokugawa Society: Development, Structure and International Relations], Tokyo: Dôbunkan.

Kobata, Atsushi (ed.) (1956), *Okamoto son-shi* [The History of Okamoto Village], Okamoto mura: Okamoto Sonshi Kankôkai, Fukui Prefecture.

—— Toyoda, Takeshi, Hôgetsu, Keigo, and Mori, Katsumi (eds.) (1966), *Tokushi sôran* [Reading History], Tokyo: Jimbutsu Ôraisha.

Kobayashi, Shigeru (1963), *Kinsei nôson keizaishi no kenkyû* [Studies in the Economic History of Early Modern Agricultural Villages]. Mirai-sha.

Kobori, Keiichi (1974), *Sakoku no shisô*, Tokyo: Chûô Kôron-sha.

Kodama, Kôta and Kitajima, Masamoto (eds.) (1977), *Hanshi sôran* [An Outline of Domainal History], Tokyo: Shin Jimbutsu Ôraisha.

Koizumi, Kesakatsu (1977), *Doryôkô no rekishi* [The History of Weights and Measures], Tokyo: Hara Shobô.

Konta, Yôzô (1977), *Edo no hon'yasan: kinsei bunkashi no sokumen* [Edo Booksellers: An Aspect of Early Modern Cultural History], Tokyo: Nihon Hôsô Shuppan Kyôkai.

Kornicki, Peter F. (1998), *The Book in Japan: A Cultural History from the Beginnings to the Nineteenth Century*, New York: E. J. Brill.

Koyama, Shûzô and Gotô, Yoshiko (1985), *"Nihonjin no shushoku no rekishi"* [The History of the Staple Foods of the Japanese], Ishige, Naomichi (ed.), *Ronshû: Higashi ajia no shokuji* [Essays on East Asian Foods], Tokyo: Heibonsha.

Kudo, Kyôkichi et al. (1983), *"Kinsei no yôsan seishigyô* [Sericulture and Silk-reeling Industry of the Early Modern Era]," Nagahara, Keiji, et al. (eds.), *Nihon gijutsu no shakaishi* [A Social History of Japanese Technology], Vol. 3, Tokyo: Nihon Hyôronsha.

Kuranami, Shôji (ed.) (1976), *Kaiho Seiryô zenshû* [The Collected Works of Kaiho Seiryô], Tokyo: Yachiyo Shuppan.

―― (1990), *Kaiho Seiryô no keizai shisô no kenkyû* [The Economic Thought of Kaiho Seiryô], Tokyo: Yûzankaku.

Kuroda, Hideo (1986), *"Yomi, kaki, soroban: shutaiteki nôryoku"* [Reading, Writing and the Abacus: Subjective Abilities], *Shûkan Asahi Hyakka: Nihon no rekishi*, Vol. 24.

Kusama, Naokata (1930), *"Sanka zui,"* Takimoto, Seiichi (ed.), *Nihon keizai taiten*, Vol. 42, Tokyo: Keimeisha.

Kuznets, Simon (1959), *Six Lectures on Economic Growth*, The Free Press of Glenco.

―― (1971), *Economic Growth of Nations: Total Output and Production Structure*, Cambridge, MA: Belknap Press of Harvard University Press.

Lamoreaux, Naomi R. (1986), "Banks, Kinship, and Economic Development: The New England Case," *Journal of Economic History*, Vol. 46, No. 3.

Lee, Dongun (1980), *"Tokugawa kôki kokudainô ni tsuite no ichi kôsatsu"* [On Substitutions for Rice in Tax Payments in the Latter Half of the Tokugawa Period], *Rokkôdai Ronshu* [Rokkôdai Essays], Vol. 27, No. 3.

Livi-Bacci, Massimo (1992), *A Concise History of World Population*, Carl Ipsen (trans.), Oxford: Blackwell.

Masuda, Shirô (1959), *Seiyô hôken shakai seiritsuki no kenkyû*, Iwanami Shoten.

Masuda, Yoshio (1967), *"Futatabi bunkashizô no keisei ni tsuite"* [A Reconsideration of the Formation of Cultural History Images], Tokyo: *Chûô kôron*, Vol. 82, No. 6.

―― (1936), *"Yôsanshi"* [A History of Sericulture], Honda Iwajirô (ed.), *Nihon Sanshigyôshi* [A History of the Silk Reeling Industry in Japan], Vol. 3, Tokyo: Dainihon Sanshikai.

Matsumoto, Shirô (1983), *Nihon kinsei toshiron* [Early Modern Japanese Cities], Tokyo: Tokyo Daigaku Shuppankai.

Matsuo, Mieko (1979), *"Kinsei kôki ni okeru daimyô jônôkin"* [Warlords' Payments of Gold to the Shogunate in the Late Edo Period], Tokugawa Rinseishi Kenkyûjo (ed.), *Kenkyû kiyô*, Tokyo: Tokugawa Reimei kai.

Matsuyoshi, Sadao (1964), *Sengoku no gunshikin*, Jimbutsu Ôraisha.

McClain, James L. (1982), *Kanazawa: A Seventeenth Century Japanese Castle Town*, New Haven: Yale University Press.

——Merriman, John M. and Ugawa, Kaoru (eds.) (1994), *Edo and Paris*, Ithaca, New York: Cornell University Press.

——and Wakita, Osamu (eds.) (1999), *Osaka: The Merchants' Capital of Early Modern Japan*, Ithaca, NY: Cornell University Press.

McEvedy, Colin and Jones, Richard (1978), *Atlas of World Population History*, New York: Penguin Books, Ltd.

McMullin, Neil (1984), *Buddhism and the State in Sixteenth Century Japan*, Princeton: Princeton University Press.

Medick, Hans (1981), "The Proto-industrial Family Economy," Peter Kriedte, et al. (eds.), *Industrialization before Industrialization: Rural Industry in the Genesis of Capitalism*, Cambridge: Cambridge University Press.

Meiji Zaiseishi Hensankai (ed.) (1904–05), *Meiji Zaisei-shi*, Vol. 5, Tokyo: Maruzen Shoten.

Melton, Frank T. (1986), *Sir Robert Clayton and the Origins of English Deposit Banking, 1658–1685*, Cambridge: Cambridge University Press.

Mendels, Franklin (1972), "Protoindustrialization: The First Phase of the Industrialization Process," *Journal of Economic History*, Vol. 32, No. 1: 241–61.

Mikami, Ryûzô (1989), *En no tanjô, zôhoban* [The Birth of the Yen] Supplemented edition, Tokyo: Tôyô Keizai Shimpôsha.

Miki, Yûsuke (1964–1965), "*Awa hansatsu kô*" [On Domainal Notes in Awa], *Shigaku*, Vols. 37 and 38.

Mitamura, Engyo (1933/1975), *Edokko* (Edoites), *Mitamura Engyo Zenshû 7*, Tokyo: Chûô Kôronsha.

Mitsuke shiyakusho (ed.) (1981), *Mitsuke-shi shi, Jôkan 2* [The History of Mitsuke City, the First Volume, Part 2], Mitsuke-shi, Niigata Prefecture.

——(ed.) (1983), *Mitsuke-shi shi, Gekan 1* [The History of Mitsuke City, Final Volume, Part 1], Mitsuke-shi, Niigata Prefecture.

Miura, Toshiaki (1982), "Kinsei Ban-shû ni okeru men-orimono," Kaneko, Seiji (ed.), *Jiba sangyô no kenkyû*, Tokyo: Hôritsu Bunkasha.

Miyamoto, Mataji (ed.) (1963), *Kinsei Osaka no bukka to rishi* [Prices and Profit in Early Modern Osaka], Tokyo: Sôbunsha.

Miyamoto, Matao (1976), "*Hitori atari nôgyô sanshutsudaka to seisan shoyôso hiritsu* [Per Capita Agricultural Output and Various Production Percentages]," Umemura, Mataji, Shimbo, Hiroshi, Hayami, Akira, and Nishikawa, Shunsaku (eds.), *Nihon keizai no hatten* [The Development of Japanese Economy], Nihon Keizai Shimbunsha.

——(1978), "*Kônoike Zen'emon*," Sakudô, Yôtarô, Miyamoto, Matao et al. (eds.), *Edoki shônin no kakushinteki kôdô*, Tokyo: Yûhikaku.

——(1981), "On Price Fluctuations in Late Tokugawa-Early Meiji Kyoto: 1830–1879," *Osaka Daigaku Keizaigaku*, Vol. 30: Nos. 2, 3.

——(1987a), "Shijô no dôkô," *Osaka-fu shi*, Vol. 6: 655–8.

——(1987b), "*Tanuma-ki no shôgyô to kin'yû*" [Commerce and Finance during the Tanuma Era], *Osaka Fu-shi* 6.

——(1988a), "*Edo jidai bukkashi: seika to mondaiten*," Odaka, Kônosuke and Yamamoto, Yûzô (eds.), *Bakumatsu meiji no keizai*, Tokyo: Nihon Keizai Shimbunsha.

——(1988b), *Kinsei Nihon no shijô keizai* [The Market Economy in Early Modern Japan], Tokyo: Yûhikaku.

——(1989), *"Bukka to makuro keizai no hendô,"* Shimbo Hiroshi and Saito Osamu (eds.), *kindai keizai seichô no taidô* [The Initial Movement to the Modern Growth], Tokyo: Iwanami Shoten, 67–126.

Miyamoto, Tsuneichi and Ushioda Tetsuo (1978), *Shoku seikatsu no kôzô* [The Structure of Food Lifestyle], Tokyo: Shibata Shoten.

Mori, Sugio (1993), *Kinsei chôsohô to nômin seikatsu* [Early Modern Tax Law and the Lives of Peasants], Tokyo: Kashiwa Shobô.

Morinaga, Shuntarô and Yasuda, Ken (1977–85), *"Edo jidai chûki ni okeru shohan no nôsakumotsu: Kyôho-Gembun shokoku sambutsuchô kara"* [Crops of the Various Domains in the Middle of the Edo Period: From Various Regional Products Records of the Kyôho–Gembun Era], *Nôgyô*, Vols. 1111–98.

Moriya, Takehisa (1990), "Urban Networks and Information Networks in the Edo Period," Nakane, Chie (ed.), *Tokugawa Japan*, Tokyo: Tokyo University Press, 97–123.

Morris-Suzuki, Tessa (1989), *A History of Japanese Economic Thought*, London: Routledge.

——(1994), "Creating the Frontier: Border, Identity and History in Japan's Far North," *East Asian History*, Vol. 7.

Mosk, Carl (1983), *Patriarchy and Fertility: Japan and Sweden, 1880–1960*, London: Academic Press.

Murakami, Masana (1978), *Fukuyama no rekishi, jôkan* [The History of Fukuyama], Vol. 1, Tokyo: Rekishi Toshosha.

Nagano, Hiroko (1986), *Bakuhan-sei kokka no keizai kôzô*, Tokyo: Yoshikawa Kôbunkan.

Nagazumi, Yôko (1987), *Tôsen yushutsunyûhin sûryô ichiran, 1637–1833* [An Overview of the Volume of Exports and Imports on Chinese Ships, 1637–1833], Tokyo: Sôbunsha.

Nagoya-shi kyoiku iinkai (ed.) (1964), *Kambun muramura oboegaki*, Nagoya: Nagoya-shi kyoikuiinkai.

——(ed.) (1964), *Owari junkôki*.

Naitô, Konan (1976), *Nihon bunkashi kenkyû, ge* [Studies in the Cultural History of Japan], Vol. 2, Tokyo: Kôdansha.

Naimushô Sômukyoku Kosekika (ed.) (1992), *"Meiji jûkyûnen jûnigatsu sanjûi-chinichi shirabe—Nihon teikoku minseki kokôhyô,"* Hayami Akira (comps.), *Kokusei chôsa izen Nihon jinkô tôkei shûsei 2*, Tokyo: Harashobô, (reprint).

Najita, Tetsuo (1970), "Ôshio Heihachirô (1793–1837)," Craig, Albert and Shively, Donald (eds.), *Personality in Japanese History*, Berkeley: University of California Press, 155–179.

——(1974), *Japan: The Intellectual Foundations of Modern Japanese Politics*, Chicago: University of Chicago Press.

——(1987), *Visions of Virtue in Tokugawa Japan: The Kaitokudô, Merchant Academy of Osaka*, Chicago: University of Chicago Press.

——(1988), "Political Economy in Thought and Practice Among Commoners in Nineteenth-century Japan," *The Japan Foundation Newsletter*, Vol. 16, No. 3: 13–18.

Nakai, Nobuhiko (1961), *Bakuhan shakai to shôhin ryûtsû*, Tokyo: Hanawa Shobô.

——(1971), *Tenkan-ki bakuhansei no kenkyû* [Studies of the Shogunal-Domainal System in its Transition Period], Tokyo: Hanawa Shobô.

Nakamura, Satoru (1968), *Meiji ishin no kiso kôzô* [The Basic Structure of the Meiji Restoration], Miraisha, chapter 5.

386 References

Nakamura, Satoru (1990), "The Development of Rural Industry," Nakane, Chie and Ôishi, Shinzaburô (eds.), Conrad Totman (trans.), *Tokugawa Japan: The Social and Economic Antecedents of Modern Japan*, Tokyo: University of Tokyo Press.

Nakamura, Takafusa (1985), *Meiji Taishôki no keizai* [The Economy of the Meiji and Taishô Periods], Tokyo: Tokyo Daigaku Shuppankai.

Nakayama, Tomihiro (1986), "*Kinsei kôki ni okeru kashitsuke shihon no sonzai keitai,*" *Hiroshima Daigaku Shigaku kenkyû*, Vol. 172: 1–20.

Narimatsu, Saeko (1985), *Kinsei tôhoku nôson no hitobito—Ôshû Asaka-gun Shimomoriyamura* [People in Early Modern Tôhoku Japan], Kyoto: Mineruva Shobô.

—— (1992), *Edo jidai no tôhoku nôson—Nihonmatsuhan Niitamura* [A Rural Village in the Tokugawa Period], Dôbunkan.

—— (2000), *Shôya nikki ni miru Edo no sesô to kurashi* [Life in the Tokugawa Society through Diary of Village Officer], Kyoto: Mineruva Shobô.

Naruto-shi shi henshû iinkai (ed.) (1976), *Naruto-shi shi, v. 1* [A History of Naruto City], Naruto: Naruto-shi.

Nihon Ginkô Chôsakyoku (ed.) (1974), Tsuchiya, Takao and Yamaguchi, Kazuo (comps.), *Zuroku Nihon no kahei 5* [An Illustrated History of Japanese Currency], *Kinsei shin'yô kahei no hattatsu 1*, Tokyo: Tôyô Keizai Shimpôsha, 280.

—— (ed.) (1975), Tsuchiya, Takao and Yamaguchi, Kazuo (comps.), *Zuroku Nihon no kahei 6* [An Illustrated History of Japanese Currency], *Kinsei shin'yô kahei no hattatsu 2*, Tokyo: Tôyô Keizai Shimpôsha.

Nihon Keieishi Kenkyûjo (ed.) (1972), *Godai Tomoatsu denki shiryô, Vol. 2* [Materials for a Biography of Godai Tomoatsu, Vol. 2], Tôyô Keizai Shimpôsha.

Nishigaki, Seiji (1983), *Oise mairi* [Ise Pilgrimages], Tokyo: Iwanami Shoten.

Nishikawa, Noboru (1995), "*Kaikei soshiki to boki gihô,*" Yasuoka, Shigeaki and Amano, Masatoshi (eds.), *Nihon kei'ei-shi 1: kinsei-teki kei'ei no tenkai*, Tokyo: Iwanami Shoten: 197–232.

Nishikawa, Shunsaku (1979), *Edo jidai no politikaru ekonomii* [Edo Period Political Economy], Tokyo: Nihon Hyôronsha.

—— (1982), "*Ikôki no chôshû ni okeru kokumotsu shôhi to jinmin jôshoku* [Grain Consumption and the People's Normal Fare in Chôshû During the Time of Domainal Transfer]," *Mita shôgaku kenkyû*, Vol. 25.

—— (1985), *Nihon keizai no seichôshi* [The History of the Growth of the Japanese Economy], Tokyo: Tôyô Keizai Shimpôsha.

—— (1987), "The Economy of Chôshû on the eve of Industrialization," *The Economic Studies Quarterly*, Vol. 38, No. 4: 335.

Nishikawa, Shunsaku and Akimoto, Hiroya (1977), "*Bôchô ichien 'keizai-hyô' josetsu*" [An Introduction to the "Economic Tables" of the Bôchô Region], Shakai Keizai-shi Gakkai (ed.), Atarashii Edo jidaishizô wo Motomete: sono shakai keizaishiteki sekkin (In Search of a New Historical View to the Edo Period: A Socio-economic Historical Approximation), Tokyo, Tôyô Keizai Shimpôsha, pp. 101–25.

—— and Ishibe, Shoko (1985), "*Han Sembaisei no Hakyû ni tsuite*" [On the Diffusion of Domainal Monopolies], *Keizai kenkyû*, Vol. 36, No. 3.

—— and Saitô, Osamu (1985), "The Economic History of the Restoration Period," Nagai, Michio and Miguel, Urrutia (eds.), *Meiji Ishin*, Tokyo: The United Nations University.

—— and Tanimura, Kenji (1980), "*Hansatsu-ron saikô* [Domainal Notes Reconsidered]," *Mita gakkai zasshi*, Vol. 73.

Nishinomiya Shiyakusho (ed.) (1963), *Nishinomiyashi shi 5* [The History of Nishinomiya, Vol. 5], Nishinomiya: Nishinomiya Shiyakusho.

Nishiyama, Matsunosuke (1975), *"Edo no machi nanushi, Saitô Gesshin"* [Saitô Gesshin: City Elder of Edo], Nishiyama, Matsunosuke (ed.), *Edo chônin no kenkyû* [Studies of Edo Townspeople], Vol. 4. Yoshikawa Kôbunkan.

Niwa, Hiroshi (1982), *Jinushi-sei no keisei to kôzô: Mino shima chitai ni okeru jisshô-teki bunseki*, Tokyo: Ochanomizu Shobô.

Nôshômushô (ed.). Keiô shyobô (1959–63), *Nôshômu tôkei hyô*, Nôshômushô (reprinted).

Nômushô Kannô-kyoku (ed.) (1878–79), *(Zenkoku) Nôsanhyô*, reprinted Meiji bunken shiryô kankô-kai (ed.) (1964–65), *Meiji zenki sangyô hattatsu-shi shiryô*.

Norman, E. Herbert (1940), *Japan's Emergence as a Modern State*, New York: Institute of Pacific Relations.

North, D. C. and Thomas, R. P. (1973), *The Rise of the Western World: A New Economic History*, Cambridge: Cambridge University Press.

Numata, Jirô (1964), *"Edo jidai no bôeki to taigai kankei,"* Ienaga, Saburô et al. (eds.), *Nihon Rekishi Kinsei 5*, Tokyo: Iwanami Shoten.

Odaka, Kônosuke (1988), *"Naibu ukeoi to naibu rôdô shijô: rôdô katei henkaku no rekishi"* riron [Internal Subcontracting and the Internal Labor Market: A Historical Theory of the Transformation of the Labor Process], *Keizai kenkyû*, Vol. 39, No. 1.

——and Yamamoto, Yûzô (eds.) (1988), *"Bakumatsu Meiji no Nihon keizai* [Japanese Economy at the Last Years of Tokugawa Era and the Beginning Years of Meiji Era]," *Sûryô Keizaishi Ronshû* Vol. 4 [Collection of Theses on Quantitative Economic History Vol. 4], Tokyo: Nihon Keizai Shimbunsha.

Ôguchi, Yûjirô (1969), *"Tempo-ki no bakufu zaisei"* [Shogunal Finances during the Tempo Era], *Ochanomizu Joshi Daigaku Jimbunkagaku Kiyô*, Vol. 22, No. 2.

——(1981), *"Bunkyûki no bakufu zaisei* [Shogunal Finances during the Bunkyû Era]," *Nempô Kindai Nihon kenkyû*, No. 3, Tokyo: Yamakawa Shuppansha.

——(1984), *"Kansei Bbunka-ki no bakufu zaisei"* [Shogunal Finances during the Kansei-Bunka Era], *Nihon kinseishi ronsô*, Vol. 2, Tokyo: Yoshikawa Kôbunkan.

——(1988a), *"Goyôkin to kinsatsu"* [Forced Loans and Gold Notes], Odaka, Kônosuke and Yamamoto, Yûzô (eds.), *Bakumatsu. Meiji no Nihon keizai (Sûryô Keizai-shi Ronshû Vol. 4)*, Tokyo: Nihon Keizai Shimbunsha.

——(1988b), *"Tempo no kaikaku"* [The Tempo Reforms], Inoue, Mitsusada et al. (eds.), *Nihon rekishi taikei*, Vol. 3, Tokyo: Yamakawa Shuppansha.

Ôishi, Shinzaburô (ed.) (1969), *Jikata hanrei roku* [Rural Precedents], Tokyo: Kondô Shuppansha (reprinted Tokyo-dô Shuppan, 1995).

——(1975), *Nihon kinsei shakai no shijô kôzô* [Market Structure in Early Modern Japanese Society], Tokyo: Iwanami Shoten.

Oka, Mitsuo (1963), *"Banshû Kakogawa-gun ni okeru men ori ni tsuite"* (2) [Cotton Weaving in Kakogawa District, Banshû, 2], *Keizaigaku ronsô* [Essays in Economics], Vol. 13, No. 1, Dôshisha Daigaku.

——and Yamazaki, Ryûzô (1983), *Nihon keizaishi*, Kyoto: Mineruva Shobô.

Ôkura, Takehiko (1987), *"Yôgin ryûnyû to bakufu zaisei,"* Kamiki Tetsuo and Matsuura Akira (eds.), *Kindai ikôki ni okeru keizai hatten*, Tokyo: Dôbunkan Shuppan.

Ôkurashô (ed.) (1922–25), *Nihon zaisei keizai shiryô*, Tokyo: Zaisei Keizai Gakkai.

——(1927), *Dainippon sozei-shi*, Vols. 1 and 2, Tokyo: Chôyôkai.

Ôno, Mizuo (1971), *"Kyôho kaikakuki no bakufu kanjôsho shiryô: Ôkôchi-ke kiroku, 2"* [Historical Documents of the Shogunal Treasury during the Kyôho Reforms: The Records of the Ôkôchi Family], *Shigaku zasshi*, Vol. 80, No. 2.

Osaka Daigaku Kindai Bukkashi Kenkyûkai (ed.) (1982), *"Meiji Osaka oroshiuri bukka shiryô (7), (8)* [Materials for Osaka Wholesale Prices During the Meiji Era, 7 & 8]," *Osaka Ddaigaku Keizaigaku* [Osaka University Economics], Vol. 34, No. 4; Vol. 32, No. 1.

Osaka-shi Sanjikai (ed.) (1910), *Osakashi shi 5* [The History of Osaka, Vol. 5], Osaka-shi.

——(1911*a*), *Osakashi shi 1* [The History of Osaka, Vol. 1], Osaka-shi.

——(1911*b*), *Osakashi shi 3* [The History of Osaka, Vol. 3], Osaka-shi.

——(1912), *Osakashi shi 4* [The History of Osaka, Vol. 4], Osaka-shi.

Ôtani, Sadao (1971), *Kyôhoki kantô ni okeru kuniyaku fushin* [Kuniyaku/Fushin in Kanto during the Kyôho Era], *Kokushigaku*, Vol. 86.

Ôtomo, Kazuo (1978), *"Musashino shinden seiritsuki ni okeru shinden seisaku"* [New Field Policy during the Period of New Field Development in Musashino Province], *Shikan*, Vol. 15.

Parker, Geoffrey (1973), "The Emergence of modern Finance in Europe, 1500–1700," Cipolla, Carlo (ed.), *The Fontana Economic History of Europe*, London: Collins/Fontana.

——(1988), *The Military Revolution*, Cambridge: Cambridge University Press.

Pirenne, Henri (1987), *"Mahomet et Charlemagne,"* Pirenne, Henri et al. (eds.), *Mahomet et Charlemagne*, Milan: Jaca Book.

Platt, Brian (1998), "School, Community, and State Integration in Nineteenth Century Japan," Unpublished Ph.D. dissertation, University of Illinois.

Presnell, L. S. (1956), *Country Banking in the Industrial Revolution*, Oxford: Clarendon Press.

Rikugun Sanbôbu (ed.) (1976), *Kyôbuseihyô—Meiji hachinen hen*, Tokyo: Seishisha (reprint).

Rosovsky, Henry (1961), *Capital Formation in Japan*, New York: Free Press of Glencoe.

Rozman, Gilbert (1973), *Urban Networks in Ch'ing China and Tokugawa Japan*, Princeton: Princeton University Press.

Saitô, Osamu (1976*a*), *"Tokugawa chûki no jisshitsu chingin to kakusa"* [Real Wage and Money Supply in mid Tokugawa Japan], *Shakai keizaishigaku*, Vol. 41, No. 50.

——(1976*b*), *"Tokugawa kôki ni okeru rishiritsu to kahei kyôkyû"* [The Interest Rate and the Money Supply in the Late Tokugawa Period], Umemura Mataji, Shimbo Hiroshi, Hayami Akira and Nishikawa Shunsaku (eds.), *Nihon keizai no hatton* [The Development of Japanese Economy], Tokyo: Nihon keizai shimbunsha, 281–97.

——(1979), *"Tokugawaki no chingin kakusa kôzô to jisshitsu chingin suijun"* [Real Wage Levels and the Structure of Tokugawa Period Wage Differentials], Shimbo Hiroshi and Yasuba Yasukichi (eds.), *Kindai ikôki no nihon keizai* [Japanese Economy in the Modern Transition], Tokyo: Nihon keizai shimbunsha.

——(1980*a*), "Osaka Commodity Price Index: 1757–1915," *Mita Gakkai Zasshi*, Vol. 68, No. 10.

——(1980*b*), *"Tokugawa kôki 'infureteki seichô-ron' no saikentô"* [Re-examination to the Inflationary Growth Theory in Late Tokugawa Period], *Mita gakkai zasshi*, Vol. 73, No. 3.

——(1982), *"19-seiki Suwa chihô no nôson keizai to jinkô"* [The Economy and Population of Nineteenth Century Agricultural Villages in the Suwa Region], *Mita gakkai zasshi*, Vol. 75, No. 3.

——(1983), "Population and the Peasant Family Economy in Proto-industrial Japan," *Journal of Family History*, Vol. 8, No. 1: 30–54.

References389

—— (1985), *Puroto–kôgyôka no jidai: Seiô to Nihon no Hikaku-shi* [The Age of Proto-industrialization], Tokyo: Nihon Hyôronsha.

—— (1986), "The Rural Economy: Commercial Agriculture, By-employment, and Wage-Work," Jansen, M. B., and Rozman, G. (eds.), *Japan in Transition: From Tokugawa to Meiji*, Princeton: Princeton University Press.

—— (1987), *Shôka no sekai, uradana no sekai: Edo to Osaka no hikaku toshishi* [The World of the Merchant Family, The World Behind the Store: A Comparative Urban History of Edo and Osaka], Tokyo: Riburopôto.

—— (1988), "*Jinkô hendô ni okeru nishi to higashi: bakumatsu kara meiji e*" [Population Change in Western and Eastern Japan: From the Late Tokugawa Era to Meiji], Odaka Kônosuke and Yamamoto-Yûzo (eds.), *Bakumatsu-Meiji no nihon keizai* [Japanese Economy in the End of Tokugawa Period and Meiji Era], Nihon keizai shimbunsha.

—— (1989a), "Bringing the covert Structure of the Past to Light," *Journal of Economic History*, Vol. 49, No. 4: 992–9.

—— (1989b), "*Toshi ari jigoku setsu no saikentô—seiô no baai to Nihon no jirei*," Hayami, Akira et al. (eds.), *Tokugawa shakai kara no tembô—hatten, kôzô, kokusai kankei*, Tokyo: Dôbunkan, 239–62.

—— (1993), "*Bakumatsu-Meiji no chingin hendô saikô*" [A Reconsideration of Late Edo-Meiji Wage Fluctuations], *Keizai kenkyû*, Vol. 44, No. 4.

—— and Tanimoro, Masayuki (1989), "*Zairai sangyô no sai-hensei*," Umemura, Mataji and Yamamoto, Yûzô (eds.), *Kaiko to Ishin* [Opening the Ports and The Meiji Restoration], Tokyo: Iwanami Shoten.

Saitô, Seiji (1984), "*Edo jidai no toshi jinkô*" [Urban Population in the Edo Period], *Chiiki kaihatsu* (Regional Development), 240.

Sakudô, Yôtarô (1958), *Kinsei Nihon kaheishi*, Tokyo: Kôbundô.

—— (1961), *Nihon kahei kin'yûshi no kenkyû*, Tokyo: Miraisha.

—— (1971), *Kinsei hôken shakai no kahei kin'yu kôzô*, Tokyo: Hanawa Shobô.

Sakurai, Tokutarô (1962), *Kô shûdan seiritsu katei no kenkyû*, Tokyo: Yoshikawa Kôbunkan.

Sansom, G. B. (1950), *The Western World and Japan*, Knopf.

Sasaki, Shinzaburô (1932), *Nishijinshi* [A History of Nishijin], Kyoto: Unsôdô.

Saxonhouse, Gary and Kiyokawa, Yukihiko (1986), "*Nihon men bôsekigyô ni okeru rôdôryoku no shitsu to sono jukyû ni tsuite: Indo to no hikaku ni yoru hitotsu no hyôka* [On the Quality and Supply and Demand for Labor Power in the Japanese Cotton Industry: An Evaluation Through a Comparison with India]," Ôkawa, Kazushi (ed.), *Nihon to hatten tojôkoku* [Japanese Development and the Developing Countries], Tokyo: Keisô Shobô.

Scheiner, Irwin (1973), "The Mindful Peasant: Sketches for a Study of Rebellion," *Journal of Asian Studies*, Vol. 32, No. 4: 579–91.

Schumpeter, Joseph (1934), *The Theory of Economic Development: An Inquiry into Profits, Capital, Credit, Interest, and the Business Cycle*, Cambridge, MA: Harvard University Press.

Seki, Junnya (1960), "*Chôshû no haze to rô*" [Candles and Their Source Plants in Chôshû], Chihôshi renraku kyôgikai (ed.), *Nihon sangyô taikei 7 Chûgoku Shikoku chihô hen* [Series Japanese Industry 7: The Chûgoku and Shikoku Regions], Tokyo: Tokyo Daigaku Shuppankai.

Sekiguchi, Yoshiyuki (1983), "*Mondai teiki: kaikô no sekai keizaishi*" [A World Economic History of the Opening of the Treaty Ports], Ishii Kanji and Sekiguchi

390   References

Yoshiyuki (eds.), *Sekai shijô to bakumatsu kaikô* [World Markets and the Opening of the Treaty Ports at the End of the Tokugawa Period], Tokyo: Tokyo Daigaku Shuppankai.

Sekiyama, Naotarô (1958/69/85), *Kinsei Nihon no jinkô kôzô*, Tokyo: Yoshikawa Kôbunkan.

Shakai Keizai-shi Gakkai (Socio-economic History Society) (ed.) (1977), *Atarashii Edo jidaishizô wo motomete: sono shakai keizaishiteki sekkin* [In Search of a New Historical Image of the Edo Period: A Socio-economic Historical Approximation], Tokyo: Tôyô Keizai Shimpôsha.

——(1987), *Shakai keizaishigaku*, No. 53.

Shakai Kôgaku Kenkyûsho (1974), *Nihon rettô ni okeru jinkô bumpu no chôki jikeiretsu bunseki* [Population Distribution in the Japanese Archipelago Over the Long Term], Tokyo: Shakai Kôgaku Kenkyûsho.

Shibusawa Eiichi Denkishiryô Kankôkai (ed.) (1957), *Shibusawa Eiichi denki shiryô* [Materials for a Biography of Shibusawa Eiichi], Vol. 17.

Shimbo, Hiroshi (1967a), *Hôkenteki shônômin no bunkai katei* [The Disintegration of the Feudal Small Peasant], Tokyo: Shinseisha.

——(1967b), *"Tokugawa jidai no shôgyô kin'yû: nigawase kin'yû wo megutte* [Commercial Finance of the Tokugawa Era: On Letters of Credit]," *Kokumin keizai zasshi*, Vol. 115, No. 1.

——(1968), *"Tokugawa jidai no nobegawase kin'yû: shôgyô kinyû no ichi keitai to shiteno"* [Extended Credit in the Tokugawa Period: As One Form of Commercial Finance], *Kokumin keizai zasshi*, Vol. 117, No. 4.

——(1972), *"Han satsu ni tsuite no ichi kôsatsu: Tokugawa jidai no shin'yô seido tono kanren ni oite"* [Thoughts on Domainal Currency: On Their Relation to the Tokugawa Era Credit System], *Kobe daigaku keizaigaku kenkyu Nempô*, Vol. 19.

——(1974), *"Tokugawa jidai kôki seisetsu nôson ni okeru kahei ryûtsû: Settsu-no-kuni Yatabe-gun Hanakuma-mura no shiryô wo chûshin ni site"* [Currency Circulation in Late Tokugawa Era Agricultural Villages of Western Settsu Province: Centering on Materials from Hanakuma Village, Yatabe District, Settsu Province], *Hyôgo-ken no rekishi*, Vol. 11.

——(1978), *Kinsei no bukka to keizai hatten: zenkôgyôka shakai e no sûryôteki sekkin* [Prices and Economic Development in Early Modern Japan: A Quantitative Approach to Pre-industrial Society], Tokyo: Tôyô Keizai Shimpôsha.

——(1980), *"Edo kôki no kahei to bukka ni kansuru danshô"* [Notes on Money and Prices in the Late Tokugawa Era], *Mita gakkai zasshi*, Vol. 73, No. 1.

——(1986), *"Bakumatsuki ni okeru Edo to Osaka no bukka: kobetsu shôhin wo chûshin to shite"* [Prices in Edo and Osaka at the end of the Tokugawa Period], *Kokumin keizai zasshi*, Vol. 153, No. 5.

——and Hasegawa, Akira (1988), *"Shôhin seisan ryûtsû no dainamikkusu"* [The Dynamics of Commodity Production and Distribution], Hayami Akira and Miyamoto Matao (eds.), *Keizai Shakai no seiritsu* [The Emergence of Economic Society], Tokyo: Iwanami Shoten.

——Hayami, Akira and Nishikawa, Shunsaku (eds.) (1975), *Sûryô keizaishi nyûmon*, Tokyo: Nihon Hyôronsha.

——and Saitô, Osamu (1989), *"Gaisetsu jûkyû-seiki e"* [An Outline: Towards the Nineteenth Century], Shimbo, Hiroshi and Saitô, Osamu (eds.), *Kindai seichô no taidô* [The Initial Movement to Modern Growth], Tokyo: Iwanami Shoten.

——and Saitô, Osamu (eds.) (1989), *Kindai seichô no taidô* [The Initial Movements Toward the Modern Growth], *Nihon keizaishi 2* [The Economic History of Japan 2], Tokyo: Iwanami Shoten.

——and Yasuba, Yasukichi (eds.) (1979), *Kindai ikôki no Nihon keizai* [Japanese Economy in Modern Transitional Periods], *Sûryô Keizaishi Ronshû* [Collection of Theses on Quantitative Economic History], Vol. 2, Tokyo: Nihon Keizai Shimbunsha.

Shinohara, Miyohei, (ed.) (1967), "*Kojin shôhi shishutsu* [Individual Consumption Expenses]," *Chôki keizai tôkei 6* [Long-term Economic Statistics], Vol. 6, Tokyo: Tôyô Keizai Shimpôsha.

——(1972), "*Kôkôgyô*" [Manufacturing and Mining], Series: *Chôki keizai tôkei 10* [Long-term Economic Statistics], Vol. 10, Tokyo: Tôyô Keizai Shimpôsha.

Shiozawa, Kimio and Kondô, Tetsuo, (eds.) (1985), *Orimonogyô no hatten to kisei jinushisei* [The Development of the Textile Industry and the Parasitic Landlord System], Tokyo: Ochanomizu Shobô.

Shôji, Kichinosuke (1958), "*Sanshugyô no tenkai katei*" [The Development of the Silk Card Industry], Takahashi, Kôhachirô et al. (eds.), *Yôsangyô no hattatsu to jinushisei*, Tokyo: Ochanomizu Shobô.

——(1964), *Kinsei yôsangyô hattatsushi* [The Development of the Sericulture Industry in Early Modern Japan], Tokyo: Ochanomizu Shobô.

Sippell, Patricia (1977), "Popular Protest in Early Modern Japan: The Bushû Outburst" *Harvard Journal of Asiatic Studies*, Vol. 37, No. 2: 273–322.

Slicher van Bath, B. H. (1963), *Agrarian History of Western Europe*, Ordish, Olive (trans), London: E. Arnold.

Smith, Thomas C. (1958), "The Land Tax in the Tokugawa Period," *The Journal of Asian Studies*, Vol. 18, No. 1: 3–19.

——(1959). *Agrarian Origins of Modern Japan*, Stanford, CA: Stanford University Press.

——(1961), "Japan's Aristocratic Revolution," *Yale Review*, Vol. 50, No. 3 (March) 370–83, reprinted in Smith (1988*a*).

——(1965), *Edo jidai no nengu* [Edo Period Annual Taxes], Ôuchi, Tsutomu (trans.), Tokyo: Tokyo Daigaku Shuppankai.

——(1969/1988*c*), "Farm Family By-employments in Preindustrial Japan," *Jounal of Economic History*, Vol. 29, No. 4: 687–715 (reprinted as chapter 3 in Smith 1988*a*).

——(1973/1988*d*), "Premodern Economic Growth: Japan and the West," *Past & Present*, 60, 127–60 (reprinted as chapter 1 in Smith 1988*a*).

——(1977*a*), *Nakahara: Family Farming and Population in a Japanese Village, 1717–1830*, Stanford: Stanford University Press.

——(1977*b*), "*Zenkindai no keizai seichô*" [Premodern Economic Growth], Shakai keizaishi gakkai (ed.), *Atarashii edojidai shizô o motomete* [On the New Perspectives to the Edo Period], Tokyo: Toyokeizai Shimposha.

——(1988*a*), *Native Sources of Japanese Industrialization, 1750–1920*, Berkeley: University of California Press.

——(1988*b*), "The Land Tax in the Tokugawa Period," Smith (1988*a*), 50–70.

Suda, Keizô (1987), *Hida O Jiin kakochô no kenkyû* [A Study of the Temple Record of "O", in Hida Province] (in Suda Keizô, *Shuyô gyôsekishû dai nibu*), Gifu: Iryô hôjin Suda byôin.

Sugiyama, Shin'ya (1988), *Japan's Industrialization in the World Economy, 1859–1899: Export, Trade and Overseas Competition*, London: Athlone Press.

Suzuki, Hisashi (1971), *Kaseki kara Nihojin made* [From Fossils to Japanese], Tokyo: Iwanami Shoten.

——(1983), *Hone kara mita Nihonjin no rûtsu* [The Roots of the Japanese as Seen through Bones], Tokyo: Iwanami Shoten.

Taeuber, Irene (1958), *Population of Japan*, Princeton: Princeton University Press, 29.

Takahashi, Bonsen (1941), Nihon jinkô-shi no kenkyû, Tokyo: Sanyûsha.

Takamura, Naosuke (1987), "*Ishin zengo no gaiatsu wo meguru ichi, ni no mondai* [One or Two Problems Concerning External Pressure Around the Time of the Meiji Restoration]," *Shakai kagaku kenkyû*, Vol. 39, No. 4, Tokyo: Tokyo Daigaku Shuppankai.

Takase, Tamotsu (1979), "*Niikawa momen no hattatsu to Takaoka wataba no kakuritsu* [The Development of Niikawa Cotton Textiles and the Establishment of the Takaoka Cotton Market]," Takase Tamotsu (ed.), *Kaga-han kaiun-shi no kenkyû* [Studies in the Shipping History of Kaga Domain], Tokyo: Yûzankaku.

——(1980), "*Kaga-han no beika-hyô*" [The Rice Price Tables of Kaga Domain], Toyoda Takeshi (ed.), *Nihonkai chiiki-shi no kenkyû*, 1 [Studies in the Regional History of the Japan Sea Coast], Tokyo: Bunken Shuppan.

Takekoshi, Yosaburô (1930), *Economic Aspects of the History of the Civilization of Japan*, 3 Vols., London: George Allen & Unwin.

Takenouchi, Waka (comps.) (1943), *Kefukigusa*, Tokyo: Iwanami Shoten.

Takeuchi, Makoto (1965), "*Nôson keizai no henbô to kin'yû seisaku no tenkai* [Changes in Village Economies and the Development of Financial Policies]," *Nihon keiza-ishi taikei*, Vol. 4, Tokyo: Tokyo Daigaku Shuppankai.

——(1969), "*Kinsei zenki no shôgyô*" [Early Edo Period Commerce], Toyoda, Takeshi and Kodama, Kôta (eds.), *Ryûtsûshi I* [A History of Circulation, Vol. 1], Tokyo: Yamakawa Shuppansha.

Takeuchi, Rizô (ed.) (1973), *Tochi seido shi I* [An Agrarian History I], Tokyo: Yamakawa Shuppansha.

Takeyasu, Shigeharu (1966), *Kinsei hôken sei no tochi kôzô* [Agrarian Structure of Early Modern Feudal Society], Tokyo: Ochanomizu Shobô.

Takimoto, Seiichi (ed.) (1928), *Nihon keizai taiten* [Works on Economics in Pre-modern Japan], Vol. 6, Tokyo: Keimeisha.

Tamura, Yoshio (ed.) (1959), *Tatsuno shôyu kenkyû shiryô*, Vol. 1, Tatsuno: Tatsuno shôyu kyôdo kumiai.

Tanaka, Akira (1960), "*Bakumatsu satchô kôeki no kenkyû*" [Trade Between Satsuma and Chôshû at the end of the Tokugawa Era], *Shigaku zasshi*, Vol. 69.

Tanaka, Yasuo (1969), "*Edo jidai kôki ni okeru mitsui ryôgaeten no keiei dôkô* [Management Trends in the Mitsui Exchange House of the Late Edo Period]," *Mitsui bunko ronsô* 3.

——(1986), *Kinsei sanbutsu seisaku-shi no kenkyû* [Studies in the History of Domainal Production Policies in Early Modern Japan], Tokyo: Bunken Shuppan.

Tanimoto, Masayuki (1986), "*Bakumatsu Meiji zenki men'orimonogyô no tenkai: saita-maken irumagun wo chûshin to shite*" [The Development of the Cotton Weaving Industry in Late Tokugawa and Early Meiji: Centering on Iruma District, Saitama Prefecture], *Shakai keizaishigaku* [Socio Economic History], Vol. 52, No. 2.

——(1987), *"Bakumatsu Meijiki menpu kokunai shijô no hatten"* [The Development of the Domestic Market for Cotton Textiles in the Late Tokugawa and Early Meiji Periods], *Tochi seidoshigaku* [The Journal of Agrarian History], Vol. 115.

——(1992a), *"Chiiki keizai no hatten to suitai: 19 seiki, Niikawa momen to izumi momen no hikaku wo tsûjite"* [The Development and Decline of Regional Economies: Through a Comparison of Cotton in Nineteenth Century Niikawa and Izumi], *Nempô kindai Nihon kenkyû 14: Meiji ishin no kakushin to renzoku* [Annual Studies in Modern Japan 14: The Revolution and Continuity of the Meiji Restoration], Tokyo: Yamakawa Shuppansha.

——(1992b), "The Evolution of Indigenous Cotton Textile Manufacture Before and After the Opening of the Ports," *Japanese Yearbook on Business History*, Vol. 9, Japan Business History Institute.

Tanimura, Kenji (1981), *"Bunsei-ki Hiroshima-han ni okeru Urabe Okusuji no hinôsanbutsu to seisansei kakusa* [Differences in the Non-Agricultural Products and Productivity in Urabe and Okusuji of Bunsei-era Hiroshima Domain]," *Mita shôgaku kenkyû*, Vol. 23, No. 6.

Tashiro, Kazui (1976), "Tsushima Han's Korean Trade, 1684–1710," *Acta Asiatica*, Vol. 30: 85–105.

——(1981), *Kinsei nitchô tsûkô bôeki-shi no kenkyû* [Studies on the History of Early Modern Diplomatic and Trade Relations Japan and Korea], Tokyo: Sôbunsha.

——(1982), "Foreign Relations during the Edo Period: Sakoku Reexamined," *Journal of Japanese Studies*, Vol. 8, No. 2.

——(1986), *"Kinsei kôki nitchô bôeki-shi kenkyû joron,"* *Mita gakkai zasshi*, Vol. 79, No. 3.

——(1989), "Exports of Japan's Silver to China via Korea and Changes in the Tokugawa Monetary System during the Seventeenth and Eighteenth Centuries," Van Cauwenberghe, Eddy H. G. (ed.), *Precious Metals, Coinage and the Changes of Monetary Structures in Latin America, Europe and Asia*, Leuven: Leuven University Press.

——(1991), "Exports of Gold and Silver during the Early Tokugawa Era, 1600–1750," Van Cauwenberghe, Eddy H. G. (ed.), *Money, Coins and Commerce: Essays in the Monetary History of Asia and Europe*, Leuven: Leuven University Press.

Taya, Hirokichi (1963), *Kinsei Ginza no kenkyû* [Studies of Early Modern Silver Mints], Tokyo: Yoshikawa Kôbunkan.

Teranishi, Jûrô (1982), *Nihon no keizai hatten to kin'yû*, Tokyo: Iwanami Shoten.

Toby, Ronald P. (1977a). "Reopening the Question of *Sakoku*: Diplomacy in the Legitimation of the Tokugawa Bakufu," *The Journal of Japanese Studies*, Vol. 3, No. 2 (Summer): 323–64.

——(1977b), *"Shoki Tokugawa gaikô seisaku ni okeru 'sakoku' no ichi duke—bakufu seitôsei kakuritsu no mondai kara mite,"* Shakai keizaishi gakkai (ed.), *Atarashii edo-jidai shizô o motomete* [On the New Perspectives to the Edo Period], Tokyo: Toyokeizai Shimposha, 21–39.

——(1984), *State and Diplomacy in Early Modern Japan: Asia in the Development of the Tokugawa Bakufu*, Princeton: Princeton University Press.

——(1993), "Changing Credit in Nineteenth-century Japan," Austin, Gareth and Sugihara, Kaoru (eds.), *Local Suppliers of Credit in the Third World, 1750–1960*, New York: The Macmillan Company & St Martin's Press, 55–90.

Togai, Yoshio (1961), *"Mitsui ômotokata no shihon chikuseki,"* *Senshû daigaku ronshû*, 27.

Tôgyô Kyôkai (ed.) (1976), *Kindai Nihon tôgyôshi jôkan* [The History of the Modern Japanese Sugar Industry, Vol. 1], Tôgyô Kyôkai.

Tokyo Daigaku Shuppankai (ed.) (1955), *Dainihon kinsei shiryô—Higo no kuni jinriku aratamechô*, 5 Vols.

——(ed.) (1956–58), *Dainihon kinsei shiryô—kokura-han jinriku aratamechô*, 5 Vols.

Tominaga, Ken'ichi (1980), "Shakai Kôzô," *Keizaigaku Daijiten* II, Tokyo: Tôyô Keizai Shimpôsha, 836.

Tonomura, Hitomi (1992), *Community and Commerce in Late Medieval Japan: The Corporate Villages of Tokuchin-ho*, Stanford, CA: Stanford University Press.

Totman, Conrad (1989), *Green Archipelago: Forestry in Pre-Industrial Japan*, Berkeley; University of California Press (reprinted Ohio University Press, 1998).

——(1995), *The Lumber Industry in Early Modern Japan*, Honolulu: University of Hawai'i Press.

Toyama, Kamtarô (1909), *Sanshuron* [Species of Silkworms], Tokyo: Maruyamasha.

Toyoda, Takeshi (1977), "The Growth of Commerce and the Trades in the Muromachi Age," Hall, John W. and Toyoda, Takeshi (eds.) *Japan in the Muromachi age*, California, 129–44.

Tsuchiya, Takao (1927), *Hôken shakai hôkai katei no kenkyû* [The Collapse of Feudal Society], Tokyo: Kôbundô.

——(1931), "*Meiji shonen no jinkô kôsei ni kansuru ichi kôsatsu*" [Population Composition of Early Meiji], *Shakai Keizaishigaku*, Vol. 1, No. 1.

Tsuda, Hideo (1960), "*Bakumatsuki no koyô rôdô ni tsuite* [On Late Tokugawa Period Hired Labor]," *Tochi Seidoshigaku* [The Journal of Agrarian History], Vol. 8.

Tsuji, Tetsuya and Matsumoto, Shirô (1964), " '*Otorika tsuji kakitsuke' oyobi 'Onengumai.Onengukin sono hoka sho muki osame watashi kakitsuke' ni tsuite*," *Yokohama Shiritsu Daigaku Ronsô (jimbun-kagaku-kei)*, Vol. 15, No. 3.

Tsuji, Zennosuke (1912/1980), *Tanuma jidai* [The Tanuma Era], Tokyo: Iwanami Bunko.

Tsukahira, George Toshio (1966), *Feudal Control in Tokugawa Japan: The Sankin Kôtai System* [East Asian Research Center], Cambridge, MA: Harvard University Press.

Uchida, Hoshimi (1982), "*Edo jidai no shigen kyôkyû shisutemu shiron*" [A Hypothesis Regarding the Resource Supply System of the Edo Period], *Jimbun shizen kagaku ronshû*, Vol. 61, Tokyo: Tokyo Keizai Daigaku.

——(1988), "Narrow Cotton Stripes and their Substitutes," *Textile History*, Vol. 19.

Uchida, Tatsuya (1985), "*Bakumatsu Kishû-han ni 'okeru ôkadaura kôeki kaisho shihô' to Kanto gyohi shijô* [The Operation of the Trading and Finance Bureau at Kada Village in Late Tokugawa Kishû Domain and the Fish Fertilizer Market in the Kanto Region]," *Chihôshi kenkyû*, Vol. 35, No. 1.

Uemura, Shôji (1986), *Kinsei nôson ni okeru shijô keizai no tenkai*, Tokyo: Dôbunkan Shuppan.

Ueno-chô Kyôikukai (ed.) (1941), *Sôkokushi 2*, [A Record of the Ise Tôdô Domain], Ueno-cho: Ueno-chô Kyôikukai.

Umemura, Mataji (1965), "*Tokugawa jidai no jinkô to sono kisei yôin*," *Keizai kenkyû*, Vol. 16, No. 2.

——(1969), "*Meiji-ki no jinkô seichô*" [Population Growth in the Meiji Period], Shakai Keizaishi Gakkai (ed.), *Keizai-shi ni okeru jinkô*, Tokyo: Keiô Tsûshin, 118–41.

——(1981), "*Bakumatasu no keizai hatten*" [Late Tokugawa Period Economic Development], *Nempô: Kindai Nihon kenkyû 3, Bakumatsu-ishin no Nihon*, Tokyo: YamakawaShuppansha, 1–30.

—— et al. (eds.) (1966), *Nôringyô* [Agriculture and Forestry], *Chôki keizai tôkei, 9* [Long-term Economic Statistics, Vol. 9], Tokyo: Tôyô Keizai Shimpôsha.

—— (eds.) (1983), *Chiiki keizai tôkei* [Regional Economic Statistics], *Chôki keizai tôkei, 13* [Long-term Economic Statistics, Vol. 13], Tokyo: Tôyô Keizai Shimpôsha.

—— Shimbo, Hiroshi, Hayami, Akira, and Nishikawa, Shunsaku (eds.) (1976), *Nihon keizai no hatten: sûryô keizaishi ronshû Vol. 1* [The Development of Japanese Economy: Collection of Theses on Quantitative Economic History Vol. 1], Tokyo: Nihon Keizai Shimbunsha.

—— and Yamamoto, Yûzô (eds.) (1989), *Kaikô to Ishin, Nihonkeizai-shi Vol. 3* [The Economic History of Japan Vol. 3: The Opening of Japan and the Meiji Restoration], Tokyo: Iwanami Shoten.

Uranagase, Takashi (1985a), *"Jûroku seiki kôhan Kyoto ni okeru kahei ryûtsû," Chihôshi kenkyû*, No. 195.

—— (1985b), *"Jûroku seiki kôhan nishi-Nihon ni okeru kahei ryûtsû: shiharai shudan no henka wo chûshin to shite," Hisutoria*, No. 106.

Vaporis, Constantine Nomikos (1994), *Breaking Barriers: Travel and the State in Early Modern Japan*, Harvard East Asian Monographs: 163, Cambridge, MA: Harvard University Press.

Varley, H. Paul (1967), *The Ônin War*, New York: Columbia University Press.

Vlastos, Stephen (1986), *Peasant Protests and Uprisings in Tokugawa Japan*, Berkeley: University of California Press.

Wakabayashi, Kisaburô (1957), *"Kaga-han shoki kaiun shiryô oboegaki: sono ni* [Memorandum on Historical Materials Pertaining to Early Marine Transportation in Kaga Domain, Part 2]," *Chihôshi kenkyû* [The Study of Local History], Vol. 13, No. 1.

Wakita, Haruko (1981), *Nihon chûsei toshiron*, Tokyo: Tokyo Daigaku Shuppankai.

Wakita, Osamu (1975), "The Kokudaka System: A Device for Unification," *Journal of Japanese Studies*, Vol. 1, No. 2 (Spring): 297–320.

Wallerstein, Immanuel (1974), *The Modern World-System: Capitalist Agriculture and the Origins of the European World-Economy in the Sixteenth Century*, New York: Academic Press.

Walthall, Anne (1986), *Social Protest and Popular Culture in Eighteenth-century Japan*, Tucson: University of Arizona Press.

—— (1994), *"Edo Riots"* McClain, Merriman, and Ugawa (eds.), *Edo and Paris: Urban Life and the State in the Early Modern Era*, Ithaca and London: Cornell University Press, 407–28.

Wanouchi-chô-shi Hensan Iinkai (ed.) (1981), *Wanouchi-chô-shi*, Wanouchi-chô Kyôiku Iinkai.

Watanabe, Hiroshi (1985), *Kinsei Nihon shakai no sôgaku* [Neo-confucianism in Early Modern Japanese Society], Tokyo: Tokyo Daigaku Shuppankai.

Watanabe, Ichirô (1965), *"Kinsei shokôgyô no hatten"* [The Growth of Various Industries in the Early Modern Period], Kodama Kôta (ed.), *Sangyôshi II* [The History of Industry, Vol. 2], Tokyo: Yamakawa Shuppansha.

Watsuji, Tetsurô (1950), *Sakoku—Nihon no higeki*, Tokyo: Chikuma Shobô.

Wigen, Karen (1995), *The Making of a Japanese Periphery, 1750–1920*, Berkeley: University of California Press.

Wrigley, E. A. (1969), *Population and History*, London: Weidenfeld & Nicolson.

—— (1988), *Continuity, Chance and Change: The Character of the Industrial Revolution in England*, Cambridge: Cambridge University Press.

Yagi, Hironori (1983), *Suiden nôgyô no hatten ronri* [Theory of the Development of Paddy Field Agriculture], Tokyo: Nihon Keizai Hyôronsha.

Yagi, Tetsuharu (1965), *Kinsei no shôhin ryûtsu* [The Early Modern Circulation of Commodities], Tokyo: Hanawa Shobô.

Yamada, Tatsuo et al. (eds.) (1981), *Nihon nôgyô zenshû* [The Encyclopedia of Japanese Agriculture], Vol. 35. Nôsangyoson bunka kyôkai.

Yamaguchi, Kazuo (1966), *"Hansatsu kenkyûshi jôsetsu"* [An Introduction to the History of Studies of Domainal Currency], *Keizaigaku ronshû*, Vol. 31, No. 4.

—— (1983), *"Hansatsu-shi no chihôbetsu kôsatsu"* [The Geographical Distribution of Domainal Notes], *Shakai keizaishigaku*, Vol. 49, No. 1: 113–42.

Yamaguchi Kenritsu Toshokan (ed.) (1960–64), *Bôchô fûdo chûshin'an* [A Report on Conditions in the Bôchô Region], 1–2.

Yamamoto, Hirofumi (1995), *Sakoku to kaikin no jidai*, Tokyo: Azekura Shobô.

Yamamoto, Yûzô (1983), *"Man'en nibukin kô,"* *Jimbungakuhô*, Vol. 54.

—— (1994), *Ryô kara en e: Bakumatsu-Meiji-ki kahei mondai kenkyû*, Mineruva Shobô.

Yamamura, Kôzô (1974), *A Study of Samurai Income and Entrepreneurship*, Cambridge, MA: Harvard University Press.

—— (1978), *"Tenkaitto no shosan—sengoku/Tokugawa shoki no keizai seichô,"* Nagahara, Keiji et al. (eds.), *Sengoku jidai*, Tokyo: Yoshikawa Kôbunkan.

—— (1981), "Returns on Unification," Hall, John W., Nagahara, Keiji, and Yamamura, Kôzô (eds.), *Japan before Tokugawa: Political Consolidation and Economic Growth*, Princeton: Princeton University Press.

—— (1991), "The Iwanami Nihon keizai-shi Series," *Journal of Japanese Studies*, Vol. 17, No. 1 (Winter): 127–42.

Yamanaka, Hisao (1965), *"Kaseiki tottori-han ni okeru momen no ryûtsû tôsei ni tsuite"* [On the Control of the Distribution of Cotton in Tottori Domain During the Kasei Period], *Tottori daigaku gakugei gakubu hôkoku* [Reports of the Department of Arts and Sciences, Tottori University], 16.

Yamawaki, Teijirô (1960), *Kinsei nitchû bôekishi no kenkyû* [Trade Between Japan and China in the Early Modern Period], Tokyo: Yoshikawa Kôbunkan.

—— (1964), *"Nagasaki no tôjin bôeki* [Trade by Chinese Merchants in Nagasaki]," Tokyo: Yoshikawa Kôbunkan.

—— (1976), *"Nagasaki bôeki-ron"* [Trade at Nagasaki], *Rekishi kôron* [Historical Debates], Vol. 2, No. 4.

—— (1980), *Nagasaki oranda shôkan*, Tokyo: Chûô Kôronsha.

Yamazaki, Ryûzô (1976), *"Nagasaki bôeki-ron"* [Trade at Nagasaki], *Rekishi Kôron* [Historical Debates], Vol. 2, No. 4.

—— (1977), *"Bakumatsu ishinki no keizai hendô"* [Late Tokugawa-Restoration Era Economic Movements], *Iwanami Kôza Nihon rekishi: kinsei 5* [Iwanami Lectures on Japanese History: Early Modern 5], new edition, Tokyo: Iwanami Shoten.

—— (1983), *Kinsei bukkashi kenkyû*, Tokyo: Hanawa Shobô.

Yasuba, Yasukichi (1980), *Keizai seichôron* [A Theory of Economic Growth], Tokyo: Chikuma Shobô.

—— and Saitô, Osamu (eds.) (1983), *Sûryô Keizaishi Ronshû* [Collection of Theses on Quantitative Economic History] Vol. 3, *Puroto kôgyôkaki no keizai to shakai*, [Economy and Society in the Proto-industrial Period], Tokyo: Nihon Keizai Shimbunsha.

Yasuda, Ken (1987), *Shokoku sanbutsuchô: Niwa Shôhaku no hito to shigoto* [Regional Product Record Books: The People and Work of Niwa Shôhaku], Tokyo: Shôbunsha.

Yasuoka, Shigeaki (1970*a*), *Zaibatsu keiseishi no kenkyû* [Studies in the History of the Formation of the *Zaibatsu*], Kyoto: Mineruva Shobô.

——(1970*b*), *Nihon shihonsei no seiritsu katei* [The Process of the Establishment of the Capitalist System in Japan], Kyoto: Mineruva Shobô.

Yasuzawa, Mine (1977), "*Kinsei kôki ni okeru nômin kin'yû ni tsuite,*" Hidemura, Senzo et al. (eds.), *Kindai keizai no rekishiteki kiban*, Kyoto: Mineruva Shobô: 63–76.

——(1980), "*Kinsei kôki ni okeru nômin kin'yû no hatten,*" *Kôbe Jogakuin Daigaku ronsô*, Vol. 26, No. 3: 266–73.

Yokohama Shiyakusho (ed.) (1959), *Yokohama-shi shi* [The History of Yokohama], Vol. 2, Yokohama: Yokohama-shi.

——(1960), *Yokohama-shi shi* [The History of Yokohama], Vol. 3, Part 1, Yokohama: Yokohama-shi.

——(1961), *Yokohama-shi shi* [The History of Yokohama], Documents, Part 1, Yokohama: Yokohama-shi.

——(1980), *Yokohama-shi shi* [The History of Yokohama], Documents, Part 2, expanded, Yokohama: Yokohama-shi.

Yokoyama, Toshio (1977), *Hyakushô: Ikki to gimin denshô* [Peasant Uprisings and the Legends of the Man of the People], Tokyo: Kyôikusha.

Yoshida, Tôgo (1910), *Ishinshi hakkô* [Eight Lectures on the Meiji Restoration], Tokyo: Fuzanbô.

Yoshida, Yoshinobu (1973), *Okitama minshû seikatsu-shi*, Kokusho Kankôkai.

Yoshinaga, Akira (1973), *Kinsei no senbai seido* [The Domainal Monopoly System in Early Modern Japan], Tokyo: Yoshikawa Kôbunkan.

Yoshizumi, Mieko (1968), "*Tetsudai fushin ni tsuite*" [On Tetsudai Fushin], *Gakushûin bungakubu kenkyû nempô*, No. 14.

Yui, Kennosuke (1935), *Tanomoshikô to sono hôritsu kankei* [The Mutual Financial Asssociations and their Juristic Development], Tokyo: Iwanami Shoten.

Yunoki, Manabu (1965), *Kinsei Nada sake keizaishi* [The Economic History of Early Modern Nada Saké], Kyoto: Mineruva Shobô.

——(1982), "*Banshûori no seiritsu*" [The Formation of Banshû Textiles], Kaneko, Seiji (ed.), *Ziba sangyô no kenkyû* [Studies of Regional Industry], Kyoto: Hôritsu Bunkasha.

——(1988), *Nihonshu* [Japan's Saké], Tokyo: Daiichi Hôki Shuppan.

Manuscripts

Bunrui kiji taikô (Tsushima Archives, National History Compilation Committee, Seoul).

Chigyô mokuroku (Tenshô 16 [1588]), Ichihashi-ke Monjo, Historiographical Institute, Tokyo University, reproduced in Wanouchi-chôshi Hensan Iinkai (1981), 785.

Goyô nikki (1835), Nishimatsu-ke Monjo, Rikkyô University Library, Tokyo.

Kahei hiroku (Secret Records of Currency).

Kingin taishaku-chô, 161 Vols., Nishimatsu-ke Monjo, Rikkyô University Library.

Mainikki (Diary of the Japanese Concession in Pusan), the Sô Family Documents, National Diet Library.

Menwarichô (Tax Registers).

Mino-no-kuni Niremata no uchi Nishijo-mura shûmon nimbetsu on-aratame-chô. (1773–1869), 97 Vols., Nishimatsu-ke Monjo, Rikkyô University Library.

Nayosechô (1660), Nishimatsu-ke Monjo, Ôgaki Municipal Library.

Reports on the Native Cotton Manufactures of Japan in "Foreign Office Miscellaneous Series," No. 49, in *British Parliamentary Papers*, 1877, LXXXII: 12.

Seisai zakki (Miscellany of Seisai), Edo sôsho kankôkai (ed.) (1917).

Shoyôdome, The Mitsui Collection, Tokyo.

Yorozu oboechô (1834, 1838, 1839), Tanahashi-ke Monjo, Gifu Kenritsu Shiryôkan.

Glossary

1. General

agemai	submission of rice from daimyo to shogunate
akamai	red rice, *Indica specy*
aratame-dokoro	inspection post
arige kemihô	examination of actual harvest
arise	basis of taxation to actually using lands
azukari	deposit
azukari tegata	exchangeable notes of deposit
bakuhan system	*bakufu* (shogunate) and *han* (daimyo) system
banmasu	see *jûgô masu*
bôeki	trade
botefuri	peddlers
buiku-kyoku	bureau of welfare
chôkô	tribute
daikan	magistrate
daikan mitate shinden	officially directed reclamations
daikanjo	magistrate's office
daimyo-gashi	lending to daimyos
debata-sei	piecework system
dekasegi	work outside of his/her village
desaku	villagers holding land outside
Edo shiirekata kaisho	Edo warehouse office
erizeni	distinction of currency
etsunenmai-daka	year-end inventory of rice
fuchimai	rations
fudai	hereditary servants
fueki	corvee
fujiki tanekashi haishakukin	loan to the village
fundô	measuring weights
furi tegata	check like notes
fushin'yaku	services to shogunate by daimyo
gekokujô	the low overthrow the high
genchi	fief reduction
genin	menial servants
gofukujaku	tailor's rule
gokenin	vassals
goketaoshi	threshing tool, literally "widow topplers"
gokuin	imprint
gônôshô	wealthy farmer-merchants
gôrikikin	money stipend

gôrikimai	rice stipends
gosanke	three direct descendent family of Tokugawa Ieyasu
gosankyô	three direct descendent family of Tokugawa Yoshimune and Ieshige
goyôkin	forced loans
gunken	originally polity to govern directly
gun'yaku	military services to shogunate by daimyo
haifuki silver	refined silver by cuppelation method
haikai	*haiku* salon
haiku	short poet using 5-7-5 *kana* letters
hakariza	scales guilds
hamako	seasonal workers
harigami-nedan	posted rice price
hatamoto	bannermen
heinô bunri	separation of warriors and peasantry
hiite	substracting
hôken	originally polity to entrust administration with local powers in China
hôkônin seido	system of servitude
honbyakushô	"original peasants"
honbyakushô kabu	membership of regular villager
honmono-gaeshi	buy back to original seller
honse	basis of taxation
hôrokumai	see *fuchimai*
irisaku	outsiders holding land in village
jiin kakochô	death registers
jinchiku aratame	survey of population and livestock
jishi	tax to urban land
jitô	stewards
jômensei	fixed tax rate system
jûgô masu	1.8 liter cubic measure
kabu nakama	licensed cartel
kabuki	drama with song and dance
kaisho	bureau
kamon	Tokugawa related
kanezashi	see *kenzao*
kanjô bugyô	finance magistrate
kanjôkata	treasury
kari	to borrow
karoku	hereditary *kokudaka* of samurai family
kashi	to lend
katakuri	arrowroot
keishû ginka	fixed value silver currency
kenzao	pole 1.8-meter-long

kimono	formal dress of Japan
kirimai	peridic rice stipends
kirisoe	newly reclamated land without report to magistrate
kô	mutual-aid societies
kôdô bunka	culture of behavior
kôeki	traffic
kogaisei	apprenticeship system
kôgi	Tokugawa government or daimyo
kokudaka	value of land assessed by rice
kokudaka system	relations between lords and vassals determined by *kokudaka*, also with peasants
kokusan kaisho	dominal yarding bureau
kokusanhin	dominal specialties
kome kitte	rice voucher
komononari	miscellaneous tax
kosode	basic form of *kimono*
kuchi-berashi	decreasing the number of dependents in the family
kudarimono	commodities coming to Edo from Osaka
kuniyakukin	collected service by money
kyôgen	comic drama with this-wordly scenario
kyômasu	see *jûgô masu*
mangoku tôshi	efficient standing sieves
mashibu kôkan hoshiki	exchanging system with premium
masu	measures
menjô	order of tax payments
miso	soybean paste
mujinkô	mutual-aid associations
muko yôshi	adoptive heir
myôgakin	offertory money
nago	indentured servants
naibu shôshinsei	internal promotion system
nanbanjin	southern barbarian, nickname for Iberians
nawanobi	stretched surveyer's rope
nayamai	rice not from tax
nengu	agrarian tax, including rent
nengumai shijô	market for tax rice
nenguritsu	tax rates
nenguwaritsukejô	see *menjo*
nenki-uri	fixed term sales
nimbetsu aratame	population survey
ninjindai-ôkogin	ancient style silver for ginseng
noh	play, dancing with masks

nômin	farmers (including peasantry)
nukemairi	pilgrimage to Ise shrine
okagemairi	see *nukemairi*
onden	concealing cultivated land
osabyakushô	powerful farmers
oshiirekata	warehouse office
osukui	relief
osukuikata	bureau of relief
osumashikata	accounts office
otetsudai fusin	daimyo's construction fees
otorika kaisei	field tax reform
rakuichi rakuza rei	order of free markets and open guilds
rekishikô	calendar mission
Ritsuryô	Ancient state's system imitated Sui and Tang
ryôgae	money exchange, banking
saké	Japanese rice brewing wine
sakutoku	land rent after tax
samurai	warriors
sanbutsu kaisho	see *kokusan kaisho*
sashigane	see kenzao
satô kawase kaisho	sugar exchange scheme
sebiki	"deducting area"
senbaisei	domain monopolies
senchu-kawase	shipper's exchange
sengoku daimyo	territorial lords in Warring States Period
sengoku tôshi	see *mangoku tôshi*
shakkin shômon	loan contracts
shakuchi	fief loan
shihon	capital
shiki	rights or role
shima-momen	stripe-woven cotton cloth
shisan	assets
shôen	land held by nobles and temples
shôya	village officials
shugo ryôgokusei	provincial constable system in Muromachi period
shûmon-aratame	religious faith investigation
sumô	Japanese wrestling
taikô kenchi	land survey by Toyotomi Hideyoshi
taikun	overlord
takamochi	landholder
taka-uke	taxed
tanomoshikô	see *mujinkô*
tatami	mat made with rush
tatara seitetsu	iron-making using forge

tenryô	shogunal fisc
tôji	winter solstice
ton'yasei kanai kôgyô	wholesale system family production
toritsugi	agent
tozama daimyo	daimyo who pledged fidelity to shogunate after 1603
tsubokari	sampling a collection of fields
uchibata-sei	small factory system
uchikowashi	house smashings
urikomi ton'ya	wholesale marketers
waito	Japanese thread
wakan	trading spot near to Pusan, Korea
wakô	Japanese pirates in the East China Sea in fourteenth to sixteenth centuries
watagae	putting out system
yaku	duties
yakunin	officials
yakuryô	rice stipends
yobu	overage
yorozuya	general store
yôshi	imported coton yarn
zaimachi	local town

2. Person

Abe Shôzo		Osaka magistrate of shogunate (in 1843)
Arai Hakuseki	(1657–1725)	scholar, senior *bakufu* official
Doi Toshikatsu	(1573–1644)	chief councillor of shogunate
Fukaeya Jimbei		merchant for Korean trade in Kyoto
Fukuzawa Yukichi	(1834–1901)	man of enlightenment, founder of Keio University
Gôdoya Bunzaemon	(early 18th century)	lumber merchant in Nagoya, Owari
Gotô Tokujô	(1550–1631)	goldsmith and treasurer of Hideyoshi and Ieyasu
Hachisuka Haruaki	(1757–1814)	daimyo of Tokushima, Awa Province
Hachisuka Shigeyoshi	(1738–1801)	daimyo of Tokushima, Awa Province

Honda Toshiaki	(1743–1820)	scholar, economist
Ito Chûbei	(1842–1903)	merchant, founder of Itochu, origin. From Ômi Province
Jin family		head of scale guild in Kyoto
Kaiho Seiryô	(1755–1817)	free scholar
Kan'o Haruhide	(1687–1753)	magistrate of finance of shogunate
Kobayashi Gin'emon		Edo kimono wholesaler, originated from Ômi Province
Kônoike Zen'emon		merchant and money exchager in Osaka
Kôshu-ya Chûemon		silk merchant in Yokohama
Kurimori Kichiemon		local merchant at Ôdate, Akita Prefecture
Kusaka Gizaemon	[1830s]	head of hansatsu office of Takamatsu domain
Kusama Naokata	(1753–1831)	economist in Osaka
Masuya Koemon		see Yamagata Bantô (pen name)
Matsudaira Nobutoki	(1686–1746)	senior councillor of *bakufu* in Kyôhô era
Matsudaira Sadanobu	(1758–1829)	chief, shogunate cabinet
Matsukata Masayoshi	(1835–1924)	finance minister of Meiji government
Matsuo Bashô	(1644–94)	poet (haiku)
Miki Yokichiriro family		indigo merchant in Tokushima, Awa Province
Mitsui family		the largest merchant and money exchanger
Miura Baien	(1723–89)	scholar of economics from Bungo Province
Miyazaki Yasusada	(1623–97)	scholar of agriculture, in Fukuoka domain, Chikuzen Province
Mizuno Tadakuni	(1794–1851)	chief councillor of shogunate
Murata Seifû	(1783–1855)	financial specialist in Chôshû domain
Muro Kyûsô	(1658–1734)	Confucian scholar, in Edo
Narita Jûbei		author of *Kogai kinu burui taisei*

Nishimatsu family		village officer, money-lender in Nishijo, Mino Province
Nomoto Dôgen		author of *Kogai yohoki*, 1702 in Tsugaru, Mutsu Province
Oda Nobunaga	(1534–82)	powerful warrior, originated from Mino Province
Ogiwara Shigehide	(1658–1713)	*bakufu's* finance magistrate
Ôoka Tadasuke	(1677–1751)	Edo magistrate of shogunate
Rai San'yô	(1780–1832)	free writer, author of *Nihon Gaishi*
Shimomura family		merchant family (Daimaru) in Osaka
Shuzui family		head of scale guild in Edo
Sufu Masunosuke	(1823–1864)	chief specialist of Chôshû domain
Takeda Katsuyori	(1546–82)	powerful warrior, originated from Kai Province
Tanahashi family		village officer, money lender in Niremata, Mino Province
Tanuma Okitsugu	(1720–88)	grand chamberman of shogunate
Tokugawa Iemitsyu	(1604–51)	the third shogun
Tokugawa Ietsuna	(1641–80)	the fourth shogun
Tokugawa Ieyasu	(1542–1616)	the first shogun, originated from Mikawa Province
Tokugawa Nariaki	(1800–60)	daimyo of Mito, Hitachi Province
Tokugawa Tsunayoshi	(1646–1709)	the fifth shogun
Tokugawa Yoshimune	(1684–1751)	the eighth shogun
Torii Yôzô	(1796–1873)	Edo magistrate of shogunate
Toyotomi Hideyori	(1593–1615)	Hideyoshi's son
Toyotomi Hideyoshi	(1537–98)	unifier of Japan, originated from Owari Province
Uegaki Morikuni	(1751–1806)	author of *Yôsan Hiroku*, 1803
Yamagata Bantô	(1748–1821)	scholar, head clerk of rice merchant
Yodogimi (f)	(1569–1615)	Hideyori's mother

3. Name of Place
(Province = Province, see Map 1. Prefecture = Prefecture, see Map 2)

Aizu	part of southern Mutsu Province
Akamagaseki	port town in Nagato Province
Akita	part of Maeyamashiro, Suwô Province
Ama	district in Kii Province
Amagasaki	castle town in western Settsu Province
Amakusa	islands off Higo Province
Ampachi	district in Mino Province
Ashina	district in Hiroshima Prefecture
Bisai	western part of Owari Province
Chôshi	town at the mouth of River Tone, Shimôsa Province
Daiya	the river in Shimotsuke Province
Dôjima	a part of Osaka City, location of the rice market
Ezochi	now Hokkaido
Fuchû	castle town in Bingo Province
Fukui	central castle town in Echizen Province
Fukuoka	central castle town in Chikuzen Province
Fukutsuka polder	polder in Ampachi District, Mino Province
Fushimi	castle town in Yamashiro Province
Gifu	commercial town in Atsumi District, Mino Province
Gotô	islands off Hizen Province
Gujô	district in Mino Province
Hakata	commercial town in Chikuzen
Hakodate	open port town trade in Hokkaidô
Hanakuma	village in Yatabe County, Settsu Province
Hayami	district in Bungo Province
Hienuki	district in Iwate Prefecture
Higashi-Aburakawa	village in Yatsushiro District, Kai Province
Higashihamachô	street in Takamatsu town, Sanuki Province
Hikone	castle town in Ômi Province
Himeji	central castle town in Harima Province
Hyôgo	port town in Settsu Province
Ibi	the river in Mino Province
Iinuma	marsh in Shimôsa Province
Ikeda	industrial town in Settsu Province
Imabari	industrial town in Ehime Prefecture
Ina Valley	valley along Tenryû River in Shinano Province
Iruma	district in Saitama Prefecture
Ise Bay	bay between Owari and Ise Provs.

Ishinomaki	port town in Mutsu Province
Itami	industrial town in Settsu Province
Izawa	district in Iwate Prefecture
Jôhana	industrial town in Etchû Province
Jûrenbô	hamlet in Nishijo village, Ampachi District, Mino Province
Kada Bura	coastal village in Ama District, Kii Province
Kagoshima	central castle town in Satsuma Province
Kakogawa	town in Harima Province
Kameda	industrial town in Niigata Prefecture
Kameoka	castle town in Tamba Province
Kamihôgunji	village in Uta District, Sanuki Province
Kamisawa	village in Azuma District, Kôzuke Province
Kanagawa	open port town trade in Musashi Province
Kanazawa	central castle town in Kaga Province
Kanô	castle town in Mino Province
Kawagoe	castle town in Musashi Province
Kirihara	village in Yamada District, Kôzuke Province
Kiryû	industrial town in Kôzuke Province
Kiso	the river in Shinano and Mino Provs
Kôfu	central castle town in Kai Province
Kojima	industrial town in Bizen Province
Kokura	castle town in Buzen Province
Komatsu	industrial town in Kaga Province
Kuga	district in Suwô Province
Kumamoto	central castle town in Higo Province
Kumano	southern part of Kii Province
Kurayoshi	industrial town in Hôki Province
Kurume	castle town in Chikugo Province
Kusatsu	post town in Ômi Province
Kuwana	castle town in Kuwana District, Ise Province
Maeyamashiro	Saiban (part of district) in Suwô Province
Matsue	central castle town in Izumo Province
Matsumoto	castle town in Chikuma District, Shinano Province
Matsuyama	castle town in Iyo Province
Miki	industrial town in Harima Province
Mito	central castle town in Hitachi Province
Mitsuke	industrial town in Niigata Prefecture
Miyazu	castle town in Tango Province
Môka	industrial town in Ibaragi Prefecture
Musashino-shinden	village in Musashi Province
Myôzai	district in Awa Province
Nada	part of western Settsu Province
Nagano	town in Shinano Province

Nagaoka	castle town in Echigo Province
Nagara	the river in Mino Province
Nagasaki	foreign trade town in Hizen Province
Nagashino	place in Mikawa Province
Nagoya	central castle town in Owari
Naha	central town in Ryûkyû
Nakamura	village in Ampachi District, Mino Province
Nakanoseki	port town in Suwô Province
Nambu	part of Mutsu Province
Nara	ancient capital in Yamato Province
Nihonbashi	a bridge, center of Edo
Niikawa	district in Toyama Prefecture
Nijô	a part in Kyoto City
Nikkô	place located Tokugawa mausoleum in Shimotsuke Province
Niremata	village in Ampachi District, Mino Province
Nishijin	a part in Kyoto City
Nishijo	village in Ampachi District, Mino Province
Nôbi	Mino and Owari Provs
Nôbi-wajû	polder in Owari and Mino Provs
Noda	industrial town in Shimosa Province
Ochi	district in Iyo Province
Odate	ex-castle town in Akita Prefecture
Ôgaki	castle town in Ampachi District, Mino Province
Okayama	central castle town in Bizen Province
Okkoto	village in Suwa District, Shinano Province
Okoshi-juku	post town in Nakashima District, Owari Province
Oriono	town in Settsu Province
Ôtsu	town in Ômi Province
Ôuchi	district in Sanuki Province
Owase	town in Muro District, Kii Province
Ôyamazaki	town in Yamashiro Province
Pusan	town in southern Korea
Saga	central castle town in Hizen Province
Sakai	ex-foreign trade town in Izumi Province
Sakata	port town in Shônai, Dewa Province
Saku	district in Shinano Province
Sanbonmatsu	village in Ôuchi District, Sanuki Province
Sanjô	industrial town in Echigo Province
Sano	industrial town in Shimotsuke Province
Sekigahara	place between Mino and Ômi Provs
Sendai	central castle town in Mutsu Province
Sennan	southern Settsu Province
Shimabara	castle town in Hizen Province

Shimo-Ôgre	village in Ampachi District, Mino Province
Shindatsu	Shinobu and Date Districts in southern Mutsu Province
Shinminatomachi	street in Takamatsu town, Sanuki Province
Shiunji	marsh in Echigo Province
Shôdoshima	island on Inland Sea, Sanuki Province
Sôma	part of southernmost Mutsu Province
Sumpu	castle town in Suruga Province
Takabatake	village in Myôzai District, Awa Province
Takada	castle town in western Echigo Province
Takamatsu	central castle town in Sanuki Province
Takefu	industrial town in Echizen Province
Takegahana	river in Shimotsuke Province
Tarui	industrial town in Osaka Prefecture
Tatsuno	industrial town in western Harima Province
Tôgane	town in Kazusa Province
Toyama	central castle town in Etchû Province
Toyobami-shinden	village in Ampachi District, Mino Province
Tsu	castle town in Ise Province
Tsugaru	northernmost part of Mutsu Province
Tsukazaki	village in Yamabe District, Kazusa Province
Tsuruoka	castle town in Shônai, Dewa Province
Ueda	town in Shinano Province
Uwajima	castle town in Iyo Province
Wajima	industrial town in Noto Province
Wakayama	central castle town in Kii Province
Yamada	village in Azuma District, Kôzuke Province
Yamaguchi	Saiban (part of district) in Suwô Province
Yamanashi	district in Yamanashi Prefecture
Yatabe	district in Settsu Province
Yatsushiro	district in Kai Province
Yokohama	city in Kanagawa Prefecture
Yokone	village in Saku District, Shinano Province
Yonezawa	castle town in Dewa Province
Yoshino	the river in Awa Province
Yuasa	industrial town in Kii Province
Yûki	town in Hitachi Province

4. Writings

Aizu nôsho, by Sase Yojiemon	agriculture in Aizu: 1684
Bôchô fûdo chûsin'an, by Murata Sefu	economic servey of Chôshû domain: from 1841 on

Denhôki, by Kishizaki Sakuji	on local administration in Matsue domain: 1682
Hanseiroku	a history of domainal government: 1868.
Jikata chikubashû, by Hiraoka Naoyuki	on embankment works: 1689
Jikata kikigaki	on the local administration: 1668
Kefukigusa, by Matsue Shigenori	a brief encyclopedia, originally for haiku: c. 1638
Keiko-dan, by Kaiho Seiryô	talk on public practice: 1813
Kenkaroku, by Murô Kyusô	an opinion to *bakufu*: 1723
Kogai kinu burui taisei, by Narita Jûbei	encyclopedia on raising silkworms and sericulture
Kogai yôhôki, by Nomoto Dôgen	techniques for raising silkworms: 1702 (the first writing on silkworms)
Kôka shunju, by Tsuchiya Matasaburô	on cultivation: 1707
Masuko-dan, by Kaiho Seiryô	talks on Masuya Kôemon, uncertain
Nihon gaishi, by Rai San'yô	an unauthorized history of Japan:
Nôgyô zensho, by Miyazaki Yasusada	on agriculture of central and western part of Japan: 1697
Nôji isho	1709
Renmin buikusho	1688
Sanka zui, by Kusama Naokata	on currency: 1815
Taigô-dan, by Kaiho Seiryô	talks on an excellent economist: 1813
Tôjin ôrai, by Fukuzawa Yukichi	
Wakan sansai zue, by Terashima Ryôan	encyclopedia: 1715
Yôsan hiroku, by Uegaki Morikuni	secrets of silkworm culture, 1803. Translated to French in 1848.

INDEX